DAVID FERRIE

Mafia Pilot, Participant in Anti-Castro Bioweapon Plot, Friend of Lee Harvey Oswald and Key to the JFK Assassination

JUDYTH VARY BAKER

Author of
ME & LEE – HOW I CAME TO KNOW, LOVE AND LOSE LEE HARVEY OSWALD

Foreword by JESSE VENTURA

David Ferrie: Mafia Pilot, Participant in Anti-Castro Bio-weapon Plot, Friend of Lee Harvey Oswald and Key to the JFK Assassination

Copyright © 2014 Judyth Vary Baker. All Rights Reserved.

Published by: Trine Day LLC
PO Box 577
Walterville, OR 97489
1-800-556-2012
www.TrineDay.com
publisher@TrineDay.net

Library of Congress Control Number: 2013937963

Baker, Judyth Vary.
David Ferrie—1st ed.
p. cm.
Includes index and references.
Epub (ISBN-13) 978-1-937584-55-9
Mobi (ISBN-13) 978-1-937584-56-6
Print (ISBN-13) 978-1-937584-54-2
1. Ferrie, David William -- 1918-1967. 2. Kennedy, John F. -- (John Fitz-gerald), -- 1917-1963 -- Assassination. 3. Baker, Judyth Vary. 4. Oswald, Lee Harvey -- 1939-1963. 4. Assassination -- Investigation -- Louisiana -- New Orleans. I. Baker, Judyth Vary. II. Title

First Edition
10 9 8 7 6 5 4 3 2 1

Printed in the USA

Distribution to the Trade by:
Independent Publishers Group (IPG)
814 North Franklin Street
Chicago, Illinois 60610
312.337.0747
www.ipgbook.com

Publisher's Foreword

This is a book like no other, written by an author like no other. We are all extremely lucky for the pluck and courage of Judyth Vary Baker. She is a first-person witness, her understanding goes beyond what can be read in books and documents. She knew and worked with David Ferrie. She met Clay Shaw, Jack Ruby, Carlos Marcello, Guy Banister, and others that sultry summer in New Orleans.

She was nineteen in 1963, and alone, having arrived in town early for her work with famed surgeon and cancer pioneer Dr. Alton Ochsner. Then a "chance" meeting changed her life forever. Judyth met a handsome young ex-Marine, Lee Harvey Oswald. They were soon working together, and later became lovers, even though both were married. It's a long story, and is told in her book, *Me & Lee: How I Came to Know, Love and Lose Lee Harvey Oswald*. We published that book in 2010, after several years of vetting her story and her abundant archive of documentation.

That her story was published by our small company speaks volumes about the state of our Fourth Estate. Most of our "free press" has been captured by what is currently being called the "Deep State," the same forces that murdered John Fitzgerald Kennedy in November of 1963. Is it any wonder that Judyth's story has been suppressed?

But then this is nothing new. After Judyth's kids were grown-up and out of the home in the late 1990s, and she began to tell her story, Judyth was contacted by *60 Minutes*. They checked out her story and had her in make-up, lights on, and in front of cameras ... when they were stopped. Don Hewitt, legendary executive producer and the man who created *60 Minutes* had this to say about Judyth's tale: "I brought that woman to New York ... Gloria and I were convinced we were about to break the biggest story of our times ... The door was slammed in our face..."

This left Judyth in limbo and open to attack. And attacked she was: her credibility, her sanity, her work, her friends ... her life. We became aware of Judyth through author Ed Haslam, when Trine-

Day published his astounding book *Dr. Mary's Monkey* in 2007. Judyth was living overseas, after too many "accidents," lost jobs, and attacks on friends and family. Ed Haslam approached us about publishing her book, and we soon received her manuscript and documentation. We were overwhelmed: there were bus tickets, trolley stubs, receipts with lipstick kisses, newspaper articles, W-2s, and, most amazing, her pay stubs from Reily Coffee Company, where she and Lee worked together – hired the same day! There were many other eye-popping items.

We asked her to come to the States for the release of her book, she wouldn't, she had been "pushed out" into too many intersections. She was afraid. Most of her friends from 1963 New Orleans were dead, many murdered. Finally with the release of her book in soft cover, we were able to get Judyth to come to North America, she came to Toronto in 2011. We celebrated Lee Oswald's birthday and were pleasantly surprised with actual news coverage: newspapers, TV, radio and Internet. Of course it didn't translate into coverage in the States, but it was a welcome change from the usual stonewall. There was hope, and Judyth began looking ahead. We started to talk about a book on David Ferrie. Judyth knew Dave, she was his friend. They spent time together, working and talking. She saw him interact with the world.

Once she started to look into Ferrie's life she found that there were many untruths and misunderstandings being promoted on the Internet. Judyth saw it as her duty to refute those claims, and give readers and researchers a place to start an honest discussion of Dave Ferrie: who he was, what he did, who he knew, and who he was working for.

Ferrie's life was not an open book, and there are many, sometimes opposing, tales told. We have used typesetting devices to try to present clearly Judyth's testimony, rebuttal and research into this fascinating individual. We hope this book helps us all along our journey of discovery – towards the truth.

Onwards to the Utmost of Futures,
Peace,

Kris Millegan
Publisher
TrineDay
September 10, 2014

That, of course, is the great secret of the successful fool – that he is no fool at all.

– Isaac Asimov, *Guide to Shakespeare.*

Dedication

To all my dear friends and supporters: I'd attempted to make a list to acknowledge all the faithful supporters, friends, witnesses, and champions of this Just Cause, but it would fill pages. Even then, it would surely be incomplete, as our ranks grow daily. Instead, I humbly dedicate this book to all of you, with particular gratitude to the people of New Orleans, without whose help, knowledge and kindness, this book would not be possible. The task to clear Lee Oswald's name has been a difficult one, but because of you (though I may not live to see it), I am now certain that Lee's standing as a true patriot and hero will be recognized and that the government's role in letting the CIA and Mafia kill Kennedy – then covering up the evil deed – will be acknowledged in tomorrow's history books. *David Ferrie: Mafia Pilot* supplants and clarifies many aspects of the Kennedy assassination that could not be fully addressed in *Me & Lee*. David Ferrie's tormented life was a very important one. This book exposes the methods used by the government, the media and associated specialists in deception to keep the truth about Dave – and about the Kennedy assassination – from being understood. We have a useful yardstick to measure how corrupt our government is and how extensively our media is controlled: just ask yourself, "What do they say about the Kennedy assassination?" Meanwhile, we still have work to do, and I am grateful that because of your courageous support, I do not stand alone. God bless you all.

Foreword

In Homer's *The Odyssey*, it takes Ulysses ten years to find his way home from the Trojan War. In this epic journey he encounters storms, sorceresses, sirens, monsters, cannibals, and even descends into Hades to consult the spirits of the dead. Eventually, he is reunited with his true love, Penelope, and regains his kingdom of Ithaca.

No such closure has been achieved in the fifty years and counting since the assassination of President John Fitzgerald Kennedy. Despite tireless efforts by modern heroes – who dare to reveal the truth – and others, the murderous monsters, the sorcerers of deception, the sirens of spin, and cannibals of history have kept us in a sea of confusion and mutual doubt. This storm of controversy has made certain that the shore of truth always remains just out of reach. And the tide of time washes away the interest of the great majority.

Still, our modern Ulysses' persevere.

One of them, possibly the bravest, is Judyth Vary Baker. When I served as a Navy Seal our missions were dangerous but straightforward. Take out the enemy, rescue the princess, and go home. But people like Judy must combat a far more elusive and influential foe. She has taken on the weight of official history and suffered the consequences for such daring folly.

I read her first book, *Me and Lee,* with a healthy amount of initial doubt. Here was a woman claiming to have been Lee Oswald's friend and lover in the six months leading up to JFK's murder, four decades and more after the event. But as the story unfolded and she brought forth facts and documents to back up her claims, I was forced to conclude that this was no charlatan or madwoman hoping to cash in on some Anastasia-like fantasy. To date, none of the conspiracy deniers have been able to disprove her assertions. And believe me, they have tried.

This new book strikes me as a perfect companion to the first. Like Ulysses, Ms. Baker has descended into Hades, and exhumed the spirit of David Ferrie, a man who was privy to the machinations of those who perpetrated our democracy's demise. Unlike other contemporary writers, she knew the man personally, in all his brilliance, eccentricity, decadence and deceit. She experienced his great loyalty along with the pain engendered by his chronic physical suffering and spiritual torment. I respect the man now as a patriotic American who was caught in the inferno of Cold War politics.

Most people know Ferrie only from the character sketched out admirably by Joe Pesci in *JFK*. For those who would dig deeper into this man's fascinating life, and his role in the events leading to what happened in November 1963, Baker's book is the place to go.

I congratulate Kris Millegan and his crew at TrineDay for another courageous stab at the windmill of mass-media indifference. On, to Ithaca!

Jesse Ventura
September 9, 2014

Table of Contents

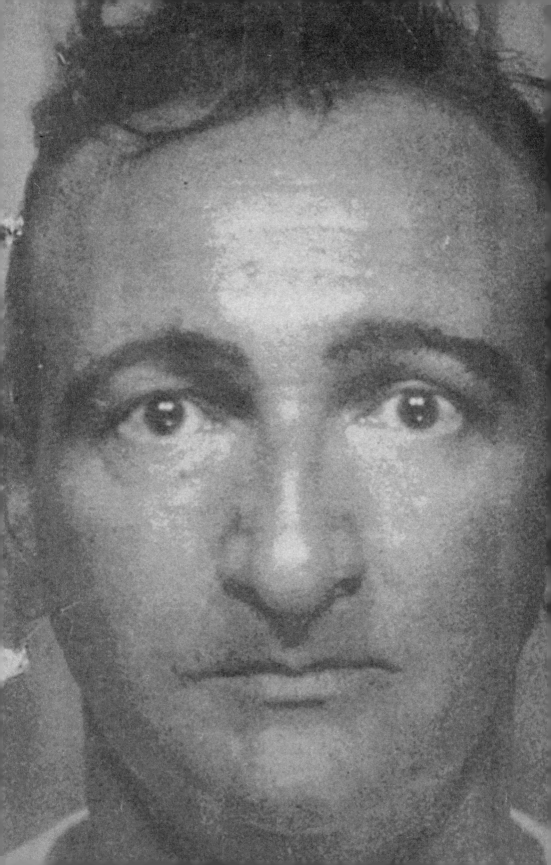

The Clown Who Wouldn't Cry

If anybody ever asks you if I have anything to do with an-
ti-Castro matters anymore, the answer is always, "No."
If anybody asks you if I have ever been associated with
the CIA, the answer is always, "No." You can say I help
out with the FBI from time to time. That's okay. But to my
boys, and everybody else, I'm just a sex fiend, a drinking
buddy, and a pilot. Let's keep it that way. Of course, I'm
just joking. Life is a joke.

                                 –David William Ferrie

David William Ferrie is one of the most mysterious and bizarre characters associated with the assassination of President John F. Kennedy.

Dave told me his parents wanted "to offer their firstborn son to God, just as Abraham offered Isaac on the altar" by making him a Catholic priest. "I especially disappointed my mother," he told me. "Spectacularly." By the end of his life, Dave was as far from an ordained priest as one could possibly get. He was a legal advisor for New Orleans Mafia Don, Carlos Marcello, a pilot for several Mafia families, a failed gas station owner, and the disappointed lover of teenage boys and young men. He also became known as a suspect in the Kennedy assassination.

His name hit the newspapers in 1967 and, soon after asking District Attorney Jim Garrison's investigators to protect him, Dave was found dead in his bed. The coroner ruled that his death was from natural causes, but you will find other evidence in these pages. Dave was my friend. I knew him from April 1963 through late 1963, when, for our mutual safety, Dave called to say he could never speak to me again. I believe he saved my life.

I first learned of the notorious David Ferrie at the tender age of nineteen, on April 26, 1963, the same day I met Lee Harvey Oswald, the falsely accused assassin of President John F. Kennedy. Lee and I met at a post office in the violent and romantic city of

New Orleans. Utterly unknown to me, at the time, the Central Intelligence Agency (CIA) was working with the Mafia in efforts to kill Cuba's Communist leader, Fidel Castro. Trained by the Office of Naval Intelligence (ONI) and loaned to the CIA for undercover operations, Lee was a bridge between the Mafia and the CIA because his family was closely associated with mob chieftain Carlos Marcello. Marcello's influence stretched across the Southern US, with New Orleans and Dallas firmly in his grip.

When I first met Dave, he was already aware that President Kennedy was in grave danger. JFK was hated for his courageous defiance of the CIA, and his interference with banking and oil interests, the military-industrial complex, secret societies, and organized crime. At the same time, Kennedy resisted going to war, infuriating his generals and breaking so-called promises to the anti-Castro rebels who had been activated by the previous administration and were inherited by Kennedy. How Dave knew that, and how he became involved, exposes the hateful underbelly of the assassination.

Today, many believe Kennedy was removed from office by a coup d'etat, using CIA assets and teams of Mafia hit men from the US and elsewhere. Many honest researchers also agree that Oswald was framed. But in 2013, during the fiftieth year 'anniversary', the major media ignored these heavily researched conclusions, again and again blaming only Lee. It was once more, "Oswald acted alone."

The preponderance of evidence points to this scenario: Elements within the CIA and the Mafia were allowed to kill Kennedy, with the co-operation of the Secret Service, all the while aided and protected by the FBI under J. Edgar Hoover, and with the approval of the military-industrial complex

When Lyndon B. Johnson placed his hand on JFK's Catholic Missal aboard Air Force One, gave the oath of office, then turned his head to smile at a winking Texas crony, Albert Thomas, our nation changed forever.

The murder and cover-up was backed by a cartel of Kennedy-haters, closely linked to government, who financially benefited. LBJ cooperated and protected the killers, because: (1) he knew that he, also, could have been killed that dark Friday, and (2) had Kennedy lived, LBJ would probably have been indicted by the Senate's Rules Committee for corruption.[1] A prison sentence was likely. The choice must have seemed clear to Johnson.

CARLOS MARCELLO

Marcello hated JFK and his crusading brother, Bobby, who tried to rid America of organized crime. Bobby had a special disdain for Marcello, who sneered at him and his brother during hearings conducted by the Senate Racket Committee in 1959. Using his power as Attorney General, Bobby was determined to end Marcello's career. As for Marcello, after the Kennedy assassination, he would brag that he cut the head off the dog to stop the tail from bothering him.[2]

Marcello pretended he'd been born in Guatemala, in order to avoid deportation to Sicily (or, worse, to Tunisia, where he'd actually been born). But his faked Guatemalan passport and visa to the US didn't fool Bobby Kennedy; so, in the fall of 1963, Marcello sent his pilot, David Ferrie, to Guatemala several times to create evidence to back up his fake birth certificate.

Marcello's real name was Calogers Minacore. The six-month visa to the USA, shown here, expiring September 15, 1961, was issued in Guatemala. Since it claimed that Marcello was a citizen of Guatemala, the visa was used on April 4, 1961 as an excuse by Robert Kennedy to deport his nemesis back to his 'native' country.

That's when Marcello's clash with Bobby Kennedy first came to a boil. The so-called tomato salesman (with U.S. military contracts) was handcuffed when he reported to his parole officer in New Orleans. Marcello found himself a piece of cargo on a plane to Guatemala. With him was his attorney, Mike Maroun.

Marcello was treated well in Guatemala, where his "tomato" business flourished, so Bobby Kennedy sent agents to change that. They snatched Marcello and Maroun and hauled them by truck deep into the Honduran jungles, where they were thrown down a steep cutoff, and expected to die. In 2000, Marcello's granddaughter, Tricia, wrote to me: "Imagine! Two overweight dagos, stumbling through the jungles for three days, with broken ribs and twisted ankles!" After reaching Honduras' capital city, Tegucigalpa, they slept for two solid days. Mike Maroun then flew back to New Orleans, where he "arranged things." Florida's Mafia chieftain, Santos Trafficante, was also probably involved. A commercial airline supposedly returned Marcello to the USA. But Tricia (and others) told me that David Ferrie flew Marcello to Miami from the remote spot where he'd been dropped off in the Everglades, thanks to Trafficante, after which Little Man made himself visible in Texas.

May 28, 1968, Laredo, Texas: Carlos Marcello, left, leaves a trial session at federal court with his attorney, Mike Maroun. Marcello had been arrested for assaulting an FBI agent at an airport.

Researcher Tom Jones summarized the situation: "To say the least, the actions of Kennedy had been arguable. He had deported Carlos on the basis of a known forged birth certificate.... Marcello was deeply offended by his treatment. Years later he told a congressional committee, "They just snatched me ... actually kidnapped me." He never forgave Kennedy and to his close friends swore vengeance against the man for the way he had been treated."[3]

On Nov. 1, 1963, only 21 days before Kennedy's assassination, Marcello paid David Ferrie, by then his family's pilot and legal advisor, $7000 for his legal services in the long, ongoing deportation trial. The sum was about $65,000 in today's funds.[4] That trial ended at 2:30 PM CST, a mere hour and a half after Kennedy died, with acquittal assured through a bribed jury. Marcello's revenge was exquisite. In Washington, DC, Bobby was advised that his brother was dead. Next, Bobby was told that Marcello was holding a victory party in New Orleans. The Mafia Don had kicked sand in Bobby's face and taken over the beach.

Tricia Marcello's story that her grandfather was grateful for Dave's help is buttressed by the fact that Marcello, who despised homosexuals, nevertheless made sure Dave got on the payroll via a job with his attorney, G. Wray Gill in March 1962, six months after Dave lost his job with Eastern Air Lines. By then, Dave was in financial trouble. That same month, Dr. Alton Ochsner's get-Castro project, eventually involving a ring of labs, began operations, with Dr. Mary Sherman as coordinator. On cue,[5] Dave moved into his apartment at 3330 East Louisiana Parkway, close to the lab animals needed for Ochsner's project. He was now located just minutes by bus from Dr. Mary Sherman's apartment.

DR. OCHSNER AND DR. SHERMAN BEGIN "THE PROJECT"

The date of March 23, 1962 is important. It's the day that Ochsner's and Sherman's research, trying to find a cure for a virulent cancer-causing monkey virus, morphed into a dedicated project to create a biological weapon to kill Fidel Castro.[6] It was the same day Ochsner distanced himself from his longtime friend, Clay Shaw, removing him from a position at International House where Shaw had held important positions for over nine years alongside Ochsner. Shaw would thus be ready to quietly assist his old friend in Ochsner's project to get Castro, as I would soon learn for myself. By May 1963, I had been influenced to join this team, which was compartmentalized so that I never knew the names of all who were involved.

Dr. Alton Ochsner

Dr. Mary Sherman

Meanwhile, Dave kept his day job with G. Wray Gill, with frequent forays to Guy Banister's office, serving as a handy link between Banister's FBI connections and the Mafia. Both sides wanted Castro dead. By May, 1963, Dr. Mary Sherman, Lee Harvey Oswald and I would be working together with Dave, and an array of doctors and scientists who were isolated from each other. The labs were in a ring – I saw initials in log-books, and sign-off sheets – but I never met everyone involved. Isolating us from each other was essential to keeping "The Project" secret.

Dr. Alton Ochsner could do almost anything he liked when it came to personal research projects, which he could easily keep secret. He was the popular CEO of both the Ochsner Foundation and the Ochsner Clinic. As CEO of International House (along with Clay Shaw) Ochsner worked closely with Shaw's International Trade Mart, which had strong anti-communist interests throughout Latin America. Ochsner, who was fiercely anti-communist, enjoyed close ties to almost every important leader in Latin America. This made him useful to the CIA. Ochsner also helped run INCA – the Information Council of the Americas, which sent anti-communist broadcasts and literature across Latin America. Ochsner was my personal mentor and sponsor. I practically worshiped him. As for David Ferrie, Ochsner was using his many talents as an untraceable asset in what would prove to be Ochsner's most important and dangerous anti-communist project – his attempt to kill Fidel Castro.

Lee first introduced Dave to me as "Dr. Ferrie," but New Orleans District Attorney Jim Garrison would call Ferrie something else – a prime suspect in the Kennedy assassination. The only thing that stopped Garrison from learning more was Dave's sudden and oh-so-convenient death, five days after his name got into the papers in 1967. But, thanks largely to Garrison, the House Select Committee on As-

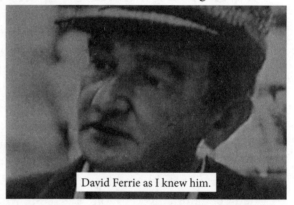

David Ferrie as I knew him.

sassinations (HSCA) was able to access evidence linking the Mafia pilot to Lee Oswald and suspects such as Clay Shaw. The HSCA learned that New Orleans was a hotbed of subversive activities against Kennedy, and (way too late) finally acknowledged the Mob's influence there and in Dallas. The HSCA, hampered by withheld evidence and lies thanks to the CIA and FBI, nevertheless determined that a conspiracy occurred – a conspiracy they failed to look further into because their time limit as a committee was expiring!

Amazingly, the U.S. government ignored the HSCA's recommendation to reopen the case. The Warren Commission's declaration that Oswald was a lone gunman was now highly questionable, but on every anniversary of the Kennedy assassination, a flood of television specials and newspaper articles nevertheless state as indisputable fact that Oswald acted alone and that there was no conspiracy. On the 50th anniversary, 38 of 39 television specials repeat the old lies, with only the Travel Channel offering up-to-date evidence that questions Oswald's guilt. The result has been that the TV and news media have lost the trust of a whole generation of young Americans, who have accessed the truth on the Internet and realized that they were being lied to. Their acid comments to CNN, ABC, NBC, Fox, etc., were overwhelmingly negative. "You must think we're idiots!" was a typical response.

RESEARCHER BIAS AND WITNESS BIAS

We who knew David Ferrie have varying opinions of him. So do the researchers who have pieced together information about Dave, sometimes selecting only what best fits their theories, or what supports the government's official story that Dave was not involved in the Kennedy assassination and was nobody special. One such researcher, rightly known as a "Ferrie specialist," is Stephen Roy, who also posts as "David Blackburst," though most are not aware that he posts as two different people. He earned the title of "Ferrie expert" due to his years of research. Several years ago, Roy wrote, "I've been studying him in detail for more than 30 years. Sometimes, I think I've found the real Ferrie, but sometimes I'm not sure."[7]

For decades, Mr. Roy promised researchers that he was going to publish a book about Dave. Mr. Roy has one troubling specialty: he is a top expert in sound-and-media editing, and as such, he can create whatever sound bytes he wishes from his many recorded interviews.

Had Mr. Roy released his interviews to other researchers, there wouldn't be a problem with the book's delay. But Mr. Roy has kept all his interviews to himself, promising "everything" when his long-awaited book is published. Mr. Roy, who is younger than almost all of us who knew Dave, has already outlived some of the witnesses he's recorded.

What troubles me is that Mr. Roy not only refused to receive copies of Dave's lectures that I offered to send him, but he also refused to meet me. Worse, he told researchers I refused to meet *him*, which Dr. Howard Platzman immediately refuted, since Mr. Roy also avoided meeting Dr. Platzman to talk about me. Though Mr. Roy wrote emails to Dr. Platzman and me between 1999 and 2004, it became clear that he was determined to do everything he could to discredit me, even though he claimed to others he was treating me fairly and without bias.

Another problem is his interview methodology. When Mr. Roy told me and Dr. Platzman that he had gathered many witnesses, who met together when he recorded their statements, alarm bells went off. I told him witnesses should not be allowed to meet and talk together.

They shouldn't even know who the other witnesses are. Which one would blurt out the misbehavior – or the lie – of another witness, when they know who is present, who might talk, who could become angry, when it came out in print? In addition, exposure to each other could also help them to "correct" their memories. I could see the consequences, as they talked to each other: "Oh, yeah, that's right – I forgot about *that!* Oh, Dave did *that,* did he? Wow, that explains why he … " and so on. Mr. Roy's response was that they already knew each other. With this violation of research methodology in mind, Mr. Roy's statements that "all" his witnesses agree on this-or-that particular point – as he has published on sundry occasions – means little.

In order to help the reader decide whether Mr. Roy's recordings and conclusions can be trusted in their entirety, I have placed Mr. Roy's quotations about various events in David Ferrie's life, along with quotes from myself and others, prominently in this book.

MAN OF A DOZEN FACES

Dave put on different faces for different people. Some women even saw him as holy, noting that he said his rosary in his office. He kindly assisted many in need, whether male or female, and was generous with his time and his planes. He was known as a psychologist, a shyster, a politician, or a pilot who had been everywhere and seen everything. To his Civil Air Patrol cadets, he was a counselor, a scientist, a soldier, a survival expert. His loyal Civil Air Patrol cadets thrilled to giddy rides in his training planes, esoteric field trips, and exciting excursions into swamps and wilderness. Many cadets followed Dave when he left an "official" CAP organization in a huff, to form their own unauthorized Civil Air Patrol. When stories of sexual misconduct, beer parties and other problems arose in the renegade patrol, worried parents learned that it wasn't legally chartered, and Ferrie got himself into a pile of trouble. In tolerant New Orleans, the wanna-be priest was soon linked to sexual misconduct with his cadets that even in the Big Easy went way too far.

To Cuban exiles, Dave was an anti-communist guerrilla trainer, a tactical specialist, a munitions expert and a daring pilot whose homosexual activities got him thrown out of its mainstream organizations. To the police, he was a leader of teens who became a disgraced child molester. They often looked the other way because of his close association with Carlos Marcello, their real boss when the chips were down. But who was the real David Ferrie? I saw so many of his many faces.[8]

Bias has always been a nagging problem in Kennedy assassination studies. Even today, the media would still like to say that Dave Ferrie and Lee Oswald never met, even after the HSCA collected witness statements that Ferrie and Oswald knew each other in the Civil Air Patrol:

For example:

> **Jerry Paradis,** a corporate attorney and a former New Orleans Lakefront Civil Air Patrol Unit Recruit Instructor, told the HSCA: "I specifically remember Oswald. I can remember him clearly, and Ferrie was heading the unit then. I'm not saying they may have been together, I'm saying it's a certainty." One FBI report states that Oswald attended sixteen meetings at the Lakefront unit, as well as at least one party at David Ferrie's house.[9]

There's really no evidence linking Lee Oswald to David Ferrie.
– John McAdams (2009)

"No! No! They never met!" WC defenders insisted. But then, in 1993, the TV program *Frontline* provided us with this photo showing Ferrie (first helmet from left) and Lee Oswald (far right).

At this CAP Bivouac, approx. July 27, 1955, Lee is 15 ½ years old. In just 16 months, he will join the Marines. David Ferrie is one of the instructors in the photo.[10] Lee Oswald is wearing a white t-shirt. A typical search-and-rescue bivouac lasted a weekend and included hands-on courses such as knot-tying and survival techniques, as well as drills in search-and-rescue operations.[11]

Mr. Roy expressed great surprise when this photo was released, despite all the important data he had collected about David Ferrie.

It's a fact that Dave's biography would be shorter and less accurate without many of Mr. Roy's contributions. But frankly, since he considers me to be a non-witness,[12] it's hard for me to properly appreciate what he has done. I do try.

JACK MARTIN AND LAYTON MARTENS – THE LIBRARY CARD, AND FALSE WITNESSES

In May 1963 I was placed in a unique position. For months, I had worked in Dave's apartment two or three afternoons a week, mostly while he was out at work, but sometimes when he was present. A few times, we spent considerably more time there, especially as The Project hit its peak after I left my cover job at Reily Coffee Company, where both Lee and I had very convenient and "flexible" employment. In the process, Dave and I had to deal with each other's radical beliefs and idiosyncrasies.

Throughout, Dave shielded me from notable encounters with his male friends, (see *Me & Lee* for details). Even so, I eventually met several of his friends and acquaintances. Only one was hostile – the alcoholic private detective, political writer, artist and sometime-cleric, Jack S. Martin. "Jackass Martin" was also David Lewis' best friend. David Lewis worked on and off for Guy Banister, often as Martin's sidekick. "Sam Spade" as we called him (there were so many 'Davids' around), played classic piano and a good game of chess. David, his wife Anna, and Lee and I did some double dating in New Orleans. Anna went on film in 2000 in New Orleans to tell the world all about that. She confirmed the close ties between her husband, Jack Martin, and their employer, former FBI Red Raider Guy Banister, a racist with ties to Bobby Kennedy, the FBI, CIA and Mafia in anti-Castro affairs in New Orleans.

Jack. S. Martin | David Lewis | Anna Lewis

Lewis spent more time with Jack Martin than he did with his wife Anna. Dave called the two of them "the comedy team of Martin and Lewis." I met Jack Martin on the last day he dared show up at Dave's place – to spy on Dave's last party until late August. David Lewis was at his side.

Jack Suggs, AKA Martin, was also a stool pigeon and private investigator for Guy Banister. He is more important in the case than most realize.[13] The night of the assassination, Martin informed authorities that David Ferrie was responsible for teaching Lee Harvey Oswald how to shoot. He also said David Ferrie's library card was found in Lee Harvey Oswald's possession.[14] Lee's name was already in the news by then as "Kennedy's assassin." Researchers make much of Martin's call from his hospital bed on Nov. 23 to media, laying blame on David Ferrie for Lee Oswald's so-called violent ways, but in fact, he had talked to the police the previous evening, after being pistol-whipped by Guy Bannister not long after JFK was shot. Did he want to bring charges against Banister for that? No – but he did want to talk about David Ferrie. At 8:32 PM an FBI report emerged about David knowing the accused assassin, Lee Oswald.

"According to Martin, Banister said something to which Martin replied, 'What are you going to do – kill me like you all did Kennedy?' An angry Banister pistol-whipped Martin with his .357 magnum revolver."[15] Martin had to be taken to Charity hospital with serious head injuries. The incident is shown in the opening minutes of Oliver Stone's influential film, *JFK*.

Martin, wanting revenge, knew that Dave Ferrie and Guy Banister were close allies. They could both could get in trouble if he said the right things. He hoped Dave would get arrested if a rumor went round that Dave's library card had been found on Oswald. But even as Jack Martin was making his phone calls and accusations, others did their best to whitewash Dave, perhaps to save themselves from suspicion by investigators, perhaps because they feared Dave's anger, but most likely because they truly liked Dave and knew Jack Martin would do anything to get Dave in trouble.

The matter of the library card involves not one, but two such cards –one of which happened to be in my possession. It's a key example of how complicated things can get, making it difficult to sort truth from fiction. Mine was no ordinary public library card. It was actually a medical library card: it could be traced back to the secret project that Dave Ferrie, Lee Oswald, Dr. Mary Sherman and I had been working on, under Dr. Alton Ochsner, because it had been issued by Ochsner Clinic to provide a means of entry to the area's medical libraries, which were off-limits for ordinary persons.

Researcher Michael T. Griffith summarized how Dave found out about the library card: "According to an FBI report, G. W. Gill, an attorney for Mafia kingfish Carlos Marcello and Santos Traffi-cante, told David Ferrie's roommate, Layton Martens, that when Oswald was arrested by the Dallas police, Oswald was carrying a library card with Ferrie's name on it. The report was based on an interview with Martens himself."[16]

G. Wray Gill

G. Wray Gill was the Mafia's most im-portant local attorney. He was also David Fer-rie's main employer in 1962-1963. When Gill learned what Jack Martin was telling author-ities from his hospital bed, he called Ferrie's apartment, where Layton Martens, a tempo-rary live-in, answered the phone. Martens had previously been involved in morals charges because of Ferrie. He had also assisted Fer-rie in stealing munitions from a Schlumberg-er bunker in a CIA-sponsored raid, and now would go on record lying for him.

As one Internet article reads, "... Ferrie met Layton when they were in the Civil Air Patrol around 1960. Layton was also involved with Ferrie in supplying weapons to anti-Castro factions in 1961. Garrison tried to bring this out during Lay-ton's Grand Jury testimony but Layton was evasive. Later all charges were dropped..."[17]

Martens told the world that David Fer-rie was a fine, upstanding man. He told that story to the end of his life. Decades after the assassination, Martens told researcher A. J. Weberman that Dave (who was arrested in 1961 for "crimes against nature") was "just your basic, good American."[18] Sometimes Martens told the truth: in 1963, he told the

Layton Martens

FBI that Dave Ferrie was "a great admirer of President Kennedy."[19] I don't know if Dave ever told Martens his secret feelings about JFK, or if Martens was just trying to protect Dave yet again, because at a party I attended, Dave posed as a Kennedy-hater right before my eyes. Only in private did Dave explain himself – that he couldn't get the latest information about Kennedy's enemies if he sang out "Hail to the Chief."

Dave was absolutely frantic when he learned that Jack Martin had told authorities that Lee Oswald was carrying his "library card." Dave's public library card, which had expired earlier in the year, was probably still in his wallet. But that wasn't the right one. He was worried about a medical library card that might have been found in Lee Oswald's wallet! His fears skyrocketed because he'd asked Lee to give the card to me. Had David Lewis – Jack Martin's best friend who was also Lee's friend *seen Lee with that card?* Dave assumed that he must have. Now Jackass Martin was using the card as a way to get Ferrie linked to the accused assassin, and arrested.

Since I had been forced to leave town, and was now working at a prestigious laboratory in Gainesville, Florida, Dave had assumed I gave the card back to Lee. Busy as Dave was, he, too, had forgotten all about it. In actuality, I'd also forgotten about the card, consumed as I was with grief and anger at being kicked out of cancer research. The destruction of my life began when I'd objected to the crime of using one or more healthy "volunteers" – prisoners who would receive injections and x-rays designed to kill them, if successful. But nobody had told the volunteers that if the experiment was successful, they'd all die. I could not abide such evil. My note of protest to Dr. Ochsner created a paper trail, and he was furious. Not only was he through with me, he yelled, but he'd make sure I never saw the inside of a cancer lab again.

Researchers were puzzled when they heard reports that Dave began desperately hunting for the missing library card the evening of the assassination. After all, that same night, he suddenly went merrily on to Houston, supposedly to go on a planned mini-vacation, without a worry in the world. They even wondered if the witnesses who said Ferrie had asked them about the card were simply seeking attention. The HSCA's intrepid researcher, Gaeton Fonzi, speculated that the witnesses had the date wrong:

" ... Oswald's former landlady in New Orleans, Mrs. Jesse Garner, told the committee she recalled that Ferric visited her home on the night of the assassination and asked about Oswald's library card. Mrs. Garner would not talk to Ferrie.

"A neighbor of Oswald's, Mrs. Doris Eames, told New Orleans district attorney investigators in 1968 that Ferrie had come by her house after the assassination, inquiring if Eames had any information regarding Oswald's library card. Mr. Eames told reporters that he had seen Oswald in the public library but apparently had no information about the library card Oswald used.

"Submitted by GAETON ,T . Fonzi, Investigator (208) Deposition of Mrs. Jesse Garner, House Select Committee on Assassinations, p. 34. Note: While Mrs. Garner believes it was the night of the assassination, it would appear, given that Ferrie left New Orleans that evening, that Ferrie may have come by her house on a later date."

Fonzi was correct. But then we must ask did Dave actually go searching for a library card at both the Eames' residence and at Garner's apartment? According to their children, he did. In 2011 and 2012, their children assured me that David Ferrie had indeed asked their parents about "Oswald's library card." Dave even searched Lee's former apartment at 4905 Magazine Street, hoping to find the card. Of course Dave didn't tell Mrs. Garner and Mr. and Mrs. Eames that the card belonged to him. Since the card carried only an ID number, linking it to Ochsner Clinic, Dave could tell these witnesses that the card belonged to the accused assassin, giving him a legitimate excuse to try to find the card.[20]

You'll soon understand how Dave and I solved the library card problem. While I can straighten out the confusion that surrounded the medical library card, and why Dave Ferrie hunted frantically for it, some witnesses have been less cooperative – especially back in the 60's when it was so dangerous to "tell all." The Kennedy assassination case is rife with falsehoods. Important witnesses who might have told the truth – and who would have been believed – were largely eliminated.[21] Witnesses such as myself, who could tell the truth, were intimidated into silence. Some of us, such as Victoria Adams, the "girl on the stairs" have finally spoken out, despite our fears. The world has been told again and again that Lee Oswald was a lone assassin, a loner who hated his life, who wanted to become important and famous by killing JFK. But I stand as a witness to the wonderful life Lee and I hoped to have, if he could only have escaped alive, after doing his best to save the President. The full, amazing story is in my book *Me & Lee*. Lee declared he didn't kill anybody and that he was a patsy. That's not a man trying to make his name in history.

THE REAL DAVID FERRIE

The truth about David Ferrie is important to help establish Lee's innocence. A mass of lies, half-truths and misinformation offered by his closest friends to the FBI, the CIA, the Warren Commission, the HSCA, and by biased researchers have made Dave's story hard to tell, which is why a book based on such sources cannot give you the full truth. As new witnesses and new evidence reach the public, the Gatekeepers have had to hide the importance of this man. He has to be portrayed as a mere felon, not very smart, with no real links to the Kennedy assassination.

Witnesses such as I, who disagree, must be discredited. Our testimonies, our integrity must be questioned, and above all, we must be ignored. Thank God, many people have now met me and realize I'm an honest person.

Judyth Vary Baker, 1963.

Yes, Dave confided in me, but why me? After all, he had boyfriends and lovers who were, from time to time, close to him. But they came and went. Did Dave sense that I could be trusted? He knew I could keep my mouth shut. In fact, I kept silent for over 35 years concerning my knowledge of Lee Harvey Oswald, David Ferrie, Jack Ruby, and many others suspected as major players in the Kennedy assassination. Even today I carry some secrets, because various minor witnesses, having read *Me & Lee*, dared tell me what they knew – as long as I promised to keep the information to myself.

Even Lee Oswald, who scarcely breathed a word about who he really was, finally opened up, though I had to injure myself to prove I wouldn't talk. Dave, who believed that most women were so hormonally driven they couldn't think straight, finally admitted, after we had worked together for months, that I was different. As he said, "One in a billion." Oh, my!

Dave could be sensitive about what women thought of him because he had very little hair on his head, and no body hair. No eyebrows, and no eyelashes, either –he was the Mona Lisa, he'd tell me, but without such beaming beauty! Dave's attempts to cope were pitiable. His bizarre false eyebrows, which he told me he needed to keep dust and dander out of his eyes while flying, were removable, usually glued on. He covered his head with ugly reddish wigs of various sizes. My friend Anna Lewis said, laughing, "It looked like he was wearin' a *rug*!" Perhaps Dave was partly color-blind, since his wigs were too red to be real.

What I did learn, right away, was that Dave appreciated my ignoring his weird appearance when his hat and sunglasses came off. I got used to it. Besides, I was fascinated with the man. He was a brilliant, charismatic individual, and I told him so. What I didn't like was his profanity. The rich wealth of Dave's mind was dark with floods of profanity suddenly shooting from his mouth, and I confronted him about it. I wasn't judging him because of his homosexuality, I told him. But that potty mouth!

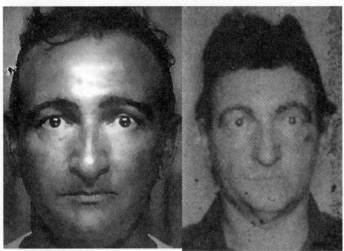

Once Lee had to reprove him, when Dave snapped at me, saying, "My God, woman, why are you such a prude?" Lee, who by then already cared for me, reminded Dave that I had wanted to become a nun, just two years earlier. That reached Dave, and he apologized. I dared challenge Dave to speak to me in the manner of the great thinkers and writers he admired, such as Aristotle, John Milton and Thomas Aquinas. Dave had yearned to become a legitimate priest and never gave up hoping that somehow he might still find a way. As I was a fellow Catholic, but had renounced my faith, Dave insisted that I listen to him about his religious beliefs. He never knew that some of his arguments eventually helped me return to a belief in God. By then, he'd been murdered.

Several times, Dave treated Lee and me to brilliant discourses. He stunned our young minds as a devious rhetorician, an erudite apologist for the Catholic Church, a medic, a probing psychologist, a social critic with dark, futuristic visions of tomorrows that turned out to be, unfortunately, pretty accurate. When Dave was thinking loftily, Lee and I felt we were in the presence of a genius whose wit, irony and epithets raised our level of being.[22] All the more sad, that he could also be shallow, brutish and foul.

Dave had his own excuses for his present condition. He spoke of turning points in his life that set aflame his overwhelming obsession with teen-aged boys (he claimed all of that was over). And I sympathized, because we were both renegades whose present lives were 100% unacceptable in the part of the country where both of us had been born and raised.

The importance of this fact should not be ignored. Like Dave, I was from the Middle West. Dave was a native of Cleveland, Ohio: I was a native of South Bend, Indiana, just four hours away by car. We spoke the same language, literally and socially. New Orleans was not only a thousand miles from Cleveland, but its Cajun traditions and Southern ways were very different from the ways of the Heartland. New Orleans, perhaps the most European of America's large cities, was filled with foreigners, was openly corrupt and did everything boldly. Its citizens were ruled under Napoleonic law and lived in parishes, not counties. In contrast, Dave and I thought of ourselves as "real Americans." You worked hard, didn't complain, went to church, minded your own business, and saluted the flag when it passed by in a parade. Hearing the National Anthem would bring a lump to your throat. Communists would go to hell, and so would homosexuals. Honesty and decency were paramount. Any radical deviance from "the norm" might be considered evil.

The cry of "the South will rise again!," flagpoles carrying the Confederate Flag, and shouts in Cajun French and Catholic Irish mingled with an influx of Cubans, Latinos and Mexicans pouring through New Orleans' international Port of Entry. The sweet vibes of Jazz and the mysteries of Voodoo promoted sexual freedom and promiscuity with every wild Mardi Gras parade.

In 1963, our Catholic-instilled morals and mores, streamlined by Puritan ethics, still dominated the two of us from within, so Dave had to provide excuses to me for his sex life. "I am cursed!" he insisted, "but, unlike you, I still trust in God." He would go on to say something like this: "God will burn it out of me in Purgatory. I'm counting on that. But He made me this way. I was born this way, and I didn't ask for this. I can't help it, damn it!"

I've been told I should have run for my life when I saw what I was getting involved with. But these people were patriots and heroes in my eyes. I had no "blueprints" as to what brave men, willing to die for their country, had to look like and act like. I'd seen plenty of rough and tough war heroes in the propaganda movies that came out before and after the big wars. In *Anchors Away* John Wayne played a hero who gave up love, family and a career to fight the foes of freedom. Audie Murphy – heroic and fearless – was a small man, soft-spoken and quiet – yet he was the most decorated man in World War II. Lee, I thought, rather resembled Murphy.

Who was I to judge these men, who were risking their lives for the sake of my country? That's the way I had been taught to look at such extraordinary men – I did not expect "the ordinary" from such men. So I overcame my inbred disgust with Dave. And I had to: we were working together, and the mission to kill Castro was important. Over time, Dave and I became real friends. I knew him well enough to ask him to draw his soul, which he took seriously, groaning over a sheet of paper riddled with dark, sharp scribbles. Dave had a soul. He'd devoted years trying to get ordained, and had failed, but this didn't stop him from shepherding young men into the priesthood or into military service. He tried to do good: he'd fly tramps back home when he could. Dave owned two small planes, and today I realize that I must have seen both of them, hangared at the Lakefront Airport, now that I know what I was looking at. I was also personally present, once, when Dave was using somebody else's (larger) plane.

Since I was then an atheist, Dave continued to do his best to argue me back into the church. Other factors pulled us together: we were deeply embroiled in a clandestine project, we had to rely on each other, we had to protect each other from contamination from a potent cancer-causing virus, and we had to make Dave's messy kitchen look normal after finishing our work there. Dave once told me, "I can't tell any of the guys I know about this stuff, because today, they might love me, but tomorrow, it can be different, and they could blackmail me."

WHY I'M SPEAKING OUT

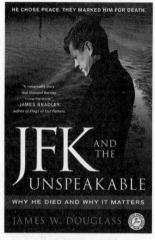

On January 1, 2008, James Douglass gave us the best book about the Kennedy assassination: *JFK and the Unspeakable: Why He Died, and Why It Matters*. Considering how our country has changed, the truth about the Kennedy assassination matters very much. It's the key to how our government was illegally taken over from within, and how the lies of the new rulers, covering up all the sins they've committed ever since, are created and defended. The cover-up is still in force because of them. I'm a living witness to that fact.[23]

TrineDay published the first edition of *Me & Lee* in 2010, including new information about David Ferrie. By then, I'd long left the country. I had to. I now only return to America on rare occasions when a bodyguard and/or lots of publicity make it foolish to target me. I also learned to have witnesses present at all times when interviewed, so I wouldn't be misquoted, having learned the hard way. I'll never stop defending Lee, but at one time, I was too afraid to do so.

Despite all my promises to Lee that I'd tell his children the truth about him, I'd originally planned to take my secrets to the grave, except for a few letters to Lee's family, to be placed in the hands of my eldest son. But things began to change in 1996. Nostalgia was the sole reason I accepted an offer to teach at a Louisiana university (Lee – I missed you so much!) And just "maybe" – I'd run into Anna Lewis or somebody else who would remember me and Lee from long ago (and I did!). Because of all the heartaches, though, I stayed away from New Orleans. But as my last child still at home planned her marriage, I dared to think about looking at the film *JFK*. Alone. So I could cry, for I knew I'd see "Lee" again … and not for the first time. In the college classes I taught, in Louisiana, I'd see young faces that looked hauntingly like my slain hero. Inbreeding and strong genes created many look-a-likes. Yes, friends and family, as early as 1980, knew I had worked with Lee at the Reily Coffee Company, and that we "rode the streetcars of New Orleans together," but they knew nothing more. Nor had I dared tell Lee's children, as I had promised, that he was, in his own words, "a good guy."

Now the time had come. When my daughter left for her honeymoon in December 1998, I wrote a tall stack of highly detailed letters. It slowly emerged into a book, expanded with photos, biographies of everyone involved, and supporting evidence. Today, it is called *Me & Lee*. That book also includes statements from my witnesses, who, back in January 1999, were still to be located. Originally, as the stack of letters grew, I felt I had done everything I could.

I was wrong. Watching *JFK* changed everything. It was sickening to watch. After all this time, with all the evidence that had to be out there, the real Lee Oswald had been cleverly hidden under mountains of lies! I was outraged. Oliver Stone's masterpiece sent a clear message. To remain silent was an act of cowardice![24]

But I was afraid. Could I overcome my fear? I laid out the evidence saved so many years. It took hours. I retrieved it from behind photos, from inside books nobody liked to read, and from five boxes of albums and papers about my five children. Some of that material existed in mere scraps, kept so I could construct a chronological record of every day I had known Lee. Just looking at it made me tremble. I could be killed for this.

At the very least, my children, who knew me as an upright, committed Christian, would learn that (1) I had a love affair with the accused assassin of President Kennedy (2) the mother who so often prayed on her knees had committed adultery only weeks into her marriage with their father. (3) I had been involved in a plot to murder Fidel Castro (4) I had helped develop a deadly biological weapon that was probably still being used to kill people.

It was nearly a decade before some of my family forgave me. Some never will. I'd eventually be forced to live overseas due to death threats and to avoid more hospitalizations for actual harm done to me. My reputation, my good name, and my comfortable future as a college professor were demolished. I'd be staring at poverty the rest of my life. But the truth had to be exposed. What traces remained had to be exhumed, no matter what the price. As for *JFK*, I've often been asked if Joe Pesci played the part of David Ferrie convincingly. To his credit, Pesci evoked some of the energetic essence of my old friend, despite his being too short, with a voice too high.

Warren Commission defenders who gripe about the film's inaccuracies should not be taken seriously. It wasn't a documentary. It *was* an eye-opening blockbuster, and the people of America responded by demanding justice for Kennedy. They also wanted to know more about Lee Harvey Oswald. *JFK* caused such a public uproar that the ARRB (the Assassinations Records Review Board) was created. New laws forced the release of truckloads of evidence that the ARRB's own Doug Horne organized and brought to the world in his five-volume masterpiece, *Inside the ARRB*. The new evidence has essentially exonerated Lee, opening doors to conspiracy theories that cannot be closed again.

The Warren Commission delivers its report to LBJ on September 24, 1964.

Even so, Dave Ferrie's personality and his true role in the Kennedy assassination were still hidden by Internet newsgroups fighting to keep him isolated from any association with Lee Oswald. John McAdams and his team of "Davids"– Dave Reitzes, David von Pein, Dave Perry, and David Blackburst (Stephen Roy) – posted a plethora of chatter, half-facts and facts out of context, overwhelming ordinary readers. Sometimes they posed as "fence-sitters," their writings carefully slanted to convince readers that only Oswald was involved in Kennedy's murder. Alongside them stand Larry Dunkel (AKA Gary Mack) and his co-conspirators, Dale Myers, Max Holland and Ken Rahn. The media that follow them and others exhibit a herd mentality, repeating their refutable lies without apologies, even after they're confronted with evidence disproving their statements. The latest approach is to mutter, *"Who cares? It was a long time ago!"* and *"Why does it matter now?"*

But it does matter now. Terribly. The Coup d'Etat in 1963 took control of an inconvenient two-party system to run its self-protecting corporate agenda, with the CIA, FBI, banking interests and the military-industrial complex cooperating. And when the Supreme Court recently ruled that corporations could, in essence, buy any and all political candidates through "donations," with no limit on what could be spent to influence votes, the American government became a prostitute whose services were purchased by the highest bidders.

In 2014, demonstrations of discontent were being suppressed – sometimes brutally – by heavily armed police. As Americans emerged from a devastating depression (misreported as a "recession") people were starting to wake up. They began to realize that endless wars, rising taxes, printing dollars with the value of toilet paper, long work hours, reduced benefits, the world's highest number of prisoners, and the world's most expensive health care system were the result of the government's disregard – even disdain – for their welfare.

Most people, as always throughout history, will just grit their teeth and soldier on. Many others give up trying to "get ahead" and join the growing ranks of the depressed: eat, drink and take drugs, for tomorrow, we'll still be poor! But there are a growing number of true patriots (currently that's a word listed as describing a "potential terrorist" by our own government). These patriots are getting educated. Their eyes are opening. They may be the only hope America has to regain her position as a champion of freedom, "with liberty and justice for all."

David Ferrie's story has been ignored as much as possible. My friend's life story is presented by Mr. Roy and his associates as a broken man of questionable sanity in his last days, with no connection to Kennedy's assassination or to any legitimate cancer research. My friend is said to have died of natural causes. My friend's death supposedly had no significance or meaning. But just as *Me & Lee* changed everything for thousands of readers, breaking down the walls of prejudice that once bricked away the real Lee Harvey Oswald from the world, it is my hope that the real David Ferrie will come to life before your eyes. That you will recognize the importance of his amazing and tragic life. Since the real Lee Oswald has been revealed to the world, flowers are beginning to appear on his grave – a grave once reviled and used as a urinal. On Nov. 23-24, 2013, the 50th Anniversary, over 50 people placed flowers or messages on Lee's grave,

Nov. 23/24, 2014: Lee Oswald's grave was honored.

and Hy McEnery, a former Marine and Green Beret, now a Chaplain, flew in from New Orleans to give Lee a long-awaited memorial Service, with Robert Groden and myself as speakers.

I think it fitting that Lee is, ironically, buried at "Arlington." As for David Ferrie, his grave at St. Bernard Memorial Gardens in St. Bernard Parish, Louisiana is just as humble. He purchased his own grave site, far from his family, who were deeply ashamed of him. Perhaps, after reading this book, Dave's family will have a better opinion of him.

Nevertheless, I will not cover up some sordid facts. Dave stalked and seduced men and teen-aged boys. "I commit mortal sins," he told me. "Problem is, I don't give a damn, until afterwards. It's always afterwards." Dave's feeble attempts at self-reform were tragic, not pitiful, because he understood who he was, so he never gave up trying to return to a position of grace with God. But yes, it was always "afterwards."

I don't remember nearly as much about Dave, after all these years, as I once did, such as precisely what words he said, in contrast to the details I remember about Lee. I was in love with Lee. I knew and believed he gave his life for Kennedy's sake, so I strove to remember every word he ever said to me, especially because he'd asked me to someday tell his wife and children who he really was. Because Lee became the only accused assassin of Kennedy, I swore not to forget.

With Dave, it was different. I avoided thinking about him for years. Then I realized how inextricably linked he was to Lee, and that it was important to review what I could remember. It turned out to be a lot. I was able to reconstruct almost everything. Of course I made some errors, but with time, I've been able to construct a good chronology of his life, to share with you. The words to some of our conversations returned to my thoughts, almost as vivid as if yesterday – aided by saved lecture notes and other memorabilia. I had also saved scraps of quotations, some diary entries, a wooden nickel, and other bits and pieces. I, as do quite a few others, have been gifted with what some call a phenomenal memory. I see highly detailed pictures in my mind, reproducing whole days of my life, from my memory banks.

Dave's story had to be told. By 1962, Dave, who had tried so desperately to be a good man, found himself publicly disgraced (for good reason). Distrusted and avoided by the nice folks in town, nevertheless, Dave's considerable talents and abilities were still highly valued. The trouble was, his talents and abilities were highly valued by the wrong people. I have written this book for the sake of my old friend. It was also written for my country and for you. I only ask that you judge for yourself who David Ferrie really was.

One of the last photos of David Ferrie.

Endnotes

1. http://www.jfklancer.com/pdf/LBJ-Reynolds.pdf

2. The article, below, as is convention, presents both sides of the "Mafia killed JFK" argument, citing government investigation conclusions as why 'not' to believe in this scenario, since the government wants the public to believe that only Oswald was involved. In the book, *Me & Lee, How I Came to Know, Love and Lose Lee Harvey Oswald*, I present the case for Lee Oswald's innocence and his profound dedication to trying to save Kennedy's life. It must be remembered that the Mafia was the 'plausible denial' that the CIA could use to hide its own sniper team. If Lee wasn't caught, or if evidence mounted of his innocence the Mafia could then be blamed. Today, the press sometimes tends in this direction – the mafia did it all by themselves – rather than turn their eyes to the government's role. With these considerations in mind, the following quotes are offered:

" ... In 1975 and 1976, during the course of congressional investigations of the mob and the CIA, Sam Giancana was gunned down in his kitchen, Jimmy Hoffa "disappeared," and Las Vegas mobster Johnny Roselli – who had told Jack Anderson that Ruby was ordered to silence Oswald – was dismembered, stuffed into an oil drum, and tossed off the coast of Florida.

• In 1979 the HSCA concluded that Hoffa, Marcello, and Trafficante all had the "motive, means, and opportunity" to assassinate Kennedy.

• Hoffa had told a federal informant that he would like to kill RFK but that his brother was the more desirable victim because "when you cut down the tree, the branches fall with it."

• Marcello – according to Las Vegas promoter Edward Becker – once coolly explained why it was better to target JFK than RFK: "If you cut off a dog's tail, the dog will only keep biting. But if you cut off its head, the dog will die."

• An FBI informant testified before the HSCA that Trafficante told him in 1962 that the president "was going to be hit."

• In 1992 Frank Ragano, a longtime lawyer for Hoffa and Trafficante, told the *New York Post* that the two mobsters and Marcello had agreed to kill the president. Ragano claimed that Trafficante said on his deathbed: "Carlos f—ed up. We shouldn't have gotten rid of Giovanni [John]. We should have killed Bobby."

REF: Pamela Colloff and Michael Hall. "Married to the Mob." *Texas Monthly*, November 1998. http://www.texasmonthly.com/story/married-mob.

3. Thomas Jones. "Carlos Marcello: Big Daddy in the Big Easy" http://www.trutv. com/library/crime/gangsters_outlaws/family_epics/marcello/9.html

4. HSCA: Ferrie also had his Eastern Air Lines payment, a severance pay deal, in hand by then, of $1600.

5. FBI Report Warren Commission Document 75 pp 285-297 (~Nov. 25, 1963) FBI Interview of David Ferrie by SA ERNEST WALL and SA L. M. SHEARER at New Orleans " ... FERRIE stated that his present address is 3330 Louisiana Avenue Parkway, where he has been residing since March, 1962."

6. Edward T. Haslam's book, *Dr. Mary's Monkey*, explains how he discovered that Ochsner's and Sherman's search to try to stop an outbreak of cancer, anticipated due to contaminated polio vaccines, ended, instead, with a task to create a deadly cancer with which to kill Castro. TrineDay published the 2nd edition in 2013.

7. Stephen Roy, Ferrie specialist, quotation from Education Forum, 05 April, 2007, 02:40 PM. Roy, who used the pseudonym "David Blackburst" for years, has been writing a book on Ferrie for decades. He has arguably collected more information about Ferrie than anyone else. However, he never met the man.

8. Back to Mr. Roy, who told the public that I refused to meet him. Anybody who ever met me knows I'll cross oceans to work for Lee Oswald's exoneration. I offered to fly to his own town. But – as researchers Howard Platzman and Martin Shackelford can verify, "Blackburst" would not disclose to me where he lived. Mr. Roy also told me (and others) that he was entirely neutral concerning Lee Oswald, but this 11/20/2003 article reveals the truth: (emphasis added)

"Stephen Roy of Brockton, a former conspiracy theorist ... now believes Lee Harvey Oswald may have acted alone ... Roy said that after reading books about Ferrie – who was investigated by former New Orleans District Attorney Jim Garrison for his alleged ties to organized crime and Kennedy assassination plots – he became convinced Ferrie played a role. But when he dug deeper, acquiring documents through the Freedom of Information Act, Roy said, he found evidence that could help exonerate Ferrie ... Roy said he hopes his research will culminate in the release of a book he is writing, *The Ferrie File*. Roy ... interviewed more than 50 of Ferrie's friends and associates. Most of his interview subjects say Ferrie was not involved in any conspiracies, according to Roy."

Mr. Roy, who also never met me, stated I never met Ferrie.

9. Williams and Conway. "The Don Reynolds Testimony and LBJ." http://www. jfklancer.com/pdf/LBJ-Reynolds.pdf. See also: http://www.acorn.net/jfkplace/03/ JA/DR/.dr10.html

"Author A. Steinberg writes in his book *Sam Johnson's Boy* (1), "After 1961, Johnson was never observed promoting a Kennedy bill on Capitol Hill, and in private he had complaints about several pieces of legislation and legislative tactics." Frustrated, JFK was said to have told his wife Jackie on the night of November 21, 1963 that Lyndon Johnson was incapable of telling the truth. (2) But most importantly and crucial to LBJ's political future was the current Senate investigation of Johnson's loyal aide and protégé, Bobby Baker ... Burkett Van Kirk, minority (Republican) counsel, was convinced that Reynolds' testimony would lead to Johnson's loss of the Vice-Presidency, "There is no doubt in my mind that Reynold's testimony would have gotten Johnson out of the vice presidency."(6) Evelyn Lincoln held a discussion with the President, on November 19, 1963. She says she was told by JFK that his 1964 running mate would not be Lyndon Johnson.(7) Bobby Kennedy was said to be working secretly with Van Kirk for weeks, through intermediaries, to accumulate evidence of payola against Johnson and Bobby Baker, Johnson's former Senate aide. (8) "Reynolds was still being questioned at 2:30 PM when a secretary burst into the hearing room with the news from Dallas."

10. (Nov. 2003) "FRONTLINE obtained this photograph from John B. Ciravolo, Jr., of New Orleans. Ciravolo was also a C.A.P. member in 1955 and says he was in the same unit with Oswald and was standing right in front of him in the photo. Ciravolo identified David Ferrie, while former C.A.P. cadet Tony Atzenhoffer, also of New Orleans, identified Oswald and Ferrie in the photograph, and Colin Hammer, who says he served with both men in the C.A.P., also identified both in the photograph.

FRONTLINE located the photographer, Chuck Frances, who says he took the picture for the C.A.P. Francis also said that when he was interviewed by the FBI, he told them Oswald and Ferrie knew each other, but he did not tell them about the photograph. The executor of Ferrie's estate, as well as Ferrie's godson, also picked out Ferrie.

"As dramatic as the discovery of this photograph is after thirty years," says Michael Sullivan, FRONTLINE executive producer for special projects, "The photograph does give much support to the eyewitnesses who say they saw Ferrie and Oswald together in the C.A.P., and it makes Ferrie's denials that he ever knew Oswald less credible. But it does not prove that the two men were with each other in 1963, nor that they were involved in a conspiracy to kill the president." http://www.freerepublic.com/focus/f-news/1028134/posts.

11. Weekend search-and-rescue bivouacs were held in the summer months, as was this one. http://www.caprcs.org/documents/rcsfaq.pdf.

12. Taking Care of Witnesses: Hiding Their Existence from the Public.
Mr. Roy was heavily influenced, I believe, by John McAdams, who publishes Roy's writings through Dave Reitzes. McAdams has always advertised Lee Oswald as Kennedy's killer. Hiding or discrediting new evidence and new witnesses in the case is common.

Debra Conway withheld evidence that I had living witnesses, even though

Dr. Howard Platzman, author, Debra Conway, Martin Shackelford, Anna Lewis. (Jan. 2000).

she filmed one of them herself for us, when she attended a conference I held in New Orleans right after New Year's Day, 2000. Conway withheld a film of one of my witnesses that the TV program *Sixty Minutes* had requested – a film that belonged to me. She gave up the film only when faced with a lawsuit and only after her attempts to silence my witness (Anna Lewis) had failed. Researcher Martin Shackelford confirmed these facts: he had emails from Anna complaining that Conway pressured her to recant.

As for me, suddenly my teaching skills at the University of Louisiana at Lafayette were no longer wanted. I was forced to move and start teaching at a Christian prep school in Dallas.

But Anna had it much worse. She was told that Family Services would be contacted to take her brain-damaged son from her care if she didn't recant and say she never knew me. Anna was so intimidated that she refused to be filmed again, so *Sixty Minutes* had no access to her. Nevertheless, Anna refused to recant.

Next, Conway revealed Anna's current name – Anna Vincent – after promising she would not, making it easy to locate her in the small town where she lived. It was no surprise that Anna lost her job. It would be a year and a half before they took her back. I now realized I had to protect my other witnesses from intimidation, so I refused to reveal their locations. I had their permission to use the audio tapes and photos they had already provided. That was enough.

13. Joan Mellen recognizes Martin's importance in the case. See Ch 5: "The Banister Menagerie" in her book *A Farewell to Justice*, Potomac Books.

14. The library card incident will be discussed in full later in this book.

15. http://en.wikipedia.org/wiki/List_of_people_involved_in_the_trial_of_Clay_Shaw accessed 1/12/2014.

16. http://www.mtgriffith.com/web_documents/justfacts.htm.

17. http://www.flickr.com/photos/isle_of_paradise/6428454755/ This is just one of many similar articles available.

18. Nodule 24. Coup D'Etat in America, A. J. Weberman.

19. http://ajweberman.com/.

20. Their personal statements are available on request but are to be kept private.

21. See Dr. Richard Charnin's important work at his blog, http://richardcharnin. wordpress.com/category/jfk/ (accessed Jan. 5, 2014) and at http://richardcharnin. wordpress.com/2013/10/14/jfk-witness-deaths-graphical-proof-of-a-conspiracy/.

22. Ferrie, seducer of teen-aged boys, mafia pilot, private investigator and anti-Castro activist – was not known to those persons as Ferrie the linguist/dialectician/philosopher/futurist/cancer researcher. I saw all sides of the man.

23. Both before and after the filming of the History Channel documentary, "The Love Affair," in 2003, I was threatened, robbed, and ended up hospitalized due to four auto "accidents." Twice I reported being harassed by a van that followed me and finally hit me, and once I reported a threat by phone I received at 5:30 AM via an early morning email to friends: they told me, "Don't be paranoid!" So I went on to work. I was struck that night when a black van forced a car against me, and once

again I landed in the hospital. For years after I spoke out, my mail was opened, the steel doors of my mailboxes in apartment complexes were ripped off, I received hate mail, and finally, the History Channel began airing (and still does!) an Internet video about Kennedy assassination conspiracy theories where they say I claimed to have helped invent AIDS. I receive death threats from that source alone, but the History Channel has ignored my requests to remove me from that video.

Due to such harassment and all the so-called "accidents" I was forced to flee overseas, on crutches. In the end, I was threatened so severely that eventually I applied for political asylum. As a citizen of the US I was told I'd be immediately deported but after Hungary would not take me back (proving I had been threatened there – EU law required political asylum cases to be handled in the first EU country of entry – but I had fled Hungary due to death threats there. I was allowed to stay for over ten and a half months in Sweden with the deportation order suspended. Critics err when they say I was forced to leave. I could have filed two more appeals and gained more time: some appeals are not settled for years).

But I left of my own free will without filing an appeal, because by then family and friends obtained places where I could stay safely overseas. I have been living overseas ever since, relying on donations to help with medical and heating bills that my small pension can't cover. No Medicare is available overseas.

24. I also realized there were so many lies out there that my son would not be able to adequately defend the book. So I wrote a second book, *Comrade Lee* – renamed *Lee, My Love* by my London-based literary agent. It was filled with utter nonsense, but I had heard horror stories about stolen manuscripts in the Kennedy assassination saga. I hoped the teaser book would open a door with honest publishers, at which time I'd show them the evidence and tell them what more was available. My agent, however, wrecked those plans when he erased the electronic links (in bold face) to the real book. A hint of the electronic link security I attempted, to protect the real book, exists on the cover page of the teaser manuscript. After my agent was fired for this and other hi-jinks, such as claiming that I was hiding in Europe (ironically, today I *am* incognito in Europe!) , I was grateful when Dr. Howard Platzman, using my emails, tried to write a version that would take the place of the teaser book (*Deadly Alliance*). As I was correcting that book due to its numerous errors, since Platzman lived in New Jersey and I was living in Dallas, Platzman gave a partially corrected copy of the manuscript to a researcher posing as our friend – Debra Conway. *Deadly Alliance* was never fully corrected for errors or completed, but it has been used by McAdams, Conway and David Lifton to try to claim I changed my story where certain details now differ from *Me & Lee*, even though my own pages of that manuscript carry massive corrections, of which Conway was aware, since a few of the pages she had copied were also marked, sometimes entirely filling the margins. A two-volume book published in 2005 on my birthday, without my knowledge, by Harrison E. Livingstone, constituted most of the original manuscript I'd written for my son via a stack of letters, with much supporting evidence and speculations from outside sources added. Because Livingstone would not allow me to view his final edit of that book, I stopped its publication. I estimate that only 80 copies of the book published by Livingstone were ever printed.

Last Call

LATE NOVEMBER 1963

David was now reluctant to call me until he exhausted all other options. He no longer trusted the special mafia phone line he set up for the three of us.

I cannot again write of all that I went through. It is in my book, *Me & Lee*. In my depression and shock, I kept no initial records of those last efforts of my friend to guide and protect me. In this book, I'll describe Dave's first phone call to me after Lee was arrested later, but here, I wish to elaborate on what was probably his third call, because it shows how closely David Ferrie, Lee Oswald and I interacted with each other and those around us.

I believe this call came late in the evening, but I simply can't remember the time. However, what I write here could not have happened prior to this date, after reading all the witness statements regarding Dave's frantic search for the medical library card.

As always at PenChem, it was my job to close the lab down. It was after 5:00, but I was still busy trying to make up for my poor work that day. And yesterday. Lee had been killed just two days ago. Seeing him die had plunged me into a darkness from which I was only now emerging. I literally cannot recall how I had survived the past 48 hours. My last coherent memory was screaming and vomiting when I saw Lee murdered. Only now – two days later – did I begin to see my own hands in front of my face.

Now I was outside, standing by the compressed gas tanks again, anxiously waiting for Dave's scheduled call. When the phone rang, Dave's voice came at me like a sledgehammer.

"Do you have my library card?" he demanded, in a frantic voice. "Jackass Martin called the police and told them Hector had my library card!" Then it struck me, in the blink of an eye.

Dave wasn't talking about his New Orleans public library card. He had ceased to use that card, since he had an extensive private library of his own and had been borrowing only from medical and legal libraries for the past few years. Dave had to be talking about the special library card he used to get into Tulane's medical library. Busy himself, now, on so many fronts, Dave had given the card to me to use, until I would be issued my own in the fall, as a student at Tulane Medical School.

Dave's card had been issued by the Ochsner Clinic for his use at Tulane, and for any "associates" he might place on a list. The card only carried a number, but a call to Ochsner Clinic would reveal my name and any other name that Dave or Ochsner had ever listed as an "associate." We could all be exposed! The Project could be exposed!

I was no longer using Dave's card regularly – that's how the problem started. On one occasion, when I met Lee at Palmer Park, we had played a game of chess, which we were forced to resume later at Thompson's Restaurant. But I arrived at Thompson's first, carrying medical journals that needed to be returned to Tulane's medical library. There, David Lewis, who also played chess, challenged me to a game. I had wanted to try out a new strategy to clobber Lee, so I told David we could resume the game Lee and I had started, to see how he would do. At the same time, I could test my new strategy, to see if it would defeat David.

When Lee arrived, I was about to wallop David Lewis, who was protesting that he had started one pawn down. Because David wanted to play a second game from scratch, I asked Lee if he would go on ahead to Tulane and return the medical journals for me. I'd join him there as soon as I finished walloping Dave again. Laughing, Lee agreed (he was in a merry mood, seeing David sweating over the game). "Here's Dave's library card," I told Lee, handing him the medical library card and the journals. "I want you to keep it from now on."

By then, I had been at Tulane's Medical library so many times that all I had to do was sign the card's number, which I knew by heart, to check out anything from the stacks. Nobody asked to look at the card anymore. If Lee kept the card, he could hand in journals and books for me anytime. But later, when I met him at Tulane's library, Lee handed the card back.

"I don't mind being your slave, hauling your books back and forth," Lee told me. "I don't mind climbing Mount Everest for you, or swimming the length of the Pacific Ocean for you. But the card's a link to Ochsner. I shouldn't be carrying it around."

He then took on the voice of The Scarlet Pimpernel. "Good Gawd, Lady Blakeney!" he drawled, "I'm demned stupid about all that medical stuff, you know. Why, I can scarcely tie my own cravat! So I shan't be seen in the medical library very often." As Lee and I laughed, we agreed that we should only meet in the music listening rooms at Tulane's main library.

All of this came to me in an instant. And with the memory of Lee's laugh, I could not keep my voice steady. Almost gagged by my emotions, I managed to tell Dave what had happened. After a pause, as it all sank in, Dave simply exploded. "That idiot, David Lewis!" Dave fumed, "That blundering fool! So he was there! He was there when you gave Lee that card. *'Here's Dave's library card, honey!'* he mocked. "*He doesn't need it back!* And so you drooled, to your One and Only – and gave me a nervous breakdown!"

"I'm sorry!" I snapped. "It was Lewis who broke his promise not to talk to Jackass!"

"And then Martin told the police," Dave said. "Because Banister put him in the hospital, for shooting off his mouth. He's mad as hell at us. So – do you have it?" Dave demanded. "I've even been to Hector's apartment. It wasn't there!"

"I have it," I replied. "I'm sorry. I forgot to give it back, that last day, when Ochsner gutted me. And I never saw you again."

"I want you to burn it!" Dave demanded. "Right now! While I'm on the phone!" Here I was, standing between a huge liquid nitrogen tank and a liquid oxygen tank, with "No Smoking" signs posted all around. I described the scene to Dave over the phone.

"Then dissolve it in sulfuric acid!" he commanded. I agreed to do just that, though I actually just ripped it into tiny pieces and buried it in the sand under a pine tree.

"Thanks, J," Dave said, sounding a bit more relieved. "I'm okay now. I'll deny knowing anything about the card."

What we talked about after that was much harder to handle.

My life was saved, I believe, due to the combined efforts of Lee, Dr. Sherman, and Dave, and because of the fact that Carlos Marcello knew I couldn't remember a face – for the life of me. Frankly, at this point, I couldn't remember my right hand from my left.

In this terrible call, Dave began by bursting in tears, insisting that Jack Ruby never wanted to shoot Lee. He was forced to, Dave said, "or they would have cut off every protruding part of his body and fed it to his own dogs." Dave tried to comfort me then, for I was shaking all over. When we both had better control of ourselves, Dave

31

was intent on convincing me that Jack's shooting Lee was almost a mercy killing, because of what his captors and the CIA intended to do to him to get him to talk. Dave went to such lengths trying to excuse Ruby, I now know, because he thought I knew him. I did, but I didn't know it. I'd met him not once but twice. He obviously liked Lee, and had known him since he was a boy. But neither Lee nor Dave had ever told me that Jack Ruby and Sparky Rubenstein were the same person.

When I saw Lee shot, I could not see the assassin's face, and after that event, I could not bear to read another newspaper.

Next, Dave told me to brace myself, because he had found out details about what had happened to Lee when he was in custody. Dave said Lee was "given CPR – Dallas Police style." Lee's chest had been pumped up and down – after the gunshot wound! Then they struck blows against his side, where the bullet had entered, to try to get him to confess, and to make certain he would bleed to death. Dave then told me more. He had found out details about what had happened to Lee when he was in custody. Cuts, a huge bruise under his arm … bruises on his back. Some came from his beating in the Texas Theater. Others came later. Dave was an expert at analyzing autopsies. He knew Lee had been tortured.

Finally, we knew the call had to end.

"I can't talk to you again, J," Dave said. "You know that. You know why. But I think one day you will turn to God again. And if you do, pray for me. I never had a child," he said, rather sadly. "My brother – I always wanted to be like my brother. That's why I wanted to be a fighter pilot. And look at all the kids he has. What I would have done –" Dave's voice cracked with emotion, "God, what I would have done to have his life! In some ways, J," he said, "You've been my little girl. Don't laugh."

I was silent, as a sense of our loss began building up inside.

"Now, J," said Dave, "listen up. For all of our own good, we must never, ever, speak to each other again. Trafficante insists that you keep your head down. You must become a 'vanilla girl.' Smell sweet, eat curds and whey, sit on your tuffet, and never again use your bright little head for anything, if you expect to stay alive."

I told him I wanted to die.

"Then who's going to tell June and Rachel that their daddy didn't kill Kennedy?" Dave argued. "Frosty, the Snowman?" Dave made a grunt. "Even my friend, the Puppeteer, thinks Lee killed the Chief."

My maiden name, Dave stressed, must not be seen in the papers. It was bad enough that "Mary," "Ferrie" and "Vary" had ever been spoken, but we were all in danger now.

"I stuck out my neck again, by calling you," Dave said. "And I'm worried about how long I might be hanging around in this world. It's getting uglier every day ... notice?"

"Well, thank you for calling," I said, in a flat voice.

"You are really out of it, aren't you?" Dave snapped, disgusted. "Go ahead, feel sorry for yourself. Think only of yourself. That's going to go down real well if Lee's looking down now at you, from heaven, counting on you to stay alive. Damn it!" he said, and I heard his hand smack against something hard, as he cursed. "Ochsner's kicked me out of whatever he's put Mary to work on, and she's being told to stay away from me, or else. So now it's up to you, J. You've gotta be that vanilla girl. Act as normal as you can. Don't get your name in the papers. *Don't!*"

"Thanks, Dave," I said. "I love you, Dave," I told him, and meant it.

"I don't believe in love anymore," he said, "but maybe I have to re-evaluate, after seeing you two. That's why I called," he told me. "Lee would have wanted me to. Now, throw away the Call Wheel," he said. "It's had its last tick-tock. Bye, J." Then Dave hung up. My extraordinary life in this incredible underground world was over.

David Ferrie at St. Charles Seminary

CHAPTER ONE

Origins and Early Years

"I read 'The Lives of the Saints,'" Dave told me, "when I was only six years old." (So had I.) "Did it do you any good?" I asked. "It God-damned well did!" he replied.

1894: David's grandfather, Patrick T. Ferrie, joins Cleveland's Fire Department and serves 45 years. He is Fire Warden the last 20 years of service.

David William Ferrie: The most attractive photograph of him.

March 28, 1918: David William Ferrie is born in Cleveland, Ohio, into a respectable Scotch-Irish family. David's parents were James Howard Ferrie (born 1890), and Burdette Couts Goldrick. James serves 23 years with the Cleveland Police department, rises to the rank of Captain, and becomes Chief Detective, with a law degree.

1920: David's father, James, earns an LLB degree from Cleveland Marshall Law School (within Baldwin-Wallace College). David's uncle, William R. Ferrie, serves 50 years with the Cleveland fire department, rising to the rank of battalion chief. He retires in 1961.[1]

Oct. 30, 1924: David's only sibling, Parmely Thomas is born in Cleveland. David is six-and-a-half.

Young David's home, at 5411 Clark Avenue, Cleveland, Ohio.

1928: The Ferrie family moves to 17302 LaVerne Drive, Cleveland.

David remembered that his father said the Irish Mafia was better than the Italian Mafia.

1929-1932: David is molested by a priest at St. Patrick's Catholic Church, where he served in the choir and as an altar boy. The molestations, David told me, continued for several years. He was warned not to tell his parents, because they would punish him for lying.

1930: David becomes physically and emotionally ill from his experiences with the priest.

17302 LaVerne Drive.

> **Stephen Roy**: The family move brought him to a new parish and a new school, St. Patrick's. Evidence suggests that Ferrie may have been molested at that church, which may have had a bearing on his own orientation later in life.

1931: Unsuccessful in an attempt to implicate the priest at St. Patrick's in immoral conduct, David told me he was labeled a liar. He consequently dropped out of school, suffering from his first bout of alopecia and depression. He could not get out of bed. His father later wrote a letter[2] stating that his ailing son was treated with ultraviolet radiation and quartz light treatments for alopecia, which were not useful for that condition. David's thyroid may have been undergoing radiation treatment instead, since a thyroid condition is also mentioned (the father could have mixed up what the treatments were for).

St. Patrick's Catholic Church.

1932: David remains ill for about a year, spending much time playing the piano. A sympathetic priest, David told me, restored his faith. He practices on the organ at church, gains approval for his talent, and returns to school.

Big brother David with Parmely.

> **Stephen Roy**: ...At St. Ignatius High School, an all-male Catholic institution, he was a writer for the school newspaper, a champion

debater, and a budding actor. In the class play, a murder mystery, he played the victim, a district attorney whose murder is solved by a man named Gill! As he was given to signing papers with his full initials (dwf), he was nicknamed "dwarf" by a fellow Ignatian.

David makes up for his lost year, and does well. He graduates from high school soon after turning 18, along with his classmates.

Sept. 1935: David enters John Carroll University as a freshman. He is mentioned on p. 4 of the university's newspaper: "... Dave Ferrie and other Carroll frosh were Good Samaritans along the road to Tiffin a week ago Friday night..."

Oct. 30, 1935: *The Carroll News* says "James H. Ferrie Donates Altar":

> Police Captain James H. Ferrie of the Cleveland Police Force and father of David Ferrie, '39 has donated an altar for the Students Sodality Chapel at Carroll. The altar, which is strictly liturgical, is in solid black with chrome finishings. The top is of solid mahogany and weighs approximately one hundred and fifty pounds. The altar stone which is sunk in the top is one of those used at the Congress and was procured especially for the Chapel. The Credence Table, Sanctuary Lamp and the main candlesticks are being made to match the altar. Behind the altar there will hang a huge curtain on which will be suspended a large crucifix.[3]

Note: When David Ferrie was found dead in New Orleans, a curtain was discovered upon which was suspended a large crucifix.

Comments, below, by Stephen Roy, posted to The Education Forum on Jan. 19, 2005,[4] and again in his article on David Ferrie's life on April 29, 2011 (unchanged) represent his summary of David's experiences at John Carroll University, constituting almost the only exposure the public has had to David's experience at John Carroll U.

> **Stephen Roy**: Ferrie's first higher-education experience was at John Carroll University, a Jesuit institution. He was involved in the Glee Club and school newspaper, and again excelled at debate. But the school forced him to repeat a year due to certain emotional issues. They wrote: "Industrious and ambitious. Is somewhat socially immature. Is an enthusiast, wants attention and distinction. Wholly lacking in common sense; hard to direct or control."[5]

We assume this negative assessment comes from FAA records obtained from the university. Mr. Roy says David failed a year of college. Newspaper articles below described David as "Class of 1939" consistently. There is no hint of Dave's failures in these articles, which generally praise him.

THE CARROLL NEWS

The university's newspaper, *The Carroll News*, offers a comprehensive view of David's many talents and a glimpse of his popularity with both students and instructors, in stark contrast to the report received years later. *The Carroll News* describes David Ferrie as a normal, bright student:

Freshman Year:
March 23, 1936: David is a fund-raiser. *The Carroll News*, Vol. 16, No. 10, mentions David as Gesu Parish's "captain" in a fundraising campaign for university faculty housing. There are 23 parishes with captains in charge of fundraising throughout the area.[6]

May 20, 1936: The student body votes for David Ferrie. These articles appeared in *The Carroll News*:[7]

> (p. 1) "Dean Bracken Gives Medal" When the finals of the Freshman Oratorical Contest were held today ... the winner was selected by decision of the entire student body.... The contestants, ... were: David Ferrie, "A Great American;" Paul Cassidy, "The American Merchant Marine;" Mark Blinn, "An Appeal to Arms;" Richard White, "Politics in College;" and Carl Burlage...
> (p. 2):"Frosh Debaters Conclude Season" ...the Freshman Debating Society of John Carroll has just concluded a short but entirely successful

season. In the first month of its existence the society held a round robin tournament. Jerome Clifford and David W. Ferrie were the winners of this tournament...

Sophomore Year:
Oct. 9, 1936: David Ferrie is put in charge of a debate contest. On this date, the newspaper (Vol. VXII) praises Ferrie's debate team, saying, "On October 9, 1936, this organization held a banquet at Kent State University.... David Ferrie has been placed in charge of the [March 20] contest.... This endeavor by the Carroll Oratorical Society climaxes a brilliant season of debating by members of that society. Successful in home debates, undefeated on a tour of midwest universities, and now ready to play host to the most active debating organization in the country, it is fitting that Carroll students doff their hats to this smoothly functioning forensic group."

March 10, 1937: David remains in charge of debate activities. In his sophomore year, David is in charge of arranging the university's debate tournament, as reported by *The Carroll News*:[8] "Carroll to Play Host to Northeast Ohio Debate Tournament....When the members of the Northeastern Ohio Debate conference meet on the Carroll campus on Saturday, March 20, more than fifteen Ohio universities will enter representatives in the annual debate tournament. According to David Ferrie, Carroll sophomore in charge of arrangements.... Four rounds of debate will be held through the day..."

April 7, 1937: David helps run the glee club. *The Carroll News*, Vol. 17, No. 11, p. 2: David is a committee member of the Glee Club, in charge of obtaining patrons (advertising support). On p. 3, David is also listed as a "veteran" contender who must write his own five-minute oration and present it for the annual Oratorical Medal.[9]

Junior Year:
Dec. 17, 1937: David is a writer for his newspaper. In *The Carroll News*, Vol. 18, No. 5. David is listed as a feature writer.[10]

Jan. 19, 1938: *The Carroll News*, Vol. 18, No. 6. David is again listed as a feature writer.[11]

March 9, 1938: David becomes assistant director of the glee club and gives an organ concert. *The Carroll News*, Vol. 18. No. 9. As well as becoming an assistant, David is also shows his competence as a musician, as evidenced by this newspaper comment on p. 1, regarding the university's annual Spring Concert to be held May 8, 1938: "Present plans for the musical program include an organ solo by David W. Ferrie, one of the assistant directors of the organization."[12]

March 30, 1938: David continues to be active in debating and public speaking. *The Carroll News*, Vol. 18, No. 10: "David Ferrie remains active as of this date in the Carroll Oratorical Society and is expected to participate in debate tournaments. "It is presumed that the following students , active during the year, in debating and public speaking, will enter: Blinn, Burlage, Corrigan, Cosgrove, Deal, DeFranco, Dinmone, Ferrie, Fogarty, Fornes, McCaffrey, McGannon, McManus, Nichols, Osborne, Rambousek, James Smith, and Victory."[13]

So, who penned the statement, "wholly lacking in common sense; hard to direct or control..." that was obtained years after David left this university? Mr. Roy will hopefully reveal the answers when his book is published.

The Carroll News, Page 2, (Vol. 18, No. 10): David's sense of humor did not go unappreciated. "For some really amusing anecdotes, listen in on Dave Ferrie when he's in a story telling mood. The other day he kept us in stitches for over an hour."

March, 1938: David is appointed by his class president to head an important, historic committee for the university (p. 3, Vol. 18, No. 10): "For several years various persons have asked if there was any memorial to the patron of the school on the premises ... there was

[nothing] about John Carroll save an unreliable painting.... Mr. James Wilson, President of the Class of '39 appointed a committee headed by Mr. David W. Ferrie, with the following members: Philip Lawton, Gene Kirby, Paul Seliskar.... The statue will measure about seven feet in height, resting on a four foot pedestal."

David Ferrie headed the committee that made this statue of Bishop John Carroll a reality at John Carroll University. Rather than a full-length figure, which already existed at Georgetown University (also founded by Bishop Carroll), the university settled on a well-designed bust of the Bishop.

May 20, 1938: David is again favorably mentioned. *The Carroll News*, Vol. 18, No. 13. [14] Under the column "Double Talk," p. 3:

> FIRST, let's toss a great, big, well deserved bouquet at Father Kiefer ... and our own Glee Club for a most excellent concert. Many favorable comments, from both students and outsiders alike ... [later, at dinner] Dave Ferrie, local virtuoso of the organ, completely dominating the conversation at his table ...

> **Edward T. Haslam**: He entered John Carroll University, a Catholic, Jesuit university, where he did well, studying Greek, Latin, History, and Government with all A's and B's. [15]

> **John Carroll U**: John Carroll is a private, coeducational, Catholic and Jesuit university providing programs in the liberal arts, sciences and business at the undergraduate level and in selected areas at the master's level. [16]

DAVID TRIES FOR THE PRIESTHOOD

Sept. 1938: Instead of going on to finish his senior year, David enters Saint Mary Seminary. (In that era, a young man who felt a calling, or "vocation" could finish his college education in a seminary.)

> **Stephen Roy**: Over his two year stay, the rector ... considered [him] unsuitable for the priesthood: Brashness, a compulsive leadership complex, excessive criticism of superiors, and most important, he "came to be regarded among his associates as rather antinomian" (one who believes that faith is enough for salvation, that adherence to a moral code is not necessary.) He was asked to leave the seminary. The stress and depression once again caused an occurrence of hair loss.

> **Edward T. Haslam**: Ferrie later reapplied for admission, but Saint Mary's would not take him back. [17]

We don't know what causes alopecia to this day. David said that while he was trying to become a priest, his homosexuality became fully developed. "God created me this way," Dave declared." I couldn't fight it any more." [18]

1940: David's father rescues his 22-year-old son by getting him into Baldwin-Wallace College, where he had successfully attended college to get his law degree. David transfers over many of his credits from John Carroll. He needs very few to graduate.

Stephen Roy: [David] took a part-time job pumping gas and entered Baldwin-Wallace College, his father's alma mater. He was assigned to student-teach at Rocky River High School,[19] but he still felt a calling to the priesthood. He applied for admission to the Society of the Precious Blood at St. Charles Seminary in Carthagena. The war was heating up, and his correspondence indicates that he asked for a hurry-up admission to avoid the draft, while his younger brother enlisted.

David, who was about to graduate, feared he would get drafted before he could be accepted into St. Charles. He was not trying to avoid the draft out of cowardice, or a lack of patriotism, but because he still had a sincere desire to become a priest, as his record the next few years will make clear.

1940-1941: David is teaching at Rocky River High School.

Frances McKee

Edward T. Haslam: Frances McKee, supervisor, said at that time, "His interest in teaching students is very closely tied up with his religious faith." When questioned years later ... she was less charitable ... he was "the poorest teacher they ever had" [and was] "tricky, a bluffer, shrewd, and probably a liar." She added that she received "complaints about his psychoanalyzing his students." ... [but she never had] "complaints involving moral problems."

June 9, 1941: David graduates with high grades from Baldwin-Wallace College with a B.A. in Philosophy.

Wikipedia ignores David's B.A. degree: Ferrie attended St. Ignatius High School, John Carroll University, St. Mary's Seminary, where he studied for the priesthood, and Baldwin-Wallace College. He next spent three years at the St. Charles' Seminary in Carthagena, Ohio.[20]

HSCA: David Ferrie received his BA degree in Philosophy from Baldwin-Wallace with high grades, as indicated by these HSCA references: (24) pp. 18-19, FAA, vol. III, exhibit. (25) Ibid., FAA, vol. III. exhibit, transcript of grades from Baldwin-Wallace College, Berea, Ohio, June 9, 1941 ; lists all courses...

Fall, 1941: David, who has applied to enter St. Charles Seminary, is accepted into its special program of studies, overseen by priests of The Society of the Precious Blood. David is also involved in community service.

Dec. 1, 1941: The Civil Air Patrol is now an official organization; Ohio has CAP squadrons.

Dec. 7, 1941: Pearl Harbor is attacked. On Dec. 11, Earle Johnson pulls a stunt in Cleveland:

> Johnson … [s]eeing the potential for light aircraft to be used by saboteurs … took it upon himself to prove how vulnerable the nation was. Johnson took off in his own aircraft from his farm airstrip near Cleveland, Ohio, taking three small sandbags with him. Flying at 500 feet (150 m), Johnson dropped a sandbag on each of three war plants and then returned to his airstrip. The next morning he notified the factory owners that he had "bombed" their facilities. The CAA apparently got Johnson's message and grounded all civil aviation until better security measures could be taken. Not surprisingly, the Civil Air Patrol's initial membership increased along with the new security.[21]

Late Dec. 1941: David begins to take flying lessons sponsored by the CAP. He will remain associated with the CAP in this area until 1949.

1941-1944: David lives in "a Society of Apostolic Life." Members revere "The Precious Blood of Jesus," dedicate themselves to a study of scriptures and academic subjects, and serve the poor, living a life of poverty while practicing good works. For three years, David leads a strict, abstemious, Spartan lifestyle in a dedicated and sincere effort to become a permanent member, and then a priest.

> **HSCA**: "…[his] intellectual ability was satisfactory," [said] a spokesman for the seminary in Carthagena…. "But his actions and attitudes were not just what we needed in a priest. There was nothing serious or outstanding, either good or bad."[22]

June 1942: Parmely graduates from Cathedral Latin High School in Cleveland, Ohio.

October 30, 1942: Parmely enlists in the Army Air Corp on his 18th birthday and trains as a pilot. He will become a war hero. [Obituary, Jan. 1, 2013]: "Lt. Ferrie flew the B-24 Liberator in the European Theater for the duration of WWII. He baled [sic] out during one mission and sent his parachute home to Cleveland to his fiancé, Rosemary Catherine Egan, who had it made into her wedding dress."

DAVID FERRIE: AN INTENSE, EMOTIONAL MAN.

David's father, James, had written to St. Charles mentioning his son's medical problems, including a hypothyroid condition, which can cause emotional problems.[23] Later in life there is little doubt that David suffered from a hyperthyroid condition, as evidenced by "bug eyes" – exophthalmia. He also had high blood pressure, as reported by Dr. Richard Bagnetto, his physician in New Orleans. High blood pressure is a side effect of a hyperthyroid condition, and the exophthalmia and autopsy report[24] suggest David suffered from a relatively rare auto-immune disorder of the thyroid. If so, he likely tried to balance his thyroid swings with a thyroid hormone, such as Proloid, to feel better. This disorder, combined with the alopecia problem, could have influenced David's emotions.

Rev. Francis B. Sullivan, "... professor of theology at St. Charles Seminary (Sullivan was David's philosophy professor) feels Ferrie to be a preconditioned psycho, impresses people by pretending to be an expert on everything, definitely has a talent for character assassination...." (citation from p. 115, HSCA Vol. X part XII).[25]

The "character assassination" reference might have been related to David's telling me that he was sexually assaulted by an important priest at St Charles. If Dave had attempted to report the deed to higher-ups, this is where the accusation of "character assassination" might have originated. The priest was highly regarded, and exhibited great piety, to the extent that Dave tried to convince himself that this priest must still retain a high standing in the eyes of God. This fit Dave's "antinomian" code that faith and good intentions can save one, despite personal sins that recur after the sinner's best efforts to stop. David will follow his "antinomian" code throughout the rest of his life. This could explain the true reason for David's expulsion and the true reason for his consequent nervous breakdown.[26]

1943: Late this year, David learns that he will not receive Perpetual Membership in the Society. He is warned that he cannot become a priest without a radical change in his behavior, with more humility and submission to authority.

David described his years in seminaries like this: "My great hope was destroyed in a desert filled with narrow minds." His expulsions, he said, were the culmination of a series of inhumane punishments to "break" his spirit to full conformity. Upon being questioned, Dave bitterly described incidents at St. Charles, where he said a high-level priest demanded that he bow to the priest's sexual demands, masked as "acts of humility" – or face expulsion. David ended up needing psychiatric treatment.

1943-1944: David returns to the seminary after psychiatric treatment and spends a year "of horror" trying to re-establish himself, but the faculty votes to turn down David's request to return for his fourth year.

1944: This is when David's father, wrote to Fr. Rohling, rector of St. Charles Seminary, in his son's defense. The letter, obtained in 1961 by the FAA in its court case against David, mentions David's alopecia problem, and David's thyroid problems are also mentioned. Proloid, used to treat hypothyroidism, was reported by New Orleans District Attorney Jim Garrison to be among Ferrie's effects at his death (Garrison: *On the Trail of the Assassins*).

Nov. 27, 1944: David is told to leave St. Charles. Denied Perpetual Membership in the Society before the end of 1943, David reacts with shock to the order to leave the society. In his mind, he believes he has successfully met the relentless demands of a seminary life.[27, 28] David will retain his priestly robes, keeping them wherever he goes, the rest of his life.[29]

1944: Despair drives David to another nervous breakdown. He attempts suicide.

> **Stephen Roy:** Among other things, he had engaged in a "doctrinal dispute" with others at the seminary and actually caused a split amongst faculty and staff. When he was declined Perpetual Membership in the Society in late 1943, he had a nervous breakdown and was ordered to seek psychiatric help. By late 1944, he was again forced out, and suffered a full breakdown.

David said he was so ashamed that he tried to kill himself by hanging, but did not succeed. He was given emergency psychiatric care at a hospital, and the incident was hushed up.

Endnotes

1. Ref: article on David Ferrie's life, Cleveland Press, Feb. 23, 1967 p A-4.

2. To St. Charles seminary: see 1941-1944 entries.

3. http://collected.jcu.edu/cgi/viewcontent.cgi?article=1045&context=carroll-news (Retrieved June 12, 2013).

4 http://educationforum.ipbhost.com/index.php?showtopic=2890&page=2 (Retrieved June 3, 2013).

5. Under http://blackburstblog.blogspot.se/2011/04/david-ferrie-biography-part-1.html on Thursday, April 28, 2011, in an article titled "David Ferrie Biography, Part I" written under his name 'Blackburst," Mr. Roy posted the same words and quotations about David Ferrie at John Carroll University that he posted back on 19 Jan., 2005 to The Education Forum.

6. http://collected.jcu.edu/cgi/viewcontent.cgi?article=1054&context=carroll-news (Retrieved June 4, 2013) Vol. 16, No. 10.

7. http://collected.jcu.edu/cgi/viewcontent.cgi?article=1055&context=carroll-news (Retrieved June 4, 2013) Vol. 16, No. 14.

8. http://collected.jcu.edu/cgi/viewcontent.cgi?article=1066&context=carroll-news (Retrieved June 4, 2013) Vol. XVII, No. 9.

9. http://collected.jcu.edu/cgi/viewcontent.cgi?article=1060&context=carroll-news (retrieved June 4, 2013) Vol. 19.

10. http://collected.jcu.edu/cgi/viewcontent.cgi?article=1062&context=carroll-news (Retrieved June 4, 2013) Vol. 18, No. 5.

The Carroll News: Edited For and By the Students of John Carroll University
PUBLISHED bi-weekly from Oct. I to June I, except during Christmas and Easter vacations, by the students of John Carroll University from their editorial and business offices at University Heights, Ohio; telephone YEllowstone 3800. Subscription rate $1 per year.

Moderator: Prof. E. R. Mittinger Editor-in-Chief: Paul F. Minarik, '38 Sports Editor: Charles W. Heaton, '38 Assistant Editors-Bernard R. Sallot, '39; Charles R. Brennan, '39; Robert E. Tryon, '38; Martin McManus. Feature Writers-Jack Lavelle, '38; Louis Horvath, '38; David Ferrie, '39; Thomas Osborne, '39; Robert Debevec, '40; Valentine Desle, '38. Sports Writers-George Otto. '40; Joseph Follen, '40; William O'Connor, '41. Cartoonist: Norm Peritore '40 Business Manager: Armos J, Loyer, '38.

11. http://collected.jcu.edu/cgi/viewcontent.cgi?article=1111&context=carroll-news (Retrieved June 4, 2013) Vol. 18, No. 6 : same information as in Vol. 18, no. 5.

12. http://collected.jcu.edu/cgi/viewcontent.cgi?article=1075&context=carroll-news Vol. 18, No. 9 (Retrieved June 4, 2013).

13. http://collected.jcu.edu/cgi/viewcontent.cgi?article=1076&context=carroll-news (Retrieved June 4, 2013) Vol. 18, No. 10.

14. http://collected.jcu.edu/cgi/viewcontent.cgi?article=1078&context=carroll-news (Retrieved June 4, 2013). Vol. 18, No. 13.

15. *Dr. Mary's Monkey*, TrineDay, 2007, 2014. by Edward T. Haslam: from outline of David Ferrie's life, pp. 93-96.

16. Ref: http://www.jcu.edu/about/ (Retrieved June 11, 2013.)

17. *Dr. Mary's Monkey*, TrineDay, 2007, 2014. by Edward T. Haslam: from outline of David Ferrie's life, pp. 93-96.

18. I'm approximating Dave's words, made easier because we hailed from the same geographical area and commonly used many of the same turns of phrase.

19. Mr. Roy's statement that David was student teaching at this date, at this high school, is in conflict with reports by the HSCA. Until we have more information, we don't know who is correct.

20. http://en.wikipedia.org/wiki/David_Ferrie. But HSCA states David Ferrie received his BA degree in Philosophy from Baldwin-Wallace with high grades, as indicated by these references: pp. 18-19, FAA, vol. III, exhibit, transcript of grades from Baldwin-Wallace College, Berea, Ohio, June 9, 1941 ; lists all courses. Ref: HSCA, Vol XII "David Ferrie" : http://www.aarclibrary.org/publib/jfk/hsca/reportvols/vol10/pdf/HSCA_Vol10_AC_12_Ferrie.pdf (Retrieved May 10, 2013).

21. http://en.wikipedia.org/wiki/History_of_the_Civil_Air_Patrol (Retrieved June 1, 2013).

22. The HSCA cites: Cleveland Press February 23, 1967 Page A-4.

23. HSCA: SR-11-N-224, Dec.19, 1962, p.19, Ferrie was treated for emotional problems in 1944, FAA, vol. 2, HSCA: "Letter of J.H.Ferrie to St. Charles Seminary."

24. Ferrie's autopsy also revealed nodules in his thyroid: "The thyroid gland is nodular on both sides and weighs 35 grams. There is one large nodule in the left lobe of the thyroid measuring 1 cm in diameter. It is firm and gray-white in color and appears poorly encapsulated." Online Ref: http://mcadams.posc.mu.edu/ferrie_autopsy.htm "The *thyroid gland* has a right lobe and a left lobe connected by a narrow isthmus. The normal *weight* of the thyroid is 10 to 30 grams." Endocrine Pathology. See Appendix to view Ferrie's autopsy. http://library.med.utah.edu/WebPath/ENDOHTML/ENDO015.html.

Ferrie's thyroid gland was enlarged – a fact that should have been mentioned in his autopsy.

For more technical information, see, for example, "The link between Graves' disease and Hashimoto's thyroiditis: a role for regulatory T cells."

McLachlan SM, Nagayama Y, Pichurin PN, Mizutori Y, Chen CR, Misharin A, Aliesky HA, Rapoport B. Source:L Cedars-Sinai Medical Center, 8700 Beverly Boulevard, Los Angeles, CA 90048, USA. mclachlans@cshs.org.

Ferrie's autopsy revealed nodules on an enlarged thyroid – as found in Graves-Hashimoto thyroiditis. Thus, Ferrie could have experienced bouts of hypo-and-hyperthyroidism creating exophthalmia and high blood pressure. He may have decided to self-medicate, using varying doses of thyroid hormones, depending on his symptoms, which would indicate to him where he was in recurring cycles of hypo-and-hyper thyroid states.

Proloid was reported by New Orleans District Attorney Jim Garrison to be among Ferrie's effects at his death (viz: Garrison: *On the Trail of the Assassins*).

25. These records are widely available. This copy was accessed at http://www.aarclibrary.org/publib/jfk/hsca/reportvols/vol10/pdf/HSCA_Vol10_AC_12_Ferrie.pdf (Retrieved May 1, 2013).

26. A recent list of sexually abusive priests in the Cleveland Diocese includes one from the 1960's; surely hundreds of abused persons never spoke up. Some priests in this group committed suicide after their misconduct was revealed.

http://bishop-accountability.org/priestdb/PriestDBbylastName-L.html   (Accessed 1/29/2014).

27. Ferrie's regimen in both seminaries would have been rigorous and challenging, as this Catholic Encyclopedia article explains: "The ordinary working day is divided between prayer, study, and recreation. Summer and winter, the student rises at 5 or 5.30 AM., makes his meditation for a half-hour, hears Mass, and usually receives Communion. Breakfast is about two hours after rising. In the forenoon there are two classes of one hour each, while two hours also are devoted to private study. After dinner, there is about an hour of recreation. In the afternoon four hours are divided between class and study, and as a rule another hour of study follows supper. A visit to the Blessed Sacrament, the recitation of the Rosary, and spiritual reading take place in the afternoon or evening; and the day closes with night prayer. Thus the student has devoted about three hours to exercises of piety and nine hours to work. After six years of this mental and moral training in retirement from the world, and in the society of fellow students animated by the same purpose and striving after the same ideals, he is deemed worthy of receiving the honor and capable of bearing the burden of the priesthood: he is an educated Christian gentleman, he possesses professional knowledge, he is ready to live and to work among men as the ambassador of Christ." New Advent Catholic Encyclopedia, http://www.newadvent.org/cathen/13694a.htm.

28. HSCA Vol. 3, exhibit XX, Ferrie file from St. Charles Seminary, December 1, 1961. (Ferrie was described as "critical of authority," "careless about observing rules," "ignored authority," "indulges freely in criticism of his superiors").

29. FAA, vol. 4, Robey report, p. 10, interview of Col. Joseph G. Ehrlicher: "resented authority"(19) Ibid.and SR-1-N-224, November 19, 1962, FAA, vol. 2, interview of George Piazza, who told investigators "Ferrie is the type of individual who fancies himself an expert in all matters and, hence, believes himself infallible. To this end Ferric would express his philosophical ideas in no uncertain terms."

CHAPTER TWO

Taking Off

1942-1945: HSCA says David took flying lessons at Sky Tech Airway Service in Cleveland.

August 10, 1945: With David's father encouraging him to fly, David earns his student pilot license.

> **Stephen Roy:** He now secured a job teaching Aeronautics at the Catholic all-male Benedictine High School ...

1946: David's father purchases a brand-new Stinson Voyager 150 4-seater plane for his son.

His dad's extraordinary act of love – making a down payment on a brand-new airplane – went far to lift Dave's depression. His wise father knew Dave would do almost anything to keep it – including holding down a steady job. Dave told me flying was his passion – and that it saved his life.

1946: David continues to undergo psychiatric care, including hypnotism. He continues to teach.

> **Stephen Roy:** Ferrie ... developed a fascination with psychiatry (and in 1946, a fascination with hypnosis.) His depression cannot have been helped by the fact that, while he dodged the draft, his younger brother had been shot down over France and parachuted to safety and was honored in the Cleveland VE-day parade.

Mr. Roy is not being very charitable. First, there is no evidence that Dave's "depression cannot have been helped" because Parmely became a hero. Dave spoke of his brother with pride, even in 1963, after Parmely had ceased to have anything to do with him. Second, Mr. Roy says Dave "dodged the draft." But Dave's sincere efforts to become a priest were followed by a deep depression requiring psychiatric intervention. This condition rendered him "4-F"– unfit for military duty.

1947: David continues to teach.

Sept. 1947: David becomes a Civil Air Patrol Cadet Instructor at Cleveland Hopkins Airport, 14 miles southwest of Cleveland.

> **HSCA**: Ferrie was a Senior Member of the Fifth Cleveland Squadron at Hopkins Airport.

Early 1948: Aviatrix Jean Helen Naatz hires David as a trainee pilot for Jeda Oil and Drilling.

> **Edward T. Haslam**: ... [it was] a firm active in South America. As Ferrie gained experience flying, Naatz continued to be impressed, praising him as a gifted pilot. Ferrie was probably her co-pilot on trips Naatz made between Cleveland and Texas.[1]

> **Jean Helen Naatz** described David thus: ... an excellent pilot, and one of the best male pilots I ever knew.... His ability as a pilot was above reproach.

July 27, 1948: Parmely marries his longtime fiancée, Rosemary, in St. Patrick's Church, Cleveland. Her wedding gown is made of the parachute that he mailed to her after his successful bailout of his plane during combat. They will have six children, and a happy life together.

1948: David is fired from Benedictine High School.

> **Stephen Roy**: [... for,] among other things, rolling a car over in the driveway of the school and stealing school property.

> **HSCA**: ... he was fired in 1948 for psychoanalyzing his students instead of teaching them.

PRAISE FOR DAVID FERRIE'S YEARS WITH CAP (1941-1949)

> **James Olmstead** (1995 post): The CAP that Ferrie helped develop in Ohio was a vital link in the Civil Defense effort of the period. He was considered a key leader in the Ohio CAP.

> **HSCA**: Jean Naatz, an aviatrix of national renown, stated, "He had done more for the Civil Air Patrol than anyone else and built up the squadron to one of the biggest squadrons in the State of Ohio."

From this organization Ferrie helped develop astronauts James Lovell and Neil Armstrong. Lovell was from Cleveland and Armstrong took his first flight in Warren, Ohio, from the same airfield used by Ferrie. This same field by the way was also used by Ernie Hall, one of the first to solo after the Wright Bros. Eddie Rickenbacker, highly impressed with the effort of Ferrie in Ohio, was from Akron, which was part of the, Cleveland, Warren, Akron triangle, which plays a major role in other aspects of the death of JFK.[2]

> **Stephen Roy**: Col. Harry A. Webb of the Cleveland CAP and others found reasons to disparage him, [but] Naatz ascribed their disapproval to jealousy. Meanwhile, Ferrie, determined to become a commercial pilot, obtained a pilot's license, possibly taking advantage of the greatly reduced fee system then offered by the CAP.

> **FAA file**: FAA, vol.4, Robey report, p.9 (J.F.K. document No. 014904), interview of Colonel Harry A. Webb: [he] had ability to get affection of the cadets ... they would do almost anything for him.

Naatz said David's letters of recommendation were stolen out of pure spite.

MINIMIZING DAVID FERRIE'S INTELLECTUAL ACHIEVEMENTS

History, as the cliché goes, is written by the victors. David Ferrie (as happened also to Lee Oswald) has suffered from a minimizing of his good points, with an exaggeration of the bad, in government reports. Example: The HSCA stated that David Ferrie's education was "not extensive" though he was considered "intelligent, even brilliant."[3]

Dave was educated in an era when only 25% of males in the United States graduated from high school.[4] Here is what Dave achieved:

> (1) Five years of university and college education.
> Nearly six years of college-level seminary education (ethics, homiletics, apologetics, two yrs. each of humanities and philosophy, with four years of theology).

> (2) Training in avionic engineering and aeronautics.

> (3) Mastery of languages and linguistics, with fluency in a total of seven languages (Spanish, French, Italian, German, English, New Testament Greek, and Classic and Medieval Latin).

> (4) Trained cadets and soldiers in martial arts, first aid, search-and-rescue, survival, and guerrilla-style combat techniques.

(5) Obtained a B.A. in Philosophy from Baldwin-Wallace in Berea, Ohio.

(6) Pursued two+ years of correspondence courses in psychology from an unaccredited Italian college.

(7) Trained in insurance investigation techniques.

(8) Trusted to interpret autopsy reports.

(9) Additional proficiency as a professional pilot and as an instructor in English, meteorology and aeronautics (including teaching aeronautics at Tulane).

(10) Hobbies were hypnosis, playing classical music and cancer research

The HSCA's description of Ferrie's education as "not extensive" is obviously false.

1948: David takes over most payments on the Stinson Voyager his father purchased for him.[5]

July 31, 1948: (FAA records) David, flying a Cessna T-50, gets certified to fly multi-engine planes.

Stephen Roy: [The Cessna] … a plane often used by Jeda. Ferrie, now flying planes for Jeda on a regular basis, was accumulating letters of recommendation for his skill as a pilot, but the company was in

David Ferrie, possibly with his mother and brother, Parmely.[6]

financial trouble.[7] ... He was also chased out of the CAP for some unorthodox flying activities and taking a group of underage boys to a whorehouse. His father apparently hushed up some criminal charges over these incidents, and David again had a nervous breakdown.

Dec. 1948: HSCA: "Although Ferrie's exact movements are not known, it appears he had gone to Tampa, Fla., where he received his instrument rating at Sunnyside Flying School."

> (Former FBI agent) **William W. Turner**: In the late 1940s and early 1950s he flew light planes commercially in the Cleveland, Ohio area, and was rated by his colleagues as an outstanding pilot. In the middle 1950s there is an untraceable gap in his career. Then he turns up as an Eastern Air Lines pilot. Although he supposedly obtained an instrument rating at the Sunnyside Flying School in Tampa, Florida, there is no record that any such school ever existed.[8]

> **Stephen Roy**: By December, he was living in Tampa and experiencing signs of instability.[9] He claimed to be married with two dependents, but he was actually single and living out of the YMCA on Zack Street. There is an unconfirmed report that Ferrie, who had been under psychoanalysis since 1944, suffered a nervous breakdown while in Florida.

Mr. Roy fails to mention *who* said David was "experiencing [sic] signs of instability" in Tampa. If David had two "nervous breakdowns" in 1948, one must ask, *when?* In 1948, David acquired the respect and admiration of Jean Helen Naatz, who described David as an excellent pilot, and in July, was certified to fly multi-engine planes. Mr. Roy says David was then flying "on a regular basis" for Jeda Oil. How did he do that with a nervous breakdown? *"The definition of a nervous breakdown is to describe an illness that is so severe that it renders someone unable to participate in their own life."*[10] Mr. Roy reports that the other "nervous breakdown" occurred in December 1948, based on an "unconfirmed report." We need more facts before assigning two nervous breakdowns to David Ferrie in a single year filled with both accomplishments and scandalous behavior. As for the false information David gave, he probably wanted to hide what had happened in Cleveland.

And by the way, what is a "nervous breakdown"?

> **Medical code, ICD-9-CM**: "Nervous Breakdown": ... a vague term ... Nervous or mental breakdown refers to a sudden deterioration in mental and emotional function brought on by severe stress the term is currently

used in popular culture ... and is of little medical utility ... many medical and psychiatric conditions ... could be referred to with the term ...[11]

DAVE MISBEHAVES: CIVIL AIR PATROL

1949: HSCA: "In 1949, Ferrie left the Cleveland area after rumors, that he had taken several young boys to a house of prostitution, circulated through his neighborhood. Although Ferrie's exact movements are not known, it appears he had gone to Tampa, Fla., where he received his instrument rating at Sunnyside Flying School."

Stephen Roy: There is little known about this 5-month period in his life.

Records show that, while in Tampa, David worked part-time in training as an insurance examiner. Perhaps he picked up his Cuban-style Spanish in Ybor City.

Edward T. Haslam: In the first case, he appropriated a squadron airplane which had been grounded by the US Air Force and flew it, after dark and without landing lights, from Columbus to Cleveland. Identifying himself as a lieutenant in the US Air force during the incident got him into even more hot water. The CAP commander [Col. Harry A. Webb] tried to have Ferrie dismissed from the CAP, but the paperwork was "lost." So, Ferrie was still on their books in 1950, when two CAP cadets signed papers reporting that Ferrie, their instructor, had taken them to a house of prostitution in a nearby town.[12]

DAVID FERRIE IN TAMPA AND THE KEFAUVER COMMITTEE (THE SO-CALLED "MISSING" FIVE MONTHS)[13]

The Kefauver Committee was created May 3, 1950. Organized crime had become so visible that there was national pressure to form the commission, FBI Director J. Edgar Hoover did his best to shut it down. Since I had lived in nearby St. Petersburg just a few years after Dave had lived in Tampa, he felt comfortable talking to me about Tampa's Mafia, where Trafficante held absolute power. The city leaders knew it, but were "paid off," according to Dave.

At one point, Dave worked with an insurance examiner who was quietly looking into Mafia activities there, because a big-shot Mafia honcho, Jimmy Velasco, had been murdered. His killer was going on trial. Hillsborough County's corruption was getting exposed, and the Kefauver Committee could no longer ignore it. David said he was working with someone in Tampa who said Cleveland was going to be one of the cities targeted for hearings.[14]

Dave arrived in Tampa at the height of the furor over the murder. He was there during the entire course of the murder trial that followed. When his boss became "an informant," Dave learned a lot about the Mafia and became fascinated by the complexities of its underworld.

The Murder Trial: "On the evening of Dec. 12, 1948, Jimmy Velasco was shot five times with a .38 revolver and killed by an unknown assailant…. The gunman hit him in the heart, left shoulder, left side, left arm, and the left side of his head. Jimmy was the main political liaison for the mob, as well as a gambling figure. He made regular payoffs to Sheriff Hugh Culbreath and then-Mayor Curtis Hixon. Underworld figure Joe Provenzano was tried for Velasco's murder. He was acquitted on April 1, 1949. The murder remains unsolved."[16]

In Tampa, David learned how to conduct an investigation, for an insurance company. But he also learned how organized crime worked. Hired as an insurance examiner trainee, as a means to pay for more flying lessons, Dave was mentored by an insurance examiner who also collected information against organized crime in Tampa. This information was used in the trial of Joe Provenzano,

> **WHAT AN INSURANCE EXAMINER DOES:**
>
> "The main responsibility is to assess the validity of a claim against an insurance policy and determine the value of the settlement. *The examiner will conduct an investigation* and, based on the results, offer the claimant a reasonable settlement after liability has been determined."
>
> **Interviews:** *The examiner will interview the claimant and other witnesses to the loss,* in person or by phone. The examiner will also order records documenting the loss, such as hospital records, *police reports and credit reports where necessary.*[15] (Author emphasis)

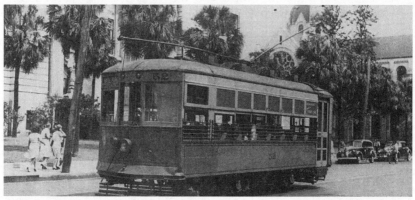

David attended daily Mass in the heart of Tampa's court district, a 4-minute walk from the YMCA on Zack St. 1941 photo shows streetcar, in front of Federal Courthouse, with Sacred Heart Catholic Church to the right. Hillsborough County Courthouse was next door.

the murderer of Tampa gang leader Jimmy Velasco. While David had mentioned his need for psychiatric intervention – the topic came up as we discussed our problems with religion (due to his encounters with abusive priests) – he said his life in Tampa ignited his interest in doing investigative work. David told me, "Sacred Heart [church] was filled with Mafia families."[17]

April 1949: David returns to Cleveland after a five-month absence. He has gained a life-long interest in organized crime and investigative work.

He hadn't planned to return to Cleveland for a long time, but Dave changed his mind after Velasco's murder trial concluded on April Fool's Day with an acquittal, due to a rigged jury.[18] Dave now feared for his and his family's safety, as well as for his father's health, and returned to Cleveland. But now he was hooked: David soon obtained work as an insurance examiner in Cleveland.

April 13, 1950: David joins the US Army Reserve for a three-year term.

> **James Olmstead**: [Ferrie] joined the USAR in 1950, served at Fort Hayes in Columbus, Ohio and/or Cleveland MI unit ... I don't think DWF tried to enlist during WWII, I think he was helping form CAP security considerations for Ohio airstrips. Cleveland was the starting point for CAP security operations prior to WWII, I believe that some of the pilots in the area recruited DWF. I have access to most of the 1940-1960 Ohio airstrips ... every chance I get I stop to look at old logs and talk to some of the "old" aces or those that remember them. Ohio had about 17 WWI Aces.

> **Stephen Roy**: ... he reportedly became an insurance inspector for two companies ... he was fired from the first company for using his private plane in violation of rules. He served the second admirably.

The HSCA calls David's position "inspector," which others have picked up to describe David's job, though technically, the position was "insurance examiner."

May 3, 1950: The Kefauver Committee is created. The Committe's hearings will be televised An estimated 30 million Americans will tune in to watch live proceedings in March 1951.

June 25, 1950: The Korean War begins.

July 1950: David's father, James H. Ferrie, dies.

Dave, seeking a commission with the Air Force, writes letters to the Secretary of Defense and Commander of the First Air Force, offering to train fighter pilots. Researchers have considered the possibility that this offer may have been interesting to the CIA.

> **David Ferrie:** There is nothing I would enjoy better than blowing the hell out of every damn Russian, Communist, Red, or what-have-you.... We can cook up a crew that will really bomb them to hell.... I want to train killers, however bad that sounds.[19]

Dave told me he tried to join the Air Force, but because of his medical records, he was turned down. He wrote these letters in an attempt to find another way to help in the war effort.

> **Stephen Roy** (posting as Blackburst to 'Bill B'):
> BILL B: With war on, why just train ?
> BLACKBURST: I dunno, that's what Ferrie seemed to want. He always fancied himself a teacher and flying instructor, and I guess he thought he could be of maximum value training fighter pilots, sort of in the Steve Canyon/Terry and the Pirates mold.[20]

August 1950-Jan. 1951: David offers to help an investigator for the Kefauver Committee in Cleveland. He begins to surreptitiously collect information for him while working full time as an insurance examiner. His job gives him access to buildings where hidden gambling is big business in Cleveland.

January 17, 1951: The Kefauver Committee begins hearings in Cleveland. The Committee, under pressure from J. Edgar Hoover, will disband in April. Around this time, David acquires information about Hoover's homosexual activities with Clyde Tolson.

April 1951: David applies for employment with Eastern Air Lines, using recommendations from other pilots, but (understandably) hiding his nervous breakdowns and his being fired from River High School.

April 16, 1951: Eastern Air Lines hires David. Though he will need additional training, so many pilots are engaged in the Korean War that there's a commercial pilot shortage.

April-May 1951: Eastern Air Lines sends David to Miami for training. After he completes a 3-week course learning how to fly large aircraft, he is assigned to LaGuardia.

1951-1952: After flying as a co-pilot for about a year, Dave becomes a pilot.

May 1, 1951: The Interim Report #3 of the Kefauver Committee is released.

David Ferrie's stock photo. He will never look better.

> The [Kefauver] commission's report on Tampa as one of the most corrupt cities in the nation has remained a stain on its history ever since.[21]

May 21, 1951: Eastern Air Lines receives Retail Credit Co.'s background, financial and character report on David Ferrie, with supplementary information going back to 1939. When Airline officials realize that Ferrie obscured his true background, they seriously consider firing him, but reports of his flying ability and good behavior make them change their minds.

> **FAA memo from G. E. Thomas to Captain F. A. Stone**: I have had him with a couple of captains here and their reports are nothing but the best...
>
> **Stephen Roy**: ...he managed to talk his way out of it.[22]
>
> **HSCA**: The New Orleans branch was advised to keep Ferrie only until a replacement could be found and a "close watch" on Ferrie's progress was recommended. Initial reports, however, were favorable. Ferrie was considered by his fellow pilots to be doing a good job, although he was "odd" at times. Eastern decided to retain him.

June 1951: Parmely earns his B.S. in Chemical engineering from Case Institute of Technology. He becomes a scientist, working as a nuclear energy system engineer.

Oct. 1951: David trains in Miami for ground school to fly the new Martin 404.

> **Stephen Roy**: Ferrie settled in to New Orleans, living on St. Louis Street, Perrier Street and Bourbon Street. One friend noted that he "liked the South but didn't like Southerners."

I never heard Dave say he didn't like Southerners. Most of his friends were Southerners.

Dec. 1951-Early 1952: David Ferrie becomes involved with the New Orleans Civil Air Patrol.

> **Stephen Roy**: Toward the end of 1951, Ferrie answered a call for "seniors" (adults) to help expand the New Orleans Cadet Squadron of the Civil Air Patrol (CAP) based at Lakefront Airport.

1952: David begins instructing cadets in aeronautics, including navigation and meteorology.

DR. ALTON OCHSNER, DR MARY SHERMAN AND POLIO

1952: Dr. Mary Stults Sherman arrives at Ochsner Clinic to become the head of the Clinic's Bone Cancer Laboratory. She will forge a strong relationship with Dr. Alton Ochsner, the Clinic's esteemed founder. Ochsner is a lung and heart surgeon with expertise in lung cancer. He works with many children paralyzed by polio who are now consigned to life in "iron lungs." Sherman, who also conducts surgeries to move tight tendons on the leg bones of children afflicted with polio, spends much time with Ochsner. One of only two members of his staff who speaks Spanish fluently, she sometimes accompanies Ochsner on his many trips to Latin America. Ochsner is creating a web of influence across the Americas and Cuba, receiving medals and honors from their leaders.

Polio victims kept alive by "iron lungs." The smaller units contain children.

Summer, 1952: The polio epidemic cancels the New Orleans Civil Air Patrol's annual summer encampment. David Ferrie remains in New Orleans with his cadets.

1952 CAP Annual Report: "High on the list of special activities held each year for CAP cadets are the summer encampments at Air Force bases. During the vacation months of 1952 42 cadet encampments were conducted at 39 bases. *All 52 wings, with the exception of Louisiana, which was in the grip of a polio epidemic, engaged in encampment activities.* Fifteen days long, the encampments supplied cadets with special academic and vocational training. Quarters, food, medical care and recreational facilities normally provided for Air Force personnel were provided..." (emphasis added)[23]

Here is where we learn that the CAP had summer encampment activities (the fifteen days would change to nine days). Cadets from New Orleans usually attended. The cadets were supposed to be members for 90 days before attending an encampment, but complaints that local leaders did as they pleased created a change in rules by 1956. This needs to be kept in mind when we try to estimate how long Lee Harvey Oswald was exposed to David Ferrie's influence in the summer of 1955.

April 1953: David receives an honorable discharge from the reserves in 1953.

1953: David becomes a Commandant in the CAP, according to an FBI interview conducted soon after the Kennedy assassination.[24]

May 23, 1953: David Ferrie is commended by Eastern Air Lines President Gen. Eddie Rickenbacker, a world-famous war hero for his exploits as a pilot in WW I.

> **HSCA**: Ferrie approached his job enthusiastically, devoting his own time to talking at schools and clubs to promote interest in aviation and travel in the Southwest area. In 1953, the president of Eastern wrote him a letter personally commending Ferrie's efforts on behalf of the company. This early record of dedication and competence may have accounted for Ferrie's longevity as an Eastern Airlines captain.

> **Stephen Roy**: He began making speeches to civic organizations about air travel to the southeast, and even appeared on a television program.... EAL actually thought he might be more valuable in Traffic and Sales than as a pilot.

But there is a notation on the file copy of Rickenbacker's letter to David that indicates Rickenbacker's praise did not primarily concern David's sales potential. The letter, "E.V. Rickenbacker to D. W. Ferrie, May 23, 1953," includes a mysteriously worded recommendation that Rickenbacker wrote onto the file copy:

This man's efforts bear watching and his qualifications justify his being used and helped whenever possible in line of duty – *and even beyond.* (emphasis added)

Summer, 1953: The New Orleans CAP participates in the annual Summer Encampment.

Typically, David devotes much time and effort during these encampment periods, now nine days long, using his summer vacation time from Eastern Air Lines to participate. David, a popular leader, is building up the CAP in New Orleans.

FERRIE, TULANE UNIVERSITY AND DR. ROBERT HEATH

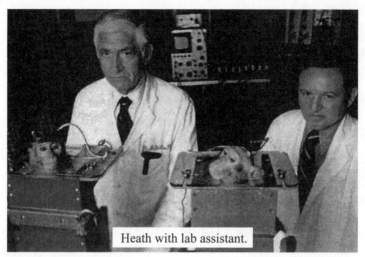

Heath with lab assistant.

1953: David audits a course in philosophy at Tulane in the fall of 1953.[25]

Don Gallant Interview, by Thomas A. Ban, New Orleans, May 7, 2001[26]

Gallant: We had an outpatient population at Charity Hospital ... where we ran a psychiatry service with LSU Medical School.... Tulane was more involved.... I was running this schizophrenic research unit at East Louisiana State Hospital up in Jackson, Louisiana...

Bob Heath was a very good politician ... and we had 120 patients, 60 male and 60 female ... not been treated by anyone, just warehoused before they came onto our unit. East Louisiana State Hospital was out in the woods, totally isolated, about 115 miles from New Orleans.... I used to go there twice a week and it took me about two and a half hours each way, five hours of travel...

Dr. Robert Heath ... was a charismatic man ... very impressive, a tall good-looking man ... *Time* magazine ... called him the Gregory Peck of psychiatry ... Dr. Heath ... asked me to start interviewing some of his patients with subcortical electrodes. The number of quintuplet electrodes would vary anywhere from 80, up to as many as 120 electrodes, implanted in the hippocampus, the thalamic nuclei, pre-frontal cortex, and the limbic system, of course. I had some fascinating experiences ... [also] there were fascinating people that used to drop by to visit us, because they had heard of Heath's research which had been mentioned in *Time* magazine.

One of those "fascinating people that used to drop by" was David William Ferrie, whose interest in psychology and physiology was endless. (Other university ties at Tulane and elsewhere: see July 23-30, 1960, and 1961.)

> **Fall, 1953: Stephen Roy**: ... during the same period [as attending Tulane] he looked into the possibility of entering the priesthood again at a seminary in Corpus Christi.[27]

1954: David begins studying by correspondence for a doctorate in psychology from the University of Phoenix at Bari, Italy, an unaccredited college.

> **1954: Stephen Roy**: Ferrie was nearly fired again after it was found that he had allowed a 15-year-old boy to fly on a pass as his "adopted son," a claim quickly proven false.[28]

1954: The New Orleans CAP holds its annual nine-day Summer Encampment. The 1954 CAP Handbook says: "... flight scholarships [can] entitle them to take actual flying instruction from local airport operators.... The Air Force is aware of the tremendous importance of an aviation-minded youth and is cooperating with the Civil Air Patrol to promote its cadet units."

> **Dec. 1954: Stephen Roy**: ...a CAP boy David trained to fly dies in a crash... Ferrie served with the Lakefront Airport squadron from 1952-April 1955, when his commander declined to renew his membership.[29]

David had been the boy's flight trainer. The boy's death was a scandalous tragedy. His commander did not tell David that he did not turn in his membership renewal material.

> **HSCA**: (A)fter one of the Cadets he was training died in a plane crash in December, 1954, Wing Commander Joe Ehrlicher refused to file Ferrie's request to renew his position as Commander, owing to public concerns about the incident. In April 1955, Ferrie learned that his application for 1955 had not been filed and was thus not renewed.... Unable to return to Lakefront, Ferrie was out of the CAP (Lakefront) for only two months before obtaining a request to serve as a summer session lecturer and aerospace trainer at the Moisant Airport CAP squadron.[30]

Tom Rozoff's 2007 photo of David's Stinson (now red and white instead of white and blue).[31]

In April, David discovered that his membership had not been renewed. But he was back as an instructor at Moisant by June 1955.

> **Stephen Roy**: When Ferrie went to Moisant June-August 1955, he added another dimension: rigorous academic standards in science, meteorology and aeronautics, and as one cadet told me, "He owned his own plane and would teach us how to fly," even though Ferrie did not get a flying instructor's ticket until 1955.[32]

DR. OCHSNER KILLS HIS GRANDSON

April 26, 1955: Ochsner, who owns stock in Cutter Laboratories (one of several companies the U.S. government licensed to produce polio vaccine), publicly inoculates his grandchildren on this date to prove the safety of the new polio vaccine. Tragically, the next day, April 27, California banned the vaccine when several children contracted polio after receiving it.

Eugene Allen Davis, Jr., Dr. Alton Ochsner's 30-month-old grandson, died of infantile paralysis (polio) on May 5, 1955. Dr. C. Harrington Snyder, who attended Eugene, insisted that polio struck the little boy by mere coincidence.[33]

Endnotes

1. Edward T. Haslam, citing the Southern Research report made on Ferrie when Ferrie petitioned to get his Eastern Air Lines job back in 1962.

2. Researcher James Olmstead, https://groups.google.com/forum/?fromgroups=#!topic/alt.conspiracy.jfk/aIzccIbaqdI%5B1-25-false%5D 10/06/1996 (Retrieved June 3, 2013).

3. David Ferrie and ancient Greek: The HSCA, composed of appointed members of Congress who were mostly lawyers educated at top universities before

obtaining their law degrees, were nevertheless unlikely to be able to translate Aeschylus or Euripedes from the ancient Greek, as Ferrie could, though they probably knew their Latin.

4. "In 1940, about one-quarter of U.S. males completed four years of high school, with the majority of males quitting school before attaining their high school diploma." Ref: "U.S. Education Attainment from 1940-2008 | http://www.realonlinedegrees.com/us-education-attainment-from-1940-2008/#ixzz1NH4GWmyf.

5. Based on David telling the author that he was initially helping to pay for his plane when he could, and that it was he who made the last payments "a couple years later."

6. Stephen Roy disagrees, though many of the facial features tend to argue that he's wrong. Roy says the woman is not Dave's mother. I saw no photos of her, so cannot say. Mr. Roy says the woman is wearing a C.A.P uniform. I haven't been able to find a uniform looking like this, and the hat she's holding is not regulation.

7. Post made June 20, 2000 to McAdams' newsgroup: https://groups.google.com/forum/?hl=en&fromgroups#!topic/alt.assassination.jfk/H5DWgF65p_4. (Retrieved June 4, 2013).

8. William W. Turner. "The Garrison Commission on the Assassination of President Kennedy" January 1968, *Ramparts* magazine. Date: reprinted 4 Aug 92 23:08:19 GMT: http://www.wf.net/~biles/jfk/ramparts.txt.

A reprint of the original article (all rights reserved) can be found here: http://jfk.hood.edu/Collection/White%20Materials/Garrison%20News%20Clippings/1968/68-01/68-01-002.pdf (Retrieved June 6, 2013).

(Retrieved June 6, 2013) Turner's work is called "outdated" but it was seminal in 1968. As a wiretap expert and investigator for the FBI, Turner's statement about the non-existence of the Sunnyside Aviation School in Tampa may have been prompted because of the school's having gone out of business, or changing its name, but Turner had the means and knowledge to trace such possibilities. David may have received some special training in Tampa just before the base there was closed down. In fact, his return to Cleveland might have been because the base was going to close down.

9. Mr. Roy does not offer any references to support this derogatory remark that David suffered another nervous breakdown in Tampa, in what he currently calls an unsubstantiated report.

10. http://www.anxiety-relief.org/2013/07/18/what-is-a-nervous-breakdown-definition-symptoms-and-treatment-options/ (Retrieved 1/25/2014).

11. "Some of the more common psychiatric causes of 'mental breakdown' include schizophrenia, depression, acute stress disorder, post-traumatic stress disorder, and bipolar mood disorder. Non-psychiatric causes commonly include glandular and metabolic disturbances (especially of the thyroid), infections, lupus, various cancers, a wide variety of neurological diseases such as stroke, multiple sclerosis, vasculitis, encephalitis, and Parkinson's disease, as well as side effects of various prescription and over-the-counter medications. There may also be complicating factors such as alcohol or drug use." http://www.mdguidelines.com/nervous-breakdown (Accessed 1/21/2014).

12. Edward T. Haslam, *Dr. Mary's Monkey*, TrineDay, 2007. P. 96.

13. From: blackburst@aol.com (Blackburst) Subject: Ferrie in Tampa, 1949 Date: 24 Jun 2000 00:00:00 GMT Message-ID: 20000624002334.05023.00000953@ng-ci1.aol.com … By the end of 1948, Ferrie's employer, Jeda Oil and Drilling, was in trouble and about to go under...He returned to Cleveland in April 1949. There is little known about this 5-month period in his life.

14. Purely by accident, David, Lee Oswald and I were discussing Ian Fleming's *Live and Let Die* – Flemings' second James Bond novel, when David told us that Tampa's Mound Park Hospital was mentioned in Fleming's book. He had that kind of esoteric knowledge. Dave then talked about Tampa, and, a little later, about the Kefauver Commission.

15. Job Description for an Insurance Examiner, eHow http://www.ehow.com/facts_5886413_job-description-insurance-examiner.html#ixzz2WWgZsQG1 (Retrieved June 7, 2013).

16. "Tampa in the 1940's" http://www.tampapix.com/tampa1940s7.htm (Retrieved June 6, 2013).

17. Sacred Heart's popularity with Mafia families is still understood today. Author Dennis Lehane (*Mystic River, Shutter Island, Live by Night*) is quoted by the *Tampa Bay Times* (June 18, 2013), concerning his character Joe Coughlin, Lehane's famous Tampa gangster in the next book. It will have more Ybor, some Davis Islands, Sacred Heart Church downtown." http://www.tampabay.com/features/books/in-ybor-gangster-tale-live-by-night-lehane-lets-it-rip/1256141 (Retrieved June 18, 2013).

18. David never named the suspect. I had to find the suspect's name many years later.

19. Available in the National Archives. Stephen Roy wrote, in 1999:

blackburst@aol.com (Blackburst)

Subject: Re: RP: Dave Ferrie told the truth

Date: 06 Jun 1999 00:00:00 GMT

Message-ID: <19990606102347.13714.00001546@ng-fv1.aol.com>

Haizen Paige wrote:>David William Ferrie was also quoted as saying: "I want to train >killers." …Train killers for what?… REPLY by Mr. Roy [as Blackburst]: "Ferrie, who had a long record of speaking in very grandiose terms, made these comments in a letter written in 1950, at the height of the Korean War anti-communist hysteria, 13 years before the assassination. The full quote can be found in the *New York Review of Books*, 9/14/67."

20. https://groups.google.com/forum/#!topic/alt.assassination.jfk/H5DWgF65p_4.

21. Kefauver Committee Interim Report #3 May 1, 1951 The U.S. Senate Special Committee to Investigate Organized Crime in Interstate Commerce. The Kefauver Committee held hearings in Cleveland between January 17, 1951 and April 1, 1951, when its commission expired, after gathering information and witnesses. In Tampa, Bolita's mob leader Jimmy Velasco was killed on December 12, 1948.

22. http://www.forumjar.com/forums/topic/David_Ferrie_biography (Retrieved March 3, 2013).

23.1952CAPHandbook:http://members.gocivilairpatrol.com/media/cms/1952_8D184B3F628D7.pdf. (retrieved 5/10/2013).

24. W.C.D. 75 FBI Interview of David Ferrie 11/25/63 by SA ERNEST WALL and SA L. M. SHEARER at New Orleans. http://www.wf.net/~biles/jfk/ferrie_FBI_1125_2.txt (retrieved June 10, 2013).

25. Reported by Stephen Roy/David Blackburst.

26. An interview with Don Gallant for the Archives of the American College of Neuropsychopharmacology. The annual meeting of the American Psychiatric Association in New Orleans, May 7, 2001. .

27. Stephen Roy, [as Blackburst], 12/14/06 McAdams' newsgroup. https://groups.google.com/forum/?fromgroups#!topic/alt.assassination.jfk/6hetWwLV2QU (Retrieved June 10, 2013).

28. http://blackburstblog.blogspot.com/2011/04/david-ferrie-biography-part-2.html (Retrieved April 10, 2013) (Note: all URLs are adjusted to '.com' for convenience, as the author, of necessity, lives in various countries).

29. Newsgroup post, Dec. 22, 1998: http://www.jfk-online.com/dbdfcapfile.html (Retrieved May 20, 2013).

30. This HSCA interview of a fellow CAP member helps verify how many times David Ferrie was lecturing at Moisant: SELECT COMMITTEE ON ASSASSINATIONS, Name Anthony Atzenhoffer Address Gretna, LA.

Interview: ... In October. Atzenhoffer stated that he believes that Ferrie was in fact instructing the Moisant CAP unit at the time that Oswald was a member.... Oswald was very quiet and was mainly friendly with Ed Voebel, who Atzenhoffer also knew. Ferrie was always around the unit during those days." Atzenhoffer also stated that the "experiments" that Ferrie tried to recruit CAP cadets for were supposedly to be conducted by the Medical School of Tulane University.

Interviewer Signature, Typed Signature Mike Ewing Date transcribed Jan 3, 1979.

31. Tom Rozoff personally photographed Ferrie's Stinson (now painted red, and in excellent condition) after it was located by researcher Stephen Roy in 2007. As of 2013, the Stinson is owned by LOMPOC, a pilot training and plane rental company in California. http://www.flylompoc.com/Fleet/ (Retrieved June 15, 2013).

32. Dec. 22, 1998, Stephen Roy, posted as David Blackburst. http://www.jfk-online.com/dbdfcapfile.htm (Retrieved Jan. 2, 2013).

33. The *Reading Eagle* newspaper, p. 34, May 5, 1955. http://news.google.com/newspapers?nid=1955&dat=19550505&id=GwcrAAAAIBAJ&sjid=TJg-FAAAAIBAJ&pg=2043,2589024.

CHAPTER THREE

David Ferrie Meets Lee Oswald

I gnoring or marginalizing witness reports and interviews, Wikipedia, Dave Reitzes (with John McAdams), Stephen Roy (with Dave Reitzes), Gerald Posner, Vincent Bugliosi, along with official government sites, have minimized the possible number of contacts between David Ferrie and Lee Harvey Oswald in 1955.[1]

> **Wikipedia**: After a Ferrie-trained cadet pilot perished in a December 1954 crash, Ferrie's annual re-appointment was declined. He was asked to be a guest aerospace education instructor at a smaller squadron at Moisant Airport, and lectured there from June to September 1955.[2] On July 27, 1955, 15-year-old Lee Harvey Oswald joined this squadron.[3]
>
> **Joseph Ehrlicher** to FBI agents: ... a record indicating that, "Oswald was enrolled as a CAP cadet on July 27, 1955, at which time he was given Serial No. 084965."[4]

But Lee had attended a number of meetings at Moisant *before* he decided to join. Previous to that, Lee attended numerous CAP meetings at Lakefront, then quit. At that time, he might have had his fight with David Ferrie (chronicled in *Me & Lee*) – it could have been later, when he attended CAP meetings at the Moisant Squadron. We know that Lee went through basic training for Cadets, which requires attendance at a number of meetings, because we have a photo of him in his Cadet uniform.[5]

Lee had to successfully complete CAP Basic to earn the right to wear the CAP uniform.

> **CAP Handbook**: Once ... passed, the CADET BASIC becomes CADET AIRMAN and has earned the first ribbon and the privilege of wearing the CAP uniform.... Cadets may work on getting their uni-

form once an application has been submitted. Only a complete uniform may be worn.

Jerry Paradis (CAP member and officer), HSCA interview (excerpted, edited for spelling): ...Paradis...stated that, "Oswald and Ferrie were in the unit together. I know they were because I was there ... I specifically remember Oswald. I can remember him clearly, and Ferrie was heading the unit then. I'm not saying that they may have been there together, I'm saying it is a certainty." Paradis stated that he liked Oswald, but that he was quiet.... He said: "I really only talked about flying with Lee.... I can't say how many times he came to the meetings, but he was there quite a few times ... at least ten or fifteen meetings."

Paradis stated that David Ferrie was present at all of these meetings, saying Ferrie never missed coming "and was always there.... Ferrie was a fairly stern, but generally likable guy ... these meetings with Ferrie and Oswald at the CAP occurred at New Orleans Lakefront Airport.... Ferrie and some of the others occasionally went to Moisant airport. He stated that Ferrie later left the Lakefront airport and worked only at Moisant with the CAP. He stated that the unit used to meet twice a week, on Friday nights and on Sunday afternoons."[6]

The photo of Ferrie and Oswald together was taken Aug. 7, 1955 at Abita Springs, LA.[7] Many such bivouacs lasted all weekend.[8] Held at Abita Springs, the event was located almost 65 miles from Moisant, as the Pontchartrain Causeway was still under construction. The photo shows five cadets wearing only t-shirts. All the cadets look dirty and sweaty. It has never been asked if Oswald

might have journeyed to and/or from New Orleans in the same car as Ferrie.

> **Stephen Roy**: In June 1955, Ferrie was approached by the Commander of the smaller (15-20 cadets) Moisant Airport CAP squadron to lecture the boys. On July 27, Lee Harvey Oswald joined the squadron.... Oswald apparently only stayed a month or two, and Ferrie didn't stay much longer, becoming peeved at having a girls' CAP group as part of the squadron. One cannot read too much into such an encounter with a 15-year old Oswald, eight years before the assassination...

But we know Lee wore a CAP uniform, the cost and trouble of which to obtain, back then, indicates his commitment. We know Lee joined the squadron, July 27, but he also had to attend enough meetings to be allowed to wear the uniform.

> **Stephen Roy**: ... in an October 1956 letter, Oswald said that he had been studying Marxism for "well over 15 months" – precisely the time he encountered Ferrie.[9]

Lee told me he studied not only the writings of Marx and Lenin, but also the writings of the great Founding Fathers of our own country, including the Federalist Papers, the writings of Jefferson, Thomas Paine and Benjamin Franklin, and such great classics as Hobbes' *Leviathan*.

> **Stephen Roy**: ... nearly everyone remembers a mesmerizing quality about him: He was very bright, well-spoken and funny, he could make complicated things understandable and he was like a buddy who showed great interest in the cadets. And Oswald probably wanted to be in a military-type situation like his brothers. His mother indicated that he leaned heavily in that direction. But why Oswald apparently quit after several weeks in unclear.[10]

Lee took a paper route to pay for his uniform. His Aunt Lil, Uncle Dutz and brother Robert also helped. Something big must have stopped Lee from attending after only "a month or two." Lee told me,with Dave present, that it was David Ferrie's physical assault that drove him out of the CAP. (However, Dave didn't sexually assault him.) By 1963, the two men had become friends. How, I don't know.

> **Anthony Marsh**: ... [in] December 9, 1978, another former CAP member recalled Oswald's participation in the New Orleans unit. Collin Hamer ... an official of the New Orleans Public Library, stated that he had attended "about ten or twelve meetings ... at Moisant ... during which Oswald was also present."[11]

Getting the Story Straight

> **Stephen Roy**: Ferrie [1963, post-assassination of JFK) ... spoke to Oswald's friend Eddie Voebel, who told Ferrie that Oswald had been a cadet in Ferrie's CAP squadron in 1955, and that he recalled Oswald attending a party at Ferrie's then-home at 209 Vinet Street.[12]

Lee described a house that did not resemble the one-story Vinet St. apartment. It was a much larger house, and Dave didn't live on Vinet St. until 1956. After Lee moved to Fort Worth in July 1956, he ceased to attend CAP meetings. The 1956 CAP Annual Report complained that, "While a three-phase training program existed prior to 1956 ... it left the criteria for advancement up to local unit commanders. The result was a program almost totally without standardization. Only the criteria for the award of the CAP Certificate of Proficiency were standardized – completion of the National Examination and attendance at one summer encampment at an Air Force base."[13]

> **Stephen Roy**: There is evidence that Oswald attended a meeting of the Lakefront squadron before settling on the Moisant squadron, all in 1955.[14]

How Mr. Roy can make such a statement when Jerry Paradis and others went on record saying Lee attended up to fifteen meetings at Lakefront is puzzling, but his understatement of how many times Lee and David Ferrie were in the same meetings pales in the face of Gerald Posner's whopper.

On Nov. 16, 1993, Posner [author of anti-Oswald book *Case Closed*] told *Frontline's* millions of viewers that David Ferrie and Lee Harvey Oswald never met – not even once.

> **NARRATOR**: Gerald Posner disputes all the sightings of Oswald and Ferrie – in the Civil Air Patrol and in 1963. He points out there has never been any hard documentary evidence linking the two men.

> **Mr. POSNER**: I discovered documents that were from the Civil Air Patrol which show that David Ferrie was suspended from the CAP in 1954 and not reinstated until 1958. He wasn't even in the Patrol in 1955, when Oswald was a member.[15]

Frontline Exposes Posner's Lies

> **Martin Shackelford**: As late as 1993, with the publication of Gerald Posner's book *Case Closed*, Garrison's critics were denying that David Ferrie was in the Civil Air Patrol in New Orleans at the same time as

Oswald (the mid-1950s), despite contrary witness testimony. Shortly after the publication of Posner's book, however, the PBS news program "Frontline" located two photographs showing Ferrie and Oswald together at a CAP barbecue...one, shown on the program "Who Was Lee Harvey Oswald?" has since been widely published.[16]

Nevertheless, *Frontline* trotted Posner out again twenty years later, for a repeat performance. In November, 2013 almost all of the TV specials called Lee Oswald "the assassin" instead of "accused assassin" – often repeating obsolete and discredited information. Only the Travel Channel refrained in one of its two programs on the subject.

As we approach the Kennedy assassination in our timeline, and surge on to the Garrison investigation and David Ferrie's death, disinformation begins to plague the record. David himself planted false notions and ideas to mask his true activities. His murder has been called a "natural death" by Gerald Posner, Stephen Roy, John McAdams, and others who support the lone gunman verdict. Indeed, researchers who only had access to redacted versions of his life might conclude that David Ferrie's demise was simply another amazing coincidence – like so many others that riddle the Kennedy assassination mystery.

Endnotes

1. In 1998, Roy/Blackburst still minimized Lee's connection with David Ferrie by making it seem Lee's only contact was "in early August' and that Dave was "a volunteer trainer only June-August 1955." For example: Subject: Re: *Live by the Sword* Date: 1998/12/12 Author: Blackburst ... it is a fact that Ferrie left hi position as Commander of the Lakefront Airport CAP squadron in April 1955, and went to the Moisant Airport CAP squadron as a volunteer trainer during June-August 1955, and it is a fact that Lee Harvey Oswald became a member of the Moisant squadron for "a few weeks" beginning on July 27, 1955. A cadet named John Ciravolo photographed both Ferrie and Oswald at a CAP bivouac in early August 1955..." oo David.

2. "While Ferrie stated during his November 25, 1963, FBI interview, that he had been a commander of the Lakefront Airport CAP unit it was not until December 10, 1963, when he provided another statement to the Bureau, that he said he had also worked with the Moisant Airport CAP." http://karws.gso.uri.edu/Marsh/Jfk-conspiracy/FERRIE.TXT (Retrieved June 2, 2013).

3. http://en.wikipedia.org/wiki/David_Ferrie (Retrieved June 11, 2013).

4. http://karws.gso.uri.edu/Marsh/Jfk-conspiracy/FERRIE.TXT (Retrieved June 6, 2013).

5. I am uncertain which squadron Lee attended when David Ferrie almost

knocked his tooth out.

6. HSCA: Name Jerry Parades Date 12/15/71a Time 3:2Q Address New Orleans law firm Place Dv phone 504/et##-*### Full interview available at "Ferrie and Oswald" as reprinted in *Probe* magazine, pp 15-16, July-Aug. 1998. http://jfk. hood.edu/Collection/Weisberg%20Subject%20Index%20Files/F%20Disk/Ferrie%20David%20William/Item%2079.pdf (Retrieved Jan. 2, 2013).

7.XXVIX: Ed Voebel said Lee had attended a party at David's house. Lee said the same thing.

8. See http://www.gocivilairpatrol.com/about/ for more information on SAR ("search & rescue") (Retrieved Jam. 2, 2013).

9. http://educationforum.ipbhost.com/index.php?showtopic=2890&page=2 (accessed 20 Jan. 2014).

10. 5 Nov. 2003 Stephen Roy, posting as David Blackburst: http://alt.assassination. jfk.narkive.com/uqFSGmWP/why-did-oswald-join-the-civil-air-patrol (Retrieved Jan. 2, 2013).

11. Hamer knew both Oswald and Voebel and said: "[Oswald began attending] CAP meetings sometime around the summer of 1955. He stated that the 10 or 12 meetings that Oswald attended were held at the Eastern Airlines hangar at Moisant Airport.... Hamer commented that he had never been interviewed by the FBI following the assassination of President Kennedy."

12. http://www.jfk-online.com/dbdflibrfile.html David Blackburst archives. (retrieved Jan. 2, 2013).

13. http://members.gocivilairpatrol.com/media/cms/1956_DE92790F03EE1.pdf (retrieved 1/12/2014).

14. Stephen Roy, posting as David Blackburst: From: blackb....@aol.com Subject: Re: Shackelford Article Date: 22 Dec 1998 00:00:00 GMT Message-ID: 19981222124033.01150.00000102@ng-ca1.aol.com. http://www.jfk-online.com/dbdfcapfile.html (Retrieved June 1, 2013).

15. Frontline TV program: "Who Was Lee Harvey Oswald?" http://www.pbs. org/wgbh/pages/frontline/programs/transcripts/1205.html (Retrieved June 1, 2012).

16. Martin Shackelford: "Garrison's Case Finally Coming Together" www.acorn. net/jfkplace/09/fp.back_issues/25th_issue/shaw.html (Retrieved May 16, 2012).

CHAPTER FOUR

Dear Dr. Ferrie ...

In April, 1955, the Supreme Court ruled Carlos "Little Man" Marcello deportable. Marcello selected France as deportation nation (Tunisia was under French control when CM was born). France refused to accept him.

David watched Marcello and his brother closely during Kefauver Committee hearings on TV. Later, David will tell Marcello all details, impressing him (This is one reason Marcello will want him as an "advisor" during Marcello's November, 1963 trial in New Orleans). Marcello fights deportation from this date, with attorneys such as Jack Wasserman, Assistant Jefferson Parish DA Dean Andrews and G. Wray Gill at his side. David knows all three men.

Oct. 26, 1956: 17-year-old Lee Harvey Oswald joins the Marine Corps in Fort Worth, Texas. Only three days earlier, he was too young to join.

> As reported by researcher **Lee Farley**, Lee's mother, **Marguerite Oswald** told radio audiences on Feb. 24, 1964: ... while [Lee] was in the Civil Air Patrol, a civilian who she believes was associated with the Civil Air Patrol, induced Lee Oswald to join the United States Marines. Mrs. Oswald said she was living in New Orleans at that time, and that her son had left school without her knowledge and tried to obtain her consent to have him enlist in the U.S. Marines. She stated that a Marine Recruiting Officer also appeared at her home and tried to get her permission to allow Lee Oswald to enlist in the Marines, however, she refused.[1]

> **Lee Farley** (Aug. 2013): I'm sure most of us would agree that she is talking about David W. Ferrie and it was he that was instrumental in "grooming" Oswald leading up to his enlistment in the United States Marines.

Dave told me he mentioned Lee to the local Marine Corps recruiting officers and, in particular, recommended him for training in the CIA because 'he could keep his mouth shut.'"

Dec. 1956: Jack Suggs Martin, who becomes an associate of David Ferrie and Guy Banister, was placed in the psychiatric ward at Mercy Hospital for alcoholism by his wife, Paula. She is the major financial support of the family, despite having a baby. In January 1957 Martin was moved to the psychiatric ward of New Orleans' Charity Hospital.

Around this time Dave received complaints from neighbors due to the smell of some 2,000 mice at 209 Vinet St. Dave tells people he is doing cancer research. He indeed may have been involved in cancer research at this time; by 1963 he exhibited a marked skill handling preclinical materials.

> Vinet St. resident **Kathy Perilloux** told me: "I was just so curious why none of what was commonly known in the neighborhood was not somewhere in print ... I lived from birth till adult in my parents house ... [at 305 Vinet Street] ... It was a close knit neighborhood ... some still live there or kids now live there ... Dave's apartment was in front of Magnolia School, which is on the corner of Central Ave. and River Road... It was commonly known [he] ... had animals and was experimenting on them on Vinet. David had many rats/mice, dogs, and monkeys ... he kept some outside along the left side of the stucco apartment building where he lived. It was always smelly, unkempt. David got teens in the neighborhood to bring him animals and to help. David walked up and down Vinet ... used the public transit (bus) on Jefferson Highway ... so walking past my house was a regular occurrence.
>
> I had a good friend who lived just around the corner from David, but I had to go a different route when I went to her house because my parents didn't want me walking past there alone.... The house was on a slab, it was a white / cream/ dirty stucco/cinder block.... It was on a narrow lot, dirty, unkempt, junk, BBQ grill, cages, buckets, screen doors....There were four apartments [four electric meters] ... skinny walkway to the left going to the back ... I saw ... a monkey (or monkeys) in a cage ... there were always a few dirty medium sized dogs around there, on and off chains ... so much trash, rubbish, and the nasty smell. The cage was rusty, with bars about 1/4 to 1/2 inch thick; it was about four or five feet high, maybe 3' x 5'.... I remember the noises they made, squeals."

> **Stephen Roy**: Bill Gurvich [Garrison detective] investigates "a theft involving a friend of Ferrie (Mike Wakeling) in 1957, he saw mice in cages, and Ferrie said he was looking for a cure for cancer."[2]

> **Joan Mellen**: These mice he at one time stored at the apartment of one of his boy-acolytes, Michael Otty Clyde Wakeling, at 209 Vinet Street,

where a "sickening odor" pervaded. Wakeling testified to Jim Garrison that Ferrie was using these mice "to develop a cure for cancer."[3]

1957: *Time* magazine runs a second story on Dr. Robert Heath. His work is funded by the US Army and the CIA

David told me he volunteered to bring "patients" to Heath's office."[4] Ferrie, who would fly from city to city, said he "used to carry" sensitive psychiatric data back and forth between Tulane's psychology department and university hospitals and departments of psychology in Houston.

> Authors **Mohr & Gordon**: "Heath's $60,000 military contract represented a deep professional involvement which became apparent in 1956, when CIA agents approached Heath to conduct human and animal tests of bulbocapnine. The Soviets were also testing it for potential mind control applications. Heath tested the drug in 1957 on several monkeys and one human – "apparently a prisoner in the state penitentiary at Angola, Louisiana." It produced symptoms similar to alcohol intoxication. Some twenty-one years would elapse before such tests "became public knowledge at Tulane, following disclosures in [the Aug. 2, 1977 issue of] the *New York Times*. [2]" [quoted and adapted from Clarence L. Mohr and Joseph E. Gordon. *Tulane: The Emergence of a Modern University*, 1945-1980, Louisiana State UP, Baton Rouge, 2001, p. 119. Ibid., p. 123.]

1957: Dangerous and unethical experiments on human beings present CIA leadership with serious concerns about their unethical and illegal behavior, a 1957 Inspector General Report, stated: "Precautions must be taken not only to protect operations from exposure to enemy forces but also to conceal these activities from the American public in general. The knowledge that the agency is engaging in unethical and illicit activities would have serious repercussions in political and diplomatic circles ..."[5]

David showed Lee and me documents linking him to MKULTRA (see *Me & Lee*).

Then there was the Tulane Electrical Brain Stimulation Program, starting in the early 1950s, Dr. Robert Heath of Tulane University performed experiments on various mentally ill patients, most of whom had schizophrenia. The experiments were funded by the U.S. Army.

An Australian psychiatrist, Dr. Harry Bailey, assisted Heath. Bailey boasted in a lecture to nurses 20 years later that the two psychiatrists had used blacks because it was "cheaper to use Niggers than cats because they were everywhere and cheap experimental animals."[6]

May-June 1957: Dave qualifies to fly the Lockheed 1049 Constellation and the L-1049C Super Constellation.

June-July 1957: David writes a thesis for his PhD in psychology about "The Psychology of Vision – the Use of Hypnotherapy in Retinitis." Having taken some two years of courses, Ferrie travels to Bari, Italy (July), where he sits for board exams for a too-easily-acquired PhD in Psychology from Phoenix University. David takes his 78-year-old mother, Burdette, on a three-week trip to Europe. He and his mother will also visit Vatican City, and Rome. This time period must be classified as vacation time-off from Eastern Air Lines. David will take a vacation in July during the Bay of Pigs invasion as well, in 1960. Dave is proud of his degree, and hangs it on his wall; from this time forward, "Captain Ferrie" also advertises himself as "Dr. Ferrie" – a psychologist – in New Orleans.

In the 1960's it was still possible to practice as a psychologist without being board certified. David knew psychology as well as any psychologist. With his skills in hypnotism, he could take advantage of young males, and did so. As for his thesis about retinitis and hypnotherapy, it's actually an entirely plausible study, though the thesis wouldn't have qualified as a doctoral dissertation in the USA. The University was coming under investigation as a diploma mill at the time.

> **Stephen Roy**: Not long after [returning from Italy], Ferrie invited his ailing mother to come live with him. She sold the family home in Cleveland to finance Ferrie's first house on Airline Park Boulevard."[7] By this time, Dave's brother Parmely and his wife have a large family.

I have criticized Stephen Roy for various reasons, but we owe a debt to him for supplying information about David's family, such as the above, surely obtained through due diligence and dedication. I could not get Parmely to speak to me. He died in 2013. When I knew Dave, he refused to talk about his mother, who I assumed was dead.

Endnotes

1. http://www.maryferre...12&relPageId=9 as cited by Lee Farley at: http://re-openkennedycase.forumotion.net/t372-david-ferrie-s-early-influence-over-lee-oswald (Retrieved 09/09/2014.

2. Posting as Stephen Roy, to The Education Forum: 30 March, 2011. http://educationforum.ipbhost.com/index.php?s=a2f1d683ef5fec9f392a9ad3d3730879&-showtopic=17536&page=2 (Retrieved June 10, 2013).

3. From Joan Mellen's book *A Farewell to Justice*. Mellen does not say that David Ferrie lived in this apartment. The Louis Ivon memo placed the Vinet Street address on Ferrie's known list of addresses. Her information about David Ferrie being friends with Dr. Mary Sherman came, she footnoted, from Jack Martin, who told Hoke May. Hoke May told Journalist Don Lee Keith the information. Keith spent decades researching the Mary Sherman case and concluded that Sherman and Ferrie were indeed friends. John H. Davis, author of *Mafia Kingfish*, and with full access to the National Archives, also reported the Ferrie-Sherman friendship tie in his book, though he may have been informed by Mr. May.

4. David said I was only twelve years old when he began to "get interested" in Dr. Robert Heath and began assisting him in finding epileptics for experiments in the Bourbon Street district.

5. David J. Rothman. *Strangers at the Bedside: A History of How Law and Bioethics Transformed Medical Decision Making*. Basic Books, 1991. He co-authored *The Oxford History of the Prison* (1995).

6. http://www.tulanelink.com/tulanelink/twoviews_04a.htm.

7. Stephen Roy, posting on his own blog as David Blackburst, Apr 28 2011. http://blackburstblog.blogspot.se/2011/04/david-ferrie-bKSiography-°©part-°©2.html (Retrieved June 3, 2013).

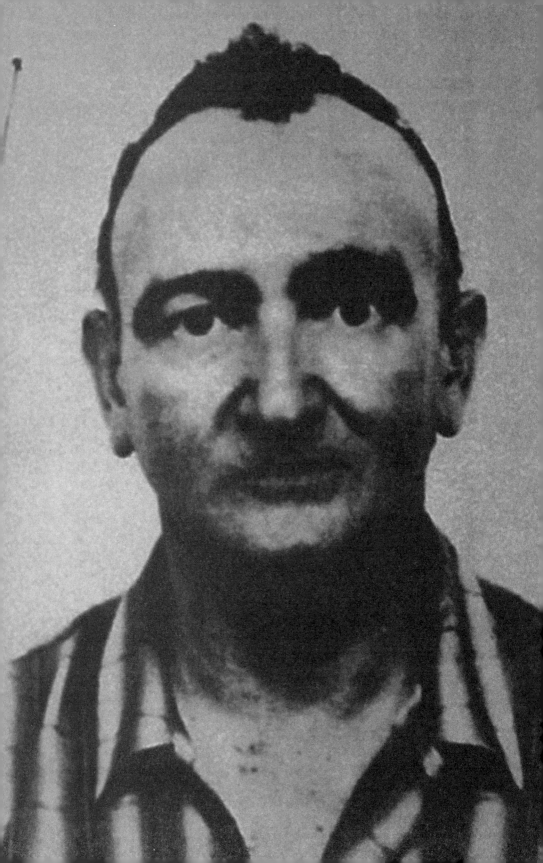

CHAPTER FIVE

David Ferrie's Strange, Clandestine World

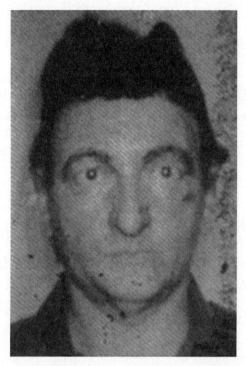

What are the marks on Dave's face? The mark on Dave's left cheekbone never went completely away, but is not mentioned in the autopsy. What other marks were not mentioned? Only one scar is mentioned on his entire body – a small mark on his leg described as resembling a burn or a healed puncture from a sharp object. (see Appendix on Autopsy) David Ferrie was no wimp. It would be nice to hear from any former CAP students if they could recall Dave's face carrying cuts and bruises, as it seems to appear in the above photo – and why.

"I WANT TO TRAIN KILLERS"

Haizen Page: [to Dave Reitzes, 1999) ... Ferrie was quoted as saying: "I want to train killers." ...Train killers for what? The ice-skating rink?

Bingo maybe? Since he has apparently been researching this case for only the last eight years, he cannot possibly know the changes this country has gone through in the last 35 years because of this awful murder, or the real heroes of this investigation, or who the villains are.

March 1958: David finally returns to instruct Civil Air Patrol Cadets of the Lakefront Squadron. He's been asked to return by a former cadet, Bob Morrell, now the Commander. Dave will eventually be reinstated to his former CAP rank, after Morrell and Dave convince Wing Executive Officer Joseph G. Ehrlicher to put aside the past (the death of a CAP cadet Dave had been training, in a plane crash).[1]

1958: The USA boycotts Cuba due to the brutal handling of student uprisings by Batista's police. Fidel Castro, his brother Raul and Che Guevara rally students and revolutionaries to join them in their struggles as New Orleans trade with Cuba plummets. There is pressure in New Orleans to support rebels in order to restore normal trade relations. The Mafia wants to help. The CIA begins to recruit Spanish-speaking assets, including pilots who can train pilots. Dave speaks fluent Spanish and has the will and desire to participate. But does he have the time?

THE CUBAN REVOLUTION AND DAVID FERRIE

It seems clear that, by 1958, David was indeed helping Fidel Castro's guerrilla movement against Batista, perhaps motivated by sympathy for students Batista had killed.

New Orleans District Attorney Jim Garrison, witnesses, and researchers agree that David Ferrie was an active supporter of Castro's guerrilla war against Cuban dictator Fulgencio Batista. But after Castro embraced Communism, David began actively supporting anti-Castro efforts, with CIA and FBI involvement.[2]

THE OFFICIAL VERSION

David Ferrie was too busy with Civil Air Patrol duties and his job as a pilot at Eastern Air Lines to get involved in anti-Castro causes. Sure, he made speeches and trained his special cadets like warriors. Yes, he worked for one of Carlos Marcello's lawyers and flew to Guatemala for Marcello, but no official records exist that David Ferrie was ever involved with the CIA or FBI, even as an informant.

Too many people who stated that David Ferrie was "CIA" were discredited, ignored, or met untimely deaths, including David himself.

Batista and his soldiers.

Castro and his guerrillas.

David Ferrie: (letter to Eastern Airlines) "It is my belief that the chronology begins in 1959. During the summer of 1959 I received my first anonymous threatening telephone call. At this time positive information had come into my hands that Fidel Castro was a Communist, and that this was known in the State Department prior to the action of the U.S. Government forcing Batista out of office."[3]

1959: David Ferrie purchases seven rifles and a revolver at Crescent Gun Shop, New Orleans, for use of cadets in the New Orleans Cadet Rifle Club that he helped organize.

> **The List**: four 1903 Model Springfield rifles, serial nos. 319961, 1371173, 367239, 803168; two .22 caliber rifles; one English rifle, serial no. 7/47 AB 5633;one flare gun, serial no. 3971; one .38 caliber revolver; one sword, and ammunition.[4]

DID DAVID FERRIE TRAIN ANTI-CASTRO GUERRILLAS? WAS HE INVOLVED IN GUN RUNNING?

The big argument is that David was too busy flying for Eastern Air Lines to find the time. But he was fired in 1961 from his job, he was unmarried and childless, and I can vouch for the fact that he spent no time cleaning his apartment.

> **Daniel Hopsicker,** quoting former CAP Cadet John Odom: One Friday evening, while we were in high school, I got a call from Barry [Seal – who would become a CIA contract pilot]... [Barry asked] ... if I'd like to fly with him in the morning over to Lacombe, a little town on the north shore across Lake Pontchartrain from New Orleans.[5]
>
> We left about 5.30 A.M. and flew over to the little airport there. And when we got off the plane there was a guy on the tarmac dressed all in black: black military fatigues, black boots, a black beret. He was sitting in a director's chair, drilling a bunch of Civil Air Patrol cadets, all carrying the old M1 rifles, standing in formation in front of him.
>
> His name was David Ferrie. He was a captain in the Louisiana Civil Air Patrol. And he had fake eyebrows, real weird, with one eyebrow turned up at a 45-degree angle. I laughed when I saw him. And Barry didn't like that, and told me to stay by the plane or he wouldn't let me fly back with him to Baton Rouge.
>
> Odom watched them confer, he said, and saw Ferrie point to the 50-or-so wooden crates staged next to the tarmac...
>
> On the way back to Baton Rouge, Barry Seal told him that he was working for Ferrie, who he said was "CIA." Ferrie's CIA link was confirmed by Victor Marchetti, former Deputy Assistant to Richard Helms. He testified that Helms disclosed, in executive discussions during the Garrison investigation, that Ferrie had in fact been employed by the CIA.
>
> "Seal said he was making $400 a week flying 'runs' of crates of weapons and ordinance for Ferrie," said Odom. He asked me, "How'd you like to make that kind of money?"
>
> Odom said he told Barry, "I'll think about it." But they never discussed it again...

Translated into today's money, [2000] Barry Seal was making $2500 weekly [now $3,200 weekly] ... on the weekends.[6]

David Ferrie's Flight Schedule

Stephen Roy/David Blackburst says Dave didn't have time for activities involving the Cuban revolution. He also says Dave was prone to lie about his own importance. Dave's flight schedules are supposedly available, but my FOIA requests were ignored. Mr. Roy has them, but to date has not published the documents. Will his book reveal all?[7]

> **Robert E. Lee,** (NOLA Assist. DA, July 12, 1967 memo to Garrison): We flew to Houston, Corpus Christi and Brownsville with stops between New Orleans and Houston, Baton Rouge, Lafayette, New Iberia, Lake Charles, Beaumont, Port Arthur, thence to Houston, Corpus Christi, Brownsville and back the same way the same day. As a rule, the flight would have about a thirty minute hangover between stops for passenger deplaning, baggage, cargo handling, etc.[8]

> **Stephen Roy** as Blackburst, arguing that Ferrie had no time for anti-Castro flights: Prior to September 1961, Ferrie was flying for Eastern Air Lines three times a week from New Orleans to Houston and other Texas cities, including two overnighters.[9] ... I have his flight and work records. He worked 5 days a week making numerous flights, but principally his 3-times weekly 379/506 run [from New Orleans] to Houston, Brownsville and Corpus Christi.[10]
>
> There would not have been a great deal of opportunity for him to have made such flights from Florida. (And the flight log on his Stinson contains no indication of any such flights.) [Mr. Roy has never released any flight logs examples.]

Lockheed Constellation, Eastern Air Lines training center, Miami. Eastern Air Lines trained David Ferrie to fly big planes here. David also took various update courses here over the years.

David initially spent weeks in Miami at Eastern Air Lines training schools and, later, he took short refresher courses. He even had opportunities to learn how to interpret autopsy reports, over an unknown stretch of time (see index entries for Dr. Joe Davis). David told me himself that he made the acquaintance of gay and anti-Castro pilots in Miami (see entry on Hemingway). Flight logs are mentioned for the Stinson, but flight logs for David Ferrie's Taylorcraft L-2 go unmentioned.

Concerning another discussion between Parson Owens and Stephen Roy about flights to Guatemala David Ferrie might have made: David did not have to fly to Guatemala, because for the weeks of interest to us, he might have trained anti-Castro guerrillas at Belle Chasse, the Naval Station only a few miles from New Orleans, which could have included some boys from his own CAP-style unit, The Internal Mobile Security Unit. With a name like that, these young men loyal to Ferrie were not sitting around drinking milkshakes.

Belle Chasse, seaboard view.

> **HSCA**: ... several of Ferrie's cadets claimed to have taken trips to Cuba in Ferrie's airplane.[11]

THE OWENS-ROY DISCUSSION

> **Stephen Roy**: Sun-Mon, Tue-Wed, Friday ... those were his main scheduled trips. He also made other runs in between.... So he gets back from an overnight trip, somehow gets to Guatemala, and trains combat pilots (at which he has had no experience) for a few hours, somehow gets back to New Orleans and gets ready for his next EAL flight? Does he get a chance to sleep anywhere in here? And why didn't Layton Martens, who lived with him, know anything about trips to Guatemala in early 1961?[12]

> **Owens**: Layton Martens has at various times said he was only Ferrie's roommate since November 17, 1963, or that he was never Ferrie's roommate. Would you classify him as a reliable source? ... It would

be helpful also if you gave the hours Ferrie worked for Eastern.(No response to Owens' request).[13]

We assume that Mr. Roy gave us a correct interpretation of David's flight schedule between March 1958 and July 1961. But when he argues that Dave had neither the time nor the ability to train combat pilots we need to define "combat pilot." Dave did not say he was training "combat pilots." He told me he was training pilots to fly "bush planes." Here is a definition of a bush plane: "A light, propeller-driven aircraft, with a high wing, designed to land on, and take off from grass airstrips or rough ground ... used in remote or hostile areas where commercial aircraft are unable to go."

Examples of bush planes: Cessna 206 Stationair (1962); Stinson Voyager (1939)[David owned one]; Douglas DC-4 (David was trained to fly this plane in 1955) In addition, the Taylorcraft L-2 was famed for its utility as a bush plane (David owned one of these, too).[14]

DID DAVID FERRIE HAVE TIME TO TRAIN BUSH PILOTS?

Between March 1958 and June 1960, David teaches CAP Cadets Friday nights and Sunday afternoons. Then he forms his own unauthorized CAP squadron, which ostensibly meets the same times, but cadets from that group said they met *many times a week*.

Problem: Mr. Roy has David flying as a pilot at those times.[15] Did Dave make a 12-hour round trip on Fridays? Supposedly these began at 11:40 AM and ended at midnight, according to information supplied by witness Robert E. Lee, a private attorney who also worked for Jim Garrison's office. Could Dave also have taught his cadets on Friday evenings, on such a schedule? We would have to discard R. E. Lee as a witness.

Mr. Roy's schedule, showing David Ferrie had no time for anti-Castro activities, also makes Dave's Friday night CAP meetings impossible. Mr. Roy also mentions Layton Martens as a roommate during this period, offering that Martens doesn't mention Dave making any flights to Cuba. But here's what Martens said about this time period:

Layton Martens, interrogated (03/12/1967), re being Dave's "roommate":

A. Well, I met him in the Civil Air patrol in 1958 when I became a C.A.P. Cadet.

Q. At this particular time, were you close to him or was he just an instructor in charge of the C.A.P. Unit or what?

A. At that time, he was just an instructor…[16]

Dick Russell: [Cuban Gen. Fabian Escalante told us] We came to know a lot of plans for exile invasions, secret overflights to provide arms to internal rebel groups. David Ferrie was the pilot for some of these flights.[17]

Jan. 1959: Fulgencio Batista flees Havana after a military coup forces him out of office. In faraway Oriente Province, Fidel Castro makes a broadcast that there will not be another coup. The people believe he's taken charge, the military leaders back down, and a week later, Castro enters Havana to cheering crowds. The seven-year guerrilla war was over.

Feb. 25: Lee Harvey Oswald takes a foreign language qualification test in Russian and scores a little less than half correct – not bad for a first year student. Warren Commission: "Most of the Marines who knew him were aware that he was studying Russian."

At this time, I also began to study Russian. In 1960, I took tests in Russian at Manatee Jr. College in Bradenton, Fl.

August: David Ferrie is placed under surveillance by Customs after a tip-off that he is smuggling guns. "Customs agents … had Pilot David William Ferrie placed under surveillance since they had a tip that Ferrie may be involved in a gun smuggling operation…. After a 26-hour surveillance and background investigation, [Customs] called to notify us that Ferrie was not involved in any nefarious acts of wrongdoing"[18]

September: David is now an Executive Officer in the CAP.

PROJECT MK-ULTRA

Many MK-ULTRA experiments have been conducted in New Orleans.

I had seen documents in Dave's possession dated from the late 1950s.[19] Dave, as previously mentioned, had been involved with MKULTRA for several years, at least partly through Dr. Robert Heath, at first regarding hypnosis, and later to locate "volunteers," and sources of drugs used in Voodoo and to produce "zombies." New Orleans had Voodoo practitioners.[20] Dave said MKULTRA turned to Haiti for better sources.

Upper Bourbon Street is a gay community, and Bourbon St. was originally a voodoo center.

> HSCA: CAP Cadet **Lawrence Marsch**: When we would spend the weekend by Dave's for these parties ... he used to practice hypnosis on us, and find out if it were working on us by using a compass or a pen and stick our arms. He was a fanatic about this hypnosis stuff."

I was surprised to read Marsch's statement, for Dave had done the same thing to me, thinking I had been hypnotized. I had no problem resisting him, but then I became determined to fool him when he brought out a long hatpin. I pretended I felt nothing, when he stuck it in my arm, but it hurt like the dickens!'

> CAP Leader **John Irion**: He fancied himself as a self-made doctor or psychologist. I personally never submitted to it, because I knew better. It's possible he hypnotized other people, but back then for kids of our age, it was more of a novelty.

> CAP Cadet, **Anthony Atzenhoffer**: [Ferrie] wanted the kids to participate in some kind of experiment for Tulane University. They didn't do it ... [Ferrie was] constantly at Tulane during those years.

SUMMER OF 1959

Jack Ruby travels to Cuba by undisclosed means. New Orleans is his base.

> **Lisa Pease** (researcher) reveals Ruby's activities in Cuba: According to Cuban travel records, Jack Ruby: Entered Cuba from New Orleans on Aug. 8, 1959 and left Cuba Sept. 11, 1959. Entered Cuba from Miami on Sept. 12, 1959; and left Cuba for New Orleans on Sept. 13, 1959. But bank records, Dallas police records, and FBI records showed Ruby in Dallas Aug. 10, 21, 31, and Sept. 4, days which fall right in the middle of his supposedly continuous stay in Cuba. Somehow, *Ruby was getting in and out of Cuba without the Cuban authorities detecting and recording such.* Why was Ruby making multiple excursions to Cuba during this time? ... and why did he choose to hide them?"(edited and emphasis added)

Eva Grant and Jack Ruby, brother and sister. Their lives are worth a book.

Jack Ruby, in Dallas, buys spy and surveillance equipment, including an apparatus so he can be wired for recording. The Dallas Office of the FBI will say Ruby applied to work as an informant for them nine times, but after finally trying him out, they received no useful information, so they didn't keep him.

So, why did Ruby keep coming back, again and again? Wasn't, "No," sufficient? Was this a lie the FBI used – pretending that Ruby's information was no good? *Something* kept bringing him back.

When I was introduced to "Sparky Rubenstein" for the first time in 1963, it was obvious that "Sparky" and David Ferrie had a long working relationship. Sparky also had known Lee since his pre-teen years, as Lee's own aunt was married to the Mob, and Lee's mother had dated Mafia members. With significant funding at this time through the CIA to finance flights to and from Cuba, it's possible that Dave provided Jack Ruby and other Mafia members with under-the–radar transportation.[22]

> **Stephen Roy**: In 1959 [David Ferrie] had found an outlet for his political fanaticism in the anti-Castro movement.

OCTOBER 1959

David purchases outright a Taylorcraft L-2 with cash. He uses it to train CAP cadets to fly.

The Taylorcraft L-2 is a bush plane. It was a favorite battle plane in WWII. New Orleans DA Jim Garrison piloted "Grasshoppers" (Piper Cubs) the

successor of the Taylorcrafts. Garrison had heard of David's skills as a pilot.

"With the outbreak of World War II, the US Army Air Corps purchased several J-3s (renumbered as an L-2) and they served faithfully as a spotter and liaison aircraft. Because of their low speed flight ability, the L-2 could land just about anywhere ... [they flew] low & slow spotter missions ... simply filling in the hole where no other aircraft could be used."[23]

> **Stephen Roy**: He was reprimanded by the FAA when the L-2 was used in a "reckless manner" by a cadet.... By now, his activities with

the boys (classified as "ephemophilia") were becoming reckless.[24]

Mr. Roy writes "ephemophilia" here, but later uses the correct term, "ephebophilia," a strong sexual attraction to teenagers between 15 and 19 years old.

Endnotes

1. Three variations of this event posted by Stephen Roy in one week (Dec.,1998) were remarked upon by the author as indicative of conflict and prejudice on Mr. Roy's part (emphasis added):

(1) Stephen Roy (posting as Blackburst): "In 1958, Ferrie weaseled his way back into the Lakefront squadron." (posted Dec. 22,1998).

(2) Stephen Roy (posting as Blackburst): In March 1958, a former cadet who had become Commander of the Lakefront CAP squadron invited Ferrie back as an advisor, and after a series of propaganda letters, he managed to be reappointed as Executive Officer. (posted 22 Dec. 1998).

(3) Stephen Roy (posting as Blackburst) : "March 1958-June 1960 DF is invited back to the New Orleans Cadet Squadron (Lakefront) as an instructor by a sympathetic former cadet who is now the commander." (posted Dec. 28, 1998).

Author: (re Stephen Roy's posts to Education Forum, 27 August, 2013): Mr. Roy considered my criticism invalid. In a thread he began, unkindly called "Baker Craziness," to which he promised to add more material on other issues later, he wrote a harmful message about me (just weeks after asking me not to put his name in my book, or he would have to write a bad book review that would hurt book sales). Hundreds of readers at The Education Forum, where I have been blocked from posting since 2005 (and therefore cannot defend myself) read this message : "There is NO conflict here. Ferrie was chased out of the squadron in 1954-5 by Wing Executive Officer Ehrlicher."

Author: Ehrlicher failed to renew David Ferrie's papers for the following year and did not tell him, to make sure David would not be able to teach. It was not so much being "chased out" as being quietly dismissed by inaction. The matter, I'm told, was over the death of a CAP Cadet David had trained to fly, who died in a plane crash, not directly connected to the CAP itself.

Roy: "In March 1958, he was invited back by new commander Bob Morrell. Ferrie came back and submitted papers for reinstatement of his CAP rank, but Ehrlicher opposed this at headquarters. Ferrie and Morrell went over his head to Wing Commander Haas and wrote him several self-serving and ass-kissing letters. By September 1959, Ehrlicher relented, Haas approved the paperwork, and Ferrie had weaseled his way back into the squadron."

Author: "Let's look at what Mr. Roy wrote. First, he says in one post that Dave *returned as an advisor.* But in another post, he says he *returned as an instruc-*

tor. Those are two different positions. Then, in two posts he says Dave was *invited back in* – while another post says Dave "*weaseled his way back in*" – with no mention that 'weaseled' concerned writing letters seeking reinstatement to his former level. Commander Morrell wanted David back. David wanted back, too. So, they petitioned Wing Commander Haas, when Ehrlicher turned them down, which was perfectly legal and acceptable. If writing letters of recommendation is "weaseling," "self-serving" and "ass-kissing" then Bob Morrell is guilty, too, though only Dave is mentioned "weaseling his way in." Mr. Roy's language was pejorative and slanted to prejudice the reader. That's why I called attention to it. The post titled "Baker Craziness" can be found here: (REF: http://educationforum.ipbhost.com/index.php?showtopic 397, Retrieved 12/21/2013).

2. Garrison: "When Castro was a guerrilla in the Sierra Maestra, Ferrie is reliably reported to have piloted guns for him. But in 1959, when Castro started to show his Marxist colors, Ferrie appears to have felt betrayed and reacted against Castro with all the bitterness of a suitor jilted by his girl." Garrison *Playboy* interview, http://22november1963.org.uk/jim-garrison-david-ferrie. (Retrieved Dec. 22, 2012).

3. Stephen Roy, posting as David Blackburst: "From: blackburst@aol.com (Blackburst) Subject: Re: Shackelford Article Date: 22 Dec 1998 00:00:00 GMT Message ID: <19981222124033.01150.00000102@ng-ca1.aol.com http://www.jfk-online.com/dbdfcapfile.html.

4. Lee Forman, from information provided by HSCA's Gaeton Fonzi and "FAA, vol.4, attachments F through I." 4 Oct. 2005, The Education Forum, http://educationforum.ipbhost.com/index.php?showtopicI39&page=3.

5. http://www.madcowprod.com/2013/11/20/barry-seal-the-cias-secret-camp-in-lacombe-the-jfk-assassination/ [author/researcher Daniel Hopsicker lives in the area, near Sarasota, Florida, where I lived as a teen, and is aware that CIA, military officers and Mafia – many of them retired to live in this area – conducted drug smuggling and secret operations in the 1960's, extending to the present era. http://www.madcowprod.com/2013/11/20/barry-seal-the-cias-secret-camp-in-lacombe-the-jfk-assassination/ (Retrieved 12/21/2013).

6. Ibid.

7. Roy/Blackburst did mention personal problems that had delayed his own book. "But we had waited years for his book: I decided we should wait no longer."

8. MEMORANDUM July 12, 1967 TO: JIM GARRISON, District Attorney FROM: ROBERT E. LEE, Assistant District Attorney RE: DAVID W. FERRIE. DAVID FERRIE was a pilot with Eastern Airlines in 1959. I was employed with Eastern Airlines while studying at Tulane in undergraduate school and completing my law studies at Tulane. During the course of my employment as a flight purser with Eastern, I had on occasion been a member of the same flight crew with DAVID W. FERRIE. After graduation from Tulane Law School, I continued to fly with Eastern, mostly at night, and practiced law out of my office on Veterans Highway in Metairie on a full time basis. I opened my law office in August of 1960. On the few occasions that I was a crew member on

FERRIE's flights, he was captain. We flew to Houston, Corpus Christie and Brownsville with stops between New Orleans and Houston, Baton Rouge, Lafayette, New Iberia, Lake Charles, Beaumont, Port Arthur, thence to Houston, Corpus Christie, Brownsville and back the same way the same day. As a rule, the flight would have about a thirty minute hangover between stops for passenger deplaning, baggage, cargo handling, etc. During this period of time, the captain would go into the station manager's operations office and check the weather ahead, fuel requirements, etc." (Note: The memo continues, including a chronological error that has David Ferrie flying in 1962 for Eastern Air Lines after he was already fired).

9. From: blackburst@aol.com (Blackburst) Subject: Re: Did Ferrie "fly missions over Cuba?" Date: 13 Feb 2000 00:00:00 GMT Message ID:) 20000213103847.01365.00000622@ng-ft1.aol.com (Retrieved June 3, 2013.

10. Posted as Stephen Roy, The Education Forum, Posted 07 March 2005 – 09:01 PM http://educationforum.ipbhost.com/index.php?showtopic413 (Retrieved June 3, 2012).

11. HSCA reference: "(100) Interview of John Irion, Oct. 28, 1978, House Select Committee on Assassinations (,J. F. K. Document 012754) : see ref. 30" http://www.aarclibrary.org/publib/jfk/hsca/reportvols/vol10/pdf/HSCA_Vol10_AC_12_Ferrie.pdf (Retrieved June 15, 2013).

12. The discussion is found at the Education Forum, Oct. 2006, Owen Parsons and Stephen Roy, at this URL: http://educationforum.ipbhost.com/index.php?-showtopic=8039&page=7.

13. The Education Forum, Oct. 2006, Parson-Roy exchange. http://educationforum.ipbhost.com/index.php?showtopic=8039&page=7 (Retrieved July 5, 2013).

14. http://en.wikipedia.org/wiki/Bush_plane (Retrieved 08/09/2013).

15. FAA rules at that time required only 8 hours rest after a day of flight – not much sleep time. Roy's schedule for David Ferrie is difficult to conform to Ferrie's known schedule teaching CAP on Friday evenings and Sunday afternoons. Since Roy/Blackburst has kept hours of flight private, for his book, we'll have to do the best we can until records can be obtained independently. Robert E. Lee says the round-trip flights he took with David Ferrie began at 11:40 AM, flying to Brownsville and back, ending at midnight in New Orleans. There were 9 stops both coming and going – a prodigious feat of professional flying. Mr. Roy places this round-trip flight on Fridays, making CAP meetings impossible for David to attend. Perhaps the flight ended a few minutes after midnight and was thus described as a Thursday-Friday flight, but Mr. Roy says he has the hours, too. Confusing, indeed! It seems that Roy's announced schedule could have worked only when David Ferrie was not teaching CAP on a regular basis. That would be between 1955-1958. 1958-1961 finds him busy with the official CAP or his own CAP squadrons. We know David attended a weekend-long bivouac when he was an ADVISOR, as shown in Ciravalo's Ferrie-Oswald photograph, July, 1955. This bivouac probably did not occur during David's vacation period, which was apparently in April, though we don't have those records (Mr. Roy should have them). Thus we can assume that David sometimes got both Saturday and Sunday off for

summer bivouacs. David's schedule must have had flexibility on some weekends. Overtime hours accumulated would allow David to arrange some days off for the bivouacs – and that's what we discover is possible, on the suggested schedule:

SUGGESTED SCHEDULE: if the flight described by Robert E. Lee occurred on SATURDAY (When Lee was free from his lawyer's office), we can assume the following: Saturday: Robert E. Lee says he and Dave made a round trip from New Orleans to Brownsville and back, 9 stops up, 9 stops back, beginning at 11:40 AM, ending at midnight back in New Orleans. Lee was free on Saturdays and Sundays from his law office. (EST. 11.5 HOURS FLIGHT TIME) – and we are just guessing.

David Ferrie is described as having "an overnighter" for Sunday-Monday by Roy/Blackburst. *But* Dave lectures CAP on Sunday afternoons. He must have at least half a day off on Sunday. NOTE: He cannot make a round trip to Brownsville and return in time on Sunday. To push the schedule as described by Roy/Blackburst, does David fly to Brownsville after Sunday afternoon lectures, spending the night there, so he can fly back by 7:00 to be available in New Orleans, as per the July 24, 1961 lecture at 8:00 PM, Monday? If so, he leaves New Orleans by 7:00 PM Sunday for Brownsville for Overnighter #1 in Brownsville. (EST. 5 HOURS FLIGHT TIME). Basically, David Ferrie probably has half of Sunday off.

MONDAY: We know David lectured The Military Order of the World Wars on Monday, July 24, 1961 (was it vacation time?) at about 8:00 PM, so we know David had to be in New Orleans no later than ~7:00 PM, when the meeting began. But even if it wasn't vacation time, he might have been able to make this meeting. His run on Monday possibly began in Brownsville with an extra flight or two, beginning at 8:00 AM, then departed for New Orleans at noon or so, with 9 stops in between, the same route from Brownsville as on Saturdays . Has time to make the 8:00 lecture on July 24, 1961 under this suggested schedule. Spends the night in New Orleans. (est. 11 HOURS FLIGHT TIME).

TUESDAY: He might fly to Brownsville 8AM-2 PM. Then he has six or more possible additional hours of flying. (we don't know where or how long he flew the extra hours), estimate 6 hours. Spends the night in Brownsville. This could be overnighter #2 in Brownsville. (EST. 12 HOURS FLIGHT TIME) But we are just guessing until Roy/Blackburst releases these records.

WEDNESDAY: After an est. 6 hours flying in the morning, at 2 PM, David flies back to New Orleans, arriving at about 7:00 PM. Spends the night in New Orleans. (Est. 11 hrs, flight time).

THURSDAY: *Roy/Blackburst says Dave has this day free.* If so, his free time is from approx. 7:00 PM Wednesday until 8:AM Friday. Miami is only 2 hours away; Cuba is just 45 minutes from Miami.

FRIDAY: David cannot make a 12 hour flight day today because he lectures Cadets on Friday nights: he must be Free by 7:00 PM For CAP evening meetings. Since they're held at the airport, David can debark immediately from his plane, if necessary, and begin teaching in the hangar. Flights on Fridays must begin and end in New Orleans, presumably at 8:00 AM and ending by 7:00 PM. (Max. time he can be flying today is approx. 11 hrs).

TOTAL FLYING TIME ON SUGGESTED SCHEDULE = 50 HOURS. This is common for pilots, but is significant overtime, so it is possible that David could arrange for free days to be with CAP cadets on summer bivouacs, in addition to his three-week vacation. This schedule, uses the data supplied by Roy/Blackburst, with the known constraints, using Robert E. Lee's testimony, the July 24, 1961 lecture, and known CAP meeting times.

16. Sunday, Mar. 12,1967, by Asst. DA Alvin Oser. James Alcock and Martens' attorney, with Milton Brenner, present. jfk.hood.edu/Collection/.../G Disk/Garrison Jim/.../Item 13.pd (Retrieved June 14, 2013).

17. 5. "JFK and the Cuba Connections" by Dick Russell Electronic Assassinations Newsletter http://www.assassinationweb.com/russell1.htm (Retrieved 12/21/2013).

18. "...Ferrie, who is a scout leader, had been trying to promote transportation to South America with the Air Force Transportation Corps. The conversation about the guns, tennis shoes and rope [that was reported] was in reference to a proposed hike at the termination of their proposed flight." HSCA, Vol. X, p. 394.

19. I described the MKULTRA documents I saw in detail before investigators, Don Hewitt, Mike Wallace and Phil Scheffler at CBS' *Sixty Minutes* in New York, Spring 2000. Questioning me was former Watergate Counsel and Senate Select Intelligence Committee member Howard Liebengood, who had personally seen many MKULTRA documents. As he questioned me, and I kept replying, finally he said, "That's enough. She's seen them." Liebengood was: (1) 1973-1974 Assistant minority counsel, Watergate Committee; (2) 1975-1976 Consultant, United States Senate, Select Committee on Intelligence (3) 1976-1977 Minority staff director, United States Senate, Select Committee on Intelligence.

20. http://keepethicallightburning.org/chris-denicola-survivor/ Testimony implicating Robert Heath, Gottlieb, etc. (Retrieved 12/12/2013)

21. A concern is that many witnesses Mr. Roy says he's interviewed are now old or deceased. Mr. Roy is a sound expert and a professional editor of audio and video tapes, so selective editing is a concern. Mr. Roy, who says he has collected everything possible about David Ferrie, refused to meet me, which itself suggests a potential to limit or selectively edit what he collects.

22. http://www.avsim.com/pages/1102/bush_adventures/pipercub/piper_story.html (Retrieved 02/11/2014).

23. HSCA reference: "(100) Interview of John Irion, Oct. 28, 1978, House Select Committee on Assassinations (,J. F. K. Document 012754) : see ref. 30" http://www.aarclibrary.org/publib/jfk/hsca/reportvols/vol10/pdf/HSCA_Vol10_AC_12_Ferrie.pdf (Retrieved June 15, 2013).

24. Stephen Roy, posting to The Education Forum, statement #4, cache accessed June 30, 2013: http://webcache.googleusercontent.com/search?qÊche:-LSV0d-8f0O4J:educationforum.ipbhost.com/index.phpshowtopic=2890&page=2+&c-d&h l=en&ct=clnk&gl=us.

MEMORANDUM FOR: LEAD FILE

RE: NOTES MADE BY DAVID FERRIE

At the bottom of FERRIE'S article on cancer, there is a portion of notes made by him but on another piece of paper. This was apparently picked up on the photostat machine when they made copies of his cancer article and obviously was not intended to be preserved. It appears that a letter or memo which he had made concerning his private activities was accidentally stuck in the photostat machine leaving us the bottom portion of his memorandum.

The portion which was reproduced reads as follows:

"...round faced - cross-filed file.

"...man - Bill Dazell (Billie Littlehorse) Some of B's microfilm were sent to Atlanta right-wingers - many of original files are at Guy Johnson's"

JIM GARRISON

Memorandum by Garrison, above, has a few words clarified due to poor legibility of original: Bill "Dazell" (Dalzell) claimed he never met Dave Ferrie, but to the Times-Picayune admitted he was CIA (http://www.wf.net/~biles/jfk/ramparts.txt – retrieved 08/08/2014); further, Billie B. Littlehorse was an alias that Dalzell used. (http://www.kenrahn.com/JFK/Issues_and_evidence/Jack_Ruby/Mob_connections.html.- retrieved 08/08/2014). Dave knew both names.

CHAPTER SIX

David Ferrie meets Dr. Sherman

OCT. 21, 1959

Dr. Alton Ochsner is cleared for a "sensitive position" with an undisclosed government agency, releasing him from a "sensitive position" with the FBI.

After the Cutter incident where he killed his grandson, through inoculating the boy, Dr. Ochsner partners with Dr. Mary Sherman, who knows the researchers in Chicago who predicted the deadly event. In their research, using radiation to create mutagens, they happen upon virulent cancer-causing viruses of such potency that Ochsner, a rabid anti-communist, considers their candidacy as a biological weapon. Thus, 'The Project' begins.

OSS Chief "Wild Bill" Donovan and Dr. Ochsner.

NEAR CHRISTMAS 1959

Dave told me he met Dr. Mary Sherman at the Crippled Children's Hospital near the campus of the US Public Health Service and its laboratories in New Orleans "around Christmas a few years ago."[1] Most of the children there suffered from polio. Dr. Sherman had operated on many of them. Dave had collected toys for a toy drive held by Jefferson Parish. He brought some to the hospital. Dr. Mary was also passing out toys. Both are both avidly anti-Castro and anti-Communist. David reveals his interest in cancer research, and his work with Dr. Robert Heath.

Dr. Mary Sherman.

Stephen Roy disputes: [Baker says] Dave Ferrie met Dr. Mary Sherman at the Crippled Children's Hospital when he brought toys from a Parish Christmas Toy Drive to children there who were suffering from polio. She was doing the same thing, and they became friends. This is not true; it's just more gratuitous inside info.

Maybe Dave didn't collect toys every year. But he did so in 1959, and he did so in 1963. In late August, Dave asked me to "look around" for toys for the toy drive.

At David's death, reporters noticed that on his front porch "piled high with debris," were "children's toys," according to a news article from the *Times-Picayune*, Feb. 22, 1967. But why?

> The Ferrie apartment was a walkup adjoining a front porch that was piled high with debris, including children's toys. Inside the living room, standing in a corner, was an American flag. Pill bottles, books and other reading matter were scattered about the living room.

On Dec. 15, 1966, David Ferrie was suddenly interviewed by John Volz, Jim Garrison's Assistant D.A. This was just before Dave would have packed up any toys he would have been collecting to deliver to the Jefferson Parish toy drive. But after the interview, David Ferrie behaved like a haunted man, and his health took a nosedive. Two months later, when he died, the toys were still there – in enough abundance to be noticed by the press.

Here is David with a baby, a stuffed toy dog in his hand. Later, anti-Castro activist Sergio Arcacha Smith declared that David Ferrie was a good man who was kind to his children.

Jan. 20, 1960: Dr. Alton Ochsner has been a consultant to the U.S. Air Force "on the medical side of subversive matters," and a personal friend of the Somoza family [Peter Dale Scott, *Beyond Conspiracy* p. 649]. He has been a consultant to the U.S. Army, and cleared by the FBI for a "Sensitive Position" for the U.S. government.[2] Dave told me he meet Dr. Ochsner through Dr. Sherman.

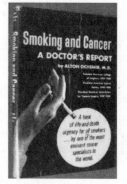

Dr. Ochsner was already assembling data to connect smoking and lung cancer. He published journal papers, articles, and books advertising the dangers of smoking. His dream was to give Fidel Castro lung cancer. Nobody could be blamed for this "natural outcome" due to smoking cigars incessantly.

ANTI-CASTRO ACTIVITIES – ESPECIALLY THOSE USING PLANES

Jan. 1960: The CIA sets up Task Force WH-4, Branch 4, Western Hemisphere Division. President Dwight Eisenhower has ordered a covert program to destroy Castro's government. Some say the program was known as "Operation 40."

A controversial picture from Barry Seal's papers. Barry (Adler Berriman Seal) a CIA connected pilot is third person on the left side. Many say it is Porter Goss, a Director of the CIA, on Seal's left. Porter has his hand on the infamous CIA agent Felix Rodriguez, laughing with a drink in his hand. The other persons have been indentified differently by various indivuals. Tosh Plumlee says he is hiding his face, others say it is Watergate burglar Frank Sturgis.

(Courtesy Daniel Hopsicker and Debbie Seal)

Jan. 12, 1960: A plane drops incendiary bombs around Bainoa, Caraballo, and San Antonio de Rio Blanco. "Another plane coming from the north, with U.S. markings, drops inflammable material on cane fields next to the Hershey factory." (*Informe Especial*. 1960)

Jan. 18, 1960: "A plane drops live phosphorous over the cane plantations of Quemados de Guines and Rancho Veloz, in Las Villas.

Seven people are detained in Sagua la Grande for trying to derail...
[a] Havana train." (*Informe Especial*: 1960)

Jan. 21, 1960: "A plane drops four one-hundred pound bombs ...
in Havana." (*Informe Especial*: 1960)

Jan. 25, 1960: President Eisenhower tells the press that Castro "begins to look like a madman."

Jan. 28, 1960: ".... a Catalina plane drops incendiary bombs that
fail to go off. The bombs have the inscription "Bristo Marines." Another plane drops incendiary bombs ... [near] the refineries of Adelaida, Violeta, Patria, Punta Alegre, and Morón ... Monati, Delicias,
and Chapana.... The incendiary devices dropped on the central
Adelaide almost totally destroy 40 million "arrobas" ["arroba" = 25
pounds] of cane." (*Informe Especial*: 1960)

Jan. 29-31, 1960: "A plane drops incendiary phosphorous bombs
on 10 districts in the area of the Chapana refinery. Other bombing
attacks take place on cane plantations in San Isidro and on houses
... in Havana. More than one hundred thousand "arrobas" of cane
are burned in Alacranes and Jovellanos in the province of Matanzas. (*Informe Especial*: 1960)

Feb. 1-13, 1960: "Planes drop bombs burning more than 17,000
arrobas of cane in Trinidad; and other bombing attacks take place
in Punta Alegre ... against the Adelaide refinery, and in the central
España." *(Informe Especial*: 1960)

Feb. 17, 1960: "A CIA briefing to the National Security Council
reports that "The USSR ... has shifted from cautious attitude to one
of active support." (CIA, Briefing, Cuba, February 17, 1960)

A Cold War Necessity: the Rolex Watch. Castro is wearing two Rolex watches, possibly confiscated from casino showcases. One watch supposedly showed Moscow time. Eisenhower and LBJ have their own, as did John F. Kennedy and his wife, Jackie. This was just before the era of good quartz watches. Rolex watches were chosen for accurate time keeping as much as for evidence of financial prosperity. Che Guevara also wore a Rolex.

Feb. 18, 1960: "A plane trying to bomb the central España, Matanzas province, explodes in mid-air. The pilot is identified as Robert Ellis Frost, an American who carries a U.S. military identification card." (*Informe Especial*: 1960)

Feb. 22-25, 1960: "A bi-motor B-25 plane takes part in burning cane fields in Las Villas. Simultaneous incursions by planes occur in Las Villas and Matanzas provinces." (*Informe Especial*: 1960)

Mar. 1960: "The CIA begins training 300 guerrillas, initially in the U.S. and the Canal Zone. ...[in June] training shifts to Guatemala. The CIA begins work to install a powerful radio station on Greater Swan Island, ninety-seven miles off the coast of Honduras." (*Gleijeses*, p.6)

Guatemala was run by a US-supported dictatorship; it was also the seat of Carlos Marcello's operations in Central America. Just as occurred in several other countries south of the border, Guatemala would endure harsh civil wars and bloodshed. More than 200,000 were killed or disappeared in the 36-year civil war, which began in 1960 and ended in 1996.[3]

Mar. 1: Psy-ops should include a "campaign directed a demoralizing the military ... based in terror," a radio and flyer campaign to identify Castro's intelligence officials and Communist spies, promoting civic resistance, and spread the word about the resistance and its operations. Among the recommendations are to "blow up Castro's radio station, the Voz del INRA, which is interfering with Radio Swans transmissions..." (*Propaganda y Guerra Psicológica* 3/60)

Mar. 4-5: The sabotage of a French ship, *La Coubre*, in Havana harbor, carrying arms into Cuba, kills about 100 people and wounds 300. The next day, while attending funerals for the victims, Fidel Castro accuses the United States of responsibility for the action. (*Informe Especial*: 1960)

Mar. 17: President Eisenhower approves a CIA project titled "A Program of Covert Action Against the Castro Regime." During the next week, US-backed rebels set fire to vast acres of cane fields while planes bomb supply routes and towns connected to oil refineries they don't want destroyed, just hobbled.

Late March: David Atlee Phillips is selected by the CIA as chief of propaganda for the Cuba project. Among other projects, Phillips will run Radio Swan, beaming anti-Castro information into Cuba.

Dave told me that he made flights into Cuba against Castro. Dave also told "runaway" Al Landry the same thing.

> HSCA: Further, several of Ferrie's cadets claimed to have taken trips to Cuba in Ferrie's airplane.[4]

April 1960: HSCA: "[Ferrie] apparently expressed his views to anyone who would listen. During an interview with an IRS auditor in 1960, Ferrie was 'outspoken' in his derogatory comments about the United States. He complained bitterly about his alleged tax persecution to such an extent that the agent reported he thought Ferrie was actually deranged, a 'psycho.'"

April 23: Cuba's Foreign Minister Raúl Roa says USA's United Fruit is using its influence in Guatemala to support the training of anti-Castro Cuban soldiers of fortune. "I can guarantee categorically," Roa says, "that Guatemalan territory is being used at this very time with the complicity of President Ydígoras and the assistance of United Fruit, as a bridgehead for an invasion of our country." (*Informe Especial*: 1960) He's right.

1960-April 1961: Stephen Roy: "[David Ferrie] pilots ... [Eastern Air Lines] Flights 573/6 and 572/9 from and to Houston three times a week, including two overnights. His co-pilots [are] Shedden and Rosasco..." (Note: Capt. H. P. "Rosy" Rosasco is listed in EAL's Retired Pilots roster for 1990.)

(1960?) FBI: "KARL LEWIS KOSTER III, was reported to have been allowed to fly FERRIE'S plane without a license and cost FERRIE a $200.00 fine."[5]

June 1960: David Ferrie leaves the Lakefront Squadron.

HSCA says David is adulated by his CAP Cadets, but has problems getting along with some of the senior (adult) CAP officials.

"... after a dispute with some CAP commanders during a bivouac, David walks out, leaving his position with the Lakefront squadron. He takes a number of young cadets with him."

> **Stephen Roy** (as Blackburst 12/22/1998) with this statement still standing in the David Blackburst Archives, as of Aug. 20, 2014): In June 1960, [Ferrie] was again forced out of the Lakefront squadron.[6] (Later, Mr. Roy posted to Education Forum that David left voluntarily, *before* he *would* have been forced out, which better conforms to the HSCA report.)

MAY 7: Two U.S. warplanes fly over Cuban territorial waters, close to the Cuban coast, and a U.S. destroyer enters Cuban waters. Two other U.S. warplanes fly over Cabo Cruz, (*Informe Especial*: 1960).

May 12: Cuban forces bring down a Piper Apache plane near Mariel, killing the pilot, a U.S. citizen named Matthew Edward Duke (*Informe Especial*: 1960).

May 13: The organizing committee of the Revolutionary Democratic Front (FRD) meets in New York City, fully funded by the CIA. They draft a manifesto to introduce the FRD to the United States and other countries, (minutes of FRD meeting, 5/13/60).

> **Cuban Information Archives**: This organization ... has received sanction and financial backing from the U.S. Government since its conception. The power behind the scenes in this political crisis is a C.I.A. agent known to the majority of the Cubans as Mr. B., an abbreviation of his name FRANK BENDER.[7]

May 19: Training of Brigade 2506 begins at Ussepa Island, off the Florida coat. In early July, the Brigadistas are flown to camps in Guatemala, (*Brigadista Diary* p. 26).

May 24: CIA Director Allen Dulles tells the National Security Council that Radio Swan will "attack [Dominican leader Rafael] Trujillo, and then later will begin to attack Castro." As usual in CIA-run media, Radio Swan will pretend to have nothing to do with CIA. (NSC, "Discussion at the 445th Meeting of the National Security Council," May 24, 1960, 5/25/60).

WHAT ABOUT DAVE?

> **Stephen Roy** (as Blackburst): Prior to April 1961, Ferrie was not fully accepted as an active participant by the anti-Castro Cubans ... Ferrie denied ever going to Cuba.[8] However, he did tell a friend about one sojourn into Cuba in August 1960, which he said was for the CIA. He

said he was wounded in the process, but his friends doubted this … the assertion that Ferrie made "flights" or extensive flights into Cuba is not strongly supported by the evidence.[9]

But how can Dave have (1) "denied" ever going to Cuba" (2) declare to a friend that he was wounded in Cuba and (3) also accept former cadets' claims that Dave flew them more than once to Cuba?

> **Stephen Roy** (to Ed. Forum, Jan 12 2005, 08:41 PM) : One of the interesting things is that when Ferrie had his IMSU [cadets] training at Belle Chasse, CIA admittedly was training UDT [Underwater Demolition Team] teams there.

July 23-30: David is listed as "faculty" by Tulane University for a two-credit hour aerospace workshop, along with distinguished names such as "Col. Maurice A. Cristadoro, Jr. USAF, Chief of the Atlas Weapon System Directorate of the Air Force," (quote: "the faculty includes…").[10]

Aug. 4: Young Albert Cheramie runs away from home and is found hiding in David Ferrie's apartment at 704 Airline Park Blvd. Lt. A. J. Scardina, Juvenile Officer for Jefferson Parish, handles the case. Things get covered up, but Dave's life is about to change for ever.

Aug. 1960: The Youth Study Center (a facility for treating problem juveniles, notorious for its abuse of juveniles) has an entry in the Visitor's Record Book of a "Dr. D. Ferrie" seeing Albert Cheramie. Written in red pencil: "NOT AN OFFICIAL VISIT."

Aug. 16: CIA focuses on Castro's cigar smoking, in efforts to assassinate him, proposing poisoned cigars, followed up with an idea to try an exploding cigar. "… this was no parlor trick – this cigar would have been packed with enough *real* explosives to take Fidel's head off. In 1967, the *Saturday Evening Post* reported that a New York City police officer had been propositioned with the idea and hoped to carry it out during Castro's United Nations visit in September 1960."

Sept. 1960: Dave, who had previously formed his own, private "CAP" group, called "The Omnipotents" now forms the Metairie Falcon Cadet Squadron, called "The Falcons" (also unaffiliated with the CAP). He eventually produces a state charter for "a business" when questions get asked. Parents at first assume it is an official CAP squadron, until Dave gets involved in a morals scandal.

Sept. 7: R. W. Tyler, acting regional counsel for Eastern Air Lines, writes David concerning use of Ferrie's plane by a student pilot carrying a passenger. The plane is not properly certificated or registered.[11]

> **Sept. 8, HSCA:** Investigations into David Ferrie's morality and character are opened by the FAA and Eastern Air Lines.[12]
>
> **Sept. 15, FBI:** Mr. Arthur W. Koon… [FAA]Tower, Moisant Airport[:] "… Mrs. John F. Barrett of Jefferson Parish, Louisiana, a former secretary in his office, had told him that her 14-year-old son had been influenced to join an organization called 'Omnipotent'[13] … the purpose of this organization was to train people concerning what they should do in the event of an all-out attack against the United States … a 'Dr. Ferrie' was behind this organization." [FBI 105-104340-1][14]

Sept. 30, 1960: The New Orleans Police department issues a background report on Guy Banister, saying Banister, a former Assistant Superintendent, can do them harm with information he gathered on police corruption before he was removed from that position.

Banister has been suspended, then demoted, after a drunken outburst of temper during Mardi Gras, involving throwing a gun and grabbing a bartender by his suspenders, at the Absinthe House Bar. Banister's friends are powerful right-wingers such as Leander Perez (Plaquemine Parish District Attorney). They defend him, but to no avail. "When [Banister's] investigation came too close to the top men, the New Orleans Police department framed him with a minor barroom incident."

At first, Banister went into various businesses, including running a CIA-sponsored anti-Castro radio program center with Jack Martin and CIA asset William Dalzell. Then he opened a private detective agency. By the time "Guy Banister Associates" relocates to Camp St. & Lafayette, his business seems to have few clients, though a swarm of anti-Castro figures pass through its doors.[15]

Oct. 3: FBI S.A. Warren C. DeBrueys requires information concerning stolen property (guns and munitions) from David Ferrie (a "Possible ITSP OO: Albuquerque.") [FBI 87-52503-6][16]

> **A.J. Weberman:** David Ferrie is being investigated for possible Interstate Transportation of Stolen Property in October 1960. The FBI Agent in charge of his case was S.A. Warren C. DeBrueys.[17]
>
> **November: Stephen Roy:** Ferrie was active with the anti-Castro FRD in New Orleans Nov 1960-August 1961.[18]

Guy Banister at the height of his power in Chicago's FBI.

Phoenix University in Bari, Italy, is investigated by the US Health Education and Welfare Department. This unaccredited school, not recognized by the US or by Italy, is issuing degrees.

HSCA: Synopsis of SBA hearing, Dr. Isadore Yager, p. 2 (J.F.K. Document 014930), and of David Ferrie, pp. 4-5. "Ferrie admitted using 'Dr.,' but for legitimate reasons. He claimed he had a Ph.D. degree from Phoenix University, Bari, Italy." vol. X, FAA file, ALPA SBA, D. W. Ferrie, 15-63-29-63, 48-63 (J.F.K. Document 014904)

Dave gets in trouble with Eastern Airlines for advertising himself as a doctor. Eastern Air Lines Exhibit 4a shows a photocopy of a telephone book with David Ferrie listed as "Dr. David Ferrie." A cadet says in FAA, vol. 2, exhibit III – "he was believed to be a medical doctor and a doctor of philosophy"; Dr. Isadore Yager testified that he confronted Dave about it (synopsis, p. 2 (J.F.K. Document 014930).

Dec. 1960: Manuel Varona sends Sergio Arcacha Smith, a Cuban exile and activist, to New Orleans without a penny. Arcacha Smith is New Orleans' official Delegate for the Frente Revolucionario Democratico (FRD). He moves into room 207, the Balter Building, named for ultra-conservative owner Col. Buford Balter, apparently free of charge. Guy Banister's office is in the same building, located at 400-404 St. Charles Street.

Dec. 5: Arcacha Smith and Manuel Quesada Castillo contact New Orleans' FBI office. On December 23, Sergio Arcacha Smith asks International Export Packers to obtain bazookas and a boat for the FRD.

Late 1960: Harold Tool (St. Bernard Parish Sheriff's Office) will inform the FBI that most of the records – including attendance records – of the Moisant CAP Squadron were stolen in late 1960,[19] while Lee Harvey Oswald is in the USSR as a "defector." Attempts to determine how many meetings Oswald attended at Moisant are thus made difficult.[19]

Thanksgiving-Christmas: David Ferrie and his friend, Dr. Mary Sherman, help support the anti-Castro cause by donating food and medical supplies to Cuban exiles and their families. Dr. Sherman told me that she and Dave had been collecting food, clothes and medical supplies to help Cuban exiles "for the last few years" during the holidays.

Endnotes

1. Dr. Mary Stultz Sherman was hired in 1952 by Dr. Alton Ochsner of the Ochsner Clinic to take charge of Ochsner's bone pathology clinic (bone cancers). She was his first female lab director. Sherman, fluent in Spanish, often accompanied Ochsner on his many trips to Latin America. Sherman, from the University of Chicago, knew Bernice Eddy and Sarah Stewart, pioneers in the polio contamination saga that led to the discovery of cancer-causing monkey viruses, whose careers were destroyed by their speaking out. See *Dr. Mary's Monkey* for the full story of how contaminated polio vaccines, loaded with cancer-causing monkey viruses (especially SV40) were administered with full knowledge that they were contaminated, infecting millions across the USA, Europe, and the USSR.

2. Edward T. Haslam, *Dr. Mary's Monkey*, TrineDay, 2007/2014, p. 182.

3. http://www.bbc.co.uk/news/world-latin-america-19636725.

4. HSCA reference: "(100) Interview of John Irion, Oct. 28, 1978, House Select Committee on Assassinations (,J. F. K. Document 012754) : see ref. 30" http://www.aarclibrary.org/publib/jfk/hsca/reportvols/vol10/pdf/HSCA_Vol10_AC_12_Ferrie.pdf (Retrieved June 15, 2013).

5. P. 3 "Sergio Arcacha." http://jfk.hood.edu/Collection/Weisberg Subject Index Files/D Disk/Dallas Records%2 0Dallas Assassination Center DMARC Copies/Item 01.pdf (Retrieved 01/01/2014.

6. From: blackburst@aol.com (Blackburst) Subject: Re: Shackelford Article Date: 22 Dec 1998 00:00:00 GMT Message-ID: <19981222124033.01150.00000102@ng-ca1.aol.com http://www.jfk-online.com/dbdfcapfile.html.

7. http://cuban-exile.com/doc_026-050/doc0032.html. (Retrieved 05/15/2013).

8. Too many witnesses stated Dave flew them to Mexico, Cuba and Miami to assume Dave "never" flew to Cuba. There are too many instances of rash and impulsive behavior on David's part to assume he would avoid Cuba. Cuba was two hours away by light plane from New Orleans, and only 45 minutes away via Miami. Dave's Taylorcraft L-2 was capable of making long flights with two 9-gallon fuel tanks, one on each wing, as well as a tank in the fuselage: "As we leveled off, the airspeed stabilized at 90-95 mph and Gary says he can flight plan 95-100 mph and be fairly close. He's generally burning around 4.5 gallons per hour and, considering his airplane has both wing tank options as well as the fuselage tank, the airplane will stay in the air far longer than he can. The ability to go long distances in a reasonable time on pennies has always been the Taylorcraft's long suit." (http://www.pilotfriend.com/aircraft performance/Taylorcraft.htm)

9. Stephen Roy, posting as David Blackburst: From: 6489mcadamsj@vms.csd. mu.edu (John McAdams) Date: 6/4/99 1:03 AM Eastern Daylight Time Message-id: 37575cac.11300416@mcadams.posc.mu.edu http://www.jfk-online. com/dbdfbackfile.html (retrieved July 1, 2013).

10. New Orleans *Times-Picayune* July 14, 1960 S3-P19 {Jerry Shinley first posted this on Internet in 2006: confirmed at Dallas library). "Space Project Faculty Listed Workshop Sponsored by Loyola, CAP Wing Faculty members for the "Aero-Space Age Education Workshop" ... July 23-30 ... [says] Rev. James F. Whelan, S. J., chairman of the department. To be held at Loyola university and nearby airports, the faculty includes Dr. Charles Webb, Assistant Director, Aviation Director, National Headquarters, Civil Air Patrol; **Captain David W. Ferrie, Civil Air Patrol**; Nash C. Roberts, Weather Consultant, New Orleans, La.; Col. Maurice A. Cristadoro, Jr. USAF, Chief of the Atlas Weapon System Directorate of the Air Force Ballistic Missile Division, Inglewood, Calif; and Col. D. R. Showen, Assistant Director of Candidate Advisory Service, U. S. Air Force Academy, Colorado. The workshop is especially designed for elementary and junior high school teachers and will be devoted to lectures and demonstrations by air-power experts as well as actual flights on Air Force and commercial aircraft. Two semester hours of graduate or undergraduate credit will be offered to those qualified persons who successfully complete the workshop.... Subjects to be covered in the aero-space laboratory include Aircraft in Flight; Power for Aircraft, Typical and Jet; Electronics; Rockets and Missiles; and Navigation. Purpose of The Project, according to Father Whelan, is to introduce teachers to the world of aero-space and to assist them in preparing classroom units."

11. HSCA: EAL Grievance hearing, FAA exhibit HHH; see ref. 11, SR-11-N-224.

12. FAA, vol. 4, exhibit A. case of "Good Moral Character"...by Richard E. Robey, summary of the report ; and FAA, vol. 3, exhibit KK, Eastern Airlines.

13. Various sources (e.g. http://www.jfk-.online.com/dbdfcapfile.html) agree that at first, some of the cadets who defected with Ferrie, following him out of the formal CAP into the unauthorized squadron started by Ferrie, called themselves "the Omnipotents."

14. A. J. Weberman Nodule 11. "David Ferrie" http://www.mcadams.posc. mu.edu/weberman/nodule11.htm.

15. FOIA records release, synopsis: http://216.12.139.91/docs/DOC_0001144061 DOC_0001144061.pdf (Retrieved 02/02/2014).

16. A. J. Weberman Nodule 11. "David Ferrie" http://www.mcadams.posc. mu.edu/weberman/nodule11.htm.

17. Ibid. (Retrieved June 24, 2013).

18. Posted as Stephen Roy, in reply to Charles Black: Jul 7 2005, 03:02 PM http:// educationforum.ipbhost.com/index.php?showtopicB73&page=3 (retrieved June 15, 2013) CIA-linked reporter Hoke May told journalist Don Lee Keith that Mary Sherman had been a close friend of David Ferrie, an associate of Guy Banister, .

19. http://karws.gso.uri.edu/Marsh/Jfk-conspiracy/FERRIE.TXT

JFK Inherits Cuba

Jan. 3, 1961: U.S. breaks off diplomatic relationships with Cuba. The CIA has already spent nine months trying to overthrow Castro.

Richard Bissell, CIA Director of Plans, meets with President Eisenhower, who "noted he was prepared to 'move against Castro' before Kennedy's inauguration on the twentieth if a 'really good excuse' was provided by Castro. 'Failing that,' he said, 'perhaps we could think of manufacturing something that would be generally acceptable.' This is but another example of his willingness to use covert action-specifically to fabricate events-to achieve his objectives in foreign policy."[1]

Jan. 6, 1961: William Dalzell helps to incorporate Friends of Democratic Cuba. Its charter is drawn up by Guy Banister. Its Vice-President is Gerard Tujague, who had employed young Lee Oswald. The group was created "to raise funds" for the Cuban Revolutionary Front (CRF), which is backed by CIA. Funds, in fact, are needed simply to feed exiles' families. The CRF's Chief Political officer is E. Howard Hunt of Watergate fame.

Later, in Garrison's Clay Shaw trial, Dalzell will claim he can't answer questions, calling on his privileges as a CIA covert contact.

Jan. 20, 1961: John F. Kennedy assumes office as President.

Jan. 21: Guy Banister's Friends of Democratic Cuba bid to purchase ten trucks from the Bolton Ford Co. The name "Oswald" is added to the bid document, and it was claimed an "Oswald" was present at the time, even though Lee Harvey Oswald is currently living as a [false] defector in the USSR. Was this the work of Gerard Tujague, who will later also claim Lee was in

the USA [HSCA, p. 143, Vol. X] ,when he was actually overseas? His claim has been used to confuse people into believing a theory that there was a "Harvey" and a "Lee" – dirtying up the true record.

Early 1961: David Ferrie is reported to be "playing soldier" before the Bay of Pigs Invasion

> **Hugh Murray**: In early 1961 Oliver [St. Pe] said he would be going to a party at David's home, for he had not seen him in a while, and he looked forward to it.... When I next saw Oliver, I asked about the party. His reply was not enthusiastic – "Oh, David was playing soldier. There were many dressed up as soldiers and with weapons." Only much later would I realize that this must have been a gathering in preparation for the Bay of Pigs invasion of Cuba.[2]

1961: David Ferrie claims to be doing physiological research at Tulane Medical School. He is also "treating" CAP cadets for medical problems. HSCA said Ferrie also told various people that he suffered from cancer and was seeking a cure for it.

> **Greg Parker**: Dr. Isadore Yager was the representative of the local medical association. In 1961, David Ferrie came to his attention due to reports of Ferrie practicing medicine without a license, in particular, [on] members of his Falcon Squad ... [at] the Grievance hearing held by Eastern Airlines in Miami during July, 1963, [Yager] stated: "He told me he had several Ph.Ds and that he was on the faculty at the Tulane Medical School and he was doing some research in the department of physiology of a very highly secretive nature, that if this works out well, it would really help us in all sorts of fields of medicine..."[3]

> **Stephen Roy**: ...he had something akin to a training lab for boys, including an ingenious skeleton with pumps, tubes and lights, nicknamed "Jonathan."[4]

Dave's medical school skeleton was put to use in First Aid courses he taught for CAP cadets. I heard about it, but never saw it. Clear plastic tubes of various diameters represented arteries and veins, through which artificial blood was pumped. The organs of the body were also shown. Cadets learned how to stop or control serious bleeds by learning pressure points and where to place tourniquets, with the help of the skeleton and its network of veins and arteries.

> **HSCA**: Ferrie spent considerable time studying medicine and psychology, especially the techniques of hypnosis which he frequently practiced on his young associates Ferrie had even set up a laboratory

over his garage, where he claimed he lost his hair, alternately attributing it to a radiation experiment, chemical explosion, and cancer research experiments. (Many friends did erroneously believe he was a medical doctor and a psychologist. This veneer of respectability and achievement could be the reason Ferrie referred to his Ph.D. degree as his most prized possession.... The committee based these findings on statements by John Johnson, Robert Morrell, Karl Koster, John Irion, Al Landry, Landry's father, Larry Adams, and Dr Yager.[5]

Feb.: Arcacha Smith informs the FBI about the FRD (Frente Revolucionario Democrático). Guy Banister runs background checks on those wishing to join the FRD.

Feb. 18: CIA activates a secret training camp at Belle Chasse Naval Base, 8 miles from New Orleans. 300 Cubans participate. After questions arise about the camp in October 1967 during Garrison's investigation, CIA official David Atlee Phillips releases a statement to the CIA describing the training camp (some parts redacted).[6]

> **HSCA Interview of John Irion**: While a member of the Falcon Squadron he joined the Internal Mobile Security Unit (IMSU). The mission of this unit was to "operate as an autonomous and self-sustaining rescue and combat unit in Cuba. This was pre-1961.... They trained with M1903-A3 bolt action rifles and 22s. Ferrie said that more equipment would be coming from the State Department, the Central Intelligence Agency through Sergio Arcacha Smith.... This training took place at Belle Chasse Naval Station south of New Orleans. The IMSU also trained in Abita Springs north of Lake Ponchartrain. Irion has photos of some of the training ... Irion stated that the training camps he went to were arranged by Ferrie and Smith but they were with North Americans at these camps, not Cubans ..."[7]

Owen Parsons (to Stephen Roy, who claimed Ferrie and Arcacha had only a slight relationship prior to the Bay of Pigs): "...whether they were "Cubans" or "North Americans," this venture was still organized jointly by both Sergio Arcacha Smith and David Ferrie prior to the Bay of Pigs and thus attests to an earlier and stronger relationship between the two."

Sergio Arcacha Smith

March 1961: Sergio Arcacha Smith and David Ferrie are now close friends.

Sat., March 18: Dr. Ralph Jones, Director of the University of Miami's School of Medicine, is the opening speaker at The American Cancer Society's elite Science Writers' Seminar, where "Top scientists from throughout the country will report on the latest advances" in cancer research this week. "Dr. Jones kicked off the seminar by reporting on a movement to rid Cuba of a political malignancy, the Castro regime."[8]

I didn't realize, when I crashed this seminar, that I'd be getting involved with doctors interested in helping the government win the Cold War. But there it is, right in the opening statement of this prestigious meeting of cancer research experts; Fidel Castro is called "a political malignancy" by the keynote speaker.

March 23: FBI creates "Clip" Bufile {Bureau File] 105-89923, New Orleans file 105-1446 when a security officer at Belle Chasse Naval base tells FBI that a training camp is "located at the Belle Chasse Ammunition Depot. He advised there were approximately 140 to 200 Cubans located at that base undergoing expert training in underwater demolition, use of sabotage techniques and combat techniques."... [He first learned of "Clip" on March 18, 1961]. [FBI 62-109060-4759]

> **CIA:** (February 1, 1977 memo from Raymond M. Reardon of CIA's Security Analysis Group/Office of Security, to the Deputy Inspector General): "This Agency training should not be confused with the infamous training activity which took place at Lake Pontchartrain circa 1962."[9]

Early 1961: Layton Martens enters the scene.

> **A. J. Weberman:** In early 1961 David Ferrie recruited a boy he had met in the Civil Air Patrol named Layton Martens, to work with Sergio Arcacha Smith and Guy Banister in the Cuban Revolutionary Front."[10]

Layton Martens

Late March: Three weeks before the April 1961 Bay of Pigs Invasion, The CRC, with CIA assistance, starts to "coordinate and direct" the activities of the Cuban Democratic Revolutionary Front. The CRC's main office is only 1.3 miles from Eastern Air Line's Miami airport headquarters.

April: David takes a three-week vacation from Eastern Air Lines and participates in anti-Castro activities. HSCA: "Ferrie's vacation in April 1961 coincided with the Bay of Pigs invasion."

New Orleans States-Item, (Apr. 25, 1967) "A source" once friends to Guy Banister reports seeing 50 to 100 boxes marked "Schlumberger" in Banister's office-storeroom early in 1961 before the Bay of Pigs.

The FBI reports that Carlos Marcello is financing Sergio Arcacha's Smith's organization – an example of Mafia and CIA cooperating with anti-Castro forces. The FBI would have been aware of CIA's involvement. The Mafia's motives: Carlos Marcello, Sam Giancana and Santos Trafficante want gambling, drug dealing and prostitution rings back in Cuba.

David works with the CAP on Fridays and Sundays, so it is possible that he is also flying for the anti-Castro movement as a pilot in Arcacha's organization on some of those days. Dave told me, "All I need is three hours to teach a pilot how to land on a beach. All I need is half a day to teach a pilot how to land on the back of a hog."

April 4: Attorney General Robert Kennedy arrests Carlos Marcello when Marcello appears before his probation officer, a visit required three times a month. He is handcuffed and taken by motorcade to Moisant Airport, where he is deported to Guatemala City.[11]

April 12: President Kennedy congratulates Khrushchev and Russia for sending the first man, Yuri Gagarin, successfully into space. While Kennedy encourages both nations to work together in an international Space program, fears of Soviet superiority in science grow.

April 15: Six B-26 bombers leave a secret airfield in Nicaragua and strike Cuba at dawn, destroying about 50% of Castro's air force. Castro, now aware of US intentions tells his pilots to "sleep under the wings of their planes." He rounds up thousands of potential rebels.

> **James Douglass**: The CIA's covert-action chief, Richard Bissell reassured [Kennedy] that there would be only a minimum need for air strikes and that Cubans on the island would join the brigade in a successful revolt against Castro.[12]

April 16: Robert Morrow claimed he and David Ferrie flew to Cuba on this date.

> **Dr. John DeLane Williams**: There, Morrow put in place equipment to collect radio signals from a mountaintop in the Camagueys. A reported large facility was under construction in a deep ravine in the Camagueys' jungle. The CIA suspected that the Soviets were moving missiles into Cuba. The intelligence they collected got back to Washington just in time for the Bay of Pigs debacle.[13]

April 17, 1961: The Bay of Pigs invasion occurs at night, with disastrous consequences that nearly create a nuclear war.

> **Jim DiEugenio**: [Sergio Arcacha] Smith's wife told the reporters that Ferrie had been at their house the day of the operation. (*Baton Rouge State-Times*, 2/27/67)[14]

April 17, 2 to 3 AM: Boats bringing troops ashore strike coral reefs. Many of them sink in the darkness, causing desperate swims for shore. A jeep that shows up is machine-gunned, waking up the nearby town. Castro is then alerted about the invasion. Cuban pilot Captain Enrique Carreras Rojas sinks command vessel "Maropa" and supply ship "Houston." The few tanks that make it ashore soon run out of ammunition and fuel, and the invading Cubans eventually surrender because they have nothing left to shoot with.

> U.S. Secretary of State **Dean Rusk** tells press conference: The American people are entitled to know whether we are intervening in Cuba or intend to do so in the future…. The answer to that question is no.

UN Ambassador Adlai Stevenson, who repeats this lie to the UN, is furious when he learns the truth.

April 17, 12:15 PM: Soviet Premier Khrushchev to President Kennedy: "It is a secret to no one that the armed bands invading this country were trained, equipped and armed in the United States of America … the bombs they are dropping are being supplied by the American Government…. The government of the USA still has the possibility of not allowing the flame of war ignited by interventions in Cuba to grow into an incomparable conflagration … there should be no mistake about our position: We will render the Cuban people and their government, all necessary help to repel an armed attack on Cuba." The expected supporting air cover by the U.S. Air Force never arrives. Critics of Kennedy's "mishandling" of the debacle will later seem to forget Khrushchev's dire warning.

> **Arthur Schlesinger, Jr**: (Kennedy said), "It's a hell of a way to learn things, but I have learned one thing from this business – that is, we will have to deal with the CIA … no one had dealt with the CIA."[15]

April 18, 1961: If David Ferrie tried to rescue any Bay of Pigs Cubans, it might have been on this day, or early on the 19th. He was on vacation at the time. Ferrie told several people (including Al

Landry and me) that he flew in to rescue Bay of Pigs survivors on a beach where a landing strip existed, when it became clear that the guerrillas were abandoned and helpless. Dave could not talk about the Bay of Pigs without getting red in the face. He said he could "sit idly by no longer" as Bay of Pigs radio operators pleaded for help and that he tried to rescue survivors. He did not indicate that he was able to save anybody.

Stephen Roy says Al Landry claimed he saw a long scar on David Ferrie's stomach from a knife wound due to his actions during the Bay of Pigs and that nobody else saw a scar. Dave told me that he was hurt in the leg.

April 19: A limited air strike is approved, too late to be effective. Four American pilots are killed.

April 19, 2:30 PM: "Brigade commander "Pepe" Perez San Roman orders radio operator Julio Monzon Santos to transmit a final message from Brigade 2506. "We have nothing left to fight with," San Roman said, his voice breaking. "How can you people do this to us, our people, our country? Over and out." Without supplies or air cover, the invading forces fell. To them, the lack of air cover was a direct betrayal. In the end, 200 rebel soldiers were killed, and 1,197 others were captured."[16]

James Douglass: The new president had bitterly disappointed the CIA and the military by his decision to accept defeat at the Bay of Pigs rather than escalate the battle. Kennedy: "They were sure I'd give in to them and send the go-head order to the [Navy's aircraft carrier] Essex," he said. "They couldn't believe that a new President like me wouldn't panic  and try to save his own face. Well, they had me figured all wrong."

New York Times (1966): President Kennedy, as the enormity of the Bay of Pigs disaster came home to him, said to one of the highest officials of his administration that he wanted to *'splinter the C.I.A. in a thousand pieces and scatter it to the winds.'*

Aftermath of The Bay of Pigs Fiasco: 1400 Cuban exiles were doomed. President Kennedy took responsibility for the disaster, but forced retirement on CIA Director Allen Dulles. CIA's second-in-command, Gen. Charles Cabell is also disgraced and fired (Cabell's brother, Earle, was former Chief of Police and Mayor of Dallas when Kennedy was shot).

April 20, 1961: Fidel Castro announces over Havana's Union Radio, "the revolution has been victorious ... destroying in less than 72 hours the army the U.S. imperialist government had organized for many months."

Captured soldiers.

April 23: Castro: "We have always been in danger of direct aggression ... we have been warning about this in the United Nations: that they would find a pretext, that they would organize some act of aggression ... so that they could intervene."

May 1: A massive May Day celebration is held in Havana, less than two weeks after the attack. Castro: "We can tell the people right here that at the same instant that three of our airports were being bombed, the Yankee agencies were telling the world that our airports had been attacked by planes from our own air force. They cold-bloodedly bombed our nation and told the world that the bombing was done by Cuban pilots with Cuban planes. This was done with planes on which they painted our insignia."

> **Legality**: U.S. involvement in the Bay of Pigs was a direct violation of Article 2, paragraph 4, Article 51, of the UN Charter, as well as of Articles 18 and 25 of the Charter of the OAS (Organization of American States). It also violated Article 1 of the Rio Treaty, where armed attacks, except for self-defense, are prohibited.

May 3-6, 1961: In Guatemala, Carlos Marcello and his family (who join him at the Biltmore Hotel) have enjoyed a luxurious twenty-nine days as the guests of President Miguel Ydígoras Fuentes, but pressure from the US mounts, and the nation's press demands Marcello's deportation.

On the night of May 3, Marcello and his attorney, Mike Maroun, are snatched by armed militia and suspicious-looking persons who are probably CIA. They are taken by a van through part of El Salvador, then cross into Honduras, where Salvadorian militia dump Marcello and Maroun deep in the Honduran jungles. Both men are injured, and it is assumed that they will perish.

> **Thomas L. Jones**: After a journey that lasted almost three days, walking up and down mountains, and in and out of jungles, the two, middle aged, overweight men, dressed in clothes more suitable for urban maneuvers than wilderness adventures, eventually staggered into a small airport and hired an aeroplane that flew them to the Honduras capital, Tegucigalpa. Battered, bruised, dirty and utterly exhausted, they checked into a hotel and slept for forty-eight hours.[17]

David with Bay of Pigs veteran Julian Buznedo (ca 1962).

May 13: Guy Banister's partner and pilot, Hugh Ward, flies Arcacha Smith to Miami in David's plane to meet Julian Buznedo Castellanos, Endrik Ceijas, and Carlos Lopez, who are Bay of Pigs veterans. Ward, who David trained to fly, will transport Lee Oswald to and from various destinations in 1963.

David's association with Hugh Ward indicates that David is also closely associated with Guy Banister by this date.

May 15, 1961: Buznedo, Ceijas and Lopez move into Arcacha Smith's small home in New Orleans. The links between Guy Banister and David Ferrie are well established by this date.

May 15, 1961: Ed Butler, with backing from Dr. Alton Ochsner, founds INCA (the Information Council of the Americas), a right-wing arm of anti-communist information, with CIA-sponsored radio broadcasts sent across Latin America. Dr. Alton Ochsner becomes President – a position he will hold, through election, for years.[18]

115

INCA was founded on my birthday and I was already aware of its existence before I moved to New Orleans due to reportage in Florida newspapers.

> "Along with founder Ed Butler, the most important member of INCA was famed physician Dr. Alton Ochsner. Ochsner, 38 years Butler's senior, formed a partnership ... which would last twenty years. Ed Butler, who didn't have a great knowledge of Latin American affairs, benefited substantially from the association with the celebrated doctor. Alton Ochsner had an internationalist outlook – especially when it pertained to the field of medicine. Ochsner ... had trained many physician exchange students from Latin America since the 1920s.
>
> "His prominence as an international physician led him to be elected to leadership of both the International Trade Mart and International House in the 1960s. Both ... promoted Latin American trade for New Orleans .... Ochsner also was elected to the presidency of the Cordell Hull Foundation, which administered a program of Inter-American university study ... Ochsner's persuasiveness helped Ed Butler recruit United Fruit's Joseph W. Montgomery, Delta Steamship Line's John W. Clark, International Trade Mart's William Salzmann and William B. Reily of Reily Coffee Company.... with Archbishop Phillip M. Hannan and Dean of Loyola University Law School A. E. Papale [were] members. INCA also received endorsements from Mayor deLesseps Morrison and Congressman Hale Boggs.
>
> "INCA's approach to anti-communism (in addition to being anti-Castro) tended to follow a practical approach of containment... Dr. Alton Ochsner [commented that] "many of Kennedy's advisors were leftists."[19]

May 23, 1961: George Lincoln Rockwell and his bodyguard Roy James fly into New Orleans to picket outside the movie premier of *Exodus*. Guy Banister is there to greet Rockwell and his Nazi followers.

May 24: Rockwell and James are arrested outside the theater due to pressure from local Jews. The police also arrest nine storm troopers with them. They are not released (on bail) until June 1.

May 28, 1961: It is rumored that Carlos Marcello is spotted in Texas. His return to the USA probably involved David Ferrie in some capacity.

> **Thomas L. Jones:** Just how he returned is a mystery. Marcello claimed he obtained a visa and bought a ticket on a commercial flight to Miami, where he had no trouble passing through immigration

Newman Building. "W. Guy Banister Associates" had a suite with an un-marked entrance – no permanent signs – near the middle car, as seen in this photo on the Lafayette side. Banister's private office within the suite provided access to the second floor, where his secretary and mistress, Delphine Roberts, said she saw Lee Oswald's office in the summer of 1963. Lee kept pro-Castro material and processed photos there. The 544 Camp St. side had two entrances. Door on left led to stairs to the second floor offices. Entrance to Mancuso's coffee and sandwich shop was at the corner. Its bathroom facility was shared with Banister's employees. The air conditioners show the depth of Mancuso's. The third floor, accessed by a fire escape and interior stairs, stored guns, rifles, tents, rations and war material in 1963.

and customs. However, a government investigation indicated that he had in fact been flown into the country aboard a Dominican Republic aircraft.

Tricia Marcello: David Ferrie helped my grandfather to return to the US.[20]

Layton Martens: Ferrie could have flown Carlos Marcello back to the United States. I wasn't there. I know he found a way to work with the Administration to get Carlos Marcello back into the country. Cause the Attorney General had boo-booed. You can't just kidnap people, even though he was late for a deportation hearing.[21]

Martens' statement that Marcello was "late" shows inside knowledge. Dave told me he helped Marcello get back to the United States.

End of May 1961: Bay of Pigs Julian Buznedo tried to make a living in New Orleans under Jack Martin's guidance – a mistake. David Ferrie and Hugh Ward did give poverty-stricken Buznedo flying lessons, just for fuel costs or for free. Buznedo has made impassioned speeches to New Orleans civic groups, helping raise funds for the FRD, with Dave arranging these talks, but will be forced to return to Miami, still impoverished.

Summer of 1961: David teaches college courses related to flying at Southeastern Louisiana College, Tulane University, and elsewhere.

> **Stephen Roy**: In 1961, according to an Eva Nettles, Ferrie also taught at a US government sponsored 3-week aerospace program at Southeastern Louisiana College at Hammond in the summer of 1961.[22] A recently-located co-pilot at Eastern said Ferrie was involved in a course at Tulane (in the late 50s) where he had students working on an Air Traffic Control system.[23]

> **Stephen Roy**: (regarding Ferrie being associated with Tulane) On the other hand, Ferrie did make some provably false claims over the years. It is hard to tell where truth leaves off and bragging begins.[25]

Summer, 1961: David is active in a variety of clandestine and public anti-Castro activities, in association with Arcacha Smith and Guy Banister.

> **Bill Davy**: (*Let Justice Be Done*) says Bill Nitschke, a Guy Banister employee, "... in a 1967 interview with a *New Orleans States-Item* reporter] ... recalled Delphine Roberts telling him that Banister, Ferrie, and ... Hugh Ward, were all involved in running guns to Miami and other places."[24]

June 1961: David's underage friend, Alexander H. Landry Jr., joins David, Arcacha Smith and others at Arcacha's home to view restricted films of the Bay of Pigs invasion.

June 1: Marcello is seen in Shreveport, LA. Authorities realize he has returned alive.

June 3: Marcello arrives in New Orleans and voluntarily surrenders to Immigration officials. In a hearing, he is ordered held at a detention center in Texas. Next Marcello is arrested by Immigration Officers in New Orleans and sent to the McAllen Texas detention center for illegal aliens.[25]

On June 11, he is ordered to be deported, but his fine team of attorneys are at work, and Marcello is soon back in Louisiana at

his office at Town & Country. Though forbidden to leave Jefferson Parish, "Little Man" regularly attends "emergency" events such as funerals and weddings in New Orleans, accompanied by his attorneys, friends, and brothers. He visits his restaurants and clubs in New Orleans at will. After all, when forced by emergencies to be away from home, a man still has to eat.

June 8: Dr. Alton Ochsner's name is prominent in the *Dallas Morning News* with two articles: "Smoking Attacked By Cancer Expert," and "Increase Seen in Fatal Cancer." Ochsner has close friendships with anti-Kennedy and anti-Castro conservatives in the oil industry and in government. This is particularly true in Dallas.

June 13: Rockwell's anti-Nazi trial begins in New Orleans and lasts two days. All ten of Rockwell's supporters are convicted on criminal mischief charges and sentenced to 30 to 60 days in jail. The next year, the U.S. Supreme Court strikes down the criminal mischief statute.

June 14: Dave brings Arcacha Smith to meet Herb Wagner Jr. about a loan. They mention "Operation Mosquito," which may have been Dave's coded term for "Operation Mongoose."

Mid-June: Operation Mongoose begins.

> **Daniel Sheehan**: … by June of 1961, Robert Kennedy had re-grouped the tattered remnants of the old Operation 40 forces and re-initiated the old, lower-profile, strategy of infiltration and guerrilla "raids" into Cuba…[now] named "Operation Mongoose." This covert "Contra" war was secretly pursued by the Kennedy Administration from June of 1961 to November of 1963.[26]
>
> **Arcacha Smith**: …we used to call Mr. Bobby Kennedy whenever we had anything to report or ask advice. He knew what we were doing all the time. But please don't use this, as it's off the record. That's the way it was. We would call Mr. Bobby Kennedy and he would take care of it.[38] Decades later Arcacha elaborated to Gus Russo, "Whenever

119

we needed, for example to send arms to the camps in Nicaragua, I'd call Bobby. The next day it would be there." (Gus Russo, *Live by the Sword*, p.142.) Shortly after the assassination, Arcacha said he called RFK with his condolences. "Little was said," Arcacha noted. "Bobby was a broken man." (Russo, p. 382.)

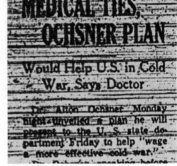

June 20: Dr. Alton Ochsner will soon meet with the U.S. State department to discuss ways for doctors to help "wage a more effective Cold War."

June 27, 1961: David gives a speech to the Exchange Club at Sheraton Charles Hotel. According to Jack Martin, Arcacha Smith introduced him to Ferrie at this time, in the hotel's coffee shop. It is likely that Jack Martin knew Dave before this and lied to the FBI when he said this was the first time the two anti-Castro activists met.

July 3: Ernest Hemingway, a Nobel Prize and Pulitzer prize-winning author, who was friendly with Fidel Castro and had two homes in Cuba, is found dead from a "self-inflicted" shotgun wound to the head. Clad in his robe and pajamas, Hemingway, it was initially surmised, must have accidentally shot himself while cleaning the shotgun. Later, the death is ruled a suicide.

A FLASH FORWARD:
DAVID FERRIE TELLS ME ABOUT ERNEST HEMINGWAY

I learned about Ernest Hemingway's virtual murder when I asked Dave if he had really killed himself. The matter had come up because Lee had told me that Hemingway was a spy in Paris and in Cuba.

"So you want my opinion about Hemingway?" Dave asked. He was helping me erase the more obvious evidence of that afternoon's lab work – cleaning test tubes, packing tumors in ice – tasks I'd recently had to take on because he was out of town so much. But Dave had returned early from Miami. "I knew you'd have an opinion," I said.

"Of course I have an opinion!" Dave snorted. "And here it is. Even though old Ernie had told the Company plenty about his 'friend' Fidel Castro, they quit playing footsies with him when he started acting paranoid."

Ernest Hemingway with Fidel Castro.

"Mental problems?"

"You'd have mental problems, too," Dave replied, "if you had FBI agents on your tail all the time. Making hang-up calls. Staring at you through binoculars. So CIA abandoned him. But first," Dave told me, "CIA made sure Ernie "got the treatment" – lots of electroshocks – lots of drugs."

"Where did that happen?" I asked.

"He had insurance, he had money," Dave replied. "So it didn't happen in a back alley somewhere. His butt ended up in Mayo Clinic. He got to bite the stick there in two different stints, five or ten shock treatments each time. Pretty much wiped him out. When they got through with him, he knew he'd never write another book."

"So he killed himself?"

"Here's how it's usually done," Dave told me, putting his hand like a gun to his head and making a 'click' sound. "You know. Fast and easy. That's what's nice about a revolver. He had revolvers. But wait," he said then. "Before you go, I'll show you something." Dave left the kitchen as I closed up a lunch pail that did not hold food. It held ice, and mouse tumors.

Dave soon returned, with a rifle. "Now watch this, J," he said. He held it at arm's length, barely able to shove the long, black end of it into his mouth. "Ish noh very eashy to do it thish way – ish it?" he said, working his mouth around the cold muzzle of the rifle. "How interesting," Dave went on, removing it from his mouth. "Consider how hard it is to reach the trigger. No matter where it's aimed. That you'll wonder if you'll miss a fatal shot, and just lay there helpless, and bleed out ... you can't easily aim the thing correctly at yourself, so you'll be sure to die quickly. But Hemingway was a master hunter, you know. Killed elephants. Lions. Himself."

As Dave set the rifle to one side, and unloaded it, a shock of horror went through me.

"It was loaded!"

"Yeah, I noticed that, too," Dave said. "But I hope I made my point. It seems these paranoid types who talk too much about CIA –or about what they know – they one and all choose shotguns or rifles to finish themselves off, for some obscure reason..."

"So it was a rifle somebody used on him?"

"Let's put it this way, chickadee," Dave told me. "Old Ernie got the full treatment. They emptied his head. Nobody would believe anything he ever said, after that – because he got the electroshocks. And as Ernie considered his options, they looked the other way, and threw him like a piece of meat to Hoover's dogs."

Dave found out that one of Hemingway's sons lived in Miami through friends at a gay bar who knew him. Gregory Hemingway was a sociable transgender type, going to medical school. He loved planes almost as much as alcohol, and was a former airplane mechanic. Dave and he ended up talking a few times.

"Once, when he was drinking," Dave said, "Gregory started to talk about hating Ernest, accusing him of killing his mother." Dave at this time was still visiting Dr. Joe Davis, the famous pathologist in Miami who ran Miami's autopsy center. He said Gregory had attended some of 'Dr. Joe's' casual seminars at the morgue, which were open to anyone who came. Dave had gained expertise in analyzing autopsy reports by visiting Dr. Joe's morgue whenever he could. Dr. Joe, Dave told me, could figure out most crime scenes.

When I asked Dave if he'd talked to Gregory Hemingway at the morgue, he fell silent.

Dr. Gregory Hemingway had himself castrated in December in 1994 and was calling himself 'Gloria' at the end of his life, though he'd married four times and had eight children.

In a separate incident, Lee told me that he used the code word "Hemingway" in a particular phrase in a letter written to John Connally, to get the attention of the State Department, because he needed strings pulled to help him to get out of Minsk. The code word meant he had to get out. The State Department then pressed for action on his request to re-enter the USA without getting arrested. Lee said he was so low on the totem pole that he'd been left behind when the Kennedy Administration took over. CIA did not want JFK's people to know all their little secrets.

"Studies in Intelligence," Vol. 56, No. 2 (June, 2012), a CIA publication, stated that though agencies such as the OSS had considered Hemingway's requests to become a spy, the Bronze Star award winner and intrepid war correspondent had always been turned down. "Ernest Hemingway," the CIA journal concludes, "may have wanted to be a spy, but he never lived up to his potential."[28]

> **The Guardian**, 3 July 2011: "Hemingway's friend and collaborator over the last 13 years of his life suggests that what was dismissed as a paranoid delusion of the Nobel prize-winning writer was, in fact, true: Hemingway was aware of his long surveillance by J Edgar Hoover's FBI, who were suspicious of his links with Cuba, and it may have helped push him to the brink."[29]

The Anti-Castro Movement in New Orleans Gets Serious
Alton Ochsner, Clay Shaw, Guy Banister, Jack Ruby, Carlos Marcello and David Ferrie

> **Michael T. Griffith**: One of Shaw's close friends was right-wing extremist Alton Ochsner. Ochsner openly admired the writings of Wilmot Robertson, who called upon citizens of Northern European extraction to take control of America from usurping racial minorities because Northern Europeans were genetically superior to minorities. Ochsner was involved in several radical right-wing organizations.[30]

> In a 1994 interview, Dan Campbell, who worked for right-wing extremist Guy Banister, said Shaw was involved with Banister in a gun running operation to the Alpha 66 Cuban exiles in Miami.... [also] A CIA document reports that Shaw and his ITM associate Mario Bermudez traveled together to Cuba in 1959 on a gun-smuggling operation."[31]

Dr. Alton Ochsner Reviews His Tragic Trust in Doctors
Dr. Ochsner is a violently anti-Castro conservative with friendships extending from Richard Nixon to oil magnate Clint Murchison. He resents the fact that Castro is now sending "his" medical students to the USSR instead of to Ochsner Clinic for training. A number of Ochsner-trained Cuban doctors agree with him. Some are close to Castro. As the President of INCA, Ochsner's rabid anti-communism is known to all.

Tainted polio vaccines have now caused some 40,000 cases of polio, leaving children with varying degrees of paralysis and killing two hundred.[32] Dr. Bernice Eddy, a friend of Dr. Mary Sherman had warned of the dangers. For being a whistler-blower, the USPHS destroyed her career.

Since then, Ochsner and Sherman have been on a quest, using radiation to mutate the viruses they've found in the polio vaccines, in an attempt to make the vaccine safer. It seems impossible to be certain that the contamination can be stopped any other way. Eventually, they discover a cancer-causing virus of such potency that Ochsner considers its candidacy as a biological weapon.

Doctors, as he has preached, must participate in the Cold War. Thus, 'The Project' is born."

In April, 1993 researcher A. J. Weberman interviewed Dr. Alton Ochsner's oldest son, "Akky" (Alton Ochsner Jr.) who confirmed that his father knew David Ferrie and "all" the area anti-communists and anti-Castro activists.

July 11: Marcello is released on bond from a Federal Detention Center in Texas. Marcello is then indicted by Bobby Kennedy for conspiracy to commit fraud by having obtained a fake birth certificate. He returns to New Orleans.

July 18: Arcacha Smith writes to Eastern Air Lines' boss, war hero

Eddie Rickenbacker, praising David Ferrie as indispensable to the anti-Castro movement. Arcacha Smith's letter proves David Ferrie placed a high priority on active and personal efforts to depose Castro. This was no Sunday afternoon hobby for "The Captain."

Eddie Rickenbacker

Arcacha Smith: ...the FRD ... was to front for the effort of the CIA to reinstate democratic government in Cuba. The effort of April 17 failed, as you know. Thereafter, the morale of the Cubans in exile and the Underground within Cuba fell to zero. Then along came Captain Ferrie. He strongly prodded our whole organization until it was revitalized.... Through him we've been able to get the best advice in affairs political, economic and military. In addition Captain Ferrie has been assisting in obtaining needed equipment.... At this time he holds in his hands so many threads which pertain to the security of the Caribbean area that no reasonable substitution can be made."[33]

Another part of the letter continued: ...Since events are approaching a climax we sorely need his advice on a day to day basis. Knowing your own often demonstrated patriotism, we are requesting that Captain Ferrie be given either a 60 or 90 day leave with pay so that the work at hand can be completed....

HSCA: ... The request was denied. Nevertheless, Ferrie's vacation in April 1961 coincided with the Bay of Pigs invasion. Ferrie's role, if any, is not known.

Mid-Summer 1961: David is active in a variety of clandestine and public anti-Castro activities, in association with Arcacha Smith and Guy Banister.

Dan Campbell, an ex-Marine that worked for Banister infiltrating left-wing groups on college campuses confirmed the gunrunning, recalling that "Banister was a bagman for the CIA and was running guns to Alpha 66 in Miami." Campbell also assisted Banister in small arms training for the Cubans and received $50 per week for his services. Campbell's recollection of Banister is telling. He describes Banister as "one of the most frighteningly violent persons I have ever known."

DAVE'S ANTI-KENNEDY SPEECH: "HE OUGHT TO BE SHOT"

On Monday, July 24 at 7:00 PM, David lectures the newly formed Military Order of the World Wars in New Orleans. It's their first meeting. "Captain D. W. Ferrie, Senior Pilot, Eastern Airlines, spoke on "Cuba: April 1961, Present, Future," shocking the seventy members and four guests present with a vehemently anti-Kennedy speech.[34] David is asked to stop speaking and leaves the podium. He is invited to speak as a private citizen after the meeting closes. Ferrie, once a sought-after speaker, will now be looked upon as a rabid radical.

What caused Dave to lose control of himself? His fury over the Bay of Pigs fiasco was aimed at Kennedy, who was taking the blame for the disaster. Dave told me he had trained "anti-Castroites" who were killed in the invasion. His visceral hatred at that time for JFK, revealed to 70 military men, would not go unnoticed by those in the CIA and FBI who despised the President.

HSCA: "Ferrie often spoke to business and civic groups on political issues. In [this] speech, Ferrie attacked President Kennedy for refusing to provide air support to the Bay of Pigs invasion force of Cuban exiles…. Ferrie admitted to the [FBI] after the assassination, that when speaking about Kennedy, he might have used the expression: "He ought to be shot." Ferrie insisted, however, that these words were just "an off-hand or colloquial expression.""

Dave told me his rage was genuine at the time. That would change. His "Kennedy ought to be shot" statement may have shocked some of the seventy military men present, but it was welcome news to others. They would not forget that this daring pilot wanted to kill John F. Kennedy – just as they did.

Endnotes

1. From Bissell's book, *Reflections of a Cold Warrior: from Yalta to the Bay of Pigs*, Yale UP, 1996.

2. Civil Rights activist Hugh Murray "My New Orleans Story, Part Four" Apr. 6, 2013: http://hughmurray.blogspot.com/2013_04_01_archive.html (Retrieved May 15, 2013).

3. Sept. 19, 2004 post by Greg Parker to the Education Forum. (Retrieved 09/09/2013) http://educationforum.ipbhost.com/index.php?showtopic74 (Retrieved June 15, 2013).

4. Jan. 2005, The Education Forum, post by Stephen Roy. http:/educationforum. ipbhost.com/index.php?showtopic(90&page=2 (Retrieved April 2, 2013).

5. Sept. 19, 2004 post by Greg Parker to the Education Forum. (Retrieved 09/09/2013) http://educationforum.ipbhost.com/index.php?showtopic74 (Retrieved June 15, 2013).

6. DAVID ATLEE PHILLIPS: WH/C 67-336 MEMORANDUM FOR: Chief, CI/R & A SUBJECT: Garrison Investigation: Belle Chasse Training Camp REFERENCE: CI/ R & A Memorandum Dated October 26, 1967 (emphasis by author)

1. Listed below is the information pertaining to the Belle Chasse training camp which was requested in reference memorandum. a. The training site was activated on February 18, 1961 and the first group of trainees arrived on February 18, 1961. b. The site was located eight miles from New Orleans at the U.S. Naval Ammunition Depot which had been inactive for five years. c. The site covered 3,500 acres of marshlands adjoining the Mississippi River. The depot consisted of ammunition magazines storage areas, warehouses, various frame and brick buildings, many miles of interlocking railroad tracks and both hard surface and improved roads and the entire site was enclosed by a chain link fence. Since much of the terrain was inaccessible and unsuitable for training purposes, due to the marshy ground and poi-

sonous reptiles, a limited area was used for actual training purposes. This area was located where the activity could neither be heard no observed. The base closed on April 21, 1961, and the training site was completely sterilized by Base and cleared Navy personnel after all demolition, ammunition, ordnance items, and field equipment was sterilized and air-lifted to a Midwest depot. Material on loan from the military was restored to original condition and returned to the appropriate military component. e. Approximately 300 Cubans were trained at the site over a six week period. The only known list of trainees which was available at Headquarters has not been located to date. A search has been initiated for this list. f. The training consisted of weapons firing, demolition, guerrilla warfare, communications, UDT, etc. One group was trained as a strike force assault battalion and was sent to Guatemala on March 22, 1961, to join the Bay of Pigs invasion strike force. g. The training camp location never came to public knowledge through press media. However, the *New York Times* and New Orleans radio and television stations reported that a Cuban training camp was located outside of New Orleans... high level military and Louisiana officials... denied knowledge of such a camp and the site was not identified... [a] representative of a leading T.V. station appeared at the main gate of the installation and requested permission to enter and take pictures. Naval authorities denied permission and there were no further inquiries. The actual training site was quite some distance from the main gates... h. The training camp was entirely Agency controlled and the training was conducted by Agency personnel.

2. During the initial phase of activation, the depot was sterilized to avoid any indication of government interest and to prevent disclosure of actual physical location of training camp to newly assigned trainees. For example, all U.S. Navy references on boxcars, buildings, etc. were painted out or destroyed. Although the first group of trainees transferred to the base from Florida knew they were going to an abandoned ammunition depot located near New Orleans, maximum precautions were taken to insure that the site location could not be pinpointed while the trainees were being transported from the airport to the camp. Despite all precautions, one incident occurred that is significant in view of the recent publication naming the Belle Chasse camp. One night, a group of trainees arriving at the Moisant Airport from Miami, were observed by Orlando Piedra, the former Chief of the Bureau of Investigation during the Batista regime. Piedra obtained the license numbers of the rental vehicles used for transporting the trainees to the camp. His license number was likewise observed by our security officer at the scene. Piedra, who is one of the individuals included in the CI R&A memorandum dated September 15, 1967 (page 3-item 21), and memorandum #5 (paragraph 4-J) may be the individual who provided the information contained in the recent publication. In any event, it would be surprising indeed of some of the 300 trainees involved have not discussed their training activities in detail over the past six years. With the clue that the camp was located at an abandoned Navy ammunition depot outside New Orleans, a long-time resident such as Piedra, Arcacha Smith, Fowler, or LaBorde, would eventually be able to narrow down the location

despite the extreme security precautions that were in effect during the training period. Although only the commanding officers of the ammunition depot and Naval Air Station were knowledgeable of the activities on the grounds, an enterprising reporter or investigator could probably surface other corroborating bits of information which would help identify the training site. For example, despite the fact the majority of supplies and equipment was procured through Navy facilities, certain items were necessarily purchased on the local market, thereby producing a sudden influx of cash in an area that had been dormant for five years. In any event, although the Garrison investigation may eventually lead to identifying the site as a government installation, there has never been any evidence or publicity identifying the Agency as the actual operators of the training camp.

3. CI/R&A may wish to discuss further aspects of the Belle Chasse training camp with Mr. (Deleted) former Base Chief, and Mr. (Deleted) former Security Officer, who are presently assigned to Headquarters. Mr. (Deleted) can be reached at this SOD office and Mr. (Deleted) can be reached at OS/SRS. Signed DAVID PHILLIPS Chief, WH/COG DDP/WH/COG/CICS/N. Gratz:ear

Distribution: Orig & 1 – Addressee 1- WH/Reg/ 1-C/WH/CO 1-WH/COG/ CICS 1-Originator [CIA OGC 67-2061]

7. Oct. 19, 1978, House Select Committee on Assassinations, p. 3 (J.F.K. document No. 012754).

8. *The Deseret News*, Mar. 20, 1961/ http://news.google.com/newspapers?nid36&-dat 610320&id÷dOAAAAIBAJ&sjid=dkkDAAAAIBAJ &pg751,3877675 (Retrieved Feb. 14, 2014).

9. The memo goes on to say: "The Lake Pontchartrain activity was run by GERALD PATRICK HEMMING as part of his Intercontinental Penetration Force (INTERPEN). There was no Agency connection with any INTERPEN activities. FRANK STURGIS of Watergate fame was also connected with INTERPEN activities." [CIA FOIA 18658 SAG Memo w/h re: H 9.10.75] Oct. 10, 2006 http://educationforum.ipbhost.com/index.php?showtopic-39&page=7 (Retrieved July 6, 2013).

10. A. J. Weberman Nodule 11. "David Ferrie" http://www.mcadams.posc.mu.edu/weberman/nodule11.htm (Retrieved June 24, 2013).

11. "... MARCELLO had a henchman go to Guatemala and enter his name in a church registry book in antique ink. Based on this entry, the Guatemalan Government was bribed into issuing a birth certificate for him." http://www.combat-diaries.co.uk/diary27/diary27chapter12/6.htm (Retrieved June 29, 2013) See also: John Davis, Carlos Marcello, Big Daddy in the Big Easy, http://www.trutv.com/library/crime/gangsters_outlaws/family_epics/marcello/9.html (Retrieved June 29, 2015).

12. James Douglass, *JFK and the Unspeakable*, Orbis Books, 2008. p. 13.

13. John DeLane Williams' Blog: 11 Dec. 2010: http://www.ofelio.com/zoom.php?id9706&lang=en&start&length (Retrieved 12/12/2012).

14. Jim DiEugenio, quoting documents examined by William Davy [*Let Justice be Done*]. http://www.ctka.net/reviews/kaiser.html. (Retrieved May 21, 2013).

15. James Douglass, *JFK and the Unspeakable*, Orbis Books, 2008. p.15.

16. "Invasion at Bay of Pigs" by Jerry A. Sierra http://www.historyofcuba.com/history/baypigs/pigslong.htm (Retrieved July 9, 2013).

17. Thomas L. Jones. *Carlos Marcello, Big Daddy in the Big Easy*. http://www.trutv.com/library/crime/gangsters_outlaws/family_epics/marcello/9.html (Retrieved Dec. 22, 2012).

18. INCA was formed one month after Ochsner met me, inspected my laboratory, and interviewed my instructor, Col. Philip V. Doyle, in Bradenton, Florida, immediately after the 4th Annual Science Writers Seminar held in St. Petersburg, FL, along with his close friend Dr. Harold Diehl, and Nobelist Harold Urey, after Dr. George E. Moore of Roswell Institute recommended his opinion, as described and documented in *Me & Lee*. It was my second meeting with Dr. Ochsner.

19. http://cuban-exile.com/doc_076-100/doc0078.html.lxii (Retrieved 02/02/2014).

20. Email, 2001, from Tricia and Steve Marcello, in the author's possession.

21. A.J. Weberman, Nodule 24, "Layton mertens" [*sic*] personal interview of Martens . http://mcadams.posc.mu.edu/weberman/nodule24.htm (Retrieved July 5, 2013).

22. Eva Nettles was a respected member of the Tangipahoa Chapter, Daughters of the American Revolution, Hammond, Louisiana See: *Hammond Daily Star*,p. 4, lower right-hand column, 03/23/66 http://newspaperarchive.com/hammond-daily-star/1966-03-23/page-4 (Retrieved Jan. 1,2013).

23. Continuing Mr. Roy's quote: 4] "Another friend of Ferrie's [name?] told me that Ferrie was close to a "man named Whitehead at Tulane and a Father Yamahuchi at Loyola." ... a Professor H. James Yamauchi, S.J., was the Chair of Loyola's Department of Religious Studies from 1956-66."

24. http://www.ctka.net/letjusticebedone/notes.htm#25. (Retrieved June 14, 2013).

25. The *Times-Picayune* online erroneously tags this photo as Marcello's arrest when he was deported to Guatemala, but that kidnapping was not made public, while his June 6 arrest after returning to New Orleans was photographed and reported. http://photos.nola.com/tpphotos/2011/11/175mob_9.html (Retrieved 02/26/2014).

26. Sheehan continues, in his deposition: "The supervisor of 'Operation Mongoose' was, then 34-year-old, Theodore Shackley. This operation, functioning in a working partnership with Mafia Lieutenant Santo Trafficante, operated from a base located in a few buildings on the campus of the University of Miami. This base – and the operation itself-came to be called "JM/Wave."

27. Gus Russo. *Live by the Sword* [Baltimore: Bancroft Press, 1998], p. 142. Quoting Richard Billings (Internal Memo for *Life* magazine, April 1967).

28. https://www.cia.gov/library/center-for-the-study-of-intelligence/csi-publi-cations/csi-studies/studies/vol.-56-no.-2/pdfs/Reynolds-Hemingway (Retrieved 2/5/2014).

29. http://www.theguardian.com/books/2011/jul/03/fbi-and-ernest-hemingway (Retrieved)2/20/2014) "... the special agent tasked with following him dutifully re-ported to Hoover in January of 1961 that Hemingway "was physically and mentally ill". That file, running to more than 120 pages, 15 of them largely blacked out for na-tional security reasons, also demonstrates quite how close an interest Hoover and his organization took in Hemingway." Hemingway went through two admissions for rounds of ECT. Thomas S. Szasz: "Law, Liberty, and Psychiatry: An Inquiry into the Social Uses of Mental Health Practices" ... 1963: How different the world might be today if only a handful of people had been sent for psychiatric "treatments," instead of being tried and sent to jail! Gandhi, Nehru, Sukarno, Castro, Hitler – ... the 'freedom riders' in the South – have been sentenced to terms in prison. Surely, the social status quo could have been better preserved by finding each of these men mentally ill and subjecting them to enough electric shock treatments to quell their aspirations."

30. Michael T. Griffith, siting *Let Justice Be Done*, p. 94 and other sources. http://www.mtgriffith.com/web_documents/russo.htm (Retrieved 02/02/2014).

31. Ibid.

32. "The National Vaccine Injury Compensation Program was introduced in 1986 to protect vaccine manufacturers from litigation on a scale that threat-ened the continuing production of vaccines." Journal of the Royal Society of Medicine, 2006 March; 99(3):156. http://www.ncbi.nlm.nih.gov/pmc/articles/PMC1383764/ (Retrieved June 1, 2013).

33. *The Road to Dallas: the Assassination of John F. Kennedy* by David E. Kaiser. Harvard UP. 2008. Also, p. 199-200 Staff Review of CIA file for Sergio Arcacha Smith, May 1, 1978, Office of Security, memo from Raymond G. Rocca, May 31, 1961, item F.

34. Here is a truncated record from Eastern Air Lines files of the "Minutes of The New Orleans Chapter of the Military Order of the World Wars:" "The Chapter held its regular meeting at Lenfant's Boulevard Room, 5236 Canal Boulevard, on 24 July 1961." (This is a Monday, at 7:00 PM.) "The meeting was called to order at 1900 hours. PRESIDING: Rear Adm. T. J. Ryan, Jr. PLEDGE: Capt. Gayle Schneidau, Jr. PREAMBLE: Capt. Francis Grevemberg. INVOCA-TION: Col. Lansing L. Mitchell.... There were 70 members and 5 guests pres-ent." [Minutes were read and business conducted, including a Flag project and incorporation protocol, all of this taking an estimated one hour] "...The speaker of the evening, Captain D. W. Ferrie, Senior Pilot, Eastern Airlines, spoke on Cuba, April 1961, Present, Future. At the opening of his presentation, he indi-cated his talk would be controversial. When partly through the presentation, the Commander rose, apologized for interrupting the speaker, and told him the tenor of his remarks, up to that point, were contrary to the preamble and objectives for which the Military Order...stands and that if he wished he could speak not as our guest speaker, but as a private citizen and to the members

present as private-citizens-after-adjournment 'of the meeting. Captain Ferrie determined he would stop his presentation. Commander Ryan then formally adjourned the meeting in accordance with the prescribed ritual at 2100. hours. FRANCIS A. WOOLFLEY Adjutant."

Bishop Carl Stanley of the America Orthodox Catholic Church ordained Dave in July 1961.

CHAPTER EIGHT

David Ferrie –
Bishop And Defrocked Priest

S atanic rites ... cups of animal blood ... and "priestly rings."
    Perry Russo (his family said he was secretly gay) reported
to Garrison's investigators that David Ferrie conducted "weekly Black Masses, wearing a black toga" and "worshiped with a chalice of animal blood [calling] himself a priest of the American Eastern Catholic Orthodox Church..."[1]

Perry Russo reports in the Kirkwood's transcript, about David's weekly Black Masses: "The chalice featured animal blood, the wafer consisted of some kind of raw flesh, instead of cake or bread. He wore a little black toga, solid black. He wore nothing underneath it.... he called it the American Eastern Catholic Orthodox Church ...

Perry Raymond Russo.

the ritual ... it's a brutal thing, a sadistic quality to it – bloodletting, chicken killing, stuff like that ..."

> **Peter Levenda** (author/occult specialist): Russo's characterization of Ferrie's Black Mass sounds more like Voudoun or Santeria than it does Satanism, and one wishes that Russo had paid a lot more attention – or [that] Kirkwood had published the transcript of his interview in full – so that we can trace the elements of Ferrie's ritual to a known progenitor ...[2]

> **Perry Russo:** (from Clay Shaw preliminary hearing, Kemp transcript) "Ferrie had shown me that he had received, I think, a doctorate of Psychology, he had received a medical degree that he could practice, and three other degrees ... and in his house ... out near the Kenner area or the Metairie area, he had surgery equipment which was kept very clean and things like that ... he gave us a demonstration in hypnotism at that time. Now, later on in talking to Al, Al Landry, Al told me that Ferrie had used hypnotism on the members of the Civil Air Patrol when he was making aggressions – sexual aggressions on them."[3]

DAVE'S INNER DEMONS

One day Dave brought out three rings to show me: an aquamarine ring that he said belonged to his mother, a small ruby ring that glowed purple under ultraviolet light, and one carved with an ugly mythological creature. "This is my priestly ring," he said. "I use it for black magic. And Satanic rituals."

"Are you serious?" I said, taking up the exotic ring.

"Of course not," Dave replied. "When I say a Mass, and sometimes I do say Mass, it isn't a Black Mass. I'm not a son of Satan, so I wouldn't wear that thing. I love God. But I use things like this to penetrate religious cults. I can go into certain places around here with that ring on, and they think I'm one of them."

Soon after I met Dave, he learned that I was, at that time, an atheist. When Dave found out that I had tried to become a nun, this deeply affected him. After all, Dave had wanted to become a priest. So we got into a big discussion.

"You have to believe in God!" he insisted, putting his face close to mine. "Dammit, God's real! Christ knows, I offered my life up – just like you – and just like you, God turned me down. But unlike you, I kept trying. I went to séances, sat in haunted houses, tried channeling. I did all the hocus-pocus. I got in with priests who said Black Masses. They were heading for hell. This last year or so, I finally gave up. That's when God proved "He" was real to me."

"What drugs did you use?" I remember asking, facetiously.

"God told me I had done enough," Dave answered. "That He had pity on me. That no matter what happened in my life, I had cared enough, and everything would be okay."

"No visions, no voices?" I pursued. "How do you know it was God, and not a figment of your imagination?"

"It was just God," Dave replied. "Nothing dramatic. Walking in, like a whisper, when I couldn't take it anymore. And I realized He was real. That He cared. And I didn't deserve it." Dave paused. He was drinking beer and smoking cigarettes. Apparently God didn't mind what a bad job Dave was doing, taking care of his body. "J," Dave went on, "you don't have what I've got. You don't know if you're going to end up OK. All you have is the emptiness. I know, because I've been there."

"I won't be bullied into having to believe in a God who can be so cruel!" I told him. The Holocaust had been going on when I was born, a mere 19 years earlier.

"I don't mean I've exorcised all my inner demons yet," Dave admitted. "But at least I know He's real, and I accept Him – right here." Dave tapped at his chest. This emotional argument left me cold, so then Dave began a long harangue based on science and philosophy. He argued that Lee and I should take the route Blaise Pascal took: that it's better to be a good person and assume God exists, and live a life devoid of evil, than to offend the only hope out there; that the chance, in such a vast universe, of a Super Being out there, was too big to ignore. That evil can't last, as it is self-destructive, with fatal flaws. Throughout this amazing discourse on God and ethics and morals, Dave sprinkled his argument with words of profanity.

If only Dave could have exorcised his inner demons! His spiritual quest was nowhere near finished in April, 1963. He was still fiercely seeking answers to handle the lust and impulses that burned inside his brain

Dave said he got involved in the occult while investigating Santeria for an un-named Agency. He showed me his "priestly ring" – given to him, he said, because he was a consecrated Bishop. He said this "priestly ring" was so ugly that some people thought it was Satanic – which helped him get better access to certain religious cults. I saw the ring twice, briefly. Imagine my surprise to find, in 2013, symbols related to Dave's church that reminded me of that ring.

Dave said he almost never wore the ring. I now believe it was a signet ring from the American Orthodox Church, with the double-headed eagle on it. Dave had removed this ring when he conducted a Roman Catholic Mass, a portion of which I witnessed – a standard Low Mass. Dave had explained that the ring was too evil, in his mind, to wear for a Roman Catholic Mass.

As for vestments, I saw what Dave had in his bedroom closet, because I kept an emergency yellow dress there, in case of a lab accident. I also saw a dress that did not belong to me. Dave had the usual Roman Catholic Church style priest's vestments and a black clerical gown, all ordinary. There was no "black toga." Today the ring signifies to me that Dave was a Bishop in the American Orthodox Catholic Church, which was filled with homosexuals, FBI informants and CIA assets. Dave was also an ordained bishop, he said, in the Old Roman Catholic Church.

Stephen Roy: "David Ferrie never owned such a ring."[4]

I have been criticized by researcher Dave Perry for saying Ferrie was an ordained bishop in the Old Roman Catholic Church. As I am only a witness, I had no answer for Perry. Then, an authority on the matter, occult expert Peter Levenda, (author of *Sinister Forces*) answered Perry: "You mention that David Ferrie was not a bishop in the Old Roman Catholic Church, and that there were very few bishops in that organization anyway. That may be true so far as it goes, but ... the claim that the Old Roman Catholic Church had few bishops is a bit misleading.

"There are several Old Catholic denominations, and others that share an Old Catholic line of succession but which are not, themselves, Old Catholic. Like most churches of the independent movement, many of these had rather more bishops than congregants ... in all fairness, bishops of the ORCC did participate in the consecrations of bishops from other denominations, thus giving rise to even further confusion. If a bishop of the ORCC assists in the consecration of a bishop of the AOCC – as happened more than once – then is that newly-consecrated bishop a "member" of the ORCC or the AOCC, or both? Or neither?"

I appreciated Levenda's remarks, which cleared up for me why Dave had a ring I now believe had significance in the American Orthodox Catholic Church. Perhaps Dave mentioned his standing in the Old Roman Catholic Church to me because I had been a Roman Catholic, and because of the name, would not see it as too 'far out' – as simple as that.

> **Peter Levenda**: His consecration by (Bishop Carl) Stanley – of the American Orthodox Catholic Church ... can be in no doubt; that there may have been others, though, is entirely within the realm of possibility. I would have dearly loved to watch "Bishop" Ferrie celebrate the Orthodox Divine Liturgy, though! What a surreal experience that would have been.[5]

Dave said he and Jack Martin had been involved in investigating weird churches. For $5.00 an applicant could get ordained. But there's a dark thread of sado-masochism that runs through the lives of Clay Shaw and David Ferrie, perhaps linked to religious beliefs that tormented them. In the 60s, homosexuality still had to be kept in the closet. Dave resented being "terrorized," as he put it, by local police concerning his being accused of "crimes against nature."

> **Greg Parker** (researcher): These fringe churches were, at times, used as cover by government agencies and private groups for various covert activities. Ollie North, for instance, used a "priest" named Tom Dow-

ling of the Celtic Catholic Church (a branch of Old Catholics) to give false testimony to counter claims of massacres conducted by Contras.[6]

Stephen Roy (2005, Education Forum, to Parker): The group Martin and Ferrie were associated with was the "Byzantine Primitive Catholic Church, Old Catholic Church in N.A., Apostolic, Orthodox, Catholic, Order of Saint John," according to the consecration certificates. The group Ferrie alone was associated with was the "Society of the Domestic Missionaries of Saint Basil the Great," according to his membership card."

In 1962-1963 David Ferrie made seven long distance phone calls from New Orleans to an unlisted number belonging to Earl Anglin Lawrence James, a bishop in the Old Roman Catholic Church of North America. In 1967, when Garrison tracked him down, a frightened Earl Anglin James said he had never been in Louisiana and that he was being smeared because he was a bishop in an unpopular church.

Levenda wrote: ... unraveling David Ferrie's religious affiliations is not a task for the faint of heart. That he was a priest and a bishop at some point in his life is beyond question.... He was definitely ordained and consecrated by others ... in fact, he was the beneficiary of several different consecrations during his lifetime. As I mention in *Sinister Forces*, Stanley died only a month after David Ferrie; one of those coincidental timings that has fallen below the radar of most conspiracy speculation but which drove Jim Garrison (and others) apoplectic. The only bishop of that entourage that managed to survive accidental death and disappearance was Jack Martin, but that's another story!

July 1961: David is ordained as a Bishop by Bishop Carl Stanley of the America Orthodox Catholic Church. Dave, who had been investigating the various sects springing from the AOCC, along with Jack Martin, became convinced that the AOCC, as an offspring of the old Roman Catholic Church, was not heretical. It was David's chance to finally hold a "legitimate" priesthood.

HSCA: Ferrie testified in August 1963 that he had helped [Jack S.] Martin on a case involving a phony religious order in Louisville, Ky. [November 1961] ...[7]

Peter Levenda: Stanley [was] himself a convicted felon with a long rap ... Ferrie's credentials were vouched for by another bishop, one quite well-known for his support of a ministry outreach to homosexuals.... That he was a priest and a bishop at some point in his life is beyond question. That he was "self-ordained" is, in my view, erroneous. He was definitely ordained and consecrated by others.[8]

Bishop Carl Stanley consecrated David Ferrie as a Bishop in the American Orthodox Catholic Church. In 1976, Stanley was canonized by the Byzantine Catholic Church (another offshoot of the Old Roman Catholic Church).[9]

July 24: Eastern Air Lines Flight 202, en route from Miami to Tampa, Florida, with 33 passengers aboard, is hijacked at gunpoint by Cuban-born Wilfredo Roman Oquendo. He forces the pilot to fly to Havana.[10]

July 25-26: The Cuban government releases the plane's passengers and five crew-members. They are flown to Miami on a Pan American Airways plane. Oquendo stays in Cuba. On July 26 Castro offers to return the hijacked plane if Cuban planes hijacked to the United States are returned. Secretary of State Rusk rejects the offer on July 27.

KERRY THORNLEY

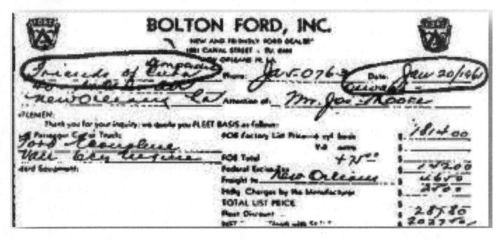

The name 'Oswald' (no 'Lee' or 'Harvey' is written) – has been used to try to "prove" a "Lee" was in New Orleans while a "Harvey" was in the Marines. Jim Garrison had an interesting theory

Kerry Thornley

about that: Kerry Thornley was impersonating Lee Harvey Oswald, using the name "Oswald" at the Bolton Ford Company at the same time he was writing about Lee as the main character in his book *Idle Warriors*. Garrison wrote that Thornley was "... one of the few men in the world who was in New Orleans around the time, who knew Lee Oswald, and who knew Oswald was in Russia. In addition, Thornley bore a striking resemblance to Oswald. They were of approximately the same height and slight build, both brown-haired and had similar facial features." Thornley claimed he never saw Lee after 1959, but many witnesses knew otherwise.

Garrison proposed that Thornley had posed as Lee in New Orleans when he lived there. Kerry would later say he had been programmed in a MK-ULTRA mind control project at Atsugi. His character assassination of Lee Oswald was thorough. The Warren Commission got thirty-three pages of testimony from Thornley (Thornley was the only Marine among the many who were interviewed who said Lee had mental problems, and that he claimed to be a Marxist).

Thornley will claim at various times that he (1) never met Lee Oswald in 1963 (2) met Lee Oswald only in the Fall of 1963 (3) will tell his supervisor, Mrs. Doris Dowell, that he and Lee Oswald "had been buddies in New Orleans" and that "he had met Oswald again in New Orleans [in the Fall]."

Lee and I met Kerry Thornley on May 8, 1963, at Lee Circle, when he came loping across the Circle to show off his new Polaroid camera to Lee. He thought I was Lee's wife because we were strolling arm-in-arm, but Lee set him straight. Kerry and Lee were obviously friends: Lee promised to go play pool with him. Not much later, they had a falling out over Lee thinking Kerry was getting too familiar with his wife (this was never fully able to be verified, because I didn't want to bring up the subject and upset Lee over it). Kerry soon left for California, swearing he would rewrite his book to blacken Lee's name "forever."

Dave's Ferrie's Relationship with Margaret Martens

Margaret Martens, Layton Martens' mother, fell in love with David Ferrie. Layton, David's musically talented friend, was a university student and roller-skating champion. Martens, despite his youth, was closely involved with Dave and Arcacha Smith in anti-Castro activities, including a patriotic raid on a Schlumberger bunker, which he will deny before a Garrison Grand Jury, perjuring himself.

> In a Facebook post to me on Sept. 17, 2013 by **Margaret's grand-daughter**: David Ferrie was my grandmother's boyfriend. They dated for some time. My uncle [Layton Martens] was involved with him as any kid would be with their future stepfather. David Ferrie may have been "bi" but I'm sure he wasn't gay. My grandmother's house blew up around 1968. Any significance? She was eventually put in a mental ward by David Ferrie and my uncle.... I've read that it was maybe to make her look crazy so no one would believe anything she had to say, or if questioned by Jim Garrison it could be considered as ramblings of someone mentally unstable.

David told me he was bisexual. He still felt attracted to women. Aviatrix Jean Helen Naatz and Margaret Martens are on record as close friends of David Ferrie. As a witness, I assert that Dr. Mary Sherman was also Dave's close friend. Edward T. Haslam, who personally knew Dr. Sherman (his father, also a doctor, was Sherman's associate), has found other witnesses who said David Ferrie knew Dr. Mary Sherman.

> **Stephen Roy**: None of the acquaintances of Ferrie I have interviewed have any recollection of Sherman by name, description or photo, and some say misogynist Ferrie was not likely to work with a woman doctor.[12]

Mr. Roy ignores me as even an acquaintance of David Ferrie. "None" is an all-inclusive word. How many "acquaintances" did Mr. Roy interview? Three? Fifteen? Will he release their names before they die, so we can independently verify such blanket statements? Or will only his friends such as Reitzes, who say Oswald killed Kennedy, be able to contact these witnesses?

Aug. 1961: David Ferrie is arrested on morals charges, which is the beginning of the destruction of his reputation.

> **Stephen Roy**: Ferrie was active with the anti-Castro FRD in New Orleans ... [until] August 1961. In that latter month, he was arrested on

morals charges, which led to a long series of legal proceedings and, by Ferrie's account, an attempt by authorities to shake him down for money.[13]

THE ALEXANDER LANDRY CASE[14]

Soon after David's consecration as a Bishop, all hell breaks loose.

When 15-year-old Al Landry runs away from home on August 2, and is found the next day at David Ferrie's home, it is the beginning of the end. Lawrence "Butch" Marsch, age 18, correctly guessed his location and returned the boy to his parents. Marsch also helped Mrs. Landry, stating he knew "that all boys go to Ferrie when they run away from home."

INFLUENCE OF DAVID FERRIE ON BOYS, USING HYPNOSIS

Lee Oswald and I personally witnessed David Ferrie placing two Cubans in their late teens into a deep hypnotic state almost with a wave of his hand. But it didn't work with everybody. Dave complained that our resistance to his efforts to hypnotize us was because neither Lee, nor I, trusted him enough, which was true.

> **Stephen Roy**: Ferrie was interested in psychology and had been interested in hypnosis since about 1947. He was fairly skilled at it, and he did practice it on his young friends, both inside and outside the CAP. (Like all hypnotists, he would do preliminary screening by giving suggestions to larger groups, watching to see who responded best, then focusing just on those subjects.)[15]

> **Daniel Hopsicker**: Ferrie was a gifted hypnotist.... After a long search I found and interviewed several of Ferrie's most prominent Civil Air Patrol acolytes ... one of them, Eddie Shearer, who knew and worked with Dave Ferrie, brought the subject of hypnotism up himself ... [Shearer said] "One time I remember, we were marching in formation – drilling – out at Lakefront Airport, getting ready to go to the CAP nationals drill competition. And this kid was twirling a 'guidon' – a metal thing, a fleur de les on the top of the pole with the units' colors – and it got away from him and it cut his hand up pretty good. I mean a real deep gash.
> "And the kid gets up, holding his hand, and there's blood running all down his arm past his elbow, and Dave walks over to him and puts his hand out in front of the kid's face, like he's giving him a stiff-arm, and says, 'Sleep. You will feel sensation but no pain,'" Shearer continued.
> "And then, while we're all waiting for an ambulance to take the kid to the hospital, the kid is bleeding all over, but he's not in pain

anymore now, okay? And then Dave goes over to him again, and says to him, 'You will stop bleeding.'

"And he did.

"Now, later, when I was in the Air Force," Shearer continued, 'I learned that this is all possible, that it can be done. But it can't be done with a subject unless you've been working, hypnotically, with that subject for a pretty long period of time. You can't just walk over to someone, in other words, and tell them to stop bleeding. So it became clear to me that Dave Ferrie had been working hypnosis with that kid for a long time ... without anyone knowing it. At least I had never heard of it before, and I spent a lot of time out there, hanging around that airport."[16] (Shearer's account is on You Tube as of 11/12/2013)

THE LANDRY CASE DESTROYS DAVE'S REPUTATION

Aug. 5: Al Landry runs away from home again. Dave is Al Landry's unit commander in the bogus Civil Air Patrol Squadron, the Falcons.

Joseph Backes (transcribing from his FOIA request packages of files): The Landrys expressed "a lack of confidence" in Capt. David Ferrie. They say that ever since their son joined the C.A.P. squadron of Capt. Ferrie that he has never been the same.[17]

Aug. 8: Landry is still gone. David Ferrie is arrested.

Joseph Backes: Ferrie wanted to know what would be done to the boy upon the boy's return. (What a humanitarian!) Ferrie harped on the idea that he was interested in the boy's welfare and felt that things were too tough for him at home. Ferrie insisted that he did not know where the boy was staying in Houston, but he was flying to Houston tonight to see if he could find him and return him to New Orleans.[18]

Aug. 11: Dave is arrested again, after two more boys attest to being sexually molested. Eric Michael Crouchet, "made a typewritten statement that Ferrie, 'committed acts of crime against nature on him on two separate occasions.'" James J. Landry, age 16, brother of Al, gave a statement that Ferrie performed sex acts on him on several occasions."

Perry Russo said David Ferrie's mother [Burdette] was present and visible in David's home during the Alexander Landry runaway scenarios. Russo said he saw Ferrie hypnotize Landry, but was eventually able to influence Landry to stay away from Ferrie, who was training youths dressed paramilitary style and accompanied by one or more Cubans.[19]

Aug. 16: As of this date, Al Landry is still missing.

Aug. 17: Al Landry calls his mother from Houston, Texas. He will return only if: 1) she allows the squadron to reform, 2) She contacts Eastern Airlines and explains this matter, as Ferrie is about to lose his job, 3) She contacts the other parents and makes them withdraw their statements about Ferrie.

Aug. 17: Arcacha negotiates on Ferrie's behalf in the matter.

Aug. 18, 3:30 PM: Officer Fournier receives a phone call about Al Landry from Arcacha Smith. Fournier can get the boy back in exchange for a notarized, signed statement from the parents indicating that they will not press charges.

> **Joseph Backes**: Amazingly, this was done. The boy was swapped for the statement. Even more amazing, Al Landry wanted to file suit against his parents for taking him away from Ferrie.[20]

David is arrested and booked. Document #180-10076-10062 is a police report to Joseph I. Giarrusso, Supt. of Police, from [Lt. Acting Commander] ... August C. Lang, Juvenile Bureau. Charge: *Contributing to the delinquency of a minor*. Runaway: Alexander Landry Jr, WM Age 15 of 5221 Arts. St. David Ferrie WM adult resides at 331 Atherten Drive, Metairie, La."

Landry says he hitch-hiked to Houston and, eventually, back. His clothing and appearance are too fresh, officials say, to be believed. Routes he says he took don't lead to Houston. He says David once took him to Mexico and to Cuba. Later, he says David took fifty boys for beer at Graci's Lounge on Homedale Ave. He says he was hypnotized and used for sex. Later, Landry recants. He says he was pressured by police and family. He then says he was pressured by David Ferrie to write his first recantation, but later writes another "as an adult," denying David ever used him sexually.

The Landry's investigate the Metairie Falcons CAP squadron. It is unknown to the national CAP and to Air Force Headquarters in Washington, D.C. They contact the FBI. They state that David took Al on flights, loaned Al his car while he was at work flying, and tried to rearrange Al's school schedule (foiled when the school contacted Al's mother).

> **Jack Martin** (to Pershing Gervais, NODA office): [Ferrie] was teaching them judo, close-order drill, extended-order drill, taking them

on camping trips … like a scout master. There was a kid involved in this mess by the name of Crouchet. Every time he flunked this kid, Crouchet, Crouchet's father got mad and came to the New Orleans Police about it.

Perry Russo testified in 1967 to Garrison investigators that he knew Landry well, that Landry went to Mexico with David at least once, and that he eventually got Landry out of David's clutches. Russo told A. J. Weberman that David "was in love with Landry."

Aug. 18, 1961: Joe Biles, "Document #180-10076-10062 is an 8-page New Orleans police report on David Ferrie giving his arrest background…. The subject: Contributing to the delinquency investigation, resulting from the runaway of Alexander Landry Jr, WM Age 15 of 5221 Arts. St. The subject alleged to be contributing is David Ferrie WM adult residing 331 Atherten Drive, in Metaire, La."

Tues., Aug. 22, 1961: David Ferrie's home at 331 Atherton Drive is searched, over objections that they have no search warrant. Passport No. 2188946 for Eumes Albert Paul Cheramie is found by New Orleans Police Sgt. Roland P. Fournier.[21]

Recall that on Aug. 4, 1960, CAP Cadet Albert Cheramie had run away. He was found living with David Ferrie at 704 Airline Park Blvd. Al Cheramie's passport's date of issuance *was two days before* "Dr. Ferrie" visited Cheramie at the Youth Study Center. Questioned, David said he "planned to do some mining in Honduras and was planning to take Cheramie along."

The Youth Study Center, a new facility, was already notorious for its harsh treatment and abuse of juveniles.

Endnotes

1. John S. Craig. *Peculiar Liaisons: In War, Espionage, and Terrorism in the Twentieth Century*. p. 217. derived from Sciambra's interview of Perry Russo at Mercy Hospital, Feb, 27, 1967.

2. Peter Levenda. *Sinister Forces*, Book I, p. 282.

3. http://jfkassassination.net/russ/testimony/russokemp.htm (Retrieved 01/13/2014).

4. From 2004 email to Dr. Howard Platzman. Mr. Roy has repeated his opinion widely, saying that he only pretended that a couple of people knew about an "unusual ring" that he later described as a "gargoyle ring" – all of which he said, years later, was just a lie he told to entrap me. He had begun this campaign by

asking me, via email, to describe a ring he said witnesses said Dave 'always wore.' I replied that *Dave almost never wore rings*. This was a difficult time, because I was aware Mr. Roy could insist he had witnesses that Dave "always wore rings," when in fact I knew better. After "Blackburst" (as he described himself at that time) insisted that I examine my memory better, I recalled the ring I'd seen under the black light, along with one of Dave's mother's rings (an ultramarine), a fossil horse tooth he found in Florida, and so on. I had also seen it sitting to one side after Dave had been saying a Mass. Blackburst then asked me to describe it, but I was unaware of that, because I was on my way by plane to *Sixty Minutes* interviews in New York, and at that time (2001) there was no Internet available to me until two days later, as I had no computer. When I was urged at CBS to describe this ring, I did so, telling everyone at *Sixty Minutes* and also Dr. Platzman that it looked like a griffin or a gargoyle, was a carved "priestly ring." Blackburst then said that Platzman *had* to have told me it was a gargoyle ring, even though he did no such thing. Blackburst then called Platzman a liar. However, when I asked who Blackburst's witnesses were, he refused to answer. Some four years went by,

and suddenly Blackburst, now Stephen Roy, announced to everyone that there 'never was' any gargoyle ring. It had been all made up. I believe the witness or witnesses were now deceased, and now Mr. Roy could with impunity declare no such ring existed. I was glad to find these symbols of the church that closely resemble what I saw carved on David Ferrie's priestly ring. For years, until now, I had no way to defend myself against Mr. Roy's claims, since he insisted that Dr. Platzman would lie in order to gain fame at *Sixty Minutes*. Since then *many* evidence files have surfaced since *Sixty Minutes* tried to film me three times.

5. http://mysite.verizon.net/dperry1943/ferrie.html. Missive to Dave Perry, who had criticized the author for stating that David Ferrie was a "Bishop," from Peter Levenda. (Retrieved 09/07/2013).

6. Greg Parker, The Education Forum, 18 Feb. 2005. http://educationforum.ipb-host.com/index.php?showtopic205&page=2 (Retrieved 02/20.2014).

7. HSCA. "David Ferrie" Vol. XII end notes.

8. http://mysite.verizon.net/dperry1943/ferrie.html {Retrieved 02/15/2014).

9. One line of thought regarding this event: "Jack Martin ... was yet another 'Bishop' as well as a drunk with, like Stanley, a long arrest record. He consecrated Thomas Jude Baumler. Baumler was a New Orleans politician and associate of Guy Bannister (sic). It was Baumler who told J. Gary Shaw that Lee Harvey Oswald worked for Guy Bannister. He also told Harold Weisberg, one of Garrison's investigators, that he had personally met Oswald. Baumler was also a Mason, allegedly belonging to the Etoile Polair Lodge of the French Grand Orient, the same lodge that Mafia don Carlos Marcello belonged to." This article names homosexual and pedophile Bishops associated with these sects. A. Branson, April, 2010. http://www.sott.net/article/207643-Down-the-Rabbit-Hole-The-Assassi-

nation-of-JFK-Bishop-Jim-Humble-And-The-Nexus-Conference (Retrieved July 25, 2013).

10. "...Oquendo [was] a former member of the Cuban secret police under the regime of ex-President Carlos Prio Socarras. Oquendo was a member of Castro's "26th of July" movement, commemorating the overthrow of Fulgencio Batista." "A Look Back, July, 1961" http://www.beartoothnbc.com/features/a-look-back/7549-a-look-back-july-1961.html?p=4 (Retrieved June 28, 2013).

11. Document # 124-90125-10013, file #62-117260-1, is Kerry Thornley's own personal letter as to his residences. *It reveals that by 1967 he did not recall ever leaving New Orleans, until after the Kennedy assassination,* even though he'd told Garrison and the FBI previously that he had been out of town for five months in 1963 and thus "never" saw Lee Harvey Oswald. He was caught lying about that by several witnesses who saw him with Lee in New Orleans in September. As to his knowing Lee Oswald in New Orleans earlier in 1963, as the author has claimed, researcher Joe G. Biles published a quote in his book, *In History's Shadow: Lee Harvey Oswald, Kerry Thornley* (p 59), that soon after the Kennedy Assassination, which Kerry celebrated with joy, he fled to Virginia, settling near CIA headquarters at a classy condo complex in Arlington, the Shirlington House, where he worked as a doorman. That's where we learn that Thornley's immediate boss, Mrs. Doris Dowell, told the FBI that about a month before he left for California.

"THORNLEY...told her that he had been in the Marine Corps with LEE HARVEY OSWALD, and also that they had been buddies in New Orleans. He said that he had met Oswald again in New Orleans, and that they had met at a place in the French Quarter that she probably would not like."

Author: Jim Garrison had witnesses who said they saw Kerry with Lee again in September. I was castigated in 1999 for saying that Lee and Kerry met in May, but Mrs. Dowell clearly states that Kerry and Lee were "buddies," in New Orleans, and then "met again" in New Orleans.

12. Posted by Stephen Roy as David Blackburst: 10/03/2012 https://groups.google.com/forum/#!topic/alt.assassination.jfk/78Eb1bl7qYA (Retrieved 6/14/2013).

13. Posted as Stephen Roy, in reply to Charles Black: Jul 7 2005, 03:02 PM http://educationforum.ipbhost.com/index.php?showtopicB73&page=3 (retrieved June 15, 2013) .

14. All information and quotations, unless otherwise indicated, are based on Joseph Backes' "The Fourth Batch" released upon order of the ARRB on October 19, 1995. http://www.acorn.net/jfkplace/09/fp.back_issues/11th_Issue/arrb_batch4.html (Retrieved June 5, 2013).

15. Posting as Stephen Roy, Lancer Forum Message #441 http://1078567.sites.myregisteredsite.com/dc/dcboard.phpaz=printer_friendly&forum&topic_id=410.

16. Daniel Hopsicker, posted Mar. 10, 2013. "Who Killed Hugo Chavez?" http://www.madcowprod.com/2013/03/08/who-killed-hugo-chavez/ (Retrieved March 15, 2013).

17. Joseph Backes. "The 11th Batch Part Two." http://www.acorn.net/jfkplace/09/fp.back_issues../20th_Issue/arrb_11a.html (Retrieved 07/11/2013).

18. Joseph Backes. ARRB Files. "The 11th Batch."

19. Ref: M E M O R A N D U M February 27, 1967 TO: JIM GARRISON FROM: ANDREW J. SCIAMBRA RE:[1st] INTERVIEW WITH PERRY RAYMOND RUSSO 311 EAST STATE STREET BATON ROUGE, LOUISIANA.

20. Joseph Backes made numerous comments about the circumstances described in files released by the ARRB.

21. When Al Landry was delivered to the Youth Study Center for problem boys, the assistant superintendent there recalled a similar incident involving another runaway boy, Albert Cheramie. The Visitor's Record Book showed a "Dr. D. Ferrie" came to see Albert Cheramie and wrote in red pencil: "NOT AN OFFICIAL VISIT." Backes: "Officer Jenau asked Ferrie if he has a Doctor's degree and was he treating any patients. Ferrie said he had a degree in psychology and that he didn't treat anyone but he did give advice. When asked about his visit to Albert Cheramie at the Youth Center in 1960 Ferrie admitted he did indeed visit Cheramie and realized he made a mistake after going."

JFK greets C.A.P. cadets at White House, May 7, 1962.

CHAPTER NINE

A Ruined Reputation

1961, David Ferrie Mug Shot. David was never convicted of any crime.

David Ferrie's CAP Capers: How "A Steady Stream of Boys," mysterious trips to Cuba and Honduras, and posing as a doctor finally gets Captain Ferrie arrested.

> **H. P. Albarelli** (author/researcher): First, a number of the boys interviewed by New Orleans police stated that they had traveled to Cuba with Ferrie and others a number of times after the island's takeover by Fidel Castro. One youth, Al Landry, according to police reports, said "that he had been to Cuba on several occasions since the revolution and stated that America should wake up because the Russians are 90 miles away." Unknown is why Ferrie took these youths to Cuba in 1960 and 1961, and what they did in Cuba while there.
>
> Another youth told police the David Ferrie had taken several boys to Honduras "to do some mining" and that additional trips to Latin America were planned by Ferrie.... Why was Ferrie taking young boys to the Honduras? What sort of "mining" were they doing there?[1]

Scammers identified by Stephen Roy as Lawrence Taylor and J. "Mac" McHenry convinced David and others to invest in the so-called "Kahunie Nut," or the "Cahone Nut" in the Honduras.[2]

> **H. P. Albarelli** (cont'd): David Ferrie, when questioned by the police on August 21, 1961, said that he had "a degree in psychology, but only gave advice" to people and treated nobody. Neighbors who lived near Ferrie's home told detectives that they "understood that Ferrie was

a psychologist" and that "a steady stream of boys were in and out of Ferrie's home" for what some thought was help with problems.

Dave counseled "his boys," helped them with homework and tests and encouraged them to go on to college or into seminary schools to become priests. He gave them money for college, or seminary school, and let them stay in his house if they were abused by their parents. There was some parental abuse going on, such as happened to Al Landry. But Dave took advantage of the most vulnerable boys. He seduced them. He tried to convince me that he switched to young adults after his arrests.

> **H. P. Albarelli** (cont'd): According to a former New Orleans resident, who is closely related to two of the boys sexually molested by Ferrie and today lives in northern New York: "The Youth Study Center has been a hotbed of corruption, sexual abuse, police brutality, and God only knows what else for decades…. Ferrie used to go there posing as a doctor of some sort, some sort of sham, to recruit kids…. He [Ferrie] took a lot of kids to Cuba, Guatemala and Honduras. Why? I don't know…. He was an amateur hypnotist … he practiced trance stuff on a lot of boys. I understand that, besides Youth Study Center visits he went to the East [Louisiana] State Hospital a lot, where some of his boys were taken for treatment. There were rumors and stories for years before I left [Louisiana] that Ferrie was in bed, no pun intended, with one of the doctors there, who was a drug addict…. Ferrie wanted the doctor to not treat the boys … the crazy rumor was that the hospital was treating the boys with LSD to stop them from becoming homosexuals and Ferrie hated that."(*A Secret Order*, pp. 79-80)

In 1999, I revealed that David Ferrie interacted with doctors and technicians at the East Louisiana State Hospital in late August 1963, teaching them how to properly inject one or more prisoners with a cancer-causing biological weapon, how and when to administer immune-system destructive x-rays, and how to keep the cancer-causing material alive. David Ferrie represented Dr. Alton Ochsner's interests there. Dr. Alton Ochsner and Dr. Robert Heath had worked together at the hospital with patients previously.[3]

In 1961, Dave would be forced to use all his wits and connections to try to extricate himself from the accusations being hurled against him.

To hear him speak of it later, a pack of piranhas had found a victim and were accusing him of everything but cannibalism. "I was a second father to my boys," he insisted. "You think I'd have fifty kids following me, if I was a monster? Do you have any idea how much damned child abuse was going on, that I stopped? They'd beat a boy with an electric cord, right out in the street, because the kid had taken a dollar bill. But according to those sons of bitches, you'd think I'd raped, killed and dismembered every boy I ever touched." Though I nodded my head in sympathy, I wondered why did Dave use the word "touch"?

David Ferrie Stands Accused:
Discoveries of Aug. – Sept. 1961:

1) David Ferrie's squadron turned out to be bogus. Parents were now worried that their sons were not getting properly trained. And would their sons be eligible for awards and certifications in the real Civil Air Patrol? The Landry's complained to the FBI.

2) Layton Martens, an underage youth, was working at the Balter Building for Sergio Arcacha Smith and had become embroiled in anti-Castro activities, including a raid on a munitions bunker.

3) A secretary at the Balter Building, Nancy Walker, recognized a photo of Al Landry and revealed she had seen Al in the building with David twice since August 5th, at the same time that the Landry's had been searching for their runaway son.

4) David took Al Landry on flights to Cuba and other foreign countries without his parents' knowledge. Under questioning, Al admitted that he had been to Cuba several times.

5) David loaned Al Landry his car while he was away on flights.

6) Mr. Landry stated that he saw David take several boys to a bar in New Orleans. He had also seen many CAP boys staying at David's home. Young Landry eventually stated that David took him and about 50 others boys to Graci's Lounge on Homedale Ave, for beer.

7) David tried to rearrange Al Landry's school schedule. The school called Mrs. Landry, who refused permission.

8) "All boys go to Ferrie when they run away from home," former CAP Cadet Lawrence "Butch" Marsch revealed.

9) Lawrence "Butch" Marsch (who found Al Landry on August 2nd and returned him to his parents) said Al will leave David only after he tires of him and finds a new boy.

10) On Aug. 17, Al Landry called his mother from Houston, Texas. He said he would come home only if certain demands were met, such as statements and actions from her and other parents to allow the Squadron to re-form and to convince Eastern Air Lines not to fire David Ferrie. Dave had created a business-type charter for the bogus squadron.

11) On Aug. 18, at about 3:30 PM, Arcacha Smith called officer Fournier. He had a notarized statement for the parents to sign. The statement, among other things, said Al Landry feared for his life at the hands of his father and grandfather and that Capt. Ferrie had done nothing wrong. All charges had to be dropped. To get their son back, the Landry's would have to sign the statement. They signed.

12) When the cover story that the boy had hitch-hiked to Houston when he ran away from home was proven a lie (Al looked too fresh to have been sleeping in ditches, and he couldn't remember the route he 'hitch-hiked' to Houston), Al tried to sue his own parents for removing him from Capt. Ferrie's possession. David again insisted that Al Landry was being abused and he had only been trying to protect him.

13) Investigators, unhappy with this coercion, found one of David's CAP members, 16-year-old Eric Michael Crouchet, who signed a typewritten statement that David "committed acts of crime against nature on him on two separate occasions." He later said Capt. Ferrie masturbated him on four or five occasions while Crouchet was under the influence of alcohol.

Crouchet also signed a statement that when Al Cheramie ran away from home, back in 1960, Capt. Ferrie had Crouchet watch Cheramie's house to see if Al would return. If he did, Crouchet was to send him by cab to David's house. David would then send Al to Corpus Christi, Texas. When David's house was raided and Albert's passport was found, it was returned to his father, Hughes Cheramie.

14) On Thursday, Aug. 24, Eric Crouchet visited the Landry home, complaining that David forced him to retract his statements. He disclosed to Officers Fournier and Juneau that on Wednesday,

Aug. 23, around 2:15 PM, Captain Ferrie said that he was delaying "M-1's and bazookas" and told him to sign a retraction. A reward was promised, if he signed. If not, Cubans would be coming after Crouchet, and he would get hurt. Crouchet signed, out of fear, and David left. Around 5:00 PM, Eric Crouchet saw David and two Cubans parked in a car outside a drug store, at which time David asked what reward he wanted from the Cubans. Crouchet suggested a motorcycle and a hideout in Miami. David said he should meet Arcacha Smith on Thursday, then said he had to rush – he had to pick up things at the "Balter Building." Crouchet said that one of the Cubans with David was described as a paratrooper who "jumped in the first invasion of Cuba."

In an August, 1993 interview, A. J. Weberman obtained a statement from Alvin Beauboeuf about Mike Crouchet:

> **Alvin Beauboeuf:** Dave ... was accused of a crime against nature with ... a real scuze-ball named Mike Crouchet. Ferrie asked me to be a character witness against him in court. It never went that far. After Dave lost his job with Eastern Airlines, the judge threw it out. It never went to trial. Dave was bisexual. No other Civil Air Patrol members came forward and said, "He did it to me too." I was a teenager back then.... My dad died when I was thirteen. Anytime I had a problem in school I went to Dave's house for some help. He had a blackboard there. He wouldn't quit until you understood what he was trying to teach you. There wasn't anything he didn't know about. He had a lot of radical beliefs. He was involved with the Cuban Revolutionary Front, Arcacha. They talked a lot. I never heard the conversations...

Records show former CAP Cadets (1958-59-60) and former Falcons (1960-1961) signed statements in 1961 accusing David Ferrie of committing crimes against nature with them. They were Mike Crouchet, James Landry, and Richard McClendon.

Perry Russo said David Ferrie's mother [Burdette, widowed] was present and visible in David's home during the Alexander Landry runaway scenarios. Russo said Ferrie would hypnotize Landry, but he was eventually able to influence Landry to stay away from Ferrie, who was training youths dressed paramilitary style and accompanied by one or more Cubans.[4]

> **HSCA:** ...a search of Ferrie's home [also revealed] priestly robes and a chalice, pills, medical syringes, blood pressure gauges ... the runaway of Al Landry [was referred] to the District Attorney, Austin Anderson. The case was never prosecuted. It was later learned that

[David's employer, G. Wray] Gil had once employed Anderson in his office some time before.

H. P. Albarelli: The investigation into David Ferrie's unlawful and perverse activities with young boys would quickly become extremely complex, involving well over 20 boys, and Ferrie and Arcacha Smith, as well as several unidentified Cubans, making strong-arm efforts to suppress evidence and threatening bodily harm to several of the young boys interviewed by detectives.... A number of the boys sexually molested by Ferrie were taken by law enforcement authorities to the Youth Study Center in New Orleans ... chartered "to provide secure detention to youth, ages 8-16 that have been arrested and are in pre-trial status." ... Since some of these boys molested by Ferrie had not been arrested, the reason for taking them to the Center is unclear and unexplained by police reports.[5]

Aug. 26, 1961: Eastern Air Lines suspends David Ferrie without pay. His ten-year career as a pilot of big planes is over.

Aug. 29, 1961: David receives a letter saying he has been removed from the Eastern Air Lines payroll as of Aug. 26, 1961.

Aug. 30, 1961: Layton Martens, Melvin Sealey[6] and Andrew Blackmon are arrested for vagrancy. They are jailed and interrogated for several days. Martens is also interviewed by the FBI. The real purpose seems to be getting more information about David Ferrie. Martens contends later that the arrest was a blatant attempt to pin a burglary charge on him, due to his association with Ferrie.

> **Arrest Reports on Martens**: (To SAG from SA Stephen Callender, 2/24/67): Layton Martens told Callender that besides David Ferrie, he was also arrested, along with Melvin Sealey and Andrew Blackmon. [Blackmon was a 'house guest' at David's home at the time.][7]

> **A. J. Weberman**: Layton Martens ... was arrested on August 30, 1961, for vagrancy pending investigation of burglary by the New Orleans Police Department. Layton Martens commented, *"No for god sakes, I was never Ferrie's roommate.* I did borrow his apartment when he was out of town, for about seven to nine days."

On November 25, 1963, Layton Martens told the FBI he had lived with David Ferrie since November 17, 1963, after his mother threw him out of her house.

"I was never arrested. I don't have any criminal record..." Jack Wasserman, a lawyer for Marcello, represented Layton Martens in this case. Layton Martens stated, "I didn't know any Jack Wasserman. It's about time I get a lawyer and start defending myself. If you print this stuff I'm going to sue! I'm a media figure. I'm a member of the Screen Actors Guild ... you're hurting me professionally..."

Except for the solitary word "activist," a multi-page tribute to Martens upon his death March 18, 2000 mentions nothing about his anti-Castro activities, David Ferrie, or the Kennedy assassination.[8] Martens played a cameo role as an FBI agent in *JFK*. He was also the phone voice threatening Garrison's daughter, and played a man who yells with pleasure in the bar scene when JFK's death is announced, in the same film.

The famous Jack Wasserman served as the attorney for David Ferrie and his young friends. Think about that. Wasserman was no ordinary attorney. Nor did his services come cheaply. Marcello may have had a hand in this, for Arcacha had no money, and neither did Dave or his cadets. Here's what famed columnist Drew Pearson wrote in a column, in Oct., 1963 about Marcello's best attorney:

> **Pearson:** The secret of his delaying tactics and the fact that he is still in the USA is Jack Wasserman, one of the smartest immigration attorneys in the business. Wasserman has handled the cases of such notorious persons as [gangster] Frankie Costello and Nicholas Malaxa [accused of genocide] ... both Costello and Malaxa are still in the United States.[9]

> **Memo:** SA Fleming, 1/24/62... LAYTON MARTENS at NOFO, 1/24/62, advised he was arrested by NOPD at his residence, 112 Egret Street ... for vagrancy and loitering and was held 3 days and released. He said he went to the Records Room of the NOPD and found out that he had been released as "case refused" by District Attorney.[10]

WEIRDNESS: AN OCCULT SYNCHRONICITY

Why were so many of Dave's boyfriends called "Al" – or the first two letters of their first or last name began with 'LA' [reversal]? Consider Al Beauboeuf, Al Landry, James Landry, Al Cheramie, Lawrence Marsch, Layton Martens. Aleister Crowley is considered to have been the epitome of the Evil Man. Crowley's Book of the Law was called LIBER AL vel LEGIS.

This of course is mere speculation, but, we must remember that David Ferrie was looking deeply into the occult. Peter Levenda notes that the famous séances attended by members of the "Round Table Foundation ... would ascend in occult prominence as "The

Nine." ... This impressive roster of America's earliest pedigreed families included, Henry Jackson, Georgia Jackson, Alice [née Astor] Bouverie, Marcella DuPont, Carl Betz, Vonnie Beck, Arthur Young [Bell Helicopter], Young's wife, *Ruth Forbes Paine Young* and [Andrija] Puharich [the séance leader]..."

The Paines were into the occult. Arthur Young went to Mexico in search of hallucinogenic drugs. Michael Paine was Young's stepson. Ruth and Michael Paine, the couple who sheltered Lee Oswald's family, seemingly out of the goodness of their hearts, also appeared to have helped to frame the innocent Lee Harvey Oswald for Kennedy's murder.

For more information on occult connections involving David Ferrie, see Peter Levenda's book *Sinister Forces*.

A GRATEFUL CARLOS MARCELLO STEPS IN

David Ferrie was in deep trouble over the Al Landry affair, backed up by accusations and statements made by Eric Crouchet, James Landry and Richard McClendon – all former CAP. It would be a financial burden, having been fired by Eastern Air Lines, to defend himself in court. Enter Carlos Marcello.

> HSCA: An unconfirmed Border Patrol report of February 1962 alleges that Ferrie was the pilot who flew Carlos Marcello back into the United States from Guatemala after he had been deported in April 1961 as part of the U.S. Attorney-General Robert Kennedy's crackdown on organized crime. This may have helped Ferrie establish an enduring relationship with the Marcello organized crime family.
>
> Another indication of any early Ferrie relationship with the Marcello organized crime family may be the legal assistance that Marcello's lawyer, Jack Wasserman ... provided to Ferrie associates, Layton Martens, who identified himself to police as Arcacha Smith's second-in-command ... and Andrew Blackmon. Both had been arrested shortly after Ferrie's arrest for indecent behavior.... Ferrie's ties to the Marcello organized crime family continued through his association with G. Wray Gill, Sr., who was also attorney of record for Carlos 'Marcello.

David often went to the four-story Balter Building on St. Charles, where Marcello's attorney and Dave's future employer, G. Wray Gill, had an office, and where Arcacha Smith's anti-Castro FRD was still located. Gill's most important client, Carlos Marcello, was highly interested in Arcacha's and David's anti-Castro affairs. David Ferrie was said to have obtained a loan from Herb Wagner to pay a $5,000 bribe to Assistant D.A. Graffagnino to defend him in court, a loan likely guaranteed by Carlos Marcello.

SOUL CITY (A BLACK NIGHT CLUB) SHUT DOWN.

Researcher Joan Mellen and others state that David Ferrie paid Jefferson Parish District Attorney Anthony J. Graffagnino $5,000 to handle the case. Graffagnino's ties to Carlos Marcello are exposed in this *Sports Illustrated* article from 1970:

> Carlos Marcello, known as the Little Man, [is] the most powerful Mafia figure on the Gulf Coast. Marcello's name doesn't appear on the title: instead, A. J. Graffagnino, a lawyer who has often represented him ... is the owner of record ... Graffagnino is a close personal friend of Marcello ... among the documents is a lease between Graffagnino and the previous tenant, Soul City, Inc., that calls for the rent to be paid at 1225 Airline Highway, which is the address of the Marcello's' Town and Country Motel as well as Carlos' headquarters.[11]

David Ferrie had saved Marcello's skin a few months earlier, and now Marcello returned the favor, and also assured David's future cooperation as a skilled pilot. Both men, after all, had a common cause – Castro's overthrow. It seems unlikely that David could have obtained $5,000 without someone like Marcello behind it.

OPERATION MONGOOSE AND BOBBY KENNEDY

> *New York Times* (November 19, 1997): Declassified Papers Show Anti-Castro Ideas Proposed to Kennedy.
>
> The Pentagon offered President John F. Kennedy an extraordinary variety of dirty tricks intended to sabotage Fidel Castro, newly declassified documents show. These plans ranged from sophomoric pranks, like faking a picture of a fat and debauched Castro to destroy the Cuban leader's image, to murderous plots, including sinking a boatload of Cuban refugees as a phony pretext for a United States military invasion. The plans were ... code-named Operation Mongoose and spurred by the President's brother Attorney General Robert F. Kennedy, to get rid of Mr. Castro by any means necessary.[12]

A sample of Mongoose mischief comes from a March 1, 1962, Army memorandum entitled "Possible Actions to Provoke, Harass or Disrupt Cuba," one among some 1,500 pages of once-secret documents made public by the Assassination Records Review Board. "In March 1962, the head of Operation Mongoose, Brig. Gen. Edward G. Lansdale, the Kennedys' personal choice for the job, asked the Joint Chiefs of Staff for their views on top-secret plans to concoct a pretext for a military invasion of Cuba. Those plans involved staging phony attacks against Americans and anti-Castro Cubans.

They included sinking an American warship.... *We could blow up a US warship in Guantanamo Bay and blame Cuba,"* the memorandum said."(Emphasis added)

HERBERT R. WAGNER, JR. AND "OPERATION MOSQUITO"

Herbert Wagner, who researcher Joan Mellen said supplied Dave with a $5000 "loan," showed up again in 1963 to provide Dave with yet another loan, at the insistence of Marcello's lawyer, (and Dave's employer) G. Wray Gill. In both cases, guarantees almost certainly came from Carlos Marcello. Wagner was one of David Ferrie's more respectable friends (Dave did have some respectable friends, believe it or not). Wagner was not a drug addict. He was not a disgruntled CAP cadet with an ax to grind. He was the respected Vice President of the St Charles Parish Credit Bureau. He owned Herb Wagner Finance Services. Wagner later supplied Garrison with information about 'Operation Mosquito, [Operation Mongoose] and Dave's activities with Arcacha Smith without malice or motive.

The statements below are taken from a scan of Garrison's D.A. Office's interview of Herb Wagner on Dec. 6, 1967:

```
I probably got to know DAVE FERRIE at the New Orleans Airport
where I have owned several airplanes.  I owned these airplanes
from 1946 on.  Sometime between 1946 and 1956 I definitely got
to know him because in 1952 when we opened the Kenner Finance
Company, I remember making direct loans to DAVE at that time.
```

Wagner also made a loan to Arcacha Smith, with David's recommendation and three references, but Wagner regretted it when Arcacha failed to repay. Later, David returned, again with Arcacha, asking for direct help from Wagner for their anti-Castro activities:

```
FERRIE came in, we sat down and we talked for a while and he told
me, "HERB, you can be real valuable to us."  FERRIE looked at me
and said, "Did you ever hear of "Operation.." And he stopped and
looked at ARCACHA and ARCACHA shook his head in an affirmative
manner and then FERRIE said, "Operation Mosquito?" I made some
little funny remark about so many mosquitos in the area and he
said, "No, HERB, with your knowledge of motors, you could be
helpful to us." Of course, he then went on to explain to me that
they were planning a sabotage campaign to Cuba to sabotage machin-
ery and transportation and so forth, in Cuba.  I stopped him at
that time and said, "Whoa, you've got the wrong man." I went on
talking to DAVE as a friend and said I was married and have
responsibilities and could not become involved in it.  He said
```

> direction gladly." DAVE then contacted me several days later and
> asked me, "HERB, did you give it any more thought?" And I told
> him, "DAVE, I just borrowed a hell of a lot of money to open this
> business up and I can't fool with this kind of stuff. I have to
> make every minute count." And he told me, "If money is the only
> thing keeping you from this, well, hell, we can get money."

But David didn't give up on Wagner. Several days later, he was back.

> He called me on another occasion later on and he came on real
> friendly this time. He said, "HERB, have you been getting any
> flying in lately?" I told him I couldn't afford to fly. And
> he said, "You're a damn fool. With what you know about navigation
> and flying, you can make money." I told him, "How in the hell can
> you make money, DAVE. Just tell me that." And he said, "We're
> taking people in and out of Cuba at nighttime." I didn't want any
> part of it.

WAGNER IS TERRORIZED

Wagner also told Garrison's people he approved a loan based on David's Stinson Voyager as collateral just prior to the Kennedy assassination, a loan which was used to provide David with funds to rent airplanes. The $400 loan was co-signed by Clay Shaw according to other sources. The official story is that David's Stinson was not flyable – worthless – but Wagner said David took him for a ride in the Stinson. He then approved the loan. Wagner's reward for his candor and loyalty to David Ferrie resulted in break-ins calculated to terrorize him.

> **Wagner,** to Garrison's people: Let me tell you this, five times since the assassination my house has been ransacked and nothing taken. Four different times my office has been ransacked and nothing taken. One time my camp on Blind River was ransacked and nothing taken. These can all be verified by police reports.

MARCELLO MAKES A DEAL

> **Dick Russell:** [FBI said] Marcello offered Arcacha Smith a deal whereby Marcello would make a substantial donation to the movement in return for concessions in Cuba after Castro's overthrow. (169) One explanation of Ferrie's ability to provide funds to Arcacha Smith may be that he acted as Marcello's financial conduit. (*The Man Who Knew Too Much.* p. 257.)

Before September 1961: At the blimp field in Houma, there were a number of storage sheds for air-freight companies to use. Dave and Guy Banister probably made one or two pick-ups of Schlumberger-marked boxes of seismic dynamite and caps before the famous heist in September. Gerry Hemming told me the pick-ups were staged to look like burglaries, so Schlumberger would get reimbursed through its insurance. I had asked Gerry about the "raids" out at Houma because the name "Schlumberger" stuck out for me.

Schlumberger supplied the plane Lee Oswald used, taking off from the same Houma blimp base, with stopovers in two Texas cities before finally landing in Houston. There, Lee caught a bus to Laredo, on his way to Mexico City. That was near the end of September 1963.

By mid-September, 1961: The famous "Schlumberger Heist" occurred. The participants were Andrew Blackmon, Rancier Blaise Ehlinger, David Ferrie, Layton Martens, Luis Rabel Nunez, Gordon Novel, Novel's wife Marlene Mancuso, Carlos Quiroga, and Sergio Arcacha Smith. Stephen Roy adds the name of "a boy" – "Woodcock." Blackmon's act of throwing an explosive cap out the window of one of the vehicles suggests what kind of material was taken. Arcacha's emerging rival was Luis Rabel, who lied to researcher A.J. Weberman, claiming that he wasn't involved in the raid, just as Layton Martens had done.

> **Stephen Roy** (posting as David Blackburst): I believe the expedition was on Sunday, September 17, 1961, and that the parties (including a boy named Woodcock) left from Ferrie's apartment at about 8:00pm and broke into the bunkers at about 10:45pm. They departed at about 11pm and arrived back at Ferrie's after midnight. The next day, Ferrie (who was skittish because his house had been searched by police several times recently) moved them to Banister's office. It appears that the arms only stayed there for a few days, until Quiroga drove them [in a U-Haul] to Miami ... Ferrie was also interested in obtaining a Douglas C-47 Skytrain transport (also known as a "Gooney Bird.") He may also have been interested in narcotics at this time.

Of all the various accounts I've read about the heist, Stephen Roy presented the best analysis of the entire matter.

This materiel was "stored on the old Houma "Blimp" field ... in a wooden shed (not a bunker) ... consist[ed] of a load of "downhole" seismographic explosive charge cartridges which Schlumberger (as well as anyone else in the seismograph industry) utilized in the oil/gas industry for mapping."

Ironically, Robert A. Baker, to whom I was married while living in New Orleans, spent the majority of his time out on "Quarter-boat Bob" replacing a man who had both his hands blown off by these same seismic charge cartridges. They were made, at that time, of dynamite. Robert wrote letters on Dixie Dynamite Distributors note-paper while out on the quarter boat that used these charges. A local address, as shown, was HOUMA, Louisiana, at the Blimp station.[13]

CARLOS QUIROGA AND DAVID FERRIE

> **HSCA:** Quiroga said, "Ferrie always had $100 bills around all the time, even after he lost his job with the airlines." He said Ferrie provided Arcacha with loans, which he never repaid.

Sixteen-year-old Carlos Quiroga (Dallas FBI Informant "NO T-5" in New Orleans) was an anti-Castro Cuban who reported on the doings of Banister, Arcacha Smith, David Ferrie and others. He was not trusted completely because his parents lived in Cuba, and his father was in prison there. Thus, he could have been a double agent.

> **Stephen Roy** (posting as Blackburst, 07/30/2000): October 1961: Arcacha ... introduces Carlos Jose Bringuier and Carlos Crusto Quiroga to Ferrie. But both men have heard about the morals charges, and decline to work with Ferrie. Ferrie's work with the FRD ends.

But Quiroga had been introduced to David prior to October, since he participated in the Houma heist along with David Ferrie and Arcacha Smith. Mr. Roy even names Quiroga as a participant, in a different post. Also, Quiroga was around David Ferrie enough to know he handed out $100 bills to Arcacha Smith. And he knew a lot more about the true role of Lee Oswald in New Orleans than he claimed, as DA Jim Garrison reminded Quiroga when he stood before Garrison's Grand Jury, concerning questions he didn't pass on a lie detector test. Quiroga took the Fifth.

```
    condition then.  But certain questions you failed, among them
                              just
    are the key matters which you/describedas having told the

    truth.   Knowing Oswald, knowing that he was not actually a

    Communist, knowing that the Fair Play for Cuba was a cover,

    in those areas the lie detector test show that you were  lying.

    Now, that is what we want to go into today, instead of stalling

    and going in other directions ....

A.  I do not want to incriminate myself, and I stand on my rights of

    the Fifth Amendment.
```
Quiroga's grand jury testimony.

AFTERMATH OF THE HOUMA HEIST

Stephen Roy: David Ferrie [was] actively involved in anti-Castro activities from November 1960 until shortly after his morals arrests, the September 1961 Houma heist being something of his "last gasp" as the Cubans ostracized him over the pederasty charges.[14]

Larry Hancock (response to Roy): ... we can make a good case that Ferrie was still involved as of 1962 with the attempt to set up the CRC sponsored camp that involved Hemming and associates. I say that because I have seen photos from that period showing Ferrie with Larry DeJoseph – and with him in planes, cars, etc. in New Orleans. Hemming says that Ferrie was helping them with his plane and that certainly appears to be true.

Dave told me he *never* stopped his anti-Castro activities. At the party I attended on April 28, 1963, a number of Cubans were present, many of them gay.

Late September: David obtains visas for travel to Argentina, Bolivia and Brazil.

Jack Martin: (to Garrison's investigator, Gervais, 1967) Two Juvenile Police Officers ... went with the Jefferson Parish Police to Ferrie's house and they made a raid and discovered a catch (sic) of arms, chemistry equipment, laboratory equipment, his library and radio equipment and other electronic devices and all this military equipment there.

HSCA inspection of police records: Two two-man submarines (made from large plane fuel tanks), a Morse code key, four model 1903 Springfield rifles, two .22 caliber rifles, one rifle, a flare gun, a .38 caliber revolver, a sword, a quantity of ammunition, three maps (of Havana Harbor, the coast of Cuba, West Indies, Cuba and North Coast).[15]

Gus Russo (*Live by the Sword*) wrote: Recalling Ferrie's bravery, Arcacha says, "He wanted to fly into Havana harbor and bomb the refineries. Ferrie had an idea to make two-man submarines, go in and just blow [the refineries] up. We actually made two of them, but we were prevented from using them." Layton Martens, who came with Ferrie to Arcacha's volunteer effort, also remembers the submarines. "Dave made them out of B-47 wing tanks," he recalls. "He kept one on his front lawn for a long time."

Don't laugh. Amateur mini-sub projects are popular. There are many photos of these on the Internet. David's project was ridiculed, but success was entirely possible.

A. J. Weberman (nodule 24), relates that an informant described Arcacha Smith's and David Ferrie's plans as of September 1961 to the FBI: ... he and his partners were taken to the residence of David Ferrie, where they were introduced to two young Cubans, and two young ex-Marines ... upon arriving at the house he was taken directly to the attic where there were maps of Cuba displayed on the walls, and a number of different types of firearms sitting in a rack. He stated in the basement of this same house were two roughly assembled two-man submarines. Source stated Smith and others excitedly discussed plans to blow up ships in Havana Harbor, sabotage key installations. He said Ferrie was to be a pilot for the organization, and they mentioned it would be about two weeks before the explosives (which were removed from a munitions bunker in Houma, Louisiana) would arrive in Cuba.

Bill Kelly (researcher): Following standard investigative procedures in the investigation of a conspiracy and homicide, DA Garrison used the Houma caper as a wedge, lever and related crime in order to 1) Convene a grand jury; 2) subpoena witnesses; 3) obtain information about Oswald and the assassination from those who could be convicted and jailed if they didn't cooperate.[16]

An Outpouring of Support at Dave's Hearing

Herbert Wagner (from his 1967 interview): When Dave became involved in a crime against nature charge in Jefferson parish, I was a character witness for him. He also had a priest from Loyola, several nuns showed up, but they were not brought in, Guy Banister showed up and many other people I didn't know. I remember talking to Banister personally and I talked to the priest personally.

Back to the grind
October 9, 1961: Arcacha Smith's FRD is absorbed into the Cuban Revolutionary Council (CRC), leaving Arcacha's organization

in chaos. He vacates the Balter Building and moves the new CRC branch into his apartment (but he has a pregnant wife and a young daughter). David Ferrie, still a close friend, would have been concerned over Arcacha's urgent need to find a new office.

October 12, 1961: Within three days, Jack Martin brings Arcacha to Sam Newman, owner of the Banister building. Newman agrees to rent room six at 544 Camp Street for $50 a month to Arcacha Smith. Rent was to be paid on based on income from fundraising drives.

Oct. 16, 1961: Senior Patrol Inspector Windle G. Roach, U.S. Border Patrol, says in September David told Eastern Air Line steward John Harris that he had an arms cache near New Orleans. He also said he was trying to buy "a C-47 airplane for $30,000."[17] Roach, as a member of the New Orleans Border Patrol, "Worked under Attorney General Bobby Kennedy and deported Carlos Marcello..."[18]

Oct. 19, 1961: Captain G. E. Grenier, Manager, Operations, Eastern Air Lines, Inc. at Moisant Airport, New Orleans, La. sends a letter to David, demanding a full chronology of events regarding the morals charges.

Oct. 22, 1961: David finds his Stinson, hangared at Lakefront, sabotaged. In 1963, Dave will tell the FBI that his Stinson has not been airworthy since spring, 1962, which his friend Herbert R. Wagner, Jr. will expose as a lie in his 1967 interview with Garrison's investigators. (Remember Dave took Wagner for a ride in his Stinson to prove its airworthiness in order to qualify the plane as collateral for a loan, just prior to the Kennedy assassination.)

> **Stephen Roy**: ... about a handful of an abrasive compound had been placed in each wing tank [and] short plastic strips [had been put into] the crankcase of the engine.... He and others say the plane was never flyable after that. His log-book seems to support it. The plane was eventually hauled to a friend's service station and disassembled. (To Education Forum) From another source, I have the 1960-1962 flight and engine logs.... There is no 1963 log as the plane was not airworthy.[19]

Was David still flying his other plane, the Taylorcraft L-2? We think so. Where are its log books? Were its log books confiscated? Stephen Roy has written: "On June 18, 1963 a student took his test flight in the Taylorcraft."[20] That's only five months before the Kennedy assassination. The Taylorcraft L-2 was flown regularly until it needed repairs late in 1962. I know it was flyable once more, after it was repaired, sometime before May 11, 1963. Dave sold it just prior to his death.

Oct. 25, 1961: FBI makes a summary statement that David is a "crackpot." FBI adds that he is "a very active member" of the CRF (Cuban Revolutionary Front), and as such, his anti-Castro activities and possession of firearms to use against Castro do not constitute a violation of the Neutrality Act, since the CRF is a creature of the CIA.[21]

A Walter Mitty Fantasy?

Stephen Roy (posting as Blackburst): Ferrie seems to have been aware of the CIA connection and romanticized it in a Walter Mitty kind of way. When he ran a training camp for his "Falcon Squadron" in early 1961, he claimed to have the backing of either the CIA or the State Department. And he claimed to Bob Boylston that, in the event of an attack on the US, he would pass along "secret orders" from the government. How much, if any, of this is true and how much might be Walter Mitty-type fantasy is unclear. But it all seems to have ended by late 1961.[22]

Anthony Marsh, son of a CIA agent/researcher: (responding to Roy/Blackburst's statement that if David Ferrie "really" was CIA, why didn't CIA protect him better and pay him better; such as, from financial troubles, the FBI assessment of being a "crackpot" and Garrison's hounding) "Sometimes the CIA tries to cut off its ties with an agent or asset when morals charges come up. Read Sheehan's *A Bright Shining Lie.*"[23]

Stephen Roy (posting as Blackburst, responds to Marsh): Ferrie's morals arrests were in August 1961, and the assassination was two years later. Why would CIA cut off ties to Ferrie (by failing to help him) after his morals arrests, but then use him as an assassin two years later?[24]

Note: Nobody was accusing Dave of being an assassin. Dave was being accused of being a getaway pilot and of being Lee Oswald's CAP gun instructor.

Anthony Marsh responds: I didn't say that CIA cut off ties to Ferrie.... But I think they maintained it to keep a pilot in reserve for Mongoose activities. Failing to help Ferrie does not signify that they cut off ties.... If you think that anyone who ever works for the CIA is automatically guaranteed to make a fortune, you need a reality check.

Stephen Roy (responding): ... Ferrie's anti-Castro activities dropped off to almost nothing a couple of months after his arrests.... I'm saying that Ferrie's post-1961 legal and financial decline does not support the idea that he was some kind of contract agent. What was Ferrie's end of the contract?

David Ferrie's "end of the contract" might have been Marcello's responsibility, through Dave's association with Arcacha Smith, whose FRD and CRC were connected to the CIA, but who was also promised funds from Marcello. David received a hefty sum equal to $65,000 in today's funds, supposedly for just two months of work during Marcello's trial, plus some flights to Guatemala. That's a lot, considering it's on top of Dave's monthly salary as a legal assistant to Marcello's attorney, G. Wray Gill.

> **Stephen Roy**, also told Marsh: As I have noted here, there is no credible evidence of a later Ferrie-CIA connection, and Ferrie's pathetic financial situation from 1962 to his death suggests that he was not paid for any such activities.

A JURY DECIDES JFK WAS ASSASSINATED BY THE CIA

A CIA veteran of 14 years, Victor Marchetti, executive assistant to CIA's Director, Richard Helms, testified that the CIA, not Lee Oswald, killed John F. Kennedy. Marchetti said Oswald was a contract agent for the CIA and that he'd been told that David Ferrie was a CIA agent at the time of the assassination.

Victor Marchetti.

Anthony Summers: (author/researcher, from *Not in Your Lifetime*) Victor Marchetti [former special assistant to CIA's Deputy Director] told me that he observed consternation on the part of then CIA Director Richard Helms and other senior officials when Ferrie's name was first publicly linked with the assassination in 1967. Marchetti claimed he asked a colleague about this and was told that "Ferrie had been a contract agent to the Agency in the early sixties and had been involved in some of the Cuban activities.

John Simkin: As a result of obtaining of getting depositions from David Atlee Phillips, Richard Helms, G. Gordon Liddy, Stansfield Turner and Marita Lorenz, plus a skillful cross-examination by [Mark] Lane of E. Howard Hunt, [a] jury decided in January, 1995, that [Victor] Marchetti had not been guilty of libel when he suggested that John F. Kennedy had been assassinated by people working for the CIA.

Money for Nothing?

As for who paid David Ferrie his big bonus, we now know the Mafia was working with the CIA, so Dave's impressive bonus payment might have been Marcello's responsibility, with backing of the CIA. Only after the Kennedy assassination was it impossible for the Mafia to give their pilot full protection, though the Marcello brothers would use Dave for contract work almost to the end of his life.

> **Stephen Roy** (as Blackburst to Marsh): Just FYI, Ferrie almost completely disappeared from anti-Castro activities after late 1961. Period.

Mr. Roy insists that Dave "almost completely disappeared from anti-Castro activities after late 1961. Period." He seems to assume that Dave's near-disappearance from overt anti-Castro activities means that he was no longer involved in any *covert* anti-Castro activities. That's not the man I knew. David was not only working for an attorney whose boss, Carlos Marcello, was actively supporting anti-Castro activities, he would soon be working with Dr. Mary Sherman, now on record as an INCA supporter and a medical aide to anti-Castro guerrillas. And Dave became involved in an underground, covert project aimed at killing Castro. That's why he became so quiet. He could still be useful in efforts to rid the planet of a hated communist without having to work with homophobic anti-Castro Cubans. However, almost to the end of his life, Dave surrounded himself with gay anti-Castro Cubans, as many witnesses mention.

October 30, 1961: Arcacha Smith awards a Certificate of Appreciation to Jack S. Martin for helping him obtain his office. From Jack Martin's interview with Garrison's Gervais: "After that [rescuing his family] Sergio trusted me more than he ever did, you know? He told me to lay off Ferrie."

David Ferrie's Lying Ways

Later, Dave will claim to the FBI that he did not know Arcacha's office was at 544 Camp St., though he was associated with Guy Banister and other anti-Castro champions in that same building at the time. He and Arcacha had remained close friends despite Mr. Roy's "timeline" for Arcacha's life, where Roy wrote:

> **August 17-18, 1961:** Arcacha intervenes on Ferrie's behalf in police matter involving Ferrie and runaway boy, Al Landry. Ferrie arrested, Arcacha begins severing relationship.[25]

This was not true. Arcacha continued to introduce David Ferrie to FRD and other anti-Castro Cubans, and of course, David was one of the leaders, with Arcacha, of the Houma heist, which occurred, according to Mr. Roy, in mid-September.

> **Roy**: I believe the expedition was on Sunday, September 17, 1961.
>
> **Stephen Roy**: (Posting as Blackburst, 07/30/2000): The time when Arcacha was at 544 Camp Street/531 Lafayette Street started just as Ferrie was being kicked out of the group, and ended just as Ferrie was beginning a relationship with Banister in that building. Could Ferrie have been telling the truth when he told the FBI that "he has never known of the [FRD] maintaining an office at 544 Camp Street, nor does he have any knowledge of Sergio Arcacha Smith maintaining an office at that address during the time that he was the head of the organization and later after he was replaced."

"Could Ferrie have been telling the truth" is a strange comment. Logic tells us that Dave was still close to Arcacha and that they had mutual friends, including Guy Banister, for whom Dave worked part-time, in the same building.

> **M. Bishop** (replying to Roy as Blackburst, above, wrote): All of this presupposes that Ferrie was so stung by his excommunication [from the FRD, after Dave's morals arrests] that he ceased to care about both the people and their cause; that he was so removed he no longer gossiped about either the people or their cause while drinking coffee at Mancuso's; that Gill, Banister, Gatlin, et al, failed to mention any further CRC/FRD/Arcacha developments to him, etc.[26]

Remember Arcacha Smith had to move the entire FRD office contents from his home to the new office.. David Ferrie was still a close friend of Arcacha's, and Dave, a frequent visitor, probably even helped in the move. Remember that fear played a role in what the FBI would be told. Example: According to Arcacha, when speaking to the *Washington Post* on Feb. 27, 1967, five days after David Ferrie was found dead, Smith couldn't quite recall if he had ever met Dave:

"I just don't know anything," Smith told a reporter over the phone. Clearly nervous and upset, Arcacha Smith refused to admit knowing Ferrie. "I can't recall," he said. "I studied the name in the papers the other day. I just can't recall him."[27] (The good news is that later Arcacha's memory improved dramatically as witnesses came forward with stories linking him to his old friend.)

David Ferrie, for his part, later claimed he had never been in Arcacha Smith's 544 Camp Street Office, though he was seen there, and his claim defies logic. The matter is a litmus test to determine the honesty of current researchers.

> **Rudolph Richard Davis**: ...had known Sergio ARCACHA for several years ... ARCACHA who introduced him to David Ferrie ... at ARCACHA'S home ... DAVIS stated he saw FERRIE three or four times, once in ARCACHA'S office at 544 Camp Street." REFERENCE: MEMORANDUM, March 22, 1967, Gurvich to Garrison, 28 Feb. 1967, interview of Rudolph Richard Davis, Jr. by Gurvich and Alcock, Houston, TX.

THE EASTERN AIR LINES LETTER

Oct. 30, 1961: David wrote a threatening and somewhat incoherent letter in his defense, with the assistance of his now-faithful Mafia-attorney, "Mr. [A. J.] Graffagnino," to Eastern Air Lines. The ever-faithful Arcacha Smith is also mentioned as being present at a "discussion."His letter is threaded with paranoia and threats against Eastern Airlines. Important parts of this long letter are shown here.[28] Some readers will find the letter fascinating. Others may wish they had never bothered to try to wade through it all. Enter at your own risk!

331 Atherton Drive Metairie, Louisiana. 30 October 1961
Captain G.E. Grenier Manager – Operations, Eastern Airlines, Inc.,
Moisant Airport, New Orleans, La.

Dear Captain Grenier:
This letter is written in response to your letter, addressed to me, dated October 19. My attorney, Mr. Graffagnino, has informed me of your request for a written report in addition to the verbal information given during the discussion between Mr. Graffagnino, Senor Arcacha, yourself, and me.

You require *"a plausible explanation of the incidents that lead to the filing of serious criminal charges" against me....* We have in hand indisputable proof for the facts cited herein. *For the composition of this letter, reports of reputable detectives have been employed.* Since your letter infers you require a chronological sequence, I shall list these events chronologically.

I must add one caution, however. The very nature of some of the information contained herein has given me considerable pause in whether I should respond to your request for information. First of all, I know of no "crime," violation of working agreement, or company rule which is violated when one individual makes a charge against another. Proven charges are another thing. *It is my opinion that it is not the business of Eastern Air Lines that some-one should make charges against me. It is another thing if these charges are proven to be true in a court of law.* In the second place, the revelation of this information to you contains a serious potential threat to my safety, as a subsequent paragraph will reveal. *I shall, therefore, hold you personally responsible if some of this information is divulged since my personal safety is involved.*

It is my belief that the chronology begins in 1959. *During the summer of 1959 I received my first anonymous threatening telephone call.* At this time positive information had come into my hands that Fidel Castro was a Communist, and that this was known in the State Department prior to the action of the U.S. Government forcing Batista out of office. Also at this time I was laboring to prevent the admission in the U.S. Air Force Academy of a candidate whose views, as well as those of his family, were anti-American, since he indicated he has no intention of supporting Amendment XIV, Section 1 of the U.S. Constitution. From that day until the present [page 2]… (at 2:15 P.M. this date) these telephone calls have continued. In some of these telephone calls I have been addressed obscenely, on some occasions as a "[…]-lover," a "Radical," a "Communist," an "Atheist," a "Religious fanatic" and so on. On other occasions polite, well-modulated voices have try [sic] to dissuade me from my activities and in particular my speeches against those persons and forces I deem subversive. Though all of these telephone calls have been anonymous, the identity of one of the voices has been established. On other occasions I receive "silent" phone calls, that in, when we answer a call, no response is made by the caller who, after a short interval, hangs up, or otherwise breaks the connection. *It became apparent that acting as a lone individual I could accomplish little, whereas with affiliation with a similar-minded group I might accomplish much more.* Therefore, I pursued several related problems:

(1) why did certain top officials deliberately cause the April 17 invasion of Cuba to fail?

(2) who is permitting millions of pieces of Communist literature to pass thru the New Orleans Post Office, at government expense, the purpose of which literature is prejudicial to the United States?

(3) who is permitting proscribed trade with Cuba to continue, which also [sic] involves a further drain on gold reserves?

(4) why are certain Communists, who enjoy high-level positions in local government, permitted to continue their activities against the United States?

(5) why are certain known communists allowed to continue dictating the placing of subversive textbooks in public and private schools?

(6) *why are certain persons in sensitive jobs, for example scheduled airlines, permitted to continue subversive activities?*

… I have been assisting in bringing Cuban refugees to the United States, and in obtaining necessities including medical care for them. I have likewise, in activities approved of and encouraged by the President of the United States and his Attorney General, – *helping to raise arms for the liberation of Cuba…*

During the month of August three persons associated with this work were arrested by a particular New Orleans policeman. We have been unable to learn what they were charged with. *They were held incommunicado for four days. During this time they were also maltreated….* In the course of the interrogations one police official tried to extract a commitment from these individuals that they would desist in their activities to assist the Cubans. *One of the officers stated that his objective was "to put Arcacha and Ferrie in jail."* In pursuance of this objective these three were interrogated to produce evidence against me of

(1) stealing an airplane;

(2) participating in acts treasonous to the United States;

(3) dealing in contraband;

(4) committing forgery;

(5) illegally dealing in arms.

Subsequent to this the New Orleans Police came to my home to search it, claiming they possessed a valid Search Warrant. They refused to produce this warrant and refused to divulge the quest of the search. These acts are in clear violation of the law. They returned a second time, and did not even claim to possess a warrant, but stated they were searching for narcotics. They returned a third time «to search» but did not search, but engaged in a day-long harassment of my mother, my guests and myself.

During this time interval I was taken to the East Bank Jail, Jefferson Parish, and interrogated relative to harboring a run-away New Orleans juvenile. Since it developed I had nothing to do with it I was released. Then I was arrested for a "crime against nature," allegedly committed with a New Orleans minor. I was held incommunicado until a friendly bondsman learned of my plight and bailed me out and summoned Mr. Graffagnino, whom I had not known prior to this time. At the time of the arrest the police refused to divulge the charge.

When I finally learned of the charge and the person allegedly making it, I took two witnesses and confronted the said New Orleans minor. He admitted that he made the charges. But, he insisted to myself and witnesses that he had been compelled to sign the charges or face a jail term. Thereafter, he signed a statement exonerating me, and indicating how he came to sign them. The following day he came, of his own volition, and signed a second statement. The New Orleans authorities were apprised of this.

Thereupon one of these same policemen returned to the New Orleans juvenile and compelled him to sign a second statement stating he had been «intimidated» by me, and these same police claimed to be able to «produce eight witnesses to the intimidation….

During this time it was learned that my telephone was tapped…. Recently a second tap occurred.

On October 24, my brother, who lives and works in the North, had pressure applied to him. One of the officials of his company summoned him and threatened his job unless it could be ascertained that our family had no further connection with any activity involving the liberation of Cuba, or other activities resisting Communist take-over in the Caribbean area.

… All of the foregoing has been climaxed by an extortion attempt, the revelation of which is dangerous to my safety. I have been told "everything will be forgotten" if

(1) I pay a substantial sum of money;

(2) leave the state of Louisiana;

(3) keep this "offer" a secret "or else."

For obvious reasons this cannot be reported to local police, and WILL NOT be reported. However, it has been reported to Federal authorities for whatever action they can take.

At this time we do not know the chain-of-command of the Communists at the local level. However, my problems have been traced with certainty to a highly placed local official…. *Whether Communists within Eastern Air Lines are involved is not known at this time.*

… We are wondering about the legality of my suspension from flying. We are curious about your statement (to Mr. Graffagnino, Senor Arcacha and myself) that someone in authority over you has indicated that my activities regarding Cuba be stopped. We are curious about your implication that Eastern has piled up other things against me. (I understand from ALPA that it is an Eastern practice to try to accumulate a file to be used against an individual as it suits the company.) Likewise, we are wondering whether the public interest would be better served if we released names of Communists and Fellow-Travelers employed by Eastern Air Lines.

Be assured that civil suits are in preparation (and probably more will be prepared) against any and every individual, organization and/or group responsible in any way for any damages that have occurred to me during this affair.

very truly,
Captain David W. Ferrie

This rude and threatening letter, of course, sealed David's fate, though he would continue to fight to get reinstated for the next two years.

HSCA: Attorney G. Wray Gill notified Eastern when the last of the charges against Ferrie had been *nolle prosequied*; Eastern responded with a letter inviting Ferrie to discuss the charges at a meeting in Miami. Ferrie did not go. Instead, several individuals, including one of the boys who had been named in a sex offense charge against him, wrote to Eastern to plead that Ferrie be reinstated."

HSCA: Jack Martin, a private investigator associated with Banister may also have been contacted by Ferrie for assistance on his case. Later, Martin wrote letters to the FAA and Eastern Airlines on Ferrie's behalf.

1961: Anti-Castro terrorist group Alpha 66 is founded by Andres Nazario Sargen and Eloy Gutierrez Menoyo. HSCA lists Alpha 66 first in a list of "over 100 ... most active anti-Castro groups ... in November 1963..."[31]

HSCA: ... the most active anti-Castro groups ... included Alpha 66, Cuban Revolutionary Junta (JURE), Commandos L, the Directorio Revolutionario Estudiantial (DRE), the Cuban Revolutionary Council (CRC), which includes the Frente Revolucianario Democratico (FRD), the Junta Gobierno de Cuba in Exilo (JGCE), the 30th of November, the International Penetration Forces (InterPen), Revolutionary Recovery Movement (MRR), and Ejercito Invasor Cubano (EIC).[32]

Dec. 1961 – Jan. 1962: Ferrie calls Guatemala City many times:
From researcher Peter Whitmey:

	Calls To	&	From
Dec. 5, 1961	Baton Rouge		New Orleans
Dec. 11, 1961	Dallas (214-RI2-5178)		New Orleans
Dec. 12, 1961	Houston		New Orleans
Dec. 12, 1961 (2)	New Orleans		Houston
Dec. 14, 1961	Guatemala City		New Orleans
Dec. 16, 1961	Guatemala City		New Orleans
Dec. 19, 1961	Guatemala City		New Orleans
Dec. 19, 1961	Brownsville, TX		New Orleans
Dec. 20, 1961	Guatemala City		New Orleans
Dec. 21, 1961	Guatemala City		New Orleans
Dec. 27, 1961	Guatemala City		New Orleans
Dec. 30, 1961	Bethesda, MD (202-DL2-3528)		New Orleans
Dec. 31, 1961	Guatemala City		New Orleans

Jan. 2, 1961	Matavaros, Mexico	New Orleans
Jan. 4, 1962	Jackson, MS	New Orleans
Jan. 6, 1962	New Orleans	Alexandria
Jan. 9, 1962	New Orleans	Houston
Jan. 10, 1962	Guatemala City	New Orleans

A 1961 $10 fundraising bond. Arcacha Smith raised funds for the FRD, with Layton Martens' assistance. Arcacha would soon be [justly] accused of keeping an undeclared portion for himself by rivals in his organization.

WHAT WAS GOING ON IN GUATEMALA?

The CIA did not want President Kennedy to get involved in Guatemala, even as the CIA interfered with the will of the people, who were in revolt. The CIA supported strong US corporate interests. Carlos Marcello's influence in Guatemala was also strong. Pro-Castro leftists, who saw their chance, began to pour in, precipitating a long and brutal civil war.

> **Document 126**: Telegram 496 from Guatemala City, April 19, 1962. Danger of a Communist takeover in Guatemala discussed with President Ydígoras. Secret. 1 p. DOS, CF, 714.00/4–1862.

> **Document 127**: Memorandum from Edwin M. Martin to McGhee, April 26, 1962. Reasons to keep the President from getting involved in Guatemalan situation for the time being. Secret. 2 pp. DOS, CF, 714.00/4–2662. (http://history.state.gov/historicaldocuments/frus1961-63v10-12mSupp/ch7)

Dec. 1961: Civil War in Guatemala: Chaos and destruction will continue for the next three decades. The US will lose diplomats to murder in the coming years in their efforts to keep puppet dictators in power for US corporate purposes, as some 200,000 citizens, mostly poor Indians, will die or go missing.

Despite the dangers, David Ferrie will personally fly to Guatemala for Carlos Marcello on numerous occasions. Several of these flights are documented by passport stamps using commercial flights.

Late December 1961: David claims he had previously helped Jack S. Martin investigate ordination scams, where for $5.00 an applicant could get ordained. This led to meetings with leaders of such sects as the Old Roman Catholic and Old Orthodox Catholic Church, and to David's eventual interest in getting ordained in one or more of the sects.

> **Peter Levenda**: Stanley told the FBI that he consecrated David Ferrie as a bishop in July of 1961, but then removed him from that office the following January when Stanley learned of Ferrie's homosexuality. When the author first read Stanley's statement, he burst out laughing. Homosexuality was never a bar to either ordination or consecration at the American Orthodox Catholic Church ... the history of the American Orthodox Catholic Church (indeed, of all the "wandering bishop" dioceses) is replete with instances of every form of sexual expression. (It's not for nothing that Propheta's headquarters – the Cathedral of the Holy Resurrection – was known as "the Cathedral of the Holy Erection" in wandering bishop circles.) ... Ferrie was never defrocked or deposed or in any way removed from office due to homosexuality, and it is doubted that he was ever removed at all, for any reason. If he was, he would have been the first (and probably only) person ever kicked out of the wandering bishops' club.[33]

January 20, 1962: Sergio Arcacha Smith is fired by vote of the CRC, but remains a member of Ronnie Caire's Crusade to Free Cuba. Since Jack Martin had created a commemorative coin idea that resulted in missing funds, Arcacha's refusal to sever his friendship with David Ferrie was the last straw. Luis Ravel takes over as the area's new CRC delegate.

Ravel will later hire Arcacha for the PR position in the CRC that Arcacha had originally given to him.

Jan. 1962: Bishop Carl John Stanley supposedly removes David Ferrie from his position as Bishop for the City of New Orleans.

> **Stephen Roy** (Feb. 19, 2005 post to Greg Parker, Education Forum): The group Martin and Ferrie were associated with was the "Byzantine Primitive Catholic Church, Old Catholic Church in N.A., Apostolic, Orthodox, Catholic, Order of Saint John," according to the consecration certificates. The group Ferrie alone was associated with was the 'Society of the Domestic Missionaries Of Saint Basil the Great', according to his membership card.

Peter Levenda: (doesn't believe David was removed, but if so) … it may have been more the legal problems Ferrie had with Eastern Airlines over his homosexual conduct that contributed to his ouster from the church, once Stanley – no stranger to the legal system – learned of them and feared that close scrutiny would be paid to his own operation…[34]

When questioned by the FBI after the Kennedy assassination, David Ferrie will claim that he never knew about the CRC, located at the Camp St. end of Banister's building, despite the fact that he often meets Arcacha, other CRC members, and Banister at Mancuso's coffee shop at the same address.

February 1962: David passes his annual medical exam for his Airman's Medical Certificate.

When Melvin Coffey, a former CAP Cadet trained by David Ferrie, is discharged from the Army, he renews his friendship with David. By November 1963, he will be a close friend. Along with Alvin Beauboeuf, Coffey will accompany David Ferrie on the suspicious trip to Houston, Texas through a rainstorm on the night of the Kennedy assassination.

Feb. 6, 1962: David hires Guy Banister as an investigator in his morals case, in exchange for investigative work for Banister. Banister will help G. Wray Gill and Jack Wasserman prepare for David's upcoming trial.

February 9, 1962: With CIA funding drying up, the CRC moves to Ravel's home. The FBI will never ask to look at Newman's lease records for the unpaid CRC office, even though Lee Harvey Oswald will be stamping "544 Camp St." – the same address as the

Lee Oswald stamped pamphlets and hundreds of "Hands off Cuba" flyers with "544 Camp St". before switching to other addresses.

CRC – on flyers handed out in 1963, and Banister will still be the main tenant there.

Feb. 16, 1962: Eric Crouchet tells Border Patrol Agent Patrick Duval that David Ferrie rescued Carlos Marcello, but since the flight was clandestine, there is no way to prove it.

Richard Billings' Journal: Information on Ferrie mug shot: 331 Atherton Dr., Metairie (address in 1961-62) – pilot, Cleveland ... ruddy, brown hair and eyes, 43, 195, 5'11" – arrested 2/16/62...[35]

Feb. 16, 1962: David is arrested and charged with extortion. He will face trial for forcing retractions of accusations made by former CAP members. By the end of February, David will be acquitted of all charges.

Feb. 27, 1962: Judge Leo W. McCune finds David W. Ferrie innocent on one of five charges of indecent behavior with a juvenile.[36] Dave is still living at 331 Atherton Drive despite mounting financial problems.

Feb. 1962: Layton Martens says David Ferrie was out of town a lot, when interrogated by Assistant D.A. Alvin Oser on Sunday, Mar. 12, 1967. He agrees that Charles Cater, a male nurse, had been living with David. Martens then states, "I think I heard Ferrie mention [Cater] concerning the trial in '61. Cater was mixed up in this some way and apparently Cater wasn't a very friendly person to Ferrie."

Assistant DA Alvin Oser with Assistant D.A. James Alcock. The two men will interrogate many of David's friends before and after the Kennedy assassination for Jim Garrison.

Oser replies, "Oh, I see. Did Dave make any trips, say in the year '63, say in the early part of '63?"

Martens replies that he asked Al Beauboeuf about this, then says "... Ferrie was probably out of town as much as he was in town at the time he was working for Gill."

Feb. 1962: Julian Buznedo Castellano, anti-Castro guerrilla and Bay of Pigs survivor who received free flying lessons from David Ferrie and Hugh Ward,[38] finally leaves New Orleans.[39]

Feb. 28, 1962: *Times-Picayune*, p. 17: "Ferrie Innocent on One Charge." "Judge Leo W. McCune of the Jefferson Parish juvenile court Tuesday found David W. Ferrie innocent on one of five charges of indecent behavior with a juvenile. Ferrie, 43, 331 Atherton Dr., Metairie, a former airline pilot, has charges against him in both Jefferson and Orleans parishes in connection with alleged indecent acts with juvenile boys, and has also been charged with extortion, intimidation of a witness and threats against a juvenile in Orleans Parish." The remaining four charges are dropped in November.

DAVE MOVES TO A NEW PAD AND TRIES TO CLEAR HIS NAME

Now that Ferrie is free of most charges, G. Wray Gill hires him as an assistant in March of 1962, doubtless due to Carlos Marcello's influence. Dave now receives a low but decent annual salary of $3,600, which would cover all his needs if he did not pump so much of it into his preferred lifestyle and anti-Castro activities. The poverty level in 1964 for a single male David's age was $1,650/yr. (Ref. US Census Bureau). David will eventually receive a $1,635.90 settlement payment [approx. $14,000 in today's funds] from Eastern Air Lines.

> **Richard Billings' Journal**: ...after [his mother's] death, Ferrie moved in March, 1962 from 331 Atherton Dr., Metairie.[40]

David Ferrie's next dwelling at 3330 Louisiana Avenue Parkway was recently re-numbered, but it's such a distinctive house that it is easily recognized. Dave's attractive second-floor apartment opened up to a large screened porch at the front, which Dave promptly began to litter. His mother's furniture and his beloved piano were moved in. A large library, with many medical

3330 Louisiana Avenue Parkway.

books, and a host of religious, scientific and unusual items, flowed from one room to the next.

RFK OK's GET-CASTRO PLOTS

March 16, 1962: "Bobby Kennedy Suggests a Plan to Assassinate Castro": (reported by *The Nation*, March 26, 2004) "[A] Pentagon document – once classified Top Secret – was released by the ARRB in late

1997 ... record[ing] a meeting of senior national security officials in the Oval Office on March 16, 1962 ... President Kennedy told the group he would not yet approve any direct US military intervention in Cuba. Next, the conversation turned to another matter. This is how {Brig. Gen. Edward] Lansdale captured it in his memorandum for the record: 'The Attorney General then mentioned Mary Hemingway [Ernest Hemingway's widow], commenting on reports that Castro was drinking heavily in disgruntlement over the way things were going, and the opportunities offered by the shrine to Hemingway

Edward Lansdale

... we were in agreement that the matter was *so delicate and sensitive* that it shouldn't be surfaced to the Special Group [an elite interagency group that reviewed covert actions] until we were ready to go, and then not in detail..." (author emphasis)

Lansdale's description of the Hemingway plan as "so delicate and sensitive" that its specifics should be hidden from the Special Group is another tip-off that the operation involved assassination. "That's the giveaway," says Peter Kornbluh, a senior analyst at the National Security Archive and a specialist on US documents regarding Cuba. "This is the closest thing to a smoking gun that has been declassified. *Only assassination would be taboo for open discussion at the Special Group,* which routinely planned sabotage, violence and chaos to undermine Castro." Samuel Halpern, who was number two to the officer who ran the CIA end of Operation Mongoose calls the document "as close as we're likely to get" to conclusive proof.

The CIA JM/WAVE station in Miami served as operational headquarters for Operation Mongoose, run by CIA's William Harvey. And as a former CIA director said, "The language of the memo speaks for itself. The only thing Robert Kennedy can be referring to is the assassination of Castro. This paragraph should never have been written."

William Harvey

The CIA now had a go-ahead to assassinate Fidel Castro. Of course CIA would support any plan that ideally could not be traced back to the CIA or to the US government – meaning Dr. Ochsner's plans would be OK, too.[41]

March 23, 1962: One week after RFK approves of plots to kill Castro, Dr. Alton Ochsner, President of International House, removes Clay Shaw as its Acting Director, where Shaw had held various positions for over nine years (Shaw remains a manager at The New Orleans Trade Mart). Dr. Paul A. Fabry (a Hungarian refugee and former CIA Voice of America, Hungary) takes Shaw's place at IH.[42]

FABRY IS NAMED AS IH DIRECTOR

Takes International House Post April 1

Paul A. Fabry, Delaware public relations counsel, has been appointed executive director of International House.

Dr. Alton Ochsner, IH president, said Fabry will assume his duties April 1.

The executive director post was held for 15 years by Charles Nutter who resigned last June. Since that time Clay Shaw, managing director of International Trade Mart, has been serving as IH acting managing director.

Fabry has been associated with the E. I. duPont de Nemours Company of Wilming-

tion since 1956 as specialist in international public relations.

From 1850 to 1851 he was connected with Radio Free Europe, heading one of its information divisions in New York and serving as editor of the monthly, News From Behind the Iron Curtain. Before returning to the United States in 1949 he was a foreign correspondent and lecturer in Istanbul, Turkey.

He has traveled widely and speaks fluently French, German and Hungarian, besides having a knowledge of Spanish, Italian and Turkish.

Dr. Ochsner said Thursday: "We are delighted to have been able to secure the services of Mr. Fabry whose background and experience will permit us to carry on the programs of our ...ation." He added that

PAUL A. FABRY

News article: "Fabry moved to New Orleans to work with International House, which later became the world's first World Trade Center. He was managing director from 1962 to 1985."

Endnotes

1. http://visupview.blogspot.com/2013/11/the-jfk-assassination-strange-and_17. html. The blog includes the Albarelli quote. (Retrieved 02/28/2014).

2. Was "Mining in the Honduras" for David's CAP Boys Based on a 'Nutty' Idea? Robert E. Lee, Assistant D.A. in Garrison's office, once worked with David on some Eastern Air Lines round-trip flights as a steward. On July 12, 1967, he revealed the following: "... FERRIE had purchased some stock in a close corporation whose headquarters were located in Honduras., In addition to buying this stock, he had flown down to Honduras to look into a "Kahunie Nut" venture. Simply it was this: "The Kahunie Nut has a juice which when squeezed out an mixed with a certain compound will harden into a mass as strong as iron, and of course, rust proof and will endure for centuries. There are only two machines available built to squeeze the juice from the Kahunie Nut – one is in Chicago and one is in Belize, Honduras. The owner of the machine in Chicago won't exhibit or sell his machine since he is preparing to move his equipment to Honduras to start production. Incidentally, there is only one area in the world where the Kahunie Nut grows, in the jungles of Honduras. So that if FERRIE acts fast ... FERRIE purchased $4,500 of stock and gave the president) of the corporation $2,000 for the machine. Neither FERRIE's money nor the machine ever got together, and FERRIE came to me."

Author: "... David had created an excuse to bring his bogus CAP boys to the Honduras, where they could go "mining" and be trained in jungle warfare, while Ferrie could also have sexual relations with some of them without worrying about parental interference. The "Kahunie Nut" is the cahune nut. While it didn't have the magical properties assigned to it, Dave knew his chemistry and would have studied its properties before making such an investment. It's likely that the nut *might* have had oils of interest to NASA. "

Original Message
From: Black….. at aol.com To: stoves at listserv.repp.org Sent: Friday, October 15, 2004 6:48 PM Subject: Cohune Nut Peter: I am researching a VERY obscure incident from 1960 or so, an apparent con game, where a promoter named Lawrence Taylor and a man named J. "Mac" McHenry took money from an investor to develop what has been described to me as the "Kahunie Nut", or the "Carosa Nut", in then-British Honduras. The nut could be crushed in a Jeep-mounted device, and the pulp would be of some value to NASA in the space program(!?!). This was supposedly complicated by the nut being protected as the "national plant", or some such thing. I did a web search for "Nut British Honduras", and I came upon your page, which mentions the "cohune nut". This is so close to "Kahunie" that I wondered if you have any additional info about it. Does any of this ring a bell? Stephen Roy (query directed to this site: http://www.bioenergylists.org/newsgroup-archive/stoves/2004-October.htm).

3. The material about Ochsner and Heath is on record in Bill Davy's book *Let Justice Be Done*, of which I knew nothing at the time. My whole family knows I never had any "JFK assassination" books. When I first brought up David's connections with Ochsner, Heath and East Louisiana State Hospital at Jackson in 1999, nobody at that time knew of any records to back this up. Davy's book was out, but mention of Heath and Ochsner was just in an obscure footnote. So nobody believed me, except Martin Shackelford, who knew about Davy's rather obscure book, and likewise knew how ignorant I was of the assassination materials published there. For example, I posted to McAdams' newsgroup, innocently believing that the hornet's nest of disinformation artists there would welcome a new witness. Instead, they began attacking me before they knew how to properly spell my name. I was quite shocked at their rudeness to both me and to Shackelford, who defended me.

4. Ref: M E M O R A N D U M February 27, 1967 TO: JIM GARRISON FROM: ANDREW J. SCIAMBRA RE:[1st] INTERVIEW WITH PERRY RAYMOND RUSSO 311 EAST STATE STREET BATON ROUGE, LOUISIANA.

5. http://visupview.blogspot.com/2013/11/the-jfk-assassination-strange-and_17.html (Retrieved 01/02/2014).

6. ARRB-released Police report says "Sealey" and Garrison Grand Jury transcript for Layton Martens(spelling errors by court stenographer possible) says "Sealing."

7. Memo, DeBrueys: 9/5/61, NO 105-1456-74: Arrest Book,3rd Dist., reflects arrest of all 3 — 8/30/61, 12:30 AM by PAT. P LEE and L RYAN for vagrancy. NO 2-112-3.

8. Fair use photo of obituary-tribute for Martens can be seen at: http://educationforum.ipbhost.com/index.php?showtopic627 as posted by Martens' friend, Daniel Meyer, 18 Sept. 2010. (Retrieved July 22, 2013).

9. Drew Pearson, "On the Washington Merry-Go-Round" Oct. 9, 1963 http://dspace.wrlc.org/doc/get/2041/50018/b18f07-1009zdisplay.pdf (Retrieved July 6, 2013).

10. See: http://jfk.hood.edu/Collection/Weisberg Subject Index Files/M Disk/Martens Layton% 20Patrick/Item 16.pdf (Retrieved July 5, 2013).

11. Morton Sharnik. "This Saint Has Been Called A Sinner" *Sports Illustrated* June 01, 1970 http://sportsillustrated.ca/vault/article/magazine/MAG1083670/index.htm (Retrieved 09/19/2013).

12. http://www.nytimes.com/1997/11/19/us/declassified-papers-show-anti-castro-ideas-proposed-to-kennedy.html (Retrieved 02/28/2014).

13. Dixie Dynamite Distributors, just as Schlumberger, was a foreign company. Registration Number: 20202430F Type: Foreign Business Corporation Status: Inactive Date of Formation: 1948-05-04 http://businessprofiles.com/details/dixie-dynamite-distributors-inc/LA-20202430F#ixzz2ugl1lPFY.

14. Posting as Stephen Roy to author Larry Hancock, The Education Forum, Jan. 12, 2005, 09:36 PM.

15. HSCA cites FAA, vol.4, attachments F through I.

16. http://educationforum.ipbhost.com/index.php?showtopic366 (Retrieved 02/14/2014).

17. A. J. Weberman ,Coup d'Etat in America, Vol. Four p. 186 http://www.scribd.com/doc/120819671/COUP-D-ETAT-IN-AMERICA-VOLUME-FOUR (Retrieved June 8, 2013).

18. Bill Broyles, Mark Haynes. *Desert Duty: On the Line with the U.S. Border Patrol.* UT Press, 2010. P. 181 "Wendy Conde."

19. Posted as Stephen Roy. http://educationforum.ipbhost.com/index.php?showtopic89 (Retrieved Nov. 3, 2012).

20. Posted as Stephen Roy to Lee Forman, 07 July 2005 -06:38 PM, Education Forum.

21. A. J. Weberman , *Coup d'Etat in America*, Vol. Four; summary of several files, e.g. FBI 105-104340-2 http://www.scribd.com/doc/120819671/COUP-D-ETAT-IN-AMERICA-VOLUME-FOUR (Retrieved June 8, 2013).

22. black....@aol.com Subject: Re: Jim Garrison vs. the CIA: TKO Date: 12 Sep 1999 00:00:00 GMT Message-ID:19990912130228.07530.00007376@ng-cj1.aol.com posting in McAdams' group. (Retrieved 04/01/2013).

23. IBID. From: Anthony Marsh Subject: Re: Jim Garrison vs. the CIA: TKO Date: 15 Sep 1999 00:00:00 GMT Message-ID: 37E00EC0.7268458E@quik.com posting in McAdams' group.

24. IBID. Besides an obvious answer to this question – that cutting Ferrie off from the CIA and then later using him as an assassin creates plausible deniability – the tag "assassin" is used instead of "asset" or "contact."

25. http://educationforum.ipbhost.com/index.php?showtopi645 (Retrieved 09/08/2013).

26. https://groups.google.com/d/topic/alt.conspiracy.jfk/wyMkDqZ5QRw [Retrieved 08/09/2013).

27. Harold Weisberg. *Oswald in New Orleans: A Case for Conspiracy with the CIA*. Ch. 14, "Garrison's Gallery."

28. Transcription by Jerry Shinely online for some 15 years. Italics for emphasis.

29. Hospital Records, Charity Hospital, New Orleans, for Jack Martin, Psychological service, 12/23/56 admitted, 1/28/57 discharged, 12 pages. Martin, an intelligent man, had received electroshock treatment for depression. 1978 examination of Garrison files found the 12-page record, contents not disclosed. http://www.copi.com/articles/connick/outside_contact_report.rtf. (Retrieved Jan. 2, 2013).

30. Jack Martin, often reviled as a lying drunkard, actually knew so much that he was allowed inside every agency and police office. This excerpt demonstrates how much Martin knew about David Ferrie. He references the Crouchet case and other incidents with an insider's knowledge: [corrected for linguistic and spelling errors of the transcriber] MARTIN:...[we met] in the Coffee Shop. So, anyway, Arcacha, tells me

-I don't trust this guy [Carlos Quiroga]. Ferrie speaks a good bit of Spanish. GERVAIS: Ferrie does? MARTIN: Oh, yeah. He can take the – of the Romans Canons...You would swear he is reading English, but he's reading Latin. He could cold turkey read Greek and he could cold turkey read Latin. I meant it and you will find out why. Well, anyway, I met Ferrie and he didn't trust him [Quiroga] after what I knew about him. <snip> Arcacha knew him;

- I had met Ferrie casually several different times. Then he got up in the St. Charles Hotel and he'd talk about Communists and Castro, Ferrie did. Now there's a record of this speech he made in … the newspaper.... This is before he got knocked off in the queer operation. He was talking about Communism, and Cuban ideas and this and that and other things. Cubans didn't like this bastard. I got along with him.... Carlos-Quiroga hated Ferrie with a passion. Arcacha used to accept Ferrie.... Arcacha was formerly with the Diplomatic Department in Cuba. Anyway, about this time, they started to close in on the Sergio Family, which was fouled up. I got hold of a friend of mine, a former FBI. I got hold of an investigator of the Naval O.N.I. (Office of the Naval Intelligence) to get his family down into the Guantanamo Naval Base and have them flown back to New Orleans and seen he got his people back. After that, Sergio trusted me more than he ever did, you know? He told me to lay off Ferrie. In the meantime, Ferrie got in on this deal where he allegedly formed a C.A.P. Squadron Civil Air Patrol)... all the authorities for C.A.P. claim that they knew nothing about it. He got a bunch of young kids in this C.A.P. and was teaching them judo, close-order drill, extended-order drill, taking them on camping trips … like a scout master. There was a kid involved in this mess by the name of Crouchet. Every time he flunked this kid, Crouchet, Crouchet's father got mad and came to the New Orleans Police about it. Two Juvenile Police Officers, I forgot their names, went with the Jefferson Parish Police- to Ferrie's house and they made a raid and discovered a catch of arms, chemistry equipment, laboratory equipment, his library and radio equipment and other electronic devices and all this military equipment there..." (from Dec. 13, 1966 Interview by Ivon and Gervais, Fontainebleau Hotel) http://

jfk.hood.edu/Collection/Weisberg Subject Index Files/F Disk/Ferrie David William Jack Martin/Item 01.pdf (Retrieved June 4, 2013).

31. "During the dictatorship of Fulgencio Batista, Andres Nazario worked with guerrillas operating independently of Castro's rebel movement. When Castro came to power Jan. 1, 1959, Nazario and other independent guerrilla leaders faced execution. They left for Miami in 1961 and joined with other Cuban exiles to form Alpha 66 – named for its 66 original members...." AP obituary for Nazario, view at: http://jacksonville.com/apnews/stories/100804/D85J734G0.shtml (Retrieved July 1, 2013).

32. HSCA Vol. X, 10a, #2. Bold face added. View online at: http://jfkassassination.net/russ/jfkinfo4/jfk10/hscv10a.htm (Retrieved June 10, 2013).

33. http://www.principiadiscordia.com/forum/index.php?topic4787.10;wap2 (Retrieved 07/17/2013).

34. Levenda's response to Perry, April, 2005.

35. http://www.jfk-online.com/billings2.html Transcribed notes. (Retrieved 03/04/2013).

36. Of the charges, Stephen Roy (as Blackburst) wrote to Marsh in Sept.1999: "Ferrie was not let-off on morals charges due to some CIA intervention. He was tried on one charge and acquitted due to a technicality about dates. The other charges were nol-prossed when Ferrie convinced witness Mike Crouchet to withdraw the charges."

37. http://jfk.hood.edu/Collection/Weisberg Subject Index Files/G Disk/Garrison Jim/Garrison Jim New Orleans To File/Item 13.pdf (Retrieved Aug. 2, 2013).

38. Stephen Roy, Feb. 5, 2005, The Education Forum: "...the picture...was taken around February of 1962... Buznedo...had moved to Denver, but on a trip to NO, he looked up Ferrie and posed for this picture." Buznedo was later investigated as to his relationship with Ferrie in 1967 by Garrison.

39. Ibid.

40. From "Richard Billings' New Orleans Journal," Entries for December 1966-January 25, 1967, as transcribed at http://www.jfk-online.com/billings2.html (Retrieved June 18, 2013).

41. Article by David Corn and Gus Russo. http://www.thenation.com/article/old-man-and-cia-kennedy-plot-kill-castro?page=0,1# (Retrieved 01/11/2014).

42. Millie Ball. "Paul Fabry: New Orleans' world traveler." Sunday, Feb. 17, 2008. http://blog.nola.com/millieball/2008/02/paul_fabry_new_orleans_world_t.html. (Retrieved June 6, 2013) A garbled scan of the CIA guidance sheet for Radio Free Hungary for 1956 can still be accessed here: http://www.faqs.org/cia/docs/102/0001426274/SUGGESTED-GUIDANCE-RE-RADIO-FREE-EUROPE.html; however, the original document (photo) is no longer available there, as of July 31, 2013.

Chapter Ten

The New Orleans Project

March 23, 1962: The New Orleans Project is born one week after US Attorney-General Robert Kennedy gives the green light to assassinate Castro. Drs. Ochsner, Sherman and others acquire the use of a secret linear particle accelerator that has come online at the U.S. Public Health Services Infectious Disease laboratories. Thousands of white mice will be tested for various secret purposes, under the eye of the CIA. The LINAC (linear particle accelerator) is guarded by armed Marines.

I was able to find the newspaper article in which Dr. Ochsner distanced Clay Shaw from himself to better compartmentalize The Project. Shaw may have been a conduit for some of the financing of the LINAC.

Edward T. Haslam found evidence that the US Public Health Service secretly installed a linear particle accelerator at its Infectious Disease Laboratory in New Orleans around 1960. Its existence was traced through massive transactions and witnesses to its construction. The linear particle accelerator would be a key to developing a biological weapon on a fast track.[1]

For an appreciation of the military aspect of the USPHS lab, to the right is a photo of the staff from 1953.

Dr. Ochsner had worked with Dr. Mary Sherman ever since SV-40, the cancer-causing virus, was found in the contaminated polio vaccine that killed his grand-

son. Now enhanced via the LINAC, on a fast-track recycling of selected fast-growing tumors, the material will soon produce a galloping lung cancer that Ochsner believes can be used to kill Castro, who is addicted to cigars, without implicating the US government.

Such assassination plans, Dave told me, had the secret approval of Bobby Kennedy.

April 1962: With a reduced income ($300 a month from Gill) David falls behind on bills and is living beyond his means. Hence, Dave is helping Arcacha "in his advertising business." To put Dave's $300 income into perspective, Lee Harvey Oswald will be paid $230 a month for himself, wife and child at Reilys, in 1963.

> **FBI**: [Ferrie] stated that … some months after he ceased his activity with the organization, SERGIO ARCACHA SMITH gave up the leadership of the organization and then went into the advertising business in New Orleans and that he had assisted SMITH in preparing letters in connection with this advertising business.[2]

Arcacha's "advertising business" was writing and publishing publicity material for the CRC, a position he was given by Ronnie Caire. In other words, David Ferrie was still connected with the CRC through Arcacha, its Public Relations manager.

For extra income, Dave gives flying lessons and promotes himself as a psychology counselor. He also contacts Dr. Mary Sherman to see if she can arrange any paramedical work for him. When Sherman, who gives Dave some professional instruction, must be out of town, Dave is finally allowed to do some genuine lab work for her. It is just the beginning.[3]

Edward T. Haslam discovered "the little lab" at 3225 Louisiana Avenue Parkway, about a block from David's new apartment, where David oversaw the care and inoculations of lab mice, and, later, marmosets and monkeys. Some processing of mice and their tumors would eventually take place in David's apartment, as The Project's schedule grew tighter in 1963.

The "Mouse House" gives some people the creeps even fifty years later. There was a full-scale incinerator behind the house as late as 2003 when I and Nigel Turner toured the property.

April 1962: By now, Jack Suggs Martin (AKA Edward Suggs) with his sidekick, David Lewis, have become fixtures in Guy Banister's office. They are involved in local politics, write a newsletter for Banister, and investigate persons Guy Banister deems communist/pro-integration. At this time, David Ferrie establishes a relationship with Martin and Lewis and is frequently seen in Banister's office.

> **Sam Newman** (owner of the building): Edward Suggs ... was in Banister's office 90% of the time; every day almost. [NARA HSCA 180-10101-10379][4]

An HSCA mug shot of Jack Martin identifies him as Suggs. David Lewis was Martin's close companion for several years. He worked for Guy Banister in 1961 and 1962 as a gofer and investigator. After that, Lewis did occasional work for Banister under the table because his wife, Anna, had asked him to get a better-paying job.

> **Anna Lewis**: Until we met in [Sept] 1962, David was Ferrie's and Martin's toy boy.[5]

Ferrie called the two men "the comedy team of Martin and Lewis."

1962-1963: David Ferrie makes seven long distance phone calls from New Orleans to an unlisted number in Toronto, Canada (406 area code).

In 1967, at DA Garrison's request, Toronto Police revealed the unlisted number belonged to Earl Anglin Lawrence James, a bishop in the Old Roman Catholic Church of North America, who will deny that he ever spoke to Ferrie. James will only admit a single telephone contact – with Jack Martin.[6]

April 2, 1962: Arcacha applies for political asylum in the US. It is granted April 11.

Apr. 16, 1962: Archbishop Joseph Francis Rummel of the Archdiocese of New Orleans excommunicates three influential, highly racist friends of Guy Banister "for defying the authority of the Church and organizing protests against the Archdiocese." This includes the notorious Judge Leander Perez.[7]

Ferrie became angry at Banister for laughing at Perez' open mockery of the aging, half-blind Archbishop Rummel.[8]

May 1962: Nikita Khrushchev and Castro begin plans to place Soviet nuclear missiles in Cuba to deter future invasion attempts.

May 4, 1962: JFK speaks in New Orleans from City Hall to a huge crowd.

Dr. Alton Ochsner was the primary person involved in handling the event.[9]

Lee told me he took the time to "stand almost where JFK stood" when he visited City Hall on Monday, July 8, 1963.

May 22, 1962: David Ferrie apparently makes a phone call to G. Wray Gill's office from Dallas. He is the only person in Gill's office who has ready access to planes and who takes care of Gill's out-of-town business.

June 30, 1962: David, again, appears to call Gill's office from Dallas. Because Gill and his secretaries and business partners do their legal work in New Orleans, David tells the FBI in November 1963, that he hasn't been in Dallas for years.

June 13, 1962: Lee Harvey Oswald, his Russian-born wife, Marina, and their infant daughter June Lee arrive in the United States. Oswald has spent almost three years in the USSR as a "defector" but inexplicably returns with a loan from the State Department, which he repays quickly. They settle in the Dallas, Texas area near family members, after first living with Lee's mother, Marguerite, who is a nurse's aide.

July 10, 1962: A New Orleans air-tel is sent to the FBI about a possible training camp in the New Orleans area. A CIA memo dated 9/10/75 will deny any connection. [CIA FOIA 18658 SAG Memo]

July 21, 1962: A *New Orleans States-Item* article by William Stuckey (he interviews Lee Oswald in 1963): speaks of an anti-Castro training camp that InterPen has established near New Orleans: "Both Fiorini [Frank Sturgis of Watergate fame] and [Gerry] Patrick [Hemming] at one time had connections with Sanchez Arrango, former Minister under President Carlos Prio.... It's an educated guess that Patrick's big backer might be Prio."[10]

> **Luis Rabel** [took over from Arcacha]: I heard of it but I never went there. I think it was in operation at one time.

> **HSCA Rabel Deposition:**

> **Question:** So did this man [Hemming] discuss with you the killing of Fidel Castro?

> **Rabel:** Oh, he had an obsession about it. In fact, he used to say, "I just come back from Cuba. I took a shot at a man who had whiskers on." We were scared of him ... he was crazy.... He said all these kinds of crazy things.

Aug. 2, 1962: FBI issues "Cuban Revolutionary Council, New Orleans, LA. IS – Cuba, NM File FRANK FIORINI," concerning Stuckey's article about the training camp. CIA chimes in with assertions that KUBARK is not involved. "KUBARK" is CIA at Langley. "AMTHUG" is Fidel Castro.

Gerry Patrick Hemming, as seen on left in this photo, is busy training INTERPEN guerrillas in parachuting. They are mostly American soldiers-of-fortune and embittered anti-Castro Cubans.

Aug. 24- Sept. 24, 1962, FBI issues negative reports about Hemming and his men, calling them rag-tag independents of no use to them. INTERPEN leaves Louisiana and returns to No Name Key, FL by mid-September; they later move to Big Pine Key, FL. On Sept. 18, Customs raids Hemming's Pine Key camp, confiscating some weapons, but making no arrests. On the 24th, FBI in Miami issues a document titled "INTERPEN."[11]

Sept. 21, 1962: Archbishop Joseph F. Rummel, who has been fighting Judge Leander Perez, Banister's friend, in the press, announces that segregation will end in all parochial schools in New Orleans in the 1962-1963 school year. Trouble is expected. Guy Banister and his mistress Delphine Roberts are furious, but David Ferrie supports the Archbishop wholeheartedly.[12]

September 26, 1962: Burdette Coates Goldrick Ferrie, David Ferrie's mother, dies of cancer in Allison Park, Penn., after a long battle with the disease.[13]

Some say Dave had flown his desperately ill mother there to get her out of the fracas he was going through, while others say he got rid of her and essentially killed her by moving her when she was too ill to fly, and that she was a woman who was devastated by the charges of immorality against her son. Though Dave never told me his mother was dead, I assumed she was because he had her furniture and was saying Masses for her and his father.

Sept. 16-17, 1962: David Ferrie calls New Orleans from Dallas, Texas.

Sept. 18, 1962: Sergio Arcacha Smith is fired from the CRC for corruption and for defending his friend, David Ferrie, after David is disgraced by his arrest for homosexual activities.

THE CUBAN MISSILE CRISIS

> **Hugh Murray:** ... during the height of the Missile Crisis in the fall of 1962, Oswald, the "defector" to the USSR with a Russian wife ... gets a job in Dallas with a corporation performing very sensitive photographic work for the US government, such as interpreting pictures of Cuban missile movements.[14]

October 14, 1962: US U-2 flyover photos reveal construction sites for medium and intermediate-range ballistic nuclear missiles

(MRBMs and IRBMs) in Cuba. On October 15, a 13-day stand off between the US and the USSR commences.

October 20, 1962: Arcacha leaves New Orleans for good, eventually ending up in Houston by 1963, but he begins his odyssey by moving his family to Miami. Two months later, he moves again, to Tampa. Soon after, his wife goes into labor and they lose the baby.

Oct. 28, 1962: The world sits on the brink of disaster, when secret negotiations suddenly defuse the time bomb. Kennedy's generals are furious with him for being "soft on Communism." Neither Kennedy nor Khrushchev will last much longer in their leadership positions. A USSR submarine captain and a US President who defies his generals, with the help of back-channel talks to Khrushchev via Bobby Kennedy, avert the annihilation of millions.

"Now they're going to find out about Cuba, they're going to find out about the guns, find out about New Orleans, find out about everything." – Jack Ruby, Lee Oswald's assassin, *HSCA Report*, vol. IX: V, p. 162. (Ruby made this comment to his former employee, Wally Weston, who was visiting him in jail.)

Fall, 1962: INCA's anti-Castro focus peaks under Dr. Alton Ochsner and Ed Butler's leadership in New Orleans, spurred on by the Cuban Missile Crisis.

Clay Shaw   Dr. Alton Ochsner

Dr. Alton Ochsner, Pres., INCA: ...when you first went to Latin America and when I started going down there, we were looked up to and respected, now everyone is against us ... because of the propaganda that has been so cleverly done by the Communists.[15]

Ed Butler, Founder, INCA: I will have to go where the communists are, and hit them where it hurts. They will retaliate in kind. Sooner or later they may kill me.[16]

Linda Minor: [researcher] The following New Orleans business executives were INCA members: coffee importer Sam Israel, Jr.; United Fruit's Joseph W. Montgomery; Robinson Lumber's Samuel G. Robinson; and Pan-American Life Insurance's G. Frank Purvis, Jr. Under Captain John W. Clark's leadership, the Delta Line reversed Kelly's position and embraced INCA; the company gave money and Clark served as a director. Among INCA's nine charter members was William G. Zetzmann, president of International Trade Mart (ITM) ... ITM also donated funds – $2,000 in 1968, for example. Also aiding INCA was the Reily family, owner of William B. Reily and Co., one of the city's largest coffee roasters. H. Eustis Reily was an INCA officer and director.[17]

Later in 1963, Delta Line, the Trade Mart, and Terry Stevedoring would cooperate to smuggle rifles from Venezuela to New Orleans. (see June 28, 1963)

Oct. 31, 1962: Carlos Marcello's attempt to nullify his 1938 drug conviction fails in Federal Court, creating yet another reason for deportation back to Guatemala (or to Tunisia, Marcello's actual birthplace).

Nov. 1962: A Southern Research background report shows two cars belong to David Ferrie. One is a 1960 Ford (to be repossessed in March, 1963). The other, a 1959 Ford, is "found registered to David W. Ferrie, Jr., 11 Prospect St. Alexandria, LA." David's friend, Alvin Beauboeuf, has relatives in Alexandria.

Stephen Roy (Aug. 1-7, 2013 – comment has since been erased): David W. Ferrie, Jr. was a young Marine whose parents would not allow him to register the car, so David Ferrie registered the car in his name. He also said reporters were told by neighbors in 1963 that David rode his motorcycle all summer, and "none of his friends" saw him driving a car between March and November, 1963. This wasn't the first time David Ferrie had pulled a stunt like this.[18]

Dave's 1960 Ford was repossessed in March, but the 1959 Ford (a rambling wreck) was still available, legally, to him. The young Marine, dubbed "Ferrie, Jr." was absent months at a time, and wouldn't keep his "adopted father's" car at his disapproving parents' address. It was almost certainly hidden from them, which is why it wouldn't be openly kept at Dave's, either. Dave did not use this vehicle regularly: he may have used it occasionally to keep the battery from running down. Perhaps this is why it had so much trouble starting (which I experienced). Of course, motorcycles make a lot of noise when used, and my presence at his apartment was discrete, so Dave would not take me anywhere on his Harley.

Nov. 1962: David's financial situation worsens. He is now being trained by Dr. Sherman for an hour or so a day, probably at the Mouse House or at her private lab on Prytania St. But Dave won't be paid much until March 1963, when Ochsner's Clinic at Prytania St. will make its massive move to Ochsner's Hospital in Jefferson Parish, after which Dave's work load will increase to a level that will require help to continue, especially as Dave's work for Marcello also starts to increase.

Nov. 16, 1962: Southern Research places surveillance on David Ferrie's apartment, using [possibly a pilot] Jack Oliphant, whose report will be in the Dec. 19, 1962 section of Eastern Air Lines' collection of information about David.

Nov. 19, 1962: Al Meister, CAP Commander, rips into David's character to Southern Research investigators for the FAA: "...Meister advised that he had heard through cadet sources 'that subject is possibly a homosexual,' and also that Ferrie "hated women." Meister called him 'officious and dictatorial' and added that Ferrie 'wears a toupee, possibly self-made.' Meister also said 'Ferrie was instrumental in persuading him to go into the seminary."" Also, Southern Research is told that David illegally "[allowed] use of [plane] rider pass to George Piazza, who Ferrie claimed was his "ward.""[19]

Dec. 19, 1962: David lies to Southern Research investigators, telling them he never applied for ordination to any church, though "he has shown such a desire since his youth."[20]

Police Lt. Francis Martello tells investigators that Arcacha's group, to which David belonged, was believed to have the "unofficial sanction of CIA."[21] Guy Banister personally testifies in David's behalf.

Dec. 31, 1962: David's Taylorcraft L-2's certificate expires. It was last flown on Sept. 9, 1962 "apparently in connection with a funeral," (Blackburst's observation). Could this be when David was visiting his mother, who was sent away? She died Sept. 26. The Taylorcraft will be taken for engine repairs to a friend's service station "in early 1963" where it will be dismantled.[22]

1963: CIA hatches plots to kill Castro without invading Cuba. Bizarre ideas abound, including exploding devices, poisons, carcinogens and other biological weapons.

> *The Atlantic*: In 1963 [the CIA] seriously examined "whether an exotic seashell, rigged to explode, could be deposited ...where Castro commonly went skin diving."... a diving suit "dusted ... with a fungus that would produce a chronic skin disease (Madura foot), and contaminated the breathing apparatus with a tubercule bacillus." ... "a ball-point pen rigged with a hypodermic needle" filled with Black-leaf-40 poison.... The CIA contact in Cuba who was given the pen, "did not 'think much of the device'," and complained that CIA could surely "come up with something more sophisticated than that."[23]

In fact, CIA did come up with something more sophisticated: a virulent lung cancer, to use as a biological weapon to kill Castro. It was being developed in New Orleans. Plausibly deniable, easily hidden, and injectable, Ochsner's lung cancer project may never be made public because cancer as an assassination tool might still be in use today.

Friends of Democratic Cuba's William Dalzell, Guy Banister's former business partner, has been placed in a mental hospital, according to an FBI report dated 6/30/1967. That made sure nobody listened to him. Placing unwanted or inconvenient informants into a mental hospital occurred again and again in this era, in New Orleans.

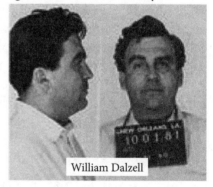
William Dalzell

Jan. 14, 1963: Arcacha moves to Houston, Texas.

Ferrie exhibits U. S. Passport Number B085860 in the name of David William Ferrie issued September 18, 1961. This passport showed that visa number 1236 was issued by the Consulate General of Guatemala of New Orleans, Louisiana, September 25, 1963; that Ferrie entered Guatemala in October 11, 1963 and departed October 18, 1963; that visa number 1406 was issued by Consulate General of Guatemala, New Orleans, Louisiana, October 29, 1963, and that Ferrie entered Guatemala on October 30, 1963 and departed November 1, 1963.

DAVE'S LIES CATCH UP WITH HIM

Feb. 1963: HSCA: "[Ferrie] went to Miami with attorney G. Wray Gill for the hearing regarding his dismissal. Eastern ruled against him; Ferrie filed another grievance."

From the beginning, the attorneys for Eastern Air Lines caught Dave in one lie after another; from his very first application form, to having a legitimate PhD, to having a legitimate CAP charter for the Falcons, to his absurd claim that he was so adept at staying out of jail that Eastern should consider that feat as a sufficient qualification to be an Eastern pilot.[24]

Feb. 15, 1963: David Ferrie writes another grievance letter to Eastern Air Lines.

March 1963: Ochsner's Clinic moves from Prytania Street to Ochsner Hospital on Jefferson Highway. The move makes the front page due to its colossal size and impact on traffic. A former FBI agent supervises.[25] Here's how the Mouse House got set up: A caravan of trucks went back and forth all day in a procession, moving the Clinic, but one truck was diverted. It delivered equipment, cages, supplies and test animals to Ochsner and Sherman's clandestine animal testing lab, close to David's apartment. Thus stocked and equipped, David Ferrie began to supervise cancer injections into weanling mice. He had at least two assistants, both Cuban.

THE SET-UP

Dave taught his assistants to care for all animals brought there. They fed, cleaned, and weighed the animals. They kept records and selected the heaviest mice (with the heaviest, most aggressive

tumors) to deliver in minutes to Dave's nearby apartment, on demand. There, Dave killed the mice, inspected their tumors under a
microscope, then created test tube cultures and extracts of a radi-
ation-altered SV40-derived cancer-causing virus. Dr. Sherman got
these materials next. Dave broke what would have been a connected chain of related labs, keeping researchers in other labs in the
dark, as to what The Project was about.

1963: David Ferrie's Neighbors: The Franz family told me who
was living in David's immediate neighborhood in 1963. In the
house to the right of David's apartment, Peter and Irma Gentile
lived upstairs. Leonard W. Franz and his wife, Irma, lived downstairs with their son, 14-year-old L.J. In the house to the left, Mr.
and Mrs. Lupo lived upstairs and Edward and Velda Kalinsky lived
downstairs. "He was nothing but a very nice man," said a Franz family member. "He rode the bus a lot."

DAVID FERRIE'S SECRET MONTHS:

Except for his Eastern Air Lines hearings, little has been reported
regarding David Ferrie's activities between March 1963 and the
end of August 1963. During this time, David, when not involved
with work for G. Wray Gill and analyzing autopsy and medical reports for Guy Banister, was being trained by Dr. Mary Sherman. By
March, he was part of Dr. Sherman's team. Beyond working part
time for both Guy Banister and G. Wray Gill, with an occasional
flying lesson and trips out of town, David was as busy as ever.

> **Stephen Roy** dismisses Ferrie's CIA connection (Posting as Black-
> burst): Ferrie's financial and social difficulties reveal no indication
> of any secret backing. He did not benefit financially, and nobody in-
> tervened to prevent his severe legal difficulties. He died an impover-
> ished broken man. A very close friend of many years said that Fer-
> rie was given to braggadocio, but was not engaged in any secret
> activities. Since Ferrie's death, a few people have come forward to al-
> lege various tales of Ferrie's involvement in such activities, but none of
> them pan out, none seem consistent with the provable record.... But
> this is by no means a final verdict ... who knows what might pop up
> someday?[26]

But was this unnamed "friend" telling the truth? Did he know
Dave's most important secrets? Even today, CIA denies that certain verified agents work for them. CIA has always abandoned

public agents who get in trouble, so David Ferrie's mounting problems don't prove that he was not with the CIA.

Here is a recent example (excerpted): "Family of Robert Levinson, American Held In Iran, Says He Was Spying for the CIA" [Dec. 13, 2013]:

> The CIA abandoned Bob Levinson and lied, saying he was never CIA: After years of secrecy, the family of the former FBI agent who disappeared in Iran seven years ago, Robert Levinson... accused the CIA, FBI and the Obama administration of – "betraying" him by not doing enough to gain his release ... David McGee, a family lawyer ... told ABC News the CIA and the FBI betrayed Levinson as it tried to hide the fact that he had a long-term relationship with the CIA, spying on Iran's nuclear program and on the terror group Hezbollah ... Levinson disappeared from Iran's Kish Island in 2007.
>
> In testimony before Congress, CIA officials gave testimony, denying any relationship with Levinson. "Absolute, bold faced lie," said McGee. Only after McGee and his paralegal obtained access to Levinson's computer files, were they able to prove the secret relationship, said McGee. 'The CIA issued a formal apology to the family,' said McGee, who then negotiated a $2.5 million settlement between the government and the Levinson family.[27]

Should we believe that, simply because David Ferrie's financial and social life declined and the CIA wasn't taking good care of him that he never worked for them?

Endnotes

1. See Edward T. Haslam's book, *Dr. Mary's Monkey*, "The Machine." Friend Romney Stubbs helped find evidence of the linear particle accelerator for Haslam.

2. Warren Commission Document 75; FBI Interview of David Ferrie 11/26/63 by SA ERNEST WALL and SA L. M. SHEARER at New Orleans. http://www.jfk-online.com/jpselffi.html (Retrieved 5 May, 2013).

3. David Ferrie, to the author, concerning his need for income and Sherman's decision to train him and use him.

4. From document as published by A. J. Weberman.

5. Anna Lewis, to the author, Jan. 3, 2001, New Orleans, in the presence of researcher Martin Shackelford.

6. Peter Wronski. "David Ferrie and Earl Anglin James / Bishop in the Old Roman Catholic Church" http://www.russianbooks.org/oswald/ferrie.htm. (Retrieved Dec. 9, 2012).

7. "The first of the three was Judge Leander Perez, 70, a parish judge from St. Bernard Parish, who called on Catholics to withhold donations to the Archdiocese and to boycott Sunday church collections. The second was Jackson G. Ricau, 44, political commentator, segregationist writer, and director of the "Citizens Council of South Louisiana". The third was Una Gaillot, 41, mother of two, housewife, and president of "Save Our Nation Inc. The excommunications made national headlines and had the tacit support of the papacy." http://en.wikipedia.org/wiki/Joseph_Rummel. (Retrieved July 16, 2013).

8. *Time* magazine, 12/12/1960 offers an example of what angered David about Perez: "...when New Orleans' Roman Catholic Archbishop Joseph F. Rummel declared that segregation was sinful, Leander Perez breathed defiance. Himself a Catholic, he accused the Catholic hierarchy of "turning against their own people." The New Orleans parochial schools remained segregated, and a fortnight ago, as Archbishop Rummel lay ill in a hospital after a fall, Perez hinted that it was all because of his stand against segregation."

9. Dr. Ochsner was in charge of Kennedy's May 4, 1962 visit to New Orleans.

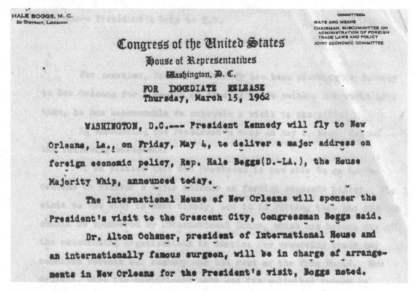

10. A. J. Weberman's material ("Hemming's Training Camp, Aug. 1962) as cited at http://www.combat-diaries.co.uk/diary27/diary27chapter12/14.htm (Retrieved June 6, 2013).

11. Ibid.

12. The September 21, 1962 issue of *Commonweal* outlines the problems to be expected. http://conciliaria.com/2012/09/the-lesson-of-new-orleans/#more-2008 (Retrieved July 11, 2013).

13. http://records.ancestry.com/Burdette_C_Goldrick_records.ashx?pidF278362 (Retrieved 09/01/2013).

14. From Murray's Feb. 13, 2014; personal email regarding his book review of Lamar Waldron's *The Hidden History of the JFK Assassination*.

15. Linda Minor. "Quixotic Joust" blog, Nov. 11, 2011. http://quixoticjoust.blogspot.com/2011/11/unbending-anti-communism.html. (Retrieved July 10, 2013).

16. Ibid.

17. Ibid. Emphasis by author.

18. Researcher Karl Kinaski and a multitude of Facebook associates saw Roy's quote before it was erased. At the time it was erased, I happened to see that Stephen Roy and Larry Hancock were both viewing the reply, (I was present as a "guest.").

19. SR 11-N-244, 11/19/1962, p.10; FAA, vol.4, p. 14, Robey report on Ferrie; SR-11-N-224, 11/19, 1962.

20. HSCA, citing SR-11-N-224, Dec. 19, 1962 (J.F.K. Document 014904).

21. A. J. Weberman and others cite EAL's Memo from Donovan E. Pratt, Sept. 28, 1967 (A, B,C, re Arcacha Smith), and an Office of Security file for David W. Ferrie re Martello, p. 10, 11-N-224, Dec. 19, 1962, Exhibit FFF (J.F.K. Document 014904).

22. Stephen Roy, to Larry Hancock. http://educationforum.ipbhost.com/index.php?showtopic(90 (Retrieved June 6, 2013).

23. Alexis C. Madrigal. "Exploding Chocolate, Poisoned Scuba Suits, and the Bulgarian Umbrella: A Survey of Strange Assassination Tech" Jul. 18, 2012. The Atlantic. http://www.theatlantic.com/technology/archive/2012/07/exploding-chocolate-poisoned-scuba-suits-and-the-bulgarian-umbrella-a-survey-of-strange-assassination-tech/260014/. (Retrieved July 7, 2013).

24. From Summary: "Before the Eastern Air Lines Pilots System Board of Adjustment" Brief of Eastern Air Lines, Inc on Grievance of David W. Ferrie. Eastern #15-43, Eastern #29-63, Eastern #48-63.

25. "...Ochsner Clinic as a wing of the Ochsner Foundation Hospital...move[d] from the Prytania site in uptown New Orleans... consolidate[ng] all Ochsner activities on the Jefferson Highway campus in 1963." Ochsner Journal, V. 7 (3) Fall 2007. PMC 3096393.

26. From: blackburst@aol.com (Blackburst) Subject: Re: Did Ferrie "fly missions over Cuba?" Date: 05 Mar 2000 00:00:00 GMT Message-ID: <20000305044552.03192.00000329@ng-fn1.aol.com> http://www.jfk-online.com/dbdfbackfile.html (Retrieved Jan. 2, 2013).

27. http://abcnews.go.com/Blotter/robert-levinson-family-american-held-iran-spying-cia/story?id!206505 (Retrieved March 3, 2014).

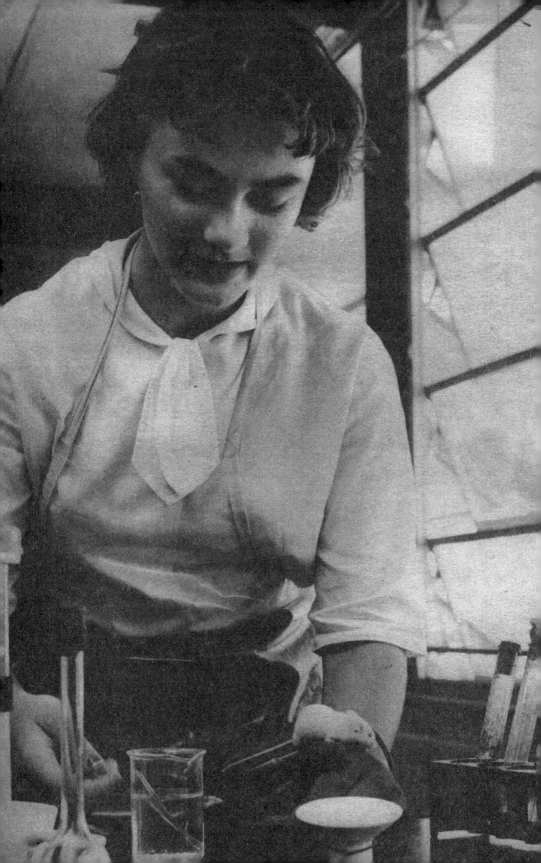

Chapter Eleven

I Join the Team

Apr. 15, 1963: Dr. Alton Ochsner phones me, after having trained me to handle cancer-causing viruses by his close friends. I had been researching how to detect cancer with a blood test. Ochsner invites me to a "summer internship" with Dr. Mary Sherman, with a fast-track entry in the fall to Tulane Medical School, all expenses paid, plus a stipend. I accept. Pre-med friends, such as Kathy Santi (who will become a doctor), hear I'll soon be leaving University of Florida to go to Tulane.

Apr. 17, 1963: I tell my lover, Robert Baker (an English Major I steered into geology and math) that I am leaving UF forever. Robert says he will follow and marry me, if it can be kept secret. Robert's parents, who are paying for his college education, will disown him if he marries before graduation. Since Robert must return to UF to finish his English degree, I don't tell him I plan to stay in New Orleans, fearing he won't marry me if he knows that. Robert, slated for summer work in his parents' real estate office, will ask permission to go. He soon starts applying for geology jobs in New Orleans.

April 18 -19, 1963: I get a pre-paid bus ticket from Dr. Ochsner. Because UF, newly on the trimester system, is shutting down, I decide to leave now, believing Ochsner has pre-arranged housing at the YWCA. Ochsner's friend, Sen. George Smathers, would have placed me in a summer research program at University of Miami, where I had many anti-Castro friends. Instead, on the 19th, I travel to New Orleans.

4:00 AM, April 20, 1963: I arrive in New Orleans. The prospect of safe sex with birth control pills – at that time not dispensed to un-married women – makes marriage look attractive, but meanwhile, I plan to stay at the YMCA, where Dr. Ochsner said he would reserve a room. But when I arrive I learn that Ochsner and Sherman are out of town, and no prepaid room exists. I select the cheapest room available, already housing four other girls. I need employment, but I'm not street-wise. The girls (two of them are strippers) soon introduce me to the seamy side of the city. Needing money, I take a part-time early-morning waitress job at Royal Castle, out on Airline Drive, by the airport.

April 22, 1963: David Ferrie realizes he can't work as many hours as he hoped on The Project. Chafing at the time it takes to safely handle what can be a dangerous cancer project, he asks for a savvy tech to help out.

Michael Riconusciuto, a young genius in electronics, biochemistry, chemistry and computers, may have been the original person who was going to be sent to help David Ferrie, but I, who have come two weeks early, will meet Lee Harvey Oswald on the 26th of April, in an encounter most researchers now believe was no accident. Naïve and vulnerable in rough, tough New Orleans, I've already seen and heard almost unbelievable things. I need to be protected until the doctors return and can set things straight.

> **Anita Langley**: Michael told me he was working with Guy Banister at this time. He says he read some of Judyth's cancer research reports [brought in to be Xeroxed].[1]

Michael was also aware that Guy Banister had one of the few Xerox machines available that we could use without having to fill out paperwork. Copiers were much rarer then.

Tuesday-Wednesday, Apr. 23-24, 1963: Lee Oswald checks some of his baggage ahead of time onto a bus to New Orleans.[2] On Wednesday, Ruth Paine, George deMohrenschildt's friend (Paine has befriended Lee's wife, Marina) comes to "visit." She will claim she's surprised to see them packed, ready to move to New Orleans. At the last moment, Ruth "persuades" Lee to allow Marina and little June Lee to live with her while Lee goes on to New Orleans by bus.

Due to his sudden transfer, Lee had so little money to live on that soon he would borrow $200 from his uncle (which he'd quickly repay). $200 was his regular CIA monthly pay. Ruth Paine has offered a suspiciously handy solution.

Apr. 25-26, 1963: Lee Oswald arrives in New Orleans after midnight on the 25th. He stores his boxes and luggage in lockers at the bus terminal, then checks into the YMCA. In the morning, he drops some boxes and three sea-bags off with his Aunt Lillian Murret. That night, Lee dines with David Ferrie.[3] On the 26th, I meet Lee at the post office at about 10:00 AM.

5/4/63	24	100	14.00	.53	.30		.30			113		12.87
PERIOD ENDING	HOURS	RATE	GROSS EARNED	F.I.C.A.	FEDERAL INCOME TAX	STATE INCOME TAX	FOOD	UNIFORMS	HOSPITAL INSURANCE	ADVANCES	TOTAL DEDUCTED	MISC.	NET PAY
		EARNINGS	*					DEDUCTIONS				

A²M 22 May

DETACH BEFORE DEPOSITING   ROYAL CASTLE SYSTEM, INC. – NEW ORLEANS, LOUISIANA

My last Royal Castle paycheck stub was issued May 4, 1963 for 14 hours of work (one week). I was hired only to cover the morning rush hour from 7:00 to 9:00 AM, but it helped pay my YWCA bill.

I have been told that the Airline Highway Royal Castle was used as a dead drop and meeting place for Bobby Kennedy's surveillance team that was keeping track of Carlos Marcello. The Town & Country Motel, behind which was Marcello's office, was visible from the Royal Castle's parking lot. The Royal Castle was open 24 hours a day.

Apr. 27, 1963: Lee Oswald eats breakfast at the Royal Castle, and later that day introduces me to David Ferrie at the Kopper Kitchen on Tulane Ave.[4] "Captain Ferrie" wears a pilot's cap and jacket, but wrinkled trousers. He wears a cheap ring that, later, I learn was made from an Eastern Air Lines pin by one of David's CAP cadets. I will not see it again.

David thinks I'm the tech he requested. He sees my ignorance of The Project as a "need to know" situation common to clandestine work. With Drs. Ochsner and Sherman out of town, coincidences and name-dropping combine to convince both him and Lee that I'm the requested tech. I am made aware that "Dr. Ferrie" is conducting some independent cancer research with Dr. Sherman. "Dr." Ferrie says he'll order anything I want or need. As for me, I'm confused. Wasn't I supposed to be working directly with Dr. Sherman?

Sun., Apr. 28, 1963: David holds a wild party at his apartment. I attend only because I'm told Dr. Sherman will be there. Though a couple of girls are present, most of the guests are Cuban and American homosexuals, showing open affection. Jack Martin and David

Lewis arrive, uninvited, and Lee plays chess with David Lewis, who, like Lee, does not drink. Martin has no such compunctions. When Dr. Sherman arrives, a tipsy Martin pesters her, trying to learn if David is being paid "big money" for his work with her. As for me, when I try to introduce myself, Dr. Sherman, shockingly, refuses to speak to me. After Sherman picks up some refrigerated tumors and leaves, David, angry at Martin's behavior, kicks him out. Soon after, the Police arrive. Dave says Martin called them in retribution. The party is shut down.

Mon. Apr. 29, 1963: I needed convincing, after all I've seen, that the cancer research project, involving plans to assassinate Fidel Castro, is legitimate and government sanctioned. Posing as Lee's wife (I spoke some Russian and resembled Marina), I met Guy Banister's secretaries and a male investigator before Banister welcomed me into his private office (he knew who I really was). I was impressed by the certificates on the wall and Banister's stern assurance that Lee Oswald and David Ferrie were dedicated patriots who could be trusted.

Anti-communist, anti-Jew, anti-Catholic, anti-Castro and anti-Kennedy, this hard-drinking racist and American patriot, whose secretary was his mistress, never realized that many of his investigators were anti-communist, anti-Castro, anti-Kennedy good American patriots, but also homosexuals.

Lee Oswald introduces me to Guy Banister:

Previously unpublished is a short conversation I had with Guy Banister soon after Lee introduced him to me, over my concerns that Dave Ferrie and his Cuban friends talked about killing both Castro and Kennedy. That made him laugh. "Compared to me," Banister said, "Ferrie's JFK's guardian angel. I'm the one who thinks Kennedy ought to be shot!" Seeing my jaw drop, he quickly added, "But I follow the law of the land. We all do, here. I'm not serious about shooting that SOB. It's just the way we talk in New Orleans." Seeing I still wasn't comfortable with what he'd just said, Banister added, soothingly, "We're a team, trying to save the country from going down the drain. We're working together, to save America from the Communists. From the nigger-lovers."

Ferrie, Banister assured me, would often float ideas like that to measure the Cubans' reactions. It was part of his job as an undercover agent working within the Cuban exile community. As for Ferrie's cancer research, his reports were photocopied on Banister's own Xerox machine, in his office, before they were "sent to some big-wig in Georgia."[5]

Ferrie's project was legitimate. Even the CIA was backing it, along with the city's crime boss, Carlos Marcello. Banister was quite serious. Marcello might have been born foreign, he said, but that Dago was a red-blooded American when it came to kicking out the Communists from Cuba. However, things could get complicated, Banister emphasized. Not for one instant should you trust Marcello.

Even so, Banister said, important people were right behind everything they were up to, even their associating with the Mob in order to get useful information. So if I saw Ferrie working with Marcello, said Banister, all I had to do was remember that even Bobby Kennedy was collecting information about Marcello from Ferrie.[6]

That was dangerous: Dave was risking his life to do that. About this same time, Lee mentioned that I had met Jack Martin and David Lewis, and that Ferrie was having a problem with Martin wanting to nose in on "The Project."

"Ferrie owes Martin," Banister said. "He's been there for Ferrie, time and again. He's the best damned investigator you'd want, when he's sober."

"That's the problem," Lee said. "He drinks too much. He bothered Dr. Sherman, too."

"I heard a different story," Banister commented. "That Ferrie cut him out of The Project."

Banister abruptly changed the subject and began talking about his special files. I was even shown where they were stored, accessible only by means of Banister's private stairs (the stairs were under construction and would soon be hard to see behind a drywall). Banister proudly explained that these were secret files that David Ferrie had been helping him with. "The police are so damned corrupt here," Banister said, "that the only way we can keep them honest is to accumulate evidence to blackmail them with, when they step out of line." Atop that, Banister had information "about every nigger and Black Muslim, especially Malcolm X" as well as on every subversive organization and their leaders. It was all handy, with index cards.

Information was his business, Banister boasted, and these files were the really important ones. Then Guy Banister told me that Lee Oswald was being groomed to do his part to save Cuba from Communism. With these comments, my concerns about Lee and Ferrie's loyalties – and Ferrie's outlandish claims about Kennedy and Castro –were put to rest, though I wasn't sure what to think about Mr. Banister.

After we left the office, I asked Lee to explain why Guy Banister had taken up the job of blackmailing the local police. Lee explained the situation: Banister came from the FBI to be the city's Deputy Chief of Police, to root out corruption, but his stay was brief. Lee intimated that Banister may have been framed because he found out too much, though Banister's quick temper could have contributed.

Dismissed and disgraced, Banister was determined to get revenge. He started a private investigation agency as a front for his real work, which focused on a variety of anti-Castro activities, but he also hired spies to gather incriminating evidence against the hated New Orleans Police and the city's corrupt politicians. Ironically, Banister ended up being paid for these efforts by Carlos Marcello's attorney. But, Lee cautioned, despite Banister's moralistic veneer, his closeness to the local FBI, and his connections to Bobby Kennedy through a trusted local FBI agent, the old man was vulnerable because he had taken Mrs. Roberts, his secretary, as a mistress, abandoning his wife. His judgment, when drinking, wasn't the worlds' best.

As for Banister's hatred of the Kennedys, it came from what he perceived as JFK's "love" of Communism, his drive to push a Civil

Rights bill into law, and the fact that the Kennedys are Catholics. Nevertheless, at last, I now understood how Dave could work for the former head of Chicago's FBI and Carlos Marcello at the same time, despite the apparent conflict of allegiance.

"And you finally understand that I am really a good guy," Lee asserted triumphantly.

I told him that I've never seen a tougher man than Banister, and his framed documents were impressive, but compared to everybody else I'd been meeting in New Orleans, Lee was looking like "Saint Oswald."

Late April 1963: David asks me to inspect his neck for cancer. The lumps were small, located on his thyroid, which, along with his exophthalmia (bug eyes) indicated hyperthyroidism, which sometimes could mean a cancerous thyroid. He had some small boils on the back of his neck, from what might have been a staph infection. He didn't seem to have cancer. I don't know why he asked me to check him. He needed to clear up the cysts. He had alopecia. His skin was very soft.

April 30, 1963: David has spoken to Dr. Sherman, who explains she didn't want to show any public acknowledgment of my relationship to her at the party. Later, intrigued by David Ferrie's eloquence, Lee and I spend all afternoon and all night at Dave's apartment. Dave

These are notes I took from the first "lecture" David Ferrie delivered to Lee and me in an all-night discussion at his apartment.

"I am disturbed about how to believe that man, life, etc. is more than a distructive (*sic*) blight that will crawl over this and other worlds with growth, disease and death its only vocabulary. I wish to believe that such processes accompany growth of a noble and more comprehensive intellect committed to a true desire for understanding, the truth and purpose of existence, an' what good can come from such – (unreadable). [Something …ance]" lectures us on philosophy, science, physics, economics, social contracts, semantics, and religion. He also explains details of the cancer project. He is now aware that I should never have known about the sinister nature of The Project. I also learn that David Ferrie and Lee Oswald had a rocky start to their friendship. In fact, it was violent.

```
PUBLIC EYE - PRIVATE EYE        REFLECTED LIGHT OF SUN
NATURAL-AND-ARTIFICIAL LIGHT
NIGHT-AND-DAY
CIRCULAR ("FELL CIRQUE") IMAGERY
FIRE-AND-WATER
WATER·CYCLE (MINE)
HOT-AND-COLD
INTERIOR-EXTERIOR SIGHT
TELESCOPING WITHIN-AND-WITHOUT: LITTLE-BIG,
EMOTION VS REASON              BIG-LITTLE
THE WOMAN & THE COQUETTE
THE CHAIN OF BEING
HYBRIS & ASPIRATIONS TO GODHEAD
TIME AND MAN, MAN IN RELATION TO ETERNAL
SIN OF PRIDE & ORIGINAL SIN
THE PILGRIMAGE - THE VOYAGE - THE QUEST
MORTALITY-IMMORTALITY
LAND-AND-SEA
CONCERNED (PATHETIC) & APATHETIC NATURE
IN-AND-OUT OF ELEMENT, PLACE, STATION
RELIGION VS NATURAL ACTIONS
TRANSCENDENCE OF ONE'S NATURE
PROBLEM OF SALVATION, THE IDENTITY AFTER DEATH
AFFIRMATION-DENIAL                          etc.
MOVEMENT BY ORGANIZATION THROUGH SEASONAL
    CYCLES, THROUGH YOUTH-TO-AGE, ETC
MANYNESS-AND-ONENESS
UNITY & DISSENSION, HARMONY & DISCORD
"METHINKS THE LADY DOTH PROTEST TOO MUCH"
```

A partial section of a page I wrote while David expounded on his second all-night lecture, based on his knowledge of philosophy. I wrote it with green ink, using a fountain pen and ink Lee Oswald had in his possession. Lee wrote (page below -partial section) in the summer of 1963 also using the same Sanford green ink. It is part of a 9-page essay comparing US and USSR political systems, revealing Lee's intelligence and his anti-communist beliefs.[11]

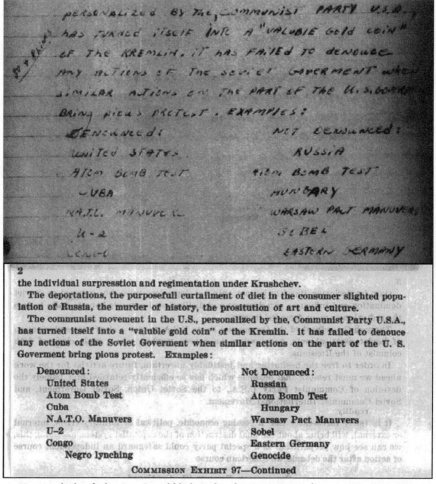

the individual surpresstion and regimentation under Krushchev.

The deportations, the purposefull curtailment of diet in the consumer slighted population of Russia, the murder of history, the prositution of art and culture.

The communist movement in the U.S., personalized by the, Communist Party U.S.A., has turned itself into a "valuble gold coin" of the Kremlin. it has failed to denouce any actions of the Soviet Goverment when similar actions on the part of the U. S. Goverment bring pious protest. Examples:

Denounced:	Not Denounced:
United States	Russian
Atom Bomb Test	Atom Bomb Test
Cuba	Hungary
N.A.T.O. Manuvers	Warsaw Pact Manuvers
U-2	Sobel
Congo	Eastern Germany
Negro lynching	Genocide

COMMISSION EXHIBIT 97—Continued

Here is a little of what Lee Oswald believed and wrote, proving he was no communist.

Also on April 30, 1963: When Robert fails to arrive as promised, Lee begs me not to marry him.

Lee shows up again at Royal Castle, and orders breakfast.[12] After he eats, he makes a bunch of phone calls, using the restaurant's popular payphone. Only later will I realize that if I had paid attention, I'd be able to figure out who Bobby Kennedy's surveillance people were, who were reporting on Carlos Marcello's activities. And only after that will I realize that Marcello would have had his own spies there, watching who used the payphone. At least today, I know better than to ask Lee what all the phone calls are about. If he's allowed to tell me, I know he will.

We talk easily as we ride the bus back to town together, and finally, Lee tells me he's also been talking to Dave Ferrie. The good news is that Dave has spoken to Dr. Sherman about her aloofness, and I'm not to worry. Everything is OK. Dr. Sherman will meet me soon, and she still wants me to work with her. Apparently, she did not want to talk at the party because I'd shown too much emotion when I came up so eagerly to meet her.

"Good grief!" I blurt out. "That's ridiculous!"

"Because you looked so happy to see her, she said she could imagine gossip from certain of Dave's friends, if she talked to you – if you know what I mean."

"Geesh!"

"If that means 'Jesus!'" Lee says, "I agree. Geesh! She said she only came to retrieve the tumors before they got too old," Lee goes on. "Dave told me that it's also fine with her, if you work in her bone lab and also at his place. Maybe on alternate afternoons."

"That would be totally weird," I reply. "His so-called 'lab' is the last place I want to work. Besides, I don't want to run into any of his friends. Ugh!"

"Nobody would be there until after he's home from work," Lee assures me. "By then, you'd be long gone. And every hour spent helping Dave will count toward your internship, so he hopes you'll do it. He says you're really the only "untraceable one" we have. That's exactly how Dave put it. *The only one. Untraceable.*"

I confess to Lee that by "acting out a role" I feel like I'm actually working for the CIA as an untraceable asset, and he smiles, shaking his head. Lee has already explained that some people who work for the CIA never know that they do. They're "unwitting." Even in the Company (that's what Lee calls it) Lee says that the names of the "case officers" are probably fake. When I ask Lee to tell me more, he clams up. I've gone too far.

When he starts talking again, he is all business. My first meeting with Dr. Ochsner will be in a few days. The good doctor will personally advise me about how it will all work out.

The news from Dr. Sherman relieves me immensely, but the internship I'm supposed to fulfill is becoming a complex matter. And how should I explain David Ferrie to Robert Baker? Or will I have to? I'm supposed to get married soon, but I'm glad so few people know about that. It gives me a chance to back out. On the bus back to town, Lee shows me a horoscope in the newspaper, entitled "Moon Messages For You." Mockingly, I read it aloud: "Today's Moon rays agitate high-strung individuals. Many contrasting opinions are expressed. In love-life, excitement and passion builds to a crescendo. Temper sentiment with common sense.

Emotional people pull situations askew." "That's you!" Lee proclaims.

"I suppose so," I agree. "After all, I'm supposed to get married tomorrow."

"He is indeed the lucky one," Lee comments.

"Apparently, you're to be invited to our wedding," I say, teasing him about his interest in the horoscope. "It says here, under Libra, 'attend a social event.' We'll need a witness, you know."

"I don't want to be there when you make your mistake," Lee says sadly, avoiding my eyes

May 2-3-4, 1963: Robert A. Baker, III marries me in Mobile, AL, where no waiting is required. (Why the hurry? He doesn't have two days, as Louisiana law requires.) By May 3rd, he leaves for the Gulf of Mexico, refusing to give me any contact details because he thinks I might follow. Robert thinks I still have my Royal Castle job, but I was fired. He thinks I still have a roof over my head, but that same night, at 1:00 AM, May 4, I am evicted during a raid (my landlady, Mrs.Webber, runs a brothel). When the police raid had carried off a lorry-load full of girls dressed in feathers, handcuffs and nail polish, I was left on the sidewalk with everything I owned, alone, in the darkness, pondering how I never had noticed that the place was a whorehouse. Penniless and abandoned, I find the St. George Episcopal Church, where Father Bill Richardson and wife, Mary, take me in.[13] Next day, Lee Oswald comes to rescue me, finding me a new apartment (1032 Marengo) not far from where he will be living a week later (4905 Magazine St). Lee tells me he will soon be living close by.

May 6, 1963: Jack Ruby (introduced to me as "Sparky Rubenstein") arrives at David's apartment from the airport in Carlos Marcello's old two-tone Chevy (Carlos' brother, Sammy, provided the vehicle). Sergio Arcacha Smith, Bill Gaudet and a pockmarked, heavyset Latino (name was not disclosed) arrive by cab.

Early that evening, "Sparky"[14] brought up some barbells with blue weights for Dave. He was athletic for his fifty-three years, walking on his hands around Dave's book-cluttered living room to show off in front of me. He then gave me $50 when he heard I had been cheated by my landlady, Mrs. Webber; who he seemed to know. The way he said, "I'll talk to her," gave me the chills.

Sparky was a health nut: when he asked Dave if he'd been using the Waring blender he'd given him, to make carrot juice, I had to warn Sparky that the stuff sitting in the blender in the refrigerator was not chopped cherries and apricots. It was mouse tumors.

Everyone – including Lee and me – would be going to a fine restaurant tonight. I would be the only girl in their party. Since Dave and Lee had advised me to act like "a dumb broad," these gentlemen welcomed my presence as a kind of showpiece for their dinner table, while at the same time, they talked indiscreetly about their plans, as if my IQ matched my bra size. Sparky was both charming and frightening. It was obvious that Sparky and David Ferrie had been friends for a while. As for Sparky and Lee, they had known each other since Lee was a boy,  playing at the picnics and parties that Marcello's family hosted. Lee's mother had even dated Marcello's driver. Her lawyer and friend, Clem Sehrt, was one of Marcello's business attorneys. Sehrt would show up on Aug. 10, 1963 to bail Lee out of jail after he was arrested for handing out pro-Castro "Hands Off Cuba" flyers and leaflets to create his pro-Castro image. Such an image would later be useful to both the CIA and to the Mafia.

Lee had volunteered to be sent to Cuba. The rumor at the table was that he'd already been there in the past, and now, thanks to David Ferrie and Marcello's ever-handy fleet of light planes, he'd been there again for a look-around. Dave even set Lee up for a free flying lesson. Lee was already halfway there, Dave said, as a co-pilot.

The passion to murder Castro had created a coalition between the Mafia and the CIA, and Lee stood with a foot in both their houses. Ironically, David Ferrie was now in the same position, in a small way: while working for Carlos Marcello, he was also working for Guy Banister. Dave told me that Banister was in touch with the Attorney General, Bobby Kennedy himself.

Dave said Banister was being driven to drink and distraction over how things were turning out. Mostly due to his own bad temper and sense of importance, Banister found himself forced into a position so alien to his nature that it was driving him crazy. The great Red Raider, the mighty anti-Communist, the FBI chieftain over 500 men in Chicago, was now working with Carlos Marcello

– mobster – and that damnable Catholic interloper – Bobby Kennedy. That was the way it had to be, if you wanted to kill Castro.

Just thinking about it, Dave said, was enough to make Banister open another bottle of Scotch. "If he realized that half the people working for him are homosexuals," Dave finished, "I think he'd shoot himself." Dave grinned. "I'm tempted to tell him, if he pisses me off one more time, just to see which blood vessels burst first – the ones on his alcoholic nose, or the ones inside his alcoholic brain."

As for Lee, Dave respected him. To me, that was some kind of triumph on Lee's part, because Dave respected fewer people than he had fingers. As for Marcello, he knew that Lee was one of the brave who dared enter the dens of lions, dressed like a sheep, but holding a sharp blade close to his chest. "

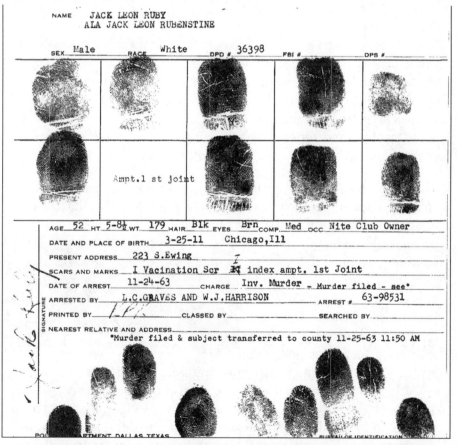

Jack Ruby's fingerprint chart shows a missing left index finger joint, a clue to the violent potential that might have earned him the nickname "Sparky." It was bitten off during a fight.

A. J. Weberman: Jack Rubenstein … changed his name to Jack Ruby in 1947…. Ruby was associated with the Marcello family soldiers, or capos, in Dallas. These men included R. D. Matthews … Joe Civello … Joe Campisi … Sam Campisi … and Ralph Paul.[15] … In June, 1961, Helen Afanace Ryan told Agents Kenneth Howe and Robert Gemberling that she knows JACK RUBY and that he is 'no good.' She stated he will not permit a girl to work for him unless she is intimate with him. [FBI DL-137-976 6.5.61

May 8 or 9, 1963: By late April, David had obtained sufficient funds to pay the bill on his Taylorcraft L-2, repaired earlier in the year. He will now be able to use it for flying lessons.

David received some funds from Jack Ruby for his work on The Project. Dave gave Lee Oswald a free flying lesson just prior to May 11, 1963. I assume it was in the Taylorcraft L-2. The Mafia and CIA are funding at least part of this "get-Castro" project.

May 10, 1963: Lee and I are hired at Standard Coffee, a small off-shoot of Reily's, where we will stay for one week while our background checks are laundered and I learn how to function as a secretary for Reily's Vice President, ex-FBI agent William I. Monaghan. A week later, we both transfer from Standard to Reily with the laundered background reports that do not mention cancer research or years spent in the USSR as a so-called defector.[16]

May 11, 1963: David Ferrie invites me to meet at Sherman's upscale apartment for lunch. David and Dr. Mary now inform me that the bioweapon project is linked to efforts to save President Kennedy's life. A broad coalition has formed to kill Kennedy, but will focus on retaking Cuba for American interests if Castro dies. If Castro isn't killed within a certain time limit, Lyndon Johnson will come to power and will invade Cuba for them, possibly precipitating World War III.

Dr. Sherman's Apartment house.

When Dr. Sherman shows me a powerful new cancer developed over the past year, I am stunned by its vigor. I agree to do what I can to stabilize the cancer and help transfer it from a mouse cancer to one that will attack human tissues. Only later will I realize that the cancer could be stolen and used to silence political enemies "forever."

I was puzzled that I'd heard Dave tell the Cubans at his party that Kennedy ought to die for what he'd done to them. He'd ranted against JFK, and I was deeply worried about that, until we started talking. "Do you think I'd have any of them coming over to my place, if I sang "Hail to the Chief?" he asked me – more than once.

My friends at University of Florida – which at that time specialized in science and engineering – had shaped a lot of my political thinking. Men greatly outnumbered the women there. They were typically staunch Republican conservatives who marched in the campus ROTC with pride, or had come in exchange programs to receive training. These were tomorrow's engineers, lawyers, scientists and psychologists. Many had fathers and grandfathers who were military men. They hoped JFK would be impeached. Many were anti-Castro Cubans who hated the President passionately. We could not guess what we were about to lose – not yet.

To both Dave and Lee, I eventually voiced my displeasure with Kennedy – the coward, the pinko – who kept giving in to Russia's leader, Nikita Khrushchev. My anti-Castro friends, in particular, believed JFK was a traitor who let hundreds die during the Bay of Pigs debacle. He had looked the other way as they begged for help on their radios. I remember how Lee and Dave just looked at me with pity and shook their heads. "They don't understand," Lee said. "He saved millions of lives by refusing to bomb Havana."

"Bomb Havana?" I was amazed. "Who said anything about bombing Havana?"

"That's what his generals wanted him to do," Dave said, making the whistling sound of a bomb falling through the air. "That's what the CIA wanted, too. If JFK had bombed Havana, we'd all be dead by now."

Lee explained that the best sources were saying that since Russian soldiers stationed in Cuba would have died, and many innocent civilians would also have died there, the USSR's Premier, Nikita Khrushchev, would have been forced to attack the US with nuclear bombs.

I argued, without much conviction, that we could shoot down anything aimed at us.

"You really want to test that theory?" Lee asked. "If they fired their missiles at us – say they fired a dozen or so – how much lead time would we have to respond?"[17]

"It depends—"

"Fact is," Lee said, "besides missiles, the Soviets could load up over a hundred bombers with atomic bombs, and send them on after the missiles. And then they have at least 50 submarines that could launch atom bombs at us."[18] Lee shook his head. "We of course would launch our own bombers, submarines and missiles. We have many more than they do. Life on the planet would be over."

"Life on this planet may be threatened by the Soviets, when Kennedy disarms us and leaves us vulnerable," I snapped back. I then sallied forth with a flotilla of reasons why I still disliked JFK.

"I see I have a mission!" Lee announced. "I must teach you to respect my Commander in Chief!" If anyone dares tell me to my face that Lee Oswald killed Kennedy, watch out.

May 31, 1963: David Ferrie invites Lee and me to meet him at Charity Hospital. He is afraid his apartment might have been bugged. Dr. Ochsner has allowed them all to meet together "this one time" because there is so much information to transmit. Ochsner has approved the use of Tulane's monkeys for The Project and Dave has been given the task of learning how to keep marmosets alive. They're cheaper than regular monkeys because of their tiny size. If the marmosets get cancer fast enough, Dave says, the next rung on the ladder is the African Green Monkey. If that works, one or more human volunteers with terminal diseases will be used to test the bioweapon's power.

Charity Hospital.

Another concern is an upcoming gun-running operation. David likes one of my ideas on how to conceal the rifles that will be coming in from Venezuela. He speculates that they might have been stockpiled there by Cuban guerrillas. He isn't sure. Before the Venezuela arms shipment arrives, Lee's job will be to help ferret out pro-Castro stevedores who might be spies, as well as FBI informants. Hoover's FBI, he says, loves to get the President in trouble by deliberately picking on anti-Castro training camps.

Lee is to offer "Hands Off Cuba" flyers, to see who takes and keeps them. Photos will be taken from a hidden location to be used to identify suspects. David gives Lee and me his schedule, which is coded, showing some commercial and personal flights.

Morning, June 4, 1963: David Ferrie and Lee join others at a meeting at Guy Banister's office, to discuss strategies on protecting the incoming arms shipment from Venezuela. Lee mentions that he could get arrested at the docks. Banister assures him it won't be like Dallas. The FBI will keep everything about Lee low key in New Orleans."[19]

June 6, 1963: Jack Ruby is in New Orleans again.

> **A. J. Weberman**: The Warren Commission found no identifying records to show that RUBY was in a hotel or anywhere else between the nights of June 5, 1963, and June 8, 1963. Was RUBY staying at Churchill Downs [sic], the multi-million dollar estate where CARLOS MARCELLO lived? [WC Hearings V14 p150; HSCA V4 p198] By June 9, 1963, RUBY was back in Dallas.

I've been out there. This was no "lap of luxury" establishment. Churchill Farms was huge. A lot of it was swamp. The big farmhouse was just that – a big farmhouse. The barns were just barns. There was a lot of space for parking. Carlos had some mansions, but not on this property. I wish I hadn't been so sore-footed that afternoon, or I would have walked around and looked for horses. Only the men were going into the farmhouse, as far as I could tell. David Ferrie would spend a number of days and nights at Churchill Farms, a safe place to meet, as Marcello's trial date drew closer.

June 6, 1963, evening: David Ferrie invites Lee and me, and David Lewis and his wife Anna to the 500 Club, compliments of Jack Ruby. (I know him as "Sparky.") Ruby greets us when we arrive, but we are seated apart from the main group. Marcello soon appears with brothers Sammy and Pete, and a bodyguard, taking one of three reserved tables. Adjoining tables are occupied by Clay Shaw seated with a married couple, Banister's pilot-partner Hugh Ward, "Sparky," an official from Terry Smith Stevedoring, and his wife. I watch Lee briefly go and meet Marcello face to face.[20]

Sunday, June 16, 1963: Lee Oswald passes out "Hands off Cuba!" flyers stamped with "A.J. Hidell" at the *USS Wasp* dock site on the Dumaine Wharf to help ferret out those pro-Castro spies. By the time he is told to leave by security authorities, he's been there several hours.[21] The *Wasp* carries 2,400 men and officers.

June 24-25, 1963: On the 24th, former Customs officer Charles Thomas flies in from Miami to expedite Lee Oswald's new passport (with a stack of others, to hide the fact). Thomas uses the name "Arthur Young." William Gaudet {CIA asset, friend of Clay Shaw, Dr. Alton Ochsner, and Guy Banister] stands just ahead of Lee in line to apply for his own new passport. On the 25th, through these connections, 64 Lee Oswald gets his new passport in only 24 hours, even though his application mentions planned visits to Cuba and the USSR, and his old passport shows that he lived in the Soviet Union nearly three years. He proudly shows it to me and introduces Thomas. Years later, I will find the Thomas family and tell them about their father's/grandfather's historic action in New Orleans.[22] (See *Me & Lee* for full story.)

Wednesday, July 10, 1963: I receive an important call at Reily Coffee from a Dr. Bowers, who tells me Dr. Ochsner asked him to relay some good news. Cells isolated from two of the lymphoma strains from the mice have produced dra-

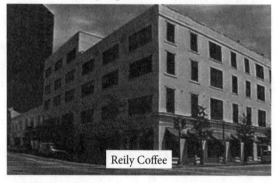

Reily Coffee

matic results in the marmoset monkeys we've started using. They suffer from not one, but two variations of a galloping cancer. We have broken through the barrier between mouse and monkey. Now we will move on to specific types of lung cancers, even though we need to keep the mouse cancers going, in case a failure occurs during our next step, when we move from marmoset monkeys to African Green monkeys. It is the first time I've heard the voice of any other doctor working in The Project. Dr. Ochsner has let a little bit of the size of the team be known to me.

I am surprised when Lee joins me at lunchtime. Instead of going directly to Dave's apartment to work, we meet Dave for lunch at Katzenjammer's, a haunt of Guy Banister's. Dave is seated in the farthest corner, wearing the familiar fatigues and sunglasses. There are several small boxes stacked on the floor beside him. As we sit down, I am told to keep my eyes and voice low. I should pretend that I can speak only Russian when the waiter comes to get our orders.

"We don't have to worry about Banister showing up," Dave says, "because he's kowtowing with some radical Christian politicos and

Minutemen right now. But it's still wise to pose as Marina, in this place. One of his secretaries might show up."

Dave says I need updating, because Lee, who is going to be working on a training film, needs my support. "You two lovebirds need to make your plans real careful," he says. "So let's talk about things."

How G. Wray Gil Got Involved with Marcello

It turns out Dave has plenty to talk about. He wants me to think better of his boss, G. Wray Gill, whom I see as a mere Mafia lawyer.

"Gill is a good man," Dave says. "So let me tell you how he got involved with the Little Man. It begins in 1934. A long time ago for a little chickadee like you. But listen." Dave tells me. "You might want to hear this, too," he tells Lee. "It all started when Gill was asked to defend a 28-year-old farmer who didn't want a livestock inspector to confiscate his mule."

"There has to be more to it than that," I interject.

"There is," Dave says. "The mule had ticks. But the mule belonged to the guy's dad. He said he didn't have a right to dip the mule for ticks. He had to wait until his dad came home. The inspector was enraged. He tried to confiscate the mule, on the spot. The young man refused to give up the mule, so the inspector came back with three deputy sheriffs. The mule was yielded up, but the sheriffs decided to arrest the young farmer. When his younger brother protested, a brawl started. They shot the brother in the stomach. He died a bit later."

"Oh!" I managed to say. David hurried on. "The young farmer, himself, was shot in the thigh. He managed to make it into the house, where he got his shotgun. He then killed one of the deputy sheriffs, as they were shooting two more of his brothers. One was just twelve years old. But there's more." We are all ears. "The deputies not only arrested the young farmer and the dying brother. They also arrested his mother, his uncle, and his sisters as well. They even arrested his dad, who wasn't even present at the time." Dave pauses to let this sink in, then says, "The young man, one of his brothers named Luther, and his mother were all charged with murder. The defense was given only three days to make its case. In the end, the young farmer was sentenced to death by hanging." Then Dave lets the blow land. "You see, they were niggers; and this was 1934."

"And Gill?" I ask.

"The NAACP knew they could save Jerome Wilson – that was his name – but only if they could find a lawyer with enough guts and compassion and skill to make a successful appeal. It wasn't easy back then to find a lawyer who would dare defend Wilson. Finally, a lawyer did step forward. He was indignant at the injustice. His name was G. Wray Gill. And this is why I like him.

"By then it was early 1935. But the same day Wilson's new trial was to begin, based on the appeal Gill won for him, the jail was stormed by a mob. They weren't about to let this thing go to trial. Wilson was clubbed to death with a hammer. They threw his body in a ditch. As for the Sheriff, he told the Press, 'They were just going about their business.' As for Gill, after that, he couldn't get much work, unless it was somebody who didn't know he was a 'nigger lover.' He finally found himself defending other victims of Sheriffs and police. More and more, that meant he found himself defending somebody in the Mob. And that's how he happened to become one of Marcello's lawyers. That's what Gill told me."

> **Senator Huey Long:** This nigger got hold of a smart lawyer somewhere and proved a technicality. He was guilty as hell. (Long to NAACP's Roy Wilkins.)[23]

Changing the subject, Dave reveals that Dr. Ochsner has corralled INCA's newest advisor, Herbert Philbrick, who will come soon to New Orleans to give a special, private lecture in a Reily boardroom. Lee is excited: this is why he had decided to take the cover job at Reily's to begin with, rather than work as a photographer. Ochsner has promised to introduce Lee to Philbrick, using a fake name for Lee. In the 1950's, Philbrick had posed as a die-hard communist, while actually secretly working for the FBI. Later, he wrote the book *I Led Three Lives*, which was turned into a TV series that mesmerized Lee when he was a young teen in New York. Lee is pleased, but then he says, "I have to get back to Reily's right away, unless you were able to pick up those ballasts for me."

Herbert Philbrick, Lee Oswald's boyhood hero.

Dave gives Lee the three small boxes that I'd spotted sitting on the floor. They're ballasts for fluorescent lights. "Thanks," Lee tells Dave, as sandwiches, iced tea, and a tall glass of beer arrive at the table. "Now," Lee says, "tell her what's going on."

"I didn't want you to know about this," Dave says bluntly. "But we've got so damned much on our plates, we can't handle it all."

"It's mostly about the training film coming up," Lee explains.

"Yes, Banister's project," says Dave. "The training film. I'm a Commander there, you might say. I'll be teaching leadership, hand-to-hand combat. Lee will be teaching stuff, too. CIA is there, too, when we're ready to film. It's how we're proving we still want to help the anti-Castroites; secretly, of course. Since Lee already told you about the training film," Dave looks disparagingly at Lee, "with that big mouth of his, you might as well hear about the rest of it."

In the following conversation, I am providing the real names in place of false ones that Lee and Dave adopted in this public place when they referred to JFK, RFK, Khrushchev, Castro, etc. Further, I am not as certain about who said what in this conversation, as I have been about the conversations in *Me & Lee*. However, I feel it's necessary to tell all I can remember.

"Kennedy has his back to the wall about Castro," Dave says, lighting a cigarette. "And it's getting worse. We've got a group that's taking things into their own hands. They're dangerous. The last thing we need, right now, is a second camp that's training anti-Castro trouble-makers. A rogue camp that's located almost on top of our own."

"But that's what we've got," Lee puts in. "Radicals who wear God on their sleeves and swastika's on their foreheads—"

"Good ole boys," Dave says. "I call them Right-wing nuts, who have bolted."

"–some dupes that have just arrived from Miami," Lee continues. "The organizers are pretending they're just training some lumberjacks to ship over to Guatemala."

"They have a company in Guatemala," Dave said.[24] "It acts as a cover. But they made a mistake. I happen to specialize in Guatemala, for Marcello's interests there."

"He's been to Guatemala," Lee puts in.

"It's my baby," Dave says. "Ochsner found out about this camp from his oil buddies, while they played poker. They're throwing good money into that particular pot. Ochsner told Shaw."

"Shaw's office is bugged, thanks to Banister's expert," Lee tells me, "which is how we happen to know about it, too.[25]

"There's just been another coup down there," I comment.

"CIA hung Fuentes out to dry when they were finished with him." Dave says.

"To start at the beginning," Lee cuts in, "JFK has ordered all funding cut off to anti-Castro organizations. For which they're mad as hell."

"The anti-Castro forces now have to regroup," Dave puts in. "With Kennedy at the top of their shit list. First, the Bay of Pigs. Next, the missile crisis last October. Now this. They lost their cash cow, so now our friendly foreigners are using JFK's photos for target practice."

"Here's the crux," Lee says. "Our enemies within can now rig things so the anti-Castro Cubans can be blamed if anything happens to JFK."[26]

They let this sink in a moment.

"As Mary and I told you," Dave says, "killing Kennedy is their ticket to getting Cuba back. A lot of money is riding on that hope. Then they can invade Cuba, and get away with it."

"Which," Lee says, "Could mean two hundred million dead Americans, Cubans and Russians."

My appetite is now gone. Our lunches sit on the table, but hunger is not on our minds.

"Bobby Kennedy knows this," Lee puts in. "Anybody in Cuba, taking Castro's place, will be offered our help to settle things down."

Dave nods in agreement. "The Russians might try to stay," he says, "but we would claim the island in the name of 'Peace.' Promising to restore order, we'll put the old regime back in power. All will be hunky-dory. Especially United Fruit, mining interests, casino owners, and drug rings. That's how you invade without dropping bombs. Unless the Russkies decide to drop them."

"Who's on the bad guys' side, around here?" I ask.

"Banister," Dave says, "Shaw. The Mob. I learn a lot, because they think I hate Kennedy's guts. Remember?"

"The Kennedy brothers see it," Lee comments. "They're playing some poker, too. By cutting off funds to the anti-Castro training camps, and so on, the President is sending a message to Castro that negotiations are possible." Lee has eaten nothing at all, he's so worked up. I push half a sandwich toward him. He takes a bite, but keeps on talking. "Also, this way, Castro might let down his guard, making it easier to assassinate him. It could be blamed on some handy lunatic. Second, with Kennedy speaking so softly, the USSR's generals might not get rid of Khrushchev."

"Khrushchev is in trouble," Dave puts in. "He backed down on Cuba. His trigger-happy generals want to dump him."

"Kennedy has the same problem here," Lee begins, but Dave cuts in. "Yeah, Kennedy is in trouble," he says, bitterly, "And it's more than some trigger-happy generals pissed off at him. More than you'd ever believe. Fact is, CIA will do as they please. With *Cosa Nostra* at their side, and the military in their pocket."

"The CIA can run the military?" I ask.

"Yes, my befuddled child," Dave says. "Ever hear of the Dulles brothers? Just the two of them ran the coups that overthrew Iran and Guatemala.[27] Allen wouldn't allow Congress to supervise his precious CIA. When he disobeyed JFK, he was fired, but his replacement, John McCone – chosen by JFK – is mostly out of the loop.[28] Truth is, Dulles is still in charge of a lot of his troops, behind the scenes. And they like LBJ."[29]

Dave makes a fake laugh. "Johnson already has more respect with the military and all the agencies than Kennedy could ever muster. Johnson's an arm-twister. He has the Senate and the House on their knees, sucking away. They will fall right in line. And because Johnson is corrupt as hell, FBI has a lot of dirt on him. CIA and FBI will ride him like a pony."

"Whereas," Lee puts in, "they can't control JFK."

Dave opines, "I'm guessing that Bobby's helping the CIA get Castro, if they can, to protect his brother."

Dave points to Lee. "He'll find out if any pro-Castro spies are hanging around out in the camps – if he can. One spy could do a lot of damage. Find out about our important camp, then tell the FBI. The FBI wants to shut down everything – to make JFK even more hated. So your Lee, here, has gotta be careful. He could get shot out there, if somebody blames him."

"You don't have to tell her stuff like that," Lee objects.

I try to act calm. "I see," I say quietly. As I realize the danger this puts Lee in, I look with alarm at the man I love.

"That's the job he signed up for," Dave says, seeing my face. "Before you came along. And yes, we could lose him, if they figure it out."

Dave says it so matter-of-factly that my blood chills. No wonder Lee isn't hungry.

"They're both rogue outfits," Lee says.

Dave makes a snort of contempt. "There's no comparison. This new camp is a half-baked Candid Camera joke that can mess up everything. Before we finish up the training film, with our authorized people, we've got to get the FBI to pop this pimple."

Dave lights a cigarette as Lee notices that his plate has been emptied by his friend. Dave shoves a dollar toward him.

"Go get some more," he says. As Lee heads to the bar, Dave says, "Even Dr. Mary's doing her bit. She's gone out to the 'good' camp, with some medical supplies. It's out in no man's land, other side of the Lake, a hard place to be. So don't talk to anybody about her, either." Lee stands up – he has to return to Reily. He reaches down and takes my hand. Dave, all wound up, has a little more to tell us.

"Banister says those rich bastards at the right-wingers' camp have their own swimming pool. They're sitting right next to a U-Haul full of explosives and war materiel," Dave says. "Usually, I'd say, let this half-assed camp just fall on its face. But since Hoover wants to break up every damned training camp he can find, and blame it on JFK—"[30]

"That's why," Lee breaks in, "we need to get the FBI on their tails. Now excuse me. I have some lights to install in Reily's warehouse."

In his famous *Playboy* interview, New Orleans District Attorney Jim Garrison explained what he understood about the anti-Castro/ Radical right situation: "...both of these groups had a vital stake in changing U.S. foreign policy – ideological on the part of the paramilitary rightists and both ideological and personal with the anti-Castro exiles, many of whom felt they would never see their homes again if Kennedy's policy of detente was allowed to succeed. The CIA was involved with both of these groups. In the New Orleans area, where the conspiracy was hatched, the CIA was training a mixed bag of Minutemen, Cuban exiles and other anti-Castro adventurers north of Lake Pontchartrain for a foray into Cuba and an assassination attempt on Fidel Castro. David Ferrie, who operated on the "command" level of the ultra-rightists, was deeply involved in this effort.[31]

Friday July 12, 1963: Dave Ferrie is back in town, and is helping us with the unpleasant task of slaughtering mice. Though we are nearly finished with mice, this last batch involves an astonishing 500 animals to process. Lee comes to Reily a half hour early today so he can get an early start at Dave's. For the first time in five weeks, I clock him out at 5:00, so we can get the work finished earlier. Even Dr. Sherman has come to help. With the summer heat and the stench of cancer, all of us get nauseated.

Later, as Dave drives me and Lee home, he tells us how he has to go back to Miami, and that Marcello's case is now taking considerable time. He's been dubbed a "Commando" out at the "good" training camp, where he's begun teaching personal self-defense.

"I haven't even had time to eat," Dave says. "Not that I want anything after this."

"I knew better than to eat today," Lee tells us. "I would have puked."

"I didn't eat before coming, either," I agree. Dave drives us up to 1032 Marengo, but I don't want to get out. Dave stops the car and turns off the engine when Lee suddenly belches, looking pale, as if he's about to vomit.

"You'll be home in a couple of minutes now, sport," Dave tells Lee, who has put his head out the window to get some fresh air. But Dave likes to tease. "Those baby mice were the saddest, most tormented little creatures I have ever seen," Dave says, in a falsetto voice, shaking his head, as we sit there. "To think that they fought so hard for their lousy little shreds of life, only to be gassed to death."

"Stop!" I cry. "Sadist! If you keep it up, I'm going to be in the same state as Lee." As I consider the slaughter we've just gone through, I have to add, "And we're trying to give Castro the same thing. It's just plain evil, Dave."

Dave's grin turns to a scowl, and he becomes angry. "Get this straight, chickadee," he snaps. "How many times do I have to tell you? This is about Kennedy, not Castro. Kennedy is surrounded by his enemies. He can do nothing right in their eyes. And he's gonna' die, unless we can stop it."

Dave throws his cigarette out the car window and lights another one. "Listen," he goes on, "...You'd better know what your boy Lee, here, is up against; and, me too. We're risking our lives to get this stuff [the biological weapon] into Cuba. Yes, we're saying we want to help them take out JFK, and they believe us. God help us, they still want to see Castro die, too. If that son-of-a-bitch Castro is eliminated, we might save more than Kennedy. We might save the whole god-damned country from becoming a fascist nation."

"Well put," Lee says. "Now I'll just go puke."

I'm angry at Dave, who thinks he knows everything. I think of all I've been taught, growing up. The Pilgrims, George Washington, who could not tell a lie. America seemed so new and clean and full of hope. Inside, I bristle. It can be that way again! At least, in my own life. In the lives of my future children. We can be honest. We can protect the land, teach people to care about each other. Can't we?

I finally get out of the car, and walk down Susie's driveway without saying goodbye.

July 15-16-17, 1963: David is in Miami again, for Eastern Air Lines hearings.

Without Dave's help, we are falling behind on finishing up our lab work at Dave's apartment. The Project has become dangerous, as well, so Dr. Sherman make a rare visit, coming with a portable lab bench. It uses inserted gloves, a filtering system, and keeps conditions sterile. We work hard; Dave is expected to return from Miami late that afternoon, in time to help with the cleanup.[32]

Wednesday July 17, 1963: A Day of Revelation – At Reily, I receive another complaint that Lee is missing, and I am required to examine his woefully incomplete work log book. I locate Lee by phone at Dave's. Lee says that Ochsner has insisted he process a final batch of mice. It makes us furious, because it's actually unnecessary. The marmosets have cancer. We should be handling marmosets. On top of this anticipated afternoon absence, Lee is late again this morning. Knowing he will be working late at Dave's on the Project tonight, Lee had decided to spend a little extra time with his family, and missed the bus.

At about noon, personnel has just about had it with Mr. Lee H. Oswald. We have been instructed to hire a replacement for Lee at once. I help Monaghan go through a list of new applicants for Lee's job, and we find a man to recommend whose background check is incomplete. That will buy Lee, at most, one more week. We only have to keep Lee employed at Reily's until next Wednesday, since he has to be in Mobile to speak at Spring Hill seminary that Friday. With Lee preparing for his pro-Castro demonstrations, right in the heart of town, his cover job at Reily's has to end soon anyway, because such activities would embarrass the company.

That will also give Lee the time he needs to deal with the training camps.

Mr. William Monaghan, my boss, is quite annoyed that I won't be returning to Reily this afternoon, but I remind him it might be the last time. With monkeys on the menu now, we'll only be seeing primate tumors. They would be brought to us ready to work with. Monaghan makes a face. It's more than he wants to know. Soon, I'm at Dave's apartment, where I find Lee and Dr. Mary working with a stack of mouse tumors in the kitchen. It's good that she's come. With Dave gone, we've fallen behind.

But this time, something is very different. The level of "laboratory precautions" has suddenly increased dramatically. Both Lee and Dr. Mary are wearing surgical masks and hats, in addition to the usual plastic aprons and surgical gloves. And they're using a germ-free isolation chamber.

Seeing that, I am concerned. Dr. Mary's hands are thrust into this "clean box" into which air is pumped in, then out, through high-grade filters to prevent airborne contaminants from floating around the kitchen and into our lungs. Dr. Mary notices that I am staring at the equipment, wondering why she has ratcheted up the precautions so suddenly. It's because our marmosets are dying. All of them. Including the control group. I ponder 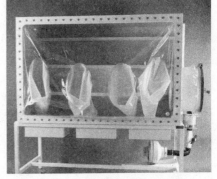 the implications. Our bioweapon has migrated between both groups of monkeys, unfettered, presenting the terrifying possibility that our mutated cancer is not only transferable, but contagious. From this moment on, we need to be concerned about catching these cancer-causing viruses.

For the next hour, I work with the microscopes, until Dave shows up. He's quite late, but that's to be expected: Dave has flown in from his Eastern Air Lines hearings in Miami, and the fact that he's made it home at all tonight is evidence of how much pressure we're under. Dave is glum and doesn't want to talk about what happened.

As my eyes get tired, I decide to help Lee, whose hands are now thrust inside the clean box gloves, leaving the microscope work to Dr. Mary

"I'm going to help," I tell him, putting on my lab coat. I can see a book in Lee's pocket through his clear plastic apron. "I see you brought along *Profiles in Courage*."

Lee replies, "I'm trying to get my hands on everything I can about the Chief. I'll read it tonight. I will also pretend I can't hear her, when Marina starts yelling at me for being late again."

As Lee says "Marina," an image of her flashes in my mind. I can almost see her, pregnant, sitting in that sparsely furnished apartment with little Junie at her side. I think about how neglected a woman can feel, and about how Robert had forgotten my birthday. Then it dawns on me.

"Oh, Lee!" I exclaim. "Didn't you tell me that today was Marina's birthday?"

Dave hears my question, and whistles like an in-bound missile. "The ding-dong bells are gonna' ring all over your poor head, boy!" he teases. Lee straightens up, steps back from the clean box, and starts peeling off his apron and lab hat. He throws the mask into the waste-basket, then looks down at his sweaty shirt.

"I need a shirt!" he cries out, urgently. "This one stinks!" He hurries past me, going through the back door of the kitchen toward the hall, to wash up.

Dave heads for his bedroom, where I, following, can see just his rear end as he goes down on his hands and knees, searching through a heap of clothes on the floor.

"Here, Oswald!" he yells, holding up something clean and white. "Okay!" Lee replies. Dave tosses him the shirt, and Lee puts it on. He kisses me on the cheek, hands me *Profiles in Courage,* and sprints down the back stairs, with Dave at his heels.

"I'll be right back!" Dave yells, car keys in his hand and his cap on, commandeering Dr. Mary's car.

"Go, go, go!" Mary calls out, from behind her surgical mask. Dr. Mary and I continue working for the next several hours, and Dave returns as promised. We finally finish around midnight, and Dr. Mary drives me home.[33] I carry *Profiles in Courage* with me to bed, and sleep with it, because Lee gave it to me. I hope it will stop me from having nightmares.

July 19, 1963: Lee Oswald is fired from Reily's a little earlier than planned, when he grabs a green glass for me out of a packing line. An ad to replace me (I am no longer needed) is then ordered. It runs the next day. However, the minimum wage pay attracts no executive secretary-type applicants (I was holding the secretary position only as a cover job). The error was discovered and the pay rate was raised to its former level, after which the ad was run again, this time attracting suitable applicants.

Endnotes

1. Anita Langley, cousin by marriage, former Black Op radio host, to author. She posted this information on newsgroups, too, adding that Michael confirmed my role in New Orleans at this time.

2. W.C. Vol. 22, p. 778. W.C. Vol. 23, p. 526.

3. Disinformation by researcher David Lifton caused some researchers to doubt my account for almost a decade. WC testimonies reveal Lee Oswald contacted

his aunt Lillian Murret April 25th. At that time, she invited him to store his things in her garage next to her washing machine. That night, Lee moved a few boxes and three seabags there, emptying one of two lockers he was renting. Several boxes were moved to 4905 Magazine St. on May 10 from the second locker. On May 11, the last of the Oswald possessions still at the bus station were moved to 4905 Magazine (often misreported as 4907) Lee's uncle Dutz used his car to move them, the same day Marina arrived, via Ruth Paine, with the rest of the Oswald belongings.

Back on the 25th, Lee told his aunt Lil he was job hunting. When she saw his clothes, she offered to get him nicer ones for his job interviews. When I met Lee the next day, the 26th, around 10:00 AM at the post office, he reluctantly broke off his conversation with me ("to get a shirt"). About one-and-a-half to two hours later, Lee appeared appropriately and neatly dressed for his first job interview. For years, David Lifton reported that I could not have met Lee Oswald on April 26 because she had described him wearing old clothes. Lifton claimed Lee had 'just arrived' in New Orleans on the 26th, wearing a suit on his bus ride from Dallas, and that he immediately went to a job interview that afternoon, ignoring the fact that Lee began his trip from Dallas on the 24.th In her Warren Commission testimony, Lilian Murret said: "...all he had on at the time was a T-shirt and pants, and I think he had only about two T-shirts with him. Mr. JENNER. You say he had no suit coat? Mrs. MURRET. No; and only one l pair of shoes." http://www.aarclibrary.org/publib/jfk/wc/wcvols/wh8/pdf/WH8_LillianMurret.pdf. In fact, many researchers accepted Lifton's claims for a decade, until I realized what he was saying behind her back. Johnson-McMillan's anti-Oswald book *Marina and Lee*, p. 382, and WC testimony indicate Lee left Dallas on the 24th. Most of Lee Oswald's activities for the two weeks between April 26 and May 10 were unknown until my book, *Me & Lee*, provided full details.

4. Lillian Murret, Lee's aunt, told the Warren Commission that when Lee moved to her home, *he never ate breakfast with the family* and would be gone all day, a pattern that continued until his wife arrived.

5. Today, photocopy machines are in every office, but in 1963 they were both rare and expensive. Virtually all were made by the Xerox Corporation, which held the patents on the technology. The few machines that existed in hospitals and medical schools were closely guarded by the secretarial staffs to make sure each copy was properly logged and accounted for. Many times this had to do with federal grant money connected to research. Personal use was seriously frowned on, and official use left a paper trail. The ability to access a photocopy machine at Banister's office meant that copies could be made for off-the-books projects without leaving a paper trail.

6. In 1999, I told researchers that Bobby Kennedy knew Lee Oswald was working for the CIA, compliments of the ONI, and that Guy Banister was using Oswald. Banister despised the Kennedys, but he despised Castro more. When Banister helped conduct operations involving CIA and Mob efforts against Castro, Bobby Kennedy's own network of informants could have been involved. I believe this has led to confusion as to Banister's relationship to RFK. The stealing of minor munitions from the Schlumberger munitions depot is an example of how Ban-

ister operated: the House Select Committee on Assassinations (HSCA) made a note of this secret operation carried out in August 1961:

"Both Ferrie and Banister were implicated in a raid in late 1961 against a munitions depot in Houma, Louisiana, in which various weapons, grenades, and ammunition were stolen. Banister's role may have been limited to storing the materiel which was reportedly seen stacked in Banister's back room by several witnesses...." [Vol 10, pp 127, 109; the month of August was specified in Garrison's indictment of Novel].

Researcher Mike Sylwester writes: "Guy Banister's employees, Jack Martin and David Lewis, explained in their affidavit that this raid was arranged by Robert Kennedy...Martin and Lewis noted in their affidavit that Robert Kennedy had established his own secret channel of communication to communicate with Banister, by-passing J. Edgar Hoover and the local FBI Special Agent in Charge.

[wrote Martin and Lewis:] "This FRD group, through Banister, was additionally serviced by an FBI Special Agent, Regis Kennedy, who we often met during this period at Banister's office. Sometimes, we would run into him several times a day. Banister once told [another of his investigators, Joseph] Newbrough and we that [Regis] Kennedy's daily reports on these activities were forwarded straight to one Assistant FBI Director Mohr, subservient only to John Edgar Hoover in Washington, always by-passing [Regis] Kennedy's own local Special Agent in Charge (resident agent) for numerous top-security reasons. From here [Washington], they were viewed by none other than Philby and RFK, the story goes.

Inasmuch as we were for many years associated with Banister, we had upon occasion engaged (independently) in some of these activities, cooperating with FRD and Dalzell operations. From time to time, our code names had been "El Gringo" and "Jauquin" during these periods. Returning to the subject, RFK allegedly tendered several documents in the form of "Letters-Marques" giving "carte-blanche" status to any and all of those about to participate in this pending pseudo-legal hijacking. These were directed to all concerned to "seize munitions or arms, the property of a foreign government, that are illegally located within the US, which might otherwise be used against nations friendly to the US, using any and all means to do so." They, of course, supposedly bore the signature of none other than RFK himself, because they were issued on Justice Department Attorney General's letterhead stationery.

Needless to say, as we recall it, everyone was overjoyed by this prospective arms hijacking. Furthermore, someone had said that either the FBI or CIA were to supply the keys to pull this "job" (robbery), so no locks would be broken.

Later on that following afternoon, we heard Banister talking over the telephone to who we were told was a Mr M.E. Loy, the South-Eastern Manager of Schlumberger in New Orleans. (Loy at this writing is the President of all Schlumberger incorporations here in the US, whose home office is in Houston, Texas.) This conversation was in regard to the pending Schlumberger operation. Banister seemed to be setting the time and date, like H hour and D date. In short, they of the Schlumberger company knew that we were coming in the fake bakery truck ...

That evening, FBI Agent [Regis] Kennedy made his daily appearance at Banister's office as usual. It was about this time that the Letters-Marque and the keys showed up. No one ever said that Agent Kennedy brought them, but they did come to light shortly after he had left.

Anyway, the story goes that it was in the dark of night that the very "chosen people" hijacked those munitions at the Houma Schlumberger bunker, transported, and stored them in their designated location, the storage area adjoining Banister's office. The following day, everyone in the "know" came to look and gloat. Boy, ol' Castro should sure catch hell now! ....

Well, at any rate, it appears that after the Houma bunker haul, Philby and company may have progressed in activity. We say this because later the next evening, apparently some other band of thieves filched those promised arms and munitions from the safety of their hiding place at Banister's office. However, no robbery report was made, nor search launched for them. Banister was ordered to do nothing about this matter and to remain silent, as were the rest of us so instructed.

Some bastard about this time circulated the rumor (we understand that it was believed by all or most of the Cubans) that Dr Arcacha had either sold or had given away these arms and munitions to the pro-Castro Cubans or others. So he engineered another hijacking of his own. On this, they only found low-yield projectiles looking like small aerial bombs, but with not much explosive power. However, the Cubans thought they were for real and [set up] ... Arcacha to a blow-out in one of the local hotels (St Charles) to celebrate the occasion... a few days later, they (the Cubans) found out that these were oil-well equipment or exploration low-yield explosive units. With this, the Cubans really believed that they'd been crossed, and Arcacha left town immediately in fear of his life. ....

Now, what happened, and where did they [the stolen arms] go? It seems that there were some others, a bunch of discontented people, who just wanted to take over Guatemala using these weapons far more than we needed them to give the "works" to Castro. Thus, via Philby and company, General Ydígoras went out of office, and Guatemala had a completely new political administration. Somebody fulfilled the vendetta for the Carlos Marcello caper in spades! JFK had gotten his revenge one way or another. ....

This left Dr. Cardona's Frente under the total command of Arcacha's former assistant, Carlos Quiroga. He claims to be an avid anti-Communist. We believe he protests far too much upon this subject. Hence, we did some checking. Quiroga says he left Cuba just at the time his father was arrested and imprisoned within the Isle of Pines near Havana. Our sources inform us that Quiroga's father may have been assisted into confinement by none other than Quiroga himself, just as he is said to have assisted Arcacha to be removed. He is truly an assistant, however, according to our information. Moreover, it is highly speculative that this subject, Quiroga, may well be as Philby, a double agent. [text rearranged slightly into chronological order; punctuation fixed]"

Sylwester continues: "Banister's secretary Delphine Roberts also indicated to Police Sgt Fenner Sedgebeer that Banister was involved with Latin American Communists who were exporting items to Central America. Sedgebeer's raw notes records Roberts' encounters with this group (Banister file, Assassination Archives, Washington DC; Sylwester: "This escapade with Ferrie apparently helped lead to the removal of Arcacha Smith from his position as chief of the CRC's New Orleans branch.

7. In a taped interview from 1999, Anna Lewis (she was now Anna Vincent), David Lewis' former wife, answered questions at random, in the presence of her daughter, Sondra. Anna and her husband had double-dated with me and Lee, and she went on film and audiotape saying so. On a 1999 tape, one of two made in 1999, in a public restaurant where we met just once, with every minute captured on the tapes, Anna expressed surprise that researchers were trying to say that Guy Banister had no access to his own upstairs office space (described as 'upstairs' by various witnesses). They insisted that he would have had to walk all the way down to the front of the long building to enter by the door on the other street (Camp St) in order to get upstairs to the second floor. "Why would he have to do that?" she commented. We told her that "Oswald-did-it" tale-tellers didn't want people to know Banister could have ever seen Oswald on the second floor, where Lee had an office for at least a month, an office later described to researcher/author Anthony Summers by Delphine Roberts ('my' Mrs. Roberts)as being full of FPCC posters and other pro-Castro materials being used by Oswald. Later, Lee used a small windowless room on the second floor as a darkroom to develop photos for both himself and Banister.

8. See Edward T. Haslam's book *Dr. Mary's Monkey* (TrineDay, 2007, 2014) for full details about these important files, and how Haslam discovered what happened to them after the Kennedy assassination.

9. J. Edgar Hoover's phone logs were made available to researchers as a result of the JFK Assassination Records Act of 1992, after Oliver Stone's movie *JFK* caused public outcries. They show that J. Edgar Hoover was communicating regularly with Guy Banister during the summer of 1963.

10. G. Wray Gill was an attorney who represented Carlos Marcello. The FBI Interviewed Gill on November 27, 1963. Gill advised the FBI that he had known David W. Ferrie since about 1961 when he represented Ferrie in a criminal matter in Jefferson Parish, Louisiana and in a grievance with Eastern Air Lines following his dismissal from that company. Guy Banister served as a character witness for Ferrie in this latter matter. Following these events, Gill hired Ferrie as an investigator. At the time, Gill's office was 1705 Pere Marquette Building, named after a famous Jesuit priest. The building was owned by the Jesuits. Gill later moved his office to the Richards building which was also owned by the Jesuits.

11. HSCA: "Undated. Handwritten speech, nine pages. Green ink: nib pen. Location: Archives. (FBI exhibit 117:CE 97: JFK F-508.)" The speech is actually an essay that is nine pages long comparing and contrasting US with USSR. Lee condemns both systems.

12. The Warren Commission … p. 136 MRS. MURRET: "You see, he went out all day. He would get up and leave early (p.137) in the morning. He wouldn't eat any breakfast. I would try to fix him an egg and bacon or something like that, but he didn't want anything to eat for breakfast and he wouldn't take a thing. We always eat a big breakfast in our family, but he wouldn't eat a thing. He would just get dressed and go out with his newspaper to look for a job..." FROM: TESTIMONY OF MRS. LILLIAN MURRET, April 6, 1964.

13. On June 24, 1973, an arsonist set a gay bar on fire, killing 32 people and

injuring many others. Only Father Bill Richardson was decent enough to hold a church service for the victims (another occurred later), for which his Bishop castigated him. Father Bill's wife, Mary, though only middle-aged, died of a sudden heart attack only 18 days after the JFK assassination (information provided by Edward T. Haslam). She was the only person who knew Lee Oswald had found an apartment for myself, who knew Lee Oswald was going to move in nearby, and who knew that I called Lee Oswald to get help (her husband was conducting a funeral service when these events occurred). For information on the fire, see: http://www.nolapride.org/upstairsloungefire.htm (Retrieved 04/09/2014).

14. Jack didn't get angry at being called "Sparky" because he was let in on the joke.

15. http://ajweberman.com/nodulex29.pdf (Retrieved June 20, 2013)

16. Essential Background Information: Reily's first non-family Vice president, former FBI agent and Standard Fruit executive Wm. I. Monaghan helped Alton Ochsner and Ed Butler create INCA, backed by Clay Shaw (General Manager of the Trade Mart and charter INCA member) and Eustis Reily (another INCA charter member) Monaghan influences Wm. B. Reily to help him and Dr. Ochsner protect Lee's and my cover jobs. At this date, Lee Oswald was investigating the bioweapon project for the CIA, and later posed as pro-Castro for Guy Banister to weed out Castro's spies. He worked with Banister on local university campuses identifying "communist" pro-integration students (a task Lee Oswald hated), a fact reported by historian and author Dr. Michael Kurtz, an eyewitness.

17. "Air Force General Curtis LeMay presented a pre-invasion bombing plan to Kennedy in September, while spy flights and minor military harassment from US forces at Guantanamo Bay Naval Base were the subject of continual Cuban diplomatic complaints to the US government." (2011). "John F Kennedy and the Cuban Missile Crisis". Retrieved February 7, 2012. BBC "History of the Cold War."

18. "At the time of the missile crisis, the Soviets had 36 intercontinental ballistic missiles (ICBMs), 138 long-range bombers with 392 nuclear warheads, and 72 submarine-launched ballistic-missile warheads (SLBMs). These forces were arrayed against a vastly more powerful U.S. nuclear arsenal of 203 ICBMs, 1,306 long-range bombers with 3,104 nuclear warheads, and 144 SLBMs – all told, about nine times as many nuclear weapons as the U.S.S.R. Nikita Khrushchev was acutely aware of America's huge advantage not just in the number of weapons but in their quality and deployment as well." Ref: http://www.theatlantic.com/magazine/archive/2013/01/the-real-cuban-missile-crisis/309190/.

19. New Orleans FBI will "inquire" to Dallas FBI about Lee Oswald [WC Vol IV, p. 443].

20. I had free evenings (That doesn't mean I was seeing Lee Oswald at night – a rare occurrence after his wife, Marina, came to New Orleans. See *Me & Lee* for evidence of Robert Baker's many and protracted absences.

21. WC, Vol. XXII, p. 806.

22. I advised researcher Joan Mellen of Lee Oswald's strong connections to Customs in 2001. Later, she interviewed Edward T. Haslam concerning Ochsner, the

bioweapon project, Dr. Mary Sherman, the linear particle accelerator, Sherman's violent death, and much more, yet never mentioned either of us as sources in her book *A Farewell to Justice.* Her book repeats what Haslam told her and goes into a long description of Lee's Customs contacts, ignoring the name of his most important Custom contact and erring when she said Lee had a Customs controller. Mellen even told researchers that all I told her was that Jim Garrison had an affair with stripper Sandra Sexton, which she said Sexton denied. Why would I call a pro-Garrison researcher just to tell her of a Garrison sin? One of my witnesses, Mac McCullough, gave me the information on Sexton: he was her bodyguard. I primarily spoke to Mellen about the important matter of Lee's links to Customs.

23. Samuel C. Hyde, editor. *A Fierce and Fractious Frontier: the Curious Development of Louisiana's Florida Parishes,* 1699-2000. USL UP. 2004. P. 177.

24. Besides Alpha-66 and the DRE, The CDP(Christian Democratic Party, also known as Moviemiento Democratica Critiano-MDC) attracted anti-Castro guerrilla forces. After the Bay of Pigs, the CDP split into factions. But HSCA investigator Gaeton Fonzi said the CDP, "...was one of the most active and effective underground groups in Cuba in the early 1960's." Richard Billings' "Garrison notes" mention two camps, one run by the CDP where the spy, Fernando Fernandez, was caught; then exposed (thanks to Lee Oswald). The other camp, which Lee and David Ferrie wanted to break up, was run by ultra-radical right wingers whose friends were known to Ochsner.

Their cover organization was the Guatemala Lumber and Mineral Corporation. The CDP camp was located on land owned by Redemptorist Fathers, of interest to David Ferrie. The radical camp used land and housing owned by William J. McLaney and would be shut down by the FBI. Many researchers now know that it was Lee Oswald who located this camp for the FBI. Peter Dale Scott (*Deep Politics and the Death of JFK*)noted that Carlos Bringuier, head of the DRE in New Orleans, said in August, 1963 (before he revised his statements for the Warren Commission)when Lee visited him, 'I thought he might be an agent from the FBI or CIA, trying to find out what we might be up to' (*Washington Post*, November 23, 1963; cf. 10 H 35; Scott, p.251.). "Bringuier's logic here is of major importance. Oswald had to be working for one side or the other; he could not have been acting alone" (Scott, Ibid.) Though DeLaney claimed the Guatemala Lumber and Mineral Co. was just trying to recruit some loggers, his partner in the business, Richard Davis, admitted being the area's CDP representative to the FBI in a highly redacted report that also released this information: "89-69-1427... N[ew] O[rleans] teletype to Director and Dallas dated 2-20-67.. page 2 XXXX Richard Davis... info that training camps had been established across the lake [near] NO. One was at the home of Davis Ferrie [sic] and the other near Mandeville. The latter camp involved several anti-communists and Davis associated with this camp."

25. This person might have been Michael Riconusciuto, who has stated he was working for Banister, installing bugging devices and electronic surveillance equipment for him in the summer of 1963. Michael also told his relative by marriage, Anita Langley, that he had seen some of my cancer research reports, which we'd Xeroxed at Banister's office. At this time, Xerox machines were mostly avail-

able in hospitals, clinics, police stations and businesses where close records were kept of copier use, due to its expense. Banister had a copy machine available for our use, without requiring a copy record.

26. A play on words is being used here. In 1960, Robert F. Kennedy published *The Enemy Within: The McClellan Committee's Crusade Against Jimmy Hoffa And Corrupt Labor Unions.* The description tells us how much we lost when Bobby Kennedy was assassinated.

27. John Foster Dulles and Allen Dulles, brothers, masterminded coups in Iran (Mossadegh, 1953), and Guatemala (Jacobo Arbenz, 1954).

28. Jim DiEugenio, as quoted on The Education Forum: "What is extraordinary about what Dulles did with the CIA is that it was too much for even certain elements of the Eastern Establishment i.e. the very people who Dulles worked with and for. In 1956, David Bruce and Robert Lovett composed the Bruce-Lovett Report on the CIA for President Eisenhower. That report is almost nowhere to be found today. RFK had access to it during his service on the board of inquiry into the Bay of Pigs debacle…Lovett told the Cuban board that, "I have never felt that the Congress of the United States ever intended to give the United States Intelligence Agency authority to conduct operations all over the earth." (ibid) Lovett's report and testimony held great sway with the Kennedys…[Lovett] told the president that the CIA was "badly organized, dangerously amateurish and excessively costly." It had to be re-organized, which wasn't possible with Eisenhower as president and Dulles as Director. (ibid p. 478) There can be little doubt that Lovett's testimony and his relationship with Kennedy's father helped convince JFK to fire Allen Dulles. How important was it? Lovett's influence was so profound that after JFK fired Dulles, Robert Kennedy was determined to find out if any other relative of Dulles was still at the State Department. When he found out that Allen's sister Eleanor worked there, he ordered Dean Rusk to fire her. Because "he didn't want any more of the Dulles family around." (Mosley, p. 473) This is the man LBJ appointed to the Warren Commission. As shown above, he became the most active member of that cover-up. And it started almost immediately. (12/16 transcript, p. 52) Dulles also backed the idea of the Commission not having independent investigators. (DiEugenio, p. 90)"

29. It is still shocking to me that Lyndon Johnson dared – and was successful – in placing Allen Dulles on the Warren Commission, which declared lee Oswald the "Lone assassin" summarily. This, despite Dulles having been fired by Kennedy and removed from his longtime position as head of the CIA. In 2010, on the Education Forum, researcher Jim DiEugenio wrote, concerning Dulles' meeting with researcher David Lifton : "It later turned out that Dulles had nothing but scorn for both the evidence and critical arguments against the Oswald-did-it hypothesis. In 1965, at UCLA, David Lifton questioned Dulles about the Zapruder film and Harold Feldman's essay entitled "51 Witnesses" about many witnesses hearing a shot from the grassy knoll. Dulles not only denied that evidence, he ridiculed Lifton for even bringing it up. He said bizarre things like "There is not a single iota of evidence indicating a conspiracy." When Lifton pointed out testimony, and even pictures, of smoke arising on the grassy knoll, Dulles derisively

replied with, "Now what are you saying, someone was smoking up there?" ...
When Lifton showed him frames from the Zapruder film arranged in sequential
order to show Kennedy's head going back toward the seat – the opposite direction of a shot from the Texas School Book Depository – Dulles said: "You have
nothing! Absolutely nothing! ... I can't see a blasted thing here. You can't say the
head goes back. I can't see it going back. It does not go back. You can't say that."
(*Best Evidence*, pgs. 34-36) When, of course, the Commission had seen the film
dozens of times. They just did not feel that powerful evidence, like Kennedy's
violent reaction backwards, merited mention in the Warren Report."

30. Some have asked why both Lee and Dave would confide in me. First, all my
life, people have chosen to confide in me. They sense that I won't tell their secrets
(they're right). Second, it was important, if anything bad happened to Lee, that
I would understand why I would have to keep silent, no matter what, since by
now, Lee and I were lovers. I can recall Dave's voice and most of what he said,
but have added a few extraneous details (such as the "U-Haul"), being unable to
remember Dave's precise words. I assume from other sources that the U-Haul
was present at the location indicated.

31. I place the history behind the "radical's camp" and its raid here, though Dave
and Lee's activities will be described later in the book. These comments come
from a variety of sources: "Researcher Dick Russell points out that "[Victor Es-
pinosa] Hernandez identified only as `A' in the congressional investigation's re-
ports was involved `with anti-Castro exiles and underworld figures who were
operating the guerrilla training camp in New Orleans in July, 1963', according
to CIA files. Then there is: "H.L. Hunt backs anti-Castro Cubans [Hinkle and
Turner, *The Fish Is Red*, P. 202]. Hunt voices his concerns about the threat of a
Kennedy dynasty in a July 11, 1963 letter to Senator Harry Byrd: `The stake is
the entire future of the nation' [Letter to Senator Byrd, Box 270, Byrd Papers,
University of Virginia Library].

From Jim Garrison's *Playboy* interview: "The CIA itself apparently did not
take the detente too seriously until the late summer of 1963, because it maintained its financing and training of anti-Castro adventurers. There was, in fact, a
triangulation of CIA-supported anti-Castro activity between Dallas where Jack
Ruby was involved in collecting guns and ammunition for the underground and
Miami and New Orleans, where most of the training was going on. But then,
Kennedy, who had signed a secret agreement with Khrushchev after the Missile
Crisis pledging not to invade Cuba if Russia would soft-pedal Castro's subversive
activities in the Americas, began to crack down on CIA operations against Cuba.

As a result, on July 31, 1963, the FBI raided the headquarters of the group of
Cuban exiles and Minutemen training north of Lake Pontchartrain and confiscated all their guns and ammunition despite the fact that the operation had the
sanction of the CIA. This action may have sealed Kennedy's fate."

32. People asked me how many times I met Dr. Sherman, and my thinking literally has got me into trouble over that. I *met* her only twice: at the party, where she
would not speak to me, and again at her nice apartment, where she awaited my
coming with David Ferrie. Had people asked me how many times I had *worked*
with Dr. Sherman, I would have said five or six times. Had people asked me how

many times I had *been in her apartment when she was also there*, I would have said a dozen times. If they had asked me *how many times we were in contact that summer*, in person or on the phone, I would have said some 25-30 times.

33. In *Farewell to Justice*, p. 51, line 40, Joan Mellen notes that witness Don Lee Keith said of Dr. Sherman, in an interview with Allen Davis (Public Relations man for Ochsner Foundation and Clinic) on June 3, 1979, that "She worked at laboratories until midnight."

President Kennedy spoke at American University's Spring Commencement on June 10, 1963. In this speech Kennedy called on the Soviet Union to work with the United States to achieve a nuclear test ban treaty and help reduce the considerable international tensions and the specter of nuclear war at that time.

Chapter Twelve

Countdown

July 26, 1963: President Kennedy announces a nuclear test ban partnership with the USSR. David is secretly delighted, but Banister is furious, convinced that Kennedy is giving in to the Communists.

July 28, 1963: Robert has been in Florida working in his parents' office, since his job in the Gulf of Mexico has ended. He now returns to live with me, though we scarcely communicate.

Robert gets a job first with Standard Coffee, with Monaghan's help, and later with Collier's Encyclopedia, both bringing in zero income, since he's far from diligent, so long as I am bringing in some money. He looks forward to starting school again at UF. He is mostly underfoot and in the way.

Ferrie's Work with Banister's Anti-Castro Activities

> **Stephen Roy** (disputes Banister and Ferrie's anti-Castro activities in the summer of 1963): It is widely believed … that Banister's office was a hotbed of anti-Castro activity in 1963. That was probably true in 1961, but I can't find much support for a high level of activity in 1963 (as regards Banister and Ferrie).[1]

Did we read that correctly? That there was no "high level of anti-Castro activity" regarding Bannister and Ferrie in 1963? I am one of several witnesses to confirm that significant anti-Castro activities, involving Guy Banister, Lee Oswald, and David Ferrie, were conducted in the summer of 1963. But first, we have to connect Lee Oswald to David Ferrie and Guy Banister to explain what kind of anti-Castro activity was going on.

Witnesses to Ferrie-Oswald-Banister Working Together

> **Bill Davy**, re Dan Campbell: Banister was a bagman for the CIA and was running guns to Alpha 66 in Miami. Campbell also assisted Banister in small arms training for the Cubans and received $50 per week for his services. The Banister menagerie, he added, were the

worst kind of fanatics. Campbell remembered seeing Oswald there, which dates his observation period fully into 1963 ...[2]

Anthony Summers: Re: William Gaudet: ...[Gaudet,] a twenty-year CIA veteran who worked out of the International Trade Mart, told Anthony Summers that "I did see Oswald discussing various things with Banister at the time," and added, "I suppose you are looking into Ferrie. He was with Oswald." Finally Gaudet said, "Another vital person is Sergio Arcacha Smith. I know he knew Oswald and knows more about the Kennedy affair than he ever admitted."[3]

William Gaudet, CIA asset/ friend of Ochsner.

I saw Arcacha Smith twice myself, while I was in New Orleans that summer.

> **Bill Nitschke** (Banister investigator): re Delphine Roberts (Banister's secretary and mistress): In a 1967 [*New Orleans States-Item*] interview ... Nitschke recalled Delphine Roberts telling him that Banister, Ferrie and sometime Banister operative and pilot, Hugh Ward, were all involved in running guns to Miami and other places. (Also interviewed for Garrison, Jan. 17, 1967).[4]

FLIGHTS WITH CUBANS

Rick Bauer, a reader in Florida, wrote online of his personal experience in 1965-66 with David Ferrie, the New Orleans pilot who has been the target of JFK conspiracy speculation for decades.

Bauer writes. "I am a graduate of Tulane University in 1966. In the fall of 1965 I commenced flight training paid for by the Department of Defense for students enrolled in various ROTC programs. I was a USN scholarship student at Tulane. My instructor was David Ferrie.... I knew Dave from Sept. 1965 until May of 1966. I passed my Private Pilot's check ride on March 27, 1966."

"He was actively engaged with Cubans. My USMC classmate recalls flights on the weekend to Picayune, Mississippi, in a DC-3 for their training."

"The company that had the government contract was called Co-mAir and was operated by a retired USAF Lt. Col whom I never met.

This sounds like CIA to those of us with a military background...," Bauer wrote.

Bauer sums up his recollections of Ferrie with these words:

"I had close contact with Dave for three quarters of a year. He was employed indirectly by the Department of Defense, had clear connections with Cubans of some stripe ... so I feel something is missing from the way he has been portrayed." Bauer thinks Ferrie's service for the U.S. military after JFK's assassination is significant.[5]

MORE WITNESSES – BANISTER, FERRIE AND OSWALD

Dr. Michael Kurtz is a crucial and credible living witness who publishes scholarly articles about the history of Louisiana in professional journals. Kurtz personally saw Guy

Dr. Michael Kurtz.

Banister and Lee Oswald working together, as did his friend, George Higginbotham. Higginbotham was employed, as was Lee Oswald, to help ferret out leftists at area colleges. Kurtz also interviewed witnesses who saw David Ferrie and Lee Oswald together in such places as the Napoleon House bar (acting critical of JFK and his handling of Cuba allowed both men to compile lists of Kennedy-haters).

Kurtz came out in 2007 and in 2013 with startling information that he had previously mentioned mostly in footnotes in his books.[6] He also obeyed requests not to release certain information until the informers were dead. That makes it hard to double-check his story.

> **Dr. Kurtz:** Twice [Ferrie and Oswald] were seen conversing in Mancuso's Restaurant. They were seen at a segregationist meeting in the late spring of that year. In August they were seen at a party in the French Quarter. According to two people who attended the party, Oswald and Ferrie discussed United States foreign policy, especially with regard to Cuba. Both men expressed strong disapproval of the failure to overthrow the Castro regime. ("Lee Harvey Oswald in New Orleans," *Louisiana History* Vol. 21, No, 1, 16.)

> **Dr. Kurtz:** During the summer of 1963, [Kurtz' friend] Van Burns worked at the Pontchartrain Beach amusement park in New Orleans. One evening, while he attended his booth, Burns saw a friend of his ... accompanied by two men, approach the booth. The friend introduced him to Lee Harvey Oswald and David Ferrie. After a few minutes of small talk, Oswald and Ferrie left and strolled down

the boardwalk together. The friend told Burns about Ferrie's having flown him over the Gulf of Mexico all the way to Cuba and told him that Ferrie had been involved in certain "missions" to Cuba.[7]

Vernon Gerdes (former Banister investigator who later worked for attorney Stephen Plotkin) "told Plotkin that he had seen Oswald and Ferrie together with Banister. Plotkin would later tell an attorney for Clay Shaw that he considered Gerdes "reliable." Gerdes signed a statement for Plotkin on Plotkin's own letterhead stationery, with two witnesses present.[8]

July, 1963: David Ferrie gives me his medical library card, which allows me to use the medical libraries at Tulane and Loyola Universities. The card, stamped "Ochsner Clinic" gave access to area medical libraries as a courtesy. I can access the latest cancer research articles from around the world. As a speed-reader I can process new information quickly, my reports are saving hundreds of hours of time for the team.

July 29, 1963: Lee Oswald tells me about a Jesuit conference he attended at Spring Hill College in Mobile, where he gave a presentation. He says Bobby Kennedy sent a spy there. However, things went badly. He has learned that "Jesus" (CIA's James Jesus Angleton) distrusts Lee because he "did not come back in a coffin" from the USSR. This is the second time I hear Lee use the same phrase. Once promised a college education, it's been denied. His place in "the Company" is "under review." Lee is trying to prove his loyalty and obedience, but he believes the CIA could murder him – the easiest way to handle an untrusted asset. He is concerned for my safety, and for the safety of his family.[9]

Lee told me, Angleton, didn't trust him because he came back alive.

July-August, 1963: During these months, David Ferrie and Lee Oswald continue to present themselves as anti-JFK to ferret out pro-Castro spies and those offering serious anti-Kennedy threats. David eventually enters Banister's inner circle, where ideas to assassinate JFK are being broached, with strong links to Texas. Dave deliberately offers assassination plans and ideas to stay credible. He keeps the pose. After Lee returns to Dallas, Dave passes on information enabling Lee to infiltrate an assassination ring in Dallas. If Dave led Lee into a trap, it was, I believe, unwittingly.[10]

LEAFLETTING, THE ANTI-CASTRO TRAINING CAMPS, AN FBI RAID, AND A TRAINING FILM

Lee and I laugh over his fake organization. There will never be a meeting. There will never be a lecture. Everyone who shows up at the stamped address, or writes to him, will be investigated by Guy Banister. They will be filmed and followed.

These pro-Castro activities will help Lee enter Cuba without getting him executed, if he's ordered to do that (now a dimming possibility). He will also look less suspicious to pro-Castro spies when he couriers the biological weapon to Mexico City (this is the current idea). He will hand off the weapon to an anti-Castro medical contact he can trust, which will require secret signs and signals. The contact also has to have some high-class skills. I've been teaching Lee how to keep "The Product" alive in the thermos system I've created for its delivery. The thermos looks like an ordinary part of a lunch kit. What looks like ordinary packets of sugar will contain the special medium needed, when reconstituted with water boiled and distilled.

A sandwich, a banana, a thermos, and a couple bottles of "7-Up" (actually sterile distilled water), along with packets of "sugar" (to make fresh medium) would disguise the bioweapon hidden in a lunch sack in Lee's blue zippered carry-on. The invisible cancer cells were alive, growing on the clear glass liner in the thermos, which had hidden vents and filters in the cap. If inspected, contents of thermos looked like chicken broth, by using a pH indicator different from the usual phenol red.

Lee's major concern is that Banister has forced him to hand a map over to the FBI – a premature step. It's led to a problem. Because Lee has helped shoot the training film at the CIA-supported camp the anti-Castroites there realize he can recognize them. Lee thinks a rumor is spreading that he supplied a map to the FBI, and the "real" camp might also have to be shut down.

Fortunately for Lee, he and Dave have found a pro-Castro spy who foolishly showed up at both camps. His name is Fernando Fernandez. Lee says they have formulated a plan to "smoke him out." Lee will go to the bars in town, where word travels fast, and make it known that Guy Banister, convinced that Fernandez was OK, had given him a map to show him how to get to the little camp, which is a private set-up. Lee tells the usual snitches who make their lunch money by informing for the FBI. The map and the upcoming raid will soon be blamed on Fernandez. Once exposed, he'll be of no use unless he gets radical plastic surgery, because Lee has taken his picture.

By the time Fernandez understands that he's been fingered, it is too late. He can't evade the net that Lee and Dave enclose around him. Ferrell's chronology describes what reached the outside world about it.

> **August 1, 1963:** Fernandez writes to Carlos Lechuga, the Cuban am-
> bassador to Mexico that, "they have to be alert from that date (8/1/63)
> until August 8." (CD 984a, pp. 2, 11)

August 1st was the first day after the raid, when Fernandez was still trying to evade being exposed. August 8th was the last day Lee could get the albatross of that map from off his neck, before his pro-Castro demonstration.[11] And he did it! All Fernandez had to do was to stay in town, looking innocent, until Lee held his demonstration, and he would have been off the hook, because the demonstration would help prove that Lee was the rat. That wasn't good for Lee's health on "demonstration day."

Instead, Fernandez bolted. By the eighth of August, Dave and Lee had forced him to flee for his life to Miami, quashing the rumor that Lee had provided the map. Fernandez' flight might have saved Lee from getting hurt in New Orleans. By the fourth of September, the *Diario Las Americas* newspaper told Miami that Fernandez was a spy for Castro. They printed his picture. The thousands of anti-Castro warriors congregated there will murder him, if they can: his career as a spy is over.

But before all that happened, I was frightened for Lee. "It seems your life is getting more complicated and risky all the time," I tell him. "What if you can't get Fernandez to leave? What if they decide it's *you* who handed over the map, after all?" Seeing my downcast face, Lee said in a cheery voice, "Don't worry, Juduffki! I'm going to have just a teensy-weensy demonstration, protected by my three helpers. Nobody will get close enough to hurt me." I think Lee told me that Dave would be helping, by staging an anti-Castro demonstration a few blocks away, at the same time."[12]

At both sites, Banister would have his people taking secret photos. Anybody who kept an FPCC flyer or who later contacts Lee will be investigated. Banister, once in charge of 500 Chicago FBI agents for a year, knows exactly how to get the skinny on every suspicious character Lee and Dave expose.

Lee always stays upbeat. He says a smack in the face from one of The Three Stooges he's arranged to 'protest' his demonstration isn't going to hurt him. I'm grateful Dave has thought up a clever way to divert the attention of some of the Cubans from Lee, so he'll be safer.

I clock in at Reily at 8 AM and begin working on an unusually high pile of credit problems, trying to avoid phone calls due to my painfully swollen lip [see *Me & Lee* for details]. After about an hour, Mr. Monaghan shows up and starts teasing me about it. Then, in a loud voice that even the hard-working clerks can hear, Mr. M. says I need to get my lip examined by a doctor. Once he's sure everyone within ear shot thinks I'm going to the doctor, Monaghan tells me I have to make a trip – immediately – "to the lab" (Dave's apartment).

"The message to give you," he whispers, "is 'Dave had to spend the night at Bedico Creek [the training camp] and now has to go out of state. So he is unable to finish the lab work." With a grimace of distaste, Mr. M says he'll cover for me.[13] *Another blasted emergency!*

"The Sleeper" Should Not Awaken

I take the bus to Dave's apartment, which is supposed to be empty during the day, especially since Dave is still at the training camp [or maybe by now, he's flying somewhere].[14] At about 9:30 AM, I enter the apartment, and find, in the refrigerator, a Waring Blender jar marked "Murine 1111FN." Murine means "mouse." These are mouse tumors! We have plunged down the monkey trail rapidly, but we still must keep the source of the most vicious cancer alive at the 'mouse level' to make sure we don't lose the original cancer source. Since these cells don't live for too many passages in test tubes, this fresh batch is going to be prepared for deep-freezing in nitrogen. That's what the "FN" part of the ID label stands for. I will never forget the '1111' – meaning this was the 1,111th experiment. And it was successful at last.

My heart sinks. I understand that the Mouse House can't risk having such mice there anymore, not with infected monkeys moving in. But deep-freezing this new backup material suggests that we aren't developing this biological weapon just for Castro. We are about to make this cancer truly immortal. Ochsner won't live forever. What if 'Murine 1111FN' gets into the wrong hands? In this same city, huge rocket parts are being built for the purpose of sending men to the moon. The city is a hot bed of Cold War operations of all kinds. The Project has required massive funding. Only one entity could afford everything happening here in New Orleans.

I remember one of Dave's comments: "Social justice and society exist not to establish an ideal, but to establish a compromise, like it or not. Man can't fulfill the perfect ideal, because man's society forces him to be evil." Dave said these weren't his original ideas, and that any philosopher who was honest would arrive at the same conclusion.[15]

Just as I'm about to do some serious mouse mincing, I hear an unusual sound. I freeze, and listen. *Someone is in the house.* The sounds are coming from Dave's bedroom, where the door is partially open. I tiptoe down the hall and look inside. There, I see a young man sprawled on Dave's bed amidst a jumble of sheets, magazines, newspapers, clothes, and pillows. He is snoring. I figure it is probably Dave's new lover, who is spending more and more time here.[16] But I am not going to be able to grind up mouse tumors in the kitchen without his hearing it!

I need to leave right away, but the tumors in Dave's refrigerator are too dangerous and important to abandon, so I quietly gather up the things I need to take to Dr. Mary's, and leave. As I ride the bus down to Dr. Mary's apartment, my frustrations are percolating. The time I need to do The Project's work is being whittled away on all fronts. I can no longer read and write reports at my place at 1032 Marengo because Robert is literally underfoot. At home, all I can do are Reily-related tasks. Stretched to the limit, working at two demanding jobs, and trying to deal with the needs of two very different lovers, I can't handle this emergency work properly because Dave has a young lover (or runaway student) sleeping in his bed!

As soon as I arrive at Dr. Mary's, I write her a note, complaining about the presence of Dave's lover and why I can't update reports on time. Then I create the tissue cultures, ready to deep freeze, doubting I'll finish in time to get back to Reily. But Lee comes to the rescue. He arrives at Mary's apartment. Now he's wearing fatigues, with a baseball cap and a white t-shirt. A blue duffel bag is slung over his shoulder. It's about 1:30 PM.

"I decided to make an appearance at the little training camp after all," he tells me. He embraces me – the best he can – slipping his arms under my protective lab tunic!

"How did you get out there, and back so quick?" I ask him.

"They drive fast," he says, smiling.

Lee took the risk that the raid wouldn't occur "quite yet." He made a point to someone at the camp that he wondered if Fernando Fernandez "was good at making maps."

Lee will soon have to go home, impressing Marina with his dirty and unkempt condition. "She hates it when I don't shave," he says, "but there's no help for it." I have seen Lee shave twice a day, but when he's out at the training camp, he hasn't time.

In Johnson-McMillan's anti-Oswald biography *Marina and Lee,* this period in Lee's life is described as occurring a month earlier than it actually did. Marina initially thought Lee was still working at Reilys, which is probably what caused the confusion.

Johnson-McMillan writes, "... by late May and early June, he had become alarmingly indifferent to the way he looked." (p. 425) This period in Lee's life actually ended with the August 1st raid. William Stuckey will describe Lee, who he meets at 8 AM, unannounced, soon after Lee's August 9 demonstration, as "clean cut."[17]

July 31, 1963: The FBI raids property owned by William Julius McLaney, former casino owner and former prisoner of Castro. Eleven men are detained briefly, including Sam Benton (McLaney's pro gambler and securities scammer) and Rich Lauchli, co-founder of the Minutemen and an arms merchant.[18] Note that William McLaney had owned the house on Magazine St. where Lee Oswald lived.

> **Larry Hancock**: The McClaney farm bust was not a training camp, it was a holding area for a parked U-haul and the FBI had full details on what was in it from an informant in Miami before they made the bust ... this is often written up in early JFK works as a full-fledged training camp – the local media coverage may have created that impression?
>
> **AP article** in the *New Orleans States-Item* (03/04/1967): Confiscated were 48 cases of dynamite ... 20 firing caps, M-1 rifles, grenades, and 55 gallons of napalm.
>
> **AP article** out of Mandeville, LA (07/31/1963): FBI agents swooped down on a house ... near here today and seized more than a ton of dynamite and 20 bomb casings. An informed source said the explosives were part of a cache to be used in an attack on Cuba. But the FBI would only say that the materials were "seized in connection with an investigation of an effort to carry out a military operation from the United States against a country with which the United States is at peace."[19]
>
> *Times-Picayune* (Aug. 1, 1963): More than a ton of dynamite, 20 bomb casings three-feet long, napalm (fire-bomb) material

and other devices were seized Wednesday by Federal Bureau of Investigation ...

Wednesday, July 31, 1963: Mid-morning, Lee calls to tell me he is safe. He says the FBI has raided the training camp across the lake. I have just finished typing a letter for Mr. Monaghan. As I hand him the letter, I tell him about the raid.

"I already know," Monaghan says. "Mr. Reily told me." Then looking at my letter, he adds, "It won't be long now before I have a real secretary again." Lee, fired July 19th, precipitated an order for an ad to replace me, published in the *Times-Picayune* on July 20th:

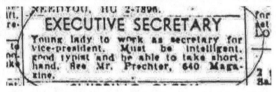

The ad ended on August 2nd, and a new ad replaced it, promising good pay, on August 1, 1963: "S2-P13 HELP WANTED – (section of paper: FEMALE Clerical) 'EXECUTIVE SECRETARY RARE opportunity! You type and take short-hand, we pay you well and give many company benefits. Interested? See Mrs. Bertucci, 640 Magazine.'"

Anxious to replace me right away, Monaghan had jumped the gun. Personnel had not changed the salary, which for my inexpert services had been reduced to minimum wage, so nobody with the proper qualifications had applied. Ochsner had also intervened and said I needed to stay longer, after I told him I didn't know what I'd do for funds if I was forced out too soon.

Now Mr. M. tells me that I'll be replaced on August 16th. I had to say something nice. "You know, I'll miss those rich timbres on your Dictaphone," I tell him.

"What I do for my country!" Monaghan mutters. "Go on to your lab, while I work with the new girl."

As I am leaving, an attractive woman arrives in Monaghan's office for training. She seems bright, is a good typist, takes shorthand, and has mature phone skills. A real secretary that he won't have to cover for! We are in high gear over at the lab, so I will be gone virtually every afternoon. I manage to get to the city library to check on quickie Mexican divorces, remembering that actress Jayne Mansfield got her divorce from her husband in one day.[20] It's just what Lee and I are hoping for!

August 1, 1963 Thursday: I trained my replacement this morning on finance reports. Now, I'm going to meet Lee at noon at Mancuso's, where I wait at a side table, watching Lee drink coffee with David Lewis and Jack Martin. When they leave, I join Lee, who complains that David Lewis has started smoking. As we reach the exit, where the door is propped open, Lee points to a well-dressed young Cuban hurrying down the sidewalk toward Banister's office. This is Carlos Quiroga. Lee distrusts him, because Quiroga's father is locked up in one of Castro's prisons and his mother still lives in Cuba. With the kind of family pressure that could be put on him, he could be forced to spy for Castro.

Lee updates me about the raid at this time. A handful of Cubans and a couple of ultra-rightwing gringos were clueless enough to keep to the house near where all the goodies were stored, which got them arrested. Newspapers have already duly reported that the FBI had confiscated arms, ammunition, and over a ton of explosives, but already, most of it is missing, Lee tells me. That's how fast Banister and his operatives got it back. Lee says he helped stack arms and ammo on Banister's third floor. As for the detainees, the FBI had already released them. Most fled the state.

Outwardly, Banister displays anger over the camp's raid, but secretly, he's glad, Lee says, because Kennedy, whom he despises, is hated as never before by the anti-Castro Cubans over the new raid.[21] As for Lee, he guesses that the traitors who want JFK dead are toasting each other over the raid. "How easily JFK could be killed now," Lee says, "with a gun that can be traced to anti-Castro renegades!"

Lee goes silent, then says, "I still don't understand how you get me to talking, the way you do. You have the same effect on Dave. It's—" he shakes his head. "Uncanny."

"Maybe it's because you know I can keep my mouth shut. And I'd take a bullet for you," I tell him. "Little things like that."

Lee then plunges on with his revelations. Fernandez is hiding out somewhere in New Orleans, and has to be found. We start walking toward Acme's oyster bar, Lee busy teaching me some phrases in Russian. We reach Acme's, where we order oyster stew (something I can eat with my sore mouth) for lunch. It's a free lunch because Acme's is "influenced" by Marcello. It's also the last time I will pose as Marina, because she's too advanced, now, in her pregnancy, and my attempt to use padding looks too weird. A few days every month I look pregnant, anyway, due to those long-ago operations and cortisone shots.

Lee has written a letter to the FPCC. Usually I help him with spelling, but this time, he's looked up most of the problem words himself. The letter is mostly about what will happen a week from now. Lee is going to mail it early, he says, because the CIA opens all his mail, and it can get delayed. Lee has already written about his membership in the FPCC to the Communist Party.[22] It will nicely link the FPCC to the communists, which is what CIA wants on paper to prove their case. Lee will soon publicize himself as a pro-Castro "Marxist."

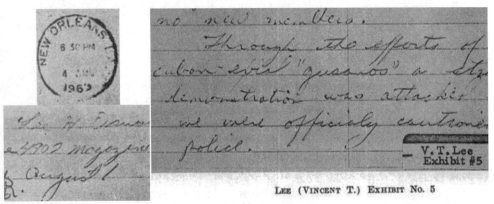

LEE (VINCENT T.) EXHIBIT No. 5

The letter itself, the date on the envelope (Aug. 4) and the date (August 1) on the letter, show Lee was planning a pre-arranged "attack" by "gusanos" and trouble with the police. That occurred August 9.

A waiter comes to us at the bar and tells Lee, "The boss wants to see you over at La Louisianne." Without a word, Lee gets up and goes next door. When he returns, I sense tension in his voice.

"I have to go. Out to the Town and Country Motel," he says bluntly. "Marcello's people need me to run an errand.[23] I'll meet you at Dave's after that." It was another "favor," as they call it, but I start to see that our free meals aren't so free, after all.

"Please," I implore in Russian, "What do you have to do with him again?" Lee looks around, then moves closer to me. "Sometimes I have to do what Little Man wants," he tells me. "But, my darling wife," he says softly, playing with a lock of my hair, "...as I've told you before, 'Either the world can be an influence on you, or you can be an influence on the world.' I decided not to let 'the world' influence me. The world I grew up in."

Lee goes on to say how his uncle Dutz, upset because Lee skipped so much school, set him to work in Marcello's restaurants as a gopher. "To make me appreciate the value of an education," Lee confides, "he set me to work after school doing menial labor." There were errands, sweeping and mopping floors, and washing cars and windows. The fallout from his work in Marcello's restaurants is that the local Mafia trusts Lee. So today, he has to take something out to Town and Country from La Louisianne.[24]

"I don't mind doing it," Lee says. "While I'm out there, I'll talk to Marcello's people about finding this Fernandez character. They'll help us flush him out, so we can finger him."

Anti-Castro Activities After the "Final Raid"

Dr. Michael Kurtz: From a Sept. 9, 1979 interview of George Wilcox of New Orleans, Kurtz says Wilcox saw: Ferrie, Oswald, and numerous Cubans, all dressed in military fatigues and carrying automatic rifles, conducting what appeared to be a "military training maneuver." This event took place near Bedico Creek, a swampy inland body of water near Lake Pontchartrain, about fifty miles north of New Orleans. This occurred in early September 1963, two months after the final government raid on anti-Castro guerrilla camps in the United States.[25]

Ferrie and Oswald as Infiltrators and Informants

Larry Hancock: ... in early JFK literature there was often speculation that it was Oswald, in his infiltrator role, who exposed the supposed camp that was busted in the McClaney raid. Perhaps he did ... [but with] the full FBI documentation on it we also have their sources – in reports written in the summer of 1963 – and their informants were exiles and not Oswald.[26]

But researchers should think twice about trusting what the FBI and CIA has given them about this incident, seeing how many lies have been thrown at them in the past. Note that the FBI reports identifying the informants were written *significantly later*, after scapegoats were finally lined up. FBI reports, as we know, identify most informants by code. The very fact that Lee Oswald is mentioned by name as *not having been the informant* means that somebody was saying that he was, and this had to be refuted. If named, an informant can become useless. A mention of multiple informants – best unnamed, or using just one as a scapegoat – keeps the true informant safer. In this game, revealing the chess piece takes it off the board. Non-participants, looking at FBI official records, can rarely piece together what happened behind the scenes.[27]

The Art of Muddying the Waters

Dave Reitzes, who works with Warren Commission apologist John McAdams, does his best to remove Lee Oswald from any equation that tends to exonerate him. But keep in mind that Lee

Oswald's name was brought up regarding this event, which itself is rather remarkable. FBI would have been better off never to have mentioned Lee's name, rather than acknowledging that someone has said Lee Oswald gave a map to the FBI.[28]

INTERPEN training.

THE TRAINING FILM: I'M ANOTHER WITNESS

Stephen Roy: On the July 1963 camp(s), we really have only Delphine Roberts (not a bad source, but not a great one) and Tannenbaum's (sic) film recollection. I would have to see the film before making up my mind.[29]

Mr. Roy ignores me as a witness. He basically calls Robert Tanenbaum – who is a credible witness and HSCA member with a sterling reputation to this day – a liar. He dismisses Colonel William Bishop as a liar, too. I suppose he adds me to that list. But Anthony Summers makes a good case for Delphine Roberts' truthfulness, and Bishop spontaneously brought up the training film, without prompting. Bishop's was an off-hand remark that meant little at the time, but along with Tanenbaum's, Delphine's and my witness statements, should carry some weight. That's four of us. I never knew if Dave went to the right-wing camp that was raided, but he went to the camp where the film was made. I saw some of the training film at his apartment.

Dave was splicing sections together. A heavyset Cuban was with him. Lee was in the film. In 1999, I told researchers that in one scene, Lee was seated in a room with a concrete floor, showing how to handle what I recalled was a rifle (Tanenbaum says it was a revolver). I had no idea Tanenbaum existed.[30]

Robert K. "Bob" Tanenbaum, HSCA's first deputy counsel, interview by Jim DiEugenio (excerpts):

JD: Another thing you've discussed ... is this incredible movie of the Cuban exile training camp.

Tanenbaum: The movie was shocking to me because it demonstrated the notion that the CIA was training, in America, a separate army ... I find that to be as contrary to the constitution as you can get.

"Bob" Tanenbaum.

JD: Was it really as you described in the book, with all the people in that film ...?

Tanenbaum: Oh, yeah. Absolutely! They're all in the film. They're all there. But ... Committee began to balk at a series of events. The most significant one was when [David Atlee] Phillips came up before the Committee and then had to be recalled because it was clear that he hadn't told the truth.... [31]

So how did Tanenbaum skirt his non-disclosure agreement with the CIA? (All HSCA members had to sign it.) He placed the film he saw in a novel – *Corruption of Blood.* Of the 8mm film, he wrote:

> The film was silent, but you could see the pinpoints of fire from the rifles and the shimmering gouts of muzzle blast from the machine guns. It cut to a mortar team firing, dropping the shells in odd silence down the tubes and shielding their ears from the blasts ... they seemed well drilled.... A white road sign loomed up.... The road sign had the shape of Louisiana and a number.

Tanenbaum names the people he recognizes: Antonio Veciana of Alpha 66, Banister, David Atlee Phillips, Lee Oswald and Ferrie.[32]

> **Larry Hancock:** ... the more I think about it the more likely it seems that a film at least somewhat like Tannenbaum (sic) describes would exist – only from the Summer of 62 not 63. We do know that Hemming and company were in New Orleans that Summer and Fall scouting out a new training camp for the CRC ... Arcacha Smith might well have been with them, at least early on. And I myself have copies of photos showing David Ferrie with Larry De Joseph...[33]

But Tanenbaum said he recognized Lee Oswald in the film. Lee was mostly in the Dallas area in the summer of 1962. Before that,

Lee was in the USSR. Tanenbaum's account cannot be twisted to fit 1962. Lee's characteristic "smirk" as described by Tanenbaum is one point. More important, he mentioned that Lee's sideburns had grown longer, in a later part of the film. I also recalled that Lee's sideburns got longer, which these photos (below) help establish.

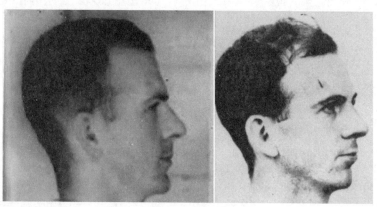

1963 arrest photos for Aug. 9, left, and Nov. 22, right, show Lee Oswald's sideburns longer in August, soon after the training film was shot. Though Lee has a new haircut, the longer sideburns are still visible. By November, they have been cut back again. Tanenbaum noticed Lee's hair and sideburns had grown longer in the last part of the training film.

Robert Tanenbaum describes Lee and David Ferrie: A man in a black T-shirt and ball cap sat at a table loading bullets into pistol magazines. He looked up for an instant, frowned, spoke briefly, and lowered his head again so that the bill of the cap obscured his face. He thought it was probably Oswald, but it had to be some time later than in the first scenes, because his sideburns [had] grown longer.... More shooting, men posing with weapons, then a close-up of a round-faced man with a fright wig and patently phony, impossibly thick eyebrows ... David Ferrie ... nobody else looked like Ferrie.

Dick Russell: Re: Colonel William Bishop: (with J. Gary Shaw present) was asked if he'd ever met Lee Harvey Oswald: Bishop said he had not, but offhandedly volunteered, "I did look into Oswald's background [in 1963]. I'd never met him, but I'd seen him in a training film in New Orleans the past summer. He just happened to be in the group out there at the Pontchartrain camp. Trying to get in with the anti-Cuban exiles."[34] [Note: Bishop, who could be an unreliable witness, died before Tanenbaum went public, so his comment was independent.]

Aug. 2, 1963: I give Lee Oswald the medical library card David Ferrie has loaned to me, so Lee can return a stack of medical journals (Lee later returns the library card to me). David Lewis is with us at the time. Lewis, not knowing the nature of the card, but seeing me hand Lee Oswald the card along with the journals, must assume it is an ordinary library card. It is he who probably tells Jack Martin, at about this date, that Lee Oswald has David Ferrie's "library card." Martin, who now hates David, will not forget this fact.

Aug. 4, 1963: Lee Oswald sends his letter to the FPCC, predicting the staged "scuffle" to take place five days later, on Aug. 9 – which will be staged to get him newspaper attention (it will actually get him arrested): "Through the efforts of some Cuban-exile 'gusanos' [worms] a street demonstration was attacked, and we were officially cautioned by police." Dave promises to help.

Aug. 5, 1963: David has told me he will be out of town, to handle his case with the FAA and Eastern Air Lines in Miami, so I leave Reily early in the morning because of the heavy load of lab work. As I have learned to do ever since I was almost "caught" by a sleeping guest, I very cautiously enter Dave's apartment.[35]

DAVID FERRIE: SAINT AND SINNER

Until now, I usually went to Dave's apartment on Wednesdays, Thursdays and Fridays after 12 noon. With Robert impeding my work at 1032 Marengo with his "idle presence" I could not write lab reports, use the microscope, or read journals there. So it means a lot that on this particular Monday, I'll be able to leave early in the morning to get in more lab time at Dave's. Ordinarily, this was impossible, due to the heavy workload on Mondays. But our salesmen took off the entire weekend, just as they had on the 4th of July, as part of their vacation package, so the usual crushing load of their sales and credit problems was delayed by a day. Monaghan, who is taking the day off, himself, has agreed that I can clock in, then go. We now have a stepped-up effort, focused on examining, classifying and propagating the first tumors being harvested from the pain-racked lungs of African Green Monkeys.

Ever since finding a snoring sleeper in Dave's bed, I've entered his apartment very quietly. I have just reached the kitchen when I happen to hear something coming from Dave's bedroom that takes my breath from me. I have just entered the kitchen when I happen to hear new sounds, coming from Dave's bedroom, of a kind that takes my breath from me. Having been beaten by my own parents, I recognize the sharp crack of a belt, and a half-smothered cry of pain – it's Dave. Then he groans. It raises the hair on my neck. Is some sick sadist beating Dave? That is my first thought. If I make a sound, will they come after me, too? My mind racing, I pick up a frying pan, then creep toward Dave's bedroom. I get close enough to see a drop of blood, like a livid punctuation mark, on the smooth surface of the door. I move a little closer and get a glimpse of him.

"Dave!" I shout out. He stiffens as if shocked, then staggers and turns to me with a haggard, glazed face. He has stripes of bleeding red on his ribs and shoulders. Tears are coursing down his cheeks. In his lowered hand, dangling almost to the floor, is a thin, black strap. Then, with a scowl, Dave reaches out and slams the door shut.

"Get out!" he orders me, through the door. "Get out!"

But I can't. With all my training in medicine, all I can think, in this moment, is that I have to fix the bleeding and the suffering. I think of the mechanical injury to his body first, revealing to myself how technically my mind works, and a part of me is stunned that I think of this, first, instead of what internal agonies have driven Dave to do this to himself. As I search for ointments, bandages, and styptic pencils in our first aid kit, that technical part is still driving me, as I yell out to Dave, "I've got to clean your wounds! You can get a cancer virus taking off in those wounds!"

Perhaps because I don't ask him why he's done this to himself, perhaps because he may suddenly realize that he could become our first "volunteer' if the virus gets into his bloodstream, Dave opens the door a crack, and asks me for rubbing alcohol. I have visions of more self-torture, if he pours it over himself, so I tell him, "I have to do it. We don't have enough alcohol to waste."

"What in hell are you doing here, at this time?" he says, as he comes slowly out, a sheet over his body. He's not naked – he has trousers on – but I ask if he has any wounds below his waist. He answers in the negative, and I begin daubing the contusions on his back with alcohol, then with antibiotic ointment. I use sterile gauze over the worst places, and sterile paper lab tape. There is a small stool in his living room, and I finally get him to sit down. We don't speak at all as I attend to what he's done to himself. The telephone rings and we ignore it.

"I have to rinse the blood out of this washcloth with acetone," I tell him. "And then I'm going to lock the doors, so nobody can just walk in on this, and embarrass you. Stay here, I'll be right back."

Dave is still seated, head down, when I return, but I sense that now he wants to talk to me, as I start working on his shoulders, first the left, then the right, both of which are covered with bleeding welts. I am not facing him: I know he couldn't bear that. Finally, he says, "You locked the doors. Aren't you afraid to do that, with somebody like me?"

"No," I tell him frankly. "You made a 'fight or flee' decision – all based on instinct – when you slammed the door and yelled at me. The psychology books say that when you slammed the door, you were fleeing. And yelling was just a defense mechanism. You are not going to hurt me."

Dave lapses almost into silence, making small sounds of discomfort when I clean out the superficial cuts, which are swelling up. "You're going to be very sore from this," I comment.

"Good," he replies. "I deserve it."

"It's your stupid religion that makes you think like that," I finally dare to say. "I know, because I whipped myself, too. I was told it would help pay for the sins of others, would help get their souls get out of purgatory. That's when I was thinking about becoming a nun."

It is something I thought nobody in the world would ever hear. I now regard it as a very sick thing to do to one's body.

"Then you understand, " Dave said blankly. "Why I have to do it."

"I know why I had to do it," I answer. "I was taught that Christ's incredible sacrifice wasn't enough to pay for everybody's sins; that we have to earn our way to forgiveness. Suffer the fires of purgatory, until we've suffered enough, or suffered enough for the sins of others. And even after all we can do, if we so much as miss a Mass, to Hell we can go. It took me a long time to get out of that trap."

"Now you don't even believe in God!" Dave says, defensively. I would again, one day, but that wasn't the case at this time. "Religion is the chief cause of human suffering," I declare. "And please don't argue with me about God existing. You may be right about God, but Jesus said, when he forgave a sinner, 'Go and sin no more.' He didn't say, 'Beat yourself to a pulp, and then go sin some more.'"

I say these things because I was raised Catholic, and I had tried to become a saint. I burned my conscience every minute with a hot iron, forbade myself meat, and was going to wear hair shirts the rest of my life. And chains, too, when I could no longer work as a doctor and scientist. As a contemplative nun, I had planned, basically, to kill myself with penances after retirement. I know that now, and I'm convinced Dave has done this to himself because of how he, too, has been taught. Despite his jokes, I don't think he's a sadist, and he's only shown kindness to me and Lee.

Dave lets me express all these ideas and admonitions in silence. It is unlike him, and I suspect that his embarrassment and feelings of humiliation are now rising to the fore. Finally, Dave says it aloud.

"No, it never stopped me from sinning again."

"You said God made you this way," I remind him. "You said you were born with a curse."

"I tried to beat it out of me," Dave says slowly. "Only, it doesn't work. Maybe you're right. Maybe," he says with a wry smile, as he puts on a clean white t-shirt, "maybe God sent you here to make me stop doing it." He knows I will never tell anybody (except Lee, who hears all things).

"Throw the stuff away that you have used to do penance!" I urge him. "Remember, the more the saints laid sufferings on themselves, the worse their temptations got. You read their lives; they all say their sufferings attracted demons. Think about that. Tell me one saint, if you can, who didn't have to fight the devil and go through what St. John the Divine called 'the dark night of the soul.'"

"My 'dark night of the soul' has never had a dawn," Dave whispered. At that time in my life, I was too young to weep over Dave's words. Today, I do.

"We're not all made of 'saint stuff,' Dave," I remind him. "Most of us aren't called to that path. I thought I was, but I wasn't. You thought you were, but you weren't. I've read *The Lives of the Saints*. I know you must have memorized them."

What Dave does next is the most extraordinary act of contrition, and if God exists, I tell him, this act of humility is genuine penance, because Dave brings out his instruments of self-torment, and lays them at my feet.

"I think you were sent by God," he says. "The right time, the right hour."

I see a rough rope made of harsh fibers, with tacks stuck into it. This is why Dave has small, inflamed red sores all around his waist, which also bears the marks of the roughness of the rope. There is a small Sterno can holder, with four sharp legs, upon which Dave had lain. He has burnt his thigh with a piece of hot screen from the same Sterno holder. He had also been holding a two-pound barbell weight in each hand, trying to keep his arms outstretched as long as possible. And he had eaten spices to burn his mouth and tongue. He has been crueler to himself than I had been to myself. There is a kind of dreadful fellowship that we now share.

Dave wraps these items in newspaper with adhesive tape so they can't be discovered, then throws them into his garbage can. He tells me that he hasn't been to confession for months. "My brother knows I wanted to be a doctor," he tells me. "Instead, he thinks I'm a pervert."

Dave tells me that he's considered suicide over his homosexual urges. "But it's the greatest sin of all," he says. "I can't do that."

"What if you try to make friends with more straight guys?" I suggest. "See how they think."

Dave shakes his head. "I have plenty of straight friends," he says. "They don't know what I am. I'm not a limp-wrist. And I used to like women." Dave puts on a nice shirt. "I'm not supposed to be here," he says. "I'm supposed to be on my way to Miami right now." Then he looks at me sharply. "And I can still have sex with a woman. I'm capable. They're not a turn-off. You're sure not a turn-off." He smiles. "Problem is, the way I look now..." his bald head with its patches of dangling hair, his lack of eyebrows and eyelashes, his dry, bugged-out eyes, and now, his reputation, have combined, he says, to ruin all his chances.

"I don't know what to do!" he says, finally. "I'm a freak. I'm just giving up."

"All I can say, Dave," I tell him earnestly, "is that there are way too many homosexuals out there for this to be called freaky. I had gay friends in high school. One of them killed himself. You know why? Because somebody told his parents. He was handsome, talented, a poet."

Dave then says something remarkable. "Maybe I can find a Catholic church congregation where gays are tolerated and forgiven. Or, maybe, I could start a church, and get a couple of gay priests to run it." Dave tells me that many priests are gay. He had been molested by one when he was in junior high school. "I had a nervous breakdown over it," he confides. "But I got over that, thanks to a decent priest. So I started trusting them again. Then it happened again. During the time I was trying to become a priest, myself. This time, it was with one of the so-called best of them. They all thought he was very, very holy." Dave gets up and starts searching through some papers on the piano. "Yes, he was holy, all right. That priest told everybody I was trying to ruin his reputation. When I tried to get help about it, from another priest, it turned out he was gay, too. You can guess what he said to everybody. So I was kicked out of the seminary. They claimed it was I who was acting immoral. My father never got over it. I think it killed him."

I'm horrified. Tears are in my eyes. "I'll always be your friend, Dave," I tell him, gripping his arm.

"Don't cry!" he admonishes me.

"I mean it! I'll always be your friend!"

"And I'll stick my neck out for you," he replies.

Then, because I have no choice, I have to start work on the horrors that await us in the form of monkey tumors, designated, in the end, to kill. How could I have fallen so low? I almost hate myself, again. It makes it easier for me to understand what has happened to Dave in his life. Dave helps me for a few minutes, then says, "I have a plane to catch." He goes hunting through papers again and finds what he's looking for. Picking up his suitcase, he asks me, "Know how this all started?" I shake my head.

"I was looking for a statement," he tells me. "That's why I'm running late. Couldn't find it. It's a statement to use for the hearing I'm going to." Dave was still trying to get his Eastern Air Lines job back.

"That statement," Dave says, "was for one of the boys to sign. Saying I'm a good man." His voice cracks with emotion. "At one time, he really did think I was a good man. I typed this out for him to sign. He refused. I begged him. He wouldn't." Dave shakes his head sadly. "Just thinking about it ... it made me ... *do* that." We look at each other helplessly. We are not having a good day, but it could have been worse.

I'm told Dave presented the boy's unsigned deposition. It was not well received.

Aug. 5, 1963: HSCA: Guy Banister testifies in David's grievance hearing (Aug. 5-8). "At the Airline Pilots board about his work with "Arcacha Smith and others." Banister said, "I had high-ranking Cuban refugees in my office asking me how to go underground and I gave them diagrams for that. I have talked to military and political leaders from the various provinces of Cuba that have slipped out and slipped back."[36]

Aug. 8, 1963: James R. Lewallen, an airplane mechanic and former roommate testifies at David's grievance hearing in his behalf.

Aug. 9, 1963: David Ferrie has returned to New Orleans in time to lead an anti-Castro demonstration a few blocks away from where Lee Oswald is distributing flyers on Canal St, near INCA. By doing so, David lures Cubans who might have potentially done harm to Lee away from the staged scene. Nobody in on the scheme wants Lee to actually get hurt.[37]

Hugh Murray, friend of Oliver St. Pe, David Ferrie's liberal activist friend, discovers FPCC flyers at Tulane. He and friends suspect it might be an FBI trap. They decide not to respond.[38]

Left: Rare green "Hands off Cuba" flyer, stamped "L. H. Oswald, 544 Camp St" (courtesy, Robert Groden). This flyer appears trimmed at the top – which is what I did. Was it also printed too far to the left? Right: An untrimmed flyer, with too much space at the top.
I gave trimmed flyers to Lee and Dean Andrews on Canal St. I left at once, but because I had been seen with Lee, Reily Co. fired me the same day.

Aug. 9-10: David Ferrie collects names and snaps photos of several Cubans and students who go to the 544 Camp St. address, but Banister is furious that the address was used. Now known as a trap, the office must be closed before more damage is done. Later, Lee will use 4907 Magazine St. (next to his apartment) and his post office box for addresses.

Mid-Aug. 1963: Soon after Aug. 9, when I lost my job at Reily Dave gives me a wooden nickel.

Zip codes came out in 1963. This wooden nickel was sent to geologists, scientists and labs that used methylene iodide, advertising the new zip code. Methyl iodide "was reported to be a direct-acting mutagen for mouse lymphoma."[39] (Yes, it was.)

"This way, you'll never run out of money," Dave jokes, "because nobody will ever take this from you." The comment was made concerning my parsimonious husband who typically kept me on a budget so tight I was unable to get a new pair of shoes (the worn-out ones created blisters). Lee sent me by cab to a shoe store to get a new pair, paying for the shoes and cab.

Aug.16, 1963: Lee Oswald distributes Hands Off Cuba flyers in front of the Trade Mart. I am there, but leave as bulky TV cameras

arrive.[40] The unemployed Lee Oswald has funds to hire two helpers to distribute the flyers. WDSU (owned by INCA charter members Edgar and Edith Stern) films the short event. David Ferrie is neither seen nor involved in the publicity that follows, although Dr. Alton Ochsner will be.

Aug. 17-18 1963: David holds a party over the weekend at his house, greatly irritating me because I wanted a sterile cleanup of the kitchen before he did so.

Aug. 21, 1963: Lee appears on "Conversation Carte Blanche" radio in a "debate" (four against one) involving Ed Butler of INCA, Carlos Bringuier, Bill Stuckey (host), and WDSU TV reporter, Bill Slatter. Present in the studio was Dr. Alton Ochsner. A record will be cut which later will be used to damn Lee in the public eye. Lee is posing as pro-Cuba and says he is a Marxist (that is, not "communist.") HUAC supplies information that Lee "defected" to the USSR, startling Lee into a statement that he *was protected* by the United States government, which he quickly corrects to say that he *was not*.

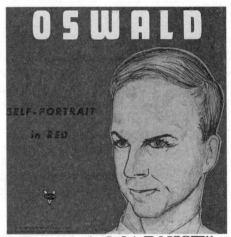

262

Aug. 23, 1963: The last of the outsourcing of the cancer project is completed. David's apartment won't see many mice again, though some cages remain. He will hold another small party soon. I will still do a little work at Dr. Sherman's, where backup mice and cancer cell strains are still accessible, in case contamination occurs. I never visit David's apartment again.

Endnotes

1. Posting as Stephen Roy to the Education Forum: 13 Jan. 2005 http://educationforum.ipbhost.com/index.php?showtopic(90 (Retrieved Jan. 15, 2013).

2. CTKA: Wm. Davy."Chapter Four: The Return of Lee Harvey Oswald" excerpted from, *Let Justice Be Done.* http://www.ctka.net/LetJusticeBeDone/chapter4.htm. (Retrieved June 10, 2013) (the quotes in this section are all from Davy's Ch. 4)

3. Ibid.

4. Ibid. (Retrieved June 10, 2013)

5. Bauer added a bit of movie criticism to his email. "By the way," he wrote, "the wig that Joe Pesci wore in 'JFK' the movie was nowhere near accurate." [Me: "I have said the same thing. I saw a sloppy reddish wig, nothing as nice as what Pesci wore, which I thought was monkey fur, and also a messy mass of a dark wig that was smaller and did not fit right, approximately like what can be seen in Dave's 1962 mug shot."] "Dave had a skin condition that meant he had no hair," Bauer went on. "That includes eye brows. He would paint ... with 'spirit gum' and then stick what looked like pubic hair shaved off and simply stuck this in place." [Author: "I was so naive and never thought of pubic hair. I saw what I thought was some greasepaint (black) full of little bits of black fuzz. Glued in place. He could rip it right off. Pubic hair? Yikes!] http://jfkfacts.org/assassination/news/a-pilot-in-training-remembers-david-ferrie/. (Retrieved Mar. 3, 2014, courtesy of Linda Minor.)

6. "Oswald and Ferrie ... frequented the Napoleon House bar, a popular hangout for college students. There they often debated Kennedy's foreign policy with the students. Accompanied by two 'Latins,' Ferrie and Oswald were observed in Baton Rouge, where they openly denounced Kennedy's foreign and domestic policies." From Kurtz' book *Crime of the Century.* Author: "I, too, have witnesses who wish to remain anonymous. Their information can be used if they have disclosed their identity to a second witness (such as, my publisher is in touch with one of my new witnesses and can vouch for her veracity).

7. Kurtz, *Crime of the Century*, xxxix-xl.

8. http://www.ctka.net/letjusticebedone/notes.html#34. Memo on Plotkin's letterhead, April 7, 1967, Interview given to Panzeca and Wilson (Wegmann files).

9. Lee told me he finally obtained crucial knowledge that almost certainly saved Kennedy's life. I and others now believe the informant named "Lee" who saved Kennedy in Chicago by contacting FBI there, was Lee Oswald. The matter is described in detail by former Secret Service agent Abraham Bolden and by James Douglass in his book *JFK and the Unspeakable: Why He Died and Why It Matters.*

10. The Warren Commission and McMillan's book *Marina and Lee* both presented the viewpoint that Lee Oswald was a "failure" regarding his leadership of the FPCC branch he started in New Orleans, avoiding the very obvious question of why Lee would pass out literature advertising its existence three times that summer, yet never hold a single meeting or lecture, despite what the flyers said. To investigate and report the truth behind Lee's fake FPCC branch would expose Lee's true identity.

11. Lee originally wanted to hold this demonstration a week later, but Banister told him the staged 'fight' had to be scheduled while District Attorney Jim Garrison was out of town, apparently doing his duty with the National Guard. Banister insisted that Lee's activity, if Garrison were in town, would have incited the D.A. to use the new and untested Communism Control Act against Lee to gain more popularity against a "Communist." But that could uncover the whole ploy. Instead, Banister – the committed racist – wanted Garrison to test the new law against the Southern Conference Educational Fund (SCEF) which openly supported local desegregation and Martin Luther King. Banister got his way: the new law was used as an excuse to raid and ruin the SCEF office in early October, with three arrests, and Garrison was right on top of it.

12. "On the day Oswald handed out pro-Castro leaflets in New Orleans, Ferrie was leading an anti-Castro demonstration a few blocks away. Guy Banister's secretary Delphine Roberts told author Anthony Summers that at least once Oswald and Ferrie went together to a Cuban exile training camp near New Orleans for rifle practice." http://spot.acorn.net/jfkplace/09/fp.back_issues/05th_issue/ferrie.html.

13. Mr. Monaghan had been advised that the cancer project was at its most important stage. I don't think he knew much else.

14. Since I wrote of this matter in *Me & Lee*, as well as in the manuscripts of 2006 and 1999, I have obtained access to phone records that suggest Dave was in Jackson, Mississippi, where he stayed until at least August 2nd. Due to my own diary and notes, I mentioned that Dave was 'still out of town" in one of them, which entered the book Me & Lee for August 1st. Dave was not mentioned as being in town in my private notes until August 4th, but I never knew where he had gone.

15. Soon, after watching the film *Lawrence of Arabia* that summer, a revival of the film after it won Academy Awards, Lee and I read *The Seven Pillars of Wisdom* together, as much as we were able, at the main public library. This magnificent book by T. E. Lawrence (which he also illustrated) could not be checked out of the library, but what we did read inspired Lee to a higher degree of stoicism. Because Lawrence carried pocket-sized books by Aeschylus, Plato and Aristotle with him on his journeys, Lee asked Dave to find the best translation he could of any of these Greek masterpieces. At the end of August, Dave would have *The Pocket Aristotle* flown in from New York, along with the usual journal articles Ochsner was always asking me to read and notate. I still have the book, which contains a few short remarks and many underlined passages spontaneously written by Lee, using a small geometry compass pencil.

16. Probably Melvin Coffey, who had his own "pad," but sometimes spent the night at Dave's. Coffey would accompany Alvin Beauboeuf out of New Orleans to the Galveston-Houston area in Dave's 1961 blue Comet station wagon the evening of

Nov. 22, 1963, the same day JFK was assassinated. They both said Dave was with them. It is certain that Dave was with them at the Winterland ice skating rink in the outskirts of Houston, not far from Hull Field in nearby Sugarland and another small airport at Alief, that both Lee and Dave told me were used by the CIA.

17. For example, Lee is described as "clean cut" by Wm. Stuckey – not as he expected – when he visits Lee at his home at 8 AM in the morning. William Kirk Stuckey on June 6, 1964, told the Warren Commission: "... instead I found this fellow who was neat and clean, watched himself pretty well...."

18. The eleven: "John Koch Gene, Sam Benton, Richard Lauchli, Earl J. Wassem Jr. Ralph Folkerts, Victor Espinosa, Carlos Eduardo Hernandez Sanchez, Acela Pedros Amores, Miguel Alvarez Jimenez, Antontio Soto Vasquez, Victor Panque. In response to FBI queries, Carlos Hernandez took the Fifth Amendment about the dynamite, and said he was associated with Manuel Artime." A. J. Weberman, Nodule 14. See quote at http://educationforum.ipbhost.com/index.php?show-topic132 (Retrieved 07/01/2013.)

19. End quote from *Washington Post*, August 1, 1963 (Weisberg, Oswald in New Orleans, 67) as supplied by www.acorn.net/jfkplace/03/JA/DR/.dr10.html This is one of the oldest such sites still alive on the Internet (accessed in 2000 by Wim Dankbaar) (Retrieved July 15, 2013).

20. I had an excellent reading memory, and recalled a newspaper article from May 1st, seen in the public library when Robert and I had gone there to look up marriage laws: the glamorous platinum blonde movie star, Jayne Mansfield, divorced weight-lifter Mickey Hargitay overnight in Juarez, Mexico. When Lee and I visited the Tulane library that week, we finally looked up the article.

21. Banister may have hated the Kennedy brothers for their desegregation policy and "softness" on Communism, but he craved Bobby's secret funds and support against Castro, which Marcello also approved, for Mafia members were raking in money supplied by the CIA to help them "get Castro." But it was not in their best interests to do much toward 'getting' Castro, or else the funding would stop.

22. joanmellen.com/wordpress/literary-matters/who-was-lee-harvey-oswald/ "In the spring of 1960, Oswald's name appears on a CIA mail opening list, meaning he was one of the two hundred most important people to them." "This list was part of the CIA's illegal HT/LINGUAL mail intercept program." www.ctka.net/reviews/newman.html.

23. "Marcello employed Oswald's uncle Charles Murret as a bookmaker in the New Orleans gambling world. In the 1970's the FBI wiretapped many of Marcello's phone conversations. ...161 reels of tape... An FBI informant, Joe Hauser, who claimed he made several of these recordings, told author John H. Davis that Marcello spoke of involvement in the assassination and that he personally knew Oswald." (Note: John Davis worked in the National Archives, giving him more information and insight as to who was who than the ordinary researcher. This makes his book, *Mafia Kingfish* of great importance.) http://spot.acorn.net/jfkplace/09/fp.back_issues/05th_issue/ferrie.html.

24. The rest of the conversation involved how Lee's mother rigged his records so he wouldn't fail a grade, after having missed so many days of school. Lee said,

"...I was caught and incarcerated in New York for my indiscretions. I was a smart ass – the despair of my mother." It was the first time I'd heard Lee refer to his mother in a positive way. "I thought she could care less, if you got an education."

"But I wasn't supposed to fail a grade, Juduff. That would have humiliated her. I didn't attend enough days, so I was supposed to be held back. Ma was smart: she used her connections. They gave out fake information so it'd be hard to trace the real me, when we moved here."

"Why New Orleans? Why didn't you go back to Fort Worth?"

"It's Yankee to say 'New Orleens,'" Lee corrected me.

"I'm sorry," I said. "My mother did it to fix my records up," Lee said.

"She could get it done here. My uncle had the contacts. But Dutz valued education, so he was mad at me." Lee's mother was dating organized crime members (friends of his uncle) in New Orleans and Covington. Meanwhile, Dutz said Marguerite was getting prematurely gray with worry over him. "To make me appreciate the value of an education," Lee said, "he set me to work after school doing menial labor." All the Murret children would attain college educations. Dutz instilled in Lee an ardent desire for the same, telling him, just before Lee moved to Texas with his mother, that he could easily join the Mob in the Dallas area, but he hoped Lee would set his goals higher.

25. Michael T. Kurtz, *Crime of the Century*, Kurtz' interview of Sept. 9, 1979; p. 203 (also see index).

26. http://educationforum.ipbhost.com/index.php?showtopic(90 (Retrieved Jan. 15, 2013).

27. Hence, on Aug. 10, Lee, having been arrested on the 9th for promoting his fake FPCC chapter for Banister, dares tell police to inform Warren DeBreuys that 'Lee Oswald has been arrested and wants an interview.' DeBrueys isn't available – it's the weekend – but FBI's S.A. Quigley comes. See *Me & Lee* for details.

28. LEE HARVEY OSWALD AS AN FBI INFORMANT: Dave Reitzes' struggle to disconnect Lee Oswald from the training camp is typical of those trying to dissociate Lee Oswald from anything to do with the CIA or the FBI. In an exchange with Robert Harris (aided by John McAdams) Reitzes tried to avoid revealing that FBI agent Warren DeBrueys, with whom Lee was working had anything to do with informing the FBI about the DeLaney house and explosives cache (remember that New Orleans FBI's Warren DeBrueys threatened witness Orestes Pena with physical harm if he mentioned that Lee was working with him) . DeBrueys made a point of stressing that Lee Oswald was *not* the informant for the raid (through the map). His denial and bringing up Lee's name means, of course, that the rumor existed. And *why* would such a rumor exist? DeBrueys tried hard to remove Lee's name from consideration. Somebody brought up the name, so DeBrueys had to insist that Oswald was not the informant. The truth is in *Me & Lee* and in the main narrative of this book.

Reitzes begins his messy attempt at a cover-up with this statement: "As a lengthy paper trail shows, the informant who led the FBI to the cache was a Cuban exile pilot codenamed MM T-1, who reported to the FBI's Miami office on the activities and plans of the exile community." However, in the ensuing debate between Reitzes and Robert Harris, it soon became obvious that Reitzes was mistaken. Reitzes then corrects himself: " Note: "As noted in my previous post, I inferred this informant to be MM T-1; I believe I was incorrect about this, although it is obviously not material to the argument that MM T-1 was not Lee Harvey Oswald.--DR

Reitzes next writes that "... On July 31, 1963, FBI agents raided the house in LaCombe. The search warrant had been based on the affidavit of S.A. DeBRUEYS. The FBI reported: "It is noted that we received information from Miami, Florida, source [MM T-1] on July 18, 1963, that Acelo Pedroso, former Cuban pilot, had gone to New Orleans about July 16, 1963, to check some bombs allegedly to be used on bombing raid over Cuba... Pedroso voluntarily accompanied Miami Agent to New Orleans on July 30, 1963, and identified house *which had been pin-pointed by New Orleans Office agents, as house where munitions were stored."*

Author: "MM T-1 was only able to locate the house, in other words, because the New Orleans FBI told MM T-1 where it was located. Keep that in mind. With MM T-1 was the Cuban pilot. But how did they find out? The FBI kindly tells us (just in case we might ask – and, by the way, why would we think to ask?) that "There are no references in the OSWALD case to any of the Subjects of the seizure matter. We have no indication that OSWALD had any connection with it." [FBI 62-109060-4760]

The HSCA, years later, identified MM T-1 as "...a Miami businessman..." (RECORD NUMBER : 180-10076-10241 8/8/63).

Gerry Hemming told A.J. Weberman that MM T-1 was Howard Kenneth Davis. OK, so we know who the guy is. So what? Reitzes then brings up A. J. Weberman's material in Nodule 12. Carlos Bringuier of the DRE told Weberman that he was upset at Lee Oswald for trying to penetrate his group, and that Lee Oswald had to know about the camp because he volunteered to train Bringuier's Cuban guerrillas. Bringuier was also aware of the spy Fernando Fernandez, described in this book [*David Ferrie-Mafia Pilot*] as an infiltrator. Bringuier compared Lee Oswald to such a spy and infiltrator. [A.J. Weberman, Nodule 12] Back in Cuba, Bringuier's own brother had spied for Castro and ruined the FRD in Cuba thereby.[WCD 1085d9; WCE 1413 p4].

But way back in 1963, Bringuier told a whopper to the FBI, as this record proves: "On December 17, 1963, BRINGUIER told the FBI that he "knew of no connection that OSWALD had with any Cubans, and that OSWALD made no mention of any Cuban training camp, and gave no indication of knowing about a training camp, or of being acquainted with any Cubans." [FBI NO 100-16601 SA John T. Reynolds].

Reitzes, knowing all of the above, amazingly again focuses on the Miami informant, citing a Weberman footnote that "The FBI informant behind the seizure of the arms cache (whose name is still classified) was himself a member of the DRE, and was reporting to the FBI in Miami, not New Orleans.(8)". Of course we know he would not be reporting TO New Orleans – he'd gotten his information FROM New Orleans. That agent from Miami learned about the cache's location *from the New Orleans FBI*, remember? Researcher Robert Harris then wrote, "Reitzes's argument was that the La Fontaines could not have been correct in their suggestion that Oswald was the informant in the Lake Pontchartrain weapons bust, since the real informant was this unnamed member of the DRE.... the first question that comes to mind, is why he didn't cite the original source ... the affidavit by SA De-

Brueys… [where DeBrueys says] "There are no references in the OSWALD case to any of the Subjects of the seizure matter. We have no indication that OSWALD had any connection with it." *IOW, this affidavit was produced by Mr. DeBrueys… the agent who has always been accused of making Oswald his informant. He physically threatened Orest Pena, another of his informants, to prevent him from telling the Warren Commission about his (DeBrueys') connection to Oswald.* Put another way, a denial by DeBrueys is about as persuasive as Carlos Marcello swearing he is an honest business man :-) Obviously, David could not convince many people, had he [directly] cited one of DeBrueys' many denials."

John McAdams didn't like what Harris said, so he made an ad hominem attack (it was all he could do, since Reitzes was exposed). He wrote: "Robert Harris is the Saddam Hussein of this newsgroup. He conceals information. He jerks people around endlessly. He welshes on his deals. Harris has learned from his mentors, the LaFontaines. But happily, he doesn't have weapons of mass destruction. John" [We do wonder what "deals" Harris "welshes on" and why McAdams complains about his being treacherous.]

Amazingly, Reitzes [encouraged by McAdams]then returns to his same error, by rephrasing it: "The error, of course, is immaterial: the McLaney cache informant was a Cuban exile and businessman reporting to the Miami FBI; not Lee Harvey Oswald, as Mary La Fontaine would have us believe." But MM T-1 (as he had to have read, above!]only *advised* Miami about the plan to bomb Cuba that he heard from the pilot, and about the cache from the FBI in New Orleans. And of course, since DeBrueys said it wasn't Lee, it couldn't have been Lee, so Mary LaFontaine was just plain wrong. Reitzes has gone down a twisted trail that just leads, as usual, back to the New Orleans FBI officer who would be in deep trouble if he ever admitted that Lee Oswald worked for him, though others there, such as Leake, said Lee did."

29. Posting as Stephen Roy to the Education Forum: 13 Jan. 2005 http://educationforum.ipbhost.com/index.php?showtopic(90 (Retrieved Jan. 15, 2013).

30. When asked what Lee wore, I remembered a striped t-shirt and a cap. So much for accuracy! However, I had seen Lee wearing a striped shirt before, and maybe that influenced my memory. I had no idea that Tanenbaum existed, having kept far away from all of that out of pure fear and the despair that would grip me if I glimpsed anything about the assassination.

31. *Probe* magazine http://www.jfk-info.com/pr796.htm From the July-August, 1996 issue (Vol. 3 No.5).

32. (Training film described from *Corruption of Blood*) www.acorn.net/jfk-place/03/JA/DR/.dr10.html (accessed in 2000 by Wim Dankbaar).

33. Lancer Forums Message #18608, "What happened to HSCA Oswald video?" (Retrieved 7/15/2013).

34. Dick Russell, *The Man Who Knew Too Much*, p. 508.

35. There is an unusual gap in the book *Me & Lee*, which has "diary entries" for most days. But there is no entry between the dates of Sunday, August 4, and Friday, August 9th. Information for August 5 was available, but not included in *Me & Lee* for two reasons: First, the original manuscript was 700 pages long and its focus was on Lee Oswald, not David Ferrie. The incident has been mentioned in live inter-

views since 2000. Second, researchers urged me not to reveal the incident because it could embarrass Ferrie's brother, Parmely. Parmely died January 1, 2013.

36. HSCA, Vol.5, EAL file, Grievances of David W. Ferrie, Aug. 5, 1963, vol.3, testimony of Banister, p.841 (J.F.K. Document 014904).

37. From Mary Ferrell's Chronology: [Also]"...on August 9, 1963 (Friday) Oswald visits his aunt, Lillian Murrett, in the hospital." [Orest Pena says he saw FBI local chief Warren DeBrueys and Lee Oswald together in August:] "On CBS documentary 11/26/75, Orestes Pena alleges he saw Oswald and FBI agent DeBrueys together at Greek restaurant in the French Quarter. (On or about 12/2/63, Pena claims DeBrueys told Pena to keep quiet about this assassination. DeBrueys denies.)"

Note by author: Later, DeBrueys will claim Lee Oswald used the alias "Hidell" and will tell the FBI *the day after the assassination to look for records under the name "Hidell."* "Lee used the fake name Hidell" in New Orleans, and DeBrueys knew it. The FBI was shown samples of Lee's handwriting on post office box application forms, which they say they used to confirm the handwriting found on the mail order rifle they linked to Lee Oswald through "Hidell." However, the handwriting samples could have been used to create the rifle order, when all other information is assembled that we now have about the order."

38. An example of researchers misreporting witness statements: Murray wrote to the author August 13, 2013, saying, "Hey Judyth, Joan Mellen interviewed me by phone but made several errors in the paragraph. Here is what she wrote in *Farewell to Justice*, p. 56-57: [Referring to how LHO seemed to have no connections to the NO Left, what Leftist would avoid the Left?} "None in history, young Bob Heller and Tulane student Hugh Murray both thought. Heller's roommate, Oliver St. Pe, took a look at the Fair Play ... leaflet, considered replying to the post office box of 'Hidell,' stamped on it, then changed his mind. It must be a trap, he decided." Judyth, There were so many errors in this one paragraph, I decided not to review her book. Even though I look upon Garrison as a hero, I distrusted her research. Let me clarify. I am the one who picked up the FPCC leaflet in the Tulane library. I then went upstairs, behind the public area to where grad students had desks, carrels. I went to Harold Alderman who had been active in the FPCC, I think in Miami or some other city, and asked him, "What are you putting out?" I thought it was his leaflet. He wanted to see the yellow flyer. He knew nothing about it. We discussed what we might do, but were cautious. I joked that if we sent a letter to the PO box, it might be the FBI. A trap. We decided to do nothing until we found out more about the source of the flyer. (This is discussed in vol.. 26 of the Warren material.) Alderman took the leaflet and placed it on the door to his dorm room, until Nov. 22, when he took it down. He was visited by the FBI, I think on Tuesday 26 November, and he told them about me, and I was visited by 2 FBI agents on that Tuesday as well."

39. DHHS (NIOSH) Publication Number 84-117 Monohalomethanes. Current Intelligence Bulletin 43 http://www.cdc.gov/niosh/docs/84-117/ (Retrieved 01/10/2014).

40. My father was half owner of a TV station. Johann Rush, who helped film, tried to say I meant big studio TV cameras. I meant no such thing. I knew what could be used in the field.

Aug. 28, 1963: Martin Luther King, Jr. stands on the steps of the Lincoln Memorial and delivers his famous "I Have a Dream" speech to over 250,000 civil rights activists at the climax of the March on Washington for Jobs and Freedom.

CHAPTER THIRTEEN

Clinton and Jackson

East Louisiana Hospital in Jackson.

On August 29, 1963 the trip to Clinton, Louisiana begins. David Ferrie, Clay Shaw and Lee Oswald leave at dawn, stopping briefly in Hammond, LA, to provide an alibi (Shaw's sick father lives there). Next, they pick up an aide who works at Jackson's East Louisiana Hospital, then travel on to Clinton where they wait to join a convoy bringing one or more prisoners from Angola Prison to East Louisiana Hospital in Jackson. Shaw must show his ID to authorities there, as the driver of a black Cadillac registered to the International Trade Mart, because they are parked near a payphone for hours. They are in full view of what they thought would be a nearly deserted courthouse, but it is swarming with blacks trying to register to vote after King's inspiring speech. Locals think the Cadillac is suspicious.

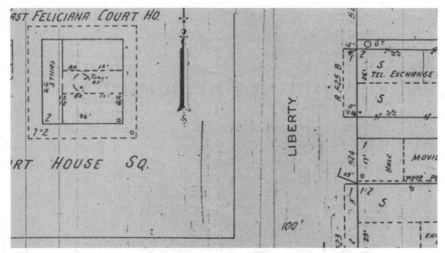

Telephone Exchange, top right, is across from Courthouse. It is probably where the pay-phone was located. This is part of an original map of the City of Clinton.

AUG. 29, 1963: A LONG WAIT IN CLINTON.

While David Ferrie and Clay Shaw remain in the Cadillac, Lee leaves the car with the aide. He stands in line a long time, is briefly able to register (winning the bet) but when Lee asks about getting employed at the hospital, since "now I'm a resident," his name is erased.[1] Registrar Henry Earl Palmer (Grand Cyclops, KKK) will not forget the joke played on him.[2] Meanwhile, David Ferrie, even under a hat, is recognizable, as is Shaw, as they wait.

> **Stephen Roy** (posting as Blackburst): "Oswald was not a resident, and was thus ineligible to vote in Clinton. Why waste all that time in line?"

The answer is that Lee, not wishing to be stared at, left the Cadillac and soon decided to stand in line to register to vote after an educated black woman had been turned away as being illiterate. He "made a bet," with Shaw, Ferrie, and the hospital employee, "that he could register without the correct ID just because he was white."[3] The registrar, Palmer, said Oswald signed his name, but it was erased when he could not produce any East Feliciana resident ID's.[4] Sometime after the registration attempt, the Cadillac drove away. The driver of the Cadillac was identified as Clay Shaw "of the International Trade Mart" by Clinton Deputy Sheriff, John Manchester.

The white man's testimony was backed up by a black man – Corrie Collins – then a local C.O.R.E. member, who by 1969 had moved to Michigan. Collins also identified Ferrie with Shaw, as well as Lee Harvey Oswald. C.O.R.E. was sponsoring a voter registration drive for black residents at the time, overlooked warily by local police and town officials, some of whom were affiliated with the racist, often violent Ku Klux Klan (KKK).

Henry Earl Palmer

Garrison's Grand Jury Court records show that Henry Earl Palmer, the Registrar, had noticed C.O.R.E. member Collins standing by the black Cadillac and had asked Manchester to investigate. Palmer himself was able to identify Clay Shaw as the driver and believed the front seat passenger might have been Ferrie.[5] Efforts to link the black Cadillac to a friend of Shaw's, Jeff Biddison, were unsuccessful.[6]

Shaw carried funds and credentials. He was also the only person who could legally drive the black Cadillac (on loan to the Trade Mart from International House), his credentials were checked in order to enter hospital grounds. Ferrie (who had expertise with cancer research) was there to advise technicians at the hospital how to handle and keep alive a dangerous cancer-causing material to be tested on the prisoner(s). Oswald was present to observe what Ferrie taught the technicians, and how and where Ferrie administered the shots. Nothing was to be written down by Lee: he was required to memorize every procedure.

Clay Shaw

The Cadillac finally joins the convoy and passes unchallenged through the gates to Jackson's mental hospital. Shaw has the money and authority, David Ferrie medical knowledge on injections and information to keep cancer cells alive, and Lee Oswald observes, so he can orally transmit the same information to a medical contact in Mexico City, where the cancer weapon, if successful, will be handed off and smuggled into Cuba. Because Lee must return with me (so I can perform a critical blood test), he fills out a job application form. This gives him an excuse to return, with me, on Saturday, Aug. 31 (a day he knows the personnel office will be closed, but Lee often plays the "stupid" card).[7]

CORRUPTION AND CRUELTY IN MENTAL HOSPITALS

At Jackson, in the small lab, I was surprised to see rows of film reels. I am convinced that Dr. Robert Heath, Dr. Frank Silva

273

(who was in charge here at the hospital) and their associates made filmed records of patient behavior during their experiments at Jackson, just as David Ferrie told me.

Backing up my belief is this quote from Dick Russell's book, *On the Trail of the JFK Assassins*, p. 266: "A paper co-authored by Heath, Silva, and a few others, and published in *Comprehensive Psychology 1960*, was titled Comparative Effects of the Administration of Taraxein, d-LSD, Mescaline, and Psilocybin to Human Volunteers." The introduction stated, "The patient donors are housed in a special Tulane University Research Unit at the East Louisiana State Hospital, Jackson." The experiments were supported by a grant from the Commonwealth Fund, later identified as a CIA front."

Description of the main building by a former patient: "Lavishly decorated, 6-8 stories (including "dungeon") building houses professional staff offices and medical records – it has "many" employees. What they do is not clear. They have no contact with patients – it appears they shuffle paper all day to justify their existence. The upper floors are full of bedrooms – with beds made up and ready – like a small hotel. Someone spends the night there occasionally. One staff said the Governor has a bedroom kept ready all the time "in case he decided to come over."... "Tulane University secret research done for the Federal Government under heavy guard (such as the now declassified project "Mind Control" for the CIA) sends the people when they are through with them – if they are still alive – directly to the "Zombie Colonies" at Jackson where they wait to die and are buried in the Jackson graveyard so that security can be maintained and the truth about what was done to them completely covered up."

I am not the only witness that prisoners from Angola were used in 1963 for medical experiments at Jackson.

William Livesay: From: William Livesay, sent: Thursday, May 06, 2004 5:51 AM To: Judyth Vary Baker Subject: Re: re Angola

Hi. I was in New Orleans Parish Prison for nearly a year awaiting trial in 1962, then sent to Angola from 1963-5.... While at Angola several others & I volunteered for medical experiments to be held at Jackson. There were 8 or 10 in my group.... The only 2 names I remember are Dan Robertson & a guy with the last name of Mayes. After we were there for 4-5 days, Mayes walked out of the ward one night after seeing one of the hospital orderlies come in from outside & forgetting to lock the door. The next morning the bus came & took us all back to Angola. I remember we were given some pills every morning but I have no idea what the experiment was about I learned later that half of us were given medicine & the other half were given placebos. Several years later I went to New Orleans at the request of Dan Robertson to testify on his behalf in a lawsuit he had brought against the State (or possibly the hospital) to show that the pills he took during that brief stay had caused him mental problems. I remember the doctor from Jackson testifying also about the experiment. If I can help further please let me know. Sincerely, Bill Livesay.

Aug. 30, 1963: My career in cancer research *ends* in minutes. I had asked Dave what kind of terminal cancer the test subject had, as I must do a blood test to check for live cancer cells. David tells me the subject is healthy. Shocked, and angry, I protest in a note to Ochsner. Soon after, Ochsner calls me at Sherman's apartment and explodes about the "paper trail," shouting that Lee and I are "expendable."

Late afternoon, Aug. 30, 1963: I take a cab and meet Lee at The Fontainebleau Hotel to discuss the emergency. Dave then drives me to Charity Hospital for my exit interview with Ochsner. Crushed by Ochsner's fury, Dave comforts me, then drives me to my apartment at 1032 Marengo. Lee soon arrives, and David leaves. In my distress, I forget to give David the medical library card. Lee gives me $400 in $20 bills (equals approx. $3700 in today's funds) so I will have a means to reach him in the future.

Lee had asked David for a copy of a pocket-sized Aristotle after reading, with me, *The Seven Pillars of Wisdom* in which T. E. Lawrence, whom Lee admired, talked about carrying around a pocket-sized book of plays by Aeschylus. Lee, while waiting for Robert to leave and, later, twice in the car, wrote comments in the margins, and underlined sections, in *The Pocket Aristotle*. The concern is about ethics.

David Ferrie gave me the book *Modern Greek Self-Taught* (property of the 'Consolidated Library Eglin Field, Fla') to provide my ticket into Eglin AFB's library, where I was slated to meet anti-Castro CIA asset Alex Rorke and his pilot Geoffrey Sullivan. They would have flown me to the Yucatan but their plane was shot down the same day Lee crossed the border into Mexico, making it impossible for me to meet Lee as planned.

CONSOLIDATED LIBRARY
EGLIN FIELD, FLA

The bottom of the book is stamped "Consolidated Library, Eglin Field, FLA." It is also stamped inside.

August 31, 1963: Lee Oswald mails letters to the Communist Party, and to the Party's nemesis, the Socialist-Workers Party, stating his intentions to move to the Washington-Baltimore area. He has also written other letters about plans to move to Philadelphia, New York, and even back to the USSR. Instead, in less than a month, Lee will be going to Mexico City, having told his wife that he intends to live in Cuba (Marina has no plan to follow him there).

Lee wrote these letters to mask his expected final destination – Mexico – where I was supposed to meet him after he handed off the bioweapon (if it worked). A medical contact would smuggle it into Cuba. Lee mailed the letters the same day we traveled to Jackson. "As Dave would put it," Lee said, "let them keep guessing." Because I was a new face in this scenario, Dave gave Lee a password for me to use to enter the area where the medical records and blood-work of the prisoner(s) could be accessed at the mental hospital. Dave had all kinds of contacts at Jackson. Lee told me Dave had rescued a couple of young adults from this institution, as well as several kids from Mandeville.

Aug. 31, 1963: (true date of Lee Oswald viewings in Jackson) Lea McGehee and Reeves Morgan estimated the date of Lee Oswald's visit to Jackson in the Clay Shaw trial as "the last part of August" and "in late August or early September."

Aug. 31, 1963: Lee drives me after noon to the hospital at Jackson to conduct essential blood tests to determine if the cancer bioweapon is working.[8]

Lee would later be tested by Dave for accuracy. If the experiment(s) on the injected prisoner(s) turned out successful (killing them) Lee Oswald would eventually go to Mexico City with the live materials. There, he would verbally instruct a medical contact in Mexico City as to what he had observed, and the biologically engineered materials, designed to cause lung cancer, would be on their way to Fidel.[9]

Castro, who smoked cigars constantly, would seem to die of natural causes if the bioweapon worked, thanks to cooperative Cuban doctors who resented their careers being taken over by the new revolutionary government. Lee had been trained in methods to keep the materials alive for transport.[10] He only pretended to seek work at the hospital to provide a motive for the trip to bring me back there, 72 hours later, when I had to do some blood counts and initiate blood tests, should he be noticed and remembered.[11]

At least two witnesses remembered seeing Lee Oswald in Jackson associated with an old car and a woman sitting in the old car (the Jackson incident) – Louisiana State Representative Reeves Morgan's daughter Mary, and the town barber, Lea McGehee. Neither Ferrie nor Shaw were seen by any of the Clay Shaw trial witnesses in the Jackson incident. In the Clinton incident, Hospital employee Estus Morgan (or possibly another hospital employee) had been brought along to help guide Dave and Lee to the White Men's Clinic behind the main building, which would have been difficult to identify and enter without assistance. The same person who was with Lee, David, and Clay Shaw on the trip to Clinton let us in at the gate two days later around 6:00 PM.

THE JACKSON SIGHTINGS

On the way up to Jackson, Lee and I had to make a stop due to some minor car trouble. On the way back to New Orleans, we had to stop again for the same reason, but it gave Lee a chance to spread story that he was job-hunting, which would help explain our presence, especially if the car broke down so seriously we'd need help to get back to new Orleans.

In nearby Jackson, Louisiana, town barber Edwin Lea McGehee had also seen Lee. He testified that Lee entered his barbershop about the same day the Clinton incident occurred. Tightly associated with Lee's visit was the appearance of an old car McGehee had

My photo, Jackson. Barbershop is to left. Note high curb, left. The barber would have been able to see into the car. He said he saw a bassinet. The "bassinet" was actually a large wicker basket that was going to be used as a bassinet by Anna Lewis, David Lewis' wife. The Kaiser-Frazier was a general-use vehicle that year for persons in The Project. It was considered a reliable vehicle, but Lee and I had problems with it.

never seen before in the village of Jackson, in which a woman was sitting.[12] After Oswald left the barbershop, the car also left, though McGehee didn't see Oswald get into the car. McGehee said he had advised Lee to visit a friend, Reeves Morgan, for information about getting employment at the nearby East Louisiana State (Mental) Hospital, about which Oswald had inquired.[13]

Reeves Morgan, who worked as a guard at the state mental hospital in Jackson, said he also received a visit from Lee just after sunset that same day. His daughter, Mary, still home on vacation from college, saw Lee, the old car, and a woman sitting in the old car – just as McGehee had.[14]

Lee indeed made excuses for his two separate appearances at the hospital, both times saying he was interested in a job. He had filled out a job application when he had come with Clay Shaw and David Ferrie, and an employee there who saw the application eventually reported it.[15] Lee also told me that a friend of the hospital employee – and aide – that they had picked up on the way to Clinton joined the registration line at one point to talk to the hospital employee. This person might have been Winslow Foster, who was also employed by the East Louisiana State Hospital.[16] In 1979, the HSCA's Final Report stated the HSCA was "inclined to believe" that Lee Oswald had been in Clinton "in the company of David Ferrie, if not Clay Shaw."[17]

> **Dr. Howard Platzman:** (researcher/author) Conflict rose among researchers because Jackson witnesses had reported seeing Oswald in an old car, with a woman, in the late afternoon and early evening, while Clinton witnesses reported seeing Oswald in a late model black Cadillac with Clay Shaw and David Ferrie in the morning and afternoon in Clinton. Nobody could satisfactorily reconcile two different cars until this explanation came to light in 1999. Nor could it be understood, until now, why Oswald would travel with Shaw and Ferrie so far from New Orleans.

Some researchers continue to speculate that Shaw and Ferrie were trying to manipulate Lee to get him a job at the mental hospital, presumably so he could later be charged with mental instability after Kennedy's assassination as part of efforts to frame Oswald.[19] But there are two problems with this theory. (1) Employment records cannot be transformed into mental hospital medical records. (2) There was no need to sit openly – being stared at – for hours, if Lee just needed to register. (3) And why didn't Lee have the correct ID, if all this time and effort was expended to drive him over a hundred miles and wait so long, only to see Lee turned away? Reason and logic shows this was a spontaneous act, to pass the time spent waiting. Lee Oswald was known to carry fake ID cards, and should have had fake ID, if this was the purpose of a trip so far from New Orleans. But that wasn't the purpose of the trip. (4) And what about the old car seen in Jackson, both times that Lee was seen in the Jackson area, with a woman sitting in it?

MARY MORGAN'S ORIGINAL STATEMENT

We are on our way back from the mental hospital at Jackson. It is near sunset, and a strong, cool breeze rises, but now the car's engine is hissing from a pinhole leak, which we temporarily fix. Since the engine still needs to cool down, Lee turns into a long driveway, saying he'll talk to Reeves Morgan, a state representative who works at the hospital, and then he'll add water to the radiator. He parks under a big tree, near a nice house with a large front porch.

"I'll be right back," Lee says, commenting that it is best that I stay in the car, so I don't complicate things. "Sorry about the mosquitoes," he adds. Lee then walks up to the house, knocks on the door, and is promptly invited inside. I sit in the car, in the deepening twilight, working on the charts and checking the temperature of the blood samples in the cooler. At one point, I look up and see a girl about my age standing on the porch. She's looking in my direction. This is Reeve Morgan's daughter, Mary. She will later tell Garrison investigator Andrew Sciambra that she remembered seeing a woman in an old car when Lee came. Her presence there will later be corroborated by her father. Importantly, Mary is still on her summer break from college – more proof that the date Lee was seen in Jackson was prior to September 2nd, at which time most colleges in 1963 began their Fall Semester. Mary Morgan is the second witness to report my presence in "an old car" "at the end of August or the first of September."[28]

Below is an excerpt from the original Clay Shaw trial testimony of Reeves Morgan.

> Q: ... how long did you talk to Oswald that day?
>
> A: Well, it wasn't too long, I would say maybe 20 minutes or 25, just talked along there.
>
> Q: Was anybody at home when Oswald was at your house, besides yourself?
>
> A: Yes, sir, my daughter was there...
>
> Q: Mr. Morgan, you say that this conversation took place either in late August or early September?

A: To the best of my recollection. <snip>...I was burning trash out of my fireplace, and it didn't feel too bad, it wasn't cold, it wasn't hot.

Q: Was he clean and neat looking?

A: Clean and neat, very well appearing fellow, nice appearance."

And from an interview with Morgan's daughter:

> **Andrew Sciambra interviewed Reeves Morgan's daughter, Mary, for Garrison privately on June 3, 1967. Here is an excerpt from his January 29, 1968 report of that interview**: I ... talk(ed) with his daughter, Mary Morgan, who had been at home at the time of the Oswald visit. Mary Morgan ... told me that when Oswald was in the house talking with her dad, she happened to walk towards the screen door and went onto the porch and just casually noticed that there was a dark colored car parked under the tree in front of the house. It was rather dark and she didn't really pay much attention to the car ... it was an old car and the model was somewhere in the Fifties. She says that she remembers seeing a woman in the car.[21]

The Beginning of the End

We have acquired powerful and dangerous enemies. From now on, we must be very careful. My main benefactor, Dr. Ochsner has declared me expendable. What does that mean?

We plan to be in touch: Dave is going to help with arranging free phone calls, using his Mafia contacts. Lee says that he has already made it plain to Marina that he would leave, never to return. "I told her she had a hundred people in Dallas who would take care of her. She'd be happy there. Or she could live with me, and never be happy." Lee feels divorce from Marina is inevitable. They should go ahead and get it over with, while the kids are young, so they won't have a lot of bad memories of fights and arguments. Lee cries as he tells me these things. He understands the weight of his actions, and they grieve him. I can see that his love for me is as deep as mine is for him. We seize our right to say good-bye to each other one last time, planning to be together tomorrow at our favorite hotel, The Roosevelt.

> **Anthony Summers**: The FBI and the CIA, often historically at loggerheads, were cooperating to an unusual extent at this time. In September 1963, a CIA officer and a senior FBI official met to discuss new plans for action against the pro-Castro Fair Play for Cuba Committee. The CIA "advised that it was "giving some consideration to countering the activities of [the Committee] in foreign countries .... and giving thought to planting deceptive information which might embarrass the

Committee." The day after that memo was written, Oswald applied for a Tourist Card for a visit to Mexico. A new passport had been issued to him within twenty-four hours – even though his application stated he might wish to return to the Soviet Union. Funny that, you may think – given Oswald's background as a defector and traitor. (email)

Endnotes

1. Why would Lee, who could claim residency from April in Orleans Parish, wish to move to a new, faraway parish where he and his pregnant wife, Marina, and his little girl would not be able to obtain free medical care, whereas the family would soon qualify at New Orleans' Charity Hospital in October, when the new baby was due? Ruth Paine will soon fake residency records for Marina Oswald so she can receive reduced-fee care at Parkland Hospital in Dallas. In a letter (WCE 90, p.1), Paine offered to pay Marina, for teaching her Russian, cash, free room and board, and all of Marina's medical and dental bills. Paine removed Marina Oswald and Oswald's daughter, June, taking them to Irving (a suburban town near Dallas) late in September, after which Lee left for Mexico City.

2. The registrar, Henry Earl Palmer, showed Garrison investigator Anne Dischler the page where an "O" could still be seen, overwritten after Oswald's name was erased, by another registrant. The record, however, soon disappeared. Dischler's credibility is considered unquestionable by honest researchers. See the book *Me & Lee*, for complete details regarding the Clinton and Jackson incidents.

3. Oswald's active support of civil rights was reported by his friend, George deMohrenschildt in his book (*I Am a Patsy!*) published by the HSCA, and by Johan Rush, Carlos Bringuier, and others who observed that when Oswald paid his fine for "disturbing the peace" when he handed out Pro-Castro literature and pro-Cuba flyers, he chose to sit with "the negroes" on "the colored side" of the New Orleans courtroom.

4. Palmer : "...two white men [were] in line with the colored people," who "were very conspicuous as they were the only two white people in the line. Speaking to them, he found they were Lee Harvey Oswald and Estes [sic] Morgan."

5. In the Clay Shaw Trial, P. 97-99 of Palmer's testimony (http://www.maryferrell. org/mffweb/archive/viewer/showDoc.do?docId73 we learn that Palmer never saw the faces of the car's occupants. Therefore, it is misleading that some Warren Commission apologists such as Dave Reitzes (published by John McAdams) have written: "Registrar of Voters Henry Earl Palmer testified that ...two men [were] inside: the passenger had heavy eyebrows "and his hair needed combing." When Sciambra displayed a photograph of David Ferrie, Palmer said, "I can't recognize the individual, but the hair and the eyebrows are similar."(6) He was more certain about the defendant, Clay Shaw, whom he positively identified as the driver of the Cadillac.(7) The apologists then argue that surely Ferrie would be recognized. However, Palmer had only seen a profile of the passenger, including just one "bushy eyebrow" and "messed-up hair" – probably not enough to identify even Ferrie.

6. The HSCA was able to extract more details from the witnesses because they were no longer under pressure. While there is no evidence that the Cadillac was registered to the International Trade Mart, Manchester had no reason to lie. The International Trade Mart hosted important visitors worldwide, often housing them at International House, an organization connected to the Trade Mart for close to a decade by Clay Shaw and Dr. Alton Ochsner, who headed International House in 1963. Ochsner was given Cadillacs annually by Texas oil magnates such as Sid Richardson and the Murchisons. These incoming Cadillacs were used for fund-raising for Ochsner Clinic. See *Surgeon of the South*, Ochsner's official biography, for details about how Ochsner disposed of some of the Cadillacs.

7. Once led to believe that Shaw and Ferrie spent half a day trying to get Lee Oswald 'registered' to help Lee get a job at the mental hospital, so that later his job there could be used to help show he was mentally unstable, researchers had no explanation for why Clay Shaw, a very busy man, was there, or why the long wait to get Lee registered occurred at all, since Lee had no ID for East Feliciana Parish – ID that could have been easily faked. Shaw and Ferrie were not idiots. They were trapped by a delayed phone call. Lee, avidly pro-civil rights, simply made a bet and got his name briefly on the registrar's rolls. Some researchers tried to claim that because witnesses in Clinton didn't speak out until 1967, the blacks and whites cooperated to make up the story, as if KKK and C.O.R.E. members would cooperate in such a thing. In addition, some witnesses such as McGehee stated they *did* try to contact FBI, and were ignored.

8. Barber Lea McGehee and Mary Morgan, daughter of Reeves Morgan, both remember an old car with a woman sitting in it associated with Lee Oswald on this trip to Jackson, due to a stop before and after the visit Lee and I made to the hospital. Because some witnesses saw Lee in the Cadillac and others saw him associated with the old car and a woman, researchers offered various theories, such as that the trip with Shaw and Ferrie must have lasted at least two days, not one. Efforts by researcher Joan Mellen, to push McGehee to add a Cadillac to his memories, and to remove Mary Morgan, Reeves Morgan's daughter, from the record, continue to the present day. Full details and witness statements can be found in *Me & Lee*.

9. For a full explanation of the development of the biological weapon and how Ferrie was involved, see *Dr. Mary's Monkey* and *Me & Lee*.

10. See more information in *Me & Lee* (2010); also, "The Love Affair," Episode 8, last segment, the banned documentary produced for the History Channel (A&E) by Nigel Turner, 2003, in the once-popular, now-removed series *The Men Who Killed Kennedy*. Oswald was a logical choice because he had been posing as pro-Castro in New Orleans and would not be suspected of carrying biological materials to hand off (or take into Cuba himself, if necessary). With no paper trails allowed, Lee was required to observe and memorize how the material was to be handled and used on a prisoner, in order to pass on the information. When the contact failed to show, Oswald tried to enter Cuba himself. Failing in that attempt, he left Mexico City days before his tourist visa expired, because the materials, having a short shelf life, would soon die. In Dallas, Lee never attempted returning to Mexico City even though his transit visa to do so arrived on his birthday (Oct. 18). He had been assigned to a different mission by then.

11. Lee drove me from and to New Orleans: at least two witnesses reported seeing a woman at that time sitting in a an old car associated with Oswald in and near Jackson (McGehee and Morgan). Numerous witnesses reported Lee could drive, although Marina Oswald and Ruth Paine insisted otherwise. If considered unable to drive, Lee's actual activities using a car would be harder to trace or anticipate.

12. Edwin Lea McGehee testified Feb. 6, 1969 that "in the last of August [or] the early part of September … along toward the evening…. I had my door open, the air-conditioning was off and it was rather cool … an old, battered, dark colored car … drove up, and … might have been dark green…[it]resembled a Kaiser or a Frazer or an old Nash.…. There was a woman sitting on the front seat," he recalled, "and in the back seat" he noticed what "looked like a bassinet."

13. There is some evidence of collusion between McGehee and Reeves Morgan on what and when they told Oswald about job opportunities at the hospital.

14. Documented by Sciambra memos and brought forth by Garrison prosecutors in the opening statements of the Clay Shaw trial, where the woman was stated *not* to be Marina Oswald, Oswald's wife. Morgan's daughter Mary, a student at Louisiana State University in 1967: "…when Oswald was in the house talking with her dad, she happened to walk towards the screen door and went onto the porch and just casually noticed that there was a dark colored car parked under the tree in front of the house." It was "an old car and the model was somewhere in the Fifties." She remembered "seeing a woman in the car."

   In her most recent book, Joan Mellen removed Mary's statement from her own description of Lee's visit to Morgan's home and said a Cadillac picked Lee up there, citing her brother, who was then a small boy. She also said McGehee told her he saw Lee get into a Cadillac after he left the barber shop. Original testimonies said no such things, and McGehee complained to me and witness Kelly Thomas that he had been harangued by Mellen to say he saw a Cadillac. This substitution of "new material" for the original testimonies was shocking to me Lee told me that he did not want it known that he could drive for various reasons.

15. Clay Shaw trial records show State Hospital employee Mrs. Bobbie Dedon testified in 1969 that she'd spoken briefly with Lee Harvey Oswald in 1963 and had directed him to the personnel office in the facility's administration building. She placed this encounter at lunchtime – too early. She was also unable to describe Lee convincingly, but her testimony is significant because she worked in the White Male Clinic where Lee first came upon arriving at the hospital, and she had no reason to fabricate her story. Maxine Kemp, a secretary in the State Hospital's personnel office, also testified that in September 1964 she found a job application filled out by a "Harvey Oswald," but by 1967, it had disappeared. Her supervisor denied that Kemp had seen anything. While some may find it "odd" that neither Dedon nor Kemp mentioned Lee's visit to the hospital earlier, when considered along with so many others who saw Ferrie, Shaw and Oswald together, and who testified that Oswald inquired about getting a job there, who also did not speak out until later (after all, New Orleans and its FBI offices were far from these small, sleepy towns), a convincing number of people from different walks of life spoke out, obviating opportunities for collusion.

16. This person, as well as Morgan, might have been wearing white clothing because both men worked at the mental hospital, whereas Lee would likely have been wearing slacks. McGehee and Morgan both described Oswald as neatly dressed.

17. I have explained that a second trip to the hospital was needed to check on the viability of the injected cancer, using a variety of a blood sedimentation test I had developed, and that Lee drove me to the hospital less than 72 hours after the Clinton incident, during which the encounters with McGehee and Reeves Morgan occurred where I was seen sitting in the old car.

18. Notably, researcher Joan Mellen, an apt defender of Garrison, who has in other instances provided important information concerning CIA/FBI interference with Garrison's investigation.

20. Mary's report has some details, such as the estimated age of the car, and Mary's original account – and some aspects of the barber's report – that have been removed from books such as Joan Mellen's, who adds testimony from Mary and her brother some 45 years later. Ever since I identified myself as the woman in the car, Mellen opposed this, apparently because it wrecked her theory that Lee was brought to Clinton to register to vote and then to Jackson so he could be more easily framed. She has to therefore delete me altogether from everything else as well, so in 2004, she invents Gladys Palmer as Lee's girlfriend, later (in 2013) abandoning poor Gladys, who she said was "40 but still hot" for Gloria Wilson, who she says was murdered and was a Clinton resident. Before I'd spoken out, the two different cars were mentioned by anti-Oswald writers trying to prove that the Clinton and Jackson witnesses were not reliable, since one group saw a Cadillac with Shaw and Ferrie and Oswald, and the other group, at about the same time, insisted they saw an old car with a woman sitting in it, associated with Oswald in Jackson sightings. My explanation – that two trips were involved – was unwelcome to anti-Oswald writers and to researchers whose theories I disrupted, so evidence of me had to vanish. I consider the removal, ignoring or distortion of this information dishonest and self-serving.

21. The Warren Commission did not look into these events. In fact, they claimed that they did not know where Lee was during this time. The Clinton Incident, as it is called, was discovered and documented in the late 1960's by the Garrison Investigation and again in the 1970's during the HSCA Investigation. Some of the related documents were kept secret until the 1990s. Lee's true activities were unknown and unsupported for years, but are clearly supported today. A few details were also gleaned from witnesses who testified either in the Clay Shaw Trial or the House Select Committee on Assassinations to present a more complete picture of the events.

The Jackson-Clinton scenario has been a thorny issue for researchers. Why would Shaw and Ferrie be seen with somebody like Oswald, for example? Researchers pushing their theories have to convince readers that both Clay Shaw and David Ferrie for some reason needed to sit in Clinton for hours, visible to the whole town, as they waited for Lee to register to vote. In a real-life situation, Shaw and Ferrie would simply have dropped Lee off and gone to a place where they wouldn't be seen –that is, if you can believe that *both* Shaw and Ferrie were needed for this time-consuming foray. Meanwhile, Lee is making a spectacle of himself, but is unable to register, ultimately, because he has no proper ID. The bright minds of Shaw and Ferrie seem to have failed them on this very basic matter. They have wasted almost half-a-day with no results. And were visible to everybody.

22. A recent claim has been made by Joan Mellen, who over the past fifteen years has offered the names of two different women (one in her 40's, and, a decade later, a younger woman) as Lee's 'real' girlfriend, without providing any evidence, is the only person who has also reported that Morgan's very young son was supposedly up in a tree at the time Lee made his visit in the old car. The boy supposedly saw Lee get into a Cadillac that came suddenly roaring up. Such a statement must be weighed against witnesses telling the author, when she visited New Orleans in Oct. 2013, that the boy, now a grown man, could have been manipulated into saying almost anything.

Judyth Vary Baker, 1964.

CHAPTER FOURTEEN

Final Days – Then Exile

MY LAST TALK WITH DAVID – "DR. JOE" AND GAINESVILLE

We all have times when we know we've made a turn in life that is going to change everything. That time had come for me. Dave and I conversed for the last time together in Susie Hanover's side yard, sitting on those aluminum folding-chairs with their harsh nylon weave. Dave was doing his best to calm me down until Lee could arrive and take over. I was about to be forced to return to Gainesville, and was still in shock from Ochsner's hate-filled thunder, ringing in my ears. I was now banned from cancer research! Only Lee's love, the thoughtful ministrations of dear old Susie, and darned ol' Dave, kept me from falling apart.

Dave told me, as I shook all over, "Listen up, chickadee, I have some contacts in Gainesville, remember? I'm going to help you." One of them, he said, knew a doctor they both trusted. The contact would give the message to Carlos, my pocked-marked anti-Castro friend who wore green sunglasses and worked at the Craft Shop.[1]

"For your information," Dave went on, "It is my friend, Dr. Joe Davis. I've told you about him." In fact, Dave had, but I'd been under the impression that "Dr. Joe" lived in New Orleans. I knew he had taught Dave how to analyze autopsies. Dave had established a friendship with Dr. Joe in Miami for various reasons related to his CAP positions, before he lost his job as a pilot with Eastern Air Lines.

Now Dave gave me more details about the man. Dr. Joe had interned at the US Public Health Service Hospital in New Orleans, where he eventually met Dr. Mary Sherman.[2] Her expertise on bones intrigued him, and Dr. Joe spent time in her bone lab, observing the different kinds of trauma and diseases that could cause bones to break or deform, including bones stressed by cancer, polio or amputations. Dr. Joe was mentored by Dr. Stanley Durlacher, who did autopsies for New Orleans Parish Coroner Dr. Nicholas Chetta.

"Durlacher and Joe saw so many strange deaths and murders," Dave said, "that they decided to do autopsies for a living." Years later, I would learn that Dr. Joe said he started doing autopsies at $50 a head for Chetta, and got hooked.[3]

Around 1955 Dr. Chetta recommended Dr. Durlacher for the position of medical examiner in Miami. Durlacher brought his protégé, Joseph Harrison Davis, to assist him. Durlacher died shortly after, and young Joseph took over.

THE IMPACT OF DR. JOSEPH H. DAVIS ON DAVID FERRIE

Dave flew between New Orleans and Miami every once in a while, most often to attend training update sessions in Miami, where Eastern Air Lines had its main offices. There is also reason to believe he made some anti-Castro flights out of Miami. It seems that after Dr. Joe moved to Miami, Dr. Mary Sherman asked Dave to give Dr. Joe an unusual autopsy report. Dave told me his association with Dr. Joe began when he delivered the report, at which time he was invited to drop by "any time" with more of the same. From then on, Dave took unusual autopsy reports to Dr. Joe for examination whenever he could.[4] Some of them reflected gangland murders, but others involved unusual tropical diseases brought in by Latino and Indian immigrants – highly valued by Dr. Joe.

With characteristic magnanimity, Dr. Joe taught Dave how to analyze these reports. "He's a tremendous teacher – a Sherlock Holmes," Dave said. Dave also observed autopsies on occasion. Dr. Joe was unusual in that he allowed "the public" to attend his autopsy sessions.[5] For the curious "Dr." Ferrie, whose brother Parmely once said Dave wanted to be a doctor, these lessons were irresistible.

Dave never told the FBI details on how he was trained in the forensic sciences, or why his opinion might be trusted. To do so might have led to Dr. Joe, Dr. Sherman, and even me. Guy Banister, however, verified that Dave Ferrie analyzed autopsy reports for him: "... he ... [entered an] arrangement in February 1962 with Guy Banister ... a former FBI agent who ran a private investigative firm.... By the terms of the agreement, [Banister said] Ferrie's work for Banister included analyzing autopsy reports in payment for Banister's investigative services."[6]

Dr. Joseph H. Davis became one of the most famous forensic pathologists in America. He was also one of the few medical experts selected by the HSCA to examine forensic details in the assassination cases of President Kennedy, Robert Kennedy, and Martin Luther King. Dr. Davis' assessment of the JFK assassination may be gauged by a remark he made to a distinguished audience on Nov. 18, 1999: "...the first thing medical examiners are supposed to talk about is the drama of mystery in knowing the outcome of who-done-its. For example: What killed Elvis Presley, or is he really dead? Who fired the shot from the grassy knoll at JFK?"[7]

> **Dr. Joseph H. Davis**: ... you have to look at the community in terms of its subsets ... one of the greatest indicators for a subset of population at risk is the untimely death of a member of that subset... I noticed this in New Orleans ... [in the deaths of drunk drivers]...[8]

It is my belief that Dr. Joe's interest in these historic assassinations was secretly fueled by his relationship with Ferrie and other anti-Castro people.

For those who wonder if such a strange-looking fellow as Dave would have been allowed in Davis' office, this statement by a former police officer can put their minds at rest: "Doctor Davis ... served as Miami-Dade County's Chief Medical Examiner for forty years, between 1957 and 1996, conducting over 10,000 autopsies and mentoring hundreds, maybe thousands, of other pathologists, forensic technicians, cops, lawyers, politicians and media personnel around the world.... He was just as respectful and friendly to a rookie cop as he was to a state governor. I seriously doubt there is one human being on the planet – though he was known by thousands – who ever had a negative word to say about Doctor Joseph H. Davis."[9]

JACK MARTIN'S ENDLESS HOSTILITY TO FERRIE EXPLAINED

David Ferrie once explained to me Jack Martin's hostility towards him in some detail. "It went something like this," Dave said. "Jack's wife, Paula, has a little kid, and at one point, I got to feeling sorry for her and the baby, because I saw Martin go straight to a booze joint as soon as he got his pay. So I brought over some groceries, and milk for the kid."

Dave said Paula was grateful for the groceries, as her own paycheck wouldn't be coming in for a few more days. "Just then," Dave said, "in busts Martin, drunk and wobbly. He gets mad because he's the provider, not me. When he raised his fists at me, Paula said she'd call the police and have him "sent to Jackson" – that she had that kind of power if he wouldn't behave himself. And the Jackass curled up in a ball and started to cry." Dave added, "That's when I found out that Paula never realized that getting him 'dried out' at Charity would mean the electroshocks."

Dave laughed bitterly. "J," he went on, "do you know how many kids I've rescued from [Dr.] Heath and Company's clutches? You'd be surprised. A few of them had ended up at Mandeville. They'd been raped with mop handles, were forced to eat their own feces, and got beat up. They were electroshocked zombies by the time I got a couple of them out of there. But Jackson was even worse. Martin knew if he ever got sent to Jackson, he'd never get out of there alive. Jackson has a graveyard. Just numbers, not names, on the graves. And those numbers vanish from the record books."

Dave went on to say that Jackson had something like 3,000 inmates, but so far this year, according to the record books, not a single one of them had died. "But there were all those fresh mounds out there," he said.

Soon after that, Dave and Martin had another tangle, and when Dave threatened to call the 'Thought Police.' Martin knew exactly what Dave meant. "He went tearing over to Gill," Dave said, "and told him to fire me, that I needed a psychiatrist, that I should be hauled off to Jackson. He made up a puke story about me. I heard him yelling, and Gill told me to get rid of him. I physically removed him from the office. From then on, we've been total enemies."

I realize now that Jack S. Martin was willing to say and do anything to get David Ferrie locked up, if he possibly could. I had forgotten all about this part of David's life story until a researcher asked me, in 2013, if David had ever been to the mental hospital at Jackson before the incident in late August. I replied that I didn't know, but he had been to Mandeville a few times, and rescued a few kids out there who had been cut off from the outside world. Dave used his influence with Gill to provide attorney's writs to get them out of there. It is sad and infuriating that at the end of his life, when Dave needed people the most, almost everybody deserted him. Even the kids he saved.

MY LAST DAY WITH LEE

On September 1, 1963, around noon, Lee and I meet in the lobby of the glorious Roosevelt Hotel in downtown New Orleans. We spend almost the whole day together in our suite. Though we love to talk, we spend several hours doing everything we can think of to express our love, without words. I wear the black necklace he gave me, and just a little bit more. There is joy, laughter, and a kind of desperate mask overlaid to stop the tears. I give Lee a black and gold hunting knife, in anticipation of our meeting in the wilds of Mexico. Lee returns the love letter I had written to him. He can't keep it safely with his things, but couldn't bring himself to destroy it. He also asks me to keep the nice brown Vesuvio tie his uncle Dutz had given him after their secret talk, so he could wear it at our marriage ceremony. I fold it carefully, not realizing that it will remain folded up for fifty years.

Because of Lee, New Orleans is transformed from a dark nest of evil into an incredibly romantic city filled with life, energy, and music. I can see it through his eyes – and it is beautiful. As our last hour together approaches, Lee and I hold each other as if our hearts will break. Finally, we must part.

Robert isn't there when I arrive at 1032, so I call Dave on Susie's phone and ask him to tell Dr. Mary that I'm leaving in the morning. Dave said, "If I tried to run, like you and Lee plan to do, how could I hide, the way I look?" I hang up the phone with a heavy heart, realizing that my dream of finding a cure for cancer is dead, and that death, in fact, is now closing in on us from every side.

Dave told me he might have to go to Texas to personally set up his, mine, and Lee's phone numbers in a cut-out system run by the Mafia that allowed them to use the phones for free. His first call to me fits well with Sept. 10. Was Dave in Ft. Worth?

From researcher Peter Whitmey's list of Ferrie's long distance calls:

DATE	CALLING TO	CALLING FROM
Sept 10, 1963 ?	New Orleans	Ft. Worth
Sept. 12, 1963 ?	New Orleans	Houston
Sept. 20, 1963	New Orleans	Houston

Sept. 20, 1963	Houston (713-CA7-7273)	New Orleans
Sept. 24, 1963	Chicago (312-WH4-4970) (Aase)	New Orleans
Sept. 24, 1963	Washington DC	New Orleans

September 1963: Lee retained his contacts with Dr. Mary Sherman and David Ferrie on a discrete basis. There were final steps being taken to perfect the bioweapon for The Project. Because I had protested to the use of healthy "volunteers;" I was expelled and forced to return to Florida. I believe this move saved my life. To convince Ochsner that he didn't have to worry about me, Lee waited several weeks until he felt it was safe to be in contact again.

My First Call to David Ferrie

Robert and I arrived in Gainesville late in the evening of September 5. I got up early the next morning and scouted out the neighborhood, locating payphones. This was fine with Robert, who didn't want to have to pay for a home phone. We drove to University of Florida, where Robert went off to meetings and I called Senator Smathers' office from the Student Union. When Smathers' secretary told me not to call again, and hung up on me, I knew Ochsner had lied about a scholarship arrangement with the senator. I had been blackballed, even to Smathers. I was dumped, without any hope of ever getting into any medical school, or ever having another scholarship.

Almost in tears, but knowing Dave had promised I'd be getting a full-time job at a chemical research laboratory, I paid late fees and signed up for two night classes.[10] Now I could apply for a part-time job at the Craft Shop, providing an excuse – just as Lee had done at the hospital at Jackson – for showing up there. Only I'd be begging to be hired again. I never dared approach any lab at UF itself, for fear they'd contact Ochsner or Smathers. Soon, the precious enrollment paper was in my hand. Trembling, I called Dave.

He answered on my second attempt, but had only a minute to talk. "I have to go to Texas to set this thing up," he said, apologizing that it would take so long. I gave Dave the second and third numbers we would need for Lee's end of the "Call Wheel."[11] One of my numbers was a payphone sitting on a high curb, all by itself, in an older neighborhood near the tiny, roach-infested hovel Robert's parents obtained for us. The other number was for a payphone located at a Seven-Eleven store a few blocks from the 'cottage' (so dubbed by Robert's mother). Later, I'd give Dave and Lee a fourth number, from PenChem, where a job was to be arranged for me.

Dave had previously informed me that for security reasons, Lee would be called 'Hector' on the phone, and I would be (what else?) 'J.' "Unless you prefer Bonnie and Clyde," he joked.

My suitcase was packed, ready to go, kept under the bed. As soon as the prisoner(s) died, Lee was to leave New Orleans. Eventually I would learn much more from Lee: he would be routed to Mexico City through Dallas and Houston, carrying the bioweapon. (All the details of that secret and remarkable journey are in *Me & Lee*.) As for me, when the right phone call came, I would head to Mexico, too. I'd be back in Lee's arms!

September 10, 1963: Dave called me for the first time using part of the Call Wheel schedule. At the same time I also received information about my upcoming prearranged job at Peninsular ChemResearch. Later, when Lee felt it was finally safe to contact me, he affirmed that he had met with "Mr. B" and a man I now know was Alpha 66's Antonio Veciana. Lee also gave me additional details, such as having to eat his lunch out of a vending machine at the airport because he wasn't invited to eat with "Mr. B" and Veciana. (In November, 2013, Veciana finally officially identified "Mr. B" as David Atlee Phillips, just as Lee himself had finally guessed, back in 1963.)

THE SECOND CALL

I had only one phone number for Dave, and it could not be used again after he received my phone numbers. When Dave said, "Let's see if you remember the codes for the Call Wheel," I hung up. It was already late, but it was a test. I was supposed to know which phone would ring ('South' – phone #2), and the time, which in this case was an hour later.

When Dave made his second call, I told him we needed more codes. For example, "I'll call you tomorrow, same time" might actually mean an hour later that same night, but at the next phone on the compass. A phone would be skipped simply by asking, "Can I reach you at this same number next time?" (no matter what the answer was).

We had to work up new codes because so much of my time, at first, was spent in only two places. I was at UF on Tuesday and Thursday nights, while Robert was at UF every night. That's because he preferred to study in a nice, well-lit carrel that UF provided for seniors and grad students. A sensible choice, since the only lighting we had in the "cottage" was a lamp with a paper plate for a shade, unless we kept the refrigerator door open. I took a bus home after working on campus, those first few weeks.

After we put together the extra codes, Dave updated me on the civil rights unrest in New Orleans, which was making Guy Banister foam at the mouth. Finally, Dave told me the big news. "Hector is in Dallas," he told me. This was probably Tuesday, September 10. (If Dave said, "All is well" it actually meant there were problems.).

"I wasn't supposed to tell you," he said. "But I think you need to know what's going on."

So, in the contorted language we utilized, Dave told me that Hector (Lee) had been flown to Dallas for a quick trip in preparation for his upcoming journey to Mexico City.[13] There, Lee was introduced by his handler, "Mr. B," to a man who was supposed to be in charge of his medical contact in Mexico City, so the bioweapon would not fall into the wrong hands. But Dave said there were problems with the meeting. First, Hector had been forbidden to speak to this man. Second, the meeting was suddenly called off. Third, "Mr. B" was calling himself "Mr. Bishop" now. At this point, Dave shut down the call. He felt he had already said too much.[14]

Today, I think Dave called so often to keep an eye on me. He knew I was an emotional person – just as he was – and that I needed emotional support during the time Lee and I could not communicate. So he made sure I was kept up to date on what Lee was doing. It was some kind of comfort. On this call, of which I remember little, Dave did tell me that Hector (Lee) was keeping nice and quiet in New Orleans, in contrast to all his pro-Cuba activities and his seeming obsession with promoting Uncle Fidel. It was a great relief. No more publicity – *thank God!* He must not be noticed leaving town … he must be forgotten, now …

Until I spoke out in 1999, nobody had a logical explanation for Lee's suddenly "giving up" on the FPCC. All his frenetic public activity supporting the FPCC and pro-Cuban interests had come to a screeching halt. Now, he hunkered down. Weeks would pass without a peep from Lee Oswald. He was waiting for an important event that would shape our future forever. As soon as the prisoner died – and the prisoner was doing quite poorly – Lee would then have to travel immediately. It was important that a sudden departure would not be noticed by the media. Lee still attended certain meetings, requiring quick trips to Sulphur, Louisiana (a very small town with its own airport outside of Lake Charles), some trips to Baton Rouge, and perhaps a flight to Florida.

While waiting, Lee read books. He loved to read. Marina would later say he spent lots of time dry-firing his rifle: click … click-click … Clunk … aiming it at the street – though not another soul ever saw a rifle. And those nosy neighbors saw a lot: they said Lee wore yellow trunks and flip-flops most of the time, as he sat reading on the porch, using a little lamp as it got dark.

THE THIRD CALL

In our third call, Dave felt free to reveal more. Because "Hector" had been told to say nothing, he could not speak when he was quietly waved away at the meeting with "Mr. B" and the contact we now know was Antonio Veciana. "The contact never heard his voice," Dave said. "Not good. Somebody else could pose as him on the phone to this contact. Then he had to fly back to New Orleans on an empty stomach, while the other guy was invited to lunch."

From Dave's tone, I knew this was bad news, as well. "Keeping Hector silent, showing him off to somebody, then calling off the meeting is sloppy trade craft, Dave said. "And not feeding him shows disrespect."

I remembered what Lee told me about being held back by The Company, because he hadn't come back to the USA in a coffin. When I asked for more clarification, Dave said, "Hector had to leave without any information, but the other guy stayed. He's the one that's getting information. The guy came there to ID Hector. Why?"

Soon, Lee gave me more details. I would flesh out the rest many decades later. Lee had met one of the CIA's most clever and dangerous leaders, David Atlee Phillips. Antonio Veciana, a notorious anti-Castro leader, the other individual, was the boss of Alpha 66. Even I had seen his photo, and certainly Lee had. After hearing this information, I purchased a .22 caliber pistol with a brown handle.[15]

"Mr. B's" poor treatment of Lee would remain a nagging concern for us. After a quick meeting, Lee had been returned to New Orleans almost at once, without knowing for sure who he would meet in Mexico City. Now wary, Lee was doubly concerned because shortly after returning to New Orleans, he was driven to Baton Rouge, where, as he stood guard (supposedly to keep a meeting safe) he found himself "inspected" by a military officer prior to the officer's entering the meeting.[16]

Sept. 15, 1963: According to (then 22 yr. old) Perry Russo, "Leon Oswald" becomes David Ferrie's room-mate. Perry believes this is Lee Harvey Oswald. (He's wrong)

295

Sept. 17, 1963: Blue Boxes — Dave established a phone connection through a Mafia racing line so all three friends could communicate with each other. "Blue Boxes" were probably used. The Mafia constantly rigged up free telephone calls for betting purposes and private communications. Blue Boxes could be portable for use at a payphone, or installed into a switchboard, where it could be activated by hand or by the caller (using a code). Such boxes were used well into the late 1970's. In the side bar, read example of dozens of such cases prosecuted by the FBI.

THE FOURTH CALL

Lee urgently wanted his family out of New Orleans before he left to courier the bioweapon to Mexico City. Ruth Paine was reliable: she would be on time, as promised. All that was set up. But what if the prisoner died before Paine arrived? There was no longer any doubt about the bioweapon's power. In Dave's fourth call, which was to me, and which had

---

HORSE RACE BETTING LINES, ETC. USED BY THE MAFIA FOR FREE CALLS

FBI File 92-HQ-4957 Serial #10: Myron Julian Deckelbaum, aka AR. 1961-11-30 "3 local men accused, 13 Indicted in New Orleans." From "about November, 1952 and continuously until about July 31,1959" when discovered, Mafia such as Albert Bagneris, Vincent Caminita, and Frank Marino "conspired" and concealed from the IRS "their widespread horse race betting and other gambling activities by securing free unauthorized long distance telephone service." [FBI via FOA]

(FBI Case #161 in series): "2 Attempted Murders, Suicide Link Mafia to Phone Company" 1975-03-30 John Moulder, *The National Tattler*: "Two lawyers… were shot while investigating Southwestern Bell and the attempt to connect Bell to the Mafia…" Involved: "Carlos Marcello (aka Little Man, mafia don, New Orleans); T.O. Gravitt; wiretapping; James H. Ashley; U.S. Rep. Charles Wilson, Dem. TX (alleged SBTCo wrongdoing for years); Fort Worth, TX; J. Randall Henderson (lawyer, shot while investigating SBTCo); James Sims (lawyer, shot while investigating SBTCo); C.L. Todd (SBTCo VP); J.M. Good (SBTCo VP); miniframe wiretapping device; FBI."

---

to be before September 23rd, he said the prisoner's death was only a matter of days. He also confirmed that Ruth Paine's job was to take care of Marina and Junie in Texas.

The days crawled by as I waited anxiously to hear Lee's voice again. Dave seemed just as jumpy. He, too, was being quiet as a church mouse. "Just don't have a nervous breakdown on me," Dave said. "Let me have it for you." He thought that over, then said, "I'll have one for you, and one for me."

On September 20, while Dave was apparently in Houston (see call record, page 251), Ruth arrived at 4905 Magazine St. with her small children. She parked her station wagon, which had a boat on top, in front of Lee's apartment on Magazine Street for the next few days. It couldn't be ignored. After three days of packing, and a visit to Bourbon Street (Lee didn't go) Ruth and Marina were ready to leave.

Meanwhile, Dave was going to meetings himself, even as he ostensibly was doing work for only Carlos Marcello, whose upcoming trial was taking up more and more of his time, including yet more trips to Guatemala and days spent at Churchill Farms – Marcello's inner sanctum for "taking care of business."

Dave's phone record shows it was almost surely he who went to Houston twice and Ft. Worth Dallas once during the waiting period.[17] At least one of those visits established the final links so Lee could call me from either Houston or Dallas, since he would be briefly visiting both cities on his way to Mexico City. DA Jim Garrison penned in his notes that Dave called Washington, DC, on September 24, when Lee was seen "leaving New Orleans." As I have reported in detail in *Me & Lee*, an emissary of Lyndon Johnson's most powerful aide, Tommy "the Cork" Corcoran, flew to New Orleans the next day. Early the morning of Wednesday, September 25, the emissary gave Lee a large envelope to deliver to a government office in Austin, Texas, as part of his travels prior to crossing the border.

Tommy "the Cork" Corcoran.

Sept. 24, 1963: Lee supposedly leaves New Orleans on the 24th, on a Greyhound bus headed for Houston, Texas. David Ferrie calls Washington, DC.

Sept. 25, 1963: At dawn, Lee Oswald, at [Ochsner's] International House, meets with Guy Banister, Hugh Ward, Clay Shaw and the envoy from Tommy "the Cork" Corcoran. David Ferrie is not present. Lee will carry money to Austin. A DeHaviland Dove awaits Lee and pilot Hugh Ward at Houma. Lee will fly to Austin and Dallas before ending up in Houston to catch a bus traveling to Laredo, TX. Only then will witnesses claim they saw him. The bus ticket leaves a trail that indicates Lee was never in Austin or Dallas. Decades later, researchers will wonder if there was a "second Oswald" due to this ploy. They will also puzzle over conflicting reports about the "lone nut's" library books being returned after he's "left town," a cashed unemployment check, and the bus schedule that makes these acts impossible. The Warren Commission never considers access to private planes.

Sept. 25, 1963: Eastern Air Lines Board announces it will not rehire David Ferrie, but awards him $1,635.90 to settle all claims (close to $14,500 in today's funds). EAL Capt. C.F. Hamer in New Orleans receives a memo to that effect on Oct. 11.

Sept. 25, 1963, Dave obtains Guatemalan visa #1236 from the Consulate general of Guatemala to use for flights to Guatemala, where Marcello had falsely claimed to have been born. In the upcoming trial, Bobby Kennedy's team will try to prove the Guatemalan birth records for Carlos Marcello were faked.

Evening, Sept. 25, 1963: Lee phones me, just prior to catching the bus to Laredo, to tell me Rorke and Sullivan's plane is missing. He says to wait in Gainesville until he learns more and it is safe to join him in Mexico.

$25,000 REWARD
Offered For Two Missing Americans

THE FIFTH CALL

As we entered the latter part of September, I knew Lee was awaiting Ruth Paine's arrival in New Orleans, so she could transport Lee's pregnant wife and their child back to Dallas. People have asked, "How could he abandon Marina like that?" Actually, Lee made sure Marina was in good hands. Ruth Paine's letter to Marina in July is mind-blowing: it shows she will pay Marina $10 a week (equal to $90 a week in today's funds), with free room and board, and all hospital

9:30 p. m.
July 14

Dear Marina,
   Oh, I made a mistake. Michael explained to me that deduction ($600 per person) should be taken out of earnings, not out of the tax. When earnings are smaller, the State wants less taxes. But not $1,800 less, as I wrote. (It is best not to write letters at 2 a. m.) But it seems that Michael would pay $450 less every year if he had 3 more people dependent upon his salary.
   No, we are not as rich as I thought. But we can arrange it this way if you wish to live with me with your children: we would pay you $10.00 a week. Out of this you could buy what you wish—clothes, stamps, etc. But not food. I will buy this and also pay for the doctor, medicines, etc.
   You do not understand how useful and pleasant it would be for me to live with

you. I want to learn Russian very much, but how can I? It is very difficult to study at home with children and I have little practice.
   We do not have to live and eat like rich people. We can live simply but wholesomely. I would consider that it would cost me little to buy groceries (food, soap, etc.) and pay for the doctor and hospital in return for acquiring the knowledge of the Russian language, and to get help with my mistakes in speech and letters.
   Calcium tablets are for you, of course. I found out that when a person eats yeast (?) all day (?) he needs more calcium.* You particularly need more calcium now. Nine tablets a day, please, with milk, if you can. Of course, you need more milk, at least one quart a day, better two. Forgive me for this extra advice.
   I am anxious to hear news from you.

/s/ Ruth

298

and medical bills! In return, Marina is to teach Ruth Russian. Paine had been speaking and writing Russian for years by now, and while it sounds like a good hobby, Paine never told the world that she would pay Marina to perfect her language skills. Instead, she told the Warren Commission that Lee never offered her a dime, though his family lived with her, leaving the impression that Lee was an ungrateful creep who left his wife penniless at the Paine's house.[18]

Fall of 1963: David Ferrie is busy on many fronts. He advertises himself as a psychologist, with an office on Perdido St, in addition to investigative work he is doing for Guy Banister. He has made multiple trips to Miami to defend himself in his doomed appeal to be reinstated as a pilot with Eastern Air Lines, and his assistance in the Carlos Marcello case is also taking up a lot of his time.[19]

Clinging to Lies Made in Fear

David Ferrie was indeed getting involved in the Kennedy assassination. Later, that possibility frightened his friends. When faced with attorneys, trials, reporters and Grand Juries, they often lied. Even under oath. Then they had to stick by their lies, even if interviewed years later. David Ferrie's true story was in danger of being forever lost, or distorted by biographers who never met him. Here is a single example of how far some of David's closest friends would go to protect themselves:

Layton Martens lied to Garrison's grand jury[20] regarding stealing explosives from a Schlumberger cache at the Houma Blimp site in 1961, in an event that reached the newspapers, involving Dave, Martens, Arcacha Smith, Gordon Novell, and others.

After a page or two of trying to refuse to testify, Martens told the jury: "I don't recall ever taking a trip to Houma or anywhere in the vicinity of Houma with David Ferrie..." But by page 16 of the transcript, having declared he could remember nothing, he finally admitted there *was* a trip, and :" ... the only person I could actually say I know was present was Ferrie." That angered a juror.

Why? Over and over, Martens had insisted he recalled no such trip. Having finally admitted the trip occurred, he couldn't remember when it happened. *He couldn't remember* why he came along, or where they went. He didn't know what they stole. He couldn't remember who was driving. Martens could not remember a single person by name or face, for pages and pages. He couldn't remember that a dynamite cap exploded when it was thrown from the vehicle. Exasperated with Martens, the Jurist blurted out:

Let me make a statement, Mr. Martens. You must think these men are stupid. If I were in a car – and it happened 50 years ago, I would remember every person in the car with me, where it happened, I would know where I had the stuff in it, I would know everything else. You must think we are a bunch of kooks to sit down and let you tell us that. This is ridiculous. That you don't know what caused an explosion and you are telling an intelligent group of people like this that you don't remember who was in the car, where you were going, where you were sitting, what you did – you must think we are really kooks to sit down and tell us that. To sit down and lie to us like that does not make sense ... I want you to know that I think you are a d— liar when you say that you are sitting in a car with an explosion and you don't remember the car, who you were with – you are too intelligent a boy. You know good and well you have to know all about it....

To which **Layton Martens** replied: I just never thought of this incident, nor had I any reason to think of it until now.[21]

Some researchers (they're usually Oswald-did-it trolls) say you should believe Layton Martens' statements because they "prove" David Ferrie had nothing whatsoever to do with the Kennedy assassination. So remember what he told the Grand Jury, under oath. I do.

In 1967, Perry Russo, a young man who had an on-and-off relationship with David, said he was introduced in September 1963, to a "Leon Oswald." Perry described his first meeting of "Leon" this way: "...upon entering the house ... I walked up and Oswald is sitting down fooling with a rifle, cleaning it or doing something with it. And I ...stuck out my hand to shake hands. He jumped up and lunged at me and said "What in the fuck is he doing here?" And I backed up and I said, "Fuck you" and with some other expletive and then Dave Ferrie jumped in between and told Oswald "he's alright."

Perry Russo: David Ferrie *wanted* to kill Kennedy.

Leon's reaction, as described, shows he knew Perry Russo. Layton Martens and I agree that this man was not "Leon Oswald" but James Lewallen, someone Perry hadn't seen very often. Even Perry, years later, finally admitted it might have been Lewallen. Layton Martens himself didn't mention seeing Lewallen much. In 1961, Perry Russo had tried to "rescue" young Al Landry during the scandal that cost David Ferrie his job. Dave was furious, but later forgave him. Lewallen is probably reacting to this bad memory, upon seeing Perry for the first time in several years.

Peter Whitmey (a researcher who kept in touch with Perry for years): ... he downplayed the threat made by Ferrie towards him, and felt he had simply forgotten what was behind it ... when he invited Ferrie over.

...Walter Sheridan [wanted Russo] to retract his allegations, along with an offer to move [him] to California, where he would be given a good job. To his credit, Russo refused to retract or even substantially change his testimony, although he slightly wavered as to whether the discussion to kill JFK was a serious one or just a "bull session." ... Russo was still certain that both Shaw and Oswald were at the party (even though LHO was supposedly on his way to Mexico by then), and that Shaw and Ferrie knew each other both before and after the assassination ... (supported by several other witnesses, including a couple whose son had taken flying lessons from Ferrie, who was seen in the company of Shaw at the airport.)

Russo startled Whitmey by writing, when JFK was shot: "I was shocked but satisfied. Kennedy destroyed this country."

Whitmey: At this point, I realized that I was dealing with someone who had no love for JFK, who sounded quite bitter, but who at least was honest about his feelings."

Perry's brother, (via Whitmey): ...Perry had been under psychiatric care as a college student for 18 months as alleged during the trial" (Whitmey suspects this was related to an earlier suicide attempt in 1960...)

Perry was threatened by suspected FBI informant and writer, Jim Phelan: "[Phelan]had come back from the dead trying to (stop) the movie [*JFK*]. That guy is a real asshole. He called me with threats, etc., 8-10 times, Jan-July, 1991."

Whitmey: Russo told him he'd asked if [Garrison] "... knew where in Canada Ferrie had taken Perry's friend, Al Landry, but he didn't know."

Whitmey: "Perry seemed to feel that Ferrie was training Landry and others in jungle warfare in order to invade Cuba..."

Perry Russo also said (via Whitmey): "Banister seemed paranoid; never turned lights on and stayed inside most of the time up to his death in June, 1964." Witness Anna Lewis said the same thing. Perry said he had seen Clay Shaw once at David's gas station (Dave -Al's). Perry felt David Ferrie had been murdered, "possibly with chemical Ferrie had devised that would make a person appear to have died from an aneurysm."

Perry's "Outlaw friends" and David Ferrie: (via Whitmey): "His mother ...died [of cancer] Jan. 31, 1963... his father had been sentenced to six months in jail for tax evasion ... while his father was away, he had "a wild sex life" – living in the house by himself; cleaning lady came in several times a week; had lots of "outlaw" friends over, including Ferrie – lots of parties; drank a lot of wine; didn't care about school – describes in great detail his arrest for theft, which he indicated was actually the work of several young friends, who left a stolen key in his living room; eventually found not guilty ... won a $3500 settlement against the local newspaper in 1983, after they called him a convicted burglar – stated that by 1969 he had been "threatened, bugged, ridiculed, slandered, libeled, etc. "My life, because of the publicity, was a shambles...I regret I ever got involved."

Excerpts from Perry Russo's last interview: "[David Ferrie] was an adventuresome type of person. There wasn't anything that he wasn't ready to attempt to conquer or challenge that he wouldn't take. But he was obsessed with the Latin type for himself, sexually and otherwise. ... the Latin type was something he was very interested in."

"... Dave Ferrie was the center axis of a wheel and all the spokes moved from Dave Ferrie and none as you pointed out, none ever touched the other. He had a relationship with me....He had a relationship with the Cubans. He had a relationship with the others and they did not have interrelationships. You dealt with Dave Ferrie to Dave Ferrie and outward from him."

"... Dave Ferrie ...on this particular night was absolutely obsessed with Cuba. He was pacing back and forth and ranting and raving... on his coffee table, which sat in the middle of the room, always you could find one cup stuck on top of another cup full of cigarette butts. You'd find beer cans here and there. He was a bachelor. He had absolutely no sense of keeping things in order. And everything in his home ... there were little cages with mice and rats and so on ... he had doctorate degrees on the wall from universities."

"... [in] the *Times-Picayune*... you will see that all of the places that were raided no arrests were made. Because, what are you doing arresting people who are patriots storing munitions for no other reason than to blow a communist head off in Cuba? Why would you arrest somebody? You couldn't do that. So all you did was confiscate the weapons."

"... at that time you could buy anything you wanted at the local military store. You could buy hand grenades, you could buy rifles, you can buy bazookas. You can buy anything you had money for. There were no laws against it... "

"I distinctly remember a map of Cuba and ...an old phonograph machine with a 78, I guess, record album on there of a speech by ... probably Fidel ... and the Cubans here were just absolutely incensed by everything said out loud on this record.... And then over the evening there was Ferrie parading around ... "we cannot invade, we don't have any guns, what are we going to use ... bows and arrows? You know this is really the shits"...he's back and forth, back and forth

... upset. And then by contribution from everybody around it was ... we got to assassinate Castro. That's it! That'll work! Assassinate Castro. That'll work! OK."

Perry Russo described a scruffy-bearded, filthy-dirty "Leon" as David Ferrie's "roommate." But in September, Lee is seen most of the time at his residence at 4905 Magazine looking normal. If he had been wearing a beard, neighbors would have reported it. Eyewitness Victoria Hawes describes Lee as neatly dressed and shaved. James Lewallen was known to wear a beard and look scruffy. Furthermore, his nickname was "Leon." This person could have passed as a "Lee look-alike."

James 'Leon' Lewallen might have been Perry Russo's "Leon Oswald." (photo courtesy of Ken Murray)

> **Whitmey** reported: ...in March, 1992 ... Perry ... continued to feel "burned out" and also was recovering from injuries sustained in a car accident.

Note that Perry Russo, who often seemed depressed, shot himself "accidentally" a year after author Ed Haslam interviewed him.[23] Whitmey wrote, "After writing to Perry ... I received what turned out to be his last reply in a letter dated August 17, 1994 (in an unidentified friend's handwriting).... He continued to feel "burned out," and was again recovering from an injury sustained after accidentally shooting himself in his cab back on May 28, 1994." Ed Haslam's book *Mary, Ferrie & the Monkey Virus* was published in 1995. Perry's cab is in one of the photos. Haslam's book was updated in 2007 as *Dr. Mary's Monkey*.

> **Whitmey**: Perry died as a result of an apparent heart attack in the fall of 1995, which was reported in *Probe*... He will be greatly missed by those members of the JFK research community who still believe in the validity of the Garrison investigation.[24]

James Lewallen was seen in Dave's apartment in 1963, according to Layton Martens, who was questioned by Garrison's Grand Jury. John Irion, Dante Marochini, and George Piazz also saw Lewallen there.

Martens was asked an interesting question by the grand jurors about David Ferrie (emphasis added):

Q: Martens, did Ferrie ever hypnotize you?

Martens: *He – at least once, he said he did once.*

Q: You believe that he did?

Martens: *No. You know these compasses that you draw circles with? He claims to have just put one of those right through here – this flesh here – and it's very peculiar ... I woke up, and he said, "You know what I did? And I said I felt something but I didn't feel anything in my hand ...*

Q: Who were the other people around?

Martens: *Some of the Cadets – I remember there were some of the CAP people around .... No, it was very curious.... The thing started hurting and then bleeding, so he said, "Wait a minute." And very quickly, he put me back under – I knew the whole time what was happening ... then he said, "Heal the wound. Absolutely heal the wound." That's what he said. And then he said, "Wake up again." And there was no wound, no blood, no hole, no nothing. It was very curious."*

LAYTON MARTENS' NBC INTERVIEW:

Q: You were, in 1963, from the period of at least September through November, closely associated with David Ferrie?

A: That's correct.

Q: You knew practically everyone associated with him at that time, is that correct?

A: That's correct–

...

Q: There has been testimony recently about a roommate of Ferrie's who was unkempt or wore a beard. Do any of the people you knew and who knew Ferrie fit this description?

A: James Lewallen could possibly fit that description very well. I remember at that time Lewallen did have some sort of beard, and I wouldn't necessarily call him unkempt, but to some people this might represent being unkempt. But one of the things I've noticed, remembering Lewallen, he bears a striking resemblance to this mock picture of Oswald [sketched by the NODA at Perry Russo's direction].

Q: Could he have been considered a roommate of Ferrie's?

A. Yes, he could have, possibly, I think he and Ferrie did room together sometime maybe prior to that, maybe around that time.

Q: Did you know anyone at the time associated with Ferrie by the name of Leon?

A: Well, Jim Lewallen's last name, sometimes people would address him as, "Hey, Lou," "Lee," something like that."[25]

MEXICO: LEE OSWALD'S SAGA

After Marina was taken to Texas, Dave said Lee spent the night of Sept. 24 at Ochsner's International House, in tactical meetings. He slept in a fancy room there. Dave was not privy to everything, because by the 26th, Lee was unable to communicate. Later, I would learn more details in conversations with Lee. Dave was aware, however, of Lee's general movements. He even told me, in his phone call on October 3rd, after Rorke and Sullivan had vanished, "I wish I could function as an emergency pilot for you, but I don't dare."

Dave would have loved our modern cell phone world. I never met a man more addicted to phone calls. If Dave were alive today, he would probably be texting to one person, talking on a cell phone to a second, and writing emails with his pinky while conversing with somebody sitting in front of him. And he could be doing it in German, Spanish, French or Italian, as well as in English, all at the same time. Dave was a master of communication.

It was important that Lee should not remain in Mexico City after the hand-off of the biological weapon, so that he would not be remembered. That's why Lee was supposed to be able to meet me somewhere in the Kankun region of the Yucatan (now spelled "Cancun"). I would actually be his "excuse" for leaving the city. Then we'd go visit the famous Chichen-Itza pyramid. It would be much taller than New Orleans' famous Monkey Hill,[26] Lee had joked. I told Lee I had purchased a revolver, since I didn't want anybody to force me out of a plane over the Gulf, and we could use the weapon in an emergency in the wilderness. Lee laughed and said that "they" would have finished me off before now, if "they" thought I was any problem.

Then, in a far more serious vein, Lee gave me the bad news. Alex Rorke and his pilot were missing. I could hear the stress in his voice. Lee said he had planned to meet Alex in Mexico City to discuss Cozumel as a meeting place, or the area near Chichen-Itza (There was a hard beach there, suitable to land a plane, and it was conveniently remote). In the meantime, I should be ready to go to Eglin AFB. Our hopes were still high, but the call was short. Lee said he did not have any more time to talk. "I love you, Juduffki," he told me, as he so often did. Then he hung up.

Sept. 27 – Oct. 2: Anthony Summers: Oswald did go to Mexico City, and his six-day visit remains one of the most mysterious – yet telltale – episodes of the entire story.... Oswald's ostensible purpose in Mexico, of course, was to go to the Cuban and Soviet embassies

– armed with his credentials as a pro-Castro activist – to try to get a visa for travel to Cuba. He failed. The Cubans – I went to Mexico and Cuba and talked to relevant witnesses – suspected he might well be a CIA agent provocateur.[27]

With Lee in Mexico City, the plot to frame him began in earnest. For example, an impostor posed as Lee, speaking poor Russian, by telephone. The CIA even sent out photos of a "fake" Oswald at the Cuban Consulate. After admitting their "mistake" they went on to claim their cameras were broken when Lee was there.

False witnesses would say Lee talked to Russia's Valeriy Kostikov – an assassin – when Lee visited the Russian Embassy, that Lee bragged about his shooting skills, that Lee took a bribe of $6500 to kill Kennedy. The impostors made sure Lee was in Mexico City so he could be framed. The CIA must have anticipated that Lee was willing to take some risks to fulfill his mission. They

"Oswald" photo from Mexico.

counted on his loyalty. As Lee made desperate attempts to get the bioweapon into Cuba personally, his zeal made him look like a pro-Castro fanatic. That would make him easy to frame in Dallas.

Oct. 3, 1963: In Dave's seventh phone call, after he told me that Rorke and Sullivan were probably dead, he said additional precautions had to be taken to break any final links between me and my time in New Orleans.[28] It was imperative for me to order another birth certificate immediately, even if it still said "Female Infant Vary" and was useless as ID. My fourth phone number for the Call Wheel had finally come into play that Monday. It pinpointed my position at the exterior emergency phone at Peninsular ChemResearch. This prestigious research laboratory supplied exotic new concoctions to private labs, NIH, and many other government labs, including NASA.[29] When I asked why I had to order another "Female Infant Vary" certificate, Dave explained. "That certificate was sent to New Orleans, and records in Indiana will show this as your last known address. We can't have that. Order a replacement. Now."

I already had a birth certificate dated April 26, 1963 in my possession, sent to me when I lived in New Orleans. Now I had to order it again, with no time to correct the "Female Infant Vary" designation that made it useless as ID. However, the 'last known address' in the system would then show Gainesville, Florida, disconnecting me from New Orleans at this crucial time.

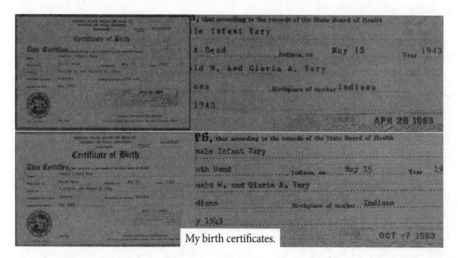

My birth certificates.

HSCA: By the fall of 1963, Ferrie had become actively involved in the defense investigation of Federal charges of a fraudulent birth certificate against Carlos Marcello. Probably.

Did the Marcello birth certificate "true address" problem cause Dave to think about my birth certificate address?

Lee's involvement in the bioweapon project was now over, as was mine. Cuba was no longer a target, or a priority. All that remained for Lee was his nagging belief that he had learned enough about Kennedy's planned assassination that he might be able to do something about it. As he obeyed the directives of the CIA in the days ahead, he stayed in Dallas because he hoped he might be able to learn more about the band of right-wing nuts – military and civilian, and the politicos and rogue elements who wanted to kill Kennedy. But what could one man do? Dave and I knew that his stubborn commitment to duty could mean Lee's death.

Oct. 9, 1963: David arranges for me (with no degree in chemistry) to be hired as a lab assistant at Peninsular ChemResearch in Gainesville, a position sought by chemistry grad students. Ochsner has been persuaded that if I leave the scientific field too suddenly, questions will be raised.

Oct. 11–18, 1963: HSCA: David takes a Delta flight to Guatemala City for Carlos Marcello. He remains there until the 18th. FBI Memo: A draft of a letter to Marcello's attorney, Jack Wasserman, states David's address in Guatemala is "Room 307, Maya Excelsior, Guatemala," a very fancy hotel.

Wed. Oct.16, 1963: Lee Oswald, with Ruth Paine's assistance, gets a job at the Texas School Book Depository, two days before his 24th birthday. Lee lives in rented rooms the rest of his life, visiting his wife and child (and soon, a new baby) on weekends. Marina remains with Ruth Paine. I am now working at Peninsular ChemResearch.

By now, Lee had moved into a safe house and had no plans to live with Marina again, though he would visit her and Junie most weekends. Lee gave me several phone numbers where he could be reached in an emergency. When Lee gets the Cuban transit visa in the mail – it comes surprisingly quickly – he ignores it. The Project is over. The transit visa is useless to us now.

The TSBD had been recently purchased by Harold Byrd, a Texas oilman close to his oil baron pals and Lyndon Johnson. Lee said it was another temporary cover job. Lee had been promised he'd be able to return to Mexico "by Christmas" so the job's low pay meant little. Mr. Roy Truly, his boss, had been told Lee was working undercover for the FBI. "I have the same kind of job freedom that I had at Reily," Lee told me. "But even better, because there's no time clock." Lee was often elsewhere, doing assignments in Dallas. His work hours were filled out by a secretary (that sounded familiar!). It didn't matter how many hours Lee actually worked there. Confirmation of this arrangement exists in Lee's last filled-out workday. It is for Friday, Nov. 22, the day Kennedy was shot and Lee was arrested. Lee left the TSBD by 12:45 PM at the latest, but his worksheet said he was "present" all day long.

Lee usually entered the building through the loading docks at the back of the TSBD, from the parking lot. That's where Buell Wesley Frazier, who usually gave Lee a ride to work, parked his car.

TSBD loading docks.

OCTOBER 18, 1963: LEE'S LAST BIRTHDAY

It was Lee's 24th birthday. Lee told me that he cried when Marina and Ruth gave him a little birthday cake. "I won't live to see another birthday cake," he told me, "unless I can get out of here. If I don't do it right, we'll all get killed." Lee said that upon his return to Dallas, he had been invited even closer into the assassination ring that was planning to take out JFK. In a later call, Lee said he wasn't good enough to be a shooter, but he'd been invited to be one, so he knew it was almost certainly a trap. "So," I said sadly, "you're going to go through with it?"

"I'm going to have to go through with it. Who else is in position to penetrate this and stop it?"

I started to cry, feeling both hopeless and helpless. Dave and Dr. Mary had been the key to Lee's learning about the assassination ring. Dave had given him names and all the information he'd collected from the wary and paranoid Guy Banister. Dave had already told me that pretending to hate JFK had eventually brought him into a ring that was dropping names, here and there. He had evidence of their plans, he said that he would pass on to Lee, since the focus had shifted from New Orleans to the kill zones of the big cities that Kennedy was slated to visit that fall.

I had needed all kinds of reassurances from Dave that he could be trusted. When I had felt the lumps on his neck, which he worried about, I said, jokingly, they weren't cancer, they were just clogged-up hair follicles. "My neck gets so stiff," he complained. "And I've had headaches ever since we lost pressure in a plane once. I think I ruptured something in my head. Or maybe I have a brain tumor. One of my school chums died from encephalitis. I have the same symptoms, sometimes."

"Stop it, Dave!" I told him. "Self-diagnosis is your worst enemy. Most of your headaches come from not drinking enough water and drinking too much coffee. When you don't have coffee, you get a headache because your brain is used to all that caffeine. Just drink more water and tone down on the coffee."

I didn't drink much coffee, so it was easy to criticize Dave, who was so hyperactive. He obviously had a high thyroid level. Today, with more knowledge, I suspect he was also taking too much Proloid – a combo of thyroid hormones – to keep feeling energetic, and this was giving him the symptoms that concerned him. Another worrying idea was that we'd worked with a cancer virus that was known to produce symptoms of encephalitis. I prayed Dave had never read the small print in any of my reports on such things.

Giving Dave medical advice about curing his problems, rather than telling him to take another pain pill, brought us closer. It would prove important.

From Banister, Dave wheedled out the names of wealthy, racist Texas oilmen closely associated with Ochsner and Lyndon Johnson. Dr. Mary was just as concerned, and also helped. Together, they could make good guesses on which plots might be serious. These nests of adders were located in Chicago, Miami, Houston, and Dallas. Using the CIA, the military, the Secret Service (SS protects the Treasury – think "bankers") the Mafia and anti-Castro agents, a webwork of plans to commit the ultimate treason was under construction, which JFK wouldn't be able to escape.

Lee was in Dallas, the most dangerous city of all. Now that he had decided to continue to penetrate the assassination ring and funnel information out, nothing could stop him. "I gave an oath as a Marine," he told me. "I swore to serve the President. I can't serve a dead President." Lee was now spending evenings with men who were plotting the death of the President of the United States – men backed by frightening power. They might even be able to blame it on Castro, thrusting America into war against Cuba, thus killing two birds with one big stone.

Dave, Dr. Mary, Lee and I all believed that an invasion of Cuba could trigger World War III, if Russia moved in to defend her. With so much at stake, there was now no way to persuade Lee to save himself. In fact, he would have thought it immoral of me to try. Lee believed that saving Kennedy was worth everything he had to offer.

Between this date and the last days of his freedom, Lee was involved with people who, I believe, lured him into position. Some of these were the very people he thought he could trust.

As for Clay Shaw, I do not know how much information Dave gave to him. None of us trusted Shaw.

THE STRANGE SYNCHRONICITY OF $7000

Joseph Milteer: Some four weeks before the Kennedy assassination, Milteer, who was taped in Miami predicting the Kennedy assassination, had made two deposits after opening an account in a Utah bank for #115376: one for $5000 (Aug 20) and one for $2000 (Sept. 24.) All $7,000 was removed Jan. 31, 1964 (52 days after the assassination)

Jack Ruby: On Oct. 7, 1963, Jack Ruby received approximately $7000 "from a Jimmy Hoffa Associate" in Chicago, in a stack of $100 bills.

Jim Braden: In Nov. 1963, Braden gets $7000 from a Louisiana oil/gas well, which never produced much income before or after. 1/31/02 1:52 PM Clark Wilkins. "

David Ferrie: On Nov. 7, David Ferrie deposits $7,093 from G. Wray Gill as a "bonus."

Mario del Rosario Molina: On November 27, 1963, someone identifying himself as Molina mailed a letter to JFK from Havana, informing him that a Castro agent in the United States named *Pedro Charles* met Oswald in Miami several months earlier and had paid Oswald *$7,000* to assassinate JFK.

Oct 24, 1963: In Dallas, U.N. Ambassador Adlai Stevenson is hissed at and jeered. Unable to finish his speech at Dallas' Memorial Auditorium, he leaves, but is struck on the head with a sign by right-wing extremist Cora Lacy Frederickson. Others assault Stevenson with boos and spittle.

Various sources describe Lee as being present here. They are correct. Lee was holding a protest sign and was marching outside the building. He was there to assess the mood of the right-wingers and to gather information. He participated in the outburst against Stevenson as well, both to present himself as an apparent "right-winger" and also to help convince JFK's Secret Service to enhance security for the President. But the Secret Service was already corrupted beyond repair.

Adlai in Dallas.

Adlai Stevenson: "Are these human beings, or are these animals?" The next day, Stevenson tells Arthur Schlesinger, Jr. "There was something very ugly and frightening about the atmosphere. Later I talked with some of the leading people out there. They wondered whether the President should go to Dallas, and so do I." JFK's staff encourages him to go to Dallas anyway. A month later in November, when JFK is slated to ride through Dallas streets in an open car, the Secret Service will decline the FBI's reported offer of assistance to help augment their staff for the impending Presidential visit. Lyndon Johnson is in political trouble: a headline story in the *Dallas Morning News* reads: "Nixon Predicts Kennedy May Drop Johnson."[32]

Oct. 29, 1963: David Ferrie obtains another Guatemalan visa and flies there.

Oct. 30 –Nov. 1: HSCA: David is in Guatemala, for Carlos Marcello's interests, again.

Endnotes

1. The message actually reached me via my boss-lady there. One of the few names from 1962-1963 I no longer remember, this sweet woman, who ran the Craft Shop, was Catholic, married, and had two sons, one of them named "Joseph"– which I linked mnemonically (to memorize) with "Dr. Joseph Davis."

2. On p. 42 of the House Select Committee on Assassinations Investigation of the Assassination of Martin Luther King, Jr. Volume 1, p. 42, we learn that "Dr. Davis received his M.D. degree from Long Island College of Medicine in 1949 and completed his residency in pathology at the U.S. Public Health Service Hospital in New Orleans." Dr. Davis retained his connections with the USPHS Hospital in New Orleans for years.

3. Dr. Davis, in his lecture "Origins of the Medical Examiner System" stated how Miami's Medical Examiner's Lab was established by recruiting New Orleans pathologist Dr. Stanley Durlacher, Dr. Davis' patron, upon the recommendation of New Orleans' Coroner, Dr. Nicholas Chetta: "... in 1955.... The Search Committee ... picked Dr. Stanley Durlacher ... Associate Professor ... at the Louisiana State University School of Medicine. He had a long illustrious career.... He had been picked by Dr. Chetta, who was elected Coroner in New Orleans way back when, to ... set up a coroner's laboratory in New Orleans. And Art Fisk, who was his sort of right hand man.... He and Stan actually physically built the office ... built it in the basement of the Courthouse in New Orleans.... One of the things that happened at Tulane Medical School and at LSU, is the young pathologists, the junior members of the department, do autopsies for the coroner. They did not have a full time coroner staff; it was done by the medical school staff at fifty dollars a head, I think it was, at the time. And you were paid just as if you had been supplying potatoes to the parish, but I found it extremely fascinating. For the first time, I was able to see disease processes, the pathology of the disease, fresh, untreated. And then I began to see other things that I had never been taught in medical school,

that was injury, and then, effects of drugs and alcohol, things you just completely ignored in medical teaching." [Re the new Medical Examiner's lab in Miami, Davis simply said, "Well, Durlacher brought me with him."]

4. Dave didn't tell me if Dr. Chetta, Mary Sherman or somebody else asked him to do this, or whether it was Dave's own idea so that he could learn more.

5. To illustrate Dr. Davis' willingness to mentor anyone who requested knowledge, as did David Ferrie, this entry in Dr. Davis' Dignity Memorial Guestbook should suffice: "March 26, 2013. When I was a lawyer handling medical malpractice cases in Miami, I called Dr. Davis to ask if I could observe autopsies at the ME's office. I thought it would be a good way to learn something about anatomy. Dr. Davis did not hesitate: 'This is a public office and you are a member of the public.' So I went, several times. It was a very useful experience. I am grateful to Dr. Davis and to the other doctors who took the time to explain things to me and to answer my questions. Dr. Davis was a great public servant." Bart Greene, Ponte Vedra Beach, Florida http://www.legacy.com/guestbook/dignitymemorial/guestbook. aspx?n=joseph-davis&pid3764790&page=5 (retrieved March 30, 2013)

6. Banister's statement concerning autopsy report analysis is recorded here: HSCA, Vol X, Sec. XII, p. 110 . HSCA cited Ref. #126: 4904) . (123) Ibid. . EAL file . grievances of David W. Ferric, Aug 5, 1963, vol. 3. testimony of Banister, p 840. (1211) Ibid., p. 825. (125) Ibid., p. 855. (126)... http://www.aarclibrary.org/ publib/jfk/hsca/reportvols/vol10/pdf/HSCA_Vol10_AC_12_Ferrie.pdf.

7. From Dr. Joseph H. Davis' remarks in his lecture "Origins of the Medical Examiner System" http://calder.med.miami.edu/gross/lecture5-main.htmlm (Retrieved March 30, 2013).

8. Ibid.

9. http://www.marshallfrank.com/articles/2013/04/dr-joseph-h-davis-m-e-remembered/ (Retrieved March 30, 2013).

10. The important document following shows I withdrew from these 7 hours of night classes the 'Winter Semester' of 1963. After Lee was shot, I was incapable of taking any final examinations and went to campus doctors, who agreed that I was ill and authorized me to receive "H" grades (unable to attend due to health). By petition, I was able to get the grade point penalties removed. This is one of the documents proving how distressed I was after the assassination. Because I also have my checks for Peninsular ChemResearch issued at the same time, proving I worked fulltime, the fact that these were night classes is thus established, and that establishes my pre-cognition that I would be hired fulltime by PenChem, though that didn't happen until mid-October. I was hired at Peninsular ChemResearch on Monday, October 14 as a research assistant. I began work on October 16 and worked that Saturday and Sunday as well, to get my paycheck 'in synch' – easy to do because PenChem closed only on Christmas and the 4th of July. On Nov. 22, I wept in front of people who cheered JFK's murder. A week later, on Nov. 29th, a meeting was held and I received 30 days' notice. On the 31st of December, I was terminated. I had worked overtime every week: some of the work was possibly for The Project in New Orleans, since I shipped glycol-based products I was asked to create to Mound Park Hospital, FL, which then were shipped

on to New Orleans. I worked 88 – 100+ hrs/every 80-hr.pay period. Only one job was routine: I arrived, alone, an hour early every morning to unlock the gates to the facility, then replenished liquid oxygen and nitrogen supplies needed for the day, which took half an hour. I then began working on gas chromatography, assays, laser tests and experiments assigned by Mr. Mays. His other assistant, Nancy, was a chemistry grad in her twenties, already an old-timer.

UNIVERSITY OF FLORIDA
GAINESVILLE

OFFICE OF THE REGISTRAR   August 18, 1964

Mrs. Judyth Vary Baker
213-B Flavet III
Gainesville, Florida

Dear Mrs. Baker:

We have your recent petition for

    The removal of seven hours of H grades from
    your record for the Winter Trimester 1963.

The record does reflect that you registered for these courses
and that you did not take the final examination. We are not
willing to remove this from the record. We are, however,
authorizing the removal of the seven hours from the hours
carried for that period which means that the H grades then do
not affect your average in any way.

Very truly yours,

R. S. Johnson, Secretary
University Senate Committee
on Student Petitions

RSJ:jr

cc: Dean Hollinshead
    Dean Hale
    Student's File

11. I told Robert that my friend Don Federman was now an editor of *The New Orange Peel* (UF's witty student magazine) and that he'd pay me to do some illustrations for the magazine (true). So Robert brought me along, and I stopped by the Craft Shop and picked up the phone number I could use to call Dave or Lee for free and with privacy. This got the Call Wheel started. I registered for classes after I knew I could be re-hired at the Craft Shop so Robert wouldn't have a hissy-fit about my spending money on college. Having "found" $400, and having earned $150 for art work Robert and I did together for his parents (ads for their new complex Hurlbert Arms near Eglin AFB). he could not forbid me to register. 12. For full details of Lee's trip to Mexico City, and how he arrived by circuitous means,, see *Me & Lee*. In 2000, Gerry Hemming at one point tried to tell me that Lee had been flown into Mexico by Alex Rorke – a story he

told others on 11 Feb., 2005: "Hoover's next big shot at revenge came during September 1964, upon demand by two members of the Warren Commission that: The Silvia Odio/Oswald visit issue be resolved or they wouldn't "sign-off"!! ...These two Castro double-agents were Manolo Aguilar and Enrique Molina Rivera. Molina Rivera later "disappeared?" while flying with Rorke and Sullivan during September '63 – after picking up Oswald and flying him from New Orleans to Merida, Mexico for further infiltration inside Cuba." (Viz: http://educationforum.ipbhost.com/index.php?showtopic173) Gerry knew Lee had been flown out of New Orleans, and he knew that two Latinos were with him on some legs of the trip, but he erroneously assumed Lee was flown into Merida – exactly where Lee was planning for us to go after he finished his Mexico City assignment – we'd be seeing Chichen-Itza, if we didn't have to flee to the Cayman islands – then head to Merida. Perhaps Gerry had obtained information about our plans to go to Merida.

After reading what he'd written to The Education Forum, I confronted him with the full details, since by then I had the full information of when Alex and Geoffrey were shot down. Many accounts show the event a week earlier than it actually occurred. It was in error, and I was then able to proceed with my argument from 2000. Gerry had to agree that he might have been giving out false information. He defended himself by cursing Weberman, who he said misquoted him "all the time." Regarding his 2005 statements, he then wrote, a few days later: "...my greatest focus is on the 40 years of misquotes, lies, libel and slander – aimed specifically at "The No Name Key Bunch"; as the perpetrators or support element in the assassinations of JFK, RFK, and MLK, Jr. (and they might throw in "Cock Robin" and Judge Crater also) – and the stupid bastards just can't grasp that this was engineered by faggot J. Edgar Hoover in retaliation for getting the goods on his ass and delivering same to RFK. His final queer stroke was to cover his ass on the Sylvia Odio meeting with Oswald in Dallas, Sept. 1963." He then added his feelings about A. J. Weberman: "Most of the InterPen guys aren't even aware (nor interested) in this JFK fantasy crap – and those who are don't really give a shit. However, some have been called out of retirement and are currently serving in Iraq, Afghanistan, Kuwait, etc. – and others non-military are working (even in their late 60s) for government agencies – including "Homeland Defense". They sure as hell don't need snitches like Weberman, et al. bandying their names about on the Internet at this stage in their careers." Hemming also wrote to the Forum that Weberman offered him a lot of money to make a full confession before he died. Sadly, Hemming died Jan. 8, 2008. We had become good friends, and I have tried to maintain contact with his children.

13. Researcher A. J. Weberman wrote, in his Nodule section on Veciana, "After the assassination, there was absolutely no doubt in Antonio Veciana's mind that the man he had seen was OSWALD. Marina Oswald told this researcher: "According to my file, Veciana said this meeting was in the first week of September. We were in New Orleans. Who was that man? Was it LEE OSWALD then? If there was a meeting in Dallas and we were in New Orleans, how is that possible unless he had a plane to fly back and forth?" (Viz: http://www.latinamerican-studies.org/belligerence/veciana-oswald.htm, retrieved May 1, 2013).

But Lee did have a plane "to fly back and forth." Not only did he tell me so, but on September 10, according to phone records reported by researcher Peter Whitmey, to which I did not have access when I wrote *Me & Lee*, we learn that David Ferrie almost certainly called from Ft. Worth, Texas on Sunday, September 10, the same day he called me.

14. Dave could hang up any time after the codes were exchanged.

15. I kept the revolver until I fled overseas after death threats, in 2003, at which time I sold it to help raise money for the trip.

16. After that meeting, Lee was informed by the same officer that some kind of cash account was set up for Marina and the children, so Lee could leave her behind without worry.

17. Supplied by researcher Peter Whitmey to newsgroups, the phone call record has Jim Garrison's handwriting on the side margins.

18. The world has been told, for over fifty years, that Lee Oswald was ungrateful to Ruth Paine for all her help, never giving her a penny. Ruth Paine is presented as sensitive, considerate and generous. Lee Oswald is presented as ungrateful, miserly and manipulative. When the Warren Commission asked Ruth if Lee ever helped out financially for all she had done, Paine just says he never gave her a penny, making Lee look like an ungrateful jerk. However, knowing Lee's true character, I decided to read Paine's letters and found, in Vol. XVI of the Warren Commission's 26 volumes, that Paine offered to pay Marina $10 a week, plus free room and board, and all her medical and hospital bills, in exchange for Marina teaching her Russian. Lee Oswald has been slammed for FIFTY years as an ungrateful wretch who took advantage of Ruth's kindness and hospitality, without offering any financial help. It is perhaps all the more touching, then, that Lee left Marina $170 total in cash for her (equal to about $1600 in today's funds) on the morning he knew he might be going to his death, Nov. 22, 1963, in his attempt to save JFK. I urge everyone to read the evidence in James Douglass' *JFK and the Unspeakable* and in *Me & Lee*, to get the full truth about Lee.

19. I was eventually asked to take his place doing lab work in his apartment, during Ferrie's working hours elsewhere, usually three afternoons a week.

20. http://www.aarclibrary.org/publib/jfk/garr/grandjury/pdf/Martens.pdf (Retrieved May 2, 2013).

21. Researcher Stephen Roy (David Blackburst) refused to identify any of the witnesses he says he has recorded, saying they fear their reputations could be ruined, even though they are elderly men now and could die at any time (or may already be dead). Mr. Roy should help the research community and release their names and their statements while they are still alive and are able to correct any errors! I have released the names of my witnesses, having obtained their permission. He could do the same. The excuse that their reputations could be ruined is weak against the argument that we are losing second chances to interview these witnesses due to a refusal to share information. In contrast, researcher Vincent Palamara interviewed, photographed and recorded witness statements of members of the Secret Service involved with The Kennedy Detail. Palamara

then posted his material free to all on the Internet (I have done the same for a mass of material). His book, *Survivor's Guilt* has been published by TrineDay.

22. http://www.redshift.com/~damason/lhreport/articles/perry.html (Retrieved 03/08/2014).

23. Email, March 2014,from Edward T Haslam: "I talked to Perry in New Orleans in the Spring of 1993, 2+ years before I published Mary ...He picked me up from the airport in his cab. He was overweight, but not overtly sick or wounded. He was curious about the cancer lab, and wondered how it could have been done without his seeing it ... a point that I think you explained clearly in *Me and Lee*, a book which I wish he could have read before passing...ETH."

24. Peter Whitmey. SUNY, Fredonia, 1966 lecture. http://mcadams.posc.mu.edu/prusso.htm (Retrieved 10/10/2013).

25. http://www.jfk-online.com/nbcrusso.html (Retrieved 04/17/2013).

26. During the Great Depression the Works Progress Administration built an artificial hill known as "Monkey Hill" to show the children of flat New Orleans what a hill looks like.

27. This quote from Summers (an email quote from Nov. 2013) reveals how Summers made a turnabout and has gone on to endorse the unreliable researcher Patricia Lambert's account of the Clinton and Jackson witnesses (for example, never having interviewed me and changing Anne Dischler's testimony). He actually threw out the entire Clinton-Jackson scenario, for which I have castigated him, with no response, by email. Summers also fell from grace by deciding that Lee Oswald shot Officer Tippit after all. This was another shock, for he based his conclusion on Dale Myers' outdated book *With Malice* that argues Lee Oswald killed Officer J. D. Tippit, despite convincing evidence supplied by Texas Theater Manager Butch Burroughs that he sold Lee Oswald popcorn in the Texas Theater at the time Tippit was shot (and much more). Jim DiEugenio's review of Summer's updated book is spot-on.

28. It was later determined that the same day Lee left 4905 Magazine, Alex Rorke and Geoffrey Sullivan were shot down over Cuba while on a mission. We now know they took off from Cozumel, and some speculated they had plans to land in Florida. But their plane was shot down. They would never meet me at Eglin Air Force base on the 26th.

29. A. Weberman's notes on Lee Oswald include remarks about locations that did not make sense to the FBI (unless they were for job-hunting purposes – *but* – if they were for job-hunting purposes, why were marks (plural) shown at intersections? Intersections often held a telephone booth back in the 1960's.) (1) "A mark at Irving Boulevard near Farrington Street,"...(2) "marks at the intersection of San Jacinto and Boll Streets," (3)" marks near the intersection of Ross and Olive Streets," (4) "and San Jacinto and Harwood Streets, and other marks on the map, have no known significance to personnel of the Dallas Office with respect to the known activities of OSWALD. A large Chevrolet agency is located at the intersection of San Jacinto and Boll Streets. Irving Boulevard near Farrington is in an industrial area where numerous businesses are located. Ross and Ol-

ive Streets intersection, and San Jacinto and Harwood Streets intersection, are in the downtown area where numerous office buildings, parking lots and other businesses are located." The notation that there were 'marks' at an intersection, where only one mark would be needed if it was a business, suggest that Lee may have placed marks for the four telephone numbers I'd given him at the locations he used to call me. He would have to keep track. There was also a mark at Houston and Elm – for the location of the TSBD – but in fact, I had been given that number for emergency calls. Weberman's remarks about the marks on the ENCO city map are found here: http://www.latinamericanstudies.org/belligerence/veciana-oswald.htm (Retrieved May 1, 2013).

30. Memorandum 89-61-742. From warrant-less police search of David Ferrie's apartment by New Orleans Police, reported by Lt. Raymond Comstock, copied to the FBI by SA Regis Kennedy, Mar. 21, 1964. http://jfk.hood.edu/Collection/Weisberg Subject Index Files/C Disk/Comstock Raymond Lieutenant/Item 06.pdf.

31.Ruth Paine told the Warren Commission that Lee never offered any money for all she had done for his family. (Why would he have to, since Paine had offered to pay Marina $10 a week (equal to $90 a week in today's funds), to teach her Russian, plus free room, board and medical and dental bills paid?)

32. www.dallasnews.com, News, JFK 50, "Reflect " Oct. 12, 2013. (Retrieved 10/12/2013).

Chapter Fifteen

The End Game

Nov. 2, 1963: An informant named "Lee" successfully saves Kennedy's life in Chicago (see Nov. 12, James Hosty entry and the Nov. 17 Telex entry)

> **Secret Service** Re: David Ferrie: During his last trip, in early November 1963, he flew Taca Airlines and made one stop in Mexico City. (Weberman, Nodule 24)

Nov. 4, 1963: The last phase of Carlos Marcello's deportation trial, relentlessly pursued by Bobby Kennedy, begins in New Orleans.

Nov. 5, 1963: HSCA: On the second day of Marcello's trial, David purchases a .38 revolver.

Nov. 9-10, 1963: David spends this weekend in conference at Marcello's Churchill Farms, Inc. Marcello's 6,400 acre swamp, forest and farm complex, with barns and a big house, is hardly palatial, but the holding is huge, private, and guarded.

Nov. 11, 1963: In his FAA application form for a commercial pilot's license, David says *he has use of a Cessna 206*. (Stephen Roy says this plane is "…probably owned by his longtime friend Lewis 'Buster' Abadie.") David now resumes flying commercially, this time for businesses affiliated with the Marcello crime family, such as the Marinos, and with Marcello's brothers, Joe, Sammy, etc. *David Ferrie is now a Mafia pilot.*

FBI Agent Hosty Destroys a Note from Oswald

Nov. 12, 1963: The June 13, 2011 *Sarasota Herald-Tribune* says Lee Oswald visited the FBI office [in Dallas] and left a terse handwritten note to [FBI agent James] Hosty, who was in the field at the time.

It reportedly stated: "If you have anything you want to learn about me, come talk to me directly. If you don't cease bothering my wife, I will take appropriate action and report this to the proper authorities." ... Hosty's name and number were discovered in Oswald's address book. Looking to assuage Hoover's fears that Oswald might have been an FBI informant, Hosty's supervisor, Gordon Shanklin, ordered Hosty to destroy the note. Hosty was temporarily suspended from duty when the truth came out during congressional hearings about his having misled the Warren Commission.

So, was the note to Hosty supposedly destroyed "to assuage Hoover's fears that Oswald might have been an FBI informant"? Then it couldn't have been about leaving Lee's wife alone, could it? If the note had said only what Hosty claims, there would have been no reason to destroy it. But what if the note said something like: "My wife knows nothing. Leave her alone. You need to meet me, because I have information of vital importance regarding the safety of a very important person." Such a message, having been ignored, would have had to be destroyed. Such a message could have come from an FBI informant. Such a message might have been about saving Kennedy. Ten days earlier, on Nov. 2, a person named "Lee" had successfully contacted the FBI in Chicago, saving Kennedy's life. Lee may have attempted to do the same thing with Agent Hosty.

James Hosty, FBI: Lee Oswald called him a traitor.

"THE BOMB"

Joan Mellen tells us David Ferrie began to carry around a manila file, which he nicknamed "the *Bomb*." It would "blow this city apart if he ever released it,"(this is after the assassination). She describes Jimmy Johnson, the young man who spied on Dave for Garrison, and who found Dave dead on Feb. 22, 1967, as saying he found "a loose-leaf paper with a diagram on it" in a notebook marked "Files, 1963." Antiques dealer Clara "Bootsie" Gay also saw the diagram, which Wray Gill's secretary was then intent on destroying. It was of a car, as seen from a great distance above, in what appeared to be the layout of Dealey Plaza. An image of a plane suggested that shots could come from the plane to shoot JFK. There were many photos and other diagrams as well. Author

James DiEugenio wrote, "It is hard after reading their descriptions not to conclude that Ferrie had some advance knowledge of how the actual circumstances of the assassination in Dealey Plaza were going to occur."[1]

Since I had seen a manila folder, and MKULTRA papers in Dave's possession, in what was probably Dave's 'strongbox' at the time, I have speculations, as do others, about "The Bomb." I can only theorize, but suspect that Dave made, or had copies made, of the ideas that were being presented to get rid of Kennedy. Handwriting on such diagrams could identify the plotters.

David Ferrie often used the coffee shop at the Lakefront Airport as an "office" to recruit students interested in flying lessons. Around 1961, the whole building was fitted with thick sheets of concrete, covering the original Art Deco façade. It was deliberately done to make the building as strong as a bomb shelter. When Dave told me that he kept his "important stuff" in a "bomb shelter" he probably meant Lakefront He said he had key information about the Kennedy assassination safely tucked away in "the bomb shelter." I didn't know where any bomb shelter was located in New Orleans until I heard about Lakefront.

Lakefront Airport, circa 1963. The airport's main building was an official nuclear bomb shelter.

Nov. 16-17, 1963: David spends this weekend in conference at Marcello's Churchill Farms, Inc.

He is working out strategies for Marcello's upcoming deportation trial. This includes ways and means to reach jurors in order to threaten and bribe them.

Nov. 17, 1963: 20-year-old Layton Martens moves into David's apartment after being kicked out of his mother's house. On Nov. 25 he tells FBI that "3330 Louisiana Avenue" (sic) is his address. He says he has known David five years, and Alvin Beauboeuf about one year. (FBI File # NO 89-69, SA Ronald A. Hoverson)

THE TELEX

Nov. 17, 1963: Lee made a Sunday call – a rarity on the Call Wheel. He said he was under pressure and could not get away to talk, because he was being watched. He would try to call later, but if it was impossible, I would have to make an emergency call [to the TSBD] to start our call wheel again.

The whereabouts of Lee Harvey Oswald on this weekend remain unknown" according to outsiders, but Lee told me he was meeting with members of the assassination ring. Coincidentally, James Files says he was with Lee Oswald this weekend. I know Lee sent a TELEX at this time, in an attempt to save Kennedy's life (and at risk of his own) to the FBI.

David Ferrie's call record shows he was likely in Houston on the 17th, the same day Lee sent the Telex: Nov.17, 1963 (call to) New Orleans (from) Houston [source: Peter Whitmey]

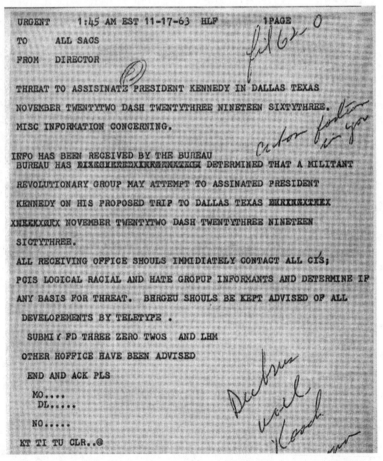

"End and ack pls": ("End and act, pls") "Assisinate" "sictythree" and "immediately" reflect the poor spelling of our very own Lee Oswald, who was dyslexic. He obviously had to type in haste, with no time to look up the correct spelling. The Telex had been destroyed but was reconstructed by New Orleans FBI Special Agent William Walter, the security clerk on duty that night.

Researchers tend to think the Telex, purportedly sent from DC, went everywhere, but it may have been sent to only a few cities – the ones where Kennedy had been or would soon visit. It would not take that much time for Hoover to remove such files from so few locations. Cities such as Chicago, Dallas, Austin, Fort Worth, New Orleans, and Miami would have received the Telex. The designation "All SAGS" might have simply meant to all SAGS at each location. The Telex numbers for the various FBI offices in the country were posted, by the way, in Banister's office, right next to his own Telex machine. Lee would have memorized the most important numbers. What has to be understood is that Lee

Accused Agent Says JFK Guards Were Lax

Abraham Bolden tried to get justice for JFK. His punishment was severe, including placement in an insane asylum.

got access to a Telex. He either sneaked into an office that had a Telex machine, or he was allowed to use one. He could even have used the Telex at the Dallas FBI office. Either way, the Telex made a racket when used. Lee may have risked his life to send it.

Nov. 18-19, 1963: Layton Martens says Alvin Beauboeuf stayed at David Ferrie's apartment both of these days, as did he. (FBI File 89-69, Nov. 25, 1963)

NOVEMBER 20, 1963, WEDNESDAY

Early afternoon: I call the TSBD person-to-person, asking for "the new janitor" Lee Oswald (the word "Harvey" is penciled into the name in the call record later, by the FBI. "J.A." are the first two letters in "janitor"– the initials for "Judyth Anne" – just as in the *Times-Picayune* message back in April. When I ask for the "new janitor" Lee knows who is placing the person-to-person call. Lee is not a janitor at the TSBD. He is a clerk in the shipping department. The time at which I placed the call told Lee when to call me back, and at what phone number, due to the Call Wheel. No actual message was exchanged because the person-to-person call (as planned) was rejected. The call appeared to have come from Covington.

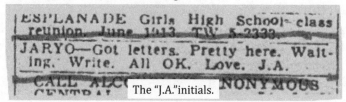

ESPLANADE Girls High School class reunion June 14-13 TW 5-2333.
JARYO—Got letters. Pretty here. Waiting. Write. All OK. Love. J.A.
CALL ALCO...NONYMOUS
CENTRAL

The "J.A." initials.

FBI: Mrs. COOPER stated that this call was placed by an adult female who was very polite, had no speech impediment, no accent, and who appeared to be familiar with the proceedings in placing long distance calls ... the answering party in Dallas, who was a female, was asked by her for LEE HARVEY [sic] OSWALD. The answering party advised she did not know who Oswald was. At this point, according to Mrs. COOPER, the calling party advised that OSWALD was a new employee. Mrs. Cooper thinks the calling party said that OSWALD was the janitor. Mrs. Cooper stated at this point the answering party said "oh" as if she knew who it was, and the call was completed.[2]

When Lee rejected this person-to-person call to the TSBD, I knew he had received it and that he would call back a certain number of hours later, according to the Call Wheel. At 11:00 PM, Dallas time, only 37 ½ hours before Kennedy was shot, Lee called and apologized for not calling me back on Sunday, saying he did not have the privacy he needed to talk to me. For the next hour and a half, we talked our hearts out. It was the most ominous call I've ever experienced. But Lee said he was no longer alone. He said an abort team had formed, and would come in to help him.

THE PLANNING MEETING AT TURTLE CREEK, DALLAS

Lee told me that a meeting was held at 3525 Turtle Creek, in Dallas, around 6:00 PM on November 20. Lee pretended to feed ducks at the pond area and creek running alongside the wooded road, while using binoculars to get the license plates of cars driving into the gated area of this posh, luxury apartment building. Later, he obtained information from the black doorman. By late that evening, Lee had been able to learn that the plan to "go ahead" with the assassination was complete. A "trophy film" was going to be made of JFK's death, "with his eyes open, and they were going to pass the film around." If the party at the Murchison's home the next night occurred (which was possible), that meeting appraised those attending of the certainty of Friday's plans."

3525 Turtle Creek.

From the 3525 Turtle Creek websites: "When it was built in 1957, 3525 Turtle Creek was the tallest and most luxurious condo building in Dallas.... Oil magnate Clint Murchison Sr. maintained an apartment on the 5th floor of 3525 Turtle Creek ... Democrat

William A. Blakey served two incomplete terms in the U.S. Senate from Texas (1957, 1961) and was succeeded in 1961 by another 3525 Turtle Creek resident, John Tower, first Republican U.S. Senator from Texas (1961-85)... Earle Cabell, mayor of Dallas (1961-64) and U.S. Congressman from Texas (1965-73) lived in the building."

THE ABORT TEAM

When Lee Oswald called me late on the 20th, Lee tells me he has joined an "abort team" that is trying to save Kennedy's life, but fears he will be killed because he has "seen too many faces. Lee also told me: "I believe I saved his life a few weeks ago."

Decades later, former Secret Service agent Abraham Bolden will reveal to author James Douglass and others that someone named "Lee" called the FBI in Chicago, which led to Kennedy calling off his trip there, resulting in the arrest of armed men. Bolden was present when the FBI called his Secret Service office and told the agents there the news by telephone. Lee had been sending warnings and even threats to get more protection for Kennedy. He was even playing the role of a willing assassin to avoid suspicion. His plans are to stay close to where he is told to be, until it is too late to replace him with somebody else. His words to that effect: "If I stay, that will be one less bullet aimed at Kennedy."[3]

Tosh Plumlee

William "Tosh" Plumlee (CIA contract pilot, who knew Lee Oswald by sight) verifies existence of an abort team:[4] "...the CIA was our support people. We were military intelligence...[John] Roselli was on board the aircraft.... Our objective ... to try to stop cross-triangulation gunfire on an ambush. We had people that filtrated out into the Plaza and the object there was ...do anything you can to eliminate the actual assassination...."[5]

In 1999, Jim Marrs told me that Tosh and I had both independently brought up the "abort team," about which nobody else had publicly spoken. Tosh later stated that the "abort mission" may have been infiltrated.

The abort team was a last-ditch attempt to make a difference. I had no idea that anyone else could confirm that an abort team existed, when I spoke to Marrs about it. At that time, he was flabbergasted that I knew about the team.

Lee had said: "Even though they're going to try to kill him, I've sent out information that might be able to save him."

Next, Lee told me, "You know how we wondered who my handler was? Mr. B? Benson, or Benton, or Bishop? Well ... he's from Fort Worth ... it has to be Phillips. Phillips is the traitor. Phillips is behind this," Lee stressed to me. "I need you to remember that name. David Atlee Phillips."[6]

Lee then said there were two other names he needed me to remember: Bobby Baker and Billy Sol Estes. He said the assassination itself was not their doing, but it was *because* of them, and I was never to forget their names. My thoughts seemed to be racing every direction at once, as I frantically sought a solution. "Is there any way you could get out of this? Something you haven't thought of?"

"They'd just get another gun to take my place," Lee said. "If I stay, that will be one less bullet aimed at Kennedy." His words seared into my soul: "*If I stay, that will be one less bullet aimed at Kennedy.*" They would haunt me forever.

When I cried out that I hated the human race, and all its evils, he corrected me.

"Stop it!" he commanded. "I can still do something. Maybe I can fire a warning shot."

I was speechless. Shocked.

"The Secret Service will react," Lee said. "The Chief might react. Even the driver." The thought of Lee firing a warning shot, and then the many guns of the Secret Service team turned towards him terrified me into silence.

After the pause, Lee said: "I'll love you as long as my heart is still beating." He told me that when he met again, he would be wearing the brown shirt I had bought for him, and that he would not be wearing "that demned wedding ring."

"Humans should live as long as oak trees!" I mourned, recalling a poem Lee had read to me called "Oak and Lily."

"But lilies are beautiful, too," he countered. "Besides, I'm no dummy. As you said, yourself, I still have some tricks up my sleeve."

Then Lee asked me to pray for him. I sorrowfully said an "Our Father" and he repeated it after me. When I finished,[7] he said, "I'm satisfied. It's a very old cry to God. Maybe He will hear it."

"I love you, Lee," I whispered, as I pressed myself against the wall of the payphone, hoping to get inches closer to the man I loved, as he spoke the last words I would ever hear him say to me: "Goodbye, Juduffki. I love you," he said. Then he hung up the phone, and the silence began. It was almost midnight, as I walked back home alone, oblivious to the darkness around me, worrying only about the dangers that Lee faced.

Much of the information in the timeline below for those fateful days (unless otherwise noted) is from the Ira Woods' chronology in *The Assassination Research Journal* (ARJ).[8] While focused primarily on assumed and speculated actions of David Ferrie, this timeline also highlights some events in Dallas and elsewhere.

11:05 AM, November 21, 1963: Air Force One leaves Andrews Air Force Base.. Aboard Air Force One today, JFK speaks to Congressman Henry Gonzalez. He is responding to Gonzalez's fears about Dallas. JFK says: "Henry, the Secret Service told me they had taken care of everything, there's nothing to worry about."

6:25 PM, November 21, 1963: Lee's last night with his family is misrepresented: The respected ARJ chronology says "Lee Harvey Oswald and Marina quarrel. Four times tonight, LHO asks Marina to move with him to a nicer apartment in Dallas. Each time, she refuses." This gives a sinister sheen to Lee's last night with Marina. After all, they quarreled four times! But did it happen? Here's Marina Oswald's Warren Commission testimony:

> **Mrs. Oswald**: He said that he was lonely because he hadn't come the preceding weekend, and he wanted to make his peace with me.
>
> **Mr. J. Lee Rankin** (Warren Commission General Counsel): Did you say anything to him then?
>
> **Mrs. Oswald**: He tried to talk to me but I would not answer him, and he was very upset.
>
> **Mr. Rankin**: Were you upset with him?
>
> **Mrs. Oswald**: I was angry, of course. He was not angry – he was upset. I was angry. He tried very hard to please me. He spent quite a bit of time putting away diapers and played with the children on the street.
>
> **Mr. Rankin**: How did you indicate to him that you were angry with him?
>
> **Mrs. Oswald**: By not talking to him.
>
> **Mr. Rankin**: And how did he show that he was upset?
>
> **Mrs. Oswald**: He was upset over the fact that I would not answer him. He tried to start a conversation with me several times, but I would not answer. And he said that he didn't want me to be angry at him because this upsets him. On that day, he suggested that we rent an apartment in

Dallas. He said that he was tired of living alone and perhaps the reason for my being so angry was the fact that we were not living together. That if I want to he would rent an apartment in Dallas tomorrow – that he didn't want me to remain with Ruth any longer, but wanted me to live with him in Dallas. He repeated this not once but several times, but I refused. And he said that once again I was preferring my friends to him, and that I didn't need him.

Mr. Rankin: What did you say to that?

Mrs. Oswald: I said it would be better if I remained with Ruth until the holidays, he would come, and we would all meet together. That this was better … we were spending less money. And I told him to buy me a washing machine, because two children it became too difficult to wash by hand.

Mr. Rankin: What did he say to that?

Mrs. Oswald: He said he would buy me a washing machine.

Mr. Rankin: What did you say to that?

Mrs. Oswald: Thank you. That it would be better if he bought something for himself – that I would manage.

Mr. Rankin: Did this seem to make him more upset, when you suggested that he wait about getting an apartment for you to live in?

Mrs. Oswald: Yes. He then stopped talking and sat down and watched television and then went to bed. I went to bed later. It was about 9 o'clock when he went to sleep. I went to sleep about 11:30. <snip>

Mr. Rankin: Why did you stay awake until 11:30? Were you still angry with him?

Mrs. Oswald: No, not for that reason, but because I had to wash dishes and be otherwise busy with the household – take a bath."

Lee told Marina that he would rent an apartment, if Marina would come to live with him, well knowing Marina would reject the idea. He even offered to get a new washing machine, but Marina turned it down. She was happy where she was. I see this as Lee making sure Marina would be okay, knowing that tomorrow, he likely could do no more for her. The next morning he would leave $170 and his wedding ring behind. There were no real quarrels.

GREG BURNHAM: EVIDENCE OF TREASON

On November 21, 1963 a "draft copy of NSAM 273 is prepared for LBJ's signature as President, by McGeorge Bundy. It will not be 'discovered' until 1991 in the LBJ Library archives. This National Security Memorandum effectively negates the withdrawal of troops and commits American support to the South Vietnamese government."

> **Greg Burnham** (author/researcher): Perhaps the most powerful evidence indicating that select Senior Administration Officials and Senior Military personnel may have had foreknowledge of the plot to assassinate … Kennedy, is found in the DRAFT of … NSAM Number 273. There are several smoking guns, but the one that initially stands out as the most obvious is the date of the DRAFT … signed by McGeorge Bundy, Special Assistant to the President for National Security. The DRAFT was written and dated November 21st, 1963 less than 24 hours before the assassination. It was ostensibly the result of the meetings that took place the previous day at the Honolulu Conference. The first sentence is indeed quite revelatory of its dubious nature: "The President has reviewed the discussions of South Vietnam which occurred in Honolulu, and has discussed the matter further with Ambassador Lodge." That is false."[9]

9:58 PM, November 21, 1963: JFK is in Houston's Coliseum. He has been busy continuously since leaving the White House.

Late evening, Fort Worth, November 21: After Johnson enters JFK's Texas Hotel suite, "an argument erupts between the two men that can be heard by the hotel staff outside in the hallway. Reportedly, they fight about Johnson's demand to change the seating position in the cars for the next morning's motorcade in Dallas. Johnson wants Governor Connally to ride with him and wants Senator Yarborough, his bitter political enemy, to ride in the Presidential Limousine with JFK. The President flatly refuses and Johnson leaves the suite 'like a pistol.'

"Jacqueline Kennedy asks, 'What was that all about? He seemed mad.'

"JFK answers, 'That's just Lyndon. He's in trouble.'

"Tonight, Jackie will sleep in a separate room in the suite, because JFK needs to sleep on a special hard mattress for his back. It is too narrow for both of them."

THE INFAMOUS "PARTY"

In a highly disputed event recounted by several witnesses, Richard Nixon and J. Edgar Hoover dined with oil baron Clint Murchison in Dallas, Texas. Also attending the party: H. L. Hunt, John Curington, George Brown of Brown & Root, former Texas Republican congressman Bruce Alger, and John J. McCloy of Chase Manhattan Bank and the Rockefeller interests.[10]

McCloy will be placed on the Warren commission within the week. Clint Murchison owns Holt, Rinehart and Winston – Hoover's publisher. The men attend with their wives and/or escorts.

After dinner, the men retire to a private room to talk. [Hoover is in Washington the next day. Richard Nixon will fly into New York.] Nixon, unlike most citizens in the country, will not quite remember "when" he heard of the assassination.

> **Madeleine Brown**, LBJ's mistress remembers: There was a real atmosphere of uneasiness at that party.

It's a social gathering, but as soon as LBJ arrives later in the evening, the women are excluded, and there ensues a private meeting of men behind the big double doors of the drawing room. As Madeleine Brown is preparing to leave, LBJ comes out of the private meeting red-faced and reportedly tells her: "After tomorrow, that's the last time those god-damned Kennedys will embarrass me again!" (LBJ's friend, convicted murderer, Mac Wallace, is also in Dallas on this day.)

The Murchison Mansion

Private Eugene B. Dinkin, Richard Case Nagell, Gilberto Alvarado Ugarte, Joseph Milteer, Rose Cherami and Abraham Bolden have all made public statements concerning the imminent assassination of JFK. Of these people, Dinkin, Cherami, Nagell, and Ugarte are threatened with being declared to be mentally unstable. Secret Service Agent Bolden will be sent to prison [part of that time, he will be drugged in a mental hospital] on a charge of discussing a bribe with two counterfeiters. He will be subsequently released and claim that he had been framed by the Secret Service and convicted in order to silence him regarding the Kennedy threat.

Ugarte. Cherami. Nagell Milteer.

Bolden, after his release, has lived an honorable and praiseworthy life. He is deep-

Abraham Bolden and author, in his home, October 2014.

ly respected by all who know him. Bolden has also reported that informant "Lee" saved JFK's life in Chicago.

Later in the evening: Jack Ruby reportedly dines at the Egyptian Lounge with his old friend and financial backer Ralph Paul. The Lounge is run by Joseph and Sam Campisi. Joseph acknowledges being very close to Carlos Marcello – each Christmas he sends Marcello and his associates 260 pounds of Italian sausage. He also makes as many as twenty telephone calls a day to New Orleans.

The last full day in John F. Kennedy's life comes quietly to an end.

Endnotes

1. http://www.ctka.net/mellen_review.html. (Retrieved 05/15/2013).

2. In tandem, Ian Griggs reported that "CE 3000 is an FBI report of an interview with Leslie Lawson, the owner and manager of Gray's Cleaners, 1209 Eldorado, Oak Cliff on 5th December 1963 … that location is only a hundred yards from Oswald's rooming house. Lawson stated … that he had seen Oswald on several occasions at Sleight's Speed Wash, 1101 North Beckley…[now]Reno's Speed Wash {August 1963]. A former Reno's employee, Joseph Johnson, was interviewed by the FBI on 28th July 1964 and stated that on the evening of 20th or 21st November 1963, Lee Harvey Oswald was 'washing laundry at Reno's Speed Wash.' Oswald, he said, remained there, reading magazines, until midnight. (CE 3001)" http://spot.acorn.net/jfkplace/09/fp.back_issues/25th_Issue/myth.html (Retrieved Dec. 15, 2012).

Lee got his laundry washed at Ruth Paine's on a regular basis. He would actually be at Paine's home the next evening. However, "doing laundry" gave him an excuse to use the payphone.

3. Lee's hour-and-a-half long call to me has never been fully transcribed. Most

of it was too personal. Some elements remain too controversial for publication.

4. William Robert "Tosh" Plumlee has suffered, as I have, at the hands of the "moderated" Education Forum. Tosh wrote this to the Deep Politics Forum Sept. 2008: (RE: two apartments used by Lee in Dallas, just as he used two apartments in New Orleans; minor edits) "Ask Jim Marrs and Peter Lemkin ... I took Jim Marrs to both of these apts, Beckley and Elsbeth, also [took] Nigel Turner and Oliver Stone's people.... The apt behind the Beckley St address, LHO visited the Cubans many times and I was there (the back building directly behind Beckley). My initials were carved in a draining board at that rear apt. and as of 1991 were still there "WRP" as confirmed by the owners. The two Cubans who rented that apt were thrown out because of the messes they made and all the late night visitors and the carved WRP on the draining board. This was also told to the Church Committee and Congressman Thomas Downing in 1975 before the HSCA was formed.... I was attacked at the time I posted most of this information [Feb. 2008 at Education Forum]and it went nowhere.... I was just trying to help researchers." https://deeppoliticsforum.com/forums/showthread.php?288-Tosh-Plumlee-posted-with-Tosh-s-permission (Retrieved Aug. 1, 2013).

5. Plumlee continued: "... or impending assassination by creating a diversion, bumping shoulders, anything that you could do ... we were looking for 9 people on cross triangulation. ..We had prior knowledge that the attempt was going to be made ... Dealey Plaza ... [was] the most logical place to make an ambush style hit ... I was there as a pilot ... a participant ... a spotter. We [had to] find out if ...

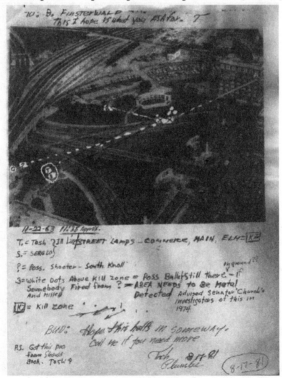

Antonio Veciana, 1963.   Tosh Plumlee with Antonio Veciana.

it was going to be a "hit" and then we would take 'em out." Post to Deep Politics Forum, July, 2008 and similar email to Judyth Vary Baker (from Wim Dankbaar) in Feb. 2000.

6. Antonio Veciana testified in 1976 to the HSCA. He was shot in the head in 1979, but survived. Tosh Plumlee has courageously filled in many blanks; Jim Marrs told me that he could confirm my statement that an "abort team" existed on Nov. 22, 1963. In late 1999/2000, I had told Marrs that Lee Oswald told me he was a member of an abort team that tried to save Kennedy's life.

Veciana finally admitted that "Maurice Bishop" was David Atlee Phillips on Nov. 22, 2013. Phillips had been Chief of Covert Action at the CIA's Mexico City Station in 1963. (See below.)

> Dear Marie Fonzi:
>
> You may publish the following statement from me:
>
> "Maurice Bishop, my CIA contact agent was David Atlee Phillips. Phillips or Bishop was the man I saw with Lee Harvey Oswald in Dallas on September 1963."
>
> Best Regards,
>
> Antonio Veciana

HSCA investigator Gaeton Fonzi and his assistant, Patricia Orr, who have been responsible for gathering the majority of the verifiable information we have about David Ferrie, helped to bring out this revelation.

7. As a Catholic, I did not put the 'Protestant' ending upon the prayer: "For Thine is the kingdom, and the power, and the glory, forever, Amen."

8. See http://www.assassinationresearch.com/v2n1/chrono2.pdf online. (Re-

trieved July 31, 2013.

9. The DRAFT was written on the evening of the 21st. JFK and Jackie left Washington aboard Air Force One for their 2-day, 5-city "whirlwind" Texas trip on the 21st ... the conference took place all day on the 20th and part of the 21st in Hawaii without the President in attendance. Since he and the First Lady were en route to Texas from Washington on the 21st, it is therefore quite clear that the President could not have reviewed the discussions conducted in Honolulu in depth, nor could he have spoken with Ambassador Lodge in a meaningful way about the conference before the DRAFT of NSAM 273 was written. For full details, see: http://jfklancer.com/NSAM273.html (Retrieved 03/03/2014).

10. Researchers Edgar Tatro and Harrison E. Livingstone knew Madeline Brown personally and obtained information convincing them that Brown's story had meat. On Sept. 3, 2014, Tatro wrote to me, regarding Joan Mellen's 2013 dissent: "The party happened."

CHAPTER SIXTEEN

The End of the Republic

NOVEMBER 22, 1963: DAY OF DOOM

At 9:00 AM Carlos Marcello's trial begins in New Orleans. Witnesses say David Ferrie is in court during Marcello's trial this morning.[1] He is not inside the courtroom, however, when President Kennedy's death is announced. George Lardner, who spoke to David by phone, (see Feb. 22, 1967 timeline) said David was sitting outside the courtroom conversing with sheriff deputies when it was announced that Kennedy was shot. A one-hour recess was then announced.

9:15 AM, Dallas: Ruth Paine says she takes her small daughter, Lynn, to the dentist and then runs errands. A car resembling Paine's will be seen minutes after Kennedy is shot, speeding away with Lee Oswald or a lookalike. Paine has left the television set on for Marina Oswald – who says she watches it all morning without getting dressed.

Ruth Paine with children Chris and Lynn, 1963

11:40 – 11:55 AM, Dallas: The Kennedy motorcade is getting assembled. The press truck which holds photographers and is usually placed in front of JFK's limo, is moved too far back in the motorcade to get photos, making it easier to hide the true assassins.

> **Vincent Palamara**: *Dallas Morning News* reporter Tom Dillard (reported): "We lost our position at the airport. I understood we were to have been quite a bit closer..."
>
> **Palamara**: ...all previous trips, incl. Florida, has press/ photographers very close in front and behind JFK's limousine.[2]

11:50 AM, Dallas: Dallas Policeman (motorcycle escort), Marion L. Baker: "When we got to the airport, our sergeant instructed me that there wouldn't be anybody riding beside the President's car."

Baker receives these instructions about five minutes before the motorcade leaves Love Field.[3]

John Stevens, Rutter Lawrence and Philip Ben Hathaway see a very tall man (6'6 or 6'7) wearing a suit carrying a rifle case "walking towards Commerce Street" past them. The man resembles Gerry Patrick Hemming, who stated it was not he, but a "doppelganger" who was in Dealey Plaza that day.(ARJ)

11:55 AM: The Kennedy motorcade leaves Love Field. The motorcade will be running late through Dallas. As the motorcade begins, film footage from ABC television's Dallas/Fort Worth affiliate WFAA shows SS agent Henry J. Rybka being recalled by shift leader (and commander of the follow-up car detail) Emory P. Roberts. As the limo begins leaving the area, Rybka's frustration – he is supposed to be riding on the back of JFK's car – is made clear as he throws his arms up several times before, during,  and after the follow-up car passes him by. The motorcade is composed of dark cars, except Vice President Johnson's car (light blue) and LBJ's secret service agents (they ride in a white car behind him). (ARJ) [In 2014, Rybka will deny, saying that his gestures only meant, "OK, I will guard the plane and go eat lunch." But his gestures were repeated – obviously a show of confusion and exasperation.]

12:29 PM: The police radio, Channel One, goes dead for at least four minutes, rendering communication in the motorcade impossible.(ARJ)

12:30 PM: JFK's limo passes a group of sheriff's deputies at Main and Houston, in front of the Sheriff's Office. (Later, the deputies will almost unanimously agree that they believe the shots came from the railroad yards behind the Grassy Knoll. Of the twenty Dallas Police deputies who will give statements "sixteen thought the assassin had fired from the area of the grassy knoll..." (ARJ) Lyndon Johnson is listening to a small walkie-talkie held over the back seat. The device is turned low. (This description comes from Sen. Ralph Yarborough who is riding with Johnson.)(ARJ)

~12:30 PM: Rose Cherami, who had been found injured, and eventually was taken to the same hospital at Jackson, LA where the cancer experiments were held, tells hospital staff Kennedy will now die. "[She] is watching television with several nurses when a spot report about JFK's motorcade comes on. Cherami says "This is when it is going to happen!" The nurses dismiss her remarks because Cherami is suffering from drug withdrawal symptoms – until moments later, when JFK is shot. Cherami has also told one of the hospital interns "…that one of the men involved in the plot was a man named Jack Rubenstein." (*Probe* magazine, Vol. 6, No. 5)

12:31 PM: Shooting begins. In seven seconds, it is over. It will take SS agent Clint Hill (Jackie's guard, who had no business riding on a different car to begin with) twelve seconds to reach JFK's limo. It takes three seconds for LBJ's Secret Service agent to cover the Vice President with his own body, because he is in the car with LBJ. Roy Kellerman, the SS agent "protecting" JFK in the front seat of JFK's limo, never moves to cover JFK. Many witnesses say Secret Service agent William Greer, the driver, puts on the brakes, perhaps fearing an ambush. (David Ferrie will later make a study of the bullets' trajectories.)

Photographer/photo retouching specialist Ike Altgens captures the JFK hit on film within two seconds of the impact of a bullet that strikes JFK's head. In the photo, a figure is visible in the background that many people think strongly resembles Lee Harvey Oswald, standing in the front entrance of the Texas School Book Depository building. If it is, in fact, Oswald, he could not have been on the sixth

The famous "Altgens photo." As first shot is heard, Secret Service agents do not look up at the 6th floor. They look ahead, or at the Dal-Tex building. Motorcade is so slow that LBJ's Secret Service agents (white car) open a door, done when speed is very slow. JFK's Secret Service agents are standing on the wrong car. Agents will be ordered to stay on the Secret Service car when JFK is hit by the next bullets. Motorcycle police are protecting the Secret Service car, not JFK's.

floor when the shots were fired. The Warren Commission identifies the man as Billy Nolan Lovelady, another building employee.(ARJ)

Controversy rages today as the Altgens photo was almost certainly retouched.

James T. Tague, standing near the concrete abutment of the tri-ple underpass, about 260 feet downhill from the President's position, is hit on his cheek by a piece of concrete blown off the street curb when it is hit by one of the bullets fired at the President, forc-ing the creation of the [patently absurd] "single bullet theory" because one rifle could not have made four shots in the time frame observed.(ARJ)

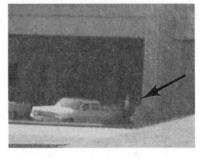

> **James Tague:** J. Edgar Hoover didn't want me to exist. I was the only proof that there were more shots fired. They said I didn't see anything that would shed any light on the assassination. I was just one man slightly injured. I was ignored. (Tague, to the author, Nov. 22, 2103. Tague died Feb. 28, 2014)

The trajectory of the bullet suggests it came from the Dal-Tex building, not the TSBD. The curb is patched and later removed. The patch, of course, made testing of the bullet's composition impossible.

Agent John D. Ready jumps off Secret Service follow-up car to dash to JFK limo. He is recalled by special Agent-in-Charge Emory Roberts. Roberts also orders all other agents not to move. Secret Service expert Vincent Palamara, in *Survivors Guilt*, shows that JFK did not order Secret Service agents off his car, and that indeed, he had no authority to do so. But during the 50th anniversary hoopla in 2013, the "Kennedy Detail" told the world in a television special that JFK was the cause of his own death by ordering them off the car.

The Grassy Knoll: Dozens of witnesses who said they heard a shot come from the Grassy Knoll are never officially interviewed. As the final shot occurs, Kenneth O'Don-nell (in the Secret Service car behind JFK) begins to bless himself. Dave Powers murmurs: "Jesus, Mary, and Joseph ..." Powers will later say that he and O'Donnell clearly heard shots come from the grassy knoll. Powers

says he felt they were "riding into an ambush," explaining why William Greer begins to slow the limo.

The Last Two Shots: Many witnesses say the last two shots were "bang-bang." (Almost simultaneous...)

> **Secret Service agent Kellerman** (JFK limo, front seat): Let me give you an illustration.... You have heard the sound barrier, of a plane breaking the sound barrier, bang, bang? That is it. It was like a double bang – bang, bang. (Responding to WC's Arlen Specter, if Kellerman could describe the sound of the last two shots.)

The JFK Limo slows down or actually stops: Fifty-nine witnesses (ten police officers, seven Secret Service Agents, thirty-seven spectators, two Presidential aides, one Senator, one State Governor, and the First Lady of the USA will attest to Secret Service Agent William Greer's de-

celeration of the Presidential limousine, as well as his two separate looks back at JFK during the assassination. Greer will deny these accusations to the Warren Commission.

~12:32 PM: Victoria Adams and Sandra Styles rush out of the back door of the TSBD. They saw nobody coming down the stairs Oswald had to take to reach the 2nd floor lunchroom, where he was seen by Marion Baker no more than 90 seconds after the shooting.

Victoria Adams proves Lee was not on the 6th floor as claimed. Victoria and Sandra descended the stairs in the TSBD building at

Victoria Adams

the same time authorities said Lee Oswald had to have done the same. In the book by Barry Ernest, *The Girl on the Stairs*, Adams, who says she was threatened into silence, makes it clear she neither saw nor heard Lee Oswald on the stairs (Victoria died of cancer soon after speaking out). Lee could not have been on the 6th floor at the time claimed because he was seen no more than 90 seconds after the first shot was fired, on the second floor, by officer Marion Baker and TSBD boss Roy Truly.

Unexplained power and communication outages: (1) The interference on police Channel 1 stops. (The microphone has been "stuck" open for at least four minutes total). But first there is an electronic beeping – *the Morse code signal for "Victory."* (2) As Officer Marion Baker and Roy Truly leave the lunchroom and run from the 2nd floor to the 5th floor, the electricity and telephone service in the TSBD is suddenly restored. The west elevator moves from the 5th floor to the 1st. (3) The telephone system in Washington, D.C. is interrupted and, in some areas, goes dead and remains out of service for an hour. (4) Aboard Air Force One, Col. James B. Swindal overhears Roy Kellerman on the Secret Service radio channel speaking from JFK's limo: "Lancer is hurt. It looks bad. We have to get to a hospital." Moments later, Secret Service communications gear on Air Force One goes dead. Swindal receives the news that JFK is dead by tuning in to network television aboard the aircraft.

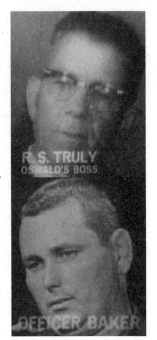

~**12:45 PM**: Eugene Hale Brading (calling himself Jim Braden) is arrested leaving the Dal-Tex building. He is an ex-con with reputed underworld ties and thirty-five arrests. He spent the previous night at the Cabana Hotel, owned by Joe Campisi, one of Marcello's men (Jack Ruby visited there at midnight). During the months preceding and after the assassination, Brading kept an office in the Pere Marquette Building in New Orleans. On the same floor, down the hall, from G. Wray Gill's office, is David Ferrie's office (#1701).(ARJ)

12:45 PM: At the Marcello trial in New Orleans, Judge Herbert W. Christenberry delivers his fifteen minute charge to the jury. Then a bailiff enters the courtroom and hands Christenberry a note. "As he reads it, a look of shock and consternation spreads over his face. Recovering quickly, he stands up and announces that President Kennedy has just been shot in Dallas and is feared dead. Carlos Marcello and his brother Joe file out of the courtroom for an hour's recess showing absolutely no emotion.... Also leaving the federal courthouse is David Ferrie."

So some say, but the best fit for when David Ferrie left the courtroom was when the judge called for an hour's recess. G. Wray Gill says he called his secretary after the verdict is given (but states the wrong hour – as he said he was told David left the office at 12:15, promising to return at 1:30) in his 1967 FBI interview. It's more likely that David reached Gill's office soon after the judge called the recess, was there until 1:15, told the secretary he would return in an hour, but did not. At about 3:30, Gill would have called his office and learned David had not returned there."

Time Gap: This is the first unaccounted-for time gap in David Ferrie's activities that day – between about 2:30 PM and when he is next reported being with personal friends.[4]

1:00 PM, Nov. 23, 1963: President John Fitzgerald Kennedy is pronounced dead, martyred for his country.

> **Larry Hancock**: …sources…indicate that although Ferrie was with Marcello in the courtroom on Nov. 22, he did not wait for the verdict but left beforehand…. shortly after the word came from Dallas…

Lyndon Johnson openly leaves Parkland Hospital with SS agent Rufus Youngblood, with no apparent worry about getting shot by a sniper.

> **Stephen Roy**: If you mean that he left the courtroom before the verdict, that is a hard thing to establish. There is a conflict and wiggle room in the few accounts in CD75.

3:20 PM: Carlos Marcello is acquitted. He walks from the courtroom showing no emotion. He will soon hold a victory party, which some people say David Ferrie briefly attended.

Dave told me Marcello had so much influence on the court system that he was able to set the end of the trial on the same day as JFK's assassination, to emotionally destroy Bobby Kennedy. It was no coincidence that Marcello's victory party was held November 22, 1963.

Nov. 22, 1963: Peninsular ChemResearch, FL

I had recently sent Dave a concoction I'd created at PenChem upon his request. It should have helped eradicate the sensation of burning at the urethral exit, in gonorrhea, which could be expedited with a catheter, using aromatic solutions I devised. Overcome by concerns looming before us, I realized I'd never asked Dave if it had done him any good. The state of Dave's ureteral tube was not my concern today. I was in anguish, worried about what would happen.

Then, soon after 1:30 PM, Florida time (12:30 PM, Dallas time), we heard "three shots" had been fired in Dealey Plaza! Soon, we learned the President had been seriously wounded. The television cut away from its regular programming. About an hour later, we heard that a priest had given last rites. This news was greeted with cheers and whistles of approval in the lab. That's when tears began running down my cheeks, despite all efforts to hide them.

"Good!" Mr. Mays said, slapping his big hand against his well-padded thigh.

"For God's sake!" I exploded, "This man is fighting for his life! What's the matter with you?" That was not the kind of language you were supposed to use with your boss, and immediately, I knew I'd crossed that invisible line. Seeing the expressions on the faces around me, I realized the terrible political error I had just made. I'd forgotten where I was, and who I was supposed to be. This was Florida! And I was a mere lab assistant. I squirmed under the malevolent glares, wiped my tears, and lowered my head. I had not only exposed myself as a Kennedy sympathizer; I could have jeopardized those who had lobbied to send me here. The poisonous whispers and sidelong glances at me continued, so I went to the sink and washed my face, put my lab coat up on a hook, and fell into a seat at the records desk, facing away from them all.

After a little while, the announcement was made: President Kennedy was dead. I could feel an aura of pure evil fill the room, like a dark presence. It was the closest I'd ever come to believing the devil existed.

Who would believe our government was being taken over from the inside? While Dave, Dr. Mary, Lee and I had done everything we could, we knew we were fighting forces much bigger than ourselves. I whispered to myself: *Remember where you are. Stay calm. You have to survive.* Finally, Lee's picture flashed on the screen. He had been beaten! I gasped. Mr. Mays noticed. "What's with you?" he shouted. "He's a God-damned Communist!"

Mays and Nancy, his main assistant, were totally puzzled at my behavior. First I cried because President Kennedy was killed, and now I was upset because they had caught the man who shot him. But I had lost more than they could understand.

And how much could Lee dare say, without exposing us? If he cried out, "I work for the CIA! I was loaned to them by the ONI!" his CIA and ONI contacts in the USSR would have been tortured for information and then executed. Marina's uncle, and Lee's ordinary friends there would probably be arrested. Lee had already told me so. He was a dead man walking. At least he had not been shot on the street, or during his arrest.

They have him. Look at his face. Un-re-touched photo with no added 'smirks.'

Perhaps police custody would provide some shield against those who wanted to silence him.

But would they try to force him to confess to a crime he not only didn't commit, but which he had tried to stop? I knew, all too well, the sickening answer to that.

Suddenly, I remembered the Call Wheel. Oh, no! I got it from my purse and checked it. Sure enough, Dave was supposed to call tonight. Thank God, I was still here! I had called Robert to take me home when everybody left, but he told me to stay (as I usually did on Fridays) to keep earning overtime money...for once, I was grateful for Robert's miserly ways! When it was time, I headed across a deserted tract of sand and crab grass to the pay phone. I looked at my watch. I am not certain of the actual time, after so many years, but I think it may have been around 5:30 PM Dallas time. I waited in the silence. When the phone rang, I didn't let it ring a second time.[5]

I have a very poor memory of all that happened to me before and after Lee's death. I used to believe that Dave called me 'right away' about the medical library card, but evidence available doesn't support it. Psychologists say that my memory loss of this time period was due to PTSS. It has taken years for me to reconstruct the exact order of things that happened between the shock of seeing Lee beaten and hounded by reporters, the shock of seeing him shot before my eyes, and the darkness of my mind for at least a day after that, but I'll do my best.

"The good news," Dave told me, in a calm, quiet voice designed to repair my frayed nerves, "is that we talked to Marcello's people, and Lee's going to get some high-powered legal help."[6] Dave said that La Cosa Nostra would not let "their boy" down. They had wanted Kennedy killed, and if they thought Lee had done them the favor, they were willing to exert some "influence."[7]

I later learned they had chosen Dean Andrews to exert the "influence" – but there was problem: Dean Andrews was in the hospital with pneumonia. His career as an assistant District Attorney in Jefferson Parish would be ruined by the reporting of the matter, which he later called a figment of his imagination due to sedatives. Token assistance to Lee Oswald would have assured Lee's Uncle Dutz Murret (who was close to Marcello) that his nephew had not been thrown to the wolves.

Marcello's attorney, Dean Andrews was called by a "Mr. Bertrand" and asked to defend Lee Oswald.

"But Dave," I protested. "Won't they arrest any of the real killers?"

"Of course not," he answered. "Besides, half of the guys they flew in wouldn't even know what city they were in. To shoot is what they do. It's just a job, to them. But we'll get Lee sprung," Dave exclaimed.

"Sprung?" I could hardly believe my ears.

"He's not the only one who got arrested," Dave said. "He's just getting all the publicity right now. You have no concept of how powerful the Mob is in Dallas. Look, Marcello got off the hook today, at the trial. Went scot-free. That's power. Marcello's lawyers are on top of it right now. And we'll be going over to Houston –me and my boys. I give you my oath – I swear – on a stack of Bibles," he went on, fiercely. "We'll get him out, or somebody will pay, big time."

I was used to Dave's hyperbole, but I did allow my hopes to rise a bit. Dave said he'd call back when he knew more. It would be to a different phone, of course, and very late. Meanwhile, he suggested that I pray to St. Jude.

Dave picked up his friend Al Beauboeuf sometime after 4:30, since he called me at 4:30 his time. His call didn't last long. I didn't know where Dave called from, and it was raining, but even so, Kohn Jr. High School was only a 15 minute drive from Dave's apartment.[8]

5:00 PM, Nov. 22: Al Beauboeuf said Dave picked him up and drove to David's apartment, reaching it at about 5:15 PM. (Stephen Roy says Layton Martens, John Irion and Johnny Johnson are there); they all watch TV as news about Kennedy's assassination unfolds. Lee Harvey Oswald, reported as arrested for shooting "a police officer" is already linked to Kennedy's murder by the media.[9]

6:00 PM, Nov. 22: Dave and Al Beauboeuf leave Dave's apartment. Layton Martens stays behind. His mom has kicked him out: perhaps he hopes she'll reconcile with him. Dave and Al drive to Melvin Coffey's place. Back in September, Coffey was arrested for giving alcohol to a minor, Ruth Kyler, who then attempted suicide. They arrive at about 6:30. Apparently while at Coffey's home, Dave calls Winterland ice rink. Presumably at Coffey's home, David also makes a reservation at [Marcello-owned] Alamotel, in Houston.

> **Stephen Roy:**(2000): (posting as Blackburst) ... the three discussed a weekend trip.... Ferrie and Alvin Roland Beauboeuf decided to take a vacation/business trip to Houston, and Coffey was invited along to help him chill out.[10]

> **Stephen Roy** (2005): At 6:30 Ferrie and Beauboeuf picked up Coffey and phoned [ice rink manager] Chuck Rolland in Houston.

> **Gus Russo** (quoting Beauboeuf): I was a former roller skating champion with dozens of medals. I wanted to see how good I'd do on ice. I had convinced Dave that ice skating was going to be the next big thing – like disco became in the seventies. We had been planning the trip for a couple of weeks.[11]

7:00 PM: David drives "the boys" to John Paul's restaurant near the airport at Kenner.

> **Stephen Roy** (posting as Blackburst) (2000): [They had]...dinner and drinks at John Paul's Restaurant, a hangout for pilots from Moisant Airport.

> **Stephen Roy** (2005): ... here Ferrie spoke with another pilot who gave him a weather update. (There had been a thunderstorm earlier.) At about 9:15 they left for Houston.

8:32 PM, November 22: As Dave and friends allegedly eat dinner at John Paul's, New Orleans Police tell FBI that David Ferrie is a pilot, was involved in anti-Castro activities and is a possible friend of Lee Harvey Oswald. This occurs before Jack Martin, out of spite, formally contacts FBI and police.

Memo: Dated 11/25/63, from ASAC J.T. Sylvester Jr. to SAC of New Orleans tells of a telephone contact at 8:32pm, 11/22/63, where David Ferrie's name is brought up in conjunction with Lee, and asks for "any information which would indicate that Oswald was friendly with Ferrie."[12] The memo was ignored.

DAVID FERRIE'S "VACATION"

David Ferrie will say he planned to skate, drink, party, and (later, says) go "goose hunting" on this day.

Dave is trying to hide his connections to Lee Oswald. His preplanned Texas "getaway" was an option based on contingency. While most of America watched the crime of the century unfold before their eyes, riveted to their TV sets, Dave and friends drove hundreds of miles in a driving rain for 'recreation.' Lee had been in contact with Dave, Mary Sherman, and me. In Houston, Dave will introduce himself to rink manager Chuck Rolland at the Winterland ice rink four or five times, by name, making sure Rolland won't forget he was there.

> **Stephen Roy** (posting as Blackburst 2000): During the trip, they checked in on radio and TV to see what was going on…
>
> **George Lardner** [*Washington Post* reporter, Feb. 22, 1967 interview]: Ferrie said he did leave for Texas on a trip with several acquaintances after leaving the courthouse but that he went to Galveston and Houston 'hunting geese,' and never set foot in Dallas.[13]

9:00 PM, Nov. 22: David Ferrie and his young friends Alvin Beauboeuf and Melvin Coffey commence a nerve-wracking 7.5-hour drive, at night, of 365 miles through on-and-off rain and road construction to Houston, Texas. One stated purpose of the trip is to look over an ice skating rink and to do some skating. His companions variously say the trip was planned two days or two weeks in advance.

> **FBI interview, Coffey**: [Coffey] said they left Kenner between 9:00 and 9:30 PM that night.
>
> **FBI interview, Ferrie:** [Ferrie] said that at approximately 9:00 PM or shortly after 9:00 PM, November 22, 1963, he, Beauboeuf and Coffey left John Paul's Restaurant to go to Houston.[14]
>
> **Stephen Roy**: (2005) As told to me, the trip had several purposes: The most important was to obtain a document from a man in Vinton …

"The most important was to obtain a document from a man in Vinton"? Then why does Dave drive all night, pass Vinton, and at 4:30 AM collapse at the Alamotel? After rest and food, he's at Winterland at 3:30 PM. Had Dave waited until 6:00 AM on the 23rd, he could have driven in good weather, picked up the document in Vinton at 10:00 AM, gone on to Houston, checked in at the Alamotel, rested some, eaten, and arrived at Winterland at the same time he actually did – 3:30 PM. Instead, he still has the client problem. Logic tells us that *getting to Houston that night* was Dave's most important goal.

> **Stephen Roy** (posting as Blackburst): [Re: Kennedy assassination] Friends recall that Ferrie was affected like most other Americans: Shock, grief at the loss of life at so young an age.[15]

But Dave makes the trip anyway. In 1967, Dave will tell DA's Andy Sciambra it was the "worst trip he ever made in his life."[16]

3:00 AM, Nov. 23 David, Alvin and Melvin arrive at the Alamotel, Houston, and check into Room 19:

> **Stephen Roy** (posting as Blackburst) : cites Jerry Shinely's post, 02 Jan. 2001: This advertisement appeared in the *Times-Picayune* July 14, 1963, classifieds section, under "Business opportunities."
>
> > **Opportunity Ice Skating Rink**: I have all machinery and equipment including skates for large Ice Rink to be located in New Orleans. Need partner active or inactive with $15,000 to finance moving and setting up. Guaranteed money return plus 20% in 6 months. For details, write C.A. Bass, 4306 Laurel Dr., Houston 21, Texas.
>
> **Stephen Roy** (posting as Blackburst): For those who find David Ferrie's interest in investing in a skating rink in New Orleans in 1963 completely unbelievable, here is evidence that such a proposition was not only possible, but offered a guaranteed return on the investment…. One wonders if Ferrie might have seen this ad, or have spoken to C.A. Bass. In Houston, of all places. Once again, an allegation of suspicious activity on Ferrie's part does not seem so suspicious when seen in context of the real events of his life.

But wait. The ad appeared July 14, 1963, one day before Dave flew to Miami to defend himself in his Eastern Airlines grievance hearing to try to get his job back. He was scrambling to collect evidence, witnesses and statements. Would he have taken the time to read "Classifieds – Business Opportunities" on the 14th? Probably not. As for speaking with Mr. Bass, in Houston, David surely would have told the FBI, because it would have helped prove he was in Houston for the right reasons.

DAVID FERRIE'S CAPACITY TO INVEST IN A $15,000 ICE RINK VENTURE: (IF HE HAD CREDIT)

> **Stephen Roy** (posting as Blackburst): Recall that David Ferrie, after a long struggle with finances, had recently come into a modest sum

of money: About $7100 from Wray Gill for his work on the Marcello case, and about $1650 in settlement of his grievance against Eastern Air Lines. He planned to partner with Alvin Beauboeuf, who would contribute a couple of thousand dollars, in a new business. Their investment capital of about $10,750 was not far from the $15,000 asked for in this ad.

Dave's 'modest sum of money' was actually substantial for the time. The $7,093 (for helping in Marcello's case), was about $54,200 in 3/2013 funds. The EAL settlement of $1,635.90, in 3/2013 funds, was ~$12,488. So Dave had ~$66,688 in 3/2013 funds. Rink cost of $15,000 was ~$114,508 (in 3/2013 funds). Al's "couple of thousand ($2000)" was ~$15,300 in 3/2013 funds. So they had ~$81,988 (in 3/2013 funds). Mr. Roy says it's ~$82,064 in 3/2013 funds. He says that's "not far from" the ~114,508 asked. *In fact, it's ~$32,444 from reality* (using Roy's figures) in 3/2013 funds. It would take Dave nine years, working for Gill, to earn the difference, with nothing left to live on.[17]

> **David Ferrie's Salary:** (FBI interview, G. Wray Gill, 11/27/63): Gill says he pays David $300 a month. Thus, David's annual income = $3,600 (average salary = $4,743 a year, but David has no dependents). Minimum wage = ~$2,100/year.[18] Poverty level in 1964 for a single male Ferrie's age was $1,650 (US Census, Bureau of Statistics).

Afternoon, Nov. 23, 1963: Jack S. Martin, hospitalized for blows

Jack S. Martin

to the head which have produced four contusions, contacts NOPD Maj. Presley J. Trosclair with accusations against David Ferrie, involving Lee Harvey Oswald, such as: they were together in the Civil Air Patrol; TV program said Oswald has Ferrie's library card; Ferrie owns a rifle such as Martin saw on TV. Martin says Ferrie, who is capable of doing anything, is currently in Texas.

12:00 noon, Nov. 23, 1963: [FBI] Alamotel ignores wake-up call request and David and friends sleep until noon. They rise, dress, eat breakfast, and go shopping at Sears, where David purchases "a jacket, a sweater and several other items." After leaving Sears, they drive directly to the Winterland Ice Skating Rink at 2400 Norfolk, which would open at 3:30 PM and close at 5:30 PM.

David Ferrie's Visit to Winterland Ice Rink

Around 3:30 PM David Ferrie, Al Beauboeuf and Melvin Coffey visit Winterland Ice Rink. Though David will say he skates here, manager Chuck Rolland will say Ferrie did not buy a ticket to skate. Though David says he talks to Rolland about operating costs, etc. of an ice rink, Rolland will deny it. Rolland will testify to FBI and in court that he observed David spending most of his time at the rink's payphone.

From R. Charles Rolland testimony (Clay Shaw trial):

> **Rolland**: Skating [at the rink] started at 3:30...
>
> **Q**: Would you approximate the time you returned?
>
> **Rolland**: Somewhere between 4:00 and 4:15. <snip>
>
> **Q**: How many times did Ferrie introduce himself to you?
>
> **Rolland**: Approximately four or five.
>
> **Q**: He mentioned his name on four or five occasions?
>
> **Rolland**: Yes, sir, he did.
>
> **Q**: Did you consider this strange?
>
> **Rolland**: Quite strange.[19]

> **Stephen Roy**: Ferrie said he spoke to the owner about the costs of equipping and operating such a rink, but manager Chuck Rolland denied that he was the person Ferrie spoke to.... Rolland also said he arrived late and did not watch Ferrie continuously, so it is not impossible that Ferrie spoke to someone else at Winterland about operating a rink.

David told the FBI he spoke to the manager, Chuck Rolland, "at length" about operating an ice rink, which Rolland denied. David never mentioned an owner. David recalled two unnamed employees – a boy and an older man. Had he spoken to the owner, he would have said so, since he did mention two unnamed employees. (See Appendix for full FBI interview Nov. 25, 1963)

> **FBI** (Nov. 25, 1963): FERRIE stated that during the time he was talking to CHUCK ROLLAND other employees of ROLLAND were present at the rink. He recalled specifically there was a young boy who was passing out skates and an older man who was on duty at the rink but he does not recall whether he was introduced to these two individuals or not.

In 2000, Mr. Roy said a researcher (unnamed) gave him a tip that Dave Ferrie "may have" contacted "another ice rink proprietor "(unnamed) with whom he discussed a "franchise" (company unnamed). He refers to this unnamed proprietor as "the Houston man."

Stephen Roy (2005): Another researcher tipped me to a contact Ferrie may have had with another ice rink proprietor and it appears that he did discuss a franchise to open a rink in New Orleans, where there were no ice rinks…. As told to me, the trip had several purposes…. The second was to talk to the Houston man about the franchise.

FBI interview of Ferrie 11/25/1963: FERRIE said he rented skates and skated at the rink for awhile …

Stephen Roy/Blackburst (2000) Ferrie tried skating, but was no good at it. His two companions continued to skate for a couple of hours.

Roy (2005): All 3 donned skates, but Ferrie was hopeless and gave up, BEFORE Chuck Rolland arrived.

MORE OF ROLLAND'S CLAY SHAW TRIAL TESTIMONY:

Q: To your knowledge did David Ferrie even rent any skates on that occasion?

Rolland: No, he did not buy a ticket of admission for skating purposes.

…

Q: Did you ever see Dave Ferrie use the public telephone?

Rolland: Yes, I did, a number of times.

Q: Did Dave Ferrie, to your knowledge, ever receive a telephone call at the skating rink?

Rolland: Yes, he did … he did not skate. He spent most of his time walking around in the lobby, looking in the Pro Shop and watching the skaters. He made a number of trips to the telephone booth and then to his two companions and he was talking to his companions and talking to me on a number of occasions.[20]

```
          On November 28, 1963, CHUCK ROLLAND, Winterland
Skating Rink, 2400 Norfolk, was interviewed, at which time
he stated that a man who introduced himself as a Mr. FERRIS
or FERRIE contacted him by telephone November 22, 1963,
and asked for the skating schedule at the Winterland
Skating Rink.  Mr. FERRIE stated that he was coming in
from out of town and desired to do some skating while in
Houston.  On November 23, 1963, between 3:30 and 5:30 PM,
Mr. FERRIE and two companions came to the Winterland
Skating Rink and talked to Mr. ROLLAND.  Mr. FERRIE had
a short general conversation with Mr. ROLLAND, but at no
time did they discuss the cost of equipping or operating
an ice skating rink.  Mr. FERRIE stated to Mr. ROLLAND
that he and his companions would be in and out of the
skating rink during the weekend.  This is the last time
Mr. ROLLAND saw FERRIE or his companions.
```

FBI report (11/28/63): Describes interview of Chuck Rolland, Winterland Skating Rink.

A. J. Weberman: … [in an] Aug. 1993 Interview, Beauboeuf said, "Dave was at the telephone at the rink. He was always on the phone with somebody."

Stephen Roy (as Blackburst): Ferrie and Beauboeuf ultimately did not invest in a skating rink in 1963. But just 2 months later, the two men DID invest their money in a business venture: Dave's Gulf Service on Veterans Highway....

Nov. 23, 1963: Attorney Dean Andrews, a patient at Hotel Dieu Hospital, is contacted by telephone by a "Clay Bertrand" who inquires if he would be interested in defending Lee Oswald.

We can conjecture that Andrews was contacted not only because he was Marcello's attorney, but because he was running for office as a judge, and could be easily manipulated to handle Lee Oswald's case the way Marcello wanted. As an out-of-state attorney, Andrews could serve in an 'advisory' capacity to one of Marcello's low-ranking attorneys in Dallas, guaranteeing Lee Oswald's fate (conviction), if one of Marcello's soldiers, or a doctor, couldn't kill Lee before he went to trial.

Afternoon, Nov. 23, 1963, FBI: "Sergeant R. Y. DAVIS, United States Army, retired, employed by ... DEAN ANDREWS ... [said Andrews] was positive that a person named CLAY BERTRAND had called him ... and asked him to represent LEE HARVEY OSWALD in Dallas, Texas.... On the afternoon of November 23, 1963, ANDREWS was periodically asleep and awake, but did not want him, DAVIS, to leave.... The chief topic of discussion ... was the progress of ANDREWS' political campaign for election as a judge in Jefferson Parish."

Afternoon, Nov. 23, 1963: When David calls Layton Martens, who has been living in his apartment about a week, Martens tells him to return to New Orleans because Police, FBI and Secret Service are looking for him.

Evening, Nov. 23 [From 11/25/1963 FBI report]: David and his two friends leave Winterland, promising to return, but they do not. They return to Alamotel. There, Dave calls New Orleans, trying to locate Gill. Dave will tell FBI they checked out of Alamotel, then drove to Houston's Bellaire ice rink, leaving after 45 minutes or so, as they were unable to speak to the owner. (Alamotel records show they do not check out, however, until 10:00 the next morning.)

SATURDAY, NOVEMBER 23, 1963 A CALL FROM DAVID FERRIE:

Waiting for Dave's phone call was taking forever. Fortunately, Robert, who had little interest in Kennedy (his parents despised JFK), was more concerned about his final exams and his GRE, just around the corner. Once again we were visiting the Zeiglars (mainly, their TV set). I said I wanted to go for a walk, to clear my head, and would be happy to pick up some cokes. They gave me some money for a vending machine down the street. As I walked to the payphone, I was on edge. Every sound in the darkness made me tense. I hoped my watch was in synch with Dave's, so I wouldn't have to wait around for his call.

The phone rang as soon as I reached it. Dave was as nervous as I was and apologized for calling a few minutes early. I told him I was glad he did. Then I heard Dave make a sound as if he were choking. I realized he was swallowing back his tears. "Oh, my God, J," he said to me. "I won't hide it from you..."

As Dave started to cry, all the wretched fear and horror and sorrow burst open inside my heart, and I began crying, too. I didn't think I had any tears left, but there they were, stinging my eyes. I was so anxious to hear what he had to say, but the darkness grew even thicker when he said, "It's hopeless. God is against us." I felt paralyzed. The cokes I had been carrying in a sack suddenly broke through the bottom, and I just let them fall. Miraculously, they didn't break. The bottles just rolled to the curb, glittering with bits of sand in the streetlight that was flickering, like a broken live wire, against the dark sky.

"If you want to stay alive," Dave warned me, with a strained voice, "it's time to go into the catacombs. Promise me you will keep your mouth shut!" he added. "I don't want to lose you, too." I felt weak all over. "If there is any chance to save him, we'll get him out of there, I swear to you," he went on. I could tell he was just trying to inject some hope. Dave said, "Play the dumb broad. Save yourself. Remember, Mr. T will watch every step you make."

Dave meant I was being watched by Trafficante, the Godfather of Tampa and Miami.

Trafficante was also the good friend and ally of Carlos Marcello. Fortunately, Marcello liked me, which is why I believed I had a chance to survive any threats from that direction. Dave added, "I'll call you once more – check the time (the Call Wheel). After that, I probably can't call you anymore. And now I have other calls to make. So, *Vale, Soror.*" ("Be strong, sister.") I returned to the Zei-glars' house with the cokes, walking like a zombie. My mind was trying to shut down. Nobody had moved from the TV set.

9:45-11:00 PM: David and friends leave the restaurant and drive 35 miles to Galveston. On the way, they stop to see NASA's manned Space Center, but it is closed.

11:00 PM, Nov. 23, 1963: Jack Ruby's close friend, Breck Wall [Bil-ly Ray Wilson], arrives in Galveston, Texas.

> **Mr. SPECTER**: What time did you arrive in Galveston?
>
> **Mr. WALL**: It would be 11 o'clock; somewhere around 11 o'clock.

Breck Wall, a homosexual and nightclub performer, also head of Dallas' AVGA union, lives in the Adolphus Hotel across from Ruby's Carousel Club in Dallas. After 44 minutes of at-tempting to reach Wall, Wall answers at 11:44 PM, at SO 3-8022 [the number of J. McKenna, Wall's adoptive father]. This is Jack Ruby's last known long-distance call before he shoots Lee Oswald the next day.[21]

Breck Wall

11:00 PM, Nov. 23, 1963: David and friends check into room 117 at the Driftwood Motel in Galveston.

11:10 PM?-1:00 AM?: David told FBI he and friends left the Drift-wood Hotel and drove "around in the vicinity of some old clubs in Galveston, Texas, returning to the motel after midnight and it could have been as late as 1:00 AM."

8:00 AM-10:00AM Nov. 24, 1963: FBI: David Ferrie says he and friends get up, eat breakfast, then check out of the Driftwood Ho-tel. (Conflicts: Driftwood Hotel records showed David Ferrie and friends checked out at 2:00 PM, Nov. 24. Alamotel records show David Ferrie and his two companions checked out at 10:00 AM.)

> **Conflicting Checkout Hours for the Driftwood and Alamotels**: [HSCA's] Gaeton Fonzi discovered "check-in and check-out times for the Alamotel Motel and Driftwood Motel conflicted. Alamotel Motel records indicated that David Ferrie and friends ... checked out at 10:00 a.m. Sunday, November 24, 1963..."[but]"Captain Ce-

cil Priest, of the Houston Police Department... [told the FBI:] that David Ferrie and his companions "registered... [in room 117 at the Driftwood Hotel at] 11:00 p.m. on November 23, 1963, and checked out at 2:00 p.m. on [Sunday] November 24, 1963."[22]

Are both records due to clerical errors? If not, did somebody alter Alamotel's records to make it look like David Ferrie stayed in Houston, far from any association with Breck Wall and Jack Ruby in Galveston?

At the time, I was freaked out. The stress was unbelievable. I couldn't sleep. Robert was surprised that I couldn't even cook. "I had no idea you liked Kennedy so much," he said. Luckily, all of America was transfixed by the tragedy. Everyone was watching their televisions, and the Zeiglars were no exception. As before, I was welcome to pop over and watch. As lunchtime approached, Ron, his wife Karen and I viewed the non-stop television coverage of the JFK assassination. As for Robert, he returned to his carrel at the university library to finish an English paper.

Lee was to be transferred from the city jail to another location, a matter announced the night before and repeatedly all morning. My outrage was intense, because I heard no friend or acquaintance put in a single good word for this man who had done no evil. He was being declared guilty, without a trial! Nobody else was being sought in connection with the crime of the century. They had their man, they knew it from the very beginning, and that was that.

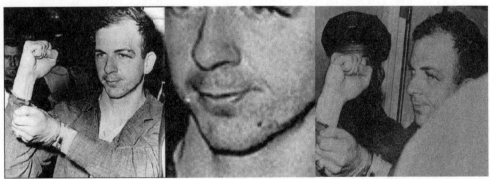

Retouched photo, left, shows 'smirk' and redrawn nose, chin and fingers. There seems to be a drop of whiteout on the right cheek. Photo to right, taken at the same moment, is un-retouched. Lee has just been brought in. He raises his handcuffed hands quickly in reply to a question as to whether he is handcuffed (rare back then). Over in a second, the gesture was touted in newspapers as a "Communist salute." It was a bold, outright lie.

There was so much danger for Lee. I could not forget how he and Dave had told me how you could be beaten without leaving any marks, tortured without anything showing. The police taped news-

At first, the glass in the door was not covered with newspapers. Inside, Roger Craig can be seen in rear. His testimony would have indicated conspirators, and that Lee had help. That kind of evidence could not be considered in the cover-up. Dallas police insisted that Craig was never inside this office, until this photo emerged.

paper over the glass windows of the homicide office. Did they have things to hide?"

Then came the time for Lee's transfer to a place out of the public eye. At first, I was relieved that they had given him a sweater to wear. Then I realized Lee was dressed all in black, like a villain or a hit man. How crowded the place was! Practically a mob scene. I could only see people in plain clothes: where were the police? I strained to see Lee as he was brought forward. You could hear the excitement rippling through the crowd in the basement. And there was Lee, handcuffed and flanked by two giant Texans restraining Lee's arms. A horn honked, there was a pause, and it honked again, as Captain Will Fritz moved quickly out of the way, leaving Lee wide open in the front. Then, as shouts mixed with the flashing of cameras, Lee glanced briefly to his left. Suddenly a hulking figure in a dark suit leapt out at him. At the same moment – a gunshot – Lee's dreadful outcry, pure agony. A bullet was tearing through his body. I screamed, as our souls were ripped apart.

Photo shows Jack Ruby restrained from shooting Lee Oswald a second time as Capt. Will Fritz (facing away, to left) is only one to stare ahead, despite gunfire. Film (from which this still was taken) shows Fritz had been walking in front of Lee, which gave Lee protection, but suddenly moved quickly away to the left, exposing Lee to Jack Ruby, who then moved in for the kill.

"My Scream." This is the kind of art that came from what I saw when Lee was destroyed on Nov. 24, 1963. Drawn with crayon and watercolor, Nov. 24, 1964, this art is still in my possession.

355

10:00 AM -12:00 noon, Nov. 24, 1963: David Ferrie and friends take the 18 minute ferry crossing at Galveston to the coastal road that leads to Port Arthur, where they stop at a Gulf station for repairs to the car. They watch TV inside the gas station lobby while the car is being repaired.

12:20 PM Dallas time: Nov. 24, 1963: Lee Oswald is fatally wounded with a gunshot wound to the abdomen by Jack Ruby, who, witnesses say, had called previously to warn police that he would do just that. David and friends observe the event as it happens.

LEE OSWALD WORE TRIPLE HANDCUFFS

Det. Jim Leavelle [to Topeka's *CJ Online*]: To keep Oswald from being snatched from custody, Leavelle [said he] handcuffed his left wrist to Oswald's right wrist. A second set of cuffs was snapped on Oswald's wrists. As Leavelle walked into the basement of the Dallas police building, he held onto Oswald's belt to control him. Leavelle was briefly blinded by TV news lights but then spotted Ruby holding a pistol by his thigh. "I saw that pistol in his hand and knew what was going to happen," he said. Ruby shoved the pistol toward Oswald and fired, mortally wounding him.[23]

When Marcello's bagman, Jack Ruby, shot Lee on Nov. 24, Marcello's "power" Dave Ferrie told me about was on raw display. Lee was assassinated in the presence of seventy Dallas police and innumerable reporters and media personnel. As for me, after screaming, and, I think, vomiting, I can remember nothing more.

1:00, Nov. 24, 1963: G. Wray Gill stops at David's apartment to tell Layton Martens that when Lee Oswald was arrested in Dallas, police found a library card with David Ferrie's name on it. Gill urges Martens to contact Dave and warn him. Gill will represent him as his attorney.[24]

Treatment of Oswald in Custody: Gus Russo tells us that Police put makeup on Lee Oswald's face to hide abuse: ... Dallas Police have officially admitted that they put makeup on his face so that he would appear unmarred when the press viewed his transfer... FBI ordered an investigation of Dallas Police to determine if abuses had occurred ... headed by agent Vincent Drain. When asked [about results] ... Drain responded, "I just wouldn't want to comment on that." (Vincent Drain, interview by Russo, 18 Oct. 1993,p 568 *Live by the Sword: the Secret War Against Castro and the Death of JFK* (Russo is no supporter of Oswald's innocence, by the way).

When viewing autopsy photos, I realized Lee had been burned behind his left ear. Since Lee was seen at the 'Midnight Conference' with cuts and bruises, one must ask what new bruising was covered up if they had to use makeup. Note the autopsy photo of Lee's feet. What are those puncture marks and cuts on both feet? The wounds look like the result of inserting electrodes to shock him. There is a bruised area next to the arch of his right foot, full of cuts such as a sharp switch would make.

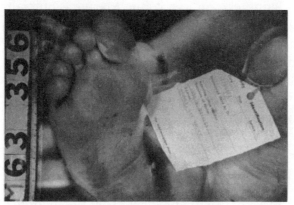

Afternoon, Nov. 24 1963: With Lee Oswald dead and unable to defend himself, Jack Martin now whips up more accusations against David Ferrie. He will call New Orleans Assistant District Attorney Herman Kohlman, a former reporter, three times. Today and tomorrow he will contact radio and TV stations, newspapers, Secret Service, and FBI with his version of David Ferrie. To wit: Ferrie taught Oswald how to shoot, Ferrie has a rifle such as the one that killed JFK, Ferrie was Oswald's mentor in the Civil Air Patrol, Ferrie hypnotized Oswald, Ferrie discussed killing JFK with Oswald, Ferrie flew Oswald to Dallas, and Ferrie was Oswald's "getaway pilot." Warren Commission Doc. # 75, p. 285, shows Martin even blames David Ferrie for the pistol-whipping Guy Banister gave him.

Nov. 24, 1963: In Dallas, Secret Service agents ask a terrified Marina Oswald if she knows a "Mr. Farry."

1:00 PM-2:00 PM, Nov. 24, 1963: FBI: David and friends drive 20 miles to Orange, Texas, then cross the state line, to Lake Charles, Louisiana. They stop at

Marina Oswald and SS agents.

Buster's Bar and Restaurant. David talks to Marion James Johnson, "a client" of Gill's, for "approximately 30 minutes" about Johnson's upcoming appeal after his conviction for perjury.

2:00-5:00 PM, Nov. 24,1963: FBI: Dave and friends arrive at Alexandria, LA, where Al Beauboeuf has relatives. David hopes to attend a party here, unless needed back in New Orleans for a murder trial on the 25th. David tries to reach G. Wray Gill by phone.

David's "adopted son" – a young Marine – officially lives in Alexandria when not on duty. According to Stephen Roy, the young Marine's parents refused to allow him to register a 1959 Ford (in poor condition). David, therefore, registered the car in his own name, adding "Jr." so his "son" could drive it. Dave probably kept his "son's" car stored in New Orleans, available whenever the young man was on leave.[25]

5:00 PM-5:15 PM? Nov. 24, 1963: FBI: David makes several [unsuccessful] pre-paid long distance calls from a gas station, trying to reach Attorney G. Wray Gill's office. Finally, he calls Layton Martens at his apartment and learns that two people from WWL-TV have come, and are still in the neighborhood. The reason: he's likely to be arrested as a suspect in Kennedy's assassination.

> **FBI**: Layton Martens tells David about the library card and all the accusations. He advises David to call Gill. (NOPD will report that ten police officers are hunting for David Ferrie in the city).

5:15 PM, Nov. 24, 1963: FBI: Shocked and worried, David leaves Alexandria. In his attempts to reach Gill, he stops "at several service stations" to use public phones. He finally reaches Gill.

> **FBI**: FERRIE said he asked Attorney GILL if he had made any attempt to verify any of this information and if he thought there was any substance to it.

> **FBI**: FERRIE said he told Attorney GILL what LAYTON MARTENS had told him ...and asked Attorney GILL for his advice. Attorney GILL advised him to continue with his plans and return to New Orleans in keeping with his original plans.

> **FBI**: FERRIE said that he proceeded directly to New Orleans, stopping at a restaurant on the west side of the highway at Baton Rouge, Louisiana, which restaurant ... specializes in steaks. He said that after eating they drove on to New Orleans...

9:00 PM, Nov. 24, 1963: David and his two friends stop the car near David's apartment, where Al Beauboeuf is dropped off. David plans to call him later to check if the house is safe. David then drops off Melvin Coffey at his home.

9:15 PM, Nov. 24, 1963: Beauboeuf and Martens are arrested at David's apartment. Without a warrant, investigators from the DA's office and the police "confiscate books, photographs and other material including a library on hypnotism, abstracts on post-hypnotic suggestion, three U.S. passports (stamped but with no pictures or descriptions) and weapons." It is presumed that both young men call G. Wray Gill to help them.[26]

10:00 PM, Nov. 24, 1963: By now, David has phoned Gill to find out what he has learned. He discovers that his apartment has been raided and Beauboeuf and Martens have been arrested and are being questioned. In a panic, David leaves town.

1:30 AM, Nov. 25, 1963: David drives 125 miles to arrive in Hammond, Louisiana, by way of Baton Rouge, perhaps afraid to risk a shorter route on bad roads off the main highway in his newly repaired car. Or, in his state of mind, perhaps he believes he is being followed.

1:30- 5:30 AM, Nov. 25, 1963: David's whereabouts are unknown.

5:30 AM, Nov. 25, 1963: Thomas Compton is wakened in his dorm bed in Holloway-Smith Hall for men at Southeastern Louisiana College in Hammond. FBI: "[FERRIE] stated that COMPTON is doing research at this school." [David also says Compton is "researching narcotics addiction." Compton is a former Moisant Squadron CAP cadet from the late 1950's.]

Thomas Compton depicts David as "hysterical and near tears" as David states "The police are at my home and have taken some of my things." David says he has done nothing wrong. They talk of "unrelated" things, then David sleeps in Compton's dorm room. In the morning, before David leaves, he calls G. Wray Gill for an update. He decides to turn himself in, hoping this will take police and FBI pressure off Beauboeuf and Martens.[27]

This day, while David is still in Hammond, the FBI is told that Dallas Police found David's library card on Lee Harvey Oswald at the time of his arrest. Ray Comstock, from Jim Garrison's office, enters Ferrie's apartment after midnight with no search warrant.

An FBI Teletype from the New Orleans field office to Director J. Edgar Hoover and the special agent in charge of the FBI office in Dallas says Layton Martens has been interviewed, that he is David Ferrie's roommate, and that "Martens said attorney G. Wray Gill visited Ferrie's residence and told Martens he was looking for Ferrie, who was then not at home. Gill remarked to Martens that, when he was arrested by Dallas Police, Oswald was carrying a library card with Ferrie's name on it.

The information by now has been mangled, having gone through so many ears and out so many mouths. David Ferrie will now wrack his brain – and will finally realize that I might still have the library card.

> **David Ferrie called Bill Wulf**: Compton (March, 1967) said somehow, David knew Lee Oswald had known "Mr. BILL WULF who headed" a high school astronomy club in 1956 that "OSWALD attempted to join … and submitted an application which was refused." [Wulf would insist that Lee was already acting 'violently pro-communist' and broke off friendship with him.] Garrison Investigator Alvin Oser reported "COMPTON related that after the assassination, MR. WULF turned over this application to the F.B.I. COMPTON stated that shortly after the assassination, DAVE FERRIE called MR. WULF and inquired if he knew anything about LEE HARVEY OSWALD. COMPTON related that he couldn't figure how DAVE FERRIE had knowledge of MR. WULF and the Astronomy Club and connecting this with LEE HARVEY OSWALD."

Lee and I had talked about astronomy with Dave. My former high-school boyfriend, Al Freeman, made me a really nice telescope. Lee told us he was ejected from his school's astronomy club meetings because he was "a mere beginner." Dave knew Wulf by name. Dave, knowing he will soon be arrested, has been contacting anyone who might have seen him with Lee, especially former CAP cadets and science-savvy people such as Compton and Wulf.

Conflict: David will tell the FBI he stayed in Hammond until 1:00 or 1:30 PM that day. Compton, however, will tell Garrison investigators in March 1967 that David left at 8:30 AM. When Compton was questioned in 1967, he said he was unable to figure out how David was able to find him. It is possible that David stopped by at Clay Shaw's parents' home at this time. By now, Shaw has returned from his "alibi trip" to San Francisco, where he invited himself as a speaker for a Trade Mart meeting on Nov. 22.

Afternoon, Nov. 25, 1963: FBI: "He [Ferrie] stated that he then drove to New Orleans and went directly to his home where he obtained a clean shirt and then proceeded to the office of Attorney GILL. He stated that from there he went to the District Attorney's office accompanied by Mr. GILL where he surrendered to the District Attorney."

HSCA: He and attorney Gill appeared at the district attorney's office around 4:30 PM He was questioned by the New Orleans police, the U.S. Secret Service, and the FBI. He denied ever seeing Oswald before.

Nov. 25, 1963: Dean Andrews is still in the hospital, but wants to defend Lee when he hears that Lee was supposed to have made an impossible shot with a rifle.

> FBI: (interview with Sgt. Davis): "On November 25, 1963, Sergeant DAVIS stated that when he visited DEAN ANDREWS, he was very much upset over a news item [on TV]… that OSWALD had fired three shots at the President of the United States from a bolt action rifle within three seconds . ANDREWS insisted that this could not be done and wanted to call the FBI and the Secret Service and furnish these agencies with his opinion. Sergeant DAVIS advised he talked ANDREWS out of this action and left the hospital."

Nov. 25, 1963: FBI interviews Layton Martens, who states, "he knows Ferrie to be a great admirer of President Kennedy and that he would classify him as a desegregationist."

I agree with Martens' assessment. Dave personally told me he had to avoid crying out "Hail to the Chief" but only to stay credible to the fanatics and radicals who wanted to see "The Man" dead. They trusted him because after the Bay of Pigs debacle, Dave had harshly criticized JFK and even talked about how easy it would be to assassinate him "from behind any bush."

Nov. 25, 1963: (Notes about the long FBI interview): David goes into detail about his Stinson, which he says is not airworthy (this is untrue, as David got a loan of $400 through his friend, Herbert Wagner) even as he hides the existence of his Taylorcraft L-2, which he owned, and flew, until mid-1964. He will claim he had access only to rental planes (with Marcello's many planes at his disposal). He will assert that he never flew Lee Oswald to Dallas or anywhere else in Texas He doesn't say he never flew Lee to any other cities (See Appendix I). David also told FBI that Jack Martin charged long distance calls to G. Wray Gill's number.

David's coffee table and couch. His Eastern Airlines Captain's cap is on the table. What looks like a logbook for recording flights is with the cap. Glasses, cigarettes, matches, and what might be a candy bar can be seen. Object to left is not a watch: it is one of two carved half-rings of wood jutting above the table's rim. What may be a Mexican blanket is draped on back of couch, under a lightweight blanket. .

Nov. 25, 1963: Sciambra (interview, 1967): "I then asked [Ferrie] if he would like to tell me some more about his trip to Hammond and he smiled and said 'Go to hell.' I then asked if he stayed with CLAY SHAW. He said, 'Who's CLAY SHAW?' I said, 'All right, if that doesn't ring a bell, how about CLAY BERTRAND?' He said, 'Who's CLAY BERTRAND?' I said CLAY BERTRAND and CLAY SHAW are the same person. He asked, 'Who said that?' I said, 'Dean Andrews told us.' He said, 'Dean Andrews might tell you guys anything. You know how Dean Andrews is.'"

Nov. 25 -26, 1963: The Library Card Fiasco

Alex and Doris Eames lived next door to the house owned by the "innocent" McLaneys. Lena Garner [Mrs. Jesse Garner] lived at 4911, managing 4907, 4905 and two apartments behind the house for them. Lee moved into 4905 on May 9, 1963, but used 4907 as his mailing address, even stamping some FPCC flyers "4907 Magazine St." which he distributed July 16. Eric Rogers (jobless) and wife moved to 4907 at that time, accepting Lee's mail and keeping 4905 safer for Lee's family. Upon vacating on September 22, Lee owed nothing for 4905, but Garner reported he owed a utility bill and two weeks' rent at 4907, where Rogers still lived (Rogers got an external job at once). Garner's hostility toward Lee is evident.[28]

> **Tom Bethell**: Monday, March 4, 1968: Did memo on "4900 Block, Magazine Street," at Garrison's request. Garrison believes that the 4900 block of Magazine Street is a "safe block," i.e. owned by the CIA, and used as a sort of parking place for agents awaiting assignments.[29]

Why Was Dave Concerned? When the FBI asked David about a "library card," he must have been stunned. His expired public library card (it had been in his wallet) was in the hands of the police. The only "library card" of concern was the medical library card linking him to me (my name was on a list, along with his, of approved 'users' of the card) – leading to Dr. Ochsner. Dave couldn't contact me until our next pre-arranged time. Since I might have given Lee the card when I left NOLA, and knowing Lee would not have kept the card in his wallet, David was in a panic. He began a search for the medical library card.

Evening, Nov. 25, 1963: The *Times-Picayune* says Alexander Eames had seen Lee Oswald at a the public library. The next day, Dave visits his home (Alexander is, however, at work.).

> **Russell Eames**: (Doris Eames' son, to the author, 2011): I remember the FBI agents in our living room [in 1967], Jim Garrison sending a limo to take my mother "downtown" for interrogation by his investigators, I remember a visit (documented) by David Ferrie and how my mother was aghast by his appearance at our front door asking questions about a library card … with … orange hair and fake eyebrows.[30]

There is no doubt that David Ferrie was looking for his "library card." In fact, it seems that Dave took significant risks in his attempts to locate it. He visited Mrs. Eames not only to see what Mr. Eames might know, but also in order to have an excuse for being in the neighborhood. Dave told me he had frantically searched Lee's apartment before contacting me. He could have been arrested for doing that, if caught.

WHEN DID DAVID FERRIE VISIT JESSE GARNER?

> **A.J. Weberman**: Mrs. Jesse Garner, OSWALD'S former landlady in New Orleans, told the HSCA that David Ferrie visited her home *on the night of the assassination* and asked about OSWALD'S library card, but she refused to speak with him: "I just opened the door and he came in, and he said, 'I'm David Ferrie.' Well, I thought he was one of the FBI men or newsmen…. He said they found his library card on OSWALD… (Weberman thinks Garner is lying).

> **Stephen Roy** (posting as Blackburst): Lena Garner's account of Ferrie's visit carries enough detail for me to accept that it may have happened. It seems consistent with the "investigation" he was conducting to clear himself after his release. The problem is the date: November 22.

Garner's story emerged after Eames' did. Garner said nothing about David's visit until 1968. When she did, the date was wrong.

Was Garner's story a lie? Perhaps. But note that everything else Garner told FBI, Warren Commission, Garrison etc. is accepted as truthful, even though she lied about Lee owing rent and utilities at 4907. Neither witness reported Dave's visit for a long time, but David wasn't important in the case until he became front-page news in 1967. I tend to believe David did visit Garner – on the 26th, the same day he visited Mrs. Eames.

After 6:00 PM, Nov. 26, 1963: David Ferrie called me at PenChem, learned that I had the medical library card, and ordered me to destroy it. I did so.[31] His panic then vanished.

Nov. 27, 1963: David visits Ed Voebel: Voebel is Lee's CAP friend and schoolmate from 1955. David asks Voebel if Lee had been in his CAP squadron. He also tells Voebel that maybe Lee stole his library card after Voebel says Lee attended a party at his house on Vinet St.

> **To Stephen Roy** (as Blackburst): Duquesne wrote (1999):[32] Oh yeah, go to someone's home and steal their library card. Yeah, that one's a keeper ... hehe. Talk about speculation![33]
>
> **Blackburst:** Well, actually, this is not my speculation. This is what Ferrie told his friends ... he heard the story that Oswald had possessed a library card with his name on it. Frantic to clear this up and clear his name, Ferrie then spoke to Oswald's friend Eddie Voebel, who told Ferrie that Oswald had been a cadet in Ferrie's CAP squadron in 1955, and that he recalled Oswald attending a party at Ferrie's.... Not knowing Jack Martin was the source of the story, he worried that Oswald might have taken an old library card. If you give Ferrie a presumption of innocence, the story is not at all unbelievable. I don't know why you find it funny.

But by now, Dave knew Jack Martin was the source, since he had talked to Gill many times by the 27th. Gill had soon learned that Hardy Davis got his information from Martin. Dave knew Davis, who was gay. Dave doesn't openly name Martin as the source about the card because Martin could do more damage if he knew how important the card was to Dave. Above all, he doesn't want Martin to bring David Lewis into the mix, though Martin will do just that after David dies in 1967.[34]

WHEN DID DAVID FERRIE VISIT DORIS EAMES?

> **Stephen Roy** (posting as Blackburst, 2001): Ferrie's friend John Irion said that Ferrie conducted his own investigation of the allegations

against him, just after he was released from custody. ... Doris Eames said Ferrie visited her asking questions about the library card after the assassination, but could not give a specific day.

The Eames' said Dave visited them the day after the newspaper mentioned that Alex Eames had seen Lee Oswald in the public library. That date was Nov. 25, so Mrs. Eames received Dave's visit on Tuesday, Nov. 26. The HSCA said Dave talked to Mr. Eames, but it was Doris to whom he spoke.[35] Once Dave knew the medical library card was no longer a problem, he shifted his focus to denying he knew Lee Oswald. On his visit to Roy McCoy, he asked if McCoy recalled photos of Lee in the CAP.[36] He had also visited Lee's erstwhile friend, former CAP cadet Ed Voebel, who reminded Dave that Lee had attended a party at Dave's house, prompting Dave to suggest that maybe Lee stole his library card from his home on Vinet St. This reduced Dave's previous frantic search to a mere comment."

The Eames' house was to the right in this 2011 photo of Lee's apartment house. Lee's house, which survived hurricane Katrina, was not repaired and is in poor condition. Efforts to save the home from destruction began in 2014.

Endnotes

1. HSCA report of Jan. 11, 1978, of CIA's Regis Kennedy and Carlos Marcello's (Immunized) testimony. Vol. X, "David Ferrie" Vol. XII.

2. From Vince Palamara's Notebook: "Gems From the 26 Volumes." For full information, read Palamara's *Survivors Guilt* (TrineDay, 2013).

3. More from Vince Palamara's notebook: "3 H 244: DPD motorcycle officer M.L. Baker testified that there was a last minute change made at Love Field – told to stay to the rear of limousine [Baker evidently interpreted this as WAY back];6 H 293:DPD motorcycle officer B.J. Martin testified that they were instructed to stay to the rear of the limousine;7 H 580-581: DPD Captain Perdue Lawrence testified that the Secret Service told them to stay to the rear on the evening of 11/21/63 [based on JFK's alleged "desires", debunked by my Secret Service interviews and previous motorcades, incl. in Texas and Florida in November 1963: how convenient – JFK's "desires" coincided with his assassination!]." Palamara has made a solid case that JFK never ordered SS off his limo and, in fact, that he did not have the authority to do so. The SS was responsible for providing the President with the protection believed to be necessary and the President could not override any such decisions.

4. G. Wray Gill, in an FBI interview on May 18, 1967, said "David was in Gill's office at 12:15 PM because he called his office to tell his secretary, Aldric Guidroz, that "the federal jury had returned a verdict in favor of Marcello. But Gill's sec-

retary told Gill that Ferrie had left Gill's office at that time (12:15 PM) stating he would return at 1:30 PM, which he failed to do." Gill was off one hour, probably because he forgot the hour of recess. Adding the hour, David's expected return at 1:30 would have been at 2:30.

5. My memory is terrible concerning the time period shortly before and after Lee was shot down in cold blood before my eyes. I had a complete blackout of memory right after Lee was shot, from which I didn't properly emerge for almost a day. I cannot remember working at PenChem, but obviously put in time there. This was the most terrible experience of my life. I now believe, from evidence provided by others, that Dave didn't question me about our medical library card until after Lee was shot. I have therefore removed that part of the conversation, and transposed it to a later call.

6. Dave might have said "will talk" rather than that he *had* talked, to Marcello's people.

7. Marcello attorney Dean Andrews at first would say a man called "Bertrand' whom many in the French Quarter to this day equate to Clay Shaw, had called him when he was in a hospital bed, asking him to arrange legal representation for Lee. Andrews never did it. He later claimed it was all a hallucination because he was on medication. But Andrews mentioned that Lee and his "gay friends" had visited him, and that he handled cases for gays. Guess what? Clay Shaw was gay. Most honest researchers assume that Shaw did make this gesture, possibly to appease Marcello, who would want to make sure that a properly designated attorney would be necessary to hide Lee's ties to the Mafia.

8. Long before I knew anything of Stephen Roy's schedule for Dave, I reported the time of about 5:30 my time and 4:30 Dave's time, as to when he called. However, I would still have been at PenChem as late as 9:00 my time on Friday nights.

9. Posted 12 September, 2005 – 06:14 PM http://educationforum.ipbhost.com/index.php?showtopicI39 (Retrieved June 3, 2013).

10. From: blackburst@aol.com (Blackburst) Subject: Ferrie's Houston Trip I Date: 16 Jun 2000 http://www.jfk-online.com/dbdfhouston.html (Retrieved June 30, 2012).

11. www.jfkassassinationforum.com/index.php?topic86.72 (repeated widely, the original quote is unable to be located).

12. Stephen Roy (posting as Blackburst) "NOPD and David Ferrie Investigation" 01 Jul 2000 00:00:00 GMT http://www.jfk-online.com/dbnopdfinv.html (Retrieved 6 Aug.2012).

13. http://jfk.hood.edu/Collection/Weisberg Subject Index Files/F Disk/Ferrie David William Stories On/Item 69.pdf (retrieved August 9, 2013).

14. http://www.jfk-online.com/dbdfhouston.html. (Retrieved 6 Aug. 2013).

15. Post to newsgroup, Apr. 2, 1999, http://www.alt.assassination.jfk. (Retrieved Aug. 1, 2013).

16. Sciambra's and Ivon's interview, Feb. 1967: "He said that all he wanted to do was relax after the MARCELLO trial and he just had the urge to go ice skating. FERRIE said, that as it turned out, it was the worst trip that he had ever made in his life. I asked FERRIE what he did in Houston. FERRIE said, "ice skate, what

else?" I said, "I don't know Dave, you tell me." FERRIE said I was a newcomer around the game and that my office knew more about the trip than he did."

17. http://www.usinflationcalculator.com/ (Accessed 03/013).

18. http://kclibrary.lonestar.edu/decade60.html Standards of Living, 1960's. (Retrieved Aug. 19, 2012).

19. P. 10, Clay Shaw trial, transcript.

20. Ibid.

21. https://deeppoliticsforum.com/forums/showthread.php?11825-The-Galveston-connection-between- Ruby-and-Ferrie (Retrieved Aug. 12, 2013) Lee David Farley posted (Jan. 2012) that Breck Wall gave Dallas mayor Earle Cabell's name as a credit reference. (http://reopenkennedycase.forumotion.net/t177-breck-wall) (Retrieved Aug. 9, 2013).

22. "...Gave as their address 618 North Pierce, New Orleans, Louisiana. Were driving four door station wagon, make unknown, Louisiana license 784-895. Also in the room with them was Melvin S. Coffey. All were white males. Also in the room was blond white female, name unknown [Beauboeuf denied this to Weberman]. While at motel placed long distance call to Alexandria, Louisiana, telephone number unknown." http://mcadams.posc.mu.edu/weberman/nodule24.htm. (Retrieved June 20, 2013).

23. http://cjonline.com/news/2013-04-20/retired-dallas-detective-recalls-ruby-killing-oswald "Retired Dallas detective recalls Ruby killing Oswald" Apr. 20, 2013. (Retrieved Aug. 8, 2013).

24. (Later, Gill says Hardy Davis told him about the library card. David will tell FBI that he got the library card information from Jack S. Martin. Martin, in turn, will claim to FBI that he and Hardy Davis speculated that Oswald got the library card from David Ferrie after watching TV programs about Oswald.

25. Synopsis, by Tolan Investigations, Inc. for Southern Research Corp. Background Check, Nov. 1962 report for Eastern Air Lines. Signed by Thomas M. Tolan. *1959 Ford found registered to David W. Ferrie, Jr. 11 Prospect St., Alexandria, LA. "...efforts to identify negative to date."* Stephen Roy stated in August, 2013, on Education Forum that this was not the first car, for some young male for whom David had faked registration papers. Mr. Roy had previously said David had no car available after his had been towed away in March, 1963 – that he had used his motorcycle only, and that I was lying about Dave's having a car at that time. It is probably this neglected car, which was unlikely to have been kept at the address of the disapproving parents. Dave used a car (though sparingly) between April and the end of August. Dave is on record as borrowing airplanes, let alone cars. I reported that Dave had a motorcycle, as well. However, the car was not reliable and David apparently used it only once in a while –possibly to keep the battery from running down. I would not have known that Dave secretly owned it for a "son."

26. Ref: James and Wardlaw; p. 44. As quoted at http://jfk.hood.edu/Collection/Weisberg Subject Index Files/F Disk/Ferrie David William/Item 85.pdf. (Retrieved Aug. 4, 2013).

27. Most information comes from March 10, 1967 interview, commissioned for Clay Shaw trial, by Alvin B. Oser. http://jfk.hood.edu/Collection/Weisberg Sub-

ject Index Files/F Disk/Ferrie David Garrison Files Miscellaneous/Item 03.pdf. (Retrieved August 10, 2013).

28. Rogers became employed by Meal-a-Minute in September and was still living at 4907 when questioned by the Warren Commission in 1964. The FBI and Warren Commission knew Lee's true address, as shown in their interviews, but advertised that Lee left New Orleans owing rent and utilities at 4907. By such means, and in other ways, they created a negative picture of Lee Oswald for their own use. It also halted inquiries into how Lee could have afforded both apartments with no visible means of support. He was unemployed from July 19 until leaving Sept. 22 for Mexico City (on what funds could he have made that trip?). In fact, Lee was being paid by both the CIA and FBI at that time. When the apartment manager [Mrs. Garner] testified to the Warren Commission on April 6, 1964, she did not mention David Ferrie's visit, but on the other hand, she was never questioned about anyone but Oswald and had no real opportunity to volunteer information about David Ferrie.

29. Thomas Bethell, Diary.

30. In March, 2011, Russell Eames, son of Oswald's landlady, Doris Eames, wrote to me about the library card (and much more – he had known Lee Oswald as a pre-teen). In the course of our IM conversation, described other details about Lee Oswald, who lived in the house next door, at 4905 Magazine St."

31. The rest of the call involved information about Jack Ruby and Lee's assassination. I have had a hard time handling the memories. They are too painful and I was in a state of shock and deep depression. At this time, I wanted to kill myself.

32. Stephen Roy, posting as blackburst@aol.com (Blackburst) Subject: Re: Why Ferrie Didn't Know LHO in the CAP Date: 08 Jun 2000 00:00:00 GMT. David Blackburst Archives. (Retrieved Jan. 15, 2013).

33. Edited for punctuation. The author also corrects almost all of Stephen Roy's typographical errors, since Roy hadn't polished his remarks for his book yet. His statements shouldn't be judged on the basis of any typos he may have made while posting to a newsgroup or published from an email.

34. Immediately after reciting his long list of problems with Martin to the FBI, Dave says: "…that he had learned through interviews with other officers that one of the allegations made against him was that when OSWALD was arrested he had his (FERRIE's) library card in OSWALD's possession and that it had been alleged that OSWALD had been using FERRIE's library card to get books at the New Orleans Public Library. FERRIE said that in his personal property located in the Property Room at the First District is his library card which expired March 13, 1963. FERRIE said that he has not made application for a new card since the above card expired and that this card has been in his possession at all times."

35. HSCA: "(457) A neighbor of Oswald's, Mrs. Doris Eames, told New Orleans district attorney investigators in 1968 that Ferrie had come by her house after the assassination, inquiring if Mr. Eames had any information regarding Oswald's library card. Eames told Ferrie he had seen Oswald in the public library but apparently had no information about the library card Oswald used.(210) (458) Ferrie also talked with several former members of the Civil Air Patrol in an

attempt to find out if any former cadets recalled Lee Harvey Oswald in Ferrie's squadron. Among those contacted was former cadet Roy McCoy, who told the FBI that Ferrie had come by looking for photographs of the cadets to see if Oswald was pictured in any photos of Ferrie's squadron.(211)."

36. HSCA says David Ferrie made a visit.

Dave's apartment at 3330 Louisiana AvenueParkway.

CHAPTER SEVENTEEN

Nowhere to Hide

O n November 27, 1963, David obtains his public library card (expired 03/13/63) from the police, who had confiscated it, and shows it to the FBI when they interview him briefly at his home. He'll repeat that Lee never had any of his library cards.

FERRIE stated he has never loaned his library card to LEE HARVEY/OSWALD or any other person at any time and that his library card, to the best of his recollection has not been out of his possession since it was issued to him. He exhibited New Orleans Public Library card # M.L. 89437 bearing the stamped lettering N.R. - P.D. in the upper left hand corner. FERRIE said the letters N.R. mean non-resident,

11/27/63 at New Orleans, Louisiana File # NO 89-69

SA'S ERNEST C. WALL, JR. &
THEODORE R. VIATER /bal Date dictated 11/27/63

ADDITIONAL NOTES FROM THE "SHORT FBI INTERVIEW":

(1)… FERRIE stated he has no recollection of knowing or having met LEE HARVEY OSWALD in the Civil Air Patrol or in any business or social capacity…"[a lie]

(2) FERRIE claimed he has owned a Stinson 150 blue and white, single engine, four passenger monoplane, registration number 8293K and that this plane has not been airworthy since the license expired in the spring of 1962. [A lie – as Wagner testified; Dave also doesn't mention his Taylorcraft L-2].

(3) FERRIE stated he has never flown LEE HARVEY OSWALD to Dallas, Texas or any other town in Texas at any time.[David only mentions "Texas." What about other cities? Other states?]

(4) He said the only planes he would have access to would be rental planes." [a lie] David has access to Marcello's many planes, as well as those of friends.

Joseph Biles: There is no doubt that Ferrie had easy access to commercial and private planes through Marcello and his family.[1]

Nov. 27, 1963: The FBI interviews David's longtime friend, James Lewallen,[2] and David's employer, G. Wray Gill. New Orleans police interview Sam Newman, who owns Banister's building.

Phone calls likely made by David (November's list was conveniently missing from Gill's records). See Appendix VIII regarding why these telephone calls were probably made by David Ferrie.

Nov. 1, 1963	Texarkana (214-794-5194) from New Orleans	
Nov. 17, 1963	New Orleans	from Houston
Dec. 2, 1963	New Orleans	from New York
Dec. 3, 1963	Jacksonville (305-EL5-7621) from New Orleans	
Dec. 7, 1963	Houston (713-JA9-0209) from New Orleans	
Dec. 14, 1963	Atlanta (404-CE3-2862) from New Orleans	

I've been told I have PTSD due to seeing Lee shot on TV. I know realize my inability to remember anything on Nov. 24 after I saw Lee shot also affected my ability to pin down the times and all details of Dave's Nov. 22 phone call, and those afterwards. Some months after his final call I had finally overcome suicidal thoughts but was depressed. I never heard from Dave again.

Nov. 27, 1963: FBI interviews "DAVID PEARCE MAGYAR, Chief Pilot, Trans Gulf Seaplane Service, Inc., New Orleans, Louisiana. MAGYAR advised that he was personally acquainted with Captain DAVE FERRIE but that this relationship was very casual."

Nov. 30, 1963: FBI SA Ernest C. Wall Jr. interviews Melvin Coffey at his home at 618 North Pierce Street.

Dec. 1963: G. Wray Gill severs his ties with David Ferrie, but Dave will still fly for the Mafia when called upon.

Dec. 1963: Garrison's District Attorney's Office secretly photograph and film Dave's apartment at this time.[3]

Dec. 1963: Clay Shaw's train trip, to a speaking engagement in San Francisco that he personally created, is examined by the FBI.[4]

Dec. 18, 1963: From this date, the Secret Service and FBI ignore Dave.[5]

Dec. 29, 1963: With the specter of a furious David Ferrie free to wreak havoc, two people now change their stories. Dean Andrews recants and says the phone call he received to act as Lee Oswald's attorney was "a dream" because he was under sedation at the hospital. Andrews does insist that Lee is just "a patsy." But he also says, "I like to live. If they can get the President, they can crush me like a bug." Next, Jack S. Martin will confess that while in the hospital from Guy Banister's pistol-whipping, he had a case of "telephonitis" and didn't know what he was talking about.

WAS DEAN ANDREWS INTIMIDATED?

Don Jeffries (friend of Andrews' son, Dean Andrews, III) wrote: "Dean's son told me someone did put out a contract on his father's life, but that Carlos Marcello, according to him a personal friend of his father's, intervened. Even after the Shaw trial, Dean Andrews grew more paranoid as time went on, and his family clearly understood he was afraid and believed the assassination was the result of a high level conspiracy."

> **David Andrews** [a son] [Sept. 12, 2012]: Manipulating LHO's legal counsel would be the real reason. It is the exact same reason Lyndon Johnson put Abe Fortas as the lawyer for Bobby Baker. And LBJ lawyer John Cofer as the lawyer for Billie Sol Estes. Control the lawyer and you can control the client for someone *else's* benefit."[6]

> **Pamela Brown** (Researcher): As everyone seems to agree, Dean Andrews could be intimidated, and he was.... Simply to dismiss everything he said as "nonsense" just allows those who intimidated Andrews in the first place to win.

> **Stephen Roy**: Who intimidated him? You sound very certain about it. I've covered much the same ground, and I am not so certain about it. That Andrews told people of a call from Washington is not a very specific intimidation. He continued to talk about the call through 1967, including under oath, so he can't have been very intimidated by it.... If people think the Andrews story falls together, I must be missing something.

> **Don Jeffries** (replying to Roy): My questions about the call from Bertrand to Andrews should not suggest that I doubt he ever received such a call. I do believe Andrews was intimidated, as he suggested in interviews ("they can squash me like a bug," "I got the shortest memory in the world," etc.) From knowing his son (and I also met and spoke with his widow), I've learned just how paranoid Andrews was in his later years.... I don't share [Stephen's] suspicions that Andrews may have invented the story.

Jan. 9, 1964: David Ferrie and Alvin Beauboeuf open "Dav-Al's Gulf Service" station on Veteran's Highway. It will go out of business by November 1964.

> **Tommie L. Clark and Dav-Al'sGulf station: interview 3/16/67**:
>
> Q: How did you have occasion to know Dave Ferrie?
>
> A: I was employed with him when he owned a filling station back in '64, I believe.
>
> Q: What was the name of the filling station?
>
> A: Dave & Al's.
>
> Q: Where was the filling station located?
>
> A: Metairie Heights and Veterans Highway. (Tommie will go on to say he quit because he wasn't paid in a timely manner and wasn't given promised work breaks.)[7]

Layton Martens tells the FBI on 10/13/67 that David Ferrie had blackmailed Carlos Marcello into buying a gasoline station for him because "Ferrie had something on him." [FBI 62-109060-251; CIA 1362-1061A; FBI 62-109060-7077 2.26.73; *Look* magazine 8.26.69; FBI 62-109060-5815 10.13.67]

Jan. 13, 1964: Amazingly, neither David Ferrie nor Carlos Marcello are mentioned in the FBI's supplemental report for New Orleans.

Feb. 13, 1964: **Raymond Comstock**, of Jefferson Parish Sheriff's Office enters Dave's home while he is out of town, without a warrant. He takes "two undated letters addressed to Jack Wasserman signed D.W. Ferrie; one letter appears to be a corrected copy of the other; an undated letter addressed to Jack signed Dave; an undated letter addressed to Jose Luis LaRoca, Guatemala, and the first page of Ferrie's bankbook with the Whitney National Bank of New Orleans."[8] It seems Dave's written connections to Marcello are being collected.

THE WINNIPEG AIRPORT INCIDENT

The same day Dave's letters were taken Canadian resident Richard Giesbrecht overhears a meeting between two men at the Winnipeg International Airport. He identifies one of the men as David Ferrie. (See Appendix XI on why Dave may have been at the airport; researcher Peter Whitmey brought together much of this material.)

Paris Flammonde: Ferrie ... was concerned over how much Oswald had told his wife about the plot to kill Kennedy. Additionally, they discussed a man named Isaacs, his relationship with Oswald, and how curious it was that he would have gotten himself involved with a "psycho" like Oswald ... Ferrie inquired about some paper, or merchandise, coming out of Nevada and the other man replied that things had gotten too risky and that the house, or shop, at a place called Mercury had been closed down, but that a "good shipment" had reached Caracas from Newport. It was also agreed that the Warren Commission would not stop its investigation, even if it did decide that Oswald was guilty.[9]

David Ferrie, Lee Oswald, Marcello, Arcacha Smith and others had rifles shipped in from Caracas, Venezuela, in the summer of 1963 using one of Delta Line's three sister ships. Where the conversation mentions Caracas, I translate that as a gun-running operation.

Feb. 14, 1964: David attends his uncle's funeral in Cleveland. [See researcher Robert Harris' argument challenging Stephen Roy's long-standing declaration that Ferrie could not have been in the Winnipeg airport on the 13th, because Ferrie was traveling in the US in a car with "a traveling companion" (who refuses to be named)]. (See Appendix XI).

Feb. 25, 1964: Flight 304, an Eastern Air Lines DC-8, crashes into Lake Pontchartrain, New Orleans. Fifty-eight people aboard the jet plane die. "A Coast Guard pilot said there were indications that the plane had exploded either in the air or on impact.[10] The aircraft crashed ... nineteen miles northeast of New Orleans International Airport, shortly after taking off."[11]

End of March, 1964: Betty Rubio says she saw Clay Shaw and David Ferrie together: "Betty Rubio worked at Lakefront Airport and knew Ferrie. Shortly before April of 1964, while standing in the ramp office, she noticed a plane taxi up to the office. Ferrie got out, talked to her for a bit, and then went back to his plane, where Clay Shaw met him. Shaw and Ferrie talked for a while and then Ferrie got in his plane as Shaw walked past her toward the terminal building."[12]

May 22, 1964: Disaster strikes again when Hugh Ward, Banister's pilot and former business partner, whom David Ferrie taught to fly, dies in a flaming plane crash with former New Orleans Mayor DeLesseps Morrison and son aboard.

June 6, 1964: Guy Banister is found naked and dead. Cause is "heart attack" but Delphine Roberts, Anna Lewis and others say he was murdered, and the fact was covered up. Banister's wife burns many of her husband's files. Other files are given away or vanish.[13]

> **Delphine Roberts**: Robert Buras says Roberts called the deaths of David Ferrie and Guy Banister murder. Delphine Roberts (Aug. 27, 1978) told investigator Earl Golz "it was made to look like a natural death."

> **Anna Lewis** (2000 videotape): Banister was hiding. He was afraid to do anything. Just like David and Jack (Martin) and the rest of us. We were all scared. He shut down his office. It was all over. Then he was found dead. He had a bullet in him, but they said it was a heart attack.[14]

July 21, 1964: Dr. Mary Sherman is brutally murdered.[15] Ed Haslam learns that Juan Valdez had fights with Sherman. Valdez will be the first person to be aware of smoke coming from Sherman's apartment at about 4 AM. Why does Valdez call the police instead of the fire department?

The same day, the Warren Commission opens in New Orleans to obtain voluntary (unsolicited) testimonies about the Kennedy assassination. It is believed that Dr. Sherman would have testified. Her murder was front page news. Dean Andrews, Jr., aware of the death of Dr. Mary Sherman on this morning's front page, offers his testimony to Wesley J. Liebeler, assistant counsel, Warren Commission. The FBI never informs the Warren Commission of any interest in David Ferrie or Carlos Marcello.

THE "PLANE TRUTH" ABOUT DAVID FERRIE'S PLANES

In mid-1964 David Ferrie sells his Taylorcraft L-2. Previously, Dave sold his beloved Stinson to Tom Brister, one of his flight students. (see below). As we've discussed elsewhere, Dave borrowed a Cessna on April 8, 1963 to transport three persons, "Lambert" "Hidell" and "Diaz," to Garland TX.[16] Dave had flown the group to Hammond, LA. "Hidell" was a name used by Lee Oswald. I myself, was introduced to Clay Shaw at Lakefront Airport when he pretended to be called "Lambert." It seems he was unaware that I had already seen him as "Clay Shaw" at the 500 Club.[17]

For such reasons as the above, researchers have tried to find records associated with the planes David Ferrie owned or could have been using. Most of the logbooks are missing. No mention can be found of flight logs for the Taylorcraft L-2. Stephen Roy says he has logbooks, but has not publicly identified which logbooks he has.

After Dave found his Stinson sabotaged, he wrote: "From this moment on I have lived in terror and with the fear that nothing could save me from these people."[18]

Jan. 1965: Dave continues in some role as a "psychologist." A Garrison Memo (Mar. 3, 1967) from Julian R. Murray says Mrs. William B. Jones, who needed a male nurse, interviewed and hired Jimmy Johnson in Jan. 1965 based on a recommendation from "a psychiatrist or psychologist whose last name was Ferrie and who lived on Louisiana Avenue Parkway."

> **Stephen Roy**: (2004) …as his temp job with G. Wray Gill…was winding down in 1963, Ferrie tried to set himself up as a psychologist, both at his home and at an office building on Perdido. Neighbors reported young teen boys coming and going from Ferrie's home, but it is unclear which were patients and which were not. By January 1964, Ferrie had pretty much abandoned this as a means of making a living, and opened a service station. I don't believe he was ever licensed. And I presume the Polk's listing was out of date …[19]
>
> **Daniel Meyer**: (in response to Roy): The 1965 Polk lists "Banister, Mary W (wid W Guy) h 7059 Argonne", and Guy Banister died in June of '64, suggesting the directory was updated at least to that month.

The FBI had paid too much attention to Dave, so Gill "let him go", as Gill's secretary made clear (Dec., 1963). As for David's standing as a psychologist, he was already in practice when new regulations came along. He was probably grandfathered-in. Dave's bogus PhD would have looked good enough, back then, to "pass."[20]

> **Stephen Roy**: …the reason for Ferrie's departure from Gill's office was embarrassment over his implication in the JFK matter, (David Blackburst, Interviews with Gill associates; E-mail to Reitzes, August 14, 1999)…. The Marcello case was over (temporarily) and Gill thought it best to gently help steer Ferrie toward the service station he had just purchased.[21]

1965: A memo from Charles Ward to James Alcock, L.P. Davies, Jr. says David Ferrie is a freelance pilot for Trans Gulf Airways in 1965. At this time, David Ferrie obtains his instructor's ticket to give flying lessons.

> **Stephen Roy**: Dave Ferrie trained MANY people, including CAP cadets, to fly between 1945 and 1965, but he never actually got his instructor's ticket until 1965."[22]

Mr. Roy is being unkind. Since Dave was trying to open his own flight school, he would want the certificate to display. David, over-qualified to be a flight instructor, with instrument rating and thousands of hours of flying as a senior commercial pilot, had trained students for years in small high performance airplanes such as his Taylorcraft L-2. At any time he could have grabbed a certificate. "Prior to 1960 (and through the early 1960s), CAA regulation 20.130 provided for private pilots to obtain a limited flight instructor certificate with as little as 200 hours total time and no instrument rating. If this private pilot instructor had an instrument rating, then he or she could also give instrument instruction to prepare and endorse applicants for their instrument rating.[23]

March 23, 1965: David Ferrie and J.O. Weilbaecher create "Professional Research Inc." There are two "Registered Agents" … J. O. Weilbaecher, III, 822 Perdido St, New Orleans, La 70112" and "… David W. Ferrie, 3330 La Ave, New Orleans, La 70115" (R Charter/ Organization ID: 26915010D). Several doctors are associated with the Weilbaecher name in the area.[24]

March 31, 1965: Jack Ruby tells reporters, "My time is running out. I am breathing toward my last breath. I was set up and tried the minute I walked down that ramp."

May 28, 1965: Maurice Gatlin, an attorney with connections to the CIA, who had worked closely with Guy Banister, falls to his death [or is pushed] from the sixth floor of The El Panama Hotel in Puerto Rico.

May 31, 1965: The *Times-Picayune* runs a front page story: "Heart Attack Kills N. O. Attorney in Puerto Rico / M. B. Gatlin Then Falls 6 Stories From Hotel"

We hear nothing about Gatlin's May 28 death until May 31, when New Orleans learns, on the front page, "the official version" – "heart attack" – as pronounced by a Puerto Rican coroner – that caused Gatlin to fall over a railing to his death.

Stephen Roy: There is no evidence[25] that Ferrie ever associated with Gatlin.[26]

Researchers **John Bevilaqua and Susan Klopfer**: (Bevilaqua posting to Ed. Forum): ... Banister used Maurice Brooks Gatlin as his attorney and confidante.... Folks, this newly coalesced information is *so big* that you may find it difficult to swallow at first gulp. And I never would have re-opened my examination of William "Guy" Banister had it not been for a posting made by Susan Klopfer on the "Mississippi Roots of the JFK Assassination", which oddly enough, was inspired by my original testimony to the ARRB about 15 years ago.[27]

Yes, Gatlin associated with Guy Banister, and since David Ferrie was frequently inside in Banister's office in 1963, he was likely to have known Gatlin, who had a flamboyant personality.

June 23, 1965: The dismembered bodies of an elderly couple are found in a refrigerator in Houston. CIA operative Charles Frederick Rogers, a friend of David Ferrie from CAP days, is a brilliant man. He is multi-lingual, a pilot, geologist, physicist, and CIA asset.[28] Last seen fleeing in a plane headed toward Mexico, Rogers is never seen again, though reports placed him, in 1986, in Guatemala "working in the Iran-Contra program." Reports of his ties to David Ferrie, Lee Oswald and the Kennedy assassination resulted in a book: *The Man on the Grassy Knoll*, by John Craig & Philip A. Rogers.

Charles F. Rogers

Stephen Roy (12 Sept. 2005): For a number of reasons, I don't buy the Rogers account. I'll provide chapter and verse for these things in my book, but I recognize that there are some who do not agree.[29]

July 11, 1965: There are various records of David flying fishermen to islands. Here is a well-documented example: Three witnesses recall that David Ferrie flew someone resembling Clay Shaw and three others out to Freemason Island for a fishing excursion. But on this date, David contacts one pilot Natt Milligan of Trans-Gulf Seaplane Service to bring Shaw and two companions back because of an upcoming storm surge that could flood the island.

William Gurvich will write a memorandum to Jim Garrison on April 5, 1967, about the event. His memo is unusually descriptive, with phone numbers, addresses, specific details and verifiable quotes. Gurvich wrote: "...Ferrie had [flown] to this island at least three times prior to Hurricane Betsy on September 9, 1965.... Both

379

Veazeys [owners] identified photograph of David Ferrie ... Ferrie's third ...visit was a day or two prior to July 11, 1965, at that time he had flown four fishermen to the island in a land plane, making two trips, On July 11, Ferrie telephoned Steve Littleton of Trans-Gulf Seaplane Service ... asking the latter to send a seaplane to Freemason to pick up three fishermen as the lowering ceiling prevented him from doing so in a land plane. At 1400 hours...pilot Natt Milligan arrived at the island ... he described [one of] these fishermen to me as -White male, 5'11", 55 - 58 years, gray hair, ruddy complexion as if sunburned.... The original Trans-Gulf log of July 11, 1965... confirms the above. [Milligan was shown photos and]... selected one of Andrew Blackmon ... Milligan then selected a photograph of Clay Shaw and said this was similar to one of the men he bad picked up at Freemason Island for Ferrie."

Sept. 4, 1965: Rose Cherami,[30] who predicted JFK's assassination before and at the moment it happened, who also told of a ride toward Dallas with two "Italians", dies in a hit-and-run incident. Author Todd. C. Elliot [*A Rose by Many Other Names*] says witness Jerry Don Moore described her luggage lined up in the center of the road along which he was speeding, forcing him to swerve. He narrowly missed striking Rose's supine body. Stopping, he saw, however, tire tread marks on her arm. She was alive: he eventually got her to Gladewater Memorial Hospital. "I surely didn't think she would die," he said. A doctor was inexplicably called in from faraway Dallas to "care" for Cherami, after which hospital personnel told Moore "she didn't live long."[31]

Oct. 11, 1965: Clay Lavergne Shaw retires as Managing Director of New Orleans International Trade Mart, a position he had held for 18 years.[32] He has been absent in Europe much of the time since the assassination. Shaw tells reporters "the new Trade Mart Building, erected at the foot of Canal St. [is] the fulfillment of [a] lifelong dream."

It's significant that Shaw stayed out of New Orleans as much as he could until 1965. See the endnote here for information on some witnesses who claimed they saw David Ferrie and Clay Shaw together.[33]

David Ferrie's Last Months

According to Tommie L. Clark, David begins working for Saturn Aviation in 1965 as a charter pilot after leaving Dav-Al's (which will be sold) and tries to organize his own flight school. He will be training students to fly until almost the end of his life, canceling his last appointment just a few days before his death. But Tommie leaves out other airlines for which David worked.

Southcentral Airlines VS "South Central" Airlines

> **Joan Mellen:** Ferrie also flew for South Central Airlines, a CIA proprietary, (*A Farewell to Justice*, p. 33).

> **Stephen Roy** [to Owen Parsons, Oct. 10, 2006, Ed. Forum]: Joan Mellen is wrong about the airline ... Southcentral Air Lines was originally Space Air Freight, chartered by Charles Wendorf and Jacob Nastasi. It was changed to Southcentral Air Lines on June 22, 1966, but had trouble being accepted by the FAA.... There is NO EVIDENCE that Southcentral had anything to do with the CIA, much less being a proprietary. Mellen was wrong to make this claim.[34]

But is "South Central Airlines" the same as "Southcentral Airlines?" Since Mr. Roy writes the name twice, it isn't a typo. South Central Airlines was doing business in Florida, North Carolina and other states by Dec. 5, 1963 and was still in business up to September, 1965, according to newspaper articles. Then lawsuits over a devastating plane crash[35] in Gainesville, where I happened to be living, on Feb. 6, 1964, basically shut South Central down by 1965. A rehearing was denied[36] Nov. 3, 1966.[37] But was this the company in Slidell, Louisiana, run by Wendorf and Nastasi? Let's see if we can figure that out.

A brochure from December 1963 shows a South Central Airlines in business at this date. This company went out of business in 1965.[38]

The name "South Central" soon vanishes (possibly due to lawsuits elsewhere) and the name "Space Air Freight" soon appears. Garrison's investigators mentioned Space Air Freight as an ongoing business operation in 1967. Space Air purchased a DC-3 in 1966 and sold it in 1969.[39]

March 9, 1966: A contract to haul strawberries is given to Space Air Freight Co. five days a week, in season, from Hammond, LA to Newark, NJ. [*Hammond Daily Star*]

So, was Space Air Freight's name changed to "South Central" on June 22, 1966, thus putting Space Air freight out of business? Actually, Space Air Freight was still up and running until at least March, 1967 (we know this because of an oblique bribe to Al Beauboeuf by Garrison investigators Lynn Loisel and Louis Ivon, which was recorded) and so conclude it wasn't.

"About 10:00 PM on Thursday, March 9th, 1967, five days before the start of the Shaw preliminary hearing, Loisel and Ivon again appeared at Beauboeuf's home... [Loisel said], "You know, Al, my boss has got unlimited money and ... we're in a position to do something for you, perhaps pay you $5,000-$10,000-$15,000 and a guaranteed job with an airline..." The next day, they mentioned Space Air Freight as the airline where a job could be arranged: "... For instance ... a small operation such as Space Air Freight. I know with one phone call he could go out to the Space Air Freight and write his own ticket, you know. That's just Space Air Freight. That's not Eastern or something else. But I feel like we have people who are stepping stones to the larger airlines and so forth." Added Loisel: "They're politically motivated, too, you know, like anything else."

So perhaps Space Air Freight did not change its name to South Central Airlines in June 1966. Now we can examine David's history in this regard, reported by the HSCA, as probably accurate.

DAVID FERRIE LOSES HIS JOB WITH SPACE AIR FREIGHT

According to the HSCA on July 23, 1966, Ferrie is fired. FAA officials say he failed to observe operational regulations at Space Air Freight.[40]

The day Dave is fired, he writes his will. His dearest friend, Alvin Beauboeuf, is the beneficiary. Dave will soon purchase a grave site in St. Bernard Cemetery. He worries that he has "encephalitis" or "cancer of the neck." The migraines he's had for so many years are now worse,[41] but his blood pressure medication could be the cause.[42] Atop that, David is apparently overdosing himself on Proloid to combat hypothyroidism. His "bug eyes" sleeplessness, nervousness, nausea and headaches are likely side effects of Proloid (see Appendix IX).

> From the **National Institute of Health**: If you have a severe headache, nausea or vomiting, bad headache, confusion ... you may have a severe and dangerous form of high blood pressure called malignant hypertension. (See Appendix IX for the official cause of death and arguments for murder versus a natural death).[43]

July 1966: HSCA says Dave previously worked for United Air Taxi (began operations 03/04/1966); "Marcello was one of the largest share-holders of United Air Taxi, for which pilot David Ferrie worked."[44] HSCA understates the Marcello connection: Marcello wasn't just a shareholder, he was "da Boss."

August 1966: Dave is quietly running his own flight school, using the airport restaurant at Lakefront as his office. He is also working as a contract pilot for Saturn Aviation, managed by Al Crouch.

> **Tommie L. Clark:** (Garrison investigation interview, March 15, 1967). Dave sold the filling station, and he asked me if I wanted to work with him as a flight instructor at the [Lakefront] airport. He was working for Saturn Aviation at that time. I agreed and more or less hung around out there and there wasn't much to do. He quit and opened his own flight school. He asked me to work with him there. This was 1966.[45]

Oct. 1, 1966: Carlos Marcello (left) strikes FBI SA Patrick Collins as Collins blocks his way at the International Airport in New Orleans.

When Carlos and his brother Joe flew from New York to New Orleans International Airport a large crowd met him, along with flashing cameras and reporters. Suddenly, finding his way blocked, Carlos punched him. "According to Collins, as he approached Carlos, the little man shouted at him, "I'm the boss around here," and then let fly. A press photographer captured the scene and the next day Carlos was arrested and charged.... Eventually, the case came to court and on May 20, 1968, Carlos went on trial in Laredo, Texas.... Yet again, he was acquitted, this time by a hung jury." But not even Wasserman, Gill, Andrews or a bribed jury could stop conviction at a final trial, in Houston, ending on August 9, 1968 with a two-year prison term (Marcello served six months in high style).[46]

Sept or Oct. 1966?: Sometime "in the fall of 1966", Stephen Roy says, Dave was sent to the hospital.

> **Stephen Roy** (Ed. Forum, 15 Feb. 2005): I now have access to most of Ferrie's medical records.... I have new information about Ferrie's medical condition. He saw a doctor and was actually hospitalized in the fall of 1966. The symptoms he was complaining of are quite interesting ... I have noted before that Ferrie had long experienced severe headaches

from 2PM to 6PM. He began complaining of head pain and other symptoms in the spring of 1966 and thought he might have encephalitis ... [47]

Concerns about autopsy photos: I was unable to obtain these records, which Mr. Roy has chosen to keep for his book. These records, along with Dave's autopsy photos, had been shown to researchers just before the Internet became available. Despite requests to place these records and photos on the Internet, they remain in the hands of Mr. Roy and a few others. Perhaps Mr. Roy will someday show them to us. It can be argued that Dave was over-medicating on Proloid (see Appendix IX), but Dave suspects, through self-diagnosis, that he has encephalitis, perhaps based on events in 1963: "Cancer or even exposure to certain drugs or toxins may also cause encephalitis."[48] (See Appendix IX) Our virus-laden lung cancer project was dangerous. David may have believed a virus in the bioweapon had infected him. Dr. Sherman was dead. He was probably no longer able to directly contact Ochsner. Dave might have thought he had a version of autoimmune encephalitis, with cancer the eventual end product.[49] [Note: Nevertheless, David still flies. He still teaches students how to fly. And they still praise his abilities.]

Oct. 1966: David is hired as a flight instructor at a flight school operated by Al Crouch at the New Orleans Lakefront Airport. [Tommy L. Clark accompanies him]. David also still works as a chartered pilot for Saturn Aviation, run by Crouch.[50] "Some time" during his work with Al Crouch at the New Orleans Lakefront Airport, Crouch finds out that David's "certificate" had expired (was this for training students?). Crouch is upset.[51]

Nov. 1966: When David requests FAA to allow him to use Buster Abadie's office as a flight school, Abadie "withdraw[s] the privilege...[as] Ferrie abused it..."[52] FAA turns down the request.

Dec. 1966: (from Richard Billings' diary) Garrison tells Billings that David Ferrie is "a helluva pilot, also a hypnotist, a defrocked priest and a fag" and was "the link between Oswald and Cubans."[53]

JACK RUBY'S ILLNESS AND DEATH FROM A GALLOPING CANCER

On Dec. 5, 1966 a judge rules that Jack Ruby's trial was held under prejudice, and a new trial is planned. Newspapers reported that Wichita Falls was selected as the new venue for Jack Ruby's trial, to be held in February.

Dec. 7, 1966: Jack Ruby slips a note into Al Maddox' hand. It says that he has been injected with cancer cells. Ruby has previously given other notes to Maddox, to give to his family, and he will do so at Parkland hospital, as well. When Maddox tells Ruby's sister, Eva Grant about the note, Grant thinks Ruby is hallucinating.

Maddox told Jim Marrs and me that a "doctor came down from Chicago" and "gave Jack penicillin shots for his cold.

"The doctor stayed on, until they took Jack to the hospital," Maddox said. "After that, he left."

Maddox, who had observed the Chicago doctor, then said, "I don't know why that doctor gave him so many shots."

"Were they all in the behind — in his buttocks?"

"Damn, I have to think about that. No. He got some in his arm. In his arm."

> **2002 INTERVIEW WITH AL MADDOX**
>
> I personally interviewed Al Maddox in July 2002. He brought out boxes of letters people had written to Jack, showed me Jack's expensive glasses, and shared hours of personal information about Jack. Al told me about Jack Ruby's life in jail, and at Parkland Hospital. In the photo, right, Al Maddox looks with awe at the rifle taken from the TSBD. He said everyone in the office wore bowties, just as did Lt. Carl Day. "We were a close bunch," he said. "It was like a fraternity."

Jim Marrs supported Maddox's claim. He told me that Policeman Tom Tilson said it was the opinion of a number of Dallas police officers that Ruby had received injections of cancer while he was incarcerated in the Dallas County Jail.

Dec. 9, 1966: Jack Ruby is admitted to Parkland Hospital. Ruby, who fatally shot Lee Oswald and who many believe was an associate of David Ferrie, through links to Carlos Marcello, was to have a re-trial in February or March 1967, in Wichita Falls, Texas. Of course a re-trial would focus on Lee Oswald as well, and on the Kennedy assassination.

> **Jack Ruby**: I have been used for a purpose (To Chief Justice Earl Warren, June 7, 1964). Ruby's interview with the Warren Commission was 120 pages long, replete with incompetent handling of information and leads that Ruby offered. Ruby's plea to be transferred out of Dallas, that he could not safely disclose what he knew with Dallas jailers present, fell on deaf ears. He then predicted (correctly) that he would never be able to testify again.

A researcher, Greg Parker, told The Education Forum that Jack Ruby was paranoid about cancer injections given to Jewish patients in New York in 1963. Certainly Ruby was paranoid about Jews being killed and tortured. But Parker summarily dismisses Ruby's having visited David Ferrie and me in New Orleans, proposing, instead, a plausible theory that beryllium – a potent carcinogen – was used to give Ruby lung cancer in jail. However, heavy metal poisoning usually sets in before cancer, and the method back in 1967 was uncertain. I repeat here that David and I had expounded to Jack – a 'health nut' – on the method to be used to kill Castro because he was curious, and Dave trusted him.

> **Greg Parker**: Deputy sheriff Al Maddox claimed to researchers in the 1980s that the doctor who gave Ruby the injections was from Chicago. Though not from Chicago, Alan Adelson said he had met with Dr Jolyon West in the Windy City to discuss the case. (Earl Ruby HSCA testimony) The last word however, probably should go to the Inspector General in reference to CIA medical experiments: "The risk of compromise of the program through correct diagnosis of an illness by an unwitting medical specialist is regularly considered and is stated to be a governing factor in the decision to conduct a given test. The Bureau officials
>
>
> Al Maddox and Jack Ruby.
>
> also maintain close working relations with local police authorities which could be utilized to protect the activity in critical situations." (July 26, 1963 memo from JS Eamon to Director, CIA).[54]

News articles said Ruby would receive surgery or chemo and radiation, but Ruby was not operated on. There is no record that he ever received any radiation or proper chemotherapy to fight the cancer.

Greg Parker published news articles: "Cancer has been found in the lining of Ruby's chest, in addition to the lymph node on his neck, where it was originally discovered. Both lungs are filled with suspicious looking nodules. The cancer spread to these areas; physicians are still looking for the place it started. The right lung was collapsed by the pressure of four quarts of fluid that were in his chest cavity when he was taken Friday from the Dallas County jail.... Dr. Barnett said it was impossible to tell how long Ruby had been suffering from cancer and declined even to speculate whether he may have had it when he killed Oswald."

Parker also posted this intriguing FBI report of a memo concerning Jack Ruby titled, "Cancer Artificially Induced":

ORIGINATOR:FBIFROM:[NoFrom]TO:[NoTo]TITLE:[NoTitle]
DATE:03/17/1967PAGES:2DOCUMENTTYPE:MEMORANDUM.
SUBJECTS : RUBY, JACK; CANCER ARTIFICIALLY INDUCED.
CLASSIFICATION : UNCLASSIFIED RESTRICTIONS : OPEN
IN FULL CURRENT STATUS : OPEN DATE OF LAST REVIEW :
06/04/1993 COMMENTS : Box 15. Section 89.

Others have recognized Dr. Jolyon West's involvement as sinister: The establishment allowed CIA programmer Dr. Louis Jolyon "Jolly" West to examine Jack Ruby in his jail cell. When Ruby

Louis "Jolly" West

refused to admit to insanity, West labeled him "paranoid and mentally ill" and Ruby was placed on pills, which were called "happy pills". Ruby believed he was being poisoned by the establishment... CIA documents show that grants were given to Dr. West for studies entitled, "Psychophysiological Studies of Hypnosis and Suggestibility" and "Studies of Dissociative States." Further, "Dr. Lois Jolyon West was cleared at Top Secret for his work on MKULTRA."[55] Jack's nephew and sister did describe some wild psychotic incidents, including suicide attempts.

But imagine Jolyon entering your jail cell, armed with needles, pills, and power!

Al Maddox told me on July 18, 2002 that Ruby was chained to his hospital bed not only while dying, but even after death "so the body could not be hauled off." Amazingly, Ruby had no elastic stockings on to stop a blood clot. Parkland Doctors told the press at first that Ruby had "pneumonia" – a common cause of the ascites fluid that drained from his lungs. One report said Ruby was in the x-ray room soon after admission for 45 minutes. The diagnosis was changed the next day to lung cancer. Doctors treating Ruby had strong links to New Orleans, Dr. Alton Ochsner, and Tulane.[56]

Jack Ruby – *Life* magazine photo, 1/04/67.

Jan. 3, 1967: Jack Ruby dies at Parkland Hospital of lung cancer, due to a pulmonary embolism that traveled to his leg.

THE DALLAS TIMES HERALD FINANCIAL EDITION

DALLAS, TEXAS, TUESDAY EVENING, JANUARY 3, 1967

Cancer Conquers

RUBY IS DEAD

Action Line

INVASION OF HAITI THWARTED

Oswald Slayer's Death Peaceful

NEW PRESIDENT Citizens Council Selects Bowles

How Ruby knew what had happened to him is fully explained in the book *Me & Lee*. He died in as few as 28 days after he said he had been injected with cancer cells. It took Dr. Earl F. Rose nearly a month, until Feb. 1, to release the cause of death:

> The autopsy studies on the above named deceased have been completed. The protocol is closed to show the cause of death as follows: Pulmonary emboli as immediate cause of death secondary to bronchiolar carcinoma of the lungs.

Ruby's fatal cancer advanced at such a rapid pace after its discovery that it is rather absurd to suggest that his cancer was a slow-growing matter of years. Ruby was described as healthy until his sister, Eva, complained he was looking bad. That was a few weeks before he was admitted to Parkland Hospital. It is possible that Ruby's illness, could have been caused by an onset of pneumonia in his poorly heated cell, which provided an excuse to bring in "the new doctor from Chicago" to give him "shots."

GARRISON PUTS PRESSURE ON DAVID FERRIE

On December 12, 1966 Jim Garrison, intent on learning more about David Ferrie, found a way to spy on his private life, using a teen who was often in trouble with the law: "... at New Orleans Lakefront Airport, Lou Ivon had located a former airplane mechanic of Ferrie's named Jimmy Johnson and had persuaded him to go back to work for Ferrie but to keep contact with our office."[57] Dave lets Jimmy move in with him.

Dec.15, 1966: David Ferrie is interviewed by Asst. DA John Volz for Garrison. This interview seems to take the place of a subpoena that had been issued by Garrison's Grand Jury. David tells Volz, among many other things, that he and the boys took shotguns for goose hunting in Galveston (Not mentioned in 1963).

I am told Beauboeuf's friends/relatives in Louisiana had shotguns to borrow. Dave tells Volz they had shotguns when they went looking for geese, first using the ferry and then driving from Texas over into Louisiana. Trouble is, they never stopped on the way *to* Texas to pick up shotguns, and friends and relatives lived further east. The logistics don't work. David was probably lying. I suspect he asked Beauboeuf and Coffey to lie about it, too.

Clay Shaw Can't Remember Where He Was....
Shaw gets an interview for a Christmas present in 1966.

> **Bill Davy**: ...when [Sciambra asked Shaw] where he was at the time of the assassination, he said he was traveling by train, on his way to San Francisco. With the exception of E. Howard Hunt, just about every American who was alive at the time of the assassination can remember where they were on that fateful day.... [In fact,] Shaw was already in San Francisco at the time of the assassination, in the company of San Francisco Trade Mart Director, J. Monroe Sullivan. After his arrest, Shaw ... [said] he was at the St. Francis Hotel at the time of the assassination. Later, under oath at his own trial, Shaw said he was invited to make a speech at the request of Sullivan. Sullivan, to this day, disputes this.[58]

Shaw told Warren Commission defender James R. Phelan, who wrote for the *Saturday Evening Post*, that he only had to stay at his desk all day to establish an alibi. But Shaw knew that FBI informants in The Big Easy's homosexual underground might say anything. We know that Shaw invited himself to speak at a Trade Mart meeting in San Francisco, and that when he was told that JFK had been shot, he showed no reaction and said he wanted to give his speech anyway.

Shaw manipulated Lee Oswald until Lee lost all trust in him. He was a key source of finance in our CIA-backed project to kill Fidel Castro. New Orleans had suffered due to Castro when half the city's most profitable trade was cut off after Cuba, which felt threatened by the world's mightiest power, turned to the USSR. Because of his prominence and proximity to many alphabet agencies, after Garrison arrests him, Shaw got backing and protection from them.

DAVID'S FLIGHT SCHOOL SETUP

In November 1966, when Dave was both a contract pilot for Al Crouch's Saturn Aviation and a flight instructor in Crouch's flight school,[59] he found himself in trouble with FAA (a familiar story). Reporters Rosemary James and Jack Wardlaw[60] say Crouch fired him, apparently regarding contract pilot assignments. This was at the same time that Tommie Clark moved in with Dave, supposedly to "watch him because he was sick." But Dave was sick in the fall. This might have been Tommie's excuse to hide David's intention to train Tommie to help with his own flight school. Tommie is probably a sex object as well. Dave needs an office at the airport, but nobody wants to rent facilities to him. He tries to use the airport's restaurant, instead, and gets caught. The FAA dislikes Dave and refuses to give him space in the Administration Building.

Briefly, after David's flying school all but shuts down, he is stressed. He's been interviewed again, too. All the old fear is beginning again. Tommie, who has a rap sheet for stealing somebody's credit card from Dave's apartment, helping to steal a car, and vagrancy, eventually admits on Mar. 16, 1967[61] that he stayed with Dave two months, leaving him two weeks before Dave died.

Dec. 31, 1966: Roy Tell, former CAP, says he and David Ferrie "exchanged greetings at the New Orleans Airport."[62] Nobody knows how Dave spent New Year's.

Jan. 18, 1967: David Ferrie comes into a large sum of cash. Jimmy Johnson, who has been calling in to Garrison's office regularly as "Agent #1" reports that he was instructed to retrieve an "8 x 10 envelope under the seat of a white Chevrolet [parked at the airport] with no license plates. David told Jimmy "I'm going to buy a new car, because I've just got hold of some cash." Funds in Dave's possession were estimated by the DA's Lynn Loisel as between $30-$40,000.[63]

While Jimmy Johnson makes some outrageous claims to the DA, Marcello's United Air Taxi jet fleet is prospering in New Orleans. I'm told Dave had bought stock in it, and almost certainly still owned shares. Did he cash in his stock? Enough money to "buy a new car" would be about $3,000 in 1967.

Though not living a life of luxury, David is not in financial distress and is now financially secure enough to start his own flight school, but there are no offices available at the airport.

Tues., Feb.7, 1967: Witness J.G. is hired by Al Campbell of Bell Helicopter, and her husband Bob is hired by Al Crouch, Director of Saturn Aviation. Both jobs are located at Lakefront Airport. Bob will be making contract flights for Al Crouch. Arriving from Ecuador around Christmas, they will not have a TV set or even a radio for a while. Of course they are unaware of the Garrison investigation, which still hasn't reached the papers. Bob is an "instrument pilot" and J.G. works as a secretary. Their little daughter is allowed to play in and around the office and hangar doors on her tricycle.

Tues. approx. 3:00 PM, Feb. 7, 1967: Al Crouch fires David Ferrie, his popular flight school instructor. James and Wardlaw say Crouch complained that, "Ferrie was violating their agreement."

Al Campbell's former secretary, J.G., says she believes Crouch rid himself of Ferrie because he was "terrified." Garrison's investigators had put Ferrie under constant surveillance and were "down at the airport all the time." Though J.G.'s husband started working for Crouch just before David was fired, and she was working for Campbell in the same airport, J.G. never got a chance to see Ferrie.

4:00 PM, Feb. 7, 1967: A training plane owned by Crouch's Saturn Aviation takes off from Lakefront. Gordon Wade needs a qualifying cross-country flight with a return and landing at 10 PM. Ferrie, fired earlier that day, was supposed to have been the pilot, but Crouch asks J.G.'s husband, Bob, to take Dave's place.

5:30 PM, Feb. 7, 1967: The training plane, with Bob G. substituting for David Ferrie, crashes in Slidell. The official report blamed the pilot, despite evidence a witness offered concerning sabotage.[64]

THE LAST DAYS OF DAVID FERRIE: A WITNESS SPEAKS OUT

Witness J. G. had tried a few times to tell her story. After she went to a researcher who misquoted her information, she almost gave up. She felt, too, that she had waited too long. Hobbled because she didn't have Internet, this discrete lady was used to minding her own business. In 2013 J.G. did not even own a cell phone. Finally she reached out to TrineDay publisher, Kris Millegan, who said I would respect what she had to say. I traveled a great distance to communicate with her on a secure telephone. It was soon clear that she was intelligent and sincere. Slowly, she began to reveal her secrets.

"We had some homosexual Cubans, taking flying lessons," she said first. "And it is about David Ferrie. But I'm afraid – I'm so afraid – to talk to you!"

"Let's start at the beginning," I suggested. J.G., as she talked, grew calmer.

"It started with Al Crouch – and then there was Allen Campbell,"[65] she told me. "I was new there. I and my husband had just come back from Ecuador, and we were out of touch with our country. We didn't know JFK had been assassinated. We arrived at Christmas, 1966, not long before they killed David Ferrie. Ferrie was working out at the Lakefront Airport. So was my husband, Bob."

I told J.G. that I knew Dave had been hired around October 1966, by Al Crouch, who ran Saturn Aviation. Dave was no longer flying for businesses owned by the Mafia. "So," I commented, "Do you think they murdered David Ferrie?"

"They most definitely did," she said firmly. J.G. has a soft, gentle voice, the voice of a lady who is comfortable baking pies and typing a letter for her boss. But as the memories crowded in, her voice became tense, and fear threaded her words like a sharp needle dipping in and out of the cloth of her story.

"What I would be hearing about, back then, would just boggle my mind," she said. "It was about David Ferrie." I wanted very much to get all the information I could from J.G., but we had to start even further back. "So, you were new at your job, as a secretary, with Allen Campbell?"

"Yes."

"Who was he?"

" Allen Campbell was the head of the Bell Helicopter port at the Lakefront Airport," she told me. The researcher who misquoted her was Joan Mellen, she said. After J.G. had talked to her, Mellen "had gone out there" and talked to Al Campbell. He had gone to school with Lee Oswald, J.G. thought. "He knew who Oswald was," she added. "He was always hanging around Guy Banister's office." I had heard of Al. Al had seen Lee at Banister's. Just as his brother Dan, Al did investigative work and college campus commie-hunting for Banister. It was similar to what Lee told me he had also done for Banister in the months of April and May 1963.

"Al was one of those people who knew too much," she said, so when news of Garrison's investigation into the Kennedy assassination hit the papers, and David Ferrie's name got plastered from one end of New Orleans to the other, Al Crouch became frightened. "Dave was fired because Crouch was scared to death," J.G. commented. "So he got rid of him."

"Ferrie – he took two gay people [pilots] with him, to our terminal," she went on. "That left Crouch needing a pilot right away. That's how my husband got hired." J.G., Bob, and their 3-year-old daughter had only been in New Orleans a couple of months. Dave would complain a day or two later to Al Campbell that, without his job at the airport, what future did he have there?

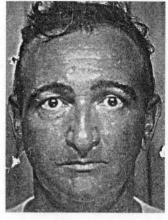

"Just watch," said Campbell to J.G. "These are David Ferrie's last days. Pay attention," he said, "because this is history." Campbell wasn't alone in his declarations. Crouch said, "I want you to go down and take a look at David Ferrie, but you'd better hurry. He'll be dead in a week." J.G. coughed, and sounded uncomfortable talking about it. "I decided not to meet him," she said. "I didn't want to get that close to a man in that kind of danger. I was worried about my little girl."

But J.G. had no idea how close, personal and hideous a turn things were about to take, just because of David Ferrie.

"When my husband – he was an instrument pilot – when my boss fired Ferrie," she said, "he said to Bob, Would you take this night flight? This guy needs a cross-country night flight. Will you take this young man up?"

J.G. explained her situation. "We were new in town still – no phone, no TV, no car. We had just moved here..." She said they fueled up the plane David Ferrie was supposed to have used – a Cessna – and, her voice breaking, she went on to say that she "waited and waited ... I kept watching the clock ... I kept waiting and waiting with my little girl, then suddenly, I sat straight up." She knew, deep inside, that her husband's plane had crashed. She could feel it. She got her daughter up and they walked toward New Orleans to find somebody with a phone, because the buses weren't running.

"So they called," she said. "And we found out a farmer saw this plane trying to land, couldn't hear a motor – it was out of gas – he said he heard it crash in thick woods, where there weren't any roads. I tried – I called the police," she went on. "They finally got to it at the crack of dawn through those thick trees and bushes. The plane was hanging upside down. Gordon's face was ruined by hanging upside down. He had to have his face reconstructed." As she fell silent, I asked her if she was okay. "Bob had a concussion," she went on. "There was blood all over him, too."

Her husband told her, from his bed in Slidell Hospital, what had happened. They had refueled. Yes, they had. But they were losing fuel at a huge rate, nonetheless. From his unique perspective, Bob, trapped as he was in the plane, could see that the fuel tank had been punctured.

I remembered at once how Dave had told me that vandals had thrown sugar into his Stinson's engine. But this wasn't mere vandalism. This was attempted murder. On David Ferrie. It was he who had just been fired. The plot to kill Ferrie had rested on the premise that he would be the pilot.

But no! Stop! You are not to think about *conspiracies!* There are no conspiracies! Nothing in the Kennedy assassination should suggest anything like that to a rational person. Right? Think again. "All of a sudden," J.G. says, "I heard a helicopter." She knew who that had to be. "Here comes Al," Bob said. But the visit wasn't a get-well sympathy call. "He looked at Bob and said, 'We gotta talk."

"They're trying to take your license away. They want to take your license."

According to officials, there was no puncture in the tank. Bob had simply made a heinous error – he had failed to refuel the Cessna, it ran out of gas, and it crashed. He would lose his license.

"Go over and look in my shirt," Bob told J.G.. The shirt had been removed and set aside. "It was all bloody," she said. "It was soaked with blood. I went over and looked into the shirt pocket. It was bloodstained, but it was there – the fuel receipt. He and Gordon had fueled up. He had proof that plane had been refueled, because of the pictures (we took)." No investigation was made into who could have punctured the Cessna's fuel tank.

11:00 PM, Feb. 7, 1967: The plane crash is reported in the news. David Ferrie will soon consult Crouch and will become aware that he was the target. Tommie L. Clark becomes frightened and moves out of Dave's apartment.

Dave had been carrying around a manila file he called "the bomb." Perhaps he was using this file as an "insurance policy." Jimmy Johnson described the file as containing diagrams and drawings, such as of Dealey Plaza, as seen from a tall building, a designation for the president's car, below, and other material seeming to indicate information about the Kennedy assassination. Bootsie Gay, who knew David, saw G. Wray Gill's secretary, Regina Franchevich, boxing up Dave's papers at Gill's office. She tried to rescue a similar diagram that was being discarded, without success.[66]

Feb. 8-16, 1967: "I'm taking all my boys with me," David told Al Crouch when he was fired. Witness J.G. says David had been Crouch's most popular flight school pilot. David was also giving flying lessons to some CAP cadets.[67] Afraid to go home, he now spent most of his time at the airport.[68] "He practically moved in," J. G. says. Dave, she said, was using the airport's pilot's lounge, with its storage, showers and rest areas, as a second home. J.G.: "They had this pilot's rest and overnight area. He was taking a bath in the bathroom, doing his laundry there, eating there, drinking there."

Airport lounge.

Feb. 14, 1967: *Life* magazine's resident investigator in New Orleans, Richard Billings, writes privately on this date that David Ferrie carries a loaded rifle ["David William Ferrie", Box 4, folder 48]. Stressed and frightened, David keeps the loaded rifle handy when he sleeps at his apartment. Surveillance on Dave's apartment is being conducted by *Life* investigators. From their vantage point in a house across the street, they can see portions of David's living room and front porch.

Feb. 15, 1967: David is still giving flying lessons. His friends, however, are withdrawing as the plane crash crisis is exposed as a plot against Ferrie. Al Crouch realizes the end is near. He tells his secretary, " ... go down and look at David Ferrie ... you'd better hurry, he'll be dead in a week," J.G. said somberly. "I never could bring myself to go take a look at him. And Al was right. David was dead a week later."[69]

A VIEW OF DAVID FERRIE'S WORLD BEFORE HIS DEATH

Bruce Nolan Interview: "There were many things that were strange about David Ferrie, beginning with his awful wigs and those changeable, glued-on mohair eyebrows, necessitated by a disease that left him hairless. But there was more: the stained, untucked shirt scorched by unfiltered Camels, his spectacularly lewd humor and his showy way of holding forth on topics like pathology, physics and organic chemistry.... He was a pilot by profession.... His associations were shadowy. There were rumors of mob connections. But there was this grudging consensus around the airport: He could really fly." (*New Orleans Advocate*)[70]

"I met him at 18, just before he became both dead and famous. In his last weeks of obscurity, Ferrie worked as the single flight instructor for a tiny flight school at Lakefront. I paid $600 in summer wages toward a private pilot's license. Early into the lessons, Ferrie and his one-armed boss had a falling out. Ferrie left; I collected a partial refund and followed him to protect my investment. Over three or four months in late 1966 and early 1967, we spent 20 or 25 hours squeezed together behind the prop of a tiny single-engine Cessna. In hourly increments over several months we flew repeated touch-and-go landings, or climbed to 2,500 feet over the empty marshes toward Chef Menteur. He taught stalls and spin recovery, crosswind landings, navigation and rudimentary instrument flying ... our relationship was commercial. We did not talk politics.... Ferrie had few students, little income and no office. At Lakefront we would meet in the lobby, sometimes have a couple of cups of coffee waiting for the weather to clear.

"That's when he would indulge his blue humor, or launch some disquisition on his amateur research in chemistry or pathology.... I recollect that once, in his persona of unrecognized scientific genius, he disparaged the clinical competence of Dr. Nick Chetta, then the Orleans Parish coroner.... Odd, I thought, that he would single out so minor an officeholder. He said something to the effect that a clever somebody could easily slip something past Chetta.... One day in early 1967, I arrived for a lesson and found Ferrie slumped over a desk, crippled by a blazing headache. He could not fly. He could barely open one eye. I shoveled him into my car. He asked to be taken to his home on Louisiana Avenue Parkway. I got him to the porch and watched him shuffle inside ..." Nolan never saw him again.

Feb. 17, 1967: The Garrison probe becomes news. An 'extra' front page story by reporters Rosemary James, Jack Dempsey and David Snyder exposes Jim Garrison's investigation into the Kennedy assassination. "Mysterious Trips Cost Large Sums... DA Here Launches Full JFK Death Plot Probe." James says she showed Garrison the story before

publication, that he read part of it, then responded with a "No comment." Snyder told readers that Garrison's office spent $8000 ($68,000 in 2014 dollars) on trips to Texas, Florida and California.

> **Garrison**: "Anyone who says I saw that story in advance is a liar."[71]

5:30 PM, Feb. 17, 1967: Davie calls the unsavory Pershing Gervais, a former investigator for Garrison. Gervais tells him to talk to the press; to give the press his side of the story.

> **Peter Whitmey**, who studied Gervais closely, wrote: Upon the death of Jim Garrison in Oct. 1992, Gervais (in a *Times-Picayune* interview) made no reference to his own lack of credibility, but was quite willing to give his assessment of Jim Garrison: "I cannot say anything but evil about him...He was a menace, and anybody who thinks he was an honest man is insane." It seems to me that this description more accurately describes Pershing Gervais.[72]

Friday, Feb. 17, 1967: Distraught, Dave invites reporter David Snyder, one of the three writers who broke the story about Garrison's investigation, to his apartment. Anti-Oswald researcher Patricia Lambert says Snyder described David as "physically ill ... his voice was barely audible, his breathing unsteady." On the way up to his second floor apartment, David's "steps were feeble ... he said he had encephalitis ... Snyder has no compassion for this sick man: his interview lasts 4 ½ hours, from 6-10:30 PM. Soon after, Sam DePino of channel 12 called. The call lasted about 20 minutes.

Feb. 18, 1967: It's another horrible day for David Ferrie. The *Times-Picayune* runs a huge front page story: "DAs Won't Confirm JFK Plot Probe On" revealing David's name and his statements, all of it penned by David Snyder. Dave is again a notorious figure. He wants to sue somebody. He calls Lou Ivon at Garrison's office: Ivon says he'll come over to conduct a fair and factual interview. Meanwhile, Garrison's staff is busy questioning Dave's friends, including Dante Marochini, Melvin Coffey and David's "godson" (addict Morris Brownlee).

David Ferrie's last photo? Feb. 18, 1967.

3:30 PM, Feb. 18, 1967: Andrew Sciambra and Lou Ivon interview David Ferrie at his apartment [See Appendix IV]. David tells them he is "sick and weak" and hasn't been able to keep any food in his stomach. Sciambra, who writes the report, thinks David is putting on an act because he "moaned and groaned with each step he took up the stairs."

Do not be fooled into thinking these are the symptoms of a bleeding aneurysm. *No* headache was mentioned. (See Appendix IX).

Most of Dave's interview covers old ground. But then he explains why the Magic Bullet Theory has problems. Sciambra is impressed: "...FERRIE went into a long spiel about JFK's neck wound. In the course of his lecture on anatomy and pathology, he named every bone in the human body and every hard and soft muscle ... FERRIE said that if the same bullet that struck JFK in the back or neck eventually struck Connally, that Connally or JFK had to be a contortionist. He then rattled off more scientific information in regards to bones and skin and how a bullet decreases in speed when it strikes an object and how the same bullet could not have possibly caused all that damage. FERRIE said that the question would never be answered because the doctor that performed the tracheotomy had 10 thumbs and left unanswered the most important question of all time..."

Andrew "Moo Moo" Sciambra was a boxer before joining Garrison's team of investigators. Garrison considered him honest, bold and intelligent.

George Lardner, as does Dave Snyder, both claimed later that David Ferrie suddenly changed his mind about the Magic Bullet Theory – that he became a "believer" after studying JFK's autopsy report more carefully. It was a well-timed change of opinion that Dave might have used in hopes of reducing suspicious, as hinted in the Sciambra interview.

> **Sciambra:** "I then said, 'In other words Dave, you don't buy the 'one-shot theory'?" FERRIE said he wasn't saying anything because he didn't want J. Edgar on his tail, that he had enough with Garrison to contend with...".
>
> **Stephen Roy** (posting as Blackburst, 4/2/99): In 1967, Ferrie studied a few assassination books and came to believe that there might have been more than one gunman.[73]

Mr. Roy doesn't give Dave enough credit. Anyone who truly knew Dave would have expected him to become a Kennedy assassination expert from Day One, because he had been implicated as Lee Oswald's getaway pilot back in November 1963. He'd been questioned by Garrison's people and the FBI about the assassination. Having been a focus of unwanted attention for weeks, Dave would have read more than "a few books." He would have read everything he could get his hands on, making sure he was safe. And he would say only those things that would keep him safe.

I can't imagine how frightened Dave had to be when he telephoned Lou Ivon to say, "You know what this news story does to me, don't you? I'm a dead man. From here on, believe me, I'm a dead man."[74]

DAVID FERRIE AND HIS HEALTH – THE DEBATE

A researcher calling himself Atlasrecrd wrote: "BTW David [Blackburst], why was Dave always complaining about that cancer in his neck?"

> **Stephen Roy** (posting as Blackburst): He complained about cancer of the neck, and also about encephalitis. The symptoms of these things are not unlike what one would experience with berry aneurysms, and might be misdiagnosed by an amateur medical person. A "doctor" who diagnoses himself has a fool for a patient…

Is Mr. Roy? Yes, a leaking "berry aneurysm" might at first cause a headache, but it will not recur every afternoon on schedule, as reported, for months at a time. Dave had suffered from migraine headaches for decades. Yes, he had some healed "leaks," reported years later (1992) but not mentioned in the autopsy (they were too small to be seen without a microscope). All good doctors know that high blood pressure can cause small bleeds, and hypertension is listed as one of the causes of Dave's death.

Dave's headaches afflicted him every afternoon around 2:00 PM. There is a tendency in this case to attribute Dave's health problems to a berry aneurysm about to burst. But Dave also had severe neck pain. Leaking aneurysms do not cause daily neck pain.

On the other hand, overdosing on Proloid, a thyroid medication, can create a daily recurrence of headaches. Dave was diagnosed as "hypo" long ago. He may have needed Proloid all these years. A little "extra" Proloid packs a feel-good effect. It can fool people. Keep doing it, and it will make you sick. If Dave took Proloid every morning, and the dose was too high, it could create high blood pressure and a headache within hours. Next, neck pain, fatigue and depression can set in. (See Appendix IX).

Dave may have been unaware of the connection because a single pill takes 5-6 hours to create such a headache. If he took a handful, his blood pressure would skyrocket in a matter of an hour or two. I, myself, once accidentally overdosed on a similar thyroid medication, and felt the effects within an hour.

If David didn't connect Proloid to his symptoms, if he thought the headache and neck pain might have resulted from an inflammation of the brain (encephalitis), knowing one of our concerns when working with the radiated monkey virus and its cancer was exactly that, he might have thought that exposure to the cancer viruses, exacerbated by his weakened immune system, had given him a case of encephalitis. This would explain why Dave told others that he was afraid he had this condition.

Feb. 19, 1967: Jim Garrison makes national front pages with the *Times-Picayune*'s stories: "Garrison Predicts Success for Probe," 'Oswald Did Not Act Alone.'" He promises a press conference on the 20th.

1:00 PM, Feb. 19, 1967: Garrison's James Alcock interviews David Ferrie's one-time friend, James Lewallen. (Note that Lewallen is still not being given the attention he deserves to this very day). In Alcock's Feb. 20 report, Lewallen said he originally met David in Cleveland in 1948 when David taught flying at Benedictine High School. By 1953 he was in New Orleans and moved in with Dave and two other Eastern Air Line pilots. He worked for EAL, as well. Lewallen lived next door to Clay Shaw at 1309 Dauphine from 1958–64, and became Shaw's friend. Lewallen made some dubious claims, such as that David Ferrie and Clay Shaw never mentioned each other, and that David Ferrie never mentioned "the Cuban situation" at any time, even though he revealed that through Dave, he met both Layton Martens and Guy Banister.

Lewallen said David called him up and asked him to help go through piles of junk, papers and books, in the presence of two FBI agents, seeking something about Lee Oswald among his possessions. But was Lewallen really there as Dave's friend? They had parted ways six months earlier, when David commandeered his plane one night.

As Garrison's investigator James Alcock reported: "They had a falling out over the use of an Ercoupe Airplane owned by [Lewallen] and WILLIAM MUNSON. [Ferrie] had flown this plane, which has a range of about 400 miles at night against the wishes of

[Lewallen] and WILLIAM MUNSON. This flight took place some-time in 1965."

The FBI later spoke "briefly" to Lewallen in his car, asking about Dave. Neither agent took any notes. With David safely dead, Lewallen could say anything. But why was Lewallen with the two FBI agents? It might have been vengeful: Lewallen used to room with Dave in 1963 and may have seen some evidence that Lee and Dave knew each other. Of course, Dave would have had to be crazy to keep any evidence of Lee after the assassination. In photos taken in 1967, a framed group photo of Lee with his CAP squadron is no longer on display on the living room wall, along with other CAP group photos. What happened to all the framed photos of Dave's many cadets?.

Sunday, Feb. 19, 1967: One of Garrison's aides, asked to locate an anti-Castro activist and Mafia man of interest, Eladio del Valle, finds him in a Miami bar. He is a friend of David Ferrie, according to several sources. In three days, del Valle will die – David Ferrie's death will be in newspapers at the same time.

> **Stephen Roy:** Ferrie misses a flight instruction appointment with Alan Shear.

David has been giving flying lessons right to the end. On weekends, he has been teaching students who work on weekdays. But Dave is now so stressed and ill that he is no longer able to keep these appointments.

WAS DAVID AFRAID FOR HIS LIFE ON FEB. 19, 1967?

David makes a telephone call in the late afternoon to Lou Ivon. Ivon and Lynn Loisel will pick up David at a bar (he's too afraid to stay at his apartment). They register him at The Fontaineb-leau Motel under an alias.

But *why* did David Ferrie call Lou Ivon? Why did Ivon and Loisel take him to the Fontainebleau?

Lou Ivon

Read how this watershed event is reported to us by 'both sides' of the debate. It's an eye-opener.

> **Stephen Roy** (Education Forum, 2005): He later calls Lou Ivon, who sets Ferrie up at the Fontainebleau, but Ferrie does not stay put.

> **Dave Reitzes**[75]: That evening, Ferrie called an assistant DA with whom he was friendly, Lou Ivon. He said that reporters were pestering him around the clock, and asked Ivon for help in temporarily getting away from them. With Jim Garrison's permission, Ivon got Ferrie a room at the Fontainebleau Motor Hotel.[76]

But Roy and Reitzes make no mention of Dave's fears. Why? If he just wishes to escape being interviewed by reporters, why did Dave make a call to reporter Dave Snyder later that night? Compare to:

> **Joan Mellen**: ... just as Ivon was sitting down to Sunday dinner, his telephone rang. "My life is being threatened," Ferrie said. "They're going to kill me!" He pleaded for protection. (*A Farewell to Justice*, p. 104).

> **Bill Davy**: (interview of Lou Ivon, whom Ferrie called) Ferrie was "very scared – a wild man." Ferrie confided to Ivon that he had done work for the CIA and had known Oswald. He admitted he knew Clay Shaw and that Shaw, too, worked for the CIA. He added that Shaw hated Kennedy. However, he did not yet admit any involvement in the assassination.[77]

If David called Ivon because "reporters were pestering him around the clock..." asking "Ivon for help in temporarily getting away from them?" Then, why did he agree to be taken to The Fontainebleau Motor Hotel? Garrison had announced that he would hold his very first press conference at The Fontainebleau *the next day*, and it was swarming with reporters. This was, in fact, the usual place Garrison's team housed witnesses.

Evening, Feb. 19, 1967: Ivon phones Jim Garrison, who reserves Dave a room in the Fontainebleau. Ivon picks up Dave at a bar, as he is afraid to go home. Garrison witnesses are often brought to this huge hotel for 'secret' questioning and to entrap suspects by making hidden tape recordings of their conversations. Trafficante uses this same huge hotel. It is Mafia-friendly, as are all big businesses in the area. Registering David Ferrie under an alias, with the well known Ivon and Loisel at his side, is like trying to smuggle in a rabbit among wolves. As long as Dave is not alone, though, he should be safe. However, that will turn out to be a problem.

The Fontainebleau Motor Hotel was illegally financed by Teamster funds. Mafia chieftain Trafficante used The Fontainebleau when he visited New Orleans.

Owen Parsons (to Stephen Roy, Oct. 2006) Under an alias, it is here, according to Ivon, that Ferrie made his partial confession.... Ferrie [only started] supporting the Single Bullet Theory *after* fleeing from the Fontainebleau.[78]

Lou Ivon interviews David at The Fontainebleau, writing notes of the interview which later, he says, vanish from Garrison's files. Ivon then goes home to his family, leaving Lynn Loisel as David's only guard. When Loisel leaves the room to get cigarettes, he will return to find David missing.

Late evening, Feb. 19, 1967: David phones reporter Dave Snyder.

Stephen Roy (Ed. Forum 2005): More Ferrie history: ...Ferrie phones Dave Snyder and tells him that, while he had had some doubts about the WC shooting scenario, he had just resolved it in his own mind [the Magic Bullet Theory]: that the autopsy "slab" distorted the positioning of the wounds. He also tells Snyder that he plans to consult an attorney about suing Jack Martin and Garrison...[79]

So, did Dave decide to phone Snyder about his change of mind? Yes. Dave, a thoroughly frightened man, has now changed his mind about the single bullet theory, and now endorses the Warren Commission version, even though it's just one day after Dave told Andrew Sciambra the exact opposite. It seems Dave got a lot of research done, very quickly, to make such a radical turnaround. Right?

Endnotes

1. Comment by Joe Biles while examining batches of records released by the ARRB. Access at: http://www.wf.net/~biles/jfk/ferrie_FBI_1125_2.txt (Retrieved May 14, 2013).

2. Lewallen knew David Ferrie back in Cleveland's CAP, and is linked (by Aynesworth) to National Auto Rentals of New Orleans. He is an example of persons able to supply a car for Dave's use "under the table" after Dave's car was repossessed in March, 1963.

3. http://jfk.hood.edu/Collection/Weisberg Subject Index Files/F Disk/Ferrie David William/Item 85.pdf (Retrieved June 30, 2013).

4. Hoover signs and sends a document from the "Latent Fingerprint Section" (ID Division)to the SAC in San Francisco, with a copy sent to New Orleans, dated December 5, 1963, regarding "five train tickets" from Southern Pacific.(Mellen, *A Farewell to Justice*, p. 128.) Shaw went by train to San Francisco to speak at J. Monroe Sullivan's San Francisco World Trade Center on November 22. He traveled from Los Angeles on November 20 to San Francisco. He testified that he took an overnight train run by Southern Pacific ('The Lark').

5. http://jfk.hood.edu/Collection/Weisberg Subject Index Files/F Disk/Ferrie David William/Item 85.pdf (Retrieved June 30, 2013).

6. http://educationforum.ipbhost.com/index.php?showtopic 485&page=2 (Retrieved 05/05/2013).

7. Thomas "Tommie" Louis Clark, Garrison Grand Jury testimony. 03/16/1967 http://jfkassassination.net/russ/testimony/clark_t.htm. (Retrieved 01/03/2013).

8. http://jfk.hood.edu/Collection/Weisberg%20Subject%20Index%20Files/F%20Disk/Ferrie%20David%20William/Item%2007.pdf. (Retrieved 09/04/2014).

9. As quoted by researcher Peter Whitmey.

10. http://en.wikipedia.org/wiki/Eastern_Air_Lines_Flight_304 (Retrieved Aug. 12, 2013).

11. http://planecrashinfo.com/1964/1964-12.htm (Retrieved Aug. 15, 2013.).

12. Bill Davy, *Let Justice Be Done* (Reston, Virginia: Jordan Publishing, 1999) p. 310n.8; p. 185-186.

13. Mrs. Mary Banister: (4/29-30/1967) to Sciambra: "... after her husband died Mrs. DELPHINE ROBERTS and her daughter took some files from GUY BANISTER's apartment and also from GUY BANISTER's office and turned them over to Mr. G. WRAY GILL ... she believes these files were in reference to an investigation concerning DAVID FERRIE and his case with Eastern Airlines ... she later on called Mr. GILL and asked him to return these files to her and he did not do so... she also burned some files because she felt, in her opinion, that these files should be destroyed as they might hurt some innocent people..."

14. Anna Lewis to Dr. Joseph Riehl, Dr. Howard Platzman, Martin Shackelford, Debra Conway, Sondra Vincent, and myself, Jan. 3, 2000, Day's Inn, New Orleans. Anna also made similar statements on film.

15. See *Dr. Mary's Monkey*, TrineDay, 2014.

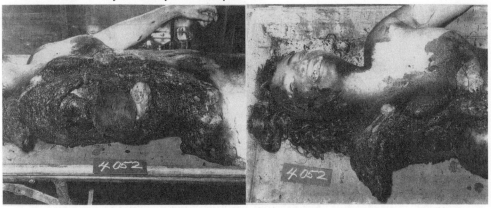

16. Records released in 1993 revealed a flight plan (HSCA RG 233) dated April 8, 1963: The flight plan ... details a pilot named Ferrie flying three passengers, Hidell, Lambert, and Diaz, from New Orleans to Garland, Texas. It is well known that Oswald used the alias of A.J. Hidell.

17. "Clay Shaw used the name "Lambert" when he rode on a plane with David Ferrie as pilot, Lee Oswald as un-recorded last-minute co-pilot, and an unknown Latino on a flight to Toronto that I observed on June 21, 1963.

18. http://educationforum.ipbhost.com/index.php?showtopic89. (Retrieved July 25, 2013).

19. http://educationforum.ipbhost.com/index.php?s7eae1f4ec1d2b3bfc7e43aaead63094&-showtopic=3 205&page=4 (Retrieved Dec. 28,2012).

20. In Florida, with my B.S. degree in anthropology (including psychology courses, culture studies, linguistics, archaeology, medical anthropology, biology, etc.) after training by the HRS, State of Florida, I was qualified to be a counselor without a degree in psychology. When the law changed a few years later, I still qualified because I was "grandfathered-in" – this was in the 1980's.

21. "Phone factoid: Tortured Connection." Dave Reitzes. http://mcadams.posc. mu.edu/factoid.htm. (Retrieved Aug, 5, 2013).

22. Jan 2005 Education Forum post: http://educationforum.ipbhost.com/index. php?showtopic(90.

23. Rod Machado Aviation Learning Center. http://www.rodmachado.com/?pd (Retrieved June 15, 2013)

24. As discovered by researcher Greg Parker.

25. See statistician Richard Charnin's well-researched analysis of mysterious deaths at http://www.lewrockwell.com/2013/04/richard-charnin/the-mysterious-deaths-of-jfk-murder-witnesses/. As of August 2014 J. McAdams' says about Gatlin, to wit: "5/65, Maurice Gatlin, Pilot for Guy Banister, Fatal fall, No connection with assassination." http://www.mcadams.posc.mu.edu/deaths.htm (Retrieved Aug. 1, 2012)

26. Stephen Roy, posting as David Blackburst, to "Bishopm" Jul 31, 2000. 9:00 am. McAdams newsgroup. In article <20000730034637.01330.00000...@ng-ci1.aol. com>;http://www.deja.com/ from original, email, 2000 from mbishop.

27. Bevilaqua: "...[Gatlin] the same lawyer used by Brig. Gen. Bonner Fellers to incorporate his For America and Ten Million Americans Mobilizing for Justice at the very same Banister complex. Fellers was involved in Cairo, Egypt with both Major Carleton S. Coon (OSS) and Brig. Gen. Hoyt Vandenberg in covert actions also involving mind control, programmed assassins and similar activities ... Gatlin, who had poor vision, could not have been a pilot.... Gatlin did fly all over the world ... in what seem to be CIA-connected activities. An attorney who specialized in Latin America, Cuban and Guatemalan affairs, with connections to France and Europe, the FBI said "[Gatlin]... General Counsel, Anti-Communist League of the Americas, a long time Castro antagonist, and Guy Banister, a former FBI agent and President of the Anti-Communist group... claimed that about 100 Jeeps were sent to Cuba through New Orleans in recent months under invoices marked as 'agricultural equipment.'"

28. *The Man on the Grassy Knoll*, by John R. Craig and Philip A. Rogers [1992] is almost the only work detailing Rogers' life. "Rogers was a brilliant recluse who lived with his parents, Fred and Edwina Rogers. On June 23, 1965, Rogers's parents were found murdered in their home, their bodies dismembered and stored in the family's refrigerator... Craig and Rogers say Rogers murdered his parents because his mother became suspicious of his alleged involvement in the Kennedy assassination...Rogers has been identified [by some] as one of the "three tramps" arrested near Dealey Plaza ...According to Watergate conspirator E. Howard Hunt's posthumously released confessions,[1][2] a gunman nicknamed "Frenchy" had been a trigger man in the assassination... "Frenchy" was alleged to be one of Rogers's CIA code names, by Craig and Rogers ... Rogers ... he was last seen piloting a light plane from Houston, in the direction of Mexico and Central America. Rogers ... is still a wanted fugitive in the United States today." http://en.wikipedia.org/wiki/Charles_Rogers_(murder_suspect). (Retrieved Aug. 5, 2013).

29. http://educationforum.ipbhost.com/index.php?showtopicI39 (Retrieved June 15, 2013).

30. "Cherami" without the 'e' is the correct spelling of her name: see Todd E. Elliot's *A Rose by Many Other Names* (TrineDay,2013).

31. The death certificate recorded death at 11AM, but Moore said he was at the hospital at 10AM and was told she was already dead. The coroner marked "DOA" in three places. The certificate was made out an astonishing five days after her death. Author Todd C. Elliott (*A Rose by Many Other Names*) found evidence that Cherami, who worked for Jack Ruby and was a heroin addict, was probably informing to the FBI, who for some reason had a long file on her, but with 1963 references missing. She was an intelligent woman: her son, Michael, became a doctor.

32. http://jfk.hood.edu/Collection/White Materials/Garrison News Clippings/1967/67-03/67- 03-006.pdf. (Retrieved Aug. 18, 2013).

33. Other witnesses: 1967 – "Banister operative Joe Newbrough recounted ... an incident that took place in the early 1960's. Banister and Ferrie were meeting in Banister's office, when Banister asked Newbrough to get Clay Shaw on the phone. Newbrough called the ITM [International Trade Mart] and reached Shaw. Banister told Newbrough to hand the phone to Ferrie, whereby Ferrie and Shaw proceeded to confer with each other." (Davy 93-94) "Betty Rubio worked at Lakefront Airport and knew Ferrie. Shortly before April of 1964, while standing in the ramp office, she noticed a plane taxi up to the office. Ferrie got out, talked to her for a bit, and then went back to his plane, where Clay Shaw met him. Shaw and Ferrie talked for a while and then Ferrie got in his plane as Shaw walked past her toward the terminal building." (Davy 185-186) http://www.wf.net/~biles/jfk/witnesses.htm.

34. http://educationforum.ipbhost.com/index.php?showtopic39&page=6 (Retrieved 03/03/2014).

35. http://www3.gendisasters.com/florida/4135/gainesville,-fl-plane-crashes-takeoff,-feb-1964 plane overloaded: http://ufdc.ufl.edu/UF00079931/00078 (Retrieved 03/03/2014).

36. http://www.leagle.com/decision/1966469191So2d278_1374 (Retrieved 03/05/2014).

37. LEEWARD & HART AERONAUTICAL CORPORATION, Appellant, v. SOUTH CENTRAL AIRLINES, INC., et al., Appellees. No. H-226, H-227. District Court of Appeal of Florida. First District. March 31, 1966. https://www.courtlistene.

38. http://www.timetableimages.com/ttimages/sca.htm (Retrieved 09/08/2013).

39. One DC-3 has a history that involved Space Air Freight Lines: Space Air Freight Lines bought this DC-3 from Flt Enterprises Inc. who had the plane in 1965. Space Air got the DC-3 in 1966. It was sold to Zephyr Aviation Inc. in Sept. 1969. It then went to Air Antilles in Nov. 1969. http://aviation-antilles.blogspot.com/2007/02/connaissez-vous-cet-avion.html Retrieved 03/04/2014).

40. [HSCA, X,XII, note 162, does use the old name, 'South Central Airlines' [1963-1964].

41. According to medical information possessed of Stephen Roy, 2005.

42. http://www.webmd.com/depression/guide/medicines-cause-depression (Retrieved Aug. 28, 2013).

43. National Institute of Health Advisory: http://www.nlm.nih.gov/medlineplus/ency/article/000204.htm.

44. http://www.insider-magazine.com/inside_the_dixie_mafia.htm (Retrieved Sept. 1, 2013).

45. http://jfk.hood.edu/Collection/Weisberg Subject Index Files/F Disk/Ferrie David Garrison Files Miscellaneous/Item 02.pdf (Retrieved Sept. 2, 2013).

46. Tom Jones. *Carlos Marcello: Big Daddy in the Big Easy*. "Punching Federele": http://www.crimelibrary.com/gangsters_outlaws/family_epics/marcello/13.html (Retrieved 01/12/2012).

---

47. http://educationforum.ipbhost.com/index.php?showtopic205. (Retrieved Sept. 1, 2013).

48. http://www.webmd.com/a-to-z-guides/understanding-encephalitis-basics.

49. II. Autoimmune/Paraneoplastic Encephalitis "Limbic Encephalitis" presents similar to viral encephalitis, ...Most frequently associated with lung cancer (especially squamous cell carcinoma), also seminomas/testicular cancers, thymomas, breast cancer, and Hodgkins lymphoma. "Rarely encephalitis develops in people who have cancer – a disorder called paraneoplastic encephalitis. What causes it is unknown...(Symptoms include) Fever, Headache,Personality changes or confusion, Seizures...People may vomit and have a stiff neck, but these symptoms tend to be less common and less severe than when caused by meningitis." http://www.merckmanuals.com/home/brain_spinal_cord_and_nerve_disorders/brain_infections/encep halitis.html. *Merck Manual*. (Retrieved August 2, 2013).

50. Rosemary James and Jack Wardlaw: *Plot or Politics? The Garrison Case and Its Cast*. 1967. "Buster Abadie."

51. Ibid.

52. Ibid.

53. http://mcadams.posc.mu.edu/jimloon5.htm. (Retrieved Aug. 2, 2013).

54. Education Forum, Nov. 23, 2006. See also: http://jfkmurdersolved.com/images/rubycancer.jpg (Retrieved 03/19/2014).

55. (Ross, 2000) "Neurofeedback and Other Interventions for Patients with Ritual Abuse, Mind Control, and Dissociative Disorders" by Susan Ford See: http://www.whale.to/b/ford5.html, and http://unitedstatesman.org/?pR9. (Retrieved Sept. 6, 2013).

56. Pg 432-33, Jim Marr's, *Crossfire* (first edition): "Deputy Sheriff Al Maddox told researchers in 1982: We had a phony doctor come in to [the Dallas County Jail] from Chicago, just as phony and as queer as a three-dollar bill. And he worked his way in through – I don't know, whoever supplied the county at that time with doctors ... you could tell he was Ruby's doctor. He spent half his time up there talking with Ruby. And one day I went in and Ruby told me, he said 'Well, they injected me for a cold.' He said it was cancer cells. That's what he told me, Ruby did. I said you don't believe that shit. He said, 'I damn sure do!' I never said anything to Decker or anybody ... [Then] one day when I started to leave, Ruby shook hands with me and I could feel a piece of paper in his palm ... [In this note] he said it was a conspiracy and he said ... *if you will keep your eyes open and your mouth shut you're gonna learn a lot*. And that was the last time I ever got to him. Maddox was not the only lawman to suspect that Ruby's death was not entirely natural ...

"Bruce McCarty operated an electron microscope at Southwest Medical School near Parkland. He told this author that he was called back to work during the holidays in 1966 to make a study of Ruby's cancer cells. McCarty explained that there are two types of cancer cells – cilia, which indicate an origin in the respiratory system, and microvilli, which indicate an origin in the digestive system.

These cells are difficult to differentiate with a regular microscope, hence the need for his electron microscope. McCarty confirmed that Ruby's cells were microvilli, indicating his cancer originated in the digestive system. He was shocked when it was announced that Ruby died from lung cancer. Could Ruby have been injected with live cancer cells, which could account for the presence of the microvilli? Traditional medical science claims this is impossible." [Author: "Jim Marrs wrote this before we met and I was able to explain to him about our project to weaponize cancer and Ruby's knowledge of our project. As I've long said, the original strain came from a pancreatic cancer – not from a lung cancer. This had nothing to do with the cancer injection project in New York where Jewish patients were injected with cancer cells. Those injections were intramuscular I myself had explained to "Sparky" (as I knew him), that the cancer cells, to stay alive, had to be injected into the bloodstream. So Jack Ruby knew what had been done to him." http://educationforum.ipbhost.com/index.php?s60a1083f9146ac226334cf40b-cf565&showtopic 18&page=3 Nov. 2006.

Trolls at Education Forum can be easily detected in this discussion, mocking the idea of injected cancer and my witness thereto. Jack Ruby was complaining of injections and said he was *told* it was cancer (this would make people think Ruby was paranoid, so it was just fine to tell him what he was getting – it would be undetectable and Ruby would be laughed at and accused of being paranoid.). However, the means to kill, by now, no doubt, was perfected. Just as Dr. Mary Sherman was from Chicago. See *Me & Lee* and *Dr. Mary's Monkey* for more information."(Ed. Forum material retrieved Sept. 5, 2013).

Greg Parker argues that the cancer was caused by thallium or beryllium. Neither heavy metal always causes cancer, and usually organ failure from heavy metal poisoning could be expected before cancer would develop. Dr. Ochsner tried to spread the idea that it "wasn't true" that Jack Ruby had come to Ochsner's Clinic in 1962 to be treated for rectal cancer, planting the seed of a "prior" cancer firmly in people's heads. But Ruby would have told doctors he had rectal cancer, if true. There is no whisper of that. He does not complain of headaches and nausea for weeks, as would be the case with heavy metal poisoning. In fact, injection with cancer cells would be easy to "disprove" as "paranoid" *because* Ruby knew about the experiments done on Jewish patients in New York.

57. Jim Garrison. *On the Trail of the Assassins*. P. 114.

58. Emphasis added. Bill Davy, *Let Justice Be Done*, pg. 63.

59. See James and Wardlaw's *Plot or Politics?* Other information comes from the HSCA and from comments posted by Stephen Roy at The Education Forum, 2005, fitted to the better dates provided by Crouch's secretary in two lengthy interviews. The plane crash of Feb. 7, 1967 in Slidell, for example, fixes the date when David was fired from Saturn Aviation as a flight instructor.

60. Rosemary James and Jack Wardlaw. *Plot or Politics?* "Buster Abadie."

61. Thomas Louis Clark, Grand Jury testimony March 16, 1967 http://jfkassassi-nation.net/russ/testimony/clark_t.htm (Retrieved Aug. 6, 2013).

62. Lou Ivon memo: "At about 3:15 P. M., Friday, February 24, 1S67, I interviewed ROY TELL at his residence." Tell is employed by Swift (foods). http://jfk.hood.

edu/Collection/Weisberg Subject Index Files/F Disk/Ferrie David G arrison Files Miscellaneous/Item 02.pdf (Retrieved Sept. 2, 2013)

63. Mellen. *A Farewell to Justice*, p. 101.

64. 39 NTSB Identification: FTW67D0457 14 CFR Part 91 General Aviation Aircraft: MOONEY M20C, Registration: N78996 NONCOMMERCIAL 3-0443 67/2/7 *TIME* 17:30 SLIDELL, LA PRIVATE, AGE 31, 300 TOTAL HOURS, 75 IN TYPE *DAMAGE*-SUBSTANTIAL NOT INSTRUMENT RATED *TYPE OF ACCIDENT* PHASE OF OPERATION HARD LANDING *LANDING*: LEVEL OFF/TOUCHDOWN NOSE OVER/DOWN *PROBABLE CAUSE(S)* PILOT IN COMMAND

-IMPROPER LEVEL OFF PILOT IN COMMAND

-IMPROPER RECOVERY FROM BOUNCED LANDING FACTOR(S) MISCELLANEOUS ACTS,CONDITIONS

- POORLY PLANNED APPROACH (Author: Authorities ignored the bloody fuel receipt as proof the plane had been refueled.)

65. "Dan Campbell, an ex-Marine that worked for Banister infiltrating left-wing groups on college campuses confirmed the gunrunning, recalling that "Banister was a bagman for the CIA and was running guns to Alpha 66 in Miami."(26) Campbell also assisted Banister in small arms training for the Cubans and received $50 per week for his services.(27) Campbell describes Banister as "one of the most frighteningly violent persons I have ever known."(28) The Banister menagerie he added "were the worst kind of fanatics."(29) ... Campbell also recalled seeing Oswald's buddy from his Marine Corps days, Kerry Thornley, pop in and out of Banister's office.(31) Strangely enough on the day Kennedy was shot Thornley was with Allen Campbell, Dan's brother.(32) Allen, like his brother, also worked for Banister. Excerpt, *Let Justice be Done* by Bill Davy, Jordan Pub. 1999 Retrieved May 20, 2013.

66. Mellen. *A Farewell to Justice*, p. 84.

67. Mentioned in a second interview with the author, Sept. 6, 2013.

68. (April 18, 1969) Letter, Sciambra to Garrison: "...O.K. HALEY of the F.A.A. [has] a list of pilots who logged time while they were being taught to fly by DAVID FERRIE. (FERRIE had a log book on every student. AL CAMPBELL... DAN CAMPBELL's brother is presently working at the Airport with Flight, Incorporated. He also said that FERRIE used to work with AL CROUCH out of the Miramont Hangar. FERRIE later left CROUCH and took most of the students with him."

69. Private communication of witness to author.

70. http://theadvocate.com/home/7557814-125/flight-instructor-david-ferrie-retains (Nov. 2013).

71. http://www.maryferrell.org/wiki/index.php/Garrison_Investigation, and http://www.www.jfk- online.com/jfk100leak.htm (Retrieved Aug. 3, 2012).

72. "Pershing Gervais and the Attempt to Frame Jim Garrison" by Peter R. Whitmey, *The Fourth Decade*, Volume 1, Number 4, May 1994, pp. 3-7. (Retrieved IT version: 01/02/2014).

73.   https://groups.google.com/forum/#!msg/alt.assassination.jfk/Kzm4vGKf-7wM/-SxF_cUfNhEJ (Retrieved Aug. 2, 2013).

74. Jim Garrison. *On the Trail of the Assassins*. p. 138.

75. Reitzes' material defending Clay Shaw is at JFK Online, a massive site. Reitzes himself makes some amazing errors, such as: (quote)" On February 20, 1967, David Ferrie, the defendant Garrison's link between Oswald and a supposed New Orleans based conspiracy to assassinate the President, died."[two days early] (http://www.jfk-online.com/christenberry2.html) (Retrieved Sept. 6, 2013). Even the Coroner's first estimate of time of death wasn't that early. Dave died before 4:00 AM, Feb. 22, but the coroner had to change the time of death to after 4:00 AM because of George Lardner's report that he interviewed David Ferrie between midnight and 4:00 AM on the 22nd.

76. http://www.jfk-online.com/jfk100ferconfess.html (Retrieved Sept. 7, 2013).

77. Bill Davy, *Let Justice Be Done* (Reston, Va. Jordan, 1999), pp. 66.

78. http://educationforum.ipbhost.com/index.php?showtopic39&page=6. (Retrieved Sept. 3,2013).

79. Again, this material comes from 2005 Education Forum posts, copied by researchers ever since. http://educationforum.ipbhost.com/index.php?showtopic205&page=2 (Retrieved Sept. 3, 2013).

Dave leaving his apartment for the last time.

CHAPTER EIGHTEEN

The Final Days

WHY DID DAVID LEAVE THE FONTAINEBLEAU?

Davemid Ferrie had called Ivon asking for protection, saying he feared for his life. He was taken to the Fontainebleau, where David was interviewed at length. Mr. Roy simply says, "Ferrie does not stay put." But, why? When Lou Ivon went home to his family and left Dave with just Lynn Loisel, and then Lynn went out "for cigarettes,"[1] Dave found himself alone at The Fontainebleau. How long did he wait for Loisel's return, before he ran? Without Loisel, Dave surely felt vulnerable. He probably spent the night of the 19th at the Lakefront Airport.

Night-to-morning, Feb. 19-20, 1967: David is probably at the Lakefront Airport. Witness J. G. says David could be seen at Lakefront Airport "practically living there, almost to the day he died."

Feb. 20, 1967: Saturn Aviation's Al Crouch, at some time shortly before David dies, hides Dave's pilot logbooks in a ground-level safe. He throws David's latest logbook onto J.G.'s desk and tells her to take good care of it. J.G. puts the logbook in her desk drawer.

THE WANDERING BISHOPS AND DAVID FERRIE

Did David find any solace in his religious beliefs? He read his priest's breviary (Roman Catholic, Latin). He said rosaries and Masses. Did he confide in any priest at this time? Raymond "Ray" Broshears, who wears a cross on his chest, says David Ferrie called him at about this time.

20 Feb. 1967: David Ferrie calls Raymond Broshears and tells him he's going to be killed.

Bishop Broshears knew David Ferrie for years.

Broshears (to Dick Russell): "He said he was going to be killed. I said, oh sure, what are you drinking. No, he says, really. I said, why don't you come out here? He said, 'I can't really leave the South. I don't want to come out there with all those Communists'. That was it. The next thing I knew, he was dead. Broshears also said David told him, "No matter what happens to me, I won't commit suicide."[2]

Stephen Roy, posting to author (as David Blackburst): Raymond Broshears… in conversations with me, was unfamiliar with Dave's apartment (in which he claimed to live) and even with the street layout in New Orleans.[3]

Some of us aren't good at recalling a street layout or an apartment's layout. I painfully recall the now discredited researcher Bob Vernon telling McAdams' newsgroup, "Baker never lived in New Orleans" because I couldn't describe the St. Charles streetcar route. I have been tested as having a powerful memory for details, but not when in motion. My brain seems to try to take in every detail and gets overwhelmed. I couldn't recognize the right bus stop after weeks of riding the same route, when Lee wasn't with me. I have met others with similar problems. As for being a roommate, do we count one night, two, five, or what? Broshears offers unpleasant information, but I cannot dismiss him just because I don't like the information. He had much to lose by talking about Dave. Hid description of Dave's activities implicated Lee Oswald in the assassination.

Dick Russell: (email, Aug. 22, 2013) Hi Judyth, I believed Broshears, had no reason to think he'd be making this up – and he was VERY nervous during our interview, unsure of how much to say, always a sign that somebody is more likely telling the truth than obfuscating it.* Best wishes, Dick. (More of Russell's interview with Broshears can be read in end note).[4]

To reconcile this, maybe Dave gave Broshears a sanitized version of why he drove to Houston and why he was standing by that payphone at the ice rink. Dave did successfully plant a seed in Broshear's head that more than one gunman was involved. At the same time he kept up his long-standing pose that he was anti-JFK. After all, there were dangerous "Bishops" out there, such as Jack Martin, Dr. Bryan, and Dr. Jolyon West, who might contact Broshears (also a Bishop).[5]

DAVID FERRIE FIGHTS BACK

According to the long-running anti-Garrison anti-*JFK* site run by Dave Reitzes and John McAdams [www.jfk-online.com/

jfk100whox.html] "Ferrie contacted David Snyder several times during the days that followed, expressing bewilderment about why the DA was targeting him. *If Garrison arrests me*, Ferrie requested of [Snyder] *try to arrange for me to take a lie-detector test.*"

This made me laugh. David would welcome such a test because he was an expert in hypnosis and a student of psychology. Dave himself told me that he knew how to beat lie detector tests and had taught some of his friends how to beat them.

Feb. 20, 1967: As Jim Garrison holds his first press conference about his investigation at The Fontainebleau Motel,[6] David visits Dr. Bagnetto, his physician, then goes to see FBI's Regis Kennedy at the FBI office. Next, he sees Carlos Bringuier (photo, right). After that, Stephen Roy says, Dave sees attorney Gerry Aurillio to discuss a lawsuit. He wants his day in court!

Feb. 21: David tries to phone Tommy Compton (the savvy student in Hammond, with whom Dave spent the night back in November, 1963). He then goes to Broadmoor Pharmacy and picks up a prescription (Is it Proloid?). Next, he encounters and visits an unknown number of people, including Jimmy Johnson, Carlos Bringuier and Orest Pena (who is later beaten up).

It's assumed Dave eats out, as usual. Dave also goes to the public library, where he peruses the 26 volumes of The Warren Commission. (Stephen Roy says Dave was looking for his name). Dave then returns home and calls Jimmy Johnson, who Roy says "then came over." After that, Roy says Dave called his "friend Les Templeton." Later, he calls Snyder, the reporter who's given him so much trouble. It's a busy day for "feeble," "groaning with every step" David Ferrie.

But wait. Dave – a fast reader with interest in the case – would have accessed the 26 volumes many times by now. I suggest David's fear comes from *not knowing what Jim Garrison knows*. He pretends bewilderment, but knows Garrison could learn, at any time, about the New Orleans project, his work with Dr. Alton Ochsner, Dr. Mary Sherman, and Lee on the CIA-sponsored kill-Castro cancer project. On May 25, 1967, Juan Valdez will be questioned about Dr. Mary Sherman. A secret report generated by the FBI on May 22,1968, confirms that Garrison planned to arrest Ochsner, a Reily Coffee executive, and others associated with the New Orleans project. It will not be the last report generated on Garrison's suspicions about Ochsner. Though Dave asked Garrison's office for protection because he fears for his life, Garrison is busy holding a press conference. He's not thinking about David Ferrie.[7]

Feb. 21, 1967: As Garrison's Press Conference makes headlines around the world, David Ferrie has only hours left to live.

THE TELLTALE NOTE

> **Stephen Roy**: At 4:30, he returns home to find a note from George Lardner Jr.

How does Mr. Roy know when Dave returned home? And we do not know who found the note. Here's why: Lardner said he slipped a note under David's door. Lardner, new in town, only knew about the front door. He didn't know there was a back entrance when he left the note. At least in 1963, Dave would enter his apartment through the back door, unless he had visitors.

The note was photographed on David's end table, after his death. That part of the photo was later poorly scanned (see note, right). But the positions of things in Dave's apartment were tampered with. Dave's rifles, for example, are shown laid out on a chair – that's not where Dave kept his rifles. The note could have been found at the front door by those entering the front way after Dave died. It could have been laid down inside, so it would not be stepped on, or it could have been planted. These are unlikely scenarios, but *we have evidence from Lardner himself that David never called him that night* (see below). While Dave, or Lardner, could have picked up the note and brought it inside when Lardner made his supposed midnight visit, I will present evidence from Lardner himself that argues he was never inside that night.

The note says: Mr. Ferrie, Sorry you were out. If at all possible, could you give me a ring at my hotel or leave a message as to where and when we might get together. George Lardner, the *Washington Post*. (Staying at New Orleans 8N Phone 573-5251).

> **Stephen Roy**: (contd.): JIMMY JOHNSON PHONES AND COMES OVER TO 3330, AND AGREES TO COME TOMORROW TO HELP FERRIE MOVE BOXES..." [Is Dave planning to move? James and Wardlaw, p. 44, reported that when Dave was arrested previously, police supposedly found three blank, stamped passports in his possession. Dave had means and ways to leave New Orleans and even the country.] "FERRIE PHONES SNYDER. AT 11PM, NODA WATCHERS SEE LIGHTS GO OUT AND LEAVE FOR EVENING. BUT FERRIE PHONES LARDNER, WHO COMES OVER AND TALKS TO HIM UNTIL ABOUT 4AM, (original in caps).

The problem with Mr. Roy's chronology is that we can show Dave didn't phone Lardner (again, see below).

GARRISON'S FAILURE TO PROTECT DAVID FERRIE: THE SO-CALLED "SURVEILLANCE" TEAM

David's apartment is reportedly under surveillance by Garrison's people until 11:00 PM, but when the lights go out, Garrison's team leaves.

In Mr. Roy's published chronology, he doesn't mention that Garrison's "NODA watchers" said Dave's lights went out at 11:00 PM, apparently soon after Dave called Dave Snyder. Ferrie had asked the DA's office for protection, but Garrison's men *stopped their surveillance* at precisely the time they should have been alert for his safety. It is an unconscionable act, under the circumstances. Their claim of "surveillance" doesn't hold water for the 22nd, either, since nobody was watching Dave's apartment when he was found dead late the next morning. Jimmy Johnson had to call Garrison to get his people over there. They arrived soon after the police. Later, Garrison will claim that his men got there first because they were already on the scene.

12:00 Midnight: George Lardner (see his interview, below, with Gurvich) says he came to interview David Ferrie at midnight – arriving by cab – *but he didn't know if Dave would agree to talk to him or not, so he had the cab wait until he was sure it was OK.*

So there was no call inviting Lardner to come over. This is our first clue that something is fishy about Lardner's account. What reporter would drop by anybody's home at midnight, without calling first? That's what Lardner says he did, and I don't buy it. The other problem is that Dave's lights were reported off at 11 PM, so why would Dave turn the lights on again? Lardner says the lights were on. Lardner's interview with Gurvich is surely available to Mr. Roy, since even I have a copy from the Internet, and I live overseas. Anyone can see the discrepancies.

Early on Feb. 22, 1967, David William Ferrie dies. He lived 48 years, ten months and 26 days.

>   **Stephen Roy** (as Blackburst): He died an impoverished broken man.[8]

David's health was broken, but not his spirit. He was assembling people in his defense. He was packing boxes and had asked Jimmy Johnson to help him move them. Was he planning on fleeing? Dave apparently hadn't purchased the new car he'd thought about, so he still had cash, if Jimmy Johnson's story is true. Even if it's not true, Dave had access to planes. He could fly to almost anywhere. Dave had been subpoenaed by the Grand Jury – not what his enemies wanted. Dave's murder could be easily disguised due to his ill health and stress. I do not see evidence of a nervous breakdown: he has overcome that monster and retains his wits. He was frightened, but not beaten. He was planning a lawsuit against his enemies. Not a plane crash, not Garrison's pressure, not his poor health, not the pressure of reporters, could combine to make him curl up in a ball, so he was killed.

11:45 AM, Feb. 22, 1967: Jimmy Johnson arrives at Ferrie's apartment to help move boxes and finds David dead.

>   **Stephen Roy** (2005): He knocks. No answer. He knocks for an additional 3 minutes or so, but still no answer. He peeks in through the missing pane of glass and pushes the curtain outward. He sees Ferrie lying in bed. He calls to him repeatedly but Ferrie…is unresponsive. Worse, Ferrie's eyes are open. At about 11:50, Johnson runs downstairs to get the landlord, and the two return to break-in the lock on the back door. They quickly determine that Ferrie appears to be deceased in his bed.

Mr. Roy's account of David's death is dispassionate. Would he have written about it differently, had he known my eccentric friend? There are no tears, no expressions of sorrow, from Jimmy or anybody else, in the standing records. But I've cried over him. Dave was a tragic figure. Despite his misdeeds, he sincerely tried to conquer his demons. I believed Dave when he said he only pre-tended to hate JFK after he learned of the treachery of Kennedy's generals and cabinet members. He gained the trust of some of the most notorious right-wingers, Cuban exiles and military men when they were going after Castro, not Kennedy. Then, when it turned ugly, Dave was able to pass on information to me, and to Lee, from his dangerous posi-tion. Having known this man, I'm split in half over him. I steadfastly believe David Ferrie was innocent of conspiracy against Kennedy, and that he helped Lee infiltrate the assassination ring in Dallas. My prayer is: "O God, give rest to David Ferrie's soul, because so many times, he meant well, and wanted to be a better man. Have mercy on him."

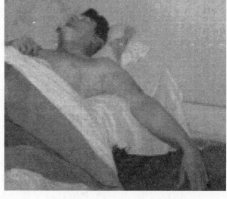

Jack S. Martin, who considered JFK a communist, at one point said, and it rings true because of what he added at the end, that "Ferrie ... was pro, pro, pro-Kennedy. He worshiped him like God ... he worshiped Kennedy. According to him, the way he preached about Kennedy, he worshiped him like God, and at the same time he [claimed] to be anti-Communist."

Now – SOME COLD, HARD FACTS:

11:45 AM: Jimmy Johnson arrives at Ferrie's apartment.

11:50 AM: Johnson peeks through door, sees body, [gets Land-lord]...breaks in door, determines Ferrie is dead. Calls NODA of-fice, line busy.

11:55 AM: Johnson calls NOPD. Again phones NODA, leaves mes-sage for Lou Ivon.

12:05 PM: NOPD arrives.

12:10 PM: Ivon arrives – other NODA people arrive shortly.

12:30 PM: Coroner's staff arrives.

12:45 PM: Coroner arrives.

1:00 PM: Ferrie is pronounced dead.

2:00 PM: Body is photographed and removed. (By 2:30, photographs have been taken of the entire apartment.

3:00 PM: Autopsy begins.[9] Instead of phoning police first, Garrison's "spy" called Lou Ivon. Years later, Garrison will write that his men were there before the police.

> **Stephen Roy** (Ed. Forum, 2005): A police officer finds an envelope taped under a dining table, marked "To be opened in the event of my death". It contains a "letter of farewell" to a friend [This is Al Beauboeuf] and a will, dated July 1966, leaving everything to Beauboeuf.[10]

Sometime later, a longer, apparently rigged, "farewell letter" is found in a pile of papers in the hall. [See Appendix XII] The *Times-Picayune* says Coroner Chetta found the letter on the dining room table. This might mean the letter was of immediate and current value to David, rather than having been relegated to a pile of papers in

> **NOTE IS FOUND**
> Ferrie was found dead at noon Wednesday in his apartment at 3330 Louisiana ave. pkwy. Dr. Chetta found a not on Ferrie's dining room table which read in part:
> "To leave this life is, for me, a sweet prospect. I find nothing in it that is desirable and on the other hand, every-
> thing that . . . . . .

the hall. A third note, apparently to his brother Parmely, was also found, and a letter written by "Tom Clark."

> **Stephen Roy** (2005): (The FBI was able to determine by about 6pm that the coroner's cause of death was a burst aneurysm, but that NODA was pressing for a finding of suicide.)... Based on a note found in Ferrie's apartment, George Lardner is called in for a statement...

Feb. 22, 1967: David Ferrie's Final Effects (Lee Forman, quoting HSCA's Gaeton Fonzi).

1961 search: [quote](97) Ibid. [Two] submarines were found in a Sept. 22, 1961 search of Ferrie's house. Also discovered among Ferrie's effects were: a Morse code key, four model 1903 Springfield rifles, two .22 caliber rifles, one rifle, a flare gun, .38 caliber revolver, a sword, a quantity of ammunition, three maps (of Havana

Harbor, the coast of Cuba, West Indies, Cuba and North Coast), plus the two submarines. FAA, vol.4, attachments F through I. Ferrie said he purchased the guns at the Crescent Gun Shop, New Orleans.[/quote]

1967 final effects: [quote] Among Ferrie's final possessions were found four rifles, an assortment of shotgun shells and .22 rifle blanks, a radio transmitter tuning unit, two Signal Corps field telephones, a 100-pound aerial-type practice bomb and – a sword.

> **Lee Forman**: That's 3 missing rifles and one missing .38 caliber revolver.[11]

> **Stephen Roy**: Ten medicine bottles are found on the coffee table in the living room...[12]

Opinions about "cause of death"

Dr. Bob Artwohl's opinion: (from McAdams' site): "Even if David Ferrie had been forced to ingest Proloid, it could not have been responsible for his death. T4, either taken orally, or injected subcutaneously, will not begin to exert a metabolic effect for about one or two days. T3 acts a little quicker, but will will [sic] not exert an effect until 6 to 12 hours after ingestion. Thus one must assume that whatever goons forced the proloid down Ferries throat, hung around his apartment 6-12 hours waiting for him to die."[13]

Dr. Artwohl said, "T3 acts a little quicker, but will...not exert an effect until 6 to 12 HOURS after ingestion." I disagree entirely, having myself accidentally overdosed on a similar thyroid product. I take a large dose, by the way. With the overdose I experienced, the effect began within an hour, with only four tablets too many, not 93. My heart raced, I counted my pills and realized what I had done. The doctor says it takes 6-12 hours for an effect (but NOT with 93 pills down your throat!). Lardner is the key here. He had motives to be cooperative: his uncle, the famed sportswriter Ring Lardner, had long ago been accused of being a communist.

Newspapers also quoted Chetta giving different estimated times of death. At first, Chetta said Dave died before midnight, "due to rigor mortis" evidence. Finally, after Lardner insisted he had seen Dave alive and cheery at 4:00 AM, the hour of death was changed to accommodate Lardner's version of events. (see "Lardner" below)

Stephen Roy, Michael T. Griffith, and the Autopsy Photos: By 1992, autopsy photos had emerged (but were kept close to the vest). They showed bruises in David's mouth, especially on the inner lips and on his gums.

Researcher Michael T. Griffith: (1995):

Recently disclosed photos from Ferrie's autopsy ...made public in 1992, show bruises on the inside of Ferrie's mouth and gums ... "perhaps to make him swallow something against his will"... The day before he died, Ferrie purchased 100 thyroid tablets.[14] However, when his body was discovered, they were nowhere to be found in his apartment. ...[Dr. and coroner]Frank Minyard theorizes that the killers may have mixed the pills into a solution and then forced it down Ferrie's throat with a tube. In this regard, it is interesting to note that one of the contusions visible in the autopsy photos of Ferrie's mouth is on the inside of the lower lip "where the tube may have struck during a struggle"...[15]

Stephen Roy (as Blackburst, 2001, ignoring Griffith's description of the photos, which were posted online since 1995). "Frank Minyard never examined the body of David Ferrie. All he has to speculate upon are the same autopsy report, the same autopsy photographs I have seen. There is no contusion in the roof of the mouth mentioned in the autopsy report or visible in the photographs."

The autopsy report mentions two areas of damage to the inner lips, including a "lesion in the upper lip...Both areas show no deep hemorrhages or swellings." A 'contusion' is an injury that does not break the skin. A 'lesion' is a wound or injury to the skin and might include breakage of the skin. A 'deep hemorrhage' is a serious bleed. By using the word 'hemorrhage', we cannot exclude a bruise, which did not involve profuse subcutaneous bleeding. Further, Dr. Frank Minyard is a highly experienced Coroner whose task has been, for decades, to rule on four types of death: "natural", "suicide", "murder" or "undetermined." As of this writing (2013) Minyard is *still* New Orleans' Coroner, the longest serving of any major city in the US. Dr. Minyard says David Ferrie was murdered.[16] His is a professional opinion, after seeing the same photographs of David's mouth that Mr. Roy viewed. But Mr. Roy says *he* is correct and the doctor is wrong.

James Richards (Education Forum, describing autopsy photos he has seen): Ferrie's head showed no visible trauma but there was an abrasion of sorts under his top lip. This poor quality image below shows Ferrie during his autopsy and the abrasion being demonstrated (photo link did not work). I am not able to post the actual and very clear series of photographs but one can get the idea here. Obviously it could be theorized that something was forced into Ferrie's mouth and down his throat.[17]

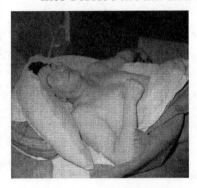

Richards was denied permission to show the clear autopsy photos. Why? Why can't the world see David Ferrie's autopsy photos? They were once available to the public. We have JFK's and Lee Oswald's autopsy photos. Why not David Ferrie's? We sought copies of these photos from a doctor holding them, without success. Mr. Roy says he has them, but does not share them online.

I never saw Dave's bedroom looking so empty. Lots of things were missing. Al Beauboeuf was said to have thrown most of Dave's boxes of books into the dump, that they were "mostly junk," according to Mr. Roy's report. But I saw wonderful books of all kinds in Dave's huge collection.

Afternoon, Feb. 22, 1967: Al Crouch of Saturn Aviation tells his secretary, J. G., "You know all those Cubans David Ferrie was training? The phones are going to be ringing off the hooks."

Feb. 22, 1967: David Talbot (*Brothers*) says Coroner Chetta received a phone call from Bobby Kennedy to verify that David Ferrie had died, with no foul play involved. Records shows LBJ telephoned Acting Attorney General Ramsey Clark to inform him of Ferrie's death. An FBI report will later disclose that LBJ was "very concerned about this matter" and wanted full details about Ferrie's death. Who would have guessed no book would be written about David Ferrie until now?

DID GEORGE LARDNER VISIT DAVID FERRIE?

(ALSO SEE APPENDICES VII AND X).

Stephen Roy (Education Forum,(2005): AT 11PM, NODA WATCHERS SEE LIGHTS GO OUT AND LEAVE FOR EVENING. BUT FERRIE PHONES LARDNER, WHO COMES OVER AND TALKS TO

HIM UNTIL ABOUT 4AM... Based on a note found in Ferrie's apartment, George Lardner is called in for a statement. At about the same time, NODA is taking a statement from Rancier Blaise Ehlinger and Gordon Novel. At 8:54pm Lardner's story runs on the wire, substantially similar to the statement he gave earlier to NODA.

9:10 PM, Feb. 22: George Lardner is interviewed by Bill Gurvich for the DA.18 Gurvich was under pressure to betray Garrison at this time (and would). He had every reason to place George Lardner in a good light. Now let's examine Lardner's interview, obtained the day David Ferrie died:

> Q. How was FERRIE dressed?
> A. Had on brown pants, white shirt open at the neck, he was barefoot. He said he was just about to go to bed when I pulled up.

Lardner told Gurvich "He said he was just about to go to bed when I pulled up." But Mr. Roy told the Education Forum that David Ferrie found Lardner's note and then called Lardner to come interview him. Next, we read this:

> Q. Did he say he noticed you pull up or was he first aware of your presence when you rang the bell?
> A. Well, he didn't make reference to my pulling up but I could I could see him looking down at the street, as I got out of the cab. I told the cab to wait until he either consented to see me or turn me away because I didn't want to get stuck

"I told the cab to wait until he either consented to see me or turn me away because I didn't want to get stuck [without a ride]."

So David Ferrie didn't know Lardner was coming, and might have rejected him.

"...Lights were on..."

> Q. How did you gain entrance?
> A. I rang the doorbell, lights were on, and as I got out of the cab I could see MR. FERRIE walking to the doors that led to the second floor porch that fronts the street.

Lardner didn't yet know that Garrison's surveillance team had left for the night at 11:00 PM when Dave's lights went off.

WHERE LARDNER SAID HE SAT, AND WHY IT'S IMPORTANT.

Focus on what Lardner tells us where he sat, while inside David's apartment:

Q: Where did you sit during your interview?

A: I sat on a sort of old chair, living room chair, single seat.

Q: Where did FERRIE sit?

A: He sat mostly on a couch opposite me and against the wall.

A surveillance view of David Ferrie's living room would not show a low coffee table.

The view in the photo above is skewed to left, but this is approx. what could be seen from across the street and photographed by surveillance. The coffee table is too low to be seen with at least ten bottles of drugs sitting there (see next photo, below). Asked if he saw any medication in the room, Lardner says he remembers a single medicine bottle on the piano. Lardner said David was on the couch, and that Lardner sat in the chair we can glimpse, at lower right in photo.

Gurvich: Did you notice any medication in the apartment?

Lardner: I noticed, particularly, a brown bottle that was standing on the piano, near where we were sitting. It had a label on it but I don't recall what the medication was.

Gurvich: Was the bottle empty?

Lardner: I couldn't tell, the label covered most of the front.[19]

Lardner could not see what was on the low coffee table because he was never inside. Had he been inside, he would have mentioned the many bottles of medicine sitting on the coffee table. He only mentioned what could be seen by surveillance from across the street.[20]

425

The Murder of David Ferrie:

News services flood America with reports of David Ferrie's death. George Lardner teletyped his story (TT) as can be seen in this list:[21]

		02/22/67	AP Wire	Ferrie Death (436pcs)	TT	Gar. - 1 Feb. 1967	
44	67-02-043	02/22/67	AP Wire	Thomas Henry Killam (503pes)	TT	Gar. - 1 Feb. 1967	
45	67-02-044	02/22/67	AP Wire	Ferrie (422pcs)	TT	Gar. - 1 Feb. 1967	
46	67-02-045	06/22/67	AP Wire	New Orleans Ferrie (734pes)	TT	Gar. - 1 Feb. 1967	
47	67-02-046	02/22/67	AP Wire	George Lardner (745pcs)	TT	Gar. - 1 Feb. 1967	
48	67-02-047	02/22/67	AP Wire	Thomas Henry Killam (748pes)	TT	Gar. - 1 Feb. 1967	
49	67-02-048	02/22/67	*San Francisco Examiner* (Final)	JFK Plot' Witness Afraid, 'Knows 5 Who Aided Oswald'	NA	Gar. - 1 Feb. 1967	
50	67-02-049	02/22/67	*San Francisco Examiner* (9 Star Edition))	Pilot in 'JFK Plot' Dead	NA	Gar. - 1 Feb. 1967	
51	67-02-050	02/22/67	ABC, Hemingway	Ferrie	Transcript	Gar. - 1 Feb. 1967	

Garrison's office [not Garrison himself] issues a statement calling David Ferrie "one of history's most important individuals."

Feb. 23, 1967: *Times-Picayune*: story of David Ferrie's death makes front page, New Orleans.

Feb. 23, 1967: Anti-Castro drug dealer Eladio del Valle has also been murdered in Florida. His death is front-page news in Miami.

It will be retold in bloody detail in the *National Enquirer*.

Feb. 23, 1967: Eladio Ceferino del Valle, ex-Cuban Congressman, described as an associate of David Ferrie, and an anti-Castro activist, is found dead in his car parked at the Commercial Plaza Shopping Center, Miami. He had been beaten, tortured, had cuts across the scalp, and was shot in the chest. Police said del Valle was involved with Santos Trafficante and Miami gambling interests.[22] There is some evidence that David Ferrie and del Valle flew some anti-Castro sorties together in the past, though reports of those activities seem to have been greatly exaggerated.

Feb. 23, 1967: American Orthodox Church Archbishop Carl John Stanley, AKA Bishop Christopher Marie, who ordained both David Ferrie and Jack S. Martin as Bishops, attacks their moral character in a meeting with the FBI.

After midnight, Feb. 23, 1967: Former CAP member (1962-63), young Philip Geraci, III,[23] is taken by Jefferson Parish Sheriff officers for questioning and is held at a relative's home within the Parish for a week. Geraci, who had ignored Garrison's subpoenas, is "severely in-

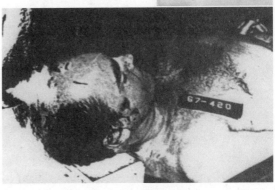

terrogated" – but not by Garrison. Geraci was interviewed by the FBI on Nov. 20, 1963, because of his association with both Carlos

Bringuier of the DRE in New Orleans and Lee Oswald. Investigator Harold Weisberg, who later interviewed Geraci III, said Geraci's connection with Bringuier had to do with the illegal sale of bonds.

Geraci was also interviewed by Weisberg after his father was electrocuted. The young man's "wrongful death" has been misreported. Numerous deaths, however, are still classified as "natural" – such as an undue number of heart attacks and sudden cancers, along with a plethora of suicides, murders and 'accidental deaths" that can no longer be ignored. A competent statistical analysis has been conducted by mathematician Richard Charnin, demonstrating that an overwhelming number of deaths of witnesses in the Kennedy assassination case have occurred passing a trillion-to-one in probability.

Feb. 24, 1967: Jim Garrison publicly announces that he has "positively solved the assassination of President John F. Kennedy." David Franklin Lewis, Jack Martin's "sidekick" now steps forth. Later, Lewis will be discredited after he is threatened, then shot at, when he lies as to the identity of the shooter. He tries to blame a suspected pro-Castro spy, Carlos Quiroga, when he originally stated in his handwritten notes that he did not know who the driver was, and on this basis, he failed a polygraph. Though Lewis, who was friends with both Lee Oswald and David Ferrie, said far less than he knew, he gave out the right names and places, which would help support the testimonies of later witnesses. His pregnant wife, Anna Lewis, is threatened and harassed. She ceased to live with Lewis after 1967.

This front page Dutch newspaper article "Moord [Death] of President Kennedy" is typical of the worldwide shock felt after David Ferrie was found dead. David Lewis (left) is shown on same page with George Lardner, (right). Defamation of Lewis began at once, including false accusations. I knew Lewis and his wife, Anna, well. Eventually the Lewis family fled New Orleans, never to return.

HOW DAVID FERRIE'S FLIGHT LOGS WERE STOLEN

J.G. wasn't thrilled when Al Crouch threw David Ferrie's most recent logbook onto her desk. She was certain there was no safe
place for it.

At this point, researcher Joan Mellen has her own version to
tell. She was the first researcher to whom J.G. had spoken.

J.G. had given Mellen some of her story, but only part of it was
printed.[24] But it's good that Mellen first heard this story, as it displays J.G.'s sincere effort to tell it.

Here is what Mellen put into print: "… new information is always
appearing: for example, I was telephoned after the publication of *A
Farewell to Justice* by a witness who observed the Gurvich brothers in New Orleans at Saturn Aviation, a company run by one Al
Crouch, and for whom David Ferrie flew. The Gurviches took away
with them, never to be seen again, the flight record showing Ferrie's
movements. These included a flight Ferrie made to Dallas the week
of the assassination. After the assassination, knowing how sensitive
they were, Crouch had put Ferrie's logbooks in a floor safe, and
they survived even a break-in. Crouch was threatened, getting an
anonymous phone call, saying, "Do you have a little girl about three
years old who rides a tricycle?" Then he turned the logbooks over
to the brothers Gurvich, one of whom, William Gurvich, had ingra-
tiated himself into the Garrison investigation. Gurvich claimed he
would deliver these records to Jim Garrison. Of course, Garrison
never saw Ferrie's log books.[25]

J.G. had more to say – much more. But first, a major correc-
tion: the three-year-old little girl was J.G.'s daughter – unrelated
to Crouch. Mellen misquoted Crouch, and she's misquoted others,
but at least she got some of the story into print. Here's how J.G. told
it to me:

"The New Orleans police knew everything that was going on,"
she said. "I think three people died in a week. David Ferrie died,
too. It was all natural causes. Then the phone calls started."

"What kind of phone calls?"

"FBI, CIA, Garrison—" I asked.

"They wanted the logbooks?"

"They wanted the logbooks. They threatened me, and Crouch,
about them. I was the one that had to take the telephone calls. They
tried to scare us. The last one was calling from Oklahoma. They had
left New Orleans, hid in Oklahoma, and wanted the log books. "Do

you happen to have a little girl about three years old?" they asked me. "We know she's riding a tricycle in and out of the hangar."

We were both mothers, and just listening to her strained voice froze my blood.

"When I got off that call," J.G. went on, "that was it. I wanted to go back to California."

Soon after that, Crouch threw a logbook on her desk. "It's David Ferrie's logbook," he told her. "I opened it up, and it was empty. I knew there were other logbooks."

Was Crouch trying to use the unused logbook as a decoy. Was this the logbook he'd thrown onto her desk? I was not going to interrupt her. I wanted her to talk and not worry about that detail,

"My boss, I thought he was going to have a heart attack," she said. "So, pretty soon, all of a sudden, somebody's at our door. (at the airport) I saw these two men, dressed in dark suits. I thought they were on our side – agents to protect us from these threats. 'I've been expecting you,' I told them."

"What did they do?" I asked.

"We're here to get the packages," they said. And my boss, he went and handed it to them...I could barely see their faces. They took those flight records."

"Did you find out who they were?"

"Yes. When RFK sent Sheridan to talk to Gurvich, that's how. I didn't know Gurvich had a brother. But there he was. Gurvich lied. He was going behind Garrison's back. He told Sheridan to tell RFK that there was no conspiracy. Forget it! And then RFK bad-mouthed Garrison, because he believed Gurvich's lie. But not long after that, I think Bobby started to realize, maybe he was the one responsible for his brother's death."

I told her I thought this idea was probably planted in RFK's brain so he'd not look into 'conspiracy' any more. That dirty word, 'conspiracy', which actually accounts for most evil-doing on the planet, is avoided most by those who perpetrate it. Maybe I should have told her more.

Feb. 23, 1967: US secret agencies and the US government react to Garrison's investigation with mockery and rumors. Their harassment and defamation of Garrison begins about a week after newspapers break the story. Not that Garrison is lily-white. Both sides will accuse each other of bribery of witnesses in the Clay Shaw trial. Both sides will be correct.

~**Feb. 23, 1967**: Al Crouch and J.G. are inundated with telephone calls. J.G.: "FBI, CIA, Garrison – they wanted Ferrie's log books."

Feb. 24, 1967: George Lardner, Jr. publishes a second story on Garrison and David Ferrie, saying, "Before Ferrie died early Wednesday morning of a cerebral hemorrhage, he told me of his fears that Garrison's investigation would prove no more than a 'witch hunt.'"[27]

Garrison's office has not given up on seeking more information about David Ferrie. Sgt. Sedsebeer gives Lou Ivon a memo regarding his interview of Roy Tell, former CAP. Tell says David Ferrie told him he "was working for the FBI" when Tell inquired about Lee Oswald and CAP days (Nov. 1963). Asked to name friends, Tell gives a list, among them "OLIVER ST. PEE [sic]"Now in the Peace Corps somewhere in Asia, ""LARRY ANDERSON – Pilot for Delta Airlines," and "GENE and RICHARD MARSHALL – GENE is traveling as a musician and RICHARD is working at Michoud."

Robert Tannenbaum, HSCA Deputy Counsel: "I remember discounting everything Garrison had said. I had a negative point of view about Garrison based upon all the reportage that had gone on. And then I read all this material that had come out of [CIA Director Richard] Helm's office, that in fact what Garrison had said was true. They [CIA agents] were harassing his witnesses, they were intimidating his witnesses."[26]

"Give Garrison nothing!"
FBI Director J. Edgar Hoover. Hoover's directive was sent to FBI field offices a week after Jim Garrison's investigation became public. In reference to the Special Agent in Charge in New Orleans, Robert Rightmyer, Hoover added: "Tell Rightmyer that I want him and all personnel in New Orleans to keep their mouths shut!"

"Goddamn the Kennedys.
First there was Jack, now there's Bobby, and then Teddy. We'll have them on our necks until the year 2000." – Clyde Tolson (J. Edgar Hoover's associate director, confidant, and roommate) cited by William Sullivan, *The Bureau: My Thirty Years in Hoover's FBI*. (Upon hearing Tolson's comment, Hoover reportedly nodded in agreement. Note: Sullivan's book about the FBI was published posthumously after Sullivan was shot dead near his New Hampshire home by a man who mistook him for a deer.

~**Feb. 24, 1967**: Saturn Aviation's Al Crouch and his secretary are now being terrorized with threatening phone calls.

Feb. 25, 1967: Jack S. Martin's wife says Martin is hiding out in Mexico to escape pressure of publicity. *LA Times* (Nelson, Chris).

February 25, 1967: Perry Russo stands forth. After reading of Ferrie's death and contacting Jim Garrison's office, Perry Russo, one-time friend of David Ferrie, who held an ongoing grudge with him later, is interviewed by Andrew Sciambra. He does not mention any conspiracy meeting to "kill Kennedy" at this time.

In a later interview, Russo says he was present at David's apartment when a New Orleans conspiracy meeting about assassinating Kennedy was held, involving Clay Shaw ['Clay Bertrand'], David Ferrie, and "Leon Oswald." Russo's credibility will be questioned due to a failed polygraph test and the use of hypnosis and sodium pentothal by coroner Nich-

Perry Russo looks at photos of "Leon."

olas Chetta and doctors. However, Russo turned down bribes from Garrison's enemies and inducements from Garrison. On the basis of Russo's testimony to the Grand Jury, Clay Shaw will go on trial.

> **Dick Russell**: "...Congressman Gerald Ford [Warren Commission]... asked to see Garrison's information and pass it on to Lyndon Johnson ... [Garrison replied] '... We're investigating a conspiracy which appeared to have occurred In New Orleans ... if they want to help me, I'll welcome their help. But I'm not reporting to anybody.' Those were strong words, and probably foolish ones. Before long, the most powerful machinery of the government had been uncorked against Garrison and his sensational charges ... the full story of how Garrison was hamstrung would fill a volume."[28]

Mar. 1, 1967: David William Ferrie is buried. A man who taught countless people how to fly, who influenced dozens to become priests or to serve their country in the Armed Services, and whose acts of charity, patriotism and courage were overshadowed by his sexual misbehavior, is buried in near-isolation. David's body had finally been claimed by his brother, Parmely T. Ferrie, of Rockford, New York. Joan Mellen: "His sole living relative, his brother Parmely, did not attend"[29] his funeral. Only two mourners attended, who refused to identify themselves to the press. David was laid to rest at St. Bernard's Memorial Cemetery. A low Requiem Mass was said for him at St. Matthias' Church, Rockford, New York, understood to be [provided by] a brother.[30]

David Ferrie was born the same year as my father. So it's not that hard for me to believe Dave when told me, before our last goodbye, that he thought of me as the daughter he never had.

Endnotes

1. Joan Mellen. *A Farewell to Justice.* p. 105, interview of Wm. Alford.

2. 1967 interview of Raymond Broshears, David Ferrie's former roommate, a cleric and gay activist then running a support organization ("Helping Hands") for gays, published in "The Vindication of Jim Garrison", *Harper's Weekly*, Sept. 6, 1976, and reprinted in *On the Trail of the JFK Assassins*, p. 107-108, by Dick Russell, with permission.

3. Re: From: Blackburst@aol.com Sent: Wednesday, June 30, 2004 3:25 PM To: elect63@xs4all.nl Me: "This email is the *sole* email where Stephen Roy/David Blackburst gave me any information. He has claimed he gave me information, but it has all come from public posts. He said he told me about Dave's car getting repossessed, but *this wasn't true*. Perhaps he had posted it somewhere and thought he'd emailed me about it. I was surprised to receive this 2004 email signed "Dave." He was angry soon after, when I outed his true name, causing his enmity. But I had an obligation. Mr. Roy was posting on Education Forum as "Stephen Roy"– but without mentioning his other name. When some readers told me "David Blackburst" was a "Ferrie expert" whose posts verified what "Stephen Roy" was posting, enough was enough. I set the record straight, despite the consequences, which turned out to be heavy: by 2012, this researcher, who had treated me deviously with slick 'tests' that even involved lying to me (such as insisting that Dave habitually wore a certain ring, when I insisted he didn't wear rings habitually – and no, Dave didn't –) was telling newsgroups I never met Dave Ferrie. Mr. Roy also said he once displayed his fake name under his real one, on a name tag at the 2000 Lancer Conference, and was hiding nothing.

4. Dick Russell, *On the Trail of the Kennedy Assassins*, 2008, p. 107-108. Me: "The rest of the quote is in Appendix XI, where Russell's important interview is quoted more thoroughly, with information on little-considered airfields in the Houston area and Me's comments, at end.

5. Ibid., p. 107-108.

6. Garrison's press conference, held at the Fontainebleau Motor Hotel on February 20, 1967, was filmed and photographed widely.

7. Reitzes-McAdams: "Inside the DA's office, it was common knowledge that there had never been any evidence of any sort linking David Ferrie to the Kenne-

dy assassination, nor had any other evidence of a New Orleans conspiracy been uncovered.(12) Garrison fanned the flames of publicity with an announcement to the press that his staff knew was not true: that the very morning Ferrie died, the DA and his men had made a decision to arrest Ferrie. In 1994, Assistant DA James Alcock, lead prosecutor at the Clay Shaw trial, broke his silence and admitted the truth. Although Garrison specifically named Alcock as one of the assistants in on the decision, Alcock states, "To my knowledge, there was no intent to arrest David Ferrie."(13) [The source for these statements: 13. Patricia Lambert, *False Witness* (New York: M. Evans and Co., 1998), p. 65.] *But wait!* Researchers have found false quotes attributed to Dischler in Lambert's book. As Jim DiEugenio critiques *False Witness*, one of his comments about her assertion that Shaw never used the alias 'Clay Bertrand' caught my eye as he quotes my longtime friend Edgar Tatro regarding the alias: "*...In fact, the number of witnesses in the files who are now on record as stating that Shaw used the alias of Clay Bertrand is well into the double digits. To illustrate just how common this knowledge was in New Orleans at the time, consider this anecdote from Ed Tatro.* Tatro was a young college student who decided to go down to New Orleans to watch the Shaw trial in person. One night he visited one of the bistros in the French Quarter. The New Orleans residents noted his Boston accent and asked him what he was there for. When he told them, the residents started giggling. He asked them what was so humorous. The reply was, "Look, everybody down here knows that Shaw uses the name Bertrand. But that poor devil Garrison can't prove it to save his soul." http://www.ctka.net/pr599-lambert.html (Retrieved 3/9/2014).

8. From: blackburst@aol.com (Blackburst) Subject: Re: Did Ferrie "fly missions over Cuba?" Date: 05 Mar 2000 00:00:00 GMT Message-ID: <20000305044552.03192.00000329@ng-fn1.aol.com>.

9. http://jfk.hood.edu/Collection/Weisberg Subject Index Files/HW Manuscripts/Inside t he Assassination Industry/ITAI Chapter 01.doc (Retrieved 09/08/2013).

10. As in other cases, Mr. Roy's information was openly presented to the Education Forum [or to the David Blackburst archives]knowing it would be freely copied, quoted and distributed to researchers and inquiring visitors to the forum. Mr. Roy says this letter was found in a pile of papers in the hall. Where did Mr. Roy get his information from? The *Times-Picayune* article, hastily written and quickly published, is the earliest source of the location of the note, on the table and it came straight from Chetta. http://educationforum.ipbhost.com/index.php?showtopic205&page=2 (Retrieved Sept. 8, 2013).

Disputing the notes as not linked to a suicide (or having feelings of immediate demise, as Mr. Roy claims), Jesse Ventura comments that the letters were typed, did not have signatures and were not dated. Ventura's inquiry into Dave's life and death brought him to the conclusion that David Ferrie was murdered. His book, They Killed Our President: 63 Facts That Prove a Conspiracy to Kill JFK, names Fact #39 as "Another Key Witness Conveniently Silenced." Researcher Dick Russell worked with Ventura to assemble the facts for this conclusion. "... Ferrie predicted his own death," Ventura notes, adding that Jim Garrison said "... witnesses in this case are bad insurance risks."

11. Oct. 4, 2005, Education Forum post by Lee Forman. http://educationforum. ipbhost.com/index.php?showtopicI39&page=3 (Retrieved June 15, 2013).

12. Changes in Stephen Roy's timeline: Roy (2005) "Ten medicine bottles are found on the coffee table in the living room. A police officer finds an envelope taped under a dining table, marked "To be opened in the event of my death". It contains a "letter of farewell" to a friend [Me: Al Beauboeuf] and a will, dated July 1966..." Representatives of the coroner's office arrive at about *12:30* [Author: in 1999 Blackburst says Coroner arrived at *12:45*)]..." Stephen Roy (contd): "Ferrie is pronounced dead at 1:00 PM. His body is removed at about *2:30* [Author: in 1999, Blackburst says the body is removed at *2:00*] ..."

13. "http://mcadams.posc.mu.edu/death1.txt. #: 23564 S2/Books & Articles [JFK]15-May-94 11:43:07 Sb: #23543-WHAT IS THE CASE???? Fm: [Dr.] Bob Artwohl 71712,2151 To: John McAdams [WPUSERS] 71333,2114 (Retrieved Sept. 4, 2013)

14. Researchers, not being doctors, sometimes thought that "thyroid pills" and "Proloid" were two separate medications. To the best of our knowledge, only one bottle of 100 pills was purchased at Broadmoor Pharmacy by David Ferrie on the 20th. 93 of these pills were missing 48 hours later.

15. Michael T. Griffith. *Hasty Judgment: A Reply to Gerald Posner –Why the JFK case Is Not Closed*, 2nd Edition (revised 11/4/01) http://michaelgriffith1.tripod. com/hasty.htm (Retrieved 07/09/2013).

16. Memo from Garrison to Alcock, "a bottle of Proloid (with only seven tablets found in it) was found in David Ferrie's apartment." The author was sent an email about a 1/31/92 interview of Dr. Minyard with Jim DiEugenio, where "Proloid" and "thyroid pills" seem to have been considered as separate medications, but the scenario is still clear, DiEugenio said "Dr. Minyard considered this a possible scenario for the murder of Ferrie: The thyroid pills [Proloid] <snip> [were mixed with some liquid and] forced down Ferrie's mouth with a tube, which caused the mouth wounds."

17. http://educationforum.ipbhost.com/index.php?showtopic205&page=4 (Retrieved Aug. 30, 2013).

18. Lardner interview here: http://jfk.hood.edu/Collection/Weisberg Subject Index Files/F Disk/Ferrie David William Garrison Stuff/Item 02.pdf. (Retrieved Aug. 31, 2013).

19. http://jfk.hood.edu/Collection/Weisberg Subject Index Files/F Disk/Ferrie David William Garrison Stuff/Item 02.pdf. (Retrieved Aug. 31, 2013).

20. Note that a coffee cup and saucer is on the coffee table, and another coffee cup and saucer is on an end table. However, David had another visitor that evening who might have been given a cup of coffee – Jimmy Johnson.

21. http://jfk.hood.edu/Collection/White Materials/Garrison Indices/67-02 Folder.xls (Retrieved Sept. 2, 2013).

22. Summers, *Conspiracy*, pp. 449-50. "Loran Eugene Hall and Santos Traffi-cante had been in jail at the same time in Cuba and were released together in July 1959. In 1963 Hall was working with Eladio del Valle's Committee to Free

Cuba. Del Valle had been a smuggling partner of Trafficante and was also a close friend and associate of David Ferrie." (See Summers, *Conspiracy*, p. 346; Anson, *They've Killed the President*, p. 197; Hinckle with Turner, T*he Fish is Red*, p. 230.) Quotes are from: http://www.acorn.net/jfkplace/09/fp.back_issues/17th_Issue/rambler3.html

23. Harold Weisberg says Philip Geraci III's father, Philip Geraci, Jr., was an electrician who had been accidentally electrocuted (not a "mysterious death"). http://jfk.hood.edu/Collection/Weisberg Subject Index Files/G Disk/Geraci Philip II I/Item 09.pdf. (Retrieved Aug. 19, 2013).

24. http://www.joanmellen.com/oswald.html Retrieved May 22, 2013.

25. Ibid.

26. Robert Tanenbaum, former Deputy Counsel for the U.S. House Select Committee on Assassinations, "The Probe Interview: Bob Tanenbaum," *Probe*, July-August 1996 (Vol. 3 No. 5).

27. http://jfk.hood.edu/Collection/Weisberg Subject Index Files/G Disk/Garrison Jim/Garr ison Jim Quotes/Item 15.pdf. (Retrieved Aug. 28, 2013)

28. Russell. *On the Trail of the JFK Assassins*, p. 100.

29. Mellen. *A Farewell to Justice* , p. 116.

30. Compiled from reports of Ferrie's obituaries.

CHAPTER NINETEEN

A Few Last Words

Mar. 1, 1967, 5:30 PM: The same day David is buried, Jim Garrison issues an arrest warrant for Clayton Lavergne Shaw, prominent New Orleans business and social figure. The DA intends to implicate Shaw in the JFK assassination. Seventeen months earlier, the City of New Orleans had bestowed upon Shaw its highest honor, a medal for the International Order of Merit.

Mar. 1, 1967: A Telex is sent: URGENT BY JOHN LANG ASSOCIATED PRESS WRITER NEW ORLEANS, MARCH 1 (AP) – DIST, ATTY. JIM GARRISON ARRESTED WEALTHY CLAY L. SHAW TONIGHT AND ACCUSED HIM OF TAKING PART IN A CONSPIRACY TO ASSASSINATE PRESIDENT JOHN F, KENNEDY. SHAW, A RETIRED EXECUTIVE, WAS BOOKED ON "CONSPIRACY TO COMMIT MURDER" AND RELEASED ON $10,000 BOND.

In his *Penthouse* interview with James Phelan, Clay Shaw said something odd. He said, "Walter Sheridan ... came down and told me there was a rumor in town that I was 'Clay Bertrand,' I told him this was silly and ridiculous, that I had never been 'Clay Bertrand.'" But wait. Instead of saying, "I never called myself 'Clay Bertrand'" Shaw said, "I had never been" Clay Bertrand. This linguistic slip suggests Shaw probably did use aliases.

> **Clay Shaw** (to Phelan): I went out to the DA's office with a perfectly clear conscience, I didn't take a lawyer with me.... Finally they began to question me about David Ferrie ... I told them I didn't know Ferrie and had never been to his place. Then suddenly they said: "What would you say if we said we had three witnesses proving that you have been there?" I told them that their witnesses were either mistaken or they were lying. At this point it was suggested that I take a lie-detector test. I said: "Certainly not. Why on earth should I take a lie-detector test?" They told me "'If you don't take a lie-detector test, we're going to charge you with conspiring to kill the President of the United States." To put it mildly, I was stunned.

Shaw further said, "I am a highly recognizable fellow" – as to why he wouldn't use an alias, but in the procurement of illegal sex, he could have used an alias, such as over the phone. Shaw denied that he called Dean Andrews using the alias.[1]

Clay Shaw with attorneys.

> **Anthony Summers** (how CIA Reacts to Shaw's arrest): Victor Marchetti [former special assistant to CIA Director Richard Helms] told me that he observed consternation on the part of then CIA Director Richard Helms and other senior officials when Ferrie's name was first publicly linked with the assassination in 1967. Marchetti claimed he asked a colleague about this and was told that "Ferrie had been a contract agent to the Agency in the early sixties and had been involved in some of the Cuban activities." (Summers, *Not in Your Lifetime*)

Mar. 1967: Clay Shaw's association with CIA-linked Permindex, first located in Rome, then in Switzerland, then in South Africa, is revealed by Italian newspaper *Paese Sera*. "Paese Sera wondered," wrote Joan Mellen, "about Shaw's leaving the United States two days after the assassination, remaining two years with only intermittent visits to America." (In his *Penthouse* interview, Shaw, at that time age 52, said he had long planned to travel before he got too old.)

Night, Mar. 1, 1967: Shaw's home at 1313 Dauphine is searched. While downstairs there is much elegance, upstairs in Shaw's bedroom big hooks, leather straps and chains hang from the ceiling, which has bloody handprints. A black cape, whips, a chain and other paraphernalia are found in a closet. [Note: Mardi Gras was Feb. 7, 1967, providing an excuse for the costumes, but Shaw's sado-masochism cannot be hidden].

By June 13, newspapers report the raid and what was found.[2] Shaw, a decorated war hero, respected businessman, socialite and man of culture, will never recover, socially, from all that is revealed about his private life.

Garrison will go off-track, wondering if Kennedy's murder was a homosexual thrill crime.

1313 Dauphine today.

438

Mar. 2, 1967: An FBI memo sent this day shows Clay Shaw was investigated in Dec. 1963, which FBI will officially deny.[3]

March 2, 1967: The FBI reports on their interview of American Orthodox Church Archbishop Carl John Stanley regarding David Ferrie. Stanley will live only six more days.

Mar. 5, 1967: Clay Shaw's former secretary, Aura Lee, after hearing on television that Shaw denied knowing David Ferrie, tells Dr. Charles B. Moore and others (including an FBI informant) that Ferrie was often seen in Clay Shaw's office at the Trade Mart, and she believes Ferrie had privileged access there.[4]

Mar. 6, 1967: FBI interviews Jack Martin, who has fled to Houston. Martin refuses to cooperate.

March 8, 1967: Two weeks after his FBI interview, the day after Dave died, Archbishop Carl John Stanley dies from a heart attack at the age of 64 in Louisville, Kentucky. His death comes at the same time the FBI report is published. He will be canonized by the Byzantine Catholic Church, to which he also belongs.

> **Peter Levenda**: At one time, there were as many as four "bishops" [in] Guy Banister's Camp Street office ... virtually all of his investigators, from David Ferrie and Jack Martin to Thomas Beckham and the lawyer Thomas Jude Baumler. Beckham was a bishop with the Universal Life Church ... [as was] Raymond Broshears ... later with one of the Orthodox sects with lines to Stanley.... In addition, Ferrie, Martin, Beckham, Broshears and Baumler all shared the same apostolic succession: that of Bishop Earl Anglin James in Canada ... and of Bishop Carl Stanley of the American Orthodox Catholic Church.[5]

Dr. William Bryan was a member of the Old Catholic Church, as was David Ferrie. Dr. Bryan made films, was an advisor for the movie *The Manchurian Candidate* and was a CIA-connected MK/ULTRA operative.

William Bryan.

> **Speculations**: Some say Bryan taught David Ferrie hypnotism. He may have hypnotized Sirhan Sirhan (who shot wildly at Bobby Kennedy from the front, as a patsy, while RFK's actual assassin shot from behind, a fatal wound behind the ear). It is also suggested that Arthur Bremer, who shot Gov. George Wallace, may have been programmed by Bryan.[6] (Jan. 29, 1965): Jack S.

Martin and Thomas Jude Baumler had started a company called "Louisiana-Psychoanalytic-Association (Inc)" a non-profit corporation.

The much-maligned Jack Martin, condemned for heavy drinking and labeled so disreputable that, for some, his statements are deemed worthless, but in 1965 he continued to show some mettle. He is a business partner with lawyer-Bishop-politician Thomas Jude Baumler. Though the name of this organization reeks of fraud, and neither man is qualified to do psychoanalysis, Dr. William Bryan is a psychoanalyst with CIA, into mind control. All three men are Bishops in the same inter-related sects, which keep getting involved in clandestine activities. David Ferrie is still advertising himself as a psychologist. The company may be a front to lure candidates for CIA-sponsored experiments.

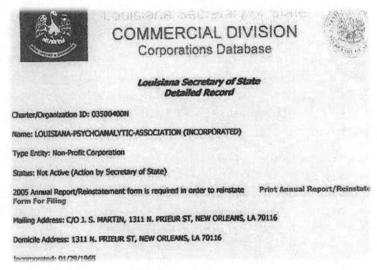

COMMERCIAL DIVISION
Corporations Database

Louisiana Secretary of State
Detailed Record

Charter/Organization ID: 03500400N

Name: LOUISIANA-PSYCHOANALYTIC-ASSOCIATION (INCORPORATED)

Type Entity: Non-Profit Corporation

Status: Not Active (Action by Secretary of State)

2005 Annual Report/Reinstatement form is required in order to reinstate   Print Annual Report/Reinstate
Form For Filing

Mailing Address: C/O J. S. MARTIN, 1311 N. PRIEUR ST, NEW ORLEANS, LA 70116

Domicile Address: 1311 N. PRIEUR ST, NEW ORLEANS, LA 70116

Incorporated: 01/29/1965

Fred Lee Crisman, whose UFO experiences have been monumentalized in the Maury Island Affair, is a Bishop via Stanley, too. His link to Dave's friend Raymond Broshears was through the same Universal Life Church.[7] Crisman could not be trusted. Broshears was in contact with Crisman and/or Bryan, which could influence what information Dave had given Broshears before he died.

Jim DiEugenio: ... Raymond Broshears, said in a Los Angeles TV interview that Ferrie actually confessed the plot to him in one of the erratic moods that then began to consume him, and which he tried to combat with pills and alcohol. (Jim DiEugenio, *Destiny Betrayed*, p. 148.)

Stephen Roy: The group Martin and Ferrie were associated with was the "Byzantine Primitive Catholic Church, Old Catholic Church in N.A., Apostolic, Orthodox, Catholic, Order of Saint John," according to the consecration certificates. The group Ferrie alone was associated with was the "Society of the Domestic Missionaries of Saint Basil the Great," according to his membership card.

March 15, 1967: Tommie L. Clark, who had worked at Dav-Al's Gulf Service station, is interviewed by Garrison's office.

> **Tommie Clark:** I lived with Dave at one time for about two months. This was right before he died. I have been to his apartment quite a few times.
>
> **Q.** Did he do much talking about the investigation? (Kennedy assassination)
>
> **A.** He said something about you all didn't know what you were doing. He was in bed – sick.

Tommie Clark is a frightened young man. He brings up Dave's illness to change the subject. He abandoned Dave the same day Dave was fired and the plane Dave was scheduled to fly was sabotaged to crash. Did Dave suddenly get "well" so Tommie could leave? Tommie fled, as a rat would from a sinking ship.

March 15, 1967: The FBI ignores a good lead: "Carroll S. Thomas, owner of Thomas Funeral Homes, Inc. in Hammond, Louisiana ... volunteered that he was a close personal friend of Clay Shaw, and that he'd met David Ferrie through Shaw. Thomas' claim remains unsubstantiated; it is not known whether he actually was friendly with Clay Shaw or not.(FBI NO 89-69-1781)

But Thomas was in charge of Clay Shaw's father's funeral. That was in the newspapers and could have been easily discovered by the FBI. Shaw and Thomas had been friends for years. Time after time, FBI fails to "substantiate" witness statements, lest they accumulate the wrong kind of evidence. No effort was made to interview any of Thomas' associates. Thomas would be one of the few persons who would attend Clay Shaw's funeral.

GORDON NOVEL DENOUNCES GARRISON

March 16, 1967: Gordon Novel is briefly questioned by Garrison's Grand Jury. He's a convicted car-jacker who some say "has to cooperate" with the CIA. But Novel, is also an electronics and bugging expert connected to Banister, a participant in the Houma Schlumberger raid with David Ferrie, Arcacha Smith, Layton Martens, and others. Later, he has links to Watergate. Papers say he is "perhaps the primary CIA contact for the New Orleans part of the anti-Castro efforts."

Dick Russell: [In Fall, 1975, Novel] met me at the airport and [took me to] … the Town and Country Motel … owned by Carlos Marcello, boss of the New Orleans Mob. "I've known Carlos since I was a little, bitty boy," Novel said. "Would you like to meet him?" [Marcello wasn't there]" …[Years later, Novel said], "Look, I know what I was paid, to interfere on Garrison, and by who."[8]

Gordon Novel

March 22, 1967: Gordon Novel gets out. He sells his share of a restaurant business in New Orleans and flees to Columbus, Ohio to avoid serious questioning by Garrison's Grand Jury. The governor is persuaded to refuse to extradite Novel after Novel (1) visits CIA headquarters (2) Novel posts bond. Next, Novel "begins a national and international junket denouncing Jim Garrison from Columbus, Ohio, McLean, Virginia, and Montreal, Canada – sidestepping Garrison's efforts to extradite him."[9]

Mar. 30, 1967: George Piazza II dies in a flaming crash that kills nineteen people. Piazza was "… counsel for James Lewallen, a former roommate of David W. Ferrie, the man Garrison alleges was part of an assassination conspiracy here. Piazza was both a lawyer and a pilot. There were no signs or calls of distress from the plane before the crash. The night was balmy with a nearly full moon."[10]

New Orleans, La. (AP) – "A DC8 jet flying a practice landing pattern cut a swath of destruction through a residential area near New Orleans International Airport early Thursday and exploded in a fiery crash into the rear of the Hilton Inn, killing 18 persons…. On board the Delta Air Line jet were five pilots and an inspector for the Federal Aviation Agency. All were killed…. The big jet had been in the air only 9 minutes."

David Pearce Magyar (see Nov. 27, 1963) told FBI that George Piazza "was one of Captain Ferrie's best friends."

April 3, 1967: Sergio Arcacha Smith, formerly of the Cuban Revolutionary Council (CRC) and manager of an air conditioner firm in Dallas, is arrested at his home in front of his family by officers sent from Jim Garrison's office. They demand that Arcacha speak with them alone, without an attorney present. After posting $1,500 bail, Arcacha is released. Garrison will seek to extradite Arcacha from Texas to Louisiana (without success, blocked by Gov. John Connally).

April 3, 1967: Jim Garrison calls a press conference to announce that he has identified the men involved in the conspiracy to assassinate JFK. Garrison says that most of the participants "are in Texas and Dallas particularly where they are protected – one, by the Dallas law enforcement establishment and two, by the federal government."

Apr. 4, 1967: A CIA document, sent to "Chief, Certain Stations and Bases" with the title "Countering Criticisms of the Warren Report," states CIA should "Employ propaganda assets to answer and refute the attacks of the critic" using "book reviews and feature articles."[11]

April 5, 1967: Clay Shaw is arraigned in New Orleans.

April 1967: Orestes Pena is beaten, then sued, by Carlos Bringuier. Orestes Pena was David Ferrie's friend. Not long after David's death, Pena was beaten up at one of the three bars he owned and was hospitalized, just after agreeing to meet an investigator from another state. Pena had said he saw Lee Oswald with FBI SAC Warren DeBrueys. Author/researcher Harold Weisberg[12] tells Garrison's Grand Jury: Pena also said he had attended "meetings including Arcacha, Ferrie and Warren DeBrueys," and "indicated Ferrie had other associates under federal employment." When Pena left the Cuban Revolutionary Front, he said he began to have trouble with DeBrueys. *After* investigator Harold Weisberg reported on what Pena told him and the Warren Commission, Carlos Bringuier filed a $350,000 civil suit against Pena, claiming Pena gave "slanderous and defamatory testimony" before the Warren Commission, portraying Bringuier as "an enemy and traitor to the United States, a Castro sympathizer and vulgar opportunist." Weisberg's article was in the April issue of *Saga Magazine*.

Weisberg collected over 250,000 government documents on the case.

April 28, 1967: former OSS agent Harold Weisberg opens some eyes on Garrison's Grand Jury: "Warren DeBrueys is fluent in Spanish, translates documents, he is one of these Spanish experts, he is one of the Oswald experts, Pena had been an informant for him reporting on those [who were] for Castro.

"When Oswald left New Orleans so did DeBrueys. When Oswald wound up in Dallas so did DeBrueys. When he was no longer in Dallas neither was DeBrueys. He came back to New Orleans when Oswald got murdered – a remarkable coincidence, gentlemen.... Warren DeBrueys from the time of his first attendance at the Cuban organizational meetings had Pena as an informer ... when things begin to get close with Cubans who might be involved or were with Oswald.... They don't want to know their names ... like the Cuban who walked out of the Cuban Embassy in Mexico City with Oswald. There is no way to see what he looked like – they sent the wrong picture up."

May 17, 1967: New Orleans' FBI boss Regis Kennedy "Reserves the privilege" when asked about David Ferrie.

Example #1:

Q: What about David Ferrie?

RK: No sir.

Q: You don't know Dave Ferrie?

RK: No sir.

[A page later KENNEDY is asked if he had met Ferrie since 1963]:

RK: In the past years?

Q: Since then (1963)?

RK: Oh yes.

Q: How often would you say?

RK: Its 'difficult, once or twice, maybe a few more times.

Q: Was this prior to your questioning him? Did you question him at any time?

RK: Would you define the word 'questioning' for me?

Example #2:

Q: Did you know anyone who knew Clay Shaw?

RK: I will reserve the privilege on that.

Q: Are you aware of the role of Guy Banister with regard to Anti-Castro Cuban activities in the early '60's.

RK: I will reserve the privilege on that.

Q: Are you aware of the fact that Dave Ferrie was very close to Guy Banister?

RK: I will reserve the privilege on that.

...

Q: Are you aware of any connection of Lee Harvey Oswald with Cubans here in New Orleans in the summer of 1963?

RK: I will reserve the privilege on that.

Q: Did you ever know anyone in any Federal Agency who saw Lee Harvey Oswald in the summer of 1963 in New Orleans?

RK: I will reserve the exception.... (Kennedy admitted he had been in Banister's office many times.)

Example #3:

Q: Do you know how many times Jack Ruby came to New Orleans in the summer of 1963?

RK: No sir.

Q: Do you know his purpose in coming here?

RK: No sir.

Q: Do you know who he met when he came here?

RK: I will reserve an exception on that.

Q: Do you have some knowledge of what Jack Ruby did when he came to New Orleans?

RK: I have to reserve an exception on that.[13]

Is there anyone reading this book who thinks FBI's Regis Kennedy would truthfully disclose what David Ferrie told him on the 20th of February 1967, two days before he died?

July 28 1967: Juan Valdez, who knew both Dr. Mary Sherman and Lee Oswald, is interviewed by William Martin (memo to Jim Garrison).[14]

Sept. 18, 1967: Edward James "Jim" Whalen, who has mental problems, is interviewed by DA James Alcock. Whalen is a career criminal and possibly a hitman, but his take is too wild to be fully truthful. According to Whalen, he was offered a large sum by David Ferrie and Clay Shaw to kill Jim Garrison in "Feb. or March of 1963." An out-of-towner, he correctly described the suspects and Dean Andrews, as well, but the scenario smacks of somebody hoping to get a reduced prison sentence based on rumors heard in New Orleans' underbelly. [F.B.I. #346-8982]

Oct. 1967: *Playboy* interviews Jim Garrison, with a long introduction that presents a balanced account of Garrison's past, his embattled status at present, and his determination to continue his investigation into the Kennedy assassination. The interview conducted by Eric Norden took 12 hours. Garrison was allowed to propose the list of questions asked.[15]

Nov. 1967: *MacLean's,* a Canadian magazine, runs a story by Jon Ruddy about the Winnipeg airport incident, saying Garrison confirmed that Ferrie had been in Winnipeg at the time. (In late September witness Richard Giesbrecht agreed tentatively to testify at Shaw trial. Now he will refuse to do so, after being threatened.)

I have no opinion about the story, but do wish to address an objection raised because the man described as being David Ferrie supposedly was also wearing thick, horn-rimmed glasses. Dave was slightly far-sighted and sometimes wore reading glasses for small print.[16]

Oct. 3, 1967: Garrison assistant Fred Williams writes a memo stating that David Ferrie's last doctor, Richard Bagnetto, says an overdose of Proloid could induce a [rupture of] a berry aneurysm.

Oct. 18, 1967: Jim Garrison contacts Dr. Edward Bruno (of New Jersey) by letter to discuss the possibility of Proloid poisoning. Dr. Bruno had come forward with his belief that it was possible.[17]

Nov. 14, 1967: Garrison's speech in Los Angeles attacks LBJ as the one person who has to be responsible for the cover-up. He discusses the symptoms of fascism, the government's attitude that it has the right to lie, and that if it can feel it's OK to lie it can feel it's OK to murder. He claims the make-up of the Warren Commission indicates it was chosen mainly to protect CIA, and that Warren was named to charm the liberals. He says Ferrie had high blood pressure and killed himself with an overdose of Proloid. *LA Free Press*, 11/17/67.

April 4, 1968: Dr. Martin Luther King, Jr. is assassinated. Riots erupt.

April 24, 1968: A confidential source advises the New Orleans FBI on April 24, 1968, that New Orleans District Attorney Jim Garrison believed: "Dr. Alton Ochsner was involved in the Kennedy assassination conspiracy. According to the source, Garrison bases his belief on the fact that Dr. Ochsner was closely involved with the Cuban element in New Orleans prior to Kennedy's assassination."

May 25, 1968: Nicholas J. Chetta, M.D., Orleans Parish Coroner since 1950, dies in Mercy Hospital of a heart attack at 10:20 P.M. He was scheduled to testify in the Clay Shaw trial.

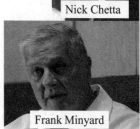

Nick Chetta

Frank Minyard

May 26, 1968: Trumpet-playing Dr. Frank Minyard becomes Acting Coroner for New Orleans Parish. After a defeat in 1969, he will be elected Coroner again and again, still holding this position in 2013, in his mid-80's. Minyard believes David Ferrie was murdered (as does this author).

Midnight, June 5, 1968: Robert F. Kennedy, brother of John F. Kennedy, has just won the California primary in his bid to obtain the Democrat Party's nomination for President when he is suddenly shot down. The deed occurs at the Ambassador Hotel in Los Angeles. Though RFK was killed by a bullet that struck him behind his ear, Sirhan Sirhan, wildly shooting from the front, will be the only person arrested and accused. Essential evidence is hauled off by LA police and never seen again. Most boxes of major evidence and witness testimonies will later be destroyed "due to the need for more storage space."

Jan. 1969: Witness Richard Giesbrecht, who says he has said enough, and people are dying, will not testify in the Clay Shaw trial. Giesbrecht had reported seeing and overhearing David Ferrie and an unidentified man as they discussed how much the "psycho" Lee Oswald told his wife, logistics, and what may have been a gun-running operation, while at lunch in a restaurant in the Winnipeg, Canada airport.

Jan. 1969: Henry Delaune, brother-in-law of coroner Dr. Nicholas Chetta, is murdered. As was the case with Guy Banister, David Ferrie and Dr. Mary Sherman, Henry DeLaune's body is found naked. *The Times-Picayune.* "New Orleans Henry M. Delaune Slain – Teacher Is Remembered. Friends Recall Peaceful, Softspoken Man

"His friends remembered him as a peaceful man who seldom raised his voice. None would have expected Henry M. Delaune, an English teacher at Thibodaux's Nicholls State College, to meet a violent death. But his nude body, its chest punctured by two bullet wounds, was found in the apartment building at 828 Burgundy, which he owned and where he lived. By Monday afternoon homicide detectives had questioned many persons, but still had no suspects..."[18]

Feb. 1969: Rev. Clyde Johnson, scheduled to testify, is severely beaten in an apparently unrelated incident.

July 1969: An angry in-law kills Rev. Clyde Johnson by shotgun in Greensburg, LA. Garrison: "Whether Johnson was a kook or the genuine article we'll never know. The jury never got the opportunity to decide on his credibility."

Johnson described a meeting involving Jack Ruby, Clay Shaw and "Leon" whom he later identified as Lee Oswald, but why he would be invited to such an important meeting remains unexplained. However, Johnson was yet another "Reverend" with ties to David Ferrie, typically offering suspicious information.[19]

1:05 AM, Mar. 1, 1969: After Jim Garrison's closing argument, Judge Haggerty charges the jury. In less than an hour, the jury finds Clay Shaw not guilty.

Nov. 1969: *Penthouse,* Nov. Vol. 4. No. 8. "Exclusive Interview With Accused Dallas Conspirator –Clay Shaw says he has been financially ruined."

Jan. 21, 1970: "CIA Killed JFK Says Garrison" *Times-Picayune*; to see how little Garrison's statement means to the newspaper, the story is run on page eight.

Aug. 14, 1974: Clay Shaw dies of lung cancer. An elaborate police report written in cooperation with a doctor from Ochsner Hospital provides evidence that Shaw died a natural death.

A close examination of Shaw's death reveals nothing suspicious concerning the cancer itself. However, there are two problems – see Appendix XIII.

A FAREWELL TO DAVID
March 28, 1918 – Feb. 22, 1967

Dave liked a poem written by a woman named "Theresa." I took the original sheet of paper, stained with coffee, and transcribed it to clean paper for him.[20] Some of its words inspired me, later, to write this about my friend, who loved to fly to the very end.

Is this man worse, than he who dies,
Who has no sparkle in his eyes?
Who knew the stature of the earth,
Traversing its blue and lofty skies?
Deep in the ground his bones were placed,
And with them, all his sins erased.
Free at last to fly to Thee,
O Pilot of Eternity.

JVB

Endnotes

1. Lie detector tests are used when a suspect is thought to be lying. Shaw was right to refuse, because to the public, taking a lie detector test means important people must doubt your statements. The use of an alias is another matter. It is used to obscure one's identity for a purpose. I used "Avary Baker" as my name in Louisiana to hide my original identity as "Judy Vary Baker" to protect myself when I returned to live in Louisiana.

2. http://jfk.hood.edu/Collection/White Materials/Garrison News Clippings/1967/67-06/67-06-034.pdf (Retrieved Sept. 8, 2013).

3. FBI's 3rd-in-command, C. DeLoach sends a memo to 2nd-in-command Clyde Tolson that the Attorney General "asked whether the FBI knew anything about Shaw. I told him Shaw's name had come up in our investigation in December, 1963 as a result of several parties furnishing information concerning Shaw. [Hoover appended the following] I hope a.g. isn't going to peddle this information we send him. H. Bill Davy. *Let Justice be Done.* p 92.

4. A. J. Weberman, Nodule 24: "...The FBI reported: "(Deleted) advised March 5, 1967, that Aura Lee (LNU) Clay Shaw's former Secretary at the International Trade Mart, New Orleans, who is employed by the heart fund at the Ochsner Clinic, stated in front of Doctor Charles B. Moore and others at Ochsner Hospital, after Shaw's press conference where he advised he never met David Ferrie, that she had seen Ferrie go into Shaw's office in the International Trade Mart Building on a number of occasions, and believed Ferrie had privileged entry into Shaw's office." [FBI-.62-109060-NR 3.9.67].

5. Peter Levenda: http://sinisterforces.info/blog (Retrieved 1 Aug. 2013).

6. A full look into Bryan can be found in H.P. Albarelli's well-.written essay on Bryan, in *A Secret Order*, Chapter Three, p. 151-155 (TrineDay, 2013). While Albarelli attacks me on Facebook, he's done good work here (that's more important than my feelings).

7. http://sinisterforces.info/blog/index.php?/archives/16-The-Bishop-and-the-Boys-Part-Two.html (Retrieved July 31, 2013).

8. Dick Russell. *On the Trail of the Kennedy Assassins*, Skyhorse, 2008. NY. p. 74-75.

9. Ibid.

10. *Avalanche Journal*, Lubbock, Texas 1967-03-31.

11. Mellen, *A Farewell to Justice*. P. 141. Mellen rightly points out that this directive is aimed at Garrison's investigation, which was making national headlines.

12. All quotes on Pena here are from the author or from Weisberg at http://www.aarclibrary.org/publib/jfk/garr/grandjury/pdf/weisberg.pdf (Retrieved 06/18/2013).

13. http://www.aarclibrary.org/publib/jfk/garr/grandjury/pdf/Kennedy.pdf (Retrieved Sept. 7, 2013).

14. Mellen, *A Farewell to Justice*, Valdez section.

15. http://22november1963.org.uk/about-this-website/ This well-organized website offers the entire article, not just the interview. (Retrieved Sept. 8, 2013)

16. I'm interested in the incident not because I believe there is enough evidence to decide if David Ferrie was there or not, but because of the exchange about the incident between Robert Harris and Stephen Roy (Blackburst), which illustrates how an error or a deliberate obfuscation can influence a debate about Ferrie. On April 27, 2010 11:49 PM an exchange commenced between Robert Harris and Stephen Roy (as Blackburst):about the Winnipeg Airport Incident (described elsewhere in this book, but in great detail online by researcher Peter Whitmey, at http://mcadams.posc.mu.edu/winnipeg.htm.) By far, the most powerful indictment of David Ferrie was his identification by a fellow named, Giesbrecht, in Winnipeg, Ontario. For years, [Blackburst –Roy] told people that Ferrie was at his uncle's funeral on the day that he was allegedly spotted at the Winnipeg airport, but during our discussion on that, I made a phone call to the Cleveland Plain Dealer and confirmed that the funeral was not Feb. 13th, but on the 14th, which means that Ferrie was at the airport at precisely the right time to catch a plane to Cleveland to be at the funeral the next day, and even attend the open casket showing that evening. David[Blackburst-Roy replied, "I stand corrected. I was working from rough notes and memory, and got the date wrong. David [Blackburst-Roy] also claims that he has spoken to one of Ferrie's associates who told him that he drove Ferrie to Cleveland that day, but he refuses to divulge the man's name or even his story. He even states that he made no effort to take notes or record his conversation with this guy, which is a strange way to research a book, IMHO. But he did say that he would contact the man for permission and then report back. That was about 7 months ago and he hasn't said a word. For those who are unfamiliar with this issue, Giesbrecht, who was an extremely credible witness, which even[Blackburst-Roy] has admitted, overheard a conversation among several men at the airport in Winnipeg, in which a man with the "oddest eyebrows" (he also called them "streaky") he had even seen, was going on about his fears that Oswald told his wife about the conspiracy and that she would tell the WC about it. He also stated that he believed that at least two of the men, including the one he later identified as Ferrie, were homosexuals. Giesbrecht had no idea who the men were, until two years later, when he saw a photo of Ferrie in the newspapers and immediately identified him. So, not only did DAVID [Blackburst-Roy] "alibi" for Ferrie fall apart, but the man Giesbrecht identified as Ferrie was in exactly the place he needed to be, to catch a flight to Cleveland in plenty of time to attend the viewing of the body that night, as well as the funeral the next day.

Interestingly, he also heard Ferrie say that he "wondered why he got involved with someone so 'psycho' as Oswald." That's exactly how Marcello described Oswald when he told an FBI informant that Ferrie introduced him to the alleged assassin, at a meeting at his brother's restaurant. The Giesbrecht incident is probably the most underrated issue in the JFK case. Because of Ferrie's unique physical appearance, it amounts to rock solid proof of conspiracy.

And even if someone is so deeply in denial that he convinces himself that Giesbrecht overheard someone other than Ferrie, we STILL have proof that people other than Oswald were involved. And yet David [Blackburst-Roy] insists on hiding both the identity of someone who might have information about this, as well as his story. Like far too many others…David [Blackburst-Roy] demonstrates the horrible consequences of taking a position of blind advocacy, rather than simply looking for the truth. Robert Harris Mr. Blackburst-Roy replied (in part): Are you asserting that Ferrie WAS in Winnipeg? To Harris' statement, "Because of Ferrie's unique physical appearance, it amounts to rock solid proof of conspiracy."

Mr. Backburst-Roy replied, "I disagree." He added, "I found the info about the funeral, and passed it along to Peter Whitmey, among others, which places Ferrie, at least, "up north", and not at home running his gas station. A guy, a community leader who doesn't want to be associated with "the homosexual stuff" went with him, and doesn't remember him being absent for any period of time (some 30 years earlier). This was for a biography, not an assassination evidence book. I have been upfront with all comers, and graciously accepted his pinpointing of the exact day of the funeral. Robert is spinning this all into "coo-coo land."Mr. Harris came back with a solid list of problems in Mr. Blackburst-Roy's position: "And he had the strangest hair and eyebrows he had ever seen." Why did an objective guy like you, just happen to forget that? David, there is no room for denial here. Alleging that *someone else* with strange, "streaky" eyebrows who was a homosexual, and was paranoically shrieking about his fears that Marina would blow the conspiracy is just crazy. And if you actually believe that, then you have someone other than Ferrie, confirming conspiracy in the JFK case. Somewhere along the line, you have to do what you guys always wind up having to do – call the witness a liar or delusional. If you don't, then how could you remain the LN advocate that you are? Yes, and that "one day" just happened to be the difference between a perfect alibi and a perfect match with Ferrie being at the airport, just in time to make it to Cleveland to attend both the viewing of the corpse and the funeral the next day.

Blackburst-Roy replied: " It didn't seem to make sense to me that Ferrie would somehow travel from New Orleans to Winnipeg, be seen at the airport, fly 1882 miles to Cleveland for the wake and funeral, and not have his absence noticed by his traveling companion."

Harris: "Of course it does. He flew to Winnipeg and called in while he was there to check on his uncle's condition. When he was told the man died, he caught a plane, right on schedule to be there when he had to. I cannot in my wildest imagination, understand how that wouldn't make sense to you.

David [Blackburst] also claims that he has spoken to one of Ferrie's associates who told him that he drove Ferrie to Cleveland that day, but he refuses to divulge the man's name or even his story." Blackburst-Roy replied: "He doesn't want to be identified by name at this time, because of the position he holds." Harris: "Uh huh. But when you told him you were writing a book, he was eager to give you a detailed story.

He even states that he made no effort to take notes or record his conversation with this guy, which is a strange way to research a book, Blackburst-Roy: "The guy put me up in a room in his home for several days on a research trip for a BIOGRAPHY of Ferrie. I didn't carry a tape recorder or note pad 24/7." Harris: "Damn! If only the guy had some paper in his house! And I guess you can't remember his story either, right? IMO. But he did say that he would contact the man for permission and then report back. That was about 7 months ago and he hasn't said a word.

Giesbrecht, who was an extremely credible witness, which even David has admitted..."Blackburst-Roy: "He may have heard such a conversation. I am not convinced it was Ferrie. "Harris: "Of course you aren't convinced, David. A DNA test and a confession by Ferrie, signed in blood, wouldn't be convincing to you.

17. It is important to note that Garrison didn't bring up Proloid at the time Dave died, though he said he picked up a bottle of Proloid at the death scene.

18. http://jfk.hood.edu/Collection/Weisberg Subject Index Files/D Disk/Delaune Henry/It em 03.pdf. (Retrieved Aug. 25, 2013).

19. Bill Davy, *Let Justice Be Done* (Reston, Virginia: Jordan Publishing, 1999) p. 310n.8.

20.

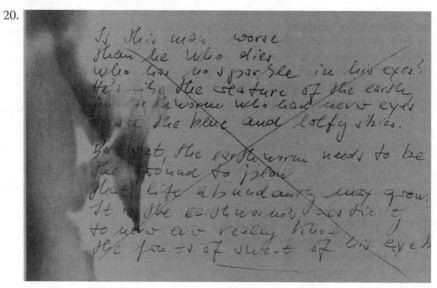

Appendices

FBI Interview of David Ferrie 11/25/63

by SA ERNEST WALL and SA L. M. SHEARER at New Orleans

DAVID WILLIAM FERRIE was interviewed at the First District Station, New Orleans Police Department. Ferrie was advised of the identity of the interviewing Agents. At the outset of the interview he was advised he did not have to make a statement, that any statement he did make could be used against him in a court of law and that he had the right to the advice of an attorney.

FERRIE advised he was born March 28, 1918, at Cleveland, Ohio. His parents JAMES HOWARD and BURDETTE C. FERRIE are both deceased. FERRIE said he received a B.A. degree from Baldwin-Wallace College, Berea, Ohio, in 1941. He also received a Ph.D. degree from Phoenix University of Bari, Bari, Italy in 1957. FERRIE stated that his present address is 3330 Louisiana Avenue Parkway, where he has been residing since March, 1962.

FERRIE stated that in 1952 he became a member of the Civil Air Patrol (CAP) in New Orleans, serving in the capacity of an instructor. He stated that in approximately 1953 he became commandant of the CAP Squadron in New Orleans, continuing in this capacity until he resigned from the CAP in 1955 with the intention of returning to school. FERRIE related that the New Orleans Cadet Squadron of the CAP functioned at Lakefront Airport. He stated that the squadron was usually made up of approximately 75 boys and the attrition rate in the squadron was approximately 20%. FERRIE stated that the squadron met twice a week. He stated that during the period he was Commander of the squadron, JERRY C. PARADIS was the recruit instructor and took all of the squadron recruits through their training. FERRIE said that PARADIS presently has offices at 225 Baronne Building and resides at 5704 Prytania street.

FERRIE stated that during the period 1952-1955 he does not recall taking any recruit class through their training program. After he became Commandant he is certain he did not instruct the recruits. FERRIE stated that he never at any time instructed either the recruits of the regular squadron members in the use of firearms, or afforded them any type of firearms training for the reason he was always able to secure the service of a qualified instructor in this type training. FERRIE related that the cadets in the squadron were instructed in the use of .22 caliber rifles with adjustable rear sights, but these rifles were not equipped with telescopic sights. He stated that the cadets received instruction in the firing of .22 caliber rifles approximately four times each year. In addition, at the annual encampment of the CAP which was held outside of the New Orleans area the cadets were permitted to fire M-1 rifles under the supervision of a qualified instructor.

FERRIE said he has never owned a telescopic sight or a rifle equipped with a telescopic sight, and to the best of his recollection he has never used a weapon equipped with a telescopic sight and would not know how to use one.

FERRIE stated that he does not know LEE HARVEY OSWALD and to the best of his knowledge OSWALD was never a member of the CAP Squadron in

New Orleans during the period he was with that group. FERRIE said that if OSWALD was a member of the squadron for only a few weeks, as had been claimed, he would have been considered a recruit and that he (FERRIE) would not have had any contact with him. FERRIE stated that he was succeeded as Commandant of the New Orleans Squadron of the CAP by a man named HINTON.

FERRIE stated that he was again associated with the CAP in New Orleans from 1958 to the end of 1960 or the beginning of 1961, serving in the capacity as instructor and later as executive officer. He said that Major BOB MORRELL was the Commandant. FERRIE stated that his applications with the CAP covering both periods he served with that unit should be on file with the CAP at Ellington Air Force Base, Houston, Texas. FERRIE related that there was a period during 1958, exact dates not recalled, in which he instructed at the CAP Squadron before he submitted his application.

FERRIE said that to the best of his knowledge he does not know any individual named LEE HARVEY OSWALD nor has he ever known the individual represented by photograph presented to him as that of LEE HARVEY OSWALD in the CAP, in any business connection or in any social capacity. He said he does not recognized the name or the photograph as being anyone he has ever had any contact with at any time.

A photograph of LEE HARVEY OSWALD, New Orleans Police Department Number 112723 taken on August 9, 1963, showing a profile, full face and full length photograph of OSWALD was exhibited to FERRIE. FERRIE upon viewing the photograph stated that the profile view has a very vague familiarity to him but the full face and full length photographs of OSWALD are not familiar to him.

FERRIE informed that since March 1962 he has been employed by Attorney G. Wray Gill in New Orleans as an investigator and law clerk. He said that since the end of August, 1963 and up until November 22, 1963 he has been working on a case involving CARLOS MARCELLO who was charged in Federal Court in connection with a fraudulent birth certificate. FERRIE stated that the trial of MARCELLO began in Federal Court in New Orleans, Louisiana on November 4, 1963 and ended on November 22, 1963 and that he was in New Orleans working with Attorney G. WRAY GILL on the case during this period. He stated that on November 9 and November 16, 1963 he was at Churchill Downs which is a farm owned by CARLOS MARCELLO, mapping strategy in connection with MARCELLO's trial. He informed that on November 11, 1963 he was in New Orleans, during the entire day and did not leave the city.

FERRIE stated that from October 11 to October 18, 1963 he was in Guatemala and again from October 30, 1963 to November 1, 1963 he was in Guatemala in connection with investigation of the MARCELLO case.

FERRIE said that prior to a very recent trip he was last in the state of Texas in August, 1962 at which time he was in Orange, Texas. FERRIE said he had planned during the trial of the MARCELLO case that immediately upon the conclusion of that case he would take a trip for the purpose of relaxing.

He said he left his home at 3330 Louisiana Avenue Parkway, New Orleans, on November 22, 1963, roughly at 6:30 PM in his light blue Comet four-door station wagon which he purchased from the Delta Mercury Company in New Orleans within the past month. He stated that CHARLES GRAHAM a salesman at Delta Mercury Company sold the Comet station wagon to him.

FERRIE related that on leaving his home he drove to the homes of ALVIN BEAUBOUEF and MELVIN COFFEY and picked them up in order that they might accompany him on the trip. He stated that at the time he left his home his did not know where he was going. He said the purpose of the trip was to merely relax and at that time he did not know whether he was going "hunting, drinking or driving." FERRIE stated he did not take any firearms with him when he left his home because he thought he might go out of the state of Louisiana and he did not know what the hunting seasons were in other states and he was also concerned about transporting firearms across the state line.

FERRIE said he had been considering for some time the feasibility and possibility of opening an ice skating rink in New Orleans. He claimed he made a telephone call, possibly from MELVIN COFFEY's home to CHUCK ROLLAND at the Winterland Skating Rink in Houston, Texas. He advised that this call to ROLLAND was charged to either telephone number [...] or [...]. Ferrie claimed he had no prior acquaintance with ROLLAND but had knowledge of the fact that the Winterland Skating Rink was located in Houston.

FERRIE related that he left MELVIN COFFEY's home between 6:30 and 7:00 PM accompanied by BEAUBOUEF and COFFEY and drove to John Paul's Restaurant, Kenner, Louisiana, where they stopped to eat. He said that at approximately 9:00 PM or shortly after 9:00 PM, November 22, 1963, he, BEAUBOUEF and COFFEY left John Paul's Restaurant to go to Houston, Texas. He informed that the route traveled was through Baton Rouge to Lafayette, Louisiana and through Lake Charles, Louisiana to Houston, Texas. FERRIE claimed they arrived in Houston between 4:30 and 5:30 AM and went directly to the Alamotel located on South Main Street, six to ten blocks south of the Shamrock Hilton Hotel, where they checked into Room 19. He stated that the three of them registered on the same card at the motel. After registering they retired for the night.

FERRIE claims that he had left a call at the motel office for 8:30 AM and another call for 10:30 AM but has no recollection of receiving a call from the motel office at either time. FERRIE said he had left the calls so that he could call Attorney G. WRAY GILL in New Orleans to tell him he had left New Orleans and was on a vacation trip. FERRIE stated that he and his companions awakened roughly at noon and after having breakfast he went down Main Street to Sears, Roebuck and Company where he purchased a jacket, a sweater and several other items. After leaving Sears, they drove directly to the Winterland Ice Skating Rink, 2400 Norfolk, which he had learned opened at 3:30 PM and closed at 5:30 PM.

FERRIE said he rented skates and skated at the rink for a while looking the situation over and also taking into consideration the amount of business at the rink. He stated that he introduced himself to CHUCK ROLLAND and spoke with him at length concerning the cost of installation and operation of the rink. FERRIE exhibited a leaflet of the Winterland Ice Skating Rink, 2400 Norfolk, Houston, Texas, which he had in his possession. FERRIE stated that during the time he was talking to CHUCK ROLLAND other employees of ROLLAND were present at the rink. He recalled specifically there was a young boy who was passing out skates and an older man who was on duty at the rink but he does not recall whether he was introduced to these two individuals or not. FERRIE claimed that he remained at the Winterland Skating Rink for a period of approximately two hours and after leaving there he returned to the motel.

After arriving at the motel he placed a telephone call to Attorney G. WRAY GILL but was unable to complete this call. He placed a second call to the Town and Country Motel in an effort to determine whether Attorney Gill was located at the Town and Country Motel. FERRIE further related that ALVIN BEAUBOUEF may have made a telephone call to his home. He said that they later checked out of the Alamotel and went to the Bellaire Skating Rink on Chimney Rock Road in the Belleview section of Houston, arriving there between 7:30 and 8:00 PM. FERRIE stated that he looked the skating rink over and tried to locate the owner but the owner was unavailable. He said that he remained at the Bellaire Skating Rink for approximately 45 minutes to 1 hour. On leaving the skating rink they drove out Old Spanish Fort Trail and stopped at a restaurant near Telephone Road. They left this restaurant at approximately 9:00 or shortly after 9:00 PM and decided to drive to Galveston, Texas. He said that while en route to Galveston, Texas, they stopped at the Manned Space Craft Center and looked around for about 20 minutes. They then proceeded to Galveston, Texas, arriving there between 10:30 and 11:30 PM. They immediately checked into Room 117 at the Driftwood Motel, 3128 Seawall Boulevard, Galveston. After checking into the motel they drove around in the vicinity of some old clubs in Galveston, Texas, returning to the motel after midnight and it could have been as late as 1:00 AM.

FERRIE stated that they arose around 8:00 or 8:30 AM on November 24, 1963. After having breakfast they took the ferry across the bay to pick up the road to Port Arthur, Texas that runs along the coast. FERRIE stated the first stop they made after reaching Port Arthur was at the Gulf Service Station on the left hand side of the highway in Port Arthur, Texas where they purchased a new set of spark plugs for the Comet station wagon. He stated that there was a television set in this station and as he walked into the station there was a picture on the television set showing the shooting of LEE OSWALD in the basement of the Dallas City Jail. FERRIE said he presumed he was looking at the original live broadcast of the shooting and that this was in the vicinity of 12:00 Noon on that date. He said the after changing the spark plugs in the station wagon he ran the car up on the rack in order that the attendant could check the transmission and differential. FERRIE estimated that he remained at this service station for approximately 20 to 30 minutes. They then left Port Arthur and drove to Orange, Texas and after crossing the Louisiana state line they stopped at Buster's Bar and Restaurant. He stated that the operator of Buster's Bar and Restaurant is MARION JAMES JOHNSON who is a client of Attorney G. WRAY GILL. He stated that he contacted JOHNSON at the bar and restaurant and talked to JOHNSON for approximately 30 minutes discussing the status of an appeal on a perjury conviction of JOHNSON in connection with an income tax case on Sheriff REID at lake Charles, Louisiana.

On leaving Buster's Bar and Restaurant they drove to Alexandria, Louisiana, arriving there at approximately 4:00 PM. FERRIE informed that ALVIN BEAUBOUEF has relatives in Alexandria. FERRIE also said that he had tentatively planned to attend a party in Alexandria and that his plans were tentative because he did not know whether or not he would be needed in New Orleans on November 25, 1963 in connection with the trial of a murder case which was scheduled to begin on that date. He stated that to ascertain whether he would be needed in New Orleans he made several pre-paid long distance calls from a gas station trying to reach Attorney G. WRAY GILL's office, but was unsuccessful.

He stated that he then telephonically contacted his home and talked to LAYTON MARTENS who at that time informed him that two WWL-TV representatives had been making inquiries at his home and in the neighborhood and he learned that he was being accused of being implicated in the assassination of President KENNEDY.

FERRIE said that as a result of the information furnished by LAYTON he was very much disturbed over the fact that he was being accused of being implicated in the assassination of the President and that he left Alexandria, Louisiana between 4:00 and 5:00 PM, possibly close to 5:00 PM. He said that he stopped at several service stations along the way to use the telephone in an attempt to reach Attorney G. WRAY GILL. He said that he was finally successful in contacting Attorney GILL by telephone and that Attorney GILL informed him that HARDY DAVIS, a former bondsman in New Orleans, had telephonically contacted GILL stating that DAVIS had been contacted by JACK S. MARTIN who claimed he had tied FERRIE in with the killing of President KENNEDY and had tipped of the Orleans Parish District Attorney's office, the FBI, the Secret Service, newspapers and radio stations. MARTIN claimed that FERRIE knew OSWALD, had trained OSWALD and had flown OSWALD to Dallas, Texas. FERRIE said he asked Attorney GILL if he had made any attempt to verify any of this information and if he thought there was any substance to it. FERRIE said he told Attorney GILL what LAYTON MARTENS had told him about the inquiries of the WWL-TV representatives and asked Attorney GILL for his advice. Attorney GILL advised him to continue with his plans and return to New Orleans in keeping with his original plans. FERRIE said that he proceeded directly to New Orleans, stopping at a restaurant on the west side of the highway at Baton Rouge, Louisiana, which restaurant is located between the Mississippi River Bridge and the Hammond Circle. He stated that this restaurant has several rooms and that one of the dining rooms is for formal attire and one is for informal attire and that this restaurant specializes in steaks. He said that after eating they drove on to New Orleans, arriving at about 9:30 PM. He stated that he dropped ALVIN BEAUBOUEF in the vicinity of his (FERRIE's) home in order that BEAUBOUEF could check his home to see if anyone was waiting for him. He then drove to MELVIN COFFEY's home and dropped him off. FERRIE said that he then telephonically contacted Attorney GILL for the purpose of trying to get GILL to obtain some more information concerning the accusations made against him. He stated that after talking to Attorney GILL he drove to Hammond, Louisiana, by way of Baton Rouge, Louisiana, and upon arriving in Hammond contacted a friend, THOMAS COMPTON at the Holloway-Smith Hall at Southeastern Louisiana College. He stated that COMPTON is doing research at this school. FERRIE claimed that he spent the balance of the night of Holloway-Smith Hall and remained in Hammond until 1:00 or 1:30 PM, November 25, 1963.

He stated that he then drove to New Orleans and went directly to his home where he obtained a clean shirt and then proceeded to the office of Attorney GILL. He stated that from there he went to the District Attorney's office accompanied by Mr. GILL where he surrendered to the District Attorney.

FERRIE said that while in Texas he had talked to waitresses, service station people, clerks, and operators of motels and that during these conversations he had speculated concerning the assassination of the President and had speculated as to whether the police had arrested the right man, whether the press was giving the complete story and had speculated as to the leftist tendencies of LEE OS-WALD and his theory of why OSWALD shot President KENNEDY. He said that it was his theory that LEE OSWALD was paranoid, probably on the psychotic side and that this act was his attempt to redress the imagined wrongs done OS-WALD in the service and was accomplished by destroying the very root of the authority he, OSWALD "bucked."

In regard to JACK S. MARTIN, FERRIE said that he also knew MARTIN had used the names of SUGGS and SCROGGS and that MARTIN lives in the 1900 block of North Prieur on the corner of North Prieur and Esplanade and that the house is located on the southwest corner of that intersection. FERRIE claimed that JACK S. MARTIN was a private detective who he first met in the Fall of 1961. He said that since that time MARTIN has attempted to insert himself into his, FER-RIE's personal affairs. He claimed that the time he first met MARTIN, MARTIN was working for a woman in the Department of Health, Education and Welfare, named CATHERINE WILKERSON or WILKINSON or some similar name. He stated that MARTIN was endeavoring to expose various frauds in the Diploma Mills and Ecclesiastical Mills and was particularly interested in CARL J. STANLEY of Louisville, Kentucky who called himself CHRISTOPHER MARIA. He stated that MARTIN was desirous of obtaining some of the phony certificates of ordination and consecration used by STANLEY and to forward them to Washington, D.C. He said that MARTIN asked his assistance in this investigation and that he accompanied MARTIN to Louisville, He stated that he received only part of his fee for the investigation conducted with MARTIN. FERRIE said that he was slow in catching on to MARTIN but determined that MARTIN was dealing in phony certificates. He said that he regarded MARTIN as being an unethical and danger-ous person. FERRIE claimed that in 1962 MARTIN disappeared from the scene and after several months suddenly re-appeared. He stated that MARTIN began visiting him at the office of Attorney G. WRAY GILL and that Mr. GILL did not want MARTIN hanging around his office. FERRIE claimed that in June of 1963 he put MARTIN out of Mr. GILL's office in an undiplomatic manner and that since that time MARTIN has bedeviled him in every manner possible.

FERRIE said that he had learned that sometime after he put MARTIN out of Mr. GILL's office MARTIN was moving around to various parts of the Unit-ed States contacting first one clergyman and then another who were connected with the old Catholic Church trying to get ordained and gave FERRIE's names as a character reference. He further determined that MARTIN was making long distance telephone calls charging these calls to Attorney GILL's office and the office of GUY BANISTER, Guy Banister Associates. FERRIE further informed that he determined that MARTIN had previously been admitted to the psychi-atric ward at Charity Hospital where he was diagnosed as a paranoid. FERRIE said he had also learned that MARTIN had been a sergeant in the U. S. Army and while in service had been mixed up in obtaining phony decrees in medicine, chiropractic and naturopathy by finding a college that was not in operation but whose charter was not defunct. FERRIE informed that he had also determined that MARTIN had been charged with murder in connection with the illegal practice of medicine in Houston, Texas. However, he believes that this charge was later dismissed.

FERRIE said that he had learned through interviews with other officers that one of the allegations made against him was that when OSWALD was arrested he had his (FERRIE's) library card in OSWALD's possession and that it had been alleged that OSWALD had been using FERRIE's library card to get books at the New Orleans Public Library. FERRIE said that in his personal property located in the Property Room at the First District is his library card which expired March 13, 1963. FERRIE said that he has not made application for a new card since the above card expired and that this card has been in his possession at all times.

FERRIE informed that he has owned a Stinson 150 single engine, blue and white four passenger monoplane, registration number 8293K, since 1948. He stated that this aircraft has not been airworthy since the license expired in April, 1962. FERRIE said that this information can be verified through the FAA Department of Airworthiness Certification in Oklahoma City, Oklahoma. FERRIE informed that he had never flown this plane to Cuba and that it has been only as far south as Miami, Florida. He claimed that the plane was flown to Dallas, Texas one time since he purchased it, which was during the year 1949.

FERRIE stated that from approximately November, 1960 until August, 1961 he was associated with the Cuban Revolutionary Front in New Orleans, Louisiana. He stated that he had been actively engaged in working for the Cuban Revolutionary Front collecting food, money, medicine and clothing for the organization as well as giving talks before various citizen's groups. He states that at the time he was associated with the Cuban Revolutionary Front the office of the organization was located in the Balter Building and that SERGIO ARCACHA SMITH was the head of this organization in New Orleans. FERRIE said that he has never known of the Cuban Revolutionary Front maintaining an office at 544 Camp Street, nor does he have any knowledge of SERGIO ARCACHA SMITH maintaining an office at that address during the time he was head of the organization and later after he was replaced. FERRIE said that the Cuban Revolutionary Front was definitely an anti-Castro organization and that all persons connected with the organization were violently anti-Castro. FERRIE started that he has not had any connection with the CUBAN Revolutionary Front or any other anti-Castro organization since August, 1961. He stated that after disassociating himself with the Cuban Revolutionary Front he continued to have contact with SERGIO ARCACHA SMITH which was purely social in nature. He stated that some months after he ceased his activity with the organization, SERGIO ARCACHA SMITH gave up the leadership of the organization and was replaced by an individual named RABEL. FERRIE related that SERGIO ARCACHA SMITH then went into the advertising business in New Orleans and that he had assisted SMITH in preparing letters in connection with this advertising business. FERRIE said that in 1962 SERGIO ARCACHA SMITH attempted to organize a fund raising committee, the name of which he does not recall, but he does not believe the this organization ever materialized. He stated that SMITH was interested at that time in issuing a commemorative coin depicting the Bay of Pigs Invasion which was to be sold to a coin company. FERRIE related that in connection with this plan SMITH obtained vendor's license from the City of New Orleans. FERRIE said that he does not believe that this plan was ever placed into effect by Smith and it is his belief that SMITH subsequently abandoned this idea.

FERRIE said that he does not have any recollection of any organization in New Orleans named the Fair Play for Cuba Committee and has never had any connection with any individual representing an organization by that name.

FERRIE recalled the following individuals were connected with the Civil Air Patrol during the period 1954 to 1955: LEON GUIDRY, Cadet Commander

//BOBBY BADELAT, Cadet Executive Officer // TOMMY McKIBBEN, Flight Leader // GEORGE BOESCH, Flight Leader // ROY CLEMMENS (or CLEM-MENTS), Rifle Instructor

FERRIE further informed that the following individuals could possibly furnish information concerning his activities and whereabouts: ALICE GUIDROZ, employee of Attorney G. WRAY GILL;

REGINA FRANCOVICH (phonetic), employee of GILL; MELVIN COFFEY; ALVIN BEAUBOEUF;

JOHN IRIAN [sic] who is employed by Curtis and Davis, Suite 400, 2475 Canal Street; JIM LEWALLEN, 1300 [Me: Actually 1309] Dauphine.

FERRIE exhibited U. S. Passport Number B085860 in the name of DAVID WILLIAM FERRIE issued September 18, 1961. This passport reflected that visa number 1236 was issued by the Consulate General of Guatemala of New Orleans, Louisiana, September 25, 1963. The passport shows that FERRIE entered Guatemala in October 11, 1963 and departed October 18, 1963. The passport further shows that visa number 1406 was issued by Consulate General of Guatemala, New Orleans, Louisiana, October 29, 1963. The passport shows that FERRIE entered Guatemala on October 30, 1963 and departed November 1, 1963. FERRIE advised that he does not know any individual by the name of JACK RUBY or JACK RUBENSTEIN.

FERRIE stated that he is not implicated in the assassination of President KENNEDY in any manner and is willing to cooperate in any manner to prove that he was not implicated in the killing of the President. He stated that he offered to the District Attorney of Orleans Parish to submit to certain examinations to prove his innocence.

The following physical examination was obtained through interview and observation:

Name: DAVID WILLIAM FERRIE
Race: White
Sex: Male
Date of Birth: March 20, 1918 [sic]
Place of Birth: Cleveland, Ohio
Height: 5 feet 11 inches
Weight: 190 pounds
Eyes: Brown
Hair: Bald; wears brownish-red toupee
Complexion: Medium
Build: Medium
Scars and Marks: Rectangular scar, outer right wrist
Marital Status: Single
Military Status: Served in Army Reserve, Cleveland, dates not recalled.

APPENDIX II

Second FBI Interview of David Ferrie, 11/27/63

Subject: Ferrie FBI Interview 11/27.63 Warren Commission Document 75 pp 199-2 **FBI Interview of David Ferrie 11/27/63 by SA Ernest C. Wall and SA Theodore Viater, New Orleans**

DAVID WILLIAM FERRIE was interviewed at his residence, 3330 Louisiana Avenue Parkway and was advised of the identity of interviewing Agents. He was advised he did not have to make a statement, that any statement he did make could be used in a court of law and he had the right to the advice of an attorney.

FERRIE stated that at the time of the Bay of Pigs invasion of Cuba, he was very embarrassed and concerned over the lack of air cover provided the Cubans who were engaged in the invasion and that he severely criticized President JOHN F. KENNEDY both in public and in private. He stated that he does not recall specifically what he said in making these criticisms and might have used an off-hand or colloquial expression «He ought to be shot» to express his feelings concerning the Cuban situation. He stated that he has never made any statement that President KENNEDY should be killed with the intention that this be done and has never at any time outline or formulated any plans or made any statement as to how this could be done or who should do it.

FERRIE stated that when it came to serious discussions, when the question of impeachment of President KENNEDY arose he opposed any impeachment proceedings. FERRIE said that within one year prior to the first Russian Sputnik he recalls being quite critical of the U.S. Space Project and the Defense Program. He said he had also been critical of any president riding in an open car and had made the statement that anyone could hide in the bushes and shoot a president. FERRIE also advised that he has been accused of being a worshiper of President KENNEDY because he is a liberal and strongly believes in President Kennedy's Civil Rights Program and Fiscal Program.

FERRIE stated that he has never loaned his library card to LEE HARVEY OSWALD or any other person at any time and that his library card, to the best of his recollection has not been out of his possession since it was issued to him. He exhibited New Orleans Public Library card # M.L. 89437 bearing the stamped lettering N.R. – P.D. in the upper left hand corner. FERRIE said the letters N.R. mean non-resident, and the letters P.D. mean paid. He related at the time he obtained this library card he was living in Metairie, Louisiana and had to pay for the issuance of the card. The library card shows it was issued in the name of Dr. DAVID FERRIE, 331 Atherton Drive, and expiration date is shown as March 13, 1963.

FERRIE stated he has no recollection of knowing or having met LEE HARVEY OSWALD in the Civil Air Patrol or in any business or social capacity.

FERRIE stated he has never owned a telescopic sight, a rifle equipped with a telescopic sight, has never used a weapon equipped with a telescopic sight and does not know how to use one. He also said he never instructed LEE HARVEY OSWALD or anyone else in the use of American made or foreign made rifles or firearms.

FERRIE said that while in the Civil Air Patrol he assisted in firearms instruction at Civil Air Patrol Bivouacs for range safety only.

FERRIE claimed he has owned a Stinson 150 blue and white, single engine, four passenger monoplane, registration number 8293K and that this plane has not been airworthy since the license expired in the spring of 1962. FERRIE stated he has never flown LEE HARVEY OSWALD to Dallas, Texas or any other town in Texas at any time. He said the only planes he would have access to would be rental planes."

Appendix III

FBI Interviews of Jack Martin

FBI Interview of Jack S. Martin   11/25/1963 by SA REGIS L. KENNEDY and SA CLAUDE L. SCHLAGERat New Orleans, Louisiana

JACK S. MARTIN, 1311 North Prieur Street, New Orleans, Louisiana, advised that he was listening to a TV program on WWL-TV reporting the life of LEE OSWALD and reporting various interviews with people in New Orleans that were acquainted with LEE OSWALD. MARTIN stated that one of the people interviewed whose name he does not know who he describes as a white male, age early 20's, wearing horn rimmed glasses, recalled that OSWALD had been active in the Civil Air Patrol with DAVID FERRIE. MARTIN stated that when he heard this he "flipped." MARTIN advised that in his occupation as a private investigator he has had occasion to develop considerable information about FERRIE and reported it to RICHARD E. ROBY, Special Agent, Investigative Division, Office of Compliance and Security, Federal Aviation Agency, Washington, D.C., who must have a big file on FERRIE as they conducted a complete investigation of his activities in New Orleans several years ago. MARTIN advised that he called WWL-TV Station and furnished the station with background information about FERRIE, particularly his homosexual tendencies and the fact that he formerly operated the Civil Air Patrol. He also told them that FERRIE was an amateur hypnotist and that it was his idea that FERRIE may have hypnotized LEE OSWALD and planted a post-hypnotic suggestion that he kill the President.

MARTIN state that has visited in the home of DAVID FERRIE and he saw a group of photographs of various Civil Air Patrol cadet groups and in this group he is sure he saw several years ago a photograph of LEE OSWALD as a member of one of the classes. He stated he did not recall the group that OSWALD was in or any other details. In addition he stated that FERRIE conducted military type drills with rifles, fatigue clothes and helmet liners of the Civil Air Patrol Cadets and he recalled that FERRIE claimed to have taught these cadets how to shoot. MARTIN stated that he observed in FERRIE's home a number of foreign made firearms and it is his opinion that FERRIE could have taught OSWALD how to purchase a foreign made firearm or possibly have purchased the gun that was shown on television. He advised that he saw similar type weapons at FERRIE's home when he visited there two years ago.

MARTIN advised that FERRIE discussed with him the charges of crime against nature which resulted in the his arrest by Jefferson Parish authorities and he recalled that FERRIE had told him that one of the «kids that was a witness against him» had moved to Mississippi from New Orleans and subsequently joined the United States Marine Corps. He heard on television that OSWALD had been in the Marine Corps therefore he surmised that OSWALD was that «kid», that he was a witness against FERRIE in the crime against nature charge that had joined the Marine Corps. Martin explained that it might have been the same individual or a very close coincidence.

MARTIN advised that he has reported this matter to Major TROSCLAIR of the New Orleans Police Department, Intelligence Division, and he felt that Major TROSCLAIR was not giving the matter sufficient concern so he called Assistant District Attorney HERMAN KOHLMAN who was a former newspaper reporter and who was very familiar with the FERRIE case as he had written various feature stories about FERRIE. MARTIN stated that he explained all of his ideas and suspicions to KOHLMAN.

MARTIN advised he was really suspicious of FERRIE's activities when he received a report from W. HARDY DAVIS, a New Orleans Bail Bondsman, who told him that G. WRAY GILL, New Orleans attorney and employer of FERRIE had called him to locate FERRIE who lives down the street from him and at the same time had denied to the TV station that FERRIE was an employee of GILL›s Office. DAVIS furnished MARTIN information that FERRIE had left town for Texas on Friday evening, November 22, 1963, which information he also made available to Mr. KOHLMAN of the District Attorney›s office. Martin stated that FERRIE is a completely disreputable person, a notorious sex deviate with a brilliant mind being highly trained in mathematics, sciences, several foreign languages including Latin, modern Greek and ancient Greek. MARTIN advised that FERRIE had been educated in a seminary and subsequently expelled from the Catholic Church and he, MARTIN, suspected him of being capable of committing any type of crime.

MARTIN stated that he felt that FERRIE›s possible association with LEE OSWALD should be the subject of close examination as he personally believed that he could be implicated in the killing of President JOHN F. KENNEDY.

Second FBI Interview of Jack S. Martin

Warren Commission Document 75 pp 217-218 FBI Interview of Jack S. Martin 11/27/1963 by SA'S L.M. SHEARER, JR. and REGIS L. KENNEDY at New Orleans, La.

JACK S. MARTIN, 1311 North Prieur Street, New Orleans, advised that he has never heard DAVID FERRIE make a statement that President KENNEDY should be killed, or outline a means by which he could be killed. MARTIN stated he had never made a state to anyone regarding this allegation.

He advised that over several years association with FERRIE, he has heard him state the Deputy Sheriffs in Jefferson Parish who had charged him (FERRIE) with a Crime against Nature offense, should be killed. His remarks were made in general conversation several years ago. MARTIN stated he had never repeated these comments to anyone.

MARTIN advised he had several phone discussions with HARDY DAVIS, a bail bondsman and [...], regarding a television program which mentioned the possibility that DAVID FERRIE was associated with LEE HARVEY OSWALD in the Civil Air Patrol, and MARTIN and DAVIS may have come to the conclusion the OSWALD had used or carried FERRIE›s library card.

He advised he had three telephone conversations with Assistant District Attorney HERMAN KOHLMAN, New Orleans, on Saturday, November 23, 1963, in which he told KOHLMAN that FERRIE had guns similar to the type used to kill President KENNEDY that had appeared on television, and further informed KOHLMAN that HARDY DAVIS had told him FERRIE possessed Cuban propaganda literature that he kept in attorney G. WRAY GILL›s office in New Orleans, but GILL made FERRIE move it approximately a year ago. MARTIN said DAVIS claimed it was Fair Play for Cuba Committee literature but MARTIN did not believe it, because he knew FERRIE was active with the Cuban Front Group that was anti-Castro. MARTIN stated he is acquainted with the leaders of the anti-Castro group that were in New Orleans before the Bay of Pigs Invasion, and was aware that FERRIE was also involved with this group. MARTIN advised he talked with JERRY PHILIP STEIN to obtain the phone number of KOHLMAN, who had recently married and obtained a new phone number, and that STEIN was the former roommate of KOHLMAN.

MARTIN admitted he had talked with STEIN about FERRIE, but did not recall specifically what information he furnished STEIN. MARTIN advised he called television station WWL, New Orleans, and told them they should contact Major PRESLEY J. TROSCLAIR of the New Orleans Police Department, who was investigating FERRIE›s connection with the shooting of President KENNEDY. He made this call immediately after he had called TROSCLAIR and furnished him with his suspicions regarding FERRIE, based on his personal knowledge of FERRIE and his observation of WWL-TV programs of the background of OSWALD.

MARTIN advised he received information from HARDY DAVIS that FERRIE was out of town and suspected FERRIE had gone to Texas. MARTIN made this information available to Assistant District Attorney KOHLMAN. MARTIN further stated he considered FERRIE to be a completely degenerate person and it was his opinion that FERRIE is capable of any crime. If was for this reason that MARTIN suspected FERRIE of being involved in the killing of President KENNEDY.

MARTIN advised that he considered the possibility that FERRIE had taught OSWALD to shoot a rifle and use a telescopic sight, in that he knew FERRIE taught military training to Civil Air Patrol Cadets and OSWALD was a Civil Air Patrol member. MARTIN insisted he told no one FERRIE had flown OSWALD to Dallas, Texas.

Sciambra Interviews David Ferrie
for Garrison, 2/18/67

MEMORANDUM February 28, 1967 TO: JIM GARRISON FROM: ANDREW SCIAMBRA AND LOUIS IVON RE: INTERVIEW WITH DAVID FERRIE

On Saturday, February 18, 1967, at approx. 3:30 P.M., Louis Ivon and I interviewed DAVID FERRIE in his apartment on Louisiana Parkway. As we approached the house, FERRIE came out on the porch and looked at us and began to walk down the steps to open the door for us. As he opened the door for us, he told Ivon that he was glad that we finally decided to come and talk with him as he had been trying to get in touch with Garrison or Ivon for several days. He told me hello and asked me what I was doing with Ivon and I explained to him that I was an Assistant DA now and thought that I would come along with Ivon since we knew each other from the airport. He told us to go on upstairs and that he would follow us, but that it would take him some time to climb up the stairs as he was sick and weak, and that he had not been able to keep anything on his stomach for the past couple of days. He moaned and groaned with each step he took up the stairs from the bottom to the top. This behavior by FERRIE impressed me as a phony act and I am sure he was not as sick as he pretended to be.

Once inside the apartment, Ivon and I sat down and FERRIE laid down on the sofa in the front room. He was wearing pants and a t-shirt and had two pillows under him. There was a young man inside the apartment in his early twenties who was a friend of FERRIE'S from the Lakefront Airport. His name is Burt Johnson and I remember him from when I was working out there. FERRIE had given him flying instructions and he told me that he had acquired his license. My first conversation with FERRIE centered around airport talk and about people we both knew from the airport. He said that he had often wondered what had happened to me and that he thought I had gone into private practice. He said that he had known a lot of ex-DAs and they were all dumb, with a few exceptions.

He said that the reason he'd called us was that he was concerned over our investigation. He had heard all kinds of rumors that he was going to get arrested and that he wanted to find out if these rumors were true. He said that as a result of these rumors, he had been asked to leave the airport and was concerned over how he was going to make a living, that flying was his only enjoyment in life. FERRIE said he was suffering from encephalitis and that he could not get any rest from the radio, TV and press boys hounding him to death. FERRIE said his phone rings from morning till night and that he had talked to Sam Depino from Ch. 12 until the early hours of the morning. FERRIE said Sam was trying to con him, but that he was too smart to fall for his line, and that all those people were "bastards." Just then the phone rang and it was a reporter from the Times-Picayune, and he said that he would positively not grant interviews and that he was tired of all those bastards calling him up. The reporter must have told him something, because he was not calling him a bastard personally, but was referring to the news media in general. He then hung up the telephone. FERRIE picked up the Picayune paper and said he wanted to show us portions of the story that really disturbed him. He said the newspapers can kill anybody when they want to, and that it was never more evident than in the cases of CARLOS MARCELLO and JIMMY HOFFA. FERRIE said the newspapers tried to frame both of these guys. He then talked about the MARCELLO trial that he was working on in 1963, and how the newspapers tried to crucify MARCELLO.

He said MARCELLO made asses out of all of them when he was acquitted. FERRIE said he wanted to know why we brought MIGUEL TORRES MIGUEL back from Angola. He said that he knew what people would do to get out of prison and he thought Garrison was trying to frame-up by using MIGUEL TORRES. FERRIE said that if this would happen, he would sue us and everybody. FERRIE said he had been contacted by some big attorneys in Washington DC, and they wanted to help him.

FERRIE also said he did not like the way Garrison was answering questions put to him by newsmen and that Garrison should make a definite statement and not say "No comment." He said the "No comment" stirs more shit than an hour's speech. FERRIE said Garrison knew this and that he was obviously using this for publicity. I assured him that Garrison was not trying to frame anybody and that he was avoiding the press and he could not say much less than "No comment." Then FERRIE said he wanted to talk to Garrison personally. We told him we would try and arrange a meeting in the near future.

FERRIE then began to curse JACK MARTIN and said MARTIN started all of this stuff. FERRIE said MARTIN was jealous of him because of his relationship with G. WRAY GILL and that MARTIN was trying to ruin him (FERRIE). He said MARTIN is a screwball and should be locked up.

FERRIE then said Garrison had better be careful because he knew that some people were trying to torpedo him; that he knew of three people on a local level and a couple people on a national level who are trying to ruin him politically and are trying to embarrass him politically with this assassination investigation. FERRIE said he did not want to mention the names of the local people, but Garrison should be smart enough to know who they were. He then began to talk about FRANK KLEIN and he inferred that this man was one of the local persons trying to destroy Garrison. However, when Ivon asked him if KLEIN was one of the people he was referring to, FERRIE said that in time we would find out. FERRIE did say that Hoover was one of the people on the national level because Garrison had dared to criticize the Bureau and has the whole country wondering if they are as smart as the Keystone Kops. However, FERRIE said he was glad about this because as far as he's concerned, all cops are bastards and that he has no use for any of them. FERRIE also said he had heard that some people in Washington were talking about the investigation and that two days before the story broke in the newspaper, some people were saying that Garrison would call a press conference Friday and give the story to the press. FERRIE said he didn't want to give out any names as he didn't want J. Edgar on his ass too.

He then asked to speak to Garrison again because he wanted to see if we were serious about this whole thing. I told him that Garrison was more than serious and that we were checking out all our leads and information. I then told FERRIE he could tell me what he wanted to say and I would tell Garrison for him. FERRIE said he wanted to talk to Garrison himself and look him in the face.

I then asked FERRIE to tell me where he was on November 22, 1963, and how he had become so involved in this. FERRIE said it was all on account of a trip he made to Houston, Texas on the afternoon of the 22nd to ice skate. He said that all he wanted to do was relax after the MARCELLO trial and he just had the urge to go ice skating. FERRIE said, that as it turned out, it was the worst trip that he had ever made in his life. I asked FERRIE what he did in Houston. FERRIE said, "ice skate, what else?" I said, "I don't know Dave, you tell me." FERRIE said I was a newcomer around the game and that my office knew more about the trip than he did. FERRIE said, "Ask your boss. He had me arrested when I got back into town. I was booked as a fugitive from Texas and I have never been to Texas." I asked him to tell me about the arrest as I didn't believe we would arrest a man who was perfectly innocent. FERRIE told me I had a lot to learn about life and that I was a starry-eyed kid right out of law school and I was still believing the inscriptions on the courthouse walls. FERRIE said that after a while, when you get a little smarter, you'll see that this is a stinking world and that what I told you at the airport is true. I told FERRIE that what he said may be true, but that still doesn't tell me about the arrest. FERRIE said, "All right, I'll go through the spiel again for your benefit."

FERRIE said that after he had taken his trip to Texas, he, [ALVIN] BEAU-BOEUF and [MELVIN] COFFEY stopped in Alexandria and he called G. WRAY GILL. GILL told him the police were looking for him and that they wanted to ask him some questions about the assassination. He said that then he drove back to New Orleans and dropped BEAUBOEUF off at his apartment on Louisiana Avenue Parkway so that he could go upstairs and call some girls for them. He said that he and COFFEY then went to the grocery store. He said that when he and COFFEY were returning to the apartment he noticed a bunch of cars around his apartment and a lot of people. FERRIE said he figured it was the police and so he went back to the store and telephoned. FERRIE said some dumb ox answered the phone and tried to suck him into a conversation, but he just hung up. He said he then dropped COFFEY off and went to Hammond, Louisiana. I asked him "where in Hammond?" FERRIE said, "by a friend." I asked him what friend and he burst out laughing and said, "I'll say one thing for you, you sure try hard." He then told me not to try and investigate him because he could show me and my whole office how to investigate. I didn't press the issue any further, but later on he told me he did not stay in a motel, but with a friend who will remain anonymous. "Besides," he said, "I've got friends all over the world."

I said that was very interesting, but that I wanted his opinion on one other small matter. He asked, "What?" I said,"Dave, who shot the President?" He said, "Well, that's an interesting question and I've got my own thoughts on it." FERRIE then sent his friend into another room to get an anatomy book and a pathology book and he pulled out a sheet of paper and began to sketch on it. FERRIE drew a sketch of the Texas School Book Depository and of the parade route and of the area in general. FERRIE said that before he would definitely draw a conclusion, he would have to have more information and facts. FERRIE then went into a long spiel about the projectory of bullets in relation to height and distance. He said that different guns and shells have different projectories and that bullets tend to drop (missing). He said the Warren Commission did not have enough pertinent scientific information to come to an objective conclusion. He said he did not read the Warren Report, but what he had read proved to him that the

470

Commission did not know what they were doing. FERRIE went into a long spiel about JFK's neck wound. In the course of his lecture on anatomy and pathology, he named every bone in the human body and every hard and soft muscle are. He talked extensively about the dermis and epidermis. FERRIE said that if the same bullet that struck JFK in the back or neck eventually struck Connally, that Connally or JFK had to be a contortionist. He then rattled off more scientific information in regards to bones and skin and how a bullet decreases in speed when it strikes an object and how the same bullet could not have possibly caused all that damage. FERRIE said that the question would never be answered because the doctor that performed the tracheotomy had 10 thumbs and left unanswered the most important question of all time. FERRIE then laughed and said that doctors are almost as stupid as lawyers, but that lawyers are worse because they are always in your pocket.

I then said, "In other words Dave, you don't buy the 'one-shot theory'?" FERRIE said he wasn't saying anything because he didn't want J. Edgar on his tail, that he had enough with Garrison to contend with. FERRIE said that in time he would work the whole thing out and then laughingly said he would contact our office. I noticed at this point that he was in very good spirits and was laughing and joking and even commented that he's feeling pretty good now and that he had had 3 cups of coffee and hadn't thrown up yet. FERRIE then received another phone call from STEVE LITTLETON and his wife and joked with LITTLETON's wife about how he knew that she had dated LEE HARVEY OSWALD and that he was going to tell Garrison on her. She must have told him that she had seen his picture in the paper and he replied that he didn't like it because it made him look unphotogenic. She also must have asked FERRIE if it was him some people identified with somebody or at some place and that he said the people are mistaken or he had a common face. After he hung up the phone, we told him we had to leave.

FERRIE said he had more to tell us about the 'one-shot theory'. We told him to save it for another day as it was dark already and we had to meet Garrison. I then asked him if he would like to tell me some more about his trip to Hammond and he smiled and said "Go to hell." I then asked if he stayed with CLAY SHAW. He said, "Who's CLAY SHAW?" I said, "All right, if that doesn't ring a bell, how about CLAY BERTRAND?" He said, "Who's CLAY BERTRAND?" I said CLAY BERTRAND and CLAY SHAW are the same person. He asked, "Who said that?" I said, "Dean Andrews told us." He said, "Dean Andrews might tell you guys anything. You know how Dean Andrews is." FERRIE then started to go into another lecture and we told him we had to go. He followed us down the stairs and walked out on the sidewalk with us. FERRIE asked Ivon to be sure and call him. Ivon assured him he would and we left.

[This was last recorded interview of David Ferrie by the New Orleans District Attorney's Office [by Sciambra and Ivons] but Lou Ivon claimed a further conversation with David Ferrie on February 19.)

Appendix V

Transcript: Garrison Team Tries to Bribe Alvin Beauboeuf

"Al Beauboeuf was one of the two men who accompanied Dave Ferrie on his infamous midnight ride from Kenner, Louisiana, to Houston, Texas, the morning of November 23, 1963. On March 9, 1967, at 2:30 PM, Beauboeuf's lawyer, Hugh Exnicios, secretly tape-recorded the following conversation with Garrison investigator Lynn Loisel."

(Excerpts)

EXNICIOS: I thought you were coming with your partner. What's his name?

LOISEL: Ivon?

EXNICIOS: Ivon. He didn't come out with you?

LOISEL: No. We've got too much to do. Now, let me bring you up to what Al [Beauboeuf] and I were talking about last night. I told him we had liberal expense money and I said the boss is in a position to put him a job, you know, possibly of his choosing, of Al's choosing. Also ... we would make a hero out of him instead of a villain, you understand. Everything would be to your satisfaction ... I mean, we can ... we can change the story around, you know, enough to.. . eliminate him, you know, [from] any type of conspiracy or what have you. The only thing we want is the truth ... no deviations on his part, you know. We want to present the truth. We want the facts and the facts of the assassination. That's what we want. And ... the thing will be typed up in such a way that Al, you know, will be free and clear.

EXNICIOS: Now, in other words, what you want him to do, he will come up and give you such evidence that you will be able to couch him in terms of being a hero?

LOISEL: That's correct.

EXNICIOS: And you'll also ... you have an unlimited expense account, you said, and you're willing to help him along?

LOISEL: I would venture to say ... [I'm] fairly certain we could put $3,000 [= approx. 25,000 in today's funds]on him just like that, you know.... I'm sure we would help him financially and I'm sure we ... real quick we could get him a job....

EXNICIOS: ... Now, about the job, what do you mean by that?

LOISEL: Al said he'd like a job with an airline and I feel the job can be had, you know.

EXNICIOS: Well, now, these are tough things to come by. What makes you feel that you would be in a position ...

LOISEL: Well, let's say that.... For instance, he was talking about a small operation such as Space Air Freight. I know with one phone call he could go out to the Space Air Freight and write his own ticket, you know. That's just Space Air Freight. That's not Eastern or something else. But I feel like we have people who are stepping stones to the larger airlines and so forth. They're politically motivated, too, you know, like anything else.

EXNICIOS: Well, now, Lynn, let me ask you this: You're speaking about the District Attorney, Jim Garrison, and his ability to place Al in a responsible pilot's position with an airline?

LOISEL: That's correct, according to Al's own ability. [The first year or two he might have to] stay in a room in the back with the charts, or something, I don't know. [Then] he advances a little further, then he's a co-pilot, then he's a pilot.

EXNICIOS: Now, let me ask you this, Lynn: Is this something that you have thought up yourself or that Garrison.... He knows about the situation?

LOISEL: That's right

EXNICIOS: And he's agreed that if we could in some way assist you, that you will be able to give him these three things?

LOISEL: That's correct.

<snip>

EXNICIOS: ... What do you think that Al has that he could help you with?

LOISEL: ... Well, we feel that Al is as close to Dave [Ferrie] as anybody could have been. [LOISEL mentions the meeting witness Perry Russo described as an assassination meeting]

LOISEL: But anyhow, the assass ... Ferrie said, "The best way in which the assassination can be done is to get the man ... to get the President in cross fire." And went on to discuss that. And then Clay Shaw and Ferrie ... I believe it was Clay Shaw and Ferrie, or maybe it was Clay Shaw and Oswald, having a little heated argument. Clay Shaw wanted some of his methods used or his thoughts, you know, used, but anyhow, that's what we have in mind, along that line.

EXNICIOS: Was Al supposed to have been at that meeting?

LOISEL: No, Al wasn't at the meeting.

EXNICIOS: Well, how is Al supposed to be able to help you with that meeting?

LOISEL:. Well, Al is in ... Al, being as close to Ferrie ...

EXNICIOS: Yes.

LOISEL: ... He has to know it.

EXNICIOS: I see. And you're convinced from all the evidence that Al could not be as close as he was to Dave without knowing something in some way?

LOISEL: That's right.

<snip>

EXNICIOS: Let me ask you this: Do you think that ... if my client, Beauboeuf, if he knew about this and didn't tell you, he's committing a crime, he's an accessory after the fact, isn't he?

LOISEL: No, he's not.... Dave Ferrie, bless his poor soul, is gone. Al was scared of Dave. Al has a family, you know. When Al first met Dave, he was a single man. Al has a family now. Al was threatened by Dave, you know, to ... never to divulge this... [or] Al or his family would be taken care of.

EXNICIOS: I see.

LOISEL: You understand, now that poor Dave is gone Al has voluntarily come forward and told of his knowledge. I mean, there's 99,000 ways we could skin that cat, you know ... that's his patriotic duty. He's ... now he's placing his family, you know, the safety of his family at the hands ... at the mercy of the District Attorney's Office because he must clear his conscience and ... as an upstanding young American.

EXNICIOS: All right.... Supposing Al in his own consciousness does not know anything ... how can that be changed?

LOISEL: When was the statement made? ... Ferrie was still living, wasn't he?

EXNICIOS: Yeah ... oh, I see.

LOISEL: He had no choice. He was scared, you know, I mean he ... married man, father-in-law, you know, wife and kids.... He's scared.

EXNICIOS: ... let me ask you this: Besides your personal opinion, have you anything really on Al Beauboeuf that he knows anything we might clear up?

LOISEL: Umm, no. Really, the only thing we're doing or have been trying to do is to have Al tell us.

EXNICIOS: Well, he's already been up there the one time. Now, what more do you want now?

LOISEL:. We don't believe him. Let's put it that way...we have no choice, you know. I mean, we are seeking the information." (tape continues with more discussion)

Beauboeuf would turn down the bribe, but would be compelled to sign a statement that Garrison's people never attempted to bribe him to offer false testimony.

"He signed it, having been assured by Lynn Loisel that if he didn't, certain files on Beauboeuf and certain photographs of Beauboeuf and Ferrie confiscated from Ferrie's apartment following his death would be circulated to the press and elsewhere. To this day, Beauboeuf insists the statement was signed only under duress." Statements in quotes from Milton Brener (author, *The Garrison Case*).

Re: Planes David Ferrie Might Have Used: Why 'Airworthiness and 'Certificates' Mean Little In Black Op Flights: Gerry Hemming

During my 50+ years as a pilot, I have flown "every" model of light aircraft in existence, and many of the heavy commercial cargo and passenger [type rated] aircraft which should never have existed. My flying of some of these "Junkers" (and brand new birds) took me all over the world. I have a few thousand hours flying all types of aircraft sans "Certificates of Air Worthiness." In the gun & drug running trade, the owner just wants to "lose" his heavily insured aircraft – which usually doesn't have said "CAW" because he is too cheap and greedy to even do "I.R.A.N." !! Much less the "major" overhaul necessary, because it will tend to diminish his expected returns from the insurance company's pay-out. Most often, I insisted upon "minimal" maintenance and repairs before even a test-flight of their birds. There are NO "Inspections Stations (@ State borders) in the Sky."

The only occasions where a pilot or owner might have to exhibit a "C.A.W." is:

[A] To the personnel of an F.O.B. (Fixed Operating Base – repairs etc., and airport located), and then only when an S.T.C. required modification is requested, or a 100 or 1,000 hour check is to be performed;

[B] To a F.A.A. designee (C.F.I. - "Certified Flight Instructor") who is there to give somebody a "Check-Ride," i.e.:

For logging "Dual Instruction," or for acquiring a "Rating" in an aircraft weighing over 12,500 lbs. (empty);

[C] To an F.A.A. "Inspector," or an N.T.S.B. "Investigator," and subsequent to a collision, failure (blown tire) which blocks a runway and causes a closure of that runway, or the entire airport, or a crash; and,

[D] When the owner, after being cited via an "Air Worthiness Directive" – has to exhibit same to the F.A.A. Representative to show compliance with same !

Every day of the year (according to the F.A.A., N.T.S.B., D.O.T., etc. websites) there are thousands of aircraft being flown without "CAWs," insurance, required "STCs," and many being flown by the hundreds of pilots with revoked, suspended, or voided "Pilot Licenses" and/or "Medical Certificates."

The F.A.A. relies on thousands of private-citizen "FAA Designees," because the Congress has refused to fund inspections over the last 60+ years !!

The few times I have ever had to show my licenses/certificates – was while undergoing "Dual Instruction," or when in a foreign country applying for one of their licenses, or validation of my U.S. or other foreign licenses.

For more than 25 years I flew "Black Ops" – where an "Alias I.D." was necessary, so I acquired quite a few licenses (U.S. & foreign) under other names. Moreover, I finally just stopped making any entries in my "Log Books," as no evidence of flights (purpose, departure & destinations, routes, etc.) could be made as a permanent record. This was the same case with parachute jumps. Since I never planned to have the "Top" rating – A.T.P. ("Airline Transport Pilot" – changed from A.T.R. "Airline Transport Rating," years ago.) in my own name; why the hell keep a record anyway ??!! **... GPH**

Appendix VII

Lardner's *Washington Post* Story, as Copied Across the Nation on Feb. 23, 1967 (Comments and corrections by JVB)

THURSDAY 'SUICIDE' PLAN UNAPPARENT
Ferrie Last Seen 'In Good Spirits'

(Editor's Note – Washington Post newsman George Lardner Jr. was one of the last people to see David Ferrie alive, interviewing him in Ferrie's apartment until 4 a. m. Ferrie was found dead at 11:40 a. m. Here is an account of what Ferrie told Lardner.) [**Author**: Lardner, if truthful, was the last person to see David Ferrie alive]

WASHINGTON (AP) – A New Orleans pilot who figured in Dist. Atty. Jim Garrison's investigation of President John F. Kennedy's assassination predicted shortly before his death that Garrison's inquiry would turn out to be a "witch hunt," the Washington Post said today. In a copyrighted interview with George Lardner Jr. of the Post, David W, Ferrie was quoted as saying he was waiting for Garrison to fall on his face. Ferrie, who was found dead in bed seven hours after the four-hour interview with Lardner, told Lardner he was sure that the FBI had investigated thoroughly Lee Harvey Oswald's activities in New Orleans."

"Ferrie told me *he* felt convinced there was no plot to kill the President, that Lee Harvey Oswald was 'a loner,' " Lardner reported in today's editions. Oswald, who lived in New Orleans during the summer of 1963, was named by the Warren Commission as Kennedy's assassin. The commission said there was no evidence Oswald did not act alone. Garrison, the New Orleans district attorney who has promised arrests and convictions in connection with his theory that an assassination conspiracy was hatched in New Orleans, said Ferrie's death was an "apparent suicide." But coroner Nicholas Chetta, who said the pilot's death was due to a ruptured blood vessel in the brain, said further tests were being made. Lardner said Ferrie "seemed in good spirits, not like a man about to kill himself" during the interview that ended at 4 a. m. yesterday.

[**Author**: Ferrie had been distraught, felt ill, and was anxious. He had called Garrison's investigators, saying due to the newspapers he was a dead man, only days earlier, and had begged Garrison's investigators to protect him. Unaccountably, after protecting Ferrie at The Fontainebleau, Garrison's investigators left him alone in the room for a period of time and Ferrie returned to his home. Surveillance of Ferrie's apartment ceased at 11:00 PM when "the lights went out" and Ferrie was again left alone. His body was found by a friend and his landlord at 11:40 AM the next morning.]

Ferrie's body was found covered by a sheet [sic] at 11 a. m. "Ferrie said he never knew Oswald and had no recollection of ever having met him," Lardner reported. Ferrie complained to Lardner that Garrison had him "pegged as the 'getaway pilot' in an elaborate plot to kill Kennedy." He previously called this a "big joke."

[**Author**: Was Lardner's interview constructed from earlier accounts? Further, Lardner's interview could have been conducted by telephone earlier in the evening of the 21st, rather than in person, since the coroner originally said Ferrie died before midnight. The time of death was re-set to 4:00 AM only because Lardner insisted he had been present until then. Unexplained is how long it took Ferrie to get back upstairs and inside his apartment, then get totally undressed (in his living room, where clothing is draped? In the hallway, where his fatigues are hanging?). He removes his dentures in the wrong room, and gets into bed with his wig and fake eyebrows on, which he usually stripped off before retiring. Then there is the nudity issue in the February cold. Lardner also said Ferrie scoffed at reports that the pilot had flown Oswald to Cuba around 1959. "I've never even been to Cuba," Lardner quoted Ferrie as saying.]

Within 72 hours after the assassination, Garrison's men picked up Ferris as a "fugitive from Texas" and questioned him about reports he might have been in Dallas the afternoon of the killing. "FERRIE said he was sitting on a courthouse bench outside a federal district courtroom in New Orleans, shooting the bull with a couple of federal agents' " at the time of the shooting, Lardner reported.

[**Author**: This complaint of Ferrie's was available in his FBI interview]

"Ferrie said he did leave for Texas on a trip with several acquaintances after leaving the courthouse but that he went to Galveston and Houston 'hunting geese,' and never set foot in Dallas," Lardner added.

[**Author**: Ferrie had only two people with him, not "several." He had never referred to them previously as "acquaintances." Did Lardner assume a third person, apparently Layton Martens, was along? The goose-hunting reference was available from one of Ferrie's last interviews.]

Lardner said Ferrie told him he had been conducting his own investigation of the assassination to counter Garrison's.

[**Author**: This reference is identical to Ferrie's earlier statements in 1963 to his former CAP members. Ferrie was investigating the Warren Commission's work and had been perusing the 26 Volumes issued by the Commission at the public library. He was also planning lawsuits to fight the investigation.]

George Lardner would support the Warren Commission's findings for decades at the Washington Post. He would attack Oliver Stone's movie JFK, having been given its film-script. Carl Oglesby (*Lies of Our Times*, Sept. 1991) :"Lardner next poked fun at the pirated first-draft version of Stone's screenplay for suggesting that as many as five or six shots might have been fired in Dealey Plaza. "Is this the Kennedy assassination," Lardner chortled, "or the Charge of the Light Brigade?" Ref: http://www.ratical.org/ratville/JFK/JFKloot.html.

APPENDIX VIII

RE: David Ferrie's
long distance phone calls

Nov. 25, 1963: David told FBI that Jack Martin charged long distance calls to G. Wray Gill's number:

> "...MARTIN was making long distance telephone calls charging these calls to Attorney GILL's office and the office of GUY BANISTER, Guy Banister Associates..."

Note: Gill never mentioned any long distance calls from Martin. Gill told Garrison that David Ferrie's long distance calls cost him a fortune and that 90% of his business was local. Every lawyer in Gill's office had his own extension.

> **Peter Whitmey**: "...Keep in mind that Gill worked for Carlos Marcello... Coincidentally, Gill's office was in the same building as another lawyer, Clem Sehrt, who also had close connections to Marcello. In addition, as author Peter Noyes discovered, Eugene Hale Braden, a.k.a. Jim Brading, who was arrested but released in Dealey Plaza shortly after the assassination, had spent several months working for an oil company in the fall of 1963, located on the very same floor as Gill's law office."

> [**Author**: Sehrt arranged Lee Oswald's bail on Aug. 10, 1963.]

WHO USED GILL'S TELEPHONE NUMBER?

> **Peter Whitmey** (June 4, 2000) wrote: "I was able to obtain photocopies of G. Wray Gill's long distance phone records, which had been subpoenaed by Garrison. I methodically went through them and typed out a list of all the calls made by David Ferrie (those which the secretary had drawn a line through had been made by other members of Gill's staff, and were mostly calls within Louisiana).

> **Stephen Roy** (posting as Blackburst): "...I respectfully disagree on this. Secretary Alice Guidroz examined and marked the phone bills in January 1967, THREE YEARS after the assassination. She drew a line through all the calls she could identify as having been made by other staff in reference to office business. It is fair to say that some of the remaining calls were probably made by Ferrie, but it is not fair to presume that any specific call was made by him, considering there were nearly a dozen people working in the office..."

> **Jim Garrison**: "....Gill instructed the secretary to draw a penciled line through every call made by the office, leaving exposed the calls made by Ferrie. "They're easy to pick out," he said. "Those cities there didn't have a damned thing to do with this office. You know better than anyone that about ninety percent of my business is right here in New Orleans." (p. 109-110, *On the Trail of the Assassins*).

Stephen Roy (posting as Blackburst, continuing his argument from above): "I wish I could be as certain as Peter that Ferrie made all the unidentified calls. I wish I could be certain that they were not made by Gill, Gilbert Bernstein, Gerard Schreiber, George W. Gill Jr., Alice Guidroz, Regina Francovich, Morris Brownlee, or a client who was sitting in the office, or some other party who happened to be there 3 years earlier, but I cannot. Maybe Ferrie made the calls. But maybe he didn't."

Author: "The argument is that Gill was in business with several other lawyers and thus it would be difficult to separate out David's phone calls. But let's use some common sense. There were four lawyers (Gill, Bernstein, Schreiber, and Gill, Jr.). Each lawyer had his own office room in the suite. Each office room had its own phones on extension lines. Gill's secretary would log Gill's incoming calls and any calls she personally made going out. Her telephone was probably a Bell Call Director.

These phones came out in 1958. I had one at Reily. They were in most downtown New Orleans offices.

Each lawyer was billed only for calls to or from his own extensions. Normally, these lawyers didn't use each other's phones (that could be a privacy issue for clients and could create bills to pay to each other). Gill's bills showed calls charged only to or from his extensions. Those extensions were probably (1) the phone on Gill's own desk, (2) a phone for use of investigators such as David Ferrie or Morris Brownlee (a drug addict who pounded the sleazy parts of town for Gill) and (3) an extension for use by his secretary, to reach other offices, especially if Gill's phone line was busy. Bernstein's secretary might have managed the main Call Director. It would be an easy matter to pick out David Ferrie's long distance calls, as the call records on Gill's bills were just for Gill's office. The main number was advertised under the listing "Bernstein and Gill 1707 Pere Marquette Bldg 156 Baronne. 524-0147."

David Ferrie's Death: Natural Causes, Suicide, Or Possible Murder? Debate And Comments.

AUTOPSY PROTOCOL

ORLEANS PARISH CORONER'S OFFICE

No. W67-2-255 .

Name: David W. Ferrie Age: Color: W Sex: M

Date and Time of Death: 2-22-67 at 1:00 P.M.

Date and Time of Autopsy: 2-22-67 at 3:00 P.M.

FINAL DIAGNOSES

1. Rupture of berry aneurysm of Circle of Willis with massive left subdural hematoma, subarachnoid hemorrhage, and secondary pontine hemorrhages.

2. Hypertensive cardiovascular disease.

3. Pulmonary edema and congestion.

[Author: this triad means all three factors played a role in David Ferrie's death. His symptoms, for weeks, represented every symptom of malignant hypertension, which can be fatal. Pulmonary edema and hypertension can result from over-medication. Dave, with his Catholic beliefs, would not commit suicide (Dave told Ray Broshears he wouldn't kill himself). A berry aneurysm, according to the NIH's website, shows few symptoms until it leaks – and those symptoms do not match what David Ferrie's symptoms were. Scroll down to end of autopsy report for more comments).]

Classification of Death: Natural
  Nicholas J. Chetta, M.D. **Coroner**
  Autopsy Protocol
  David Ferrie
  W/M

EXTERNAL EXAMINATION: The body is that of a well developed white male measuring 5 ft. 9 in. in length and weighing 182 ½ lbs.

[Author: David has lost about 9.5 pounds since Nov. 1963; he is an inch shorter than when measured by FBI because he is shoeless.] There are no external marks of violence on the body at any point. The face is heavily cyanotic, as are the shoulders and portions of the back.

[Author: Photos of Dave when found in his bed do not show a "heavily cyanotic" face. Since his shoulders and portions of the back are described as livor mortis "posterior" we have a duality of distribution, important because it means the body was turned over long enough to turn the face purple after it was discovered. A purple face would hide bruises to the face. David apparently was laid face-down for some time before the autopsy. The words "heavily cyanotic" are inappropriate, as this can cause some to think asphyxia was involved.]

Livor mortis appears posterior. The scalp is covered with a false wig, which is easily removed. [**Author: David did not normally go to bed with his wig and eyebrows still on. Perhaps he was too tired to remove them, though apparently, he was not too tired to remove all his clothes.**]

There are no evidences of trauma or contusions to the scalp at any point. A few residual normal hairs are still present, particularly around the right occipital region and along both sideburn areas. There is a small 1/32 in. residual unshaven beard on the inferior aspect of the chin but the overall body hair is markedly absent. There are false eyebrows present. These are easily removed leaving a shiny skin. There is absence of axillary hair and pubic hair. No hair is present on the arms or legs.

The pupils are equal. The ears, nose and mouth show no abnormlities.[sic] There is a small area of dryness of the inner aspect of the upper lip on the right side. This area measures ¾ in. in length and is somewhat reddish brown in color. There is a less well defined area on the lower lip immediately inferior to the lesion in the upper lip. Both areas show no deep hemorrhages or swellings.

[**Author: The "small area of dryness" is as wide as a finger. It is a lesion – and is described as such when the second lesion is described as 'less well defined'. A lesion is an injury to living tissue, involving damage or a wound to the skin. 'No deep hemorrhages' does not mean these lesions did not bleed. It means any bleeding was superficial. Not much consolation to anyone who has ever had a 'superficial' wound to the mouth. Lack of swelling means the damage was very recent.**]

Researcher **Jim Hargrove**, 3/6/99: "Dr. Frank Minyard [who succeeded Chetta as Acting Coroner] some years ago distributed photographs from Ferrie's autopsy. Photos of the inside of Ferrie's mouth revealed recent wounds…In a 1/31/92 interview with Jim DiEugenio, Dr. Minyard considered this a possible scenario for the murder of Ferrie: …[thyroid] pills were mixed with the Proloid [sic]and forced down Ferrie's mouth with a tube, which caused the mouth wounds." http://www.jfk-online.com/ferriedeath2.html. Retrieved Aug. 29, 2013)

[**Author: "Proloid and thyroid pills are one and the same. Proloid is a combination of two thyroid hormone sources – T4(Levothyroxine) and T3 – the bioactive thyroid hormone. This probably caused the confusion of "thyroid" and "proloid" as separate pills."**]

The mouth is edentulous in the upper area. [**no teeth**] The lower front teeth are present but in a poor state of condition. There are no burns or hemorrhages in the oral cavity. The neck is symmetrical. There are no contusions in the neck. The chest is slightly increased in its anterior posterior diameter. The abdomen is not protuberant. The external genitalia are normal male. The upper and lower extremities show no abnormalities. There are no venipuncture marks at any point in the extremities on the body.

[Author: There are no venipuncture marks at any point in the extremities on the body means the arms, legs, hands and feet weren't punctured where veins were. There is no mention of venipuncture anywhere else, such as in the neck. There is no particular examination of the oral cavity that would assure us that no puncture of the roof of the mouth occurred.]

Rigor mortis is just beginning in the distal aspects of the extremities. The body is tagged with NOPD identification tag #1440.

BODY CAVITIES: The usual Y-shaped incision is made. The vicera[sic] lie in their usual positions. There is no abnormal accumulation of blood or fluid.

CARDIO-VASCULAR SYSTEM: The heart is enlarged and weighs 490 grams. [Author: Normal weight is up to about 425 grams. David's heart is indeed enlarged.]

The coronary arteries show only mild to moderate atherosclerosis. There is no significant narrowing at any point, nor is there any occlusion. Sections through the myocardium demonstrate marked hypertrophy of the left ventricle measuring 3 cm. in thickness at its mid level

[Author: David's heart reveals he was suffering from hypertension so severe it was killing him "Pulmonary hypertension (PH) is often associated with left heart failure.... patients can progress to pulmonary edema ... [and] left atrial enlargement, left rather than right ventricular hypertrophy." Ref: "Diagnosis and management of pulmonary hypertension associated with left ventricular diastolic dysfunction" http://www.pulmonarycirculation.org/article.asp?issn=2045-8932;year=2012;volume=2;issue=2;spage=163;epage=169;aulast=de (Retrieved Aug. 30, 2013).]

There is no evidence of infarction, old or recent. The valves are normal. The coronary ostia are patent. The aorta shows mild to moderate atherosclerosis.

RESPIRATORY SYSTEM: The neck contents are carefully removed. There is no evidence of hemorrhage in the musculature of the neck. There are no hemorrhages in the tongue, hypopharynx or pharyngeal mucosa. There are no fractures of the hyoid bone, thyroid cartilage or criccid bone. There are no hemorrhages in the mucosa of the trachea or larynx.

[Author: Why are 'no hemorrhages' used to describe tongue, larynx and pharyngeal 'mucosa' instead of saying these areas are "unremarkable"? Why doesn't it read, for example, as "the laryngeal mucosa is smooth and unremarkable"? What aren't we being told?]

The thyroid gland is nodular on both sides and weighs 35 grams. There is one large nodule in the left lobe of the thyroid measuring 1 cm in diameter. It is firm and gray-white in color and appears poorly encapsulated.

{Author: Males in David's age range had an average thyroid weight of less than 20 grams. [Ref: "Adult Human Thyroid Weight" NIH: www.ncbi.nlm.nih.gov/pubmed/4077513, Retrieved Aug. 30, 2013) . David's thyroid gland is at least 57% larger than normal. The autopsy fails to identify this alarmingly big thyroid as evidence of hyperthyroidism, also a cause of high blood pressure. The presence of thyroid medication or Proloid among David's drugs was probably related to lifelong treatment of his hypothyroid condition beginning many years earlier. His bug-eyes – exophthalmia – show us David was taking too much thyroid medication, probably because it made him feel better and kept his weight down. Sudden ingestion of many pills could kill within hours. I know: I accidentally overdosed when I was suffering from a concussion and had short term memory loss. It took only a couple of hours to make my heart race and my blood pressure zoom."]

The left lung weighs 650 grams. The right lung weighs 700 grams. Both lungs show marked congestion with increased fluid on cut section. There are no emphysematous blebs demonstrable. The mainstem bronchi [contain] a rather abundant mucus. The pulmonary arteries are normal. [**Author: David's lungs weigh more than expected due to fluid. The right lung, as is the usual case, is heavier. The congestion reflects congestive heart failure/high blood pressure that could have been caused by thyroid poisoning.**]

GASTRO-INTESTINAL SYSTEM: The esophagus is intact. There is no hemorrhage or ulceration of the esophagus. The stomach contains approx. ½ pt. of a brownish turbid fluid in which particles of vegetable matter are still identifiable.

[**Author: "Particles of vegetable matter" do not appear in a cup of coffee, which is all that George Lardner said David Ferrie ingested. But "particles of vegetable matter" [cellulose, microcellulose] were used in the 1960's to hold pills together. The stomach contents should not have had any 'vegetable matter' and should have been analyzed. I was surprised to learn that David had this fluid in his stomach. ½ pint is a cup. It should have exited his stomach quickly. Instead, fluid was still present – probably due to gastroparesis, a failure of the stomach to move contents out, often provoking nausea and vomiting, all of which can be caused by hypothyroidism. "The primary gastroparesis symptoms are nausea and vomiting. ... [and can be] caused by...thyroid disease." http://www.medicinenet.com/gastroparesis/page2.htm. (Retrieved Aug. 31, 2013) I feel so sorry for David. It looks as if hyperthyroidism was the base cause of all his distress.**]**

There is no hemorrhage or ulceration of the stomach mucosa, although the fundus of the stomach is showing early greenish discoloration from post mortem digestion. The duodanum,[sic] small intestine and colon shows no hemorrhage or ulceration.

The liver is red-brown in color and weighs 2400 grams. [**Author: This weight is near the limit for normal and is significantly heavier than the average liver.**] There are slight mottled areas of yellowish change beneath the capsule. On cut section the overall coloration is red-brown with mild congestion. The gall bladder and pancreas are normal.

SPLEEN: The splean (sic) is congested and weighs 300 grams. On cut section the pulp is very soft. [**Author: The spleen is close to the normal limit in weight and is significantly heavier than average.**]

ADREANALS (sic) These show no hemorrhage or nacrosis (sic) or adenomas or tumors. [**Author: Either this doctor, his typist, or the Internet publisher of this document cannot spell**]

GENITO-URINARY SYSTEM: The left kidney weighs 230 grams. The right kidney weighs 240 grams. Both kidneys are somewhat larger than normal, and congested. They have a granular cortical surface. On cut section they show congestion. There is no hemorrhage or infection.

[**Author: The kidneys are affected by hypertension. Both kidneys are overweight, which the pathologist does recognize. Enlargement is a renal function matter, related to David's thyroid condition, which, as evidence accumulates, can scarcely be ignored, considering the size of the thyroid gland and the presence of nodules. Ref: (NIH):"The kidney is an important target of thyroid hormone action. "Correlation between severity of thyroid dysfunction and renal function" Clin Endocrinol (Oxf). 2005 Apr;62(4):423-7. http://www.ncbi.nlm.nih.gov/pubmed/15807872 (Retrieved Aug. 31, 2013)**]

The ureters are normal. The bladder contains 200 cc of clear straw colored urine. The prostate is normal.

CENTRAL NERVOUS SYSTEM: The scalp is reflected and the calvarium is removed in the usual manner.

[**Author: "Joan Mellen cites David's doctor, Martin Palmer, complaining that "...they did not even open the braincase..." [*A Farewell to Justice*, p.106-107. If this is true, then the autopsy is a total fabrication, since this record plainly states "the calvarium is removed in the usual manner." Did Palmer examine David's body before its burial? These are questions we must ask.**]

There are no contusions in the scalp. [**Author: Why is this repeated? We were told this at the beginning of the autopsy.**] There is no fracture of the calvarium. The dura is stretched tightly over the left cerebral hemisphere and a large subdural hematoma is visible beneath the dura at this area. The right cerebral hemisphere is markedly compressed and flattened. The total volume of the subdural hematoma on the left side is measured at 95ml. The brain is removed and weighs 1480 grams.

[**Author: David's brain weighs somewhat more than average, probably because of edema from the hemorrhage. We assume the blood clots have been removed, which should have exposed any visible healed, prior bleeds. No previous bleeds are mentioned, even though this would give us a partial explanation for David's headaches. Hypertension and pulmonary edema, causing congestive heart failure, with severe headaches, nausea and vomiting due to high blood pressure, hyperthyroidism and resultant gastroparesis, creating weakness and sleeplessness, might explain David's full set of symptoms.**]

Dissection of the Circle of Willis demonstrates a small berry aneurysm at the anterior communicating artery between the two anterior cerebral vessels. This ansurysm [sic] measures 1/8 in. in maximum diameter. There is a frim (sic) blood clot adherent to it, and a much larger fresh blood clot lying between the frontal lobes communicating with the area of the aneurysm.

> [Author: David's aneurysm was so small that it was actually unlikely to leak or rupture. "...the rupture rate per year was 0.05% for patients with small aneurysms (less than 5mm diameter)[David's aneurysm was in this category] and 0.5% per year for patients with large aneurysms (greater than 10mm diameter)." "The Aneurysm and AVM Foundation" http:// www.taafonline.org/ba_about.html. (Retrieved Aug. 30, 2013) NIH: "The mean size of all ruptured aneurysms (10.8 mm) was significantly larger than the mean size of all unruptured aneurysms (7.8 mm, p < 0.001); the median sizes were 10 mm and 5 mm, respectively." http://www.ncbi.nlm. nih.gov/pubmed/11794606 (Retrieved Aug. 3-, 2013)]

Multiple sections through the brain show no evidence of contusion foci in the contex. The white matter is normal. The basal ganglia shows no changes. The lateral ventricles are slightly compressed. There is a marked edema and flattening of the right cerebral convolutions. There is uncinate herniation on the left side. There are numerous hemorrhages in the rostral pons and thalamic region. Therse [sic] hemorrhages lie mostly in the tegmental area of the pons but some are in the basilar substance in the midline. The medulla and cerebellum show no changes. The dura is stripped from the base of the skull and no fractures are found.

> [Author: All from the presence of the ruptured aneurysm and the pressure of the blood clots deforming the brain, accompanied by swelling. Unfortunately, the blood clots were not weighed, which would have offered proof of the mass of the hemorrhage.]

An unhealed hemorrhage (fatal) showing brain tissue death around it. Small bleeds that had healed should have been visible by eye (when the brain was washed and weighed) and by tissue section.\
PROVISIONAL ANATOMICAL DIAGNOSIS:

1. Rupture of berry aneurysm of Circle of Willis with massive left subdural hematoma, subarachnoid hemorrhage, and secondary pontine hemorrhages.

2. Hypertensive cardiovascular disease.

3. Pulmonary edema and congestion.

ADDENDUM TO EXTERIAL EXAMINATION: On the right leg on its lateral aspect overlying the head of the fibula there is a pigmented ovoid area measureing(sic) 1 1/4 x 1 in. in diameter that shows a grid like stippling. This does not appear recent. [Author: This might be a healed contact burn.] [Signature] **Ronald A. Welsh, M.D., Pathologist** (typed by: smk)

(Ref: as posted at http://mcadams.posc.mu.edu/ferrie_autopsy.htm.)

Appendix X

Summary
(HSCA Records and Multiple Sources)

Letters show thyroid deficiency from early age: Three letters from James H. Ferrie, David's father (1/29/44, 2/2/44 and 4/4/44) mentioned a thyroid deficiency to authorities at St. Charles Seminary. Ferrie had very high blood pressure, for which he was being treated by Dr. Richard Bagnetto, according to New Orleans District Attorney Jim Garrison. (sources incl .Stephen Roy and HSCA)

Acute (sudden) Overdose of Thyroid Medication: Too much Proloid can cause high blood pressure. A vasodilated shock state can be induced in a relatively short period of time by a sudden, large overdose of Proloid due to its T3 content. T4 would take much longer to build up what could also be a fatal reaction. Ferrie's refilled prescription for Proloid, according to Garrison, was "not prescribed" by his pharmacy (Broadmoor Pharmacy), but a pharmacy record saying merely "thyroid pills" as mentioned by Dr. Frank Minyard could account for that. 93 (of 100 tablets) were missing. New Orleans District Attorney Jim Garrison recognized the kind of symptoms an overdose could cause because he, too, had taken Proloid briefly. (See Michael T. Griffith's essay :http://karws.gso.uri.edu/jfk/the_critics/griffith/Hasty_Judgment.html.) (Retrieved Sept. 1m 2013)

The opinion of Dr. Ronald A. Welsh: Dr. Ronald A. Welsh was the pathologist who botched the autopsy by not testing for T3 and T4, not testing the spinal fluid, not checking the blood for same despite the enlarged thyroid, hypertension and pulmonary edema, and who also neglected to analyze the particle-filled liquid in David Ferrie's stomach – though he knew knowing there were suspicions of suicide. Patricia Lambert interviewed Welsh in 1993. Welsh told Lambert (author of *False Witness*) that he had made slides of Ferrie's brain tissue and examined them under the microscope. In addition to the burst berry aneurysm, he told her "scar tissue indicat[ed] that Ferrie had had another bleed, a small one, previously ... at least one or two of them at least two weeks before he died. This is a common occurence [sic] with Berry aneurysms...people have one or two before they blow out completely ... His headaches were from the early bleeds" (p. 302 .).

Garrison Suspected Proloid Poisoning: Garrison confiscated the tablets, but Chetta told him it would take a long time for Proloid to have any effect. However, Proloid has T3 in it, not just T4. The coroner did not test Ferrie for Proloid poisoning, nor were stomach contents analyzed. Proloid, of itself, could look like a suicide, since David "KNEW MEDICINE."

David (Unaccountably) Not Checked for T3 and T4 levels in his Blood after Death: The lack of extensive forensic testing – not only of his stomach contents, but of Ferrie's spinal fluid and blood for T4 and T3 denotes incompetence at the least, since David's thyroid gland was clearly enlarged and he presented symptoms of hypertension and hyperthyroidism (Me: " I have personally accidentally overdosed on thyroid medication myself and suffered a rapid heart rate, sweating, and alarmingly high blood pressure as a result of taking 6 pills containing only T4.").

Problem with Time of Death: All discussions of David's death should include an inspection of other possible scenarios. Journalist George Lardner related that Ferrie was in good spirits at 4:00 AM when he left Ferrie quite well and alive. The time of death was changed from before midnight to 4:00 AM based solely on Lardner's statement. Without headache symptoms and death occurring quickly after Lardner's departure, Ferrie's demise from a sudden "bleed" may have occurred naturally, but Ferrie still had "coffee" in his stomach when he died. The stomach should have been empty. It wasn't. Is gastroparesis a possible cause for his vomiting and nausea, clinically observable due to an overdose of Proloid? Ferrie had been complaining of nausea and vomiting, additional signs of chronic Proloid poisoning. Atop all this, David seems to have been living on coffee (too much caffeine could cause David to experience causes headaches as blood pressure rises. David's nausea had apparently reduced him to a diet of coffee, alcohol, jello and possibly vitamin tablets, hardly conducive to lowering his high blood pressure and getting healthy again.

David Ferrie's problems were known to his doctor and were in his hospital records. He was under surveillance. He was going to be required to testify about the Kennedy assassination and what he knew. Pure stress could be the culprit, but the wounds in the mouth lead us to a different conclusion.

Misinformed Newsgroup Opinions on Ferrie's Death Mislead Readers.

Example #1: Greg Parker Confronts Stephen Roy (as David Blackburst)

Parker: "… For someone with high metabolism, an OD of Proloid would cause a massive heart attack or a brain hemorrhage."

Blackburst: "No one has established that a **Proloid** OD would cause any life-threatening problems. Or that Ferrie was already hyperthyroid, for that matter… the first mention of Proloid seems to be in the October 3 Bagnetto interview. I have found no earlier mention. I am certain that Garrison's account of a 2/22/67 interest in Proloid is not accurate. oo David"

Author (interposing here): "Why quibble that it took months to think about Proloid again, after Chetta said it wasn't a factor? Though Garrison didn't mention Proloid before Oct. in any formal documents, that doesn't mean he had no suspicions about Proloid. *He did, or he would not have picked up the bottle and counted the pills and kept the bottle.* That's common sense. We thought of a doctor's word as gold back then. When Chetta said Proloid wouldn't work fast enough, Garrison believed him. It is remarkable that later he actually decided to get a second medical opinion, from David's doctor."

Example #2: Dr. Pitelli Confronts Stephen Roy (as Blackburst) and Dave Reitzes: NOTE: PItelli is a psychiatrist. This means he is also a medical doctor. A portion of their exchange displays positions held by Blackburst (Stephen Roy) and Dave Reitzes (acolyte of pro-Warren Commission advocate John McAdams) as they debate the doctor (edited):

Reitzes and Blackburst: "The absence of venipuncture wounds precludes the possibility the Ferrie was killed by a sharp thin object being pushed through the roof of his mouth."

Dr Pittelli; "Just for Clarification: A venipuncture wound is basically a needle puncture directly into a vein to draw blood or give a direct venous injection or place an I.V. line ... A puncture to the roof of the mouth would not be considered a venipuncture, as no one would try to find a vein on the roof of the mouth. So if this puncture had occurred, it would not have been described as a venipuncture. **Reitzes**: He complained of headaches for approximately two years prior to his death; numerous people were aware of this. He was complaining of headaches to George Lardner the night he died. Both David Blackburst and I have posted about this over the past two or three days. He had several "minor bleeds" before the final rupture; this is documented. David and I have posted about that as well. Have you read any of my posts or the especially well informed posts of David Blackburst on this subject? There have been two threads on this in the last few days alone. You're speculating; we are not. Do you want another re-post? Just say the word."

Dr. Pitelli: "The well informed David Blackburst did not even know what a venipuncture was.

Is he the autopsy expert that proves your point. Nice try..."

Reitzes: "Death by Proloid ingestion would come many hours after ingestion, it is easily detectable cause of death."

Dr. Pitelli: No. The cause of death would have to do with what the Proloid did to the person. For example, it could cause a fatal heart arrhythmia. That would be a cause of death then. It might also cause severe hypertension which leads to a ruptured berry aneurysm. I agree that that would generally take several hours to kick in ...[but] it would depend a lot on the person, how quickly the blood pressure responds... and how weak the vessel wall was at the time...."

Reason for Chronic Overdoses: Even intelligent people might believe that taking 'more' of the feel-good thyroid medication would help relieve symptoms of fatigue, but the opposite is true. Over-medication with Proloid could cause every symptom David Ferrie had. The T3 component in Proloid could drastically raise blood pressure quickly if a very large dose was taken. With David's high metabolism, a dose of some 97 pills [as mentioned in a memo from Garrison to Alcock) could have a devastating effect as it began to be absorbed by the bloodstream; David Ferrie's mouth showed trauma, **negating suicide.**

What About Lardner? With proloid forced down his throat, Dave's berry aneurysm burst before his heart could fail. All that was required of George Lardner, anxious to overcome his famous uncle's Communist reputation, was to say he was interviewing Ferrie face-to-face during those fatal hours. Lardner could have interviewed Ferrie, but it was possibly by phone, since his description of the drugs he said he saw in Ferrie's apartment casts doubts he ever entered it. He ignores the big stash of drugs supposedly in his line of sight, present on Dave's coffee table, only recalling a single bottle sitting on the piano – which is what surveillance photos would show from the perch across the street. Lardner only describes the furniture and piano visible by surveillance. He says he used Dave's bathroom (!) but did not comment on its truly epic filthiness (unless Dave's housekeeping habits had made a stellar leap forward). Read *Dr. Mary's Monkey* and *Me & Lee* to learn why some doctors might have wanted David Ferrie to die, just as Dr. Mary Sherman, Guy Banister, Hugh Ward, Jack Ruby and Lee Oswald also had to die.

Over-medication on Synthroid/Proloid: Comments

"I felt terrible this past summer. I had terrible headaches, muscle aches in my neck and shoulders, constant fatigue, and extreme pain in my feet to the point I didn't want to get out of bed in the morning." (over-medicated on Synthroid) http://community.babycenter.com/post/a2218075/feeling_better_after_stopping_synthroid_.

"I felt horrible! At one point last night I thought about going to the hospital. My heart was pounding and I had a terrible headache, along with being nauseated, spacey, and having hot flashes (and I'm a guy lol!). Wasn't sure if I was having a heart attack, or only suffering side-effects from being over-medicated- an uneasy feeling to say the least. Feel 100% better." http://index.healthboards.com/thyroid/synthroid-side-effects-headache/1/.

I was just upped from 1 to 125 and only 3 days ... I was up all night ... could not sleep, nausea, headache, and rumbling stomach ... I am thinking too much as well... "http://index.healthboards.com/thyroid/synthroid-side-effects-headache/1/.

(edited) "...Severe depression, mood changes, irritability, emotional sensitivity. Brain Fog. ... Headaches...NOTE- I have never been depressed in my life or even had any signs of mental conditions. Since starting Synthroid, I am so sad all the time and have feelings of hopelessness. "

http://www.askapatient.com/viewrating.asp?drug=21402&name=SYNTHROID&sort=timelength&page=8&PerPage=60

A Proloid website: Signs of overdose include insomnia, heart palpitations, jitteriness, rapid heartbeat, increased sweating, higher blood pressure...tremor, headache, diarrhea, and weight loss. http://www.healthcentral.com/peoplespharmacy/408/drugs/brand/62_sideeffects/proloid.html.

THYROGLOBULIN IS THE GENERIC NAME FOR PROLOID. "Symptoms of high thyroid levels include headache, chest pain, rapid or irregular heartbeat, shortness of breath, trembling, sweating, diarrhea, weight loss." http://www.patientassistance.com/G11487-thyroglobulinoral.html.

POISONING BY THYROID MEDICATIONS HAS ITS OWN MEDICAL DIAGNOSIS CODE: 2013 ICD-9-CM Diagnosis Code 962.7 Poisoning by thyroid and thyroid derivatives. ICD-9-CM 962.7 is a billable medical code that can be used to specify a diagnosis on a reimbursement claim.

http://www.icd9data.com/2013/Volume1/800-999/960-979/962/962.7.htm

An anti-Garrison, pro Warren Commission website describes symptoms of Proloid over-medication:

"Ferrie was aware of his failing health, [and had] expectation that he would soon die – but not by his own hand. Journalist David Snyder reported that Ferrie told him that he had encephalitis, that Ferrie's voice was barely audible, his breathing unsteady and his "steps were feeble." Not only had he been complaining about headaches, when two Garrison aides visited him the Saturday before his death, he "moaned and groaned with each step he took up the stairs" and told them that he had not been able to keep food on his stomach for a couple of days (Patricia Lambert, *False Witness*, pp. 57, 62-63)."

Author: "The autopsy shows an enlarged thyroid, pulmonary edema, evidence of high blood pressure, and an enlarged heart, all pointing to hyperthyroidism. David's stomach contained "coffee" with particles in it, suggesting many pills were thrust down his throat, the aggressive act of which also created lesions on both interior aspects of his lips, and gums. The stomach contents are not analyzed. His upper false teeth were removed so he couldn't bite, but his clothing may have had to be removed. Stephen Roy said he 'retired for the night' naked in bed on a cool night (yes, he has some covers) in an inadequately heated apartment. Oddly, he kept his wig and eyebrows on.

David leaves a small blood clot on the pillow, characteristic of a gag reflex from so many pills, or possibly, a clot of blood issued from an injured lip or pharynx (not enough to be called a hemorrhage). The autopsy did not describe the pharyngeal and laryngeal areas as "unremarkable," instead saying they did not exhibit hemorrhages. Where are the words, "clear" "smooth" or "normal" one would expect? Why wasn't Dave's thyroid described as enlarged? Why was 'time of death' over an hour *after* the body was found? There are problems with this autopsy. The autopsy obscured the fact of David's hyperthyroidism. Or was that diagnosis quashed because of the lesions in David's mouth? They threw away David's blood samples, too, instead of freezing them in case more tests were needed. It is shocking to read of such carelessness. In any case where suicide might be suspected, all known medications should have been listed as evidence. Instead, Garrison pockets one of the bottles personally. Where's the protection of evidence in this case? It doesn't exist."

APPENDIX XI

Dick Russell's Interview of Raymond "Ray" Broshears, From, *On The Trail Of The Kennedy Assassins*, With Comments On "The Getaway Pilot"

"There is another long silence as Broshears considers the question about Ferrie's sudden trip to Texas through a driving rainstorm on November 22, 1963. "David was to meet a plane. He was going to fly them on to Mexico, and eventually to South Africa." [Me: Wm. Davy, in Destiny Betrayed,p. 1248 (quoted through an Education Forum post, June, 2005 at http://educationforum.ipbhost.com/index. php?showtopic=8039&&page=7) wrote: "Raymond Broshears, said in a Los Angeles TV interview that Ferrie actually confessed the plot to him in one of the erratic moods that then began to consume him, and which he tried to combat with pills and alcohol. He stated that his function was to fly the assassins from Houston to South America. From there they would fly to South Africa, which had no extradition treaty with the United States. [Interestingly, Johannesburg is where the CIA front, Permindex, co-directed by Shaw, had recently been relocated, following its expulsion from Italy.]

BROSHEARS , TO RUSSELL, CONTD: "They had left from some little airfield between Dallas and Fort Worth, and David had a twin-engine plane ready for them, and that was the purpose of his mad dash through a driving rainstorm from New Orleans. But the plane crashed off the coast of Texas near Corpus Christi. That was what David was told in the telephone booth that day. Apparently, they had decided to try to make it to Mexico on their own. They did not." Had Ferrie ever told Broshears who was on that plane? "They had code names. The only one I remember was Garcia." Another pause. "He told me Lee Harvey Oswald did *not* kill the president. He was very adamant about it, and I believed him. All the things he told me about Oswald, I doubt he could have shot a rabbit 50 feet away. He said four people were going to shoot. It was a very patriotic thing to David. I don't think it was any great long drawn-out conspiracy. It was a conglomerate of different right-wing ideologies pushing on a few people, and it all came together at the same time. I think they were manipulated very cleverly – by somebody pulling the strings."

Comment by Author: "Broshears has elsewhere made statements that I find off the wall. But Dave probably fed Broshears some misinformation. Why? Because Dave had been pretending to be anti-JFK with some dangerous characters, such as Dr. William Bryan, and with fanatics such as Guy Banister and his mistress, Delphine Roberts. Dave told me he didn't dare reveal his true feelings about Kennedy in the midst of so many who hated JFK.

I find myself concerned: what if David lied to me? He certainly lied to others. However, he had to have lied to Dr. Mary Sherman, as well, and I am certain that she trusted him. There is a possibility that Dave transmitted information from Dr. Sherman to Lee Oswald that allowed him to reach the right contacts in Chicago (Mary's 'hometown' area} so Lee was able to pass on information that probably saved Kennedy's life in Chicago three weeks before the assassination, when someone named "Lee' informed FBI, which produced arrests of armed gunmen (see *JFK and the Unspeakable*, by James Douglass – Abraham Bolden's testimony).

Dave knew how to investigate. That's the key. He knew what to say, what would reach certain people, to keep himself secure while investigating. He knew how to seem what he was not. Either that, or he totally fooled me, after all his praises of Kennedy and after all we had done to try to kill Castro together. When Stephen Roy tells me that many people never guessed Dave was gay, saying I am presenting a David Ferrie that was openly gay, when he was "in the closet" (but with his very public record of 'acts against nature' in the papers, and newspaper accounts of sexual mishandling of teen-aged boys, Dave was known for what he was.) However, Dave could put on many faces to many different people. I believe Broshears was given some false information because of the "wandering bishops" that Dave had reason to fear. "Bishop" Jack Martin turned on him, for example. I conclude that Dave dared not communicate concerning his true feelings about Kennedy, but wanted Broshears' comfort at a dark time. Still, he didn't dare give Broshears information that made him look like he was pro-JFK. But he tells Broshears the conspirators' plane 'crashed near Corpus Christi.' No record of that crash has ever emerged, but by revealing more than one gunman, Dave plants the seed of conspiracy, probably all he dared to do. As for what he told me, fresh from Marcello's victory in New Orleans, Dave seemed to really believe Marcello could spring Lee and that he could fly him to Laredo, where Lee was supposed to have another plane waiting to take him into Mexico. So I was told to be alert – I might still be able to join Lee in Mexico, after all. Could the mafia have got Lee out? Why did Dean Andrews get the mystery call, asking if Andrews would serve as Lee's lawyer? But Marcello was using this as a backup plan. Lee had to be killed before the link between CIA and Mafia, who orchestrated the hit on Kennedy with the blessings of the soon-to-be-legal new government and its many backers, would be exposed. Dave got kids out of jail all the time himself, due to corrupt judges, and he knew the same corruption was rampant in Dallas, where Marcello also had great power."

Bill Davy's *Destiny Betrayed*, p.46: "Air service personnel seemed to recall that in 1963 Ferrie had access to an airplane based in Houston. In this craft, the flight to Matamoros would take little more than an hour." Also the deservedly? much maligned Jack S. Martin also is on record as saying that Ferrie was to fly the assassins to Matamoros, Mexico." (quoted at Education Forum, http://educationforum.ipbhost.com/index.php?showtopic=8039&&page=7, (Retrieved August 30, 2013)

Two Other Airports of Interest: Little-Known Air Fields Only Miles from Winterland Ice Skating Rink

Author: In 1963, two little-known air fields were located close to Winterland Ice Rink. Prior to Nov. 22, 1963: "I knew that an escape plan existed to get Lee out of Dallas, by plane. I have always thought this was to involve Redbird Airport, due to the incident that occurred there (the plane seemed to wait a long time for a passenger that never came, revving its engines, waiting to take off ASAP). Lee would be wearing a policeman's jacket or uniform. The getaway plane would land at Alief Field (only 13 1/2 miles from Winterland Ice Rink), where two policemen would get off, but only one would get back on. After Lee's arrest, Dave mentioned Hull Field as a rendezvous spot if Lee could be released on bail. This was before Lee was arraigned for Tippit's murder. Dave was used to seeing people get sprung on bail through Marcello's influence, which was also tremendous in Dallas. I have reported that a Schlumberger DeHaviland Dove duo-engine plane was available from Hull Field in late September, which was appropriated for use by Hugh Ward and Lee at Houma.

In that plane, which eventually was left at Chennault Field, Hugh flew Lee to Austin, Dallas and Houston, while an alibi bus ticket hid these facts if efforts to trace Lee Oswald's actions occurred. In Houston, Lee finally boarded a bus to Laredo and then went on to Mexico City, where we now know he was impersonated and framed. In Austin, Lee delivered a package; another package was delivered by two Cubans with him to St. Edward's University. Next, Lee saw Senora Odio in Dallas with another pair of Cubans, who, I believe, wittingly or unwittingly maneuvered Lee into being introduced to her (he was originally seeking information about Rorke and Sullivan's downed plane). A call to her later helped frame Lee there, too. Then, arriving in Houston, Lee was suddenly given a "fresher" batch of the bioweapon, from M.D. Anderson Hospital. After much discussion with those more knowledgeable than I, we now believe Lee was given a fake batch in Houston, and that M.D. Anderson thus obtained what Lee brought from new Orleans, in a clever swap that hid the fact that only then did they obtain a live specimen of the bioweapon. It seems Lee was never meant to entrust such a weapon to anti-Castro dissidents in Mexico City, but he was lured into going there thinking otherwise. While there, it was easy to impersonate him and frame him.

Hull Field (now Hull Regional Airport) is located in Sugar Land, TX, 19 miles from Winterland Ice Rink, but only 7 miles from Alief Field. In 1977, as a reporter, I interviewed Don Hull, deliberately obtaining and inserting into my news story the fact that the field was used for FREE by government entities, and that Hull handled flights from Mexico. Here is a portion of the interview, as published in Houston's Suburbia newspaper. Below it, a large portion of the interview is presented:

Of the planes, 75-80 per cent are owned by businesses in Fort Bend County. But the airport also has a great deal of use by government agencies.

The Department of Public Safety, the Major Crime Task Force, the State Department of Health, and the State Attorney General, among many others, use the airport facilities at no charge.

Security personnel with guard dogs patrol the airport regularly. Hull has two sniffer dogs which can detect contraband and illicit drug shipments. Many aircraft from Mexico and South America land at Hull Airport. "We believe in prevention," said Hull, who's never had a drug or contraband incident at his airfield.

Cancer patients from a number of countries and states are brought here en route to M.D. Anderson Hospital. And resident doctors are flown in to the Richmond State School to give the children there good medical care.

The Air Ambulance Service can handle four persons on stretchers or

Suburbia, June 15, 1977, Page 9 East

Hull Airport

First-class treatment at a first-class establishment

by *Judy Baker*

Snoopy and the Red Baron are at home here — and so are 130 aircraft which are based at Sugar Land's Don Hull Airport.

Meet Don Hull: he's middle-aged, unassuming, and he holds a steady rein on the airport's operations. The airport is tight, safe and clean.

Hull is married, with two daughters also, but they didn't care to learn about the trade. "When you're around it all the time, it doesn't seem so exciting," Hull said.

It seemed plenty exciting to be at the airport, where expansion plans are in the works, and everyone's hopping.

There was a telephone call

> 'We have never had an accident in any plane here for 23 years.'

"Even the visitors bend down and pick up cigarette butts," Hull said, with a nearly every minute that the interview was being conducted, and personnel

planes gleam and glitter in the sun. There isn't a spot on them.

The fragile-looking private planes are built of aluminum, which Hull assured us was for lightness, fuel conservation, etc. "We have never had an accident in any plane here for 23 years," he said. "The only kind of thing that has happened has been a couple of times when out-of-state visitors landed and forgot to put their wheels down." Even so, there was only minor damage.

Of the planes, 75-80 per cent are owned by businesses in Fort Bend County. But the airport also has a great deal of use by government agencies.

The Department of Public Safety, the Major Crime Task Force, the State Department of Health, and the State Attorney General, among many others, use the airport facilities at no charge.

and laid out by the Texas Aeronautics Commission to qualify us as a basic transport airport," Hull said. The airport has a capacity of 40 to 50 planes in an hour, although actual traffic is not nearly so heavy.

The restoration of a number of planes of World War II vintage has been accomplished here. "We turned them into licensed, airworthy craft," Hull said with a real modest pride. "For instance, we've restored a German Focke-Wulf, a British Spitfire, an Aircobra, some Mustangs. . . ."

Some of the restored planes fly with the Confederate Air Force Museum at Arlington.

Don Hull is the kind of person who does not like to talk about himself. But we noted that Cub Scouts and other groups are frequent visitors to the airport, where

Government agencies use for free, "many aircraft from Mexico," M.D. Anderson cancer patients...

Researcher Robert Howard posted the following on Education Forum in the same debate as above: (http://educationforum.ipbhost.com/index.php?show-topic=8039&&page=7): **CIA file on David Ferrie**:

Home/Archive/Documents/JFK Assassination Documents/JFK Documents – Central Intelligence Agency/HSCA Segregated CIA Collection/HSCA Segregated CIA Collection, Box 14/

NARA Record Number: 1993.07.31.11:22:43:680028

REVIEW OF 201 FILE ON U.S. CITIZEN DAVID W. FERRIE

DAVID FERRIE

REVIEW OF 201 FILE ON U.S. CITIZEN DAVID W. FERRIE categories listed and codes SHOULD BE CLOSED UNWITTING COLLABORATOR 01 CODE A7 WITTING COLLABORATOR 01 CODE A1 POTENTIAL WITTING COLLABORATOR RELATIONSHIP TERMINATED 01 CODE A3 01 CODE A4 COUNTER-INTELLIGENCE CASE 01 CODE A5 ALL OTHERS 01 CODE A6

Re: Two Undated, Typed Notes Found After David Ferrie's Death on Feb. 22, 1967, with Evidence Of Tampering

A typed letter to "Al" with Dave's will was supposedly found taped under the table at his apartment. The other typed note was found by Coroner Nicholas Chetta, according to extant newspaper articles.

Question: Were the two letters tampered with to provide a better basis for "suicide"?

Did somebody *tamper with* two letters David Ferrie had previously typed, using his typewriter? The typewriter was on the piano stool at the piano. Dave never kept it there when I knew him, as he not only played the piano, but people used the stool to sit on. Both notes support suicide as cause of death. Tampering with these letters would be a sophisticated act, but Proloid poisoning is also a sophisticated way to kill, making the kill look like suicide.

View from dining room. Typewriter is in wrong place.

Dave would never have committed suicide. It was against everything he believed in, so support for suicide would have to be manufactured. Both "found" notes were undated and one was signed by typewriter, the other left unsigned. *The only 'proof' that Dave wrote them is his typewriter.* Photos show the typewriter placed on Dave's piano stool *instead of on his dining room table,* where I saw it. This was a Royal typewriter, as I recall. Dave played the piano. Why would he haul his typewriter from the dining room over to the piano stool? Did somebody ask for Dave's typewriter, unwilling to leave the living room because Dave was sit-

Though the view is skewed to left, this is approximately what could be seen from across the street and photographed by surveillance.

ting there, bound and dying? Had they found a short letter that could be retyped or altered using Dave's own typewriter? Had they found another letter where it was easy to just add a "death sentence" line at the top?

The "Dear AL" note was found in an envelope, taped under the table along with his will. But Dave used to keep his important papers in his "strongbox" in 1963. After reading the first letter, take a good, hard look at Letter #2, along with us.

Dear Al: [Beauboeuf]

When you read this I will be quite dead and no answer will be possible. I wonder how you are going to justify things. Tell me you treated me as you did because I was the one who always got you in trouble. The police arrest. The stripped car charge. The deal at Kohn School. Flying Barragona in the Beech. Etc.

Well, I guess that helps ease your conscience, even if it is not the truth. All I can say is that I offered you love, and the best I could. All I got in return in the end was a kick in the teeth. Hence I die alone and unloved. You would not even straighten out Carol about me, though this you started when you were going steady. I wonder what your last days and hours are going to be like. As you sow, so shall you reap. Goodbye. Dave (typed signature) (the note below was typed on a full sheet of paper)

THE SECOND LETTER

W as a "death sentence" added to this letter? Read the letter, then look at something interesting ...

"To leave this life is, for me, a sweet prospect. I find nothing in it that is desirable, and on the other hand everything that is loathsome.

"Daily we are propagandized more and more about a rising crime rate. But how do we know it is true? We don't, for we Americans have little or no access to the truth. Today I went to the police headquarters to see these "public records" of this rising crime rate and nearly wound up in jail for my trouble. I was searched, interrogated, verbally abused, had my record checked, and finally threatened. Needless to say, I did not see the "public records."

"Still more irking is to hear a superintendent of police, who rose through the ranks (thus proving that zero equals super zero) stating that the solution to the crime problem was tightened and more stringent laws. A somewhat messianic district attorney concurred. Together these men prove themselves utterly unfit for office, just as they proved that an electorate cannot be depended on to pick the right man. The problems of crime rest deep in society. The problems exist in the existence of divorce and the absence of regulations.

"No parents would send him [sic] child to an amateur for dental work, nor a quack for an appendectomy. Yet what atrocious negligence is permitting other amateurs to raise children. Mere kids are allowed to marry because they have the "urge." How stupid can you get? Every expert tells in detail how children must be cared for physically, emotionally and intellectually. Yet society lets girls and boys, not yet capable of lover [sic] begat [sic] children who, love-starved, turn to crime for some sort of identification. However, I don't think we will often see a district attorney or a police chief with brains to realize this.

"We pay so much attention to the law. I have not figured out the reason. I have watched judges like Cocke at work. The various police and district attorneys and the like get to bend the judge's ear long before the trial. These judges of today deny defendants due process of the law. They permit the court to try the case in chambers, to have district attorneys form their opinions and decisions long before the defense gets a chance. Further, these same judges (and I am afraid it pertains to nearly all of them) then comment, by word, glance, gesture or remark, on the evidence in front of a jury. If the defendant wins, these judges take it as a personal insult.

"When I was a boy my father preached that in the "American way of life" you are innocent till proven guilty. No greater lie has been told. The man charged before the court has flat got to prove his innocence. Go witness a criminal trial and watch. The state is supposed to prove guilt beyond a reasonable doubt. If you read decisions of the various courts of appeal and the Supreme Court you discover that truth and falsehood, right and wrong have no place in court. All the state needs is "evidence to support a conviction." If this is justice, then justice be damned.

This letter resembles a letter to a newspaper.

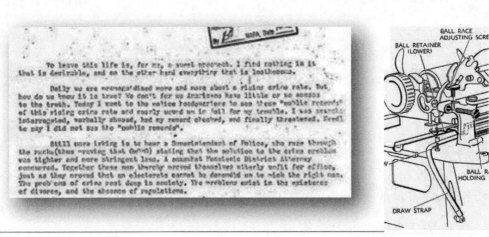

The carriage return on a typewriter is set, and does not change for the whole letter, paragraph by paragraph. It will line up. But the carriage return can get 'less tight' over time, as it is on a draw strap, so it can 'creep.' A "creep bar" to help control this tendency is part of the machine, but creep still occurs. A letter typed somewhat later on the same typewriter can show a carriage return point slightly more to the left. Is this important concerning letter #2? Yes.

At left, we have lined up the first letter of each new paragraph in the letter #2. Result: the "T" in "To" is *one letter more to the left*. It was almost certainly written sometime *after* the rest of the letter. The 'o' is where the "T" should be. In addition, there is a peculiar vertical line between Paragraph #1 and Paragraph #2. It looks like a "spacer" mark to make sure the typewriter is lined up just right to place the "death sentences" at a correct distance from the second paragraph. See for yourself: The "To" is at the top right, misaligned, showing "To." The other letters (D,S,W,W) are properly aligned, so the first two sentences of this letter were likely cleverly added to the original.

At the far left, the vertical line could have functioned as a 'spacer.' at the near left, the "T" has drifted left in the carriage return. The first sentence was added later. It then handily served as a "suicide note."

Appendix XIII

The Death of Clay Shaw

Aneighbor saw mysterious people removing his body from the home and called the coroner's office. By the time their investigators arrived, Shaw's body was gone. After inquiring into the matter for a full day, they were finally told that Shaw had been buried. Frank Minyard, the coroner of New Orleans, called for the exhumation of Shaw's body. He wished to conduct an autopsy, but was viciously attacked in the New Orleans press for this reasonable request. Minyard backed down, and no autopsy was ever performed. " Me: "Though cancer was the obvious cause of death, an autopsy should have been done to determine its origin and to set reasonable questions to rest."

An elaborate police report written in cooperation with a doctor from Ochsner Hospital provides evidence that Shaw died a natural death, with two problems: (1) Shaw's pain control and his care in his final days by unskilled, untrained "sitters" reflect negligence and a lack of concern for Shaw's sufferings on the part of his doctor (2) Upon death, the body was immediately embalmed and a funeral was held a day later, making it impossible for Shaw's many friends to be apprised of his death in time to attend. Was this done to keep people from gathering together and comparing notes? Concerned neighbors basically watched Shaw vanish from his house.

Clayton E. Cole (from book review):

5.0 out of 5 stars my friend, clay July 26, 2012 By Clayton E. Cote Format:Hardcover

i met james kirkwood when he was in n.o. interviewing, for his great book, very well written. i was friends with clay shaw, until his death on aug.15, 1974. i was outside his front door the evening before, and saw an ambelance leaving. i did not see clay that evening. the next morning very early, an amblance was out side his front door. i could never understand why it was there if, as i learned later he was dead! my friend clay,and i spent many evenings siting out back of the swimming pool, on seats available. many times i would take care of him, in the resturant i worked at, accross from the federal court house.where the trial was going on. clay laverne shaw will alway's have a place in my thoughts, and my heart. a great read american grotesque. of cource [sic] my copy is signed inside the hard cover, for clay- with affection and regards clay shaw mar. 1972 my first name being,clayton, always called clay, many times he would open my mail, and write on the envelope, sorry,-clay, again!

http://www.amazon.com/American-grotesque-account-Shaw-Jim-Garrison/dp/0671206842

(EDITED FOR BREVITY. FOR ENTIRE DOCUMENT. NO SIGNIFICANT INFORMATION HAS BEEN REMOVED.)

New Orleans Department of Police HOSPITALIZATION CASE REPORT .1 Death ... 7. Location: 1022 St. Peter Street 8. Date-Time Occurred 8-15-74 12:30 AM 9. Day of Week Occurred Thursday 10. Date-Time 8-16-74 3:00 PM 11. Name of Victim Shaw, Clay Race W Sex M Age 61 2. Residence Address 1022 St. Peter Street 13. Residence Phone - - - 14. Business Phone - - - [Coroner's Office Reported Death] 19. Person Who Discovered Victim Doody Don Race W Sex M Age 46 20. Residence Address 1022 St. Peter Street ... Victim Conveyed To: Funeral Home By:...Ambulance [House of Bultman Funeral Home] Attending Physician Hugh Batson 33 Tentative Diagnosis ... Natural--Terminal Cancer 35. Physician Pronouncing Death Fatality Dr. Hugh Batson Time 1:00 AM 36. Detective Bureau Notified Dillmann Date -Time 8-16-74 3 PM 40. Witness Julian WAYNE Race W Sex M Age 25 41. Residence Address 818 Moss Street, Apt. 202 42. Residence Phone None 43. Business Phone - - -

50. Narrative: Dets. John Dillmann and Fred Dantagnan, assigned to the Criminal Investigation Division, report that on Friday, August 16, 1974 they were instructed by Chief of Detectives Henry M. Morris to initiate an investigation into the death of one Clay L. Shaw, White Male, age 61, formerly residing 1022 St. Peter Street...the victim expired on August 15, 1974 about 12:40 AM at his residence, 1022 St. Peter Street. The death certificate was signed by Dr. Hugh M. Batson, with the cause of death reflecting Methstatic [METASTATIC] Lung Malignancy, Brain and Liver. Also furnished was a statement obtained by the Orleans Parish Coroner's Office from Mr. William Acosta, Manager of the House of Bultman Funeral Home. A review of this statement reflected that the House of Bultman received a telephone call about 1:30 AM on August 15, 1974 from Mr. E. Wegmann, Attorney at Law, representing the deceased, Clay Shaw. Mr. Wegman stated that Mr. Shaw had expired and requested the House of Bultman to pick up the remains. Mr. Acosta went on to say that he and Mrs. Frances Bultman, who were personal friends of the deceased, proceeded directly to 1022 St. Peter Street, arriving there about 1:55 AM. Upon entering the residence, Mr. Acosta observed Mr. Shaw's remains lying in a bed in the rear bedroom, clad in a hospital gown. A night table was at the foot of the bed. The body was lying with the head to the north and the feet to the south. Mr. Acosta added that upon his arrival, he was met by Mr. Wegman, Dr. Batson, and a sitter, named Don. The hearse arrived at the residence about 2:00 AM manned by a Mr. Englehart and Mr. Vickers. The body was then removed to the funeral home and the normal procedure of arterial injection and aspirating of the body cavities took place. Mr. Acosta closed by stating that while at the Shaw residence, he did not observe any evidence of violence or any abnormalities. There was nothing to indicate to Mr. Acosta that this death was anything other than normal. Dets. Dillman and Dantagnan then proceeded to the law offices of Mr. E. Wegman, where at 3:10 PM [P. 3] an oral interview was conducted. It was learned from Mr. Wegman that he has been Mr. Shaw's attorney since 1949 and since that time has become a close and personal friend. He added that on August 15, 1974 about 12:40 AM he was notified by Mr. Shaw's sitter (Don Doody) that Mr. Shaw had expired.

[NOTE BY AUTHOR: in the Clay Shaw trial, Doody testified. Mary Ferrell file card: 3/25/67 Houston Chronicle, Plot or Politics, James, p. 146. As-

sociate of Clay Shaw. Questioned by New Orleans Grand Jury 3/24/67. 35-yrs old. Tall, slim, red-bearded. (Named in Shaw's notebooks) Donald H. Carpenter, writing a book about Shaw, comments: "Don Doody served in the Air Force in an intelligence position. He also knew Russian. He had traveled to Cuba, and in 1963, he traveled to Mexico City. For several months before Shaw's death, Doody filled the job of a sitter while Shaw rapidly declined in health." Doody was alive in 2005, according to Carpenter. (Ref online at: http://blog.donaldhcarpenter.com/2011/12/don-doodyclay-shaw.html.#sthash.7NpIklBp.dpuf)] It should be noted that Shaw went to San Francisco, where Doody lived, on the date of the Kennedy assassination and was there again in 1966.]

Mr. Doody informed Mr. Wegman that about 12:30 AM he was called to Mr. Shaw's bed and upon checking the victim, observed an amount of secretion flowing from the victim's mouth and nostrils. He attempted to clean the victim's face and while doing so, the victim gasped and apparently expired. ... Upon further questioning, Mr. Wegman stated that to his knowledge the victim had been suffering from terminal cancer and had been seen by his attending physician, Dr. Batson, the day prior to his death. To his knowledge, Mr. Shaw's condition had been progressively worsened in the last week, and it was just a matter of time until he expired. The main reason for the sitter's presence was to make certain that Mr. Shaw was comfortable and cared for. Mr. Wegman further stated that the New Orleans Police Department and the New Orleans Coroner's Office was not notified of Mr. Shaw's death because it was his understanding that it was not necessary. He elaborated by stating that he and Dr. Batson were under the impression that if a person expires and has been seen by his attending physician within 36 hours of his death, that it is not a necessity that the Coroner's. P. 4: Office be notified. [**What about Shaw's relatives? His friends? Why are no calls mentioned? Where are others?**] Mr. Wegman furnished the detectives with the names and addresses of the sitters hired to take care of Mr. Shaw, and it should be noted that Mr. Wegman was very cooperative in assisting in this investigation...Upon completing the above mentioned interview, Dets. Dillmann and Dantagnan proceeded to Ochsner Foundation Hospital where at 5:00 PM they interviewed Mr. Shaw's attending physician, Dr. Hugh Batson. Dr. Batson was very cooperative and furnished the detectives with a detailed synopsis of Mr. Shaw's condition. Dr. Batson first began to treat Shaw in May of 1973. Mr. Shaw's first complaint was of a leg condition, however, during the subsequent examination, an ulcer was detected. During the subsequent examination and treatment for Mr. Shaw's ulcer, Dr. Batson found that Mr. Shaw was suffering from acute lung cancer. Shaw then began radiation treatments for this condition. He was again hospitalized in January, 1974 for four days, at which time he continued the radiation treatments. He was released and re-admitted in February, 1974, this time suffering from seizures. A blood clot was detected in the left portion of Mr. Shaw's skull, however, this was not the cause of Mr. Shaw's seizures. [**How was that determined?**] . Shaw was admitted on February 5, 1974 and surgery was performed on February 8, 1974. During the removal of the blood clot, lesions (signs of cancer) were detected in Mr. Shaw's brain. He then began radiation treatments for the brain cancer and was released on February [illegible] 1974. During the months of March and April, Shaw continued the radiation treatments, but on April 18, 1974, he discontinued these treatments, and it was the feeling of Dr. Batson that Mr. Shaw was drinking [P. 5] heavily. [**Good for him. Some relief from the agony.**] Shaw was again admitted on June 14, 1974 and received several more radiation treatments. His condition seemed to worsen and he appeared to be incoherent at times. He was released on June 27, 1974 against the recommendation of Dr. Batson. It was during this confinement that cancer was also detected in Mr. Shaw's liver. During the time between June 27, 1974 and Shaw's death he was visited several times by Dr. y7Batson. His condition was progressively worse and according to Dr. Batson, the week preceeding (sic) his death, the victim was completely bedridden. Mr. Shaw needed constant care as he urinated without his knowledge, was at times delirious, and on occasion refused his medication. According to Dr. Batson, he visited the victim on the date preceding his death and found that his condition was to the point where he was not in touch with reality, that is, he did not recognize people and was only eating a small amount of candy. It was Dr. Batson's opinion after examining him on August 14, 1974 and receiving no response from him, that nothing could be done for him at this point, except to make him as comfortable as possible. Upon further questioning, Dr. Batson stated that to his knowledge, the sitters obtained by Mr. Shaw to care for him were personal friends and not any form of registered nurses, et cetera. Dr. Batson also furnished the detectives with a list of medications he had prescribed for Mr. Shaw, which are as follows: //DILANTAN – prescribed by Dr. Batson since February, 1974 for Mr. Shaw's seizures. To Dr. Batson's knowledge, Shaw continued the medication until the latter part of June, at which time he refused to continue. SINEQUAN AND TRIAVIL – Anti-depressants prescribed in May and June, 1974. According to Dr.[p. 6] Batson, he did not think that Mr. Shaw had taken very much of this medication.

DARVON – 65 milligrams, prescribed in the latter part of June for pain. This prescription was phoned to K & B Drug Store and picked up by one of Mr. Shaw's sitters (Mrs. Baumgarter). Dr. Batson did not know if Shaw had taken any of this medication. //

[**Author:** *Surprised to see Darvon prescribed, because if a patient has seizures, they shouldn't be on Darvon.* **Banned due to side effects many places. "Before using this medication, tell your doctor or pharmacist your medical history, especially of: brain disorders (such as head injury, tumor, seizures), breathing problems (such as asthma, sleep apnea, chronic obstructive pulmonary disease-COPD), kidney disease, liver disease, mental/mood disorders (such as confusion, depression) "Darvon (propoxyphene) is intended for the management of mild to moderate pain." Ref: http://www.rxlist.com/darvon-drug.htm.] Author: "Pain management for liver cancer is important, and tricky to handle. The doc should have kept track. Doctor was visiting, but didn't know if Shaw was getting pain relief? Poor CLS."**]

It should be noted that the investigating detectives attempted to interview Mr. Shaw's sitter, Don Doody, on the night of August 16, 1974. This interview was not conducted because Don Doody had just returned from Mr. Shaw's funeral, and it was apparent that he did not have full control at the time; therefore, an appointment was made for the following day. On August 17, 1974 about 11:30 AM detectives met with Mr. Don Doody at 1022 St. Peter Street in the presence of Mr. Wegman, victim's attorney. It was learned from Mr. Doody that he has been a close and personal friend of the victim for the past 20 years. Doody attended Tulane Law School, graduating (P. 7) in 1961 and has resided at 1214 Cole Street in San Francisco for the past few years. Doody was contacted by Mr. Shaw in late May, at which time he was told of Mr. Shaw's condition. The victim requested that Doody come to New Orleans and attend to him with the understanding that he would be compensated for this service. Doody arrived in New Orleans the latter part of June and has taken care of Mr. Shaw since his arrival...

The following is a list of medication found by the investigating detectives on the [illegible] while conducting their investigation:

//DILANTIN – prescribed on June 6, 1974, one three times daily, 46 tablets remained in bottle DARVOCET – N-100 – prescribed June 29, 1974, bottle empty DARVOCET – N-100 – prescribed July 27, 1974, one tablet every four hours when needed, 12 tablets remained in bottle SINEQUEN – 25 – prescribed March 25, 1974, one at bedtime, 48 tablets remained in bottle. BECOTIN-T – Vitamin B Complex with Vitamin C – 35 tablets remained in bottle One bottle of ALERTONIC – three quarters full One bottle of ROBITUSSIN COUGH FORMULA – bottle full//

It should be noted that 1022 St. Peter Street is a wood frame raised single dwelling, consisting of a livingroom, dining room, kitchen, bath, and two rear bedrooms. The investigating detectives conducted a thorough search of the residence, including the rear bedroom occupied by the victim. It was noted that in this room, twin single beds had been placed side by side. It was learned from Mr. Doody (P. 9) that this was done for the purpose of better observation of the victim by the medical student, Wayne Julian. No other pertinent signs were noted in the residence.

Shaw's last residence on St. Peter St. is modest compared to his former residence at 1313 Dauphine. Shaw was no longer a wealthy man: the Garrison trial had hurt him financially, just as he said.

On August 20, 1974 Dets. Dillmann and Dantagnan had the occasion to interview one Wayne Julian, who was acting as a sitter for Mr. Shaw at the time of his death. It was learned from Mr. Julian that he is in his second year at Tulane Medical School and learned of Mr. Shaw's need from the Student Affairs Office at Tulane University. Julian inquired into the job and was hired by Mrs. Gail Baumgardner, who at the time worked at Tulane University. He began acting as a sitter in the latter part of June and was paid about $3.00 an hour...Although the exact cause of Mr. Shaw's death could never be determined without the results of an autopsy, it is clearly evident that Mr. Shaw's condition was terminal. During the week prior to his death, he was seen by his attending physician and was being made as comfortable as possible. As of the completion of this report, no evidence has been found to indicate that Mr. Shaw's death was anything but natural. Final classification to be made by the Orleans Parish Coroner's Office.

//Reporting Officer Det. John Dillmann Badge 1309 Reporting Officer Det. Fred Dantagnan Badge 1534 Supervisor Approving Lt. Robert Mutz Date of Report 8-28-74 // REF: http://mcadams.posc.mu.edu/death9.htm

[Author: In my opinion, after close scrutiny of available records, no foul play occurred in the death of Clay Shaw. The only unexplained concerns are what neighbors thought they saw concerning the ambulance and their total ignorance of Shaw's condition, apparently for months. The origin of Shaw's cancer seemed to be natural, but medical treatment and care for his comfort that Shaw received was, in my opinion, well below par. No skilled nursing was supplied or attempted in the home, and so Shaw suffered before he drowned in the accumulated fluids of his own lung cancer, which should have been drained off to assist in his comfort. His sufferings before he finally lost sensibility must have been intense. It seems a "babysitter" – a good old friend with ties to the CIA – brought in a month after Shaw called him for help – was present to assure that Shaw's illness and death remained a very private affair. We can't have anyone babbling about things. And what happened to Shaw's telephone]

Appendix XIV

David Ferrie's Apartment

David Ferrie probably lived at 3330 East LA Pkwy longer than at any other address in his adulthood.

Note: The sketch of David's apartment is an approximation from memory, drawn after visiting David's apartment in 2003 with Nigel Turner, with furniture placed approximately as it was in late spring and summer, 1963, to the best of author's recollection. The living room and dining room were near the same size. Many apartments at this time had no dining room with such a large kitchen. There was a bathtub, not just a shower, in the bathroom. The large screened-in porch provided not only a good view, but also a breeze to cool the apartment in summer. David Ferrie's apartment was modern and spacious for one tenant or two. It was soon crammed with books, scientific equipment, and junk.

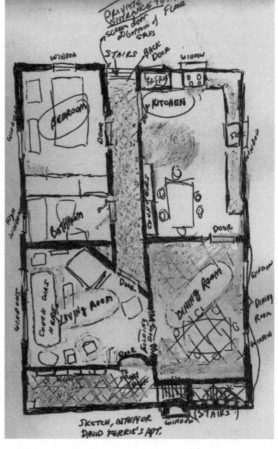

I remembered the piano as located in the dining room, but photos in 1967 show otherwise. However, it was many years ago. The apartment had retained most of the same layout as in 1963. The back entrance had changed from the way I remembered it in 1963, as well. The service road behind the apartment had also vanished. Regarding our work isolating tumors and viral materials in conducting development of the biological weapon, in that aspect of The Project, David's kitchen was relatively isolated from view and it was easier to keep contamination from reaching other areas of the apartment. The kitchen itself is not visible from the halls, the living room, or from any entrance. No surveillance from any other building can see down into the kitchen.

506

Appendix XV

Perry Russo Article
Portion Of Lardner Interview
Implicating David Ferrie

Perry Russo proposed to dress in a suit and impersonate himself as an insurance salesman (which he was, at the time), so that he could go to the door and see Clay Shaw up close to see if it was the same man. After all, it had been a few years since he'd last seen him. But didn't anybody consider the risk that Clay Shaw would fail to recognize Russo? Or that he could assert that Russo was an accessory before the fact and should go to jail for not disclosing this information before the assassination?

Author's friend "Lola J" wrote: "Perry Russo's family believed that Ferrie died of a hot shot. He was a junkie by that time and the stuff he bought on the street was always crap ... but these people are ignorant country people, so.... My first husband worked offshore and he had a friend who worked with him named Robert Russo, Perry Russo's cousin. He said Ferry was murdered, now that certainly doesn't make it true, but I still think there was some relationship between the two that was never revealed. Russo was Garrison's golden boy, the one who was going to get Shaw convicted. My friend's family was ashamed of Perry because he was gay, they, being Sicilian, didn't like that. Did anyone ever think about Shaw's death? I knew he was a chain smoker, but he died young of "lung" cancer, could he have met the same fate as Jack Ruby?" (Aug. 2013)

S T A T E M E N T   **Page five**

GEORGE LARDNER, JR.   continued

---

cause me to feel there was a second assasin and therefore
a plot. I found was the result of hastily collated material
poor cross-checking and editing, and that confusion as far
as I am concerned could have come only from the autopsy
report and nothing else.

NOTE: LARDNER in latter part of answer was quoting FERRIE.

Q. Is there more?
A. Yes. He also said QUOTE It was not until it occurred to me
that the public post-mortem should have reflected the position, not of the various wounds in a body when lying on
a slab, but rather a body sitting in a position similar to
what it was at the time of the shooting END QUOTE Parenthesis That I, FERRIE, Close Parenthesis resolve my doubts.

NOTE: LARDNER finishing quote for FERRIE.

A. (continuing) He did say he had given them a lot of leads or perhaps, more precisely points, to check out. That he had given them an exhaustive run-down of where he had been on his trip to TEXAS that afternoon:

Q. What afternoon?
A. Afternoon the PRESIDENT was killed. Said he had also given it to the DISTRICT ATTORNEY'S OFFICE and that, as I recall it, it was at his insistence that the statement be given to the FBI, SECRET SERVICE, everybody.

Q. Did he talk about his arrests of the past?
A. I gathered only illusion he was making to arrests in past was his reference to youngsters he had helped and befriended. I took that to be his answer to what seems to be a common understanding.

Q. Is there anything you can think of during your interview with DAVID WILLIAM FERRIE that might be of interest or assistance to the DISTRICT ATTORNEY?
A. No, not off hand.

Q. Did you want to add something?
A. To finish the other answer, a common understanding or rather suspicion that these friendships might in any way be improper.

Q. Will you describe your parting with FERRIE?
A. I had been asking him to agree to publication a comment he had made during the interview. It related to the time he said he was questioned by the DISTRICT ATTORNEY'S OFFICE in the recent investigation last NOVEMBER. The substance of the comment was that when he was called in the DISTRICT ATTORNEY'S OFFICE said they wanted to run over the statement he had made in 1963 on the grounds that they had lost their copy. He said he replied that he would get the statement for them from the FBI. He said that the DISTRICT ATTORNEY'S men told him QUOTE NO, DON'T DO THAT UNQUOTE. FERRIE replied that he would go to the FBI and get a copy of the statement. He said the DISTRICT ATTORNEY'S men told him QUOTE DON'T SAY WE SENT YOU UNQUOTE.

Q. Did FERRIE get that statement from the FBI?
A. He said that when he went to the FBI their immediate response was OH THAT'S JACK MARTIN

WITNESS DETAILS 'PLOT' ON KENNEDY

Says He Heard Oswald and 3 Plan Assassination

By GENE ROBERTS
Special to The New York Times

NEW ORLEANS, March 14— A life insurance agent who once denied that he had ever met Lee Harvey Oswald prior to the assassination of President Kennedy testified today that he had heard Oswald and two New Orleans men plot the assassination.

Then the witness, Perry Raymond Russo, an agent for the Equitable Life Assurance Society, left his chair in court and held his hand above the head of Clay L. Shaw to point him out as one of the participants in the alleged conspiracy.

Mr. Shaw, a retired New Orleans business executive, was arrested by District Attorney Jim Harrison on March 1 and accused of—but not formally charged with—helping to plot Mr. Kennedy's assassination.

A third conspirator, according to Mr. Russo, was David W. Ferrie, a former airline pilot who was found dead in bed here on Feb. 22.

Mr. Russo said he saw Mr. Shaw and Oswald together at Mr. Ferrie's apartment in New Orleans on three occasions in September of 1963. He said that on one occasion they carried on a detailed discussion of plans and alternate plans for assassinating President Kennedy.

They talked, he said, of "using diversionary tactics," of an "escape" route by airplane, of "selecting a kind of scapegoat" to draw attention from the real assassins and of "triangulation" —shots from three directions.

Interviewed by TV Man

On Feb. 24 Mr. Russo had said in a recorded interview with Al Crouch, news director of television station WBRZ-TV in Baton Rouge, that he had never met Oswald. The tapes of the interview are in the possession of the television station.

In the interview he said he met Mr. Ferrie in 1962 through a mutual friend, Al Landry.

"Did he [Ferrie] ever say [that] he knew Lee Harvey Oswald?" Mr. Crouch asked.

"No," Mr. Russo replied.

"Had you ever heard of Lee Harvey Oswald before the assassination?"

"No," Mr. Russo said.

In an interview with The Morning Advocate in Baton Rouge on Feb. 24, Mr. Russo did not mention Oswald but said he had once heard Mr. Ferrie say that "we will get him [President Kennedy] and it won't be long."

He also told the paper, according to its news article, that he first met Mr. Ferrie 18 months before the Kennedy

Associated Press Wirephoto
TELLS OF PLOT: Perry Raymond Russo outside hearing room. He said he heard three men plot to kill President Kennedy.

'Some Sort of Party'

District Attorney Garrison, making his third official appearance in a courtroom since assuming office five years ago, called Mr. Russo to testify before a three-judge panel today. He questioned the witness for more than three hours.

Mr. Russo gave his age as 25 and said he had graduated from high school and from Loyola University in New Orleans and had completed a year of law school.

Then he told how he visited Mr. Ferrie's apartment on Louisiana Avenue Parkway here one night in September, 1963, and found "some sort of party in progress."

The party, with about eight people, was soon over, he said, and he, Mr. Ferrie, a man he had met previously and knew as "Leon Oswald" and another man who called himself "Clem Bertrand" were left behind in the apartment.

At Mr. Garrison's request, Mr. Russo then identified Lee Harvey Oswald from a photograph as "Leon Oswald" and pointed out Mr. Shaw in the courtroom as the man he said he had known as "Clem Bertrand."

He said the three men began talking over plans and alternate plans for killing President Kennedy.

"Dave Ferrie," he testified, "took the initiative in the conversation. He paced back and forth and was talking.

"He said the assassination would have to use diversionary tactics.

"He said three people, at the very least two, would have to be there and another man would have to be a kind of scapegoat.

"If there were only two people," he continued, "then definitely one would have to be the scapegoat."

"Did he mention the phrase

Tells of 2 Proposals

Mr. Russo said Mr. Ferrie had made it clear that he had "worked up two proposals" for escaping soon after the assassination.

One involved flying to Mexico and Brazil and then perhaps to Cuba, he said, and the other involved going directly to Cuba.

According to Mr. Russo, Mr. Ferrie thought there might be danger in both plans—that they could be shot down going directly into Cuba, and that they might be picked up by Mexican authorities if they stopped in Mexico to refuel.

"Bertrand," Mr. Russo said, "offered an alternate solution on the day of the assassination —making sure they [the conspirators] had been at a certain place at a certain time."

At one point in the discussion, Mr. Russo said, Oswald told Bertrand to "shut up and leave him [Ferrie] alone—he knows what he's talking about, he's been a pilot."

"But Bertrand said as far as he was concerned Dave [Mr. Ferrie] was a washed-up pilot," Mr. Russo continued.

Later in the month of September, Mr. Russo said, he visited Mr. Ferrie's apartment again and found him "wearing baggy pants and a general's hat" and Oswald "half-shaved— there was three or four days' growth [of beard]."

He said Oswald was cleaning a rifle, which appeared to have a "bolt action" and a "hunting sight."

At this point, Mr. Garrison introduced a rifle that he identified only as "Exhibit S-14" and asked Mr. Russo to tell him how it differed from the rifle Oswald was cleaning.

Mr. Russo said Oswald's rifle appeared to have a "straight" telescopic sight, whereas the rifle Mr. Garrison exhibited was bulbous at one end.

Near the end of his testimony, Mr. Russo said Mr. Garrison's investigators took him to Mr. Shaw's apartment on Dauphine Street one night in late February and had him wait outside in a car for about two hours to get a look at Mr. Shaw if he came out of the house and determine whether he was "Clem Bertrand."

Mr. Russo testified that Mr. Shaw came out of the house briefly and that he immediately recognized him.

"I said he was the man—I am sure of it," he said.

"I asked," he went on, "if I could go to his [Mr. Shaw's] house and impersonate a Mutual of Omaha [insurance] man, which I did with the help of a member of your [Mr. Garrison's] staff."

"He said he was covered adequately as far as he thought. I was absolutely sure I had seen him before at Dave Ferrie's apartment."

Index